A Guidebook to Historic Western Pennsylvania

A Guidebook to

Historic
Western Pennsylvania

REVISED AND ENLARGED EDITION

HELENE SMITH
and
GEORGE SWETNAM

UNIVERSITY OF PITTSBURGH PRESS

Copyright © 1976, 1991, University of Pittsburgh Press
All rights reserved
Baker & Taylor International, London
Manufactured in the United States of America

Second edition, revised and enlarged

Library of Congress Cataloging-in-Publication Data

Smith, Helene.
    A guidebook to historic western Pennsylvania / Helene Smith and
George Swetnam.
    p.   cm.
    Includes bibliographical references.
    ISBN 0-8229-3630-5.—ISBN 0-8229-5424-9 (pbk.)
        1. Pennsylvania—Description and travel—1981-   —Guide-
books. 2. Historic sites—Pennsylvania—Guide-books. I. Swetnam, George. II. Title.
F147.3.S65
917.4804'43—dc20   89-16605
                                                                      CIP

The county maps were drawn by William Nelson.
Photographs, unless otherwise noted, were taken by the authors.

The publication of the first edition of this book was supported
by grants from the William K. Fitch Fund and
The Vira I. Heinz Fund of The Pittsburgh Foundation
and from The Hunt Foundation.

Grants from The James H. Beal Fund,
The Beechwood Fund, The Arthur Ebbert Fund,
and The Alice Risk Wilson Fund
of The Pittsburgh Foundation have supported the publication
of the second, revised edition.

Contents

About the Authors

George Swetnam was a staff writer for the Pittsburgh Press for thirty years. He has written over a dozen books on western Pennsylvania history, and his articles and stories have appeared in many publications. Helene Smith, a free-lance artist and writer of over half a dozen books, is co-author with Dr. Swetnam of a children's book, *Hannah's Town,* and four historical dramas, including one presented for the Westmoreland County Bicentennial in 1973, and one for the Blairsville Sesquicentennial in 1975. They have visited over twenty-five hundred locations in western Pennsylvania and have driven more than fifty thousand miles researching and photographing the sites.

Preface to the Second Edition

Historic sites generally tend to remain constant, but this is by no means true of highways and other guidance features, particularly in western Pennsylvania at this time. The state Department of Transportation has recently changed all its highway numbers; state highways and legislative routes (l.r.) have become state routes (SR). This is in addition to the many ordinary additions and alterations dictated by the passage of more than a decade since the first edition of this book. We have therefore revisited all principal sites, often changing the route numbers for locating them. It is well to note, however, that where SR numbers now begin with a zero, such as 0130 or 0008, former markers (130 or 8) have often remained unchanged. (We have retained the designation T for a local, or township, road.)

We have also taken advantage of this opportunity to include several hundred additional sites which had been previously omitted for lack of time and space. This selection was not easy considering the plethora of early buildings in each county. For example, Unity Township in Westmoreland County alone has more than 300 documented historic sites. For this edition, area and population figures have been taken from the 1980 census, as given in the 1986 *Rand McNally Commercial Atlas and Marketing Guide.*

Unfortunately, a considerable number of previously listed historic structures have been destroyed since 1976. These have been taken from the text, but are listed at the end of each chapter. Since sites are constantly being added to the National Register, listings for the most part are not given, as any attempt to include all would be quickly out of date. We have, however, listed covered bridges and a few more iron furnaces, but only where there is enough remaining to arouse the interest of the casual traveler. Although this state had (and still has) more covered bridges than any other state, many are now gone. In western Pennsylvania we discovered only six log churches remaining, a few log schools, and three lime kilns. In the entire state there are only sixteen octagonal barns left. Every effort should be made to preserve these architectural treasures.

Let us repeat two warnings: Although many sites include visiting hours, these are frequently changed; if travel of any considerable distance is required, it is wise to call ahead and confirm the hours. Also, since more than half the sites included in this guidebook are on private property, please respect owners' rights and do not feel free to go dashing in or about without asking permission.

The following counties, according to the authors' research and the response from county historical societies, have had no losses of landmarks since the last publication of the guidebook. We commend them in their efforts in preservation: Armstrong, Blair, Forest, Jefferson, Lawrence, Mercer, and Venango.

Since the 1976 edition many of the landmarks have been readapted for other uses, such as bed and breakfast inns. The new usage of early buildings through restoration is a real bonus for preservation.

For the revision of this book we would like to extend our sincere appreciation and gratitude to Frederick A. Hetzel, director of the University of Pittsburgh Press, together with the managing editor, Catherine Marshall, and the staff for their assistance and direction. A grant from the Pittsburgh Foundation enabled us to visit and photograph both old and new sites.

We also want to thank the staff in the Pennsylvania Department of Carnegie Library in Oakland for their help. Also, special thanks to Gregory Smith for his interest, assistance, and enthusiasm.

Our appreciation is given to the many organizations, especially historical societies, for answering questionnaires sent to them by the University of Pittsburgh Press. We thank them as well as various individuals and county planning commissioners for their help and response. Allegheny County: David L. Wright, B. E. Bockrath, Mary Beth Pastorius, Walter C. Kidney, Vera B. Ferree, Cynthia McLane, Eliot R. Johnson, Paul Koch, Jean G. Brown, Joseph A. Borkowski, Elizabeth M. Hunter, Deane L. Root, Alan R. Clarke, Donald E. Harper, Robert G. Larimer, Betsy Kunkle, Dorothy Sloan, and the Western Pennsylvania School for the Blind. Armstrong County: Mildred Thomas, Alice Walter, Darlene Raymont, and Grace Presbyterian Church (Kittanning). Bedford County: James B. Whisker, B. F. Van Horn, and Kay Williams. Beaver County: Vivian C. McLaughlin, Lois McKean, Robert A. Smith, Kay Williams, Robert Bonnage, and Arnold B. McMahon. Blair County: William and Mary Jane Anslinger, Peggy Field and staff at Fort Roberdeau. Butler County: Patricia A. Meyer, Fred Lochner, Beulah Frey, Francis Griffin, and Margarette Moore. Cambria County: Mr. and Mrs. Richard Davis and John D. Pryce. Clarion County: Clete L. Berner, Michael A. Bertheaud, Lagene Carrier Mayo, and Alice Walter. Clearfied County: George A. Scott. Crawford County: Vance Packard, Anne W. Stewart, and Ralph E. Pratt. Elk County: C. William Reed, Alice L. Wessman, Jean Dostal, Alice B. Beimel, and Iva A. Fay. Erie County: Bert E. Page, John R. Claridge, Susan Beates Hansen, and Elizabeth Stafford. Fayette County: Walter "Buzz" Storey, Sandra Lee Dils, William O. Fink, Mike Workman, and Karen L. Hechler. Forest County: Bette D. Walters. Greene County: Beth Goodwin Glass, W. Bertram Waychoff, and Rachel Hayward. Indiana County: William Wolford. Jefferson County: Jean K. Harriger. McKean County: Ted R. King, Mary Willson, M. B. Vernon, Larry Clark, and Aileen Burtt. Mercer County: Orris Anderson and Mary Snyder. Somerset County: Donna Glessner, Elizabeth M. Haupt, and Anita D. Blackaby. Venango County: Alice E. Morrison and Dennis L. Armstrong. Warren County: Chase Putnam. Washington County: Charlotte K. Lane, Laura M. Liggett, Roy Sarver, Terry Necciai, Bruce L. Weston, A. D. White, Richard M. Birch, William P. Young, Frank D. Kurfess, Sara M. Irwin, Sandra K. Shaw, and Rita Miller. Westmoreland County: Thomas J. Metzgar, Edward F. Nowlin, John C. Leighow, William Dzombak, Karl Koch, William Wolford, Susan Endersby, Jay Shaffer, Denver Walton, Irma S. de Carpentier, Harry J. Graham, and Donna Ferry.

Acknowledgments

Many people have helped us in preparing this book, and to them we would like to express our particular appreciation.

Our greatest debt must go to our spouses, Ruth Swetnam and Wayne Smith, who accompanied us on trips to many sites and who were patient throughout the many steps of writing and publishing this book.

In a guidebook to historic places there are an astronomical number of facts, and the chance for errors to slip by is great. The following authorities helped to eliminate these errors by checking over the material for specific counties: Allegheny County, Robert C. Alberts, Joseph G. Smith, and Helen M. Wilson, all of the Historical Society of Western Pennsylvania. Armstrong County, K. D. Colbert of the Armstrong County Historical and Museum Society Beaver County, Frank F. Carver of the Beaver Area Heritage Foundation. Bedford County, William Jordan of the Bedford County Heritage Commission. Blair County, Fred E. Long of the Blair County Historical Society. Butler County, June M. Cannard of the Butler County Courthouse and John Wise and his staff at the *Butler Eagle*. Cambria County, Betty Moyer of the Johnstown Flood Museum and Betty Mulhollen of the Cambria County Historical Society. Cameron County, Edna H. Bowser of the Cameron County Historical Society. Clarion County, Edna Jean Black of the Pennsylvania Record Press. Clearfield County, Joseph A Dague, Jr., of the Clearfield County Historical Society and George A. Scott of *The Progress*. Crawford County, Robert D. Ilisevich of the Crawford County Historical Society and James B. Stevenson of the *Titusville Herald*. Elk County, Mary C. McMahon and Alice L. Wessman, both of the Elk County Historical Society. Erie County, Helen Andrews and Clare Swisher, both of the Erie County Historical Society. Fayette County, I. N. Hagan and Eleanor Roland of the Connellsville Area Historical Society. Forest County, Ronald Childs of the Sarah Stewart Bovard Memorial Library. Greene County, Josephine Denny of the Greene County Historical Society. Indiana County, Frances S. Helman and Clarence Stephenson, both of the Indiana County Historical and Genealogical Society. Jefferson County, James H. Sterrett of Geneva College. Lawrence County, Bart Richards of the Lawrence County Historical Society. McKean County, Marian Bromeley of the Bradford Landmark Society, Joseph M. Cleary of Bradford Publications, Inc., and Merle E. Dickinson of the McKean County Historical Society. Mercer County, the *Sharon Herald* and Orvis Anderson of the Mercer County Historical Society. Venango County, James B. Stevenson of the *Titusville Herald*. Warren County, Ernest C. Miller and Chase Putnam, both of the Warren County Historical Association, and James B. Stevenson of the *Titusville Herald*. Washington County, Washington Greene County Tourist Promotion Agency, West Middletown Historical Center. Westmoreland County, Calvin E. Pollins of the Westmoreland County Historical Society.

Particular thanks go to Maria Zini and the staff of the Pennsylvania Department, Carnegie Library of Pittsburgh, and to Sara L. Rowley and her staff at Hillman Library, University of Pittsburgh.

Others who have helped in various ways include Arthur L. Altman, Ray Austin, Mae Beringer, Joe Borkowski, Eileen Clark, Patricia Cochran, John Coleman, Anna Connors, Jo Cornish, Wendy Cox, Peggy Fields, John B. Gibson, William Graff, Frank Hood, Thomas C. Imler, Jean Kautman, Karl Koch, Alvin Laidley, George Melvin, June

ACKNOWLEDGMENTS

Millison, Lester R. Mohr, Thomas Moore, Frank Piper, Joseph A. Plunkett, Michael Robbe, Peg Robinson, Lucille Senko, Paul Shatter, Dorothy Sloan, Helen Cestello Smith, John B. Snyder, Mary Snyder, Arthur Stewart, Charmaine Stickel, Helen Stuebgen, Patricia Truschel, V. E. Whisker, A. D. White, Margaret White, Edward G. Williams, and Richard Wright. There were scores of people in all twenty-six counties who helped with information pertaining to their own and nearby historic properties.

Introduction

*In days to come, when your children ask you what these stones
mean, you shall tell them.* —Joshua 4:7

It has long been recognized that succeeding generations, as well as newcomers and visitors to any area, have a proper—even laudable—curiosity about unusual or outstanding landscape features that they discover and about where to find those attractions they have heard of. This is the third historical guidebook to western Pennsylvania—an area remarkably full of history and wonders—to be published by the University of Pittsburgh Press. The first, compiled largely from correspondence during the great survey of the area's cultural history (sponsored by the Historical Society of Western Pennsylvania in the 1930s), was *Guidebook to Historic Places in Western Pennsylvania,* published in 1938. The second, a far more carefully prepared and comprehensive work, was *A Traveler's Guide to Historic Western Pennsylvania* by Lois Mulkearn and Edwin V. Pugh in 1954. Both books have been out of print for many years.

The necessity for a succession of guidebooks to the area is evident upon even brief consideration. A great many changes have occurred since Mulkearn and Pugh produced their work. Roads, road numbers, and travel patterns have changed, so that in numerous instances old directions for reaching a place no longer apply. Changes render former descriptions inaccurate; new facts are discovered; and unfortunately many historic structures have disappeared during the past twenty-two years, falling victim to the elements, fire, floods, and the wreckingball and bulldozer. Often not a trace remains. Events give interest to new places. In addition, any survey is sure to miss some locations of real worth.

This third guidebook differs from its predecessors in a number of respects. The most obvious is the omission of Potter County, thus covering twenty-six instead of the former twenty-seven counties. The reason for this change is apparent on laying a ruler over the map of Pennsylvania along the meridian of Potter's western, then along its eastern edge. The western meridian bisects Cameron County but runs along or very near the eastern edges of the other easternmost western Pennsylvania counties: McKean, Elk, Clearfield, Blair, and Bedford. The center of Potter County is appreciably nearer the eastern than the western border of the state. And a line along the meridian of Potter's eastern boundary would include all of Fulton and Huntingdon Counties, and well over half of Clinton, Centre, Mifflin, and Franklin Counties. Regretfully, but constrained by consistency, we have used the western line as our limit.

Another difference has been a sharply decreased emphasis on aboriginal, colonial, and early Federal history, in line with our conviction that history is a living and ongoing study, not simply concerned with something that happened a long time ago. While we believe we have done justice to the earlier periods and for good reason have limited the space allotted to recent matters, we feel that history is continuous and undividable, except for practical necessities.

A third difference is the greatly increased number of sites included. The first guidebook had a total of about 600, which covered nonexistent forts, stone iron furnace ruins, towns in general, and locations where events occurred, with a separate addition of travelways. Mulkearn and Pugh included 637 sites, almost half of them names and history, where nothing remained to be seen. The present book contains more than twice that number, all showing enough still remaining that the writers felt rewarded for visiting them. We omitted lists of forts and blockhouses. These are described in detail in *Report of the Commission to Locate the Site of the Frontier Forts of Pennsylvania* edited by Thomas L. Montgomery (see Bibliography). However, we did include the travelways and Indian paths in the capsule histories that introduce each county; and following the entries for each county is a list of all the Pennsylvania Historical and Museum Commission markers for the convenience of those who pass them on the highway so fast that they cannot read what site is indicated by the sign. The text of each is available in *Guide to the Historical Markers of Pennsylvania* by Henry A. Haas, available from the Pennsylvania Historical and Museum Commission, Harrisburg.

But by far the most important difference between this book and its predecessors is the outcome of our feeling that a guidebook is neither a history text nor a handbook of places and dates. Essentially a guidebook should present the reader with places where there is *something to be seen,* give a part of their story, and provide information on *how to get there.* For this reason we have omitted many sites of important events where no physical remains exist. It is discouraging to drive thirty-five miles to a spot where all you can see is a guardrail in the middle of the Pennsylvania Turnpike. The historian who is deeply concerned with every possible aspect of the event will be too well versed in his specialty to need our help in finding its exact location; most others would feel the trip only a waste of time.

No doubt critical readers will be surprised at the inclusion of certain sites and the omission of others. This is their right, as was recognized in the old proverb, "There is no arguing about tastes." We have included those places which we feel are most likely to interest the greatest number and widest variety of readers and history buffs. To a certain extent, the appeal of sites may depend on their rarity as well as their importance in other respects. In or near Pittsburgh, for instance, a log house is unusual; in Bedford County, where over five hundred log homes are still in daily use, it draws only a yawn. A mansion in the more sparsely populated counties will quickly attract attention and questions; on millionaire's row in East Liberty in Allegheny County it might not be noticed. An early stone house is a landmark in some areas; Washington County is full of them.

We have omitted many worthwhile sites in order to avoid duplication, as well as to conserve space. Only a few of the area's 184 early stone blast furnaces are included for this reason: the field has been thoroughly and accurately covered in *Guide to Old Stone Blast Furnaces in Western Pennsylvania* by Myron Sharp and William H. Thomas, available at a low price from the Historical Society of Western Pennsylvania. Material on covered bridges may be obtained from the Theodore Burr Covered Bridge Society. Many houses of principally architectural interest, especially in Allegheny County, have been passed over so as not to duplicate *The Architectural Heritage of Early Western Pennsylvania* by Charles Morse Stotz (see Bibliography) and *Landmark Architecture of Allegheny County, Pennsylvania,* by James D. Van Trump and Arthur P. Ziegler, Jr., available from the Pittsburgh History and Landmarks Foundation.

The order of the sites has proved a considerable problem, especially in the older, more populous and historically rich counties. Although it has appeared inadvisable to attempt a continuous tour arrangement, we have tried, in general, to keep places close together in the chapter if they are so geographically. However, necessary choices as to whether to turn right or left have sometimes resulted in sites not far apart in space being many pages away from one another. We hope the reader will bear in mind that the place-to-place course which may seem logical to him would have created additional problems for us.

Hours and admission charges of museums and other public buildings are subject to change. The reader might be wise to call or write before going to considerable difficulty in visiting them. Fewer than 10 percent of the sites include any charge for the visitor.

Since more than half the houses listed are private residences, we have marked them so only when requested by the owners or occupants. These have been included because at least the outside may be seen. All houses should be assumed to be private unless obviously public. Please do not think that because a house is listed in this guide, everyone has a right to go charging into it.

Those who search carefully may find some errors in this book. While we have visited every site and photographed all but a few that were not suited to pictures, we have included many about which hard documentary proof either does not exist or could not be located by a reasonable amount of searching. In such cases, we have used the best information available, combining evidence of physical facts with local tradition when the former appeared to corroborate the latter. At a tavern where one of us was asking for information on ownership of a landmark, a smart aleck butted in with, "If you want to be authentic, you ought to go to the courthouse and look up the records." We did not bother to remind him that in some counties, including the one we were in, many early records had been destroyed; or that for about 1,300 sites, such searches—for which lawyers usually charge a minimum of $500 each—would require either years of time or a budget of more than half a million dollars.

At times we have rejected previously published statements because they could not be made to agree with other known facts. The printed page is not sacrosanct. Early writers could twist facts or make mistakes as readily as later informants. We trust that our judgments in our researching and interviewing have been sound.

Many a reader, no doubt, will note omissions startling enough to make him say—as we have said of others—"How could they have missed that?" One of the hardest parts of the preparation was deciding where to draw the line between what to include and what to leave out. In a way, that is good. We do not want to rob the reader of the delight of discovering things for himself. Just keep your eyes open; there's plenty to find.

A Guidebook to Historic Western Pennsylvania

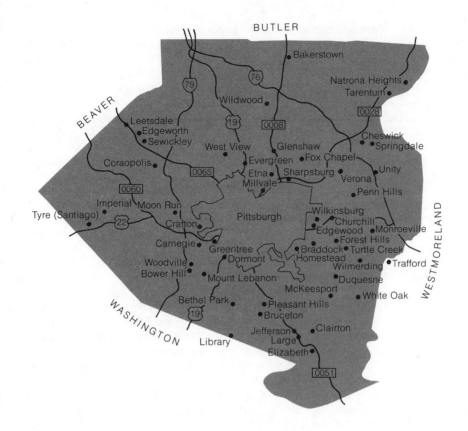

Allegheny County

Capsule History

Allegheny County took its name from the river, which in turn derived its title from the Allegewi, an early Indian tribe of the area which was vanquished by the Iroquois before the French exploration. The county, erected out of Westmoreland and Washington counties on September 24, 1788, embraced all of what was then the northwestern portion of Pennsylvania. It was soon increased by additional territory from Washington County and in 1792 by Pennsylvania's purchase of the Erie Triangle from New York. In 1800 it was reduced by the formation of the northwestern counties. Today its area is a modest 727 square miles, with a population of 1,450,195—second only to Philadelphia County.

A number of Indian trails traversed Allegheny County, most of them converging at Shannopinstown, now Lawrenceville. The four most important were the Raystown,

Kiskiminetas, Venango-Shannopin, and Nemacolin's paths. The *Raystown Path,* largely followed by John Forbes from Bedford, had two branches: one entered the county near Pitcairn, continued along the present site of the Old Greensburg Pike, going through Forest Hills to Wilkinsburg, and entered the Golden Triangle on what is now Penn Avenue; a second ran through Monroeville and followed the curving ridge through East Liberty and Bloomfield. The *Kiskiminetas Path* crossed the Allegheny River just above Tarentum and followed the right bank past the Point. The *Venango-Shannopin Path* crossed the Allegheny near its mouth and passed along the ridge near Federal Street Extension, through West View, Perrysville, Wexford, and Warrendale, thence heading toward Evans City. *Nemacolin's Path,* principally followed by the Braddock Expedition, traced Long Run into McKeesport, crossed the Monongahela below that place and again at the mouth of Turtle Creek, and passed through Braddock (site of Braddock's defeat in 1755), joining the Raystown Path at Forest Hills.

Other Indian trails included the *Catfish Path,* which ran from the Point through the West End, Carnegie, and Bridgeville, thence southwest to the Washington County line; two *Kuskusky* paths, one from below Tarentum paralleling Bull Creek to the Butler County line, and the other leaving the Venango-Shannopin trail at the headwaters of Girty's Run and running north of SR 0856 to the northeast corner of the county; the *Sewickley Old Town Path,* which ran south from Logan's Ferry through New Texas and Trafford to the Westmoreland County line; and the *Great Path* from Pittsburgh to Detroit, which followed the right bank of the Allegheny and Ohio rivers in this county.

At the time of British settlement three Indian towns existed in Allegheny County. Shannopinstown (Delaware Indian) was in the Lawrenceville area below the Washington Crossing Bridge, which memorializes the narrow escape of George Washington and Christopher Gist when their raft upset on December 29, 1753. A Delaware Indian town, home of Chief Shingas, was located at McKees Rocks. In 1752 Queen Alliquippa, the old Delaware ruler, and her following were living directly across the Ohio from that point, but she later had her village on the Youghiogheny River, near McKeesport. Chartiers Town was at the site of Tarentum until 1745, when it was abandoned by the Shawnee Indians, who moved to the Wabash River to be nearer the French.

George Croghan, "king of the traders," had a home and trading post in the upper end of Lawrenceville from before 1750 until it was burned during the Revolution. In 1749 he purchased from the Indians two immense areas including most of present day Pittsburgh, and these were confirmed in the first treaty of Fort Stanwix in 1768. But the Crown refused to approve the purchase, and the rights were worthless when he transferred them to his creditor, Bernard Gratz, in 1775. John Fraser, a blacksmith driven out of the area farther north by the French, lived at the mouth of Turtle Creek in 1753.

The Point, now Pittsburgh's Golden Triangle, was a wooded area when George Washington recommended it as a site for a fort. A company sent out by the Ohio Company of Virginia began Fort Saint (or Prince) George there early in 1754, but were driven off by the French, who rebuilt it as Fort Duquesne. They held it until 1758, defeating a British force under Maj. Gen. Edward Braddock near the mouth of Turtle Creek on July 9, 1755, but blew up the fort in November 1758, at the approach of Brig. Gen. John Forbes. Upon taking over the land, Forbes immediately named the area for William Pitt, British secretary of state, and ordered the construction of both a temporary fort and the tremendous Fort Pitt, largest British fortification in America, which was built of brick and earth in 1759–60. It withstood a siege during Pontiac's Rebellion in 1763, and Col. John Campbell laid out four blocks of a town during the following year.

During the border dispute with Virginia, Dr. John Connolly took over Fort Pitt in 1774, renaming it Fort Dunmore, for the governor of Virginia; and at the beginning of the Revolution it was occupied by Virginia troops under Col. John Neville. The dispute was settled by the two states in 1780 and was marked by the completion of the Mason and Dixon line two years later. In 1784 Col. George Woods laid out the town as far as Grant Street. After the Revolution, Fort Pitt was dismantled and sold. It was replaced in 1792 by Fort Fayette (bounded by Penn Avenue, the Allegheny River, and Ninth and Tenth streets) which was torn down just before the opening of the War of 1812 and in turn replaced by the Allegheny Arsenal in Lawrenceville.

Boat-building on the Allegheny and Monongahela rivers became the county's first industry. Barges, keel boats, and ocean-going ships were constructed in the area, and in 1811 Nicholas Roosevelt built the *New Orleans*—the first steamboat on western waters—on the Monongahela about half a mile above the Point.

Iron-making quickly became the principal industry, especially during and after the War of 1812. Since pig iron was available from nearby areas, no considerable amount of iron was smelted within the county until after the general adoption of coke as a fuel in 1859. The county had two stone blast furnaces. Glass was also a very important industry throughout the nineteenth century. In 1795 James O'Hara and Isaac Craig were the first glass manufacturers in western Pennsylvania.

Pittsburgh suffered a disastrous fire in April 1845 and severe damage from floods—especially in 1907 and 1936—until the building of a system of flood-control dams.

Improved roads and (beginning in 1828) the Pennsylvania Canal promoted Pittsburgh's growth into the second major city of the state. Plentiful supplies of coal, limestone, and ore, and the genius of Andrew Carnegie made it the steel capital of the world. Also contributing to the city's progress was the arrival of railroads in 1851–52.

Always smoky from its factories and the soft coal used for heating, Pittsburgh earned the title "hell with the lid off"; and from 1873 to 1909 when the Flinn-Magee political ring was in control, it became a city familiar with political corruption and social problems. Labor troubles such as the great railroad riots of 1877, the Homestead steel strike of 1892, and the Pressed Steel Car strike of 1910 made it even worse. Social conditions began to improve after the smashing of the ring and the Russell Sage Foundation's great Pittsburgh Survey (1907–08, published 1909–14), whose disclosures helped bring about reform.

Incorporated in 1816, Pittsburgh became a Renaissance city after World War II mainly due to the efforts of Mayor David L. Lawrence and Richard King Mellon. A fire which destroyed the old Wabash Railroad warehouses in 1946 opened the way for construction of Point State Park (1953) and Gateway Center, which wiped out the traces of much of the city's early history. Renaissance II began under the leadership of Mayor Richard S. Caliguiri (1975–88). At one time the city had the reputation of being one of the world's leading industrial cities. Today it excels in high technology and medical research. Located at the confluence of the Monongahela River (one of the few major rivers of America that flows north) and the Allegheny River, which together form the Ohio, it is the nation's largest inland navigation port, in regard to the amount of tonnage.

On December 24, 1891, the United States Board of Geographic Names ordered the removal of the final *h* from all towns ending with burgh, specifically pointing out Pittsburgh. After a long fight, the original spelling was restored on July 19, 1911, and changed on post office canceling machines by October 1 of that year.

Landmarks

A. Pittsburgh: The Golden Triangle

A1. County Courthouse was first located on Market Street. A frame structure, it was replaced by a second courthouse, of brick, which was completed in 1799 in the Diamond on the west side of Market Street and used until 1841. The third was built in 1842 by Coltart and Dilworth at a cost of $200,000 and was "the most monumental building erected in western Pennsylvania before 1860." Designed by John Chislett, this building was destroyed by fire in 1882.

The present and fourth structure (Worcester granite, brick, limestone), designed by Henry Hobson Richardson, who died before its completion, was constructed in 1884–88 on the site where a British detachment under Maj. James Grant met defeat during the Forbes expedition against Fort Duquesne in 1758. The Norman-Romanesque structure has three main entrance arches and a turreted tower. Built before the "hump" (a mound known as Grant's Hill) was cut in 1911-13, its first story was originally under ground. The present stone jail, built in 1904 in Richardsonian Romanesque style, was expanded five years later under the design of Frederick J. Osterling. It replaced the stone jail which was at the site now occupied by the Kossman Building at the foot of Forbes Avenue. It is connected to the courthouse by a "Bridge of Sighs" over Ross Street. *Location:* 436 Grant Street, bounded by Ross Street and Fifth and Forbes avenues, with jail in rear.

Note: One courtroom has been restored. *Hours:* Monday–Friday, 9 A.M.–4 P.M.

A2. City-County Building (reinforced stone) was built in 1915–17 with an arched loggia, an interior hall with gilded metal columns, and ornate detail in the supreme court room. Architects were Palmer, Hornbostel & Jones (with Edward B. Lee). *Location:* 414 Grant Street near courthouse.

A3. Allegheny County Morgue (stone) was built in 1901–03. It was designed, in character, by Frederick J. Osterling, inspired by Richardson's courthouse and jail. *Location:* 604 Fourth Avenue.

A4. Grant Building (limestone, brick, and Belgian granite) was designed by Henry Hornbostel. It is the tallest brick building in the city, having forty stories above ground and five below for parking, as well as a tunnel connecting with the courthouse. Opened in 1928, it was named for James Grant, whose advance guard in the attack on Fort Duquesne in 1758 was routed by the French. What was once the world's largest neon air beacon, blinking the city's name in international Morse code, is visible for 150 miles on a clear night. The third floor was for many years occupied by KDKA, one of the pioneer broadcasting stations of the world. (See *Conrad's Radio Station.*) A public observation deck is on the thirty-seventh floor. *Location:* 330 Grant Street.

A5. Chinatown in the early days was located in Herron Hill; when this uptown area became crowded about the turn of the century, most of the city's Chinese moved to the area around Second and Third avenues. A few Chinese families and organizations still remain there, their homes easily distinguished by the tile pagoda-type roofs. Most of these houses were built before 1925. *Location:* Between Second and Third avenues above Grant Street.

A6. Americus Club (brick), the present Pitt Building, formerly housed a very important Republican organization. *Location:* Smithfield Street and Boulevard of the Allies, northwest corner.

A7. Smithfield Street Bridge, spanning the Monongahela River, was constructed with the double sine curve truss in 1883 and enlarged to two lanes in 1889. The upstream truss was widened in 1911. About twenty-five years ago its major framework was replaced with aluminum, to lighten its self-load. Designed by Gustave Lindenthal, it was the first and largest bridge in America to employ the Pauli system of lenticular trusses. It is the oldest

6

bridge in Pittsburgh. *Location:* Smithfield Street.

A8. Dollar Savings Bank (brownstone) was built by Isaac H. Hobbs & Sons of classical design in 1868–71, with two wings added in 1906. Established in 1855, this banking company was Pittsburgh's first institution devoted to mutual banking, which operates solely for the benefit of depositors. *Location:* Fourth Avenue at Smithfield Street.

Note: Smithfield Street was named for the Indian trader and merchant, Devereaux Smith.

A9. Fort Pitt Federal Building (stone) is a five-story Richardsonian Romanesque structure built in 1890. *Location:* 301 Smithfield Street.

A10. Mellon National Bank and Trust Company (granite) of classical style, was built in 1923–24 with Doric columns and pilasters. *Location:* Smithfield Street, Oliver and Fifth Avenues.

A11. Park Building (steel and terra cotta), an eighteen-story Renaissance structure erected in 1896, is one of Pittsburgh's first steel-framed skyscrapers. *Location:* 355 Fifth Avenue.

A12. Union Trust Building (stone and terra cotta), now Two Mellon Bank Center, was built by Henry Clay Frick and designed by Frederick J. Osterling in 1915–16. This Flemish Gothic structure, modeled after a library at Louvain, Belgium, was erected on the site of the city's first Catholic cathedral, St. Paul's. This eleven-story building contains a large glass rotunda originally known as the Union Arcade. *Location:* 435 Grant Street.

A13. William Penn Hotel (brick and terra cotta), now the Westin William Penn, was designed by Janssen & Abbott and built in 1914–16. It was enlarged in 1928–29 at which time Janssen & Cocken were the architects. The Urban Room in the later addition was designed by Joseph Urban of New York. This Art Deco interior has been restored. The building has been an important Pittsburgh landmark and social center for decades. *Location:* Grant Street between Oliver Avenue and Sixth Avenue.

A14. Robert Morris College (brick) was until 1963 a business school. Its Moon Township campus was added in 1964, with the Oliver M. Kaufmann country home as a nucleus.

Since 1963 the college has sponsored the annual Pittsburgh Folk Festival, an important civic event founded in 1956 by Duquesne University and held at the Civic Arena (q.v.) late in May. *Locations:* Downtown campus, 610 Fifth Avenue; Moon Township campus, Narrows Run Road.

A15. First Lutheran Church (stone), of Gothic architecture, was organized in 1837 and erected its first structure in 1839–40. The present church, designed in the form of a Greek cross, was built in 1886 and consecrated in 1888. The north transept windows were designed by Frederick Wilson of the Tiffany Studios as a memorial to the Black family. Rev. William A. Passavant was the founder and one of the main forces behind the erection of this church. *Location:* 615 Grant Street.

A16. Pennsylvania Railroad Station and Rotunda (brick and terra cotta), designed by D. H. Burnham, was built in 1898–1903 on the site of the first Union Station of 1865, which was destroyed by fire during the railroad riots of 1877. This twelve-story, Beaux Arts, neo-Baroque building with a domed rotunda having four centered arches is one of the most outstanding railroad structures ever erected. The Pennsylvania Canal terminal at Pittsburgh was the site of this station. A branch of the canal ran through a tunnel (hence the name of nearby Tunnel Street) to locks on the Monongahela near the Try Street Terminal. (This tunnel should not be confused with the one in the same area used by the Panhandle Division of the Pennsylvania Railroad.) This station now functions as the terminus for the Port Authority East Busway, the Light Rail Transit (LRT), and the Amtrak railroad. Now called the Pennsylvanian, the building also serves as a luxury apartment complex. *Location:* 1100 Liberty Avenue at Grant Street.

A17. Gulf Building (stone and steel) was built in 1930–32 after the design by Trowbridge & Livingston, with E. P. Mellon. Its stepped, pyramidlike top is an adaptation of the mausoleum at Halicarnassus—one of the seven wonders of the ancient world. The famous beacon on top is the world's largest weather signal: red means fair with rising temperatures; blinking red, fair with falling temperatures; blue, rain or snow with rising temperatures; blinking blue, rain or snow with falling temperatures. In 1984 the building was sold to Chevron. *Location:* 435 Seventh Avenue.

A18. Koppers Building (granite, limestone, steel), constructed in 1929, has a fine lobby lined with marble. It was designed by Graham, Anderson, Probst & White, with E. P. Mellon. This structure has been called "the finest Art Deco building in Pittsburgh." *Location:* 436 Seventh Avenue.

A19. United States Steel Building, now USX Tower, 841 feet high with sixty-four stories, was once the world's second largest high-rise office building. Erected in 1967–69, it was designed to form a weathered protective steel layer (Cor-Ten). The roof was built with a heliport. Water-filled columns provide a built-in fire protection device. *Location:* Bounded by Grant Street, Bigelow Boulevard, and Seventh Avenue.

A20. Seventh Avenue Hotel (brick). Built in the middle 1800s, this building was originally a drovers' inn. It is the oldest hotel in Pittsburgh, now a commercial building. A Spread Eagle Hotel, run by a Mr. McMasters, used to be at this site. *Location:* Seventh Avenue at Liberty Avenue.

A21. German Evangelical Protestant Church (reinforced stone) was erected in 1927 and is one of the few churches remaining in downtown Pittsburgh. It occupies land granted from the Penn heirs in 1787, and the congregation is the outgrowth of the oldest religious group in the city, formed in 1782 by Rev. John William Weber. This building, now the United Church of Christ, was designed by Henry Hornbostel. It has a remarkable group of windows portraying religious and Pennsylvania history, and its cast-aluminum spire is fantastic. *Location:* 620 Smithfield Street.

A22. Alcoa Building (aluminum over steel), built in 1953, is the first skyscraper to be sheathed in aluminum. It has a charming lobby on Sixth Avenue that displays a mobile by Alexander Calder. *Location:* 425 Sixth Avenue.

A23. Harvard-Yale-Princeton Club (brick), built in 1894 in Georgian style around an interior courtyard, is one of the last vestiges of residential downtown Pittsburgh. Half of the building, remodeled in 1930–31 by Edward B. Lee, now operates as a club; the rest serves as offices. It was to have been torn down for the construction of the Alcoa Building, along with the old Nixon Theater, but was saved by strong protest. *Location:* William Penn Way near Seventh Avenue.

A24. Frick Building (granite and steel) was designed in neoclassic style by D. H. Burnham & Company of Chicago and built in 1901–02 by Henry Clay Frick, coke magnate and former steel partner of Andrew Carnegie. The annex was added in 1906. The main lobby of this building contains a stained glass window, *Fortune and Her Wheel* by John La Farge, and two bronze lions by A. P. Proctor. When Frick constructed this large building he was competing with Carnegie, who had built a smaller one next to the site. The annex is called the Allegheny Building. *Location:* Southwest corner of Fifth Avenue at 437 Grant Street.

A25. Hamilton Building (stone) was the first skyscraper built in Pittsburgh. Samuel Hamilton, who had opened a piano business in 1869, built the first structure in 1885. After it burned in 1887 he rebuilt and fireproofed it, completing it in 1889. It had nine stories (ten including the tower), 116 rooms, and the largest window glasses in America. It had a seventh-floor balcony 135 feet up and an observation deck at 185 feet. The height to the top of the flagpole was 216 feet. Now, much altered, it is a savings and loan office. *Location:* 335 Fifth Avenue.

A26. Magee Building (brick and stone), designed by Frederick J. Osterling in Romanesque style, was erected in 1895. *Location:* 334–36 Fourth Avenue.

A27. Point Park College was formed in 1960 (first as a junior college) from the Business Training College, which had resulted from a 1954 merger of two century-old business schools, Duff's and Iron City.

   a. Woodwell Hardware Store (brick) was built about 1870 by Joseph Woodwell, sculptor, artist, merchant, and patron of the arts. When the Boulevard of the Allies was widened in 1921 the Eichleay Company moved this eight-story structure north forty feet and raised it twelve inches, without ever shutting it down or cutting off services to its occupants. It is now Lawrence Hall. *Location:* Wood Street and Boulevard of the Allies.

   b. Keystone Athletic Club (reinforced brick and stone) was erected just before the 1929 crash as a fashionable athletic club. It soon fell on hard times and became, in turn, the Keystone Hotel, Sheraton Hotel, and Sherwyn Hotel, and is now a Point Park College dormitory, with a dance auditorium and other features. *Location:* Wood Street and Boulevard of the Allies across from Lawrence Hall.

A28. Colonial Trust (stone), in more recent years part of a complex known as The Bank Center (housing restaurants and shops), was built in 1902 and expanded in 1908 (remodeled in 1925). Its facade consists of marble, including four massive Corinthian columns. The interior contains one of the few solid marble self-supporting spiral staircases in the country. Frederick J. Osterling was the architect. (Other buildings in this complex include: Peoples Savings Bank, built in 1901–02 and designed by Alden & Harlow; Freehold Realty Building, 1893; and Commercial National Bank, 1897). *Location:* 310 Forbes Avenue.

A29. Benedum-Trees Building (brick and terra cotta), formerly the MacChesney Building, was designed in Beaux Arts style by Thomas H. Scott. This nineteen-story Edwardian skyscraper was built in 1905 in the financial section of the city. *Location:* 221–25 Fourth Avenue.

A30. Burke's Building (brick with stone facade) was built in 1836 of Greek Revival design by John Chislett and is one of the first office buildings constructed in Pittsburgh. This structure, built on property the Burkes purchased from the Irwin family, served at one time as a bank. *Location:* 211 Fourth Avenue.

A31. The Diamond, land set aside for public use by the Penns when Pittsburgh was laid out, is one of the city's most historic spots. Intended for a public market, it was also occupied by the county's first brick courthouse and later a city hall, where the Associate Reformed Presbyterian and Associate Presbyterian Churches merged in 1858 to form the United Presbyterian Church. During the Civil War it was used to feed and care for tired and ailing soldiers passing through the city. Its last structure, dating from 1916, was a market house which stood for about forty years. *Location:* Crossing of Market Street and Forbes Avenue (originally called Diamond Alley and then, after being widened early in this century, Diamond Street).

A32. Buhl Building (terra cotta on steel frame), a small, charming office building which dates from 1913, was purchased half-built and completed by Henry Buhl, Jr., a merchant and philanthropist whose Buhl Foundation also sponsored historical research and publication, the Buhl Science Center, Chatham Village (both q.v.), and other worthwhile projects. *Location:* 204 Fifth Avenue.

A33. Half Building (brick) received its name from the days when streets were widened and buildings were sometimes torn down, sometimes moved, and now and then cut in half. This hot-dog stand is one of the few surviving examples of the last. *Location:* Northwest corner of Forbes Avenue and Wood Street.

A34. Cast-iron Fronts, a once-popular type of commercial building, are not much in evidence today. Eight of them, built between 1840 and 1870, may still be seen downtown. One, housing a paint store, is at 101–03 Wood Street. A more ornate example may be seen on Fifth Avenue at McMaster Way, adjacent to the dime store. On Liberty Avenue are twin iron fronts at 805–07 and 927–29; other examples are at 951–53 Liberty and 308 Seventh Avenue.

A35. PPG Place (insulating glass), headquarters for the Pittsburgh Plate Glass Industries, founded in Pittsburgh in 1895. (In 1886 it had been established at Tarentum and eventually the company became the nation's primary producer of glass products.) This building complex was designed by Philip Johnson (and John Burgee) and was completed in 1983 at a total cost of $200 million. It includes a winter garden, a forty-story tower, and five buildings, all are crowned by 231 spires. The modern architecture ties in with and was inspired by the Gothic architecture of the past. It includes one million square feet of silver insulating glass—one of the world's most outstanding modern buildings, reflecting sky, surrounding architecture, and itself. *Location:* Market Square.

A36. 1902 Landmark Tavern (brick), with the building date in its modern-day title, was originally Dimling's Restaurant. The building thus still serves its original purpose. Inside is a fine tin embossed ceiling with ornate coving, together with original white tiled walls and floor. The extensive old brass rail bar and atmosphere remind people today of the old taverns in New York and Chicago. *Location:* 24 Market Square.

A37. Oyster House (brick), built in 1870, originally the Bear Tavern site, is the oldest tavern site in Pittsburgh still operating as a public house. *Location:* Market Square.

A38. St. Mary of Mercy Church (brick) was built in 1936 on the site of the first mass said at Fort Duquesne in 1754. A plaque designates the high water mark of the St. Patrick's Day flood which occurred the year it was

A35. PPG Place

erected. The architect was William P. Hutchison. *Location:* Third Avenue at Stanwix Street.

A39. World-Wide Clock, designed about 1960 by a local Bell Telephone employee, shows the time, as it revolves, of many principal cities all around the world. *Location:* Under portico of Bell Telephone Building, Stanwix Street and Boulevard of the Allies.

A40. Pittsburgh Chronicle Building (brick), of uncertain age, is the remains of an edifice in which Alexander Berkman shot Henry Clay Frick in an attempt on his life during the Homestead steel strike of 1892. *Location:* Graeme and Market streets and Fifth Avenue.

A41. Gateway 4 Building (steel and glass), located on the site of the 1905 Wabash Railroad Station, is felt by many to be the most beautiful of all the buildings erected as a result of the Pittsburgh Renaissance. The Three Rivers Arts Festival, band concerts, and other functions are held on the courtyards beside it and other Gateway Center buildings. *Location:* Stanwix Street and Commonwealth Place.

A42. The Blockhouse (brick), also called Bouquet's Redoubt, was one of two built in 1764 after Pontiac's Rebellion had shown the vulnerability of Fort Pitt's earthen breastworks facing the rivers. The last above-ground vestige of the fort, this five-sided structure mi-

raculously survived a century of neglect, during which it was the residence of Isaac Craig, assistant deputy quartermaster general of the army, and of various others, the last of whom was a woman who ran a candy store in a slum area, surrounded by lumber yards and tenements. In 1894 Mrs. Mary Croghan Schenley (who had inherited it from her grandfather, James O'Hara) gave it to the Daughters of the American Revolution, along with a 90-by-100-foot plot of ground. *Hours:* Tuesday–Saturday, 9 A.M.–4:30 P.M.; Sunday, 12 noon–4:30 P.M. Closed Monday. *Location:* Point State Park (25 Penn Avenue).

Note: Point State Park at the forks of the Ohio, site of George Washington's visits in 1753 and 1758 when the area was a forested wilderness, was begun in 1953 and completed in 1974. It was designed by Charles M. Stotz (Hess, McLachlan and Foster) for Pittsburgh's Renaissance I. The 150-foot fountain (largest in the Americas) draws water from an underground river—a (Wisconsin) glacial aquifer that is 35 feet deep and flows under about one-third of the city. More than three hundred buildings in Pittsburgh tap this "fourth river" which follows the course of the Allegheny.

A43. Fort Pitt Museum (brick) is a reproduction of the Monongahela bastion of Fort Pitt, a mammoth star fort. The other bastions were the Ohio, Music (whose base, excavated, may be seen in the park), Grenadier, and

Flag. Over sixty exhibits of the French and Indian War and of Pittsburgh's early history are on display at the museum. The redoubt and museum are administered by the Pennsylvania Historical and Museum Commission. *Hours:* Wednesday–Saturday, 9 A.M.–5 P.M.; Sunday, 12 noon–5 P.M. Closed Monday. *Admission charge.* Free to schools, scouts, and senior citizens. *Location:* Point State Park.

A44. First Presbyterian Church (sandstone) was chartered in 1788, with its first building erected in 1789 on a Penn land grant. The present Edwardian classical Gothic structure was designed by Theophilus Chandler, Jr., and completed in 1905. The central roof-support beams (84 feet long by 2 feet square) are said to be the longest timbers ever brought into Pittsburgh. A "Geneva pulpit," from which open-air services are conducted, is on the Sixth Avenue facade. Some of the windows were designed by Louis Tiffany. *Location:* 320 Sixth Avenue.

A45. Azen's Building (stone) is a fine classical building erected in the early 1900s. Fortunately it was preserved and is now used as a subway station (T). *Location:* 601 Sixth Street at Wood Street.

A46. Duquesne Club (brownstone) was founded in 1873, incorporated in 1881, and, when the present building (designed by Longfellow, Alden & Harlow) was completed, moved to this site in 1889. Additions to this Romanesque structure were made in 1902 and in 1930–31. It was severely damaged by fire in 1966. *Location:* 325 Sixth Avenue.

A47. Arbuckle Coffee Building (brick) was built about 1865 by John Arbuckle, a North Side coffee merchant, who, by inventing and using automatic weighing and packaging machines and by coating coffee beans with gelatine to prevent aging, became the world's coffee king; he even successfully challenged the Havemeyer sugar trust. In sculptured relief on the exterior wall of the building are busts of Washington, Lincoln, an Indian-head-penny Indian, and a woman often presumed to be Mary Croghan Schenley, but who may be Jane Grey Cannon Swisshelm. *Location:* Behind Duquesne Club between Wood Street, Strawberry Alley, and 808 Liberty Avenue.

A48. Trinity Episcopal Cathedral (stone), designed by Gordon W. Lloyd in 1871–72 in Gothic style, became the Cathedral of the Diocese in 1928, with Alexander Mann the first bishop. The church has a graceful tower and a pulpit designed by Bertram G. Goodhue in 1922. Adjacent to the church is Fort Duquesne Cemetery containing graves of very early Pittsburghers and others, including Chief Red Pole, who died in 1797 after visiting George Washington in Philadelphia. The Trinity congregation was formed in 1787 and became a parish in 1805. Land was given to it by the Penns in 1787, but its first church (which was round and of stone) was built at Wood, Sixth, and Liberty streets. The second church was erected at the present location in 1824–25. *Location:* 330 Sixth Avenue.

A49. Heinz Hall for the Performing Arts (brick) was built in 1925–27 as the Penn Theater. It was designed by architects Rapp & Rapp in Viennese Baroque style. Purchased by the Heinz family in 1967, it was restored and reopened in 1971. This magnificent building provides space for the Pittsburgh Symphony, live theater, and other cultural performances. Next to it is the Heinz Garden Plaza, a gift of the Howard Heinz Endowment, which features a carnelian granite waterfall, the source of which is Pittsburgh's underground river. The water-powered sculpture entitled "Quartet" was designed by British sculptor Angela Conner. *Location:* 600 Penn Avenue.

Note: The Penn-Liberty turn-of-the-century retail section was designated as a Pittsburgh Historic District in 1987.

A50. Keenan Building (brick and terra cotta), built in 1907, is an eighteen-story structure having a copper roof and bas-relief portraits of historic figures. *Location:* 643 Liberty Avenue.

A51. Benedum Center for the Performing Arts (brick and terra cotta) of classic style, was designed by Hoffman-Henon Company of Philadelphia and built in 1926–28. Originally the Stanley Theater, it was remodeled in 1985–86 at a cost of forty-two million dollars. This outstanding landmark is the home of the Civic Light Opera, the Pittsburgh Opera, the Pittsburgh Ballet Theater, and the presentations of the Pittsburgh Dance Council. The backstage area is larger than that of the Metropolitan Opera House in New York. *Location:* 719 Liberty Avenue.

A52. Grand Opera House (brick and terra cotta), which became the Warner Theater and is now a fine complex, the Warner Center, was built in 1906 and reconstructed in 1983–85. Architects for the original work were MacClure & Spahr. The old theater burned in 1917 and it was reconstructed the following year for vaudeville and movies by C. Howard Crane of Detroit. Its original features are marquis-type lighting facilities on its facade, and the lobby. *Location:* 336 Fifth Avenue.

A53. Fulton Building and Theater (brick and granite), twelve and one-half stories, designed by Grosvenor Atterbury, was built in 1906 by Henry Phipps, a partner of Andrew Carnegie. The lobby includes a skylighted interior court. The Gayety Theater preceded the Fulton at this site. *Location:* 107 Sixth Street.

A54. Armstrong Tunnel (stone), of Italian Renaissance style, was built as a highway tunnel in 1926–27 with Stanley L. Roush as the architect and Vernon R. Covell, chief engineer. This structure, with a 40-degree interior curve, is 1,300 feet long. *Location:* Connecting Forbes and Second avenues.

A55. Sixteenth Street Bridge, of steel truss with elaborate baroque adornment and stone piers, features bronze winged horses holding armillary spheres. Designed by Warren and Wetmore, it was built in 1923. *Location:* Sixteenth Street, spanning the Allegheny River.

A56. Strip District (brick buildings), originally Bayardstown, housed the wholesale food trade from the turn of the century. This section continues to provide the community with markets selling fresh fish, vegetables, and produce. *Location:* Eleventh Street to Twenty-seventh Street (Penn Manor line), including Smallman Street.
  a. Pittsburgh Police Stables (brick) were built around 1909 to house the horses for the mounted police force of the city. It later became Fort Pitt Chemical Co. In recent years it has been converted into a restaurant, the Spaghetti Warehouse. *Location:* 2601 Smallman Street.
  b. St. Stanislaus Kostka Roman Catholic Church (brick and brownstone) was built in 1891–92 in Romanesque style and named for Father Stanislaus Parzyk. The congregation was organized in 1875, the first of Pittsburgh's Polish Roman Catholic parishes and the first mother church of all western Pennsylvania parishes of Polish-American descent. The first meetinghouse was located in a former Presbyterian church at Penn Avenue and Seventeenth Street. The present structure features a large rose window, double towers, and frescoes painted by Polish immigrants. This church in 1968 was scheduled for demolition

to make way for a U.S. Postal Service facility. Fortunately it was saved by efforts of local people, mainly initiated by teenagers of the Boys' Club of Pittsburgh and Joseph Borkowski. *Location:* Twenty-first and Smallman streets.
  c. Pennsylvania Railroad Fruit Auction and Sales House (brick) is a fine example of a produce building typical of the Strip District. Today it is the headquarters for the Society for Art in Crafts. *Location:* Smallman and Twenty-first streets.

B. Pittsburgh: Lawrenceville. This community was laid out June 1, 1814, by William Barclay Foster who named it in honor of Capt. James Lawrence, hero of the War of 1812. It became a borough in 1834.

B1. Allegheny (U.S.) Arsenal was established in 1814–20 on the space now between Thirty-ninth and Fortieth streets, from Penn Avenue to the Allegheny River, land once owned by William Foster, father of composer Stephen Foster. Plans were drawn by Benjamin H. Latrobe to be used by a protégé, Thomas Pope, but they were not closely followed. Col. Abraham R. Wooley was the arsenal's first commandant. Among later ones was Maj. Thomas J. Rodman, who produced the world's largest bore cannon, shooting a twenty-inch round ball. The arsenal supplied arms and ammunition for frontier defense and for the Mexican War (1846–48). During the Civil War it produced more munitions than any other for the Union, despite an explosion on September 17, 1862, which killed more than seventy people, mostly women, boys, and girls. After about 1869 it was used only as a storage and distribution depot. Forty years later the part above Butler Street was given to Pittsburgh as a park and the rest sold in 1926. Among the few remaining structures, fast disappearing, are the stone officers' house (now a warehouse) and some storage buildings, across Butler Street from Arsenal Park and the stone powder magazine, partly underground in the park. Researchers for the Pittsburgh History and Landmarks Foundation report that existing houses in the area at 257 Fortieth Street, 5134 Carnegie Street, 5300 McCandless Avenue, 186 Home Street, and 4745 Modoc Alley, all brick and dating from 1830 to 1850, were more or less modeled on the arsenal architecture. *Location:* Arsenal Park, Fortieth and Butler Streets.

B2. Marine Hospital (brick), on land originally part of Allegheny Arsenal, opened in 1851 at Woods Run as a federal project to serve sick and injured boatmen on the rivers. It was closed in 1873. The second building, constructed in 1907–09, is now used by the Allegheny County Department of Health. *Location:* Northwest corner of Fortieth Street and Penn Avenue.

B3. Locust Grove Seminary (brick), built as a home by industrialist Alba Fisk around 1840, became the Locust Grove Episcopal Female Seminary (a boarding and day school for girls) in 1853, with William H. Clarke as rector. Apparently in financial difficulties, it was purchased for one dollar in 1856 by ironmaster J. H. Shoenberger. After the school closed, he transferred it to the (Episcopal) Church Home Association in 1862, and it is still operated as a home for the aged and sick. *Location:* Northeast corner of Fortieth Street and Penn Avenue.

B4. Washington Crossing Bridge is situated at the site where it is believed that George Washington and Christopher Gist crossed the Allegheny River on December 29–30, 1753, and nearly drowned in doing so. The bridge was built in 1923 (Janssen & Cocken, architects; Charles S. Davis, county engineer). Some say Washington crossed at Thirty-first Street (bridge spanning Herr's Island). *Location:* Fortieth Street at Allegheny River.

B5. Pittsburgh Reduction Company had its beginnings in this building, marked by an aluminum tablet, where Alfred E. Hunt, Charles M. Hall, and Arthur V. Davis produced the first commercial ingot of aluminum on Thanksgiving Day, 1888. The firm later became the Aluminum Company of America. *Location:* 3200 block of Smallman Street.

B6. Western Pennsylvania Medical College (brick), the first medical school established here, opened in 1886 near the old Western Pennsylvania Hospital. In 1902 it became the School of Medicine of the Western University of Pennsylvania (now University of Pittsburgh). In 1920 the property was sold to the Immaculate Heart of Mary Church. Part of the building has been torn down. *Location:* Brereton Avenue and Thirtieth Street.

B7. Emma Kaufmann Clinic (brick) was founded in 1896 by Isaac Kaufmann (one of the founders of Kaufmann's Department Store) as a free clinic, dispensary, and temporary hospital until 1913. It presently serves as the Polish Falcons' Home. *Location:* Brereton Avenue next to old Medical College.

B8. Reineman Hospital (frame) was established in 1893 by Adam Reineman, a jeweler, who set it up as Pittsburgh's first maternity hospital, an adjunct of the above medical school. It operated until 1911 and is now an apartment house. *Location:* 3400 block of Melwood Avenue near Finland Street.

B9. Branch Library (brick), Lawrenceville, designed by Alden and Harlow, was the first branch of the Carnegie Library of Pittsburgh (see *The Carnegie*). Its first librarian was H. Elizabeth Cory. Built in 1898 at a cost of $41,200, this was the first library in America to have a separate room for children. *Location:* 1898 Fisk Street.

B10. St. Mary's Academy (brick) is a late Greek Revival building of about 1850. Its porch features charming cast-iron decorations. Next to the academy is St. Mary's Roman Catholic Church, designed by James S. Devlin and built in 1874. In 1906 twenty stained glass windows by Mayer from Munich, Germany, were installed. In the same complex is the chapel of St. Anne, designed by John Comes in 1921. *Location:* 300 Forty-sixth Street.

Note: The Immaculate Heart of Mary Roman Catholic Church at 300 Brereton Avenue was built in 1904–06 with a copper-covered dome of late Renaissance style. It was designed by William P. Ginther.

B11. Wainwright Brewery (brick), now the Pittsburgh Brewing Company, includes a number of buildings that date from 1861 to 1873. The firm was founded in 1818 by Joseph Wainwright. (Administration Building erected 1888.) In 1899 it formed the nucleus of the "beer trust" which took in every brewery but one in or near the city. In 1962 this company, in cooperation with Alcoa, was the first to use the snap-open beverage cap. Swan Brewing Co., Inc., of Perth, Australia, took over the company in 1986. Tours by appointment. *Location:* 3340 Liberty Avenue.

B12. Allegheny Cemetery, the first and most outstanding public one west of the Alleghenies, was founded in 1844 by a group of well-known citizens, and was modeled after Mount Auburn Cemetery in Boston. The group bought 257 acres of land for $118,500 and engaged John Chislett as superintendent. He laid out the grounds and designed the Butler Street gateway, a stone Gothic Revival structure, in 1848; it was enlarged twenty years later with a chapel and offices by Barr and Moser. The Penn Avenue gates were added

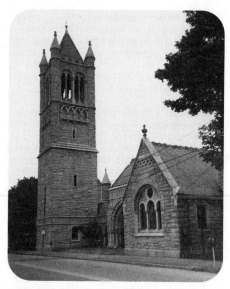

B12. Allegheny Cemetery

in 1887. The first burial, in September 1845, was that of Mrs. (Margaretta) James A. Briggs of Cleveland, daughter of George A. Bayard, who had sold the ground for the cemetery. The stained glass windows in the Temple Mausoleum were designed by Dr. Henry Lee Willet. Scenes depict composer Stephen Foster's life and his songs. Among the famous people buried here are the actress Lillian Russell, Stephen Foster, and William and Margaret (Morrison) Carnegie, parents of Andrew Carnegie. *Location:* 4734 Butler Street.

B13. St. Margaret's Hospital Building (brick) was erected in 1896–98. Endowed by John H. Shoenberger (founder of one of Pittsburgh's leading iron works) in memory of his wife, it was designed by Ernest Flagg. (The hospital, no longer in this building, has been moved to Aspinwall.) The rear of the main building has a fine baroque chapel. *Location:* 265 Forty-sixth Street.

B14. Public Baths (brick), conceived by Gertrude Thompson, wife of the rector of St. James Episcopal Church, were made available to Pittsburghers, especially steelworkers, in this building constructed with funds provided by steelman Henry Phipps in 1898. People used to stand in line for a turn at bathing and doing laundry. The name was changed in 1928 to the Lawrenceville Neighborhood House, and it closed near the end of 1961. *Location:* Thirty-fifth and Butler streets.

Note: A similar institution, Soho Public Baths, was located at 2610 Fifth Avenue (Uptown). The building was remodeled in 1988.

B15. Round Corner Hotel (brick), a former tavern, has been in continuous business as a public house since its erection in 1862 by Jacob Waidler. Years ago it was known for its "home-like meals and stabling accommodations." In 1881 Eli, Waidler's son, added the second story when he took over the business. In recent years the property was purchased by Dan Sufak. *Location:* Thirty-eighth and Butler streets.

Note: The region's first boys' club was at 4412 Butler Street.

B16. Westinghouse Air Brake Factory (brick) was the first airbrake factory, built by George Westinghouse in 1868–70. It is now a garage for Otto Milk Co. *Location:* Liberty Avenue and Twenty-fifth Street.

Note: In Lawrenceville in 1885–86 was the first successful exhibition of the transmission of electric energy at a considerable distance through the use of alternating current. It was produced by William Stanley.

B17. Zion Evangelical Lutheran Church (brick), Lawrenceville's oldest active congregation, built its second and present church in 1873–74. A two-story brick building next to it was erected in 1886 for a Sunday school and church offices. The first pastor was Rev. C. Emgelder. *Location:* Thirty-seventh and Bandera streets (the latter originally Bank Street).

Note: Since 1976 the Presbyterian Church has been occupied by the New Bethel Missionary Church at Summit and Forty-third streets. The German Reformed Adventist Church (brick), built in 1899 at 167 Fortieth Street, is now the Refuge Church of God in Christ. Both are black churches.

B18. St. Augustine's Roman Catholic Church (brick) was built in 1899-1901. It was designed by John T. Comes with two Romanesque towers and a dome. *Location:* 220 Thirty-seventh Street.

C. Pittsburgh: Uptown, Oakland, Hazelwood

C1. Civic Arena, built in 1961, 136 feet high at the center and 415 feet in diameter. The $22-million structure has a stainless-steel retractable dome three times the size of that of Saint Peter's in Rome. It is used for sports and theatrical events, for conventions, and for the Pittsburgh Folk Festival. *Location:* Uptown,

Washington Place, Center and Bedford avenues.

C2. Duquesne University (brick complex), established by the Dominican Order in 1878 as the College of Arts and Letters at Wylie Avenue and Fernando Street, was acquired three years later by the Order of the Holy Ghost. Moved to its present location, it was renamed Pittsburgh Catholic College of the Holy Ghost until 1911, when it was recognized as Duquesne University of the Holy Ghost. The administration building, oldest structure on the campus, was erected in 1883–84 and dedicated in 1885. In 1975 this brick structure was badly damaged by fire. The Richard King Mellon Hall of Science was designed by Ludwig Mies van der Rohe in 1968. *Location:* Uptown, 801 Bluff Street between Colbert and Shingiss streets.

　a. Duquesne Tamburitzans, world famous dance troupe, was founded at Duquesne University. It was organized to preserve the traditional folk songs and dances of Slavs and other peoples of Central Europe. *Location:* Duquesne University Building (brick, with mosaic mural of dancers over entranceway), 1801 Boulevard of the Allies.

C3. Mercy Hospital (brick) was first opened by the Catholic Sisters of Mercy, January 1, 1847, in a house on Penn Avenue, downtown. Land for this institution, the oldest of its kind in Pittsburgh, was bought on Boyd's Hill. The first building there, erected in 1848, partly exists in the later complex. New wings were added, notably in 1882 (now demolished), and in 1903–18 the south-wing buildings were constructed. The nurses' home was built in 1925–26, and in 1938 the southeast wing was added. *Location:* Uptown, Soho, and on the Bluff, corner of Stevenson and Locust Streets. Hospital is bounded by Pride Street, Forbes Avenue, and Boulevard of the Allies.

C4. Bethel African Methodist Episcopal Church (brick), founded in February 1827, is the oldest black church west of the Allegheny Mountains. Its first house of worship was on the northwest corner of Water (Fort Pitt Boulevard) and Smithfield streets, later the site of the famed Monongahela House. For over a century its churches were at Wylie Avenue and Elm Street, where one of its pastors was Benjamin T. Tanner, father of the artist Henry Ossawa Tanner. *Location:* Uptown, 2720 Webster Avenue.

C5. Epiphany Roman Catholic Church (brick and terra cotta), in Romanesque basili-

can style, was designed by John T. Comes and built in 1903, one of the few survivors of the Lower Hill. The church served as headquarters of the Roman Catholic diocese when St. Paul's was under construction in Oakland. Interior murals by Taber Sears are illustrated in *Mural Painting in America* (1912) by Edwin Blashfield. *Location:* Uptown, Epiphany Street.

C6. Madison School (brick) was built in 1902 with a 1929 addition. It was often called "the monkey school" because of carvings of the three moralizing monkeys around the stone lintel facade. *Location:* Uptown, 3401 Milwaukee Street.

C7. The Flag Plaza and Scout Center contains the world's largest collection of historic American flag art and a duplicate of the Liberty Bell. *Location:* 1275 Bedford Avenue.

C8. Old Passavant Hospital (brick), the first Protestant hospital built in America, was erected in 1851 and designed by Joseph W. Kerr (1815–86). This Tudor style was copied in later additions by Edward Stotz in 1898 and in 1917. The hospital in recent years moved to the North Hills. The original building, the oldest extant building in Pittsburgh, is still used. *Location:* Uptown, Reed and Roberts streets.

C9. Cinderella (ash cement), was a house erected during a bricklayers' strike in July 1903, when John Fink determined to test the use of ashes in construction. Setting up forms like those for concrete, he filled them with a mixture of ashes, cement, and water, well tamped down. The house, integrally built, is still in excellent condition, with a speckled appearance. The plan proved cheaper than brick construction, but never became popular. The Cinderella originally had a bakeshop in the cellar and apartments above. It remains an apartment house. *Location:* Uptown, corner of 263 Thirty-seventh Street and 3701 Penn Avenue.

C10. Carlow College was founded by the Sisters of Mercy in 1929 and at that time was called Mount Mercy College. In 1969 it became known by its present name in honor of a town in Ireland. *Location:* Oakland, 3333 Fifth Avenue.

C11. University of Pittsburgh (Western University of Pennsylvania, 1819–1908) dates back to the Pittsburgh Academy of 1787. It has expanded over the years to become a state-related and nationally known institution of learning. The University Art Gallery in the Henry Clay Frick Fine Arts Building contains national and international collections. *Gallery hours:* Tuesday–Saturday, 10 A.M.–4 P.M.; Sunday, 2–5 P.M. during exhibitions.

a. Cathedral of Learning (stone), a Gothic structrue forty-two stories high, was designed by Charles Z. Klauder and built in 1926–37, the only skyscraper university building in the United States and one of the greatest of its style in the country. Housed within it are the Commons Room, 87 classrooms—twenty-one of which are nationality rooms representing those groups who helped build Pittsburgh—184 laboratories, 23 lecture rooms, 19 libraries, 80 conference rooms, and 60 offices, among others. Nationality Room hours: Monday–Saturday, 9:00 A.M.–4:30 P.M.; Sunday, 11 A.M.–4:30 P.M.

Two rooms from Picnic, the manor, razed in 1949, of Mary E. Croghan Schenley, daughter of William Croghan, Jr. (brother-in-law of George Rogers Clark) and Mary O'Hara (daughter of Gen. James O'Hara), have been restored on the first floor. According to Charles M. Stotz, these rooms are "the outstanding achievement of the Greek Revival style in Western Pennsylvania." They are now the Oval Room and the Ballroom. Tours by arrangement. *Location:* Oakland, bounded by Forbes, Fifth, and Bellefield avenues, and Bigelow Boulevard.

b. Forbes Field Memorial Wall (brick) is the last remnant of the famous seven-acre ball yard (1909–70), once known as a "pitcher's ballpark" because of its distant outfield walls. It was the scene of four World Series. In 1960 Bill Mazeroski hit a home run over this wall in the ninth inning of the seventh game to give the Pirates a victory over the Yankees—their first world championship since the 1920s. *Location:* Oakland, end of Schenley Street, adjacent to the Mary E. Croghan Schenley Fountain and the Frick Fine Arts Building.

c. Stephen Foster Memorial (limestone), containing an auditorium that seats almost 700, is dedicated to Stephen Collins Foster (1826–64), a native of Pittsburgh and composer of some of America's best loved songs, including "Old Folks at Home" and "My Old Kentucky Home." (The original benefactor of the memorial was Josiah Kirby Lilly, 1861–1948.) The west wing houses the Foster Hall collection, containing more than 20,000 items relating to the musician. Foster's home site was at 3600 Penn Avenue (present headquarters for the Pittsburgh Wind Symphony). This brick house where his daughter, Mrs. Mor-

rison Foster Welch lived, replaced the original "White Cottage" birth site. A statue in memory of him is located across from the memorial. It was designed by Giuseppe Moretti (1859–1935). *Hours:* Monday–Friday, 9 A.M.–4 P.M. *Location:* Oakland, facing Forbes Avenue on Cathedral of Learning plot.

d. Heinz Memorial Chapel (limestone), built in 1938, is an outstanding example of medieval French Gothic architecture, designed by Charles Z. Klauder. The carving on the Indiana limestone was the work of Joseph Gottoni, and the stained glass windows (tallest in America), patterned after those in Sainte Chapelle, the royal church in Paris, were made by Charles J. Connick of Boston. This interfaith chapel, used for a variety of services, weddings, and organ presentations, was a gift in memory of Mr. and Mrs. H. J. Heinz from their children and grandchildren. *Hours:* Monday–Friday, 9 A.M.–4 P.M.; Saturday, scheduled weddings; Sunday, 1:30–5:30 P.M. *Location:* Oakland, east lawn of Cathedral of Learning.

e. Schenley Hotel (reinforced brick), now the William Pitt Student Union, opened in 1898. This building was Pittsburgh's first large, steel-framed skyscraper hotel. In 1956 the classical ten-story structure became part of the University of Pittsburgh and at present contains the Student Union. The famous actress Eleonora Duse died at the Schenley Hotel in 1924. In 1914, the Veterans of Foreign Wars organization was formed here. *Location:* Oakland, Fifth and Forbes avenues at Bigelow Boulevard.

–

C12. Masonic Temple (limestone and terra cotta) was built in 1914 in Greek Revival temple style. Architects were Janssen & Abbott. *Location:* Oakland, Fifth and Lytton avenues.

C13. Board of Education Building (limestone), resembling an Italian Renaissance town palace, was built in 1926–27. A fine courtyard and a fountain with a cobblestone walk around it occupy the center of the building. *Location:* Oakland, Bellefield Avenue at Forbes Avenue.

C14. St. Nicholas Greek Orthodox Cathedral (sandstone and brick), a classical building with six fluted columns, was built in 1904 as the First Congregational Church, a connection shown by the many examples of the wreath motif evident in the interior. It became Greek Orthodox in 1921 and contains much fine mosaic work and numerous icons of interest. *Location:* Oakland, Forbes Avenue and South Dithridge Street.

C15. The Carnegie (gray sandstone), in Italian Renaissance style and occupying five acres, was built in 1892–95 for $1 million, with funds donated by Andrew Carnegie for a free library. In 1907 an addition costing $5 million was dedicated; it included the museum of art, museum of natural history, and a music hall. That year the Pittsburgh Orchestra (became the Pittsburgh Symphony in 1937) performed there under the direction of Frederick Archer. Victor Herbert had preceded him in 1899 in that post. The museum includes thousands of exhibits among which is the world's most complete fossilized dinosaur skeleton.

On the stone piers of the roof are large bronze figures symbolizing art and science by J. Massey Rhind. Longfellow, Alden, and Harlow of Pittsburgh designed the original edifice, and Alden and Harlow drew the later plans which extended the building. In 1975 the Sarah Scaife Gallery of the Museum of Art was dedicated. Heinz Galleries and other galleries from endowments set up by Andrew W. Mellon are also open. The International Poetry Forum is housed at the institute and holds periodic readings. *Museum hours:* Tuesday, Wednesday, Thursday, Saturday, 10 A.M.– 5 P.M.; Friday, 10 A.M.–9 P.M.; Sunday, 1– 5 P.M. Closed Monday. *Donation. Library hours:* Monday, Tuesday, Wednesday, Friday, 9 A.M.–9 P.M.; Thursday and Saturday, 9 A.M.– 5:30 P.M.; Sunday, 1–5 P.M. (in summer, closed Sunday). *Free. Location:* Oakland, 4400 Forbes Avenue.

C16. Phipps Conservatory (iron and glass), designed by Lord & Burnham, is one of the largest indoor botanical gardens in the United States. It was given to the city in 1893 by Henry C. Phipps, steel magnate and partner of Andrew Carnegie. In 1896, Phipps added three other houses to the original nine display buildings, and in 1900 the city erected nine growing houses. The structures contain a palm court, a cactus room, an aquatic room, a Charleston garden, a cloistered sixteenth-century garden, a fern room, and an orchid room. There are new outdoor gardens. Displays are readied year round with special ones usually at Easter, Thanksgiving, and during the Christmas season. Tours available. *Hours:* Daily, 9 A.M.–5 P.M. *Location:* Oakland, Bigelow Boulevard in Schenley Park.

C17. Neil House (log) was built between 1787 and 1795 by Robert Neil. It collapsed in 1968 and was restored by the Pittsburgh His-

C17. Neil House

tory and Landmarks Foundation (sign reads Neill). The one-room structure, with a loft reached by a ladder, has a large fieldstone chimney on one end. *Hours:* By appointment. *Location:* Oakland, Schenley Park, on Serpentine Drive near Darlington Road.

Note: Schenley Park, named for Mary Croghan Schenley, was founded in 1889. It now contains 456 acres. Schenley Farms, designated a Pittsburgh Historic District in 1982, was developed by F. F. Nicola as a residential community in 1906.

C18. Carnegie Mellon University had its beginning on November 15, 1900, when Andrew Carnegie offered buildings and a $1 million endowment (increased to about $50 million in support over forty-six years) for a trade school for poor men. By 1912 trends had changed, and it became Carnegie Institute of Technology. About this time, Andrew and Richard B. Mellon supported the organization of a scientific research program called Mellon Institute. A marriage of convenience between the two produced Carnegie Mellon University in 1967. Carnegie Tech was the first institution in Pennsylvania to offer drama, music, and computer science.

a. Mellon Institute for Industrial Research (limestone), a huge structure with sixty-two monolithic Ionic columns, was built in 1931–37 (designed by Janssen & Cocken). On January 1, 1907, Robert Kennedy Duncan established the first Industrial Fellowship at the University of Kansas, and in 1911 Andrew W. and Richard B. Mellon financed him in a similar program at the University of Pittsburgh. It was incorporated as the Mellon Institute of Industrial Research in 1927, and the name was shortened to Mellon Institute in 1962. It was Pennsylvania's first independent research institute. *Location:* Oakland, 4400 Fifth Avenue.

b. Margaret Morrison College (terra cotta and brick) was named for Carnegie's mother and intended as a women's department, later phased out by coeducation. Now a general liberal arts hall, this rather flossy classical structure was built in 1906–07. *Location:* Oakland, Margaret Morrison Street on main campus.

c. Hunt Library (glass and metal) is a magnificent library building. Its top floor houses the world's largest private botanical book collection, gathered by Rachel McMasters Miller Hunt, an internationally known author, exhibitor, and lecturer on horticulture until her death in 1963. The priceless collection and building were the gift of the Hunt family in 1961. A decade later it became the Hunt Institute for Botanical Documentation. *Hours:* Daily, 9 A.M.–noon, 1–5 P.M. *Location:* Oakland, near Fine Arts Building on main campus.

C19. Episcopal Church of the Ascension (stone), an English Gothic structure with distinctive red doors, was built in 1896–98. William Halsey Wood was its architect, and the wood carving was done by Lamb Studios of Tenafly, N.J. The tower was modeled after the late Gothic tower of Wrexam Church in Wales. *Location:* Oakland, Ellsworth and North Neville avenues.

C20. Samson Funeral Home (brick), founded in 1859, was the first of its kind in the Pittsburgh area that did not also offer furniture for sale. Its founder, Hudson Samson, and his wife Susan G., came from Oswego, N.Y., and established a funeral home at 433 Sixth Street in Pittsburgh. In 1922 the building was sold to the Philadelphia Company and the business moved to the present site. Two old brick homes next to one another, the King-Jennings (left side) and the Livingston (right side), were later connected with a middle section, and in 1950 a common entranceway was built. Famous funerals at this establishment have included those of Lillian Russell and A. W. Mellon. *Location:* Oakland, 537 Neville Street.

C21. St. Paul's Roman Catholic Cathedral (stone) is a Gothic structure built in 1903–06 with double spires, designed by Egan and Prindeville. The original building, known as St. Paul's Church and located at Grant Street and Fifth Avenue, was built in 1828–34 and destroyed by fire in 1851. When the Diocese of

Pittsburgh was formed August 7, 1843, St. Paul's became its cathedral. The second church, constructed in 1851–53 on the same site, was said to be the largest brick structure in America at that time. In 1901 H. C. Frick bought the property for his Union Trust Building at a cost of $1,325,000—the largest single transaction in the history of Pittsburgh realty up until that time. While the third and present structure was being erected, services were held in the Church of the Epiphany. The cathedral was consecrated October 24, 1906, free of debt upon completion. (The stone Parish House is adjacent to the cathedral.) The organ that was donated by Andrew Carnegie for the second building and later moved to the present one was replaced by a world-famous German Beckerath organ in 1962, generally regarded as one of the finest instruments in the Americas. During its entire history, St. Paul's has had only three organists. Paul Koch was the organist and choirmaster from 1949 until 1988. *Location:* Oakland, Fifth Avenue at Craig Street.

C22. Central Catholic High School (brick complex), an impressive Victorian structure designed by Edward J. Weber, was built in 1926–27. It is composed of diaper-patterned brick and turrets. *Location:* Oakland, Fifth Avenue and Clyde Street.

Note: Across the street at 4721 Fifth Avenue, are the brick Cenacle buildings (one is Greek Revival), part of the Catholic Diocese.

C23. Holy Spirit Byzantine Church (brick) was built in 1962. The facade is faced with a multicolored mosaic mural. *Location:* Oakland, Fifth Avenue and Clyde Street, across from Central Catholic High School.

C24. First Church of Christ Scientist (limestone), in Greek Revival Style, was built in 1904. S. S. Beman was the architect. *Location:* Oakland, Clyde Street.

C25. Bellefield Presbyterian Church Tower (stone) marks the site where old-line Presbyterians met to march to the Syria Mosque for the 1958 merger which formed the new United Presbyterian Church, U.S.A. Unfortunately the church was demolished in 1985, replaced by a modern structure which houses the headquarters for the United Campus Ministries and the church of the Community of Reconciliation, among other offices.

Across Bellefield is a stone building that was once the manse of the Bellefield Presbyterian Church. It was built in 1891 as a gift to its pastor, W. F. Holland (a noted lepidopterist), from his wife, the former Carrie J. Moorhead. From a manse it became the former studio of WQED, the first successful educational television station, launched in 1954, and the first station to telecast instruction to elementary schools. The building now houses the University of Pittsburgh's Music Department. *Location:* Oakland, Fifth and Bellefield avenues.

Note: The present Bellefield Presbyterian Church is located in the former United Presbyterian Church built in 1896 at Fifth Avenue and Thackeray Street—a stone Richardsonian Romanesque structure.

C26. First Baptist Church (limestone) was erected about 1909–12 when the congregation's former home was taken for construction of the City-County Building. A fine Gothic Revival structure, it has a remarkable bronze spire and good wood carving in the chancel. It was designed by Bertram G. Goodhue. *Location:* Oakland, Bellefield Avenue and Bayard Street.

C27. Western Pennsylvania School for Blind Children (brick) was built in 1893–94 (George S. Orth, architect), five years after it was established, with funds supplied largely by two cousins, both named Jane Holmes. Civic planners had hoped to locate it in a secluded area and were dismayed when Mrs. Mary Schenley gave it one of the most desirable lots on her property. But she refused to reconsider and the school was built at the designated site. *Location:* Oakland, Bayard Street, between Bellefield Avenue and Bigelow Boulevard.

C28. Historical Society of Western Pennsylvania Building (brick and terra cotta) was erected in 1912, although the society has been active for nearly a century. Its exhibits consist of early Americana, together with an archive of old manuscripts, diaries, and letters. On the top floor of the building is a fine library containing more than seventeen thousand books and pamphlets devoted to western Pennsylvania. The structure is also the meeting place for the Western Pennsylvania Genealogical Society. *Hours:* Tuesday–Saturday, 9:30 A.M.–4:30 P.M. Tours arranged. *Location:* Oakland, 4338 Bigelow Boulevard.

C29. Twentieth Century Club (limestone) was formed in 1894 and had its first headquarters in the old James Laughlin house on Duquesne Way. It was relocated to the present building in Schenley Farms, a structure built in 1910 and remodeled completely in

C28. Historical Society of Western Pennsylvania Building

1929, with its exterior changed from brick to limestone. *Location:* Oakland, 4201 Bigelow Boulevard at Parkman Avenue.

C30. Soldiers and Sailors Memorial Hall (stone), on the former Charles J. Clark property, was built in 1907–11 as a memorial to Civil War veterans, as a part of the cultural build-up of Oakland. It is modeled after the Mausoleum at Halicarnassus, one of the seven wonders of the ancient world. Architect Henry Hornbostel felt that it needed a fine vista, but this was refused by county officials, who assigned it a rather unimportant lot, facing east. The structure was almost complete before they discovered he had built it facing south, and Hornbostel got his vista. It contains a museum—now of all America's wars—a dining hall, and a large public auditorium. *Hours:* Monday–Friday, 9 A.M.–4 P.M.; Saturday, Sunday, and holidays, 1–4 P.M. *Location:* Oakland, Fifth Avenue at Bigelow Boulevard.

C31. Syria Mosque (brick and terra cotta) was built in 1915 (Huehl, Schmidt & Holmes, architects) of Syrian Arabic style. Two bronze sphinxes at the entrance were designed by Giuseppe Moretti. *Location:* Oakland, 4423 Bigelow Boulevard near Fifth Avenue.

C32. Pittsburgh Athletic Association (stone and terra cotta), a five-story Italian Renaissance structure designed by Janssen & Abbott and built in 1909–11, is one of the finest classical buildings in the city. *Location:* Oakland, Bigelow Boulevard at Fifth Avenue.

C33. Rodef Shalom Temple (brick and terra cotta) was chartered in 1856. At the turn of the century it was located in the building later occupied by the Second Presbyterian Church on Eighth Avenue. The present square-domed structure was erected in 1906–07, with the additions of a school in 1938 and a social hall in 1956. Here also is the Biblical Botanical Garden with herbs and pharmaceuticals from the biblical world (open summer only; call for hours). *Location:* Shadyside, Fifth and Morewood avenues.

C34. Woods House (stone and frame) was erected by George Woods before 1800 and had a frame addition built about 1850. This structure, the Neil House (q.v.) in Schenley Park, and the Blockhouse at Fort Pitt (q.v.) are perhaps the only eighteenth-century buildings that still survive in Pittsburgh. *Location:* Hazelwood, 4604 Monongahela Street.

C35. First Hungarian Reformed Church (buff brick and stone) was erected in 1903–04. It has a central tower and Art Nouveau windows. *Location:* Hazelwood, 221 Johnston Avenue.

D. Pittsburgh: East End. Shadyside, originally the Thomas Aiken farm and named for the county's only charcoal iron furnace built here by George Anschutz in 1793, has many interesting houses. (Only a sampling is given here.) Other East End neighborhoods are East Liberty, Squirrel Hill, Point Breeze, Highland Park, and Bloomfield.

D1. Hunt Residence (anodized aluminum and bauxite ore) contains all that remains of the home of Roy A. Hunt, former president of the Aluminum Company of America, who died in 1966. His father, Capt. Alfred E. Hunt, was an early pioneer in aluminum-making and the founder of the family fortune. This ultra-modern town house was built around the original Hunt Library by Alfred M. Hunt, one of the heirs to the Alcoa fortune and governor of the Ligonier Rolling Rock Club. At one time the Hunt family kept seven thousand volumes and fifteen hundred prints and paintings in this specially built two-story wing of their home. *Location:* Shadyside, 4875 Ellsworth Avenue at Devonshire Street.

D2. Moreland-Hoffstot House (terra cotta and stucco), of French Renaissance style, was built about 1914. *Location:* Shadyside, 5057 Fifth Avenue.

D3. Gwinner-Harter House (brick), of Victorian Second Empire style, was built in 1870–80 (burned). *Location:* Shadyside, 5061 Fifth Avenue.

D4. Burgwin House (brick) was built between 1830 and 1870 (probably closer to the latter date). *Location:* Shadyside, 5219 Fifth Avenue.

D5. Spinelli House (board and batten) was built about 1870 in Romantic cottage style. *Location:* Shadyside, 5302 Westminster Place.

D6. Abbott and Marshall Houses (board and batten) were built about 1860. *Location:* Shadyside, 918–20 St. James Street.

D7. Hillman House (brick), a three-story Victorian mansion with twenty rooms, was built around 1878 by James Rees, a local steamboat builder. In 1919 John Hartwell Hillman, Jr., purchased the house and added a new wing with Edward Purcell Mellon as consultant architect. The structure has been resurfaced with limestone and reflects English Georgian style (remodeling began in 1924). *Location:* Shadyside, 5045 Fifth Avenue.

D8. Hunt House (brick) was the home of Capt. and Mrs. Alfred E. Hunt at the time he was involved in launching what was soon to become the Aluminum Company of America. The building at present houses a commercial business. *Location:* East Liberty, 272 Shady Avenue.

D9. Shadyside Presbyterian Church (stone), with a large central dome of Romanesque design, was erected in 1888–90, replacing an earlier building of 1874–75. For years many considered it the wealthiest and most socially acceptable Protestant church in the city. In 1892 the chapel on Westminster Place was completed; in 1937–38 the interior of the church was remodeled; and in 1952–53 a new parish hall was constructed. The congregation of this church was formed in 1860. *Location:* Shadyside, Amberson Avenue at Westminster Place.

D10. "Sunnyledge" (brick), the residence and office of Dr. James H. McClelland, a physician. A pointing hand on the stone lintel indicates the entranceway. This Romanesque house was designed in 1886 by Frank E. Alden, clerk of the works for H. H. Richardson's masterpiece, the Allegheny County Courthouse (q.v.). Ethelbert Nevin, composer of "The Rosary," used to play as a guest pianist for private concerts in this house. *Location:* Shadyside, Fifth and Wilkins avenues.

D8. Hunt House

D11. Willa Cather Residence (brick). The home of Judge Samuel McClung was one of the places where Willa Cather resided during the years near the turn of the century that she lived in Pittsburgh while working as art critic for the *Leader* newspaper. The judge's daughter, Isabelle, was her friend. Cather wrote *O Pioneers, My Antonia,* and the Pulitzer-prize-winning *One of Ours,* among numerous other novels. *Location:* Squirrel Hill, 1180 Murray Hill Avenue.

D12. Sacred Heart Roman Catholic Church (stone), of English Gothic style notable for its interior beamed roof, was constructed over a period of years between 1924 and 1953. The designer, Carlton Strong, did not live to see it finished. *Location:* Shadyside, Walnut Street at Shady Avenue.

D13. Calvary Episcopal Church (limestone) was erected in 1906–07, replacing the second church at the corner of Penn Avenue and Station Street. The parish was organized in 1855, with William H. Paddock the earliest rector. At this church the first church service ever broadcast was transmitted on January 2, 1921, through radio wireless by KDKA. Encouraged by the rector, Dr. Edwin J. Van Etten, these broadcast services continued for nineteen years.

The designer of many of the windows, as well as the building, was Ralph Adams Cram. Outstanding stained glass windows depicting western Pennsylvania history were made by William Willet of Pittsburgh. Beautiful fifteenth-century-style wood carving by Kirchmeyer of Cambridge, Mass., adorns the interior. *Location:* Shadyside, 315 Shady Avenue at Walnut Street.

D14. Chatham College was organized in 1869 by the Shadyside Presbyterian Church as the Pennsylvania College for Women, receiving its present name in 1955. Some of its more interesting buildings were originally residences of well-to-do Pittsburghers. *Location:* Shadyside, between Fifth and Wilkins avenues.

a. Mellon Home (brick and stone), of Tudor style, was built in 1897 by the Laughlin family (of Jones & Laughlin Steel). In 1917 Andrew Mellon bought the property, renovating and enlarging the building. When he became secretary of the treasury in 1921, his son Paul moved here, deeding the property to the college in 1940. *Location:* Woodland Road.

b. Greystone (later Benedum Hall) was the estate of Thomas Marshall Howe, who had built a house on the hill before the Civil War. In 1911 M. L. Benedum bought the seven-acre estate, demolished the home called Greystone, and built another one by the same name, using some of the original stone. The Claude Worthington Benedum Foundation gave the house to the college in 1960. Howe also built the spring shelter bearing his name below this house, where South Highland Avenue runs into Fifth Avenue. Donated for public use, it was a favorite drinking fountain for years but is now dry. *Location:* East Woodland Road.

c. Howe-Childs-Gateway House (frame), built around 1860 by Thomas Howe, is a three-story building in Picturesque Victorian style. Once known as Willow Cottage—Howe's home prior to Graystone—it is presently used as a Chatham College dormitory. *Location:* Shadyside, 6000 Fifth Avenue.

D15. Kaufman House (brick) is the boyhood home of playwright George S. Kaufman, born in 1889 at Station Street in East Liberty. He was the son of Henrietta and Joseph Kaufman and the grandson of one of the founders of Temple Rodef Shalom. When Kaufman was a boy he used to fill bottles of water from nearby Howe Spring and sell them on the street for a dime apiece. In 1936 the Kaufmans moved to the Barley Sheaf Farm in Bucks County. George's friend Moss Hart purchased an old stone house across the road from him. The rural experiences of these playwright collaborators inspired much of their work. Kaufman and Hart plays include *The Man Who Came to Dinner, George Washington Slept Here,* and *You Can't Take It with You.* Kaufman was a Pulitzer Prize winner and also a director. He died in 1961. *Location:* Shadyside, Walnut Street and Stratton Lane.

D16. Pargny House (brick), a Greek Revival mansion of the late 1800s, was the home of Eugene W. Pargny, one of the millionaires who formed the United States Steel Company. *Location:* Squirrel Hill, 1054 Beechwood Boulevard.

D17. Pittsburgh Center for the Arts (stucco), constructed in 1911–12 by Charles D. Marshall in Edwardian Classical style, was one of the last of the area's great millionaire mansions to be erected. It was given to the center by the Marshall family in 1944–45 and houses exhibitions, arts-and-crafts classes, and a shop where works of local artists and craftsmen are sold. Pennsylvania's largest community arts center, it also provides meeting space for many cultural organizations. The R. B. Mellon family donated the park and rose gardens around it in 1946. (Mellon had his house razed. See *Mt. St. Peter's Church*, Westmorland County.) The only remaining structure on this estate is the carriage house–garage, now part of the Pittsburgh Civic Garden Club. *Hours:* Tuesday–Saturday, 10 A.M.–5 P.M.; Sunday, 1–5 P.M. *Location:* Shadyside, Fifth and Shady avenues.

D18. Lewando House (brick) was built in the 1920s for Ralph Lewando, a violinist and music critic for the *Pittsburgh Press*. The architect was Theodore Eicholtz. It contains a winding staircase to a turret. The high peaked gables include unusual, randomly laid bricks and pieces. A house designed by the same architect at about the same period is at 1321 Cordova Road, near Highland Park. *Location:* Point Breeze, 121 Elysian Street.

D19. The Mansion (brick), an eighteen-room, three-story house including a ballroom, was built in the late 1800s in Colonial Revival style with Palladian Greek ornamentation and sandstone pillars. It was constructed for William Penn Snyder (1862–1920), one of Pittsburgh's leading industrialists. The site is part of Colonial Place Plan, the homes of which were designed by architect George Orth. Snyder, founder of the William Penn Snyder Company, an iron brokerage firm (later in partnership with Henry W. Oliver) lived here until the early 1900s. At that time Edward Vose Babcock purchased the house. (His summer estate was built at Logan Road and Babcock Boulevard.) Babcock, who owned the largest hardwood production company in the world, was the mayor of Pittsburgh from 1918 to 1922. He became known as the "father of the county parks system." At this

house famous dignitaries and royalty were entertained. In 1975 Herbert Beatty, a Pittsburgh interior designer, bought the property. *Location:* Shadyside, 5135 Ellsworth Avenue at Colonial Place.

D20. Clayton (Frick House) (brick), now a museum, was the home of Henry Clay Frick and is now owned by a foundation established by his daughter, Helen Clay Frick. Built about 1870, it was bought by Frick in 1882 and extensively remodeled in 1893 by John Osterling. (See also *Henry Clay Frick Birthplace*, Westmoreland County.) Frick's carriages of the horse-and-buggy era are still preserved here. Open to the public at a future date. *Location:* Point Breeze, 7200 Penn Avenue, at South Homewood Avenue.

D21. The Frick Art Museum nearby at 7227 Reynolds Street contains many expert copies of old masters as well as originals. *Hours:* Tuesday–Saturday, 10 A.M.–5:30 P.M.; Sunday, 12 noon–6 P.M. Tours by appointment.

D22. H. J. Heinz Carriage House (brick and stone), erected in 1900, is the only remaining building on the Heinz estate, "Greenlawn," which used to include the entire block. This building, now a private residence, is constructed of alternate rows of brick and stone. A floral arched wrought iron fence, a fine landmark in itself, marks the boundaries of the original property now divided into numerous lots. The Heinz house was demolished in 1924. *Location:* Point Breeze, 7001 North Murtland Avenue at Penn Avenue.

D23. Gladys Schmitt House (brick), originally the old Munroe House, was later the home of award-winning novelist and poet Gladys Schmitt (1909–72). In 1937 she married Simon Goldfield, a musician and her literary critic. The author, who had no children but adopted a niece, became a professor of English literature at Carnegie Mellon University (then Carnegie Institute of Technology) after she wrote *The Gates of Aulis*. Some of her other baroque works include: *David the King*, *The Godforgotten*, *Rembrandt*, *Electra*, and *Alexandra*. In 1961 she received an honorary doctor of letters degree from the University of Pittsburgh and was included in the Distinguished Daughters of America. *Location:* Squirrel Hill, 5840 Wilkins Avenue.

D24. Judge Forward House (frame with siding), of Vernacular Greek Revival design, was built in 1840. It was the country house of Walter Forward, at one time president judge of

D22. H. J. Heinz Carriage House

D23. Gladys Schmitt House

Allegheny County and later secretary of the treasury under President John Tyler. *Location:* Squirrel Hill, 2361 Tilbury Street.

D25. St. Philomena's Roman Catholic Church (stone), a huge Gothic structure, was built in 1920–21. The previous church, erected around 1846 for a German-speaking congregation, was in the Strip District until 1925. There was an early school in conjunction with the church; a later school is still in operation. *Location:* Squirrel Hill, 2740 Beechwood Boulevard.

D26. Motor Square Garden (brick), with a large dome, was built as a market house in 1898–1900. It was converted to a sports arena in 1915 and became the site of the first heavyweight boxing event broadcast over a commercial radio station (KDKA)—a ten-round, no-decision fight between Johnny Ray and Johnny Dundee, announced by Florent Gibson. At present the building is a shopping mall. *Location:* East Liberty, Center Avenue at Baum Boulevard and South Beatty Street.

D27. B'nai Israel Synagogue (stone and brick), a domed structure built in the round with a massive classical portico arched on three sides, was erected in 1923. Henry Hornbostel was the lead architect. Stained glass by Jean-Jacques Duval was added at a later date. *Location:* Highland Park, 327 North Negley Avenue.

D28. Highland Park Gate Statuary. Two identical monuments at the entrance of the park display women in classical dress; at the Stanton Avenue Gate are sculptures of men with horses. All were modeled by Giuseppe Moretti in 1896 and 1900. None of the early buildings of the Highland Park Zoo are extant. *Location:* Highland Park, Highland and Stanton avenues.

D29. Highland Towers Apartments (brick), a four-story Art Deco building erected in 1913 with cobalt blue glass decoration, was designed by Frederick G. Scheibler, Jr. This is one of his most outstanding projects. *Location:* Highland Park, 340 South Highland Avenue.
 Note: Scheibler also built, in 1905–08, the Old Heidelberg apartments and cottages on Braddock Avenue at Waverly Street.

D30. Selma Burke Art Center, founded and named in honor of a distinguished contemporary black sculptor, presents exhibitions with emphasis on black culture and art. *Hours:* Tuesday–Saturday, 11 A.M.–7 P.M. *Location:* East Liberty, 6118 Penn Circle.

D31. East Liberty Presbyterian Church (stone), fifth home of the congregation, is an immense structure that was a family memorial gift from Mr. and Mrs. Richard B. Mellon. Built in 1931–35, it was the last great effort of Ralph Adams Cram and features much fine wood and stone carving and stained glass. This was the site of a log schoolhouse-church built by Jacob Negley, Sr. *Location:* East Liberty, Penn and Highland avenues.

D32. Eastminster United Presbyterian Church (stone), now a child care center, was organized in 1856 and built in 1893. *Location:* 250 North Highland Avenue at Penn Circle.

D33. King Mansion (brick), a typical mid-Victorian, successful businessman's house, was the girlhood home of Jennie King, wife of Richard B. Mellon. A four-towered, stone and brick garden structure built by Robert King in 1898 is much dilapidated. After his death in 1954 the home became the King Mansion Conservation Center. It now houses the Pittsburgh Plan for Art. Many works of art by local artists are on display here and may be rented or purchased. Originally called "Baywood," this was the home of Alexander King, Robert's father, a glass manufacturer. It was remodeled by his wife to Second Empire style. *Location:* Highland Park, 1251 North Negley Avenue.

D34. Pittsburgh (Presbyterian) Theological Seminary (brick complex) traces its descent from the oldest separate Protestant seminary in the United States, founded in Beaver County in 1794 (see *Service Associate Presbyterian Church,* Beaver County), and from Western Theological Seminary, established in Pittsburgh in 1827. It occupies ten acres—the old Lockhart estate—and has a fine library and a small museum of artifacts from the expeditions of James L. Kelso and Melvin G. Kyle to the Holy Land. Pittsburgh-Xenia Seminary moved to the site in 1954, and the present name was adopted after the church union of 1958. *Location:* East Liberty, 616 North Highland Avenue.

D35. SS. Peter and Paul Church (block stone) was built in 1890, its parish having been founded in 1857. The structure, a fine example of Gothic architecture, contains a vaulted ceiling and a beautiful rose window. In 1911 the church was struck by lightning; the towers were saved, but the middle section and roof burned. *Location:* East Liberty, 130 Larimer Avenue.

D36. Kingsley House, Pittsburgh's first settlement house, was founded by Rev. George Hodges, Episcopalian; Rev. Charles E. St. John, Unitarian; Rev. Morgan Sheedy, Roman Catholic; and Rev. E. M. Donehoo, Presbyterian. Named for the British clergyman reformer, Charles Kingsley, it opened December 3, 1893, at 1707 Penn Avenue in the Strip, moved to Herron Hill in 1909, and finally relocated to its present site soon after World War I. *Location:* East Liberty, 220 Larimer Avenue.

D37. Immaculate Conception Church (glass and masonry) was built in 1960. The stained glass windows were designed by Hunt Studios of Pittsburgh. Other noteworthy church windows include those at the Immaculate Heart of Mary Roman Catholic Church (3058 Brereton Avenue), made in Innsbruck, Austria. Another Polish church, Holy Family (256 Forty-fourth Street), has a fine panel on Polish history by an artist named Rosen. *Location:* Bloomfield, Edmond Street.

D38. William Giffen-Vorndran-Hildebrande House (brick and stone), built in 1904 or before, has an unusual dressed-stone facade. On the second floor a series of these stones are engraved with floral and bird decorations. The house has an adaptation of a mansard roof. *Location:* Bloomfield, 608–10 South Millvale Avenue at Cypress Street.

D39. Ursuline Academy (brick), in Italianate and Second Empire style, was built in the 1860s. After 1893 it became a convent and school. An adjacent chapel, sisters' residence, and gymnasium were erected in 1913, with Carlton Strong as the architect. Other additions were constructed in 1926. *Location:* Bloomfield, 201 South Winebiddle Street, near Friendship Avenue.

D40. St. Francis General Hospital (brick) was erected in 1871 with additions in 1891, 1907–10, 1932, and 1964. It was founded by the Franciscan sisters. Sidney F. Heckert was one of the architects. *Location:* Bloomfield, Forty-fifth Street near Penn Avenue.

D41. Brilliant Cutoff Stone Arch Bridges were built in 1902–03. This massive complex, resembling a Roman viaduct, was designed by William H. Brown, chief engineer of the Pennsylvania Railroad. (Brown also was the architect for the stone railroad abutments at the Latrobe Railroad Station.) These structures supported the connecting link between the Allegheny Valley, the West Penn, and the main line at Fifth Avenue. *Location:* Washington Boulevard near Frankstown Avenue.

E. Pittsburgh: North Side

E1. Allegheny Post Office (granite),now the Pittsburgh Children's Museum, was built in 1894–97 as the post office of Allegheny City. This impressive building with a central dome, designed by A. W. Aiken, was marked for demolition in the 1960s but was preserved by its sponsor, the Pittsburgh History and Landmarks Foundation (headquarters at Station Square). The museum, which includes a garden of architectural artifacts, presents various shows, programs, and exhibits which change

E1. Allegheny Post Office

every few weeks. *Hours:* May–August (summer): Monday–Saturday, 11 A.M.–5 P.M.; Sunday, 1–5 P.M. September–April (winter): Tuesday–Thursday, 1–4 P.M.; Friday, 10 A.M.–4 P.M.; Saturday, 11 A.M.–5 P.M.; Sunday, 1–5 P.M. *Admission charge. Location:* Allegheny Center.

E2. Carnegie Free Library and Music Hall (granite), now the Pittsburgh Public Theater was designed by Smithmeyer & Pelz, architects of the Library of Congress. Constructed in 1888–89 at a cost of $240,000, it was given to Allegheny City by Andrew Carnegie and is situated on land donated by the city. President Benjamin Harrison spoke at its dedication in 1890. (At that time a special passageway for his convenience was made between the library and the music hall, and it has been used ever since.) Organ recitals, begun by organist Rinehart Mayer in 1890, were held in this structure over an eighty-year period. The first city organist was Leonard Wales, followed by Henry P. Ecker. From 1904 until 1954 Dr. Caspar P. Koch, a leading authority on Bach, was the city organist, followed by his son, Paul Koch, from 1954 to 1974. This was the oldest series of free weekly municipal organ recitals in America. *Location:* Allegheny Center.

E3. Rinehart House (brick) was the residence of Mary Roberts Rinehart, Pittsburgh's most prolific writer, from her marriage in 1896 to Dr. Stanley M. Rinehart until she moved to the Sewickley area in 1910. Among her many successful detective stories, the most famous was *The Circular Staircase. Location:* Allegheny and Beech avenues.

E4. Pittsburgh Aviary (brick and glass) is one of the world's finest free-flight aviaries and is operated by the city of Pittsburgh. It contains ecological exhibits, talking birds, and free-flight rooms with exotic specimens from around the world. *Hours:* Daily, 9 A.M.–4:30 P.M. *Admission charge. Location:* Allegheny Commons, west corner of West Ohio Street and Sherman Avenue.

E5. Calvary Methodist Church (stone), of late Victorian Gothic style, was built in 1892–93 with two spires and is richly carved inside as well as outside. Three large windows were made by Tiffany and before being installed were exhibited at the World Columbian Exposition of 1893 in Chicago. *Location:* Allegheny and Beech avenues.

E6. Buhl Science Center (stone) was built in 1939 by Longfellow, Alden & Harlow for the Buhl Foundation on the site of the old city hall. In addition to sky dramas and science lectures it offers a variety of programs and exhibits, including a miniature railroad and village. Of special note are the iron-industry historical murals painted by Pittsburgh artist Nat Youngblood. *Hours:* Daily (except Christmas), 1–5 P.M. (Friday, 1–9:30 P.M.; Saturday, 10 A.M.–5 P.M.). *Admission charge. Location:* Allegheny Square.

E7. Three Rivers Stadium (masonry), home of the Steelers, Pittsburgh's professional football team, and the major-league Pirates baseball team, was the first structure of its kind to have a computerized scoreboard. Museum tours by appointment. *Location:* 400 Stadium Circle.

E8. Gertrude Stein Home (brick), a three-bay Italianate house, was the early home of the internationally known writer and literary critic (1874–1946). She was born at 71 Beech Avenue. Her father owned a clothing store at the corner of Fourth Avenue and Wood Street. She spent most of her life in Paris where she was a friend of the literati. Some of her books include *The Autobiography of Alice B. Toklas, Picasso, The World Is Round,* and *Wars I Have Seen. Location:* 850 Beech Avenue.

E9. Community College of Allegheny County, founded in 1966, includes on this campus some notable buildings.

   a. Byers-Lyon House (brick and stone), French Renaissance style, was built in 1898 by Alexander M. Byers, a well-known Pittsburgh industrialist. The house (two structures fitted together to form a court) cost $500,000 to build, with an additional $90,000 for the lot.

In 1941 it sold for $15,000. It now houses offices. *Location:* 901 Ridge Avenue.

b. West Hall (brick), built in 1912, is almost the last vestige of Western Theological Seminary, founded in 1825 (see *Pittsburgh Theological Seminary*). It was built in 1875 and used as a seminary (in part) until after the Presbyterian Church merger in 1958. *Location:* 834 Ridge Avenue.

c. Jones House (brick and stone), in Tudor style, designed by Rutan & Russell, was built by B. F. Jones, Jr., son of Benjamin Franklin Jones, partner and cofounder of Jones & Laughlin Steel Company. The forty-two room building now serves as the administration center for the college. *Location:* 808 Ridge Avenue.

Note: "Fair Acres," the country estate of B. F. Jones, Jr., was in Sewickley Heights. It was demolished in 1964. A house built later on the property, called "Overlook," was once owned by the mayor of Edgeworth, John Oliver. On Chestnut Road off Irwin Drive, at the Sewickley-Edgeworth borough line.

E10. Henry W. Oliver House (stone) was built around 1891. A. H. English, who sold it to the Oliver family, had it remodeled in fifteenth-century Italianate style with Tiffany windows. H. W. Oliver was prominent in the steel industry. *Location:* 845 Ridge Avenue.

E11. William Penn Snyder House (stone), which cost $450,000, was built in 1911 in French Renaissance style by George Orth & Brother for iron and steel magnate W. P. Snyder (1862–1920). He was an associate of Henry W. Oliver in the development of Lake Superior iron ore and owner of the Shenango Furnace Company. This house contains a French ballroom and an underground automobile entrance. It has served as the headquarters (since 1969) of Babb Inc., the company that renovated it. *Location:* 852 Ridge Avenue at Galveston Avenue ("Millionaires' Row").

E12. William Thaw House (brick), a three-bay townhouse built in the 1880s, was the home of industrialist William Thaw, father of the notorious Harry K. Thaw who killed architect Stanford White. *Location:* 930 Galveston Avenue.

E13. Mattress Factory (brick), renovated in recent years, houses a little theater, art studios, and an arts center within a research and development environment. *Hours:* Wednesday, 1–4 P.M.; Saturday and Sunday, 11 A.M.–4 P.M. *Location:* 500 Sampsonia Way.

E14. Emmanuel Episcopal Church (brick), of Romanesque style, was constructed in 1885–86 by Henry Hobson Richardson, who had recently taken the contract for the county courthouse (q.v.). This structure, often called the "bake-oven church" because of its shape, has had a wide influence on Pittsburgh architecture. *Location:* Corner of North and Allegheny avenues.

E15. Mexican War Streets (Historic District) are located on a tract of land originally owned by William Robinson and developed following the Mexican War of 1846–48, as evidenced by the street names. The houses vary from simple Greek Revival to mid and late Victorian. One three-story house at 1241 Resaca Place has a Romanesque stone facade and carved stone faces on its exterior. The area has been redeveloped through the attention of the Pittsburgh History and Landmarks Foundation. *Location:* Buena Vista, Taylor, Arch, Sherman, North, Monterey, Resaca Place, Palo Alto, and Jacksonia streets, many of which commemorate battles and heroes of the Mexican War (mainly between Brighton and Arch streets and between O'Hern and West Park streets)

E16. St. Mary's Roman Catholic Church and Priory (brick), of Italianate classical design, were built in 1853–54. According to tradition, the architect was Fr. John Stibiel, the second pastor of the parish which was formed in 1848 by German Redemptorist Fathers from St. Philomena's Church. Murals by M. Lambart of New York were added in 1882. The adjoining brick house for Benedictine priests was erected in 1888. These structures received a last minute reprieve from demolition in 1981 when the path of I-279 was moved forty yards east. The property was privately purchased and in 1986 the fully restored Priory opened as a twenty-four room, European-style hotel. Plans have been made for the Priory to be converted into a bed and breakfast hotel. *Location:* 614 Pressley Street at Nash Street.

E17. New Zion Baptist Church (brick), designed by Barr & Moser, was built in 1866–67 by the Union Methodist Church (formed in 1846) which sold it to the Baptist Church in 1961. *Location:* 1304 Manhattan Street at Pennsylvania Avenue.

E18. Old Widows' Home (brick and stone), now public housing, was designed by John Chislett and established in 1860. The Allegheny Widows' Home Association took over the former Allegheny Protestant Orphan Asylum in 1866. Other buildings were added after 1873 on Sherman and Dawson avenues and in 1903 on Arlington Avenue. *Location:* 536 Armandale Street at Garfield Avenue.

E19. Western State Penitentiary (stone), now the State Correctional Institution, was built in 1876–82. E. M. Butz was the architect of this enormous complex stretching along the Ohio River. This was the first American building style to attract international attention. *Location:* Manchester area.

E20. Manchester (Historic District), consisting of a preservation district mostly made up of mid and late Victorian middle-class houses, was laid out in 1832. It became a borough in 1843; part of the City of Allegheny in 1867; and the Twenty-first Ward of Pittsburgh in 1908, when the two cities amalgamated. There are both single houses and row houses in this district (1840–1900). *Location:* Bidwell, Chateau, Franklin, Faulsey streets; Columbus and West North avenues.

E21. Allegheny Observatory (brick and terra cotta), with three domes, designed by T. E. Billquist, was built in 1900–12 and is one of the foremost observatories in the world, containing the largest (thirty-inch) spectrographic refractor telescope. Its first building was erected in 1860 near Perrysville Avenue, and in 1865 it was made part of the Western University of Pennsylvania (now the University of Pittsburgh). The ashes of John Brashear, the astronomer who built the equipment, are here, as are those of others, in the pedestal of the refractory telescope. The present site, along with the park, was donated to the city of Allegheny by David E. Parks. The institution offers lectures, movies, and on clear nights, viewing through the telescope. *Hours:* By appointment only. *Location:* Riverview Park, 159 Riverview Avenue.

E22. St. Anthony's Religious Art Museum (brick) (originally Shrine of St. Anthony of S. Padua, Roman Catholic church) with twin towers reminiscent of medieval Germany, was built in 1880 (dedicated 1883) by S. G. Mollinger, pastor of Most Holy Name of Jesus Church from 1868 to 1892. (The towers were added in 1890–92.) He purchased relics from looted European churches from a wealthy Belgian family and used $300,000 of his personal funds to build the chapel which was opened on the Feast of St. Anthony in 1892. Two days later Father Mollinger died. The stained glass windows and Stations of

the Cross came from Munich, Germany. *Hours:* Sunday (except holidays), 11 A.M.– 4 P.M.; group tours Tuesday, Thursday, Saturday, 1–4 P.M. *Location:* Troy Hill, 1704 Harpster Street at Tinsbury.

Note: The brick Second Empire rectory next to the church was built in 1875–76.

E23. Heathside Cottage (brick), a one-story Gothic Revival structure, was built between 1860 and 1865. *Location:* Fineview, 416 Catoma Street.

E24. Swedenborgian Church (brick), called the Church of the New Jerusalem, was founded by followers of Emanuel Swedenborg (1688–1772), a Swedish scientist and mystical religious leader. This 1906 building, now vacant and in need of preservation, replaced a former church which was attended by Andrew Carnegie and other family members. Carnegie gave the first organ (out of 7,689 he donated) to this church. Built in 1874 by John Roberts, it was later moved to the present church and more recently to a church in Ohio. *Location:* 120 Parkhurst Street at Sandusky Street.

E25. Max's Allegheny Tavern (brick), built in the late 1800s on the present site of the Allegheny Room, was formerly the Farmers' and Drovers' Hotel in Deutch (Dutch) Town. Drivers of wagons filled with produce for the Pittsburgh market used to lodge here. At the turn of the century George Rahn bought the old hotel. In 1903 he built the Rahn Hotel (today the main bar and dining room). The hand-carved back bar came from the St. Louis Exposition, and the original icebox is still in use. In 1914 George Rahn died from a blow on the head from his swinging bar door after he had thrown out a rowdy and inebriated customer. During Prohibition this hotel became a speakeasy. *Location:* 539 Second Street (now Suismon).

E26. St. Boniface Roman Catholic Church (limestone), designed by A. F. Link in Romanesque Byzantine style with a vaulted dome, was built in 1925–26. An earlier brick section is the Parish House. These buildings were spared after a long legal fight with the Department of Highways over I-279. *Location:* 2200–08 East Street.

E27. Eberhardt and Ober Brewery (brick) was established in 1840 and closed in the early 1900s. The main corner building was constructed in 1897. During its heyday this was one of the major industries in the Deutsch

E28 & E29. Heinz Plant and Sarah Heinz House

Town area of Allegheny City (North Side). This and other local breweries were bought out in 1899 by the Pittsburgh Brewing Company. At present a new micro-brewery (first in the state) is housed in the old E & O building. (An early bottling center and warehouse are also at this location.) Pennsylvania Brewing, founded in 1986 by Thomas Pastorius, operates this business, producing Pennsylvania Pilsner (German) beer. The building was restored in 1987 and is now open to the public with a brew pub, a brewmaster from Germany, and a glass wall for viewing the operations of the brewery. *Location:* Troy Hill, across from the H. J. Heinz factory.

E28. Heinz Plant is the largest food plant of its kind in the world. The firm was founded by the Heinz family in 1869 at Sharpsburg and moved to the present location in 1889–90. Some of the buildings display remarkable ornamental brickwork. *Location:* Corner of Heinz Street and River Avenue.

E29. Sarah Heinz House (brick and terra cotta), a neighborhood club for boys and girls, was founded by Howard Heinz in 1901. He gave the building in 1914 in honor of his mother, Sarah Young Heinz. The original Heinz home is now at the Henry Ford Museum in Dearborn, Michigan. *Location:* 923 East Ohio Street.

E30. Warhol Museum (brick), in the seven-story Volkwein music building, preserves the work of Pop artist Andy Warhol (1928–1987). Warhol, a graduate of Carnegie Institute of Technology, lived in the Soho section of Pittsburgh. He is famous for his silk-screen prints of such subjects as Marilyn Monroe and Campbell soup cans. The artist also founded *Interview* magazine and produced a number

of films. The museum, sponsored by the Carnegie Museum of Art, the Dia Art Foundation (N.Y.), and the Andy Warhol Foundation for the Visual Arts, is scheduled to open in late 1992. *Location:* Sandusky Street.

F. Pittsburgh: South Side and West End. East Carson Street, together with Allegheny West and Deutsch Town neighborhoods, have been included in the National Register.

F1. Pittsburgh & Lake Erie Railroad Station (brick and terra cotta), now Station Square, was built in 1898–1901 in Beaux Art classical style, designed by William George Burns. On the exterior is a large relief of a moving locomotive, "Number 135." The stained glass skylight is part of the Grand Concourse restaurant. Also incorporated in the building and its former freight station are the Gandy Dancer and other restaurants, offices, including headquarters for the P&LE Railroad, and at least seventy shops. *Location:* South Side, at Smithfield Street Bridge and West Carson Street.

Note: The Transportation Museum, 450 Landmark Building, includes Pittsburgh's first auto, vintage cars, and automobile memorabilia. *Hours:* Tuesday–Saturday, 11 A.M.–4 P.M.; Sunday, 12 noon–8 P.M. Station Square is also the site of an industrial and railroad museum.

F2. Morse Public School (brick), a three-story Victorian building, was erected in 1874 and still contains the original school bell. It now provides apartments and a center for senior citizens. *Location:* 2416 Sarah Street at Twenty-fifth Street.

Note: Holy Assumption of St. Mary Orthodox Church (brick, 1886), originally Russian Orthodox, is at 103 South Nineteenth Street at Sarah Street. The Tabernacle of the Union Baptist Church (brick, 1881), now Pan-Icarian Brotherhood of America, is located at 81 South Nineteenth Street at Sarah Street.

F3. Monongahela Incline, built in 1869–70 and rebuilt in 1882 and 1982, was the first of its kind erected in Pittsburgh. Today it is the oldest operating funicular in the United States. Of the twenty-three original inclines only two remain, this one and the nearby *Duquesne Incline,* built in 1877 (rebuilt of iron in 1888) at 1220 Grandview Avenue (hours: Monday–Saturday, 5:30 A.M.–12:45 A.M.; Sundays and holidays, 7 A.M.–12:45 A.M.). Chartered in 1867, the Monongahela funicular was designed by John J. Endres of Cincinnati, whose daughter Caroline lived at the Monongahela

House and supervised construction. This incline has never had a fatal accident. Originally it was constructed of wood with wire cables made by John Roebling but was later rebuilt with steel. It is 640 feet in length, extending 370 feet above West Carson Street. *Hours:* Monday–Saturday, 5:30 A.M.–12:45 A.M.; Sundays and holidays, 8:45 A.M.–midnight. *Transportation fare. Location:* Mt. Washington. Runs between Grandview Avenue at Wyoming Avenue (top of hill) and West Carson Street near Smithfield Street Bridge.

F4. Chatham Village (brick) has been described as the "first large-scale planned residential community built from the ground up in one operation to be retained in single ownership and managed as a long term investment." It was erected on a forty-five-acre tract of land by the Buhl Foundation; 129 houses were finished in 1932 and 68 in 1936. In recent years the foundation has withdrawn from the venture and houses are sold to individuals. The Bigham house, (brick) built in 1843–44 by Thomas James Bigham, serves as the community center for Chatham Village. *Location:* Mt. Washington, bounded by Bigham and Olympia roads, off Virginia Avenue.

F5. Ninth United Presbyterian Church (brick), built in 1854, was originally the First Associate Reformed Presbyterian Church of Birmingham. It was closed after the church union of 1958. *Location:* South Side, Bingham and South Fourteenth Streets.

F6. South Side Market House (brick) is one of the last two market houses in Pittsburgh, the other being in East Liberty (see *Motor Square Garden*). (A third, the North Side Market, the last to function as such, was taken down for the construction of Allegheny Center.) Built in 1893, the South Side Market House burned about twenty years later and was rebuilt in 1915. It has been a recreation center since 1950. *Location:* South Twelfth and Bingham streets.

F7. St. John the Baptist Ukrainian Catholic Church (brick) was founded in 1891 and built in 1895, with an addition in 1918–19. Its eight turquoise onion domes lend much charm to the otherwise drab landscape of the area. It is the mother church of all Eastern Rite Catholic churches in western Pennsylvania and the oldest church of the Byzantine Rite in the Pittsburgh area. Its first pastor was Gabriel Wyslecki. The parish cemetery is located in Carrick. *Location:* South Side, South Seventh Street at 109 East Carson Street.

F8. Wellersbacher's Hotel (brick), a popular saloon with a fine bar, was built about 1890 by John Wellersbacher. About 1900 it became a club and was purchased in 1918 by Simon Krom, in whose family it has continued ever since. During Prohibition days it was an eating place, becoming a tavern again after repeal. *Location:* South Side, 80 South Tenth Street.

Other noteworthy buildings on the South Side include:

a. Manufacturer's Bank (brick with partial stone facade and iron front), is an impressive corner structure with four stories and a mansard roof. This Second Empire, George III building was erected in the late 1800s. *Location:* 1739 East Carson Street and South Eighteenth Street.

b. St. Casimir's Roman Catholic Church (brick), Lithuanian, is a large corner church where parts of the movie *Dominic and Eugene* were filmed in 1987. *Location:* Sarah Street and South Twenty-second Street.

c. St. Josaphat's Roman Catholic Church (brick), Polish, has a rich, ornate interior with a copper tower. This Romanesque church was designed by architect John T. Comes and dates from 1913–17. *Location:* 2314 Mission and Sterling streets.

d. St. Michael's Roman Catholic Church (brick) is of German descent. The present building was erected in 1861, replacing a "mother church" of the Passionist Fathers built in 1848. Noteworthy features include: a beautiful 100-year-old marble altar from Italy, carved statues from Germany, and a fine covered pulpit reached by a flight of steps. The impressive organ was donated by Andrew Carnegie. St. Michael's Parish is the site of the annual passion play, "Veronica's Veil," which has been produced every year since 1919. (It was first staged at the parish in 1913). Since the 1850s St. Michael's has honored every August the patron St. Roch who, according to tradition, protected the neighborhood from the cholera plague. *Location:* 1–17 Pius Street.

e. St. Paul of the Cross Roman Catholic Monastery (brick) is the home of the Passionist Fathers. In the basement of this church is a crypt museum which houses ancient artifacts and costumes and the remains of some of the early fathers. Founded in 1853, the monastery was built in 1854 and the church in 1859. The architect was Charles Bartberger. *Location:* 148 Monastery Avenue.

f. South Side Presbyterian Church (brick), originally constructed in 1869, was rebuilt in part in 1893. *Location:* Sarah Street and South Twentieth Street.

29

g. Walton Methodist Church (brick) was built in 1882. *Location:* Sarah Street and Twenty-fourth Street.

h. Beck's Run Schoolhouse (frame), the last two-room schoolhouse remaining in the city, was built about 1888. It closed in 1939 and later functioned as an ice cream parlor. The Howard Dower family purchased it in 1954 and in this building they continue to operate a tavern. Much of the original woodwork, shutters, and blackboards are still intact. *Location:* 1000 Beck's Run Road off East Carson Street.

Note: There are enough early noteworthy buildings in South Side to constitute a historic district and preservation area.

F9. Old Stone (or Coates) Tavern was built on the Washington Pike about 1793–1800 by James Coates on land purchased by West Elliot in 1768. According to the *Pittsburgh Chronicle Telegraph* of 1903, there was then an inscription on the north side of the building that read, "Old Stone Tavern, R. Smith." Robert Smith, who was associated with Collins Forge, bought the house from Lemual Miller and operated a tavern here for nearly half a century. The Smiths had kept a store in the old house before the tavern was opened. When they moved, George Schad maintained the inn, followed by other proprietors until the Smith family returned forty years later. The stone house is still operated as a tavern.

The area surrounding the tavern was once known as Temperanceville. When Warden Alexander laid out the town, he made a restriction against buying or selling liquor, but a court soon revoked it. *Location:* West End, 434–36 Greentree Road.

F10. German Church (brick) was constructed in 1864 by a German Reformed group; it now serves a black congregation, the Jerusalem Baptist Church, organized in 1901 and reestablished in 1945. *Location:* West End, Sanctus and Steuben streets.

F11. Fire Hall (brick), built in 1874, has a cast-iron front on the first story. It is now used as a storage facility by the city. *Location:* West End, Sanctus and Steuben streets across from Baptist Church.

F12. Monongahela Valley Steel Mills includes: Jones & Laughlin's Eliza blast furnace, which was demolished despite the efforts of preservationists; U.S. Steel's Homestead Works (1881), where open hearth technology was initiated; Carrie Furnaces in Rankin; the Duquesne Works above Port Perry twin bridges, an 1886 Bessemer converter shop and a blooming mill bought by Andrew Carnegie in 1890 as well as the Dorothy furnace added in 1963 (the Duquesne plant in 1901 purchased National Tube Works of 1870); the Irvin Plant, which began operating in 1938; the Clairton Works, the nation's largest coke plant and producer of coal-based chemicals (originally St. Clair Steel, bought by U.S. Steel in 1902); and the Edgar Thomson plant where Andrew Carnegie had his first steel works, the Braddock mill.

The abandoned mills along the Monongahela River are high priority preservation projects of the recently formed Steel Industry Heritage Task Force which is working toward multifaceted adaptation for the mills and economic development opportunities.

F13. Duquesne Brewery (brick), the only Pittsburgh company which did not join the "beer trust" at the turn of the century, has been vacant since it closed half a century later. It is now the home of Pittsburgh City Theater. *Location:* South Twenty-second and Mary streets.

G. Allegheny Suburban: East

G1. Conrad's Radio Station (brick), now the Wilkinsburg Elks Club, was the site at which Dr. Frank Conrad (1874–1941), assistant chief of engineers at the Westinghouse Corporation, built a small radio receiver to hear time signals from transmitters at Arlington, Va., in 1916. A year later he built a transmitter, station license 8XK, over his garage. In 1917 his facilities were used to test military radio equipment being built at East Pittsburgh for the United States and British governments. The outcome of the experiments was one of the first practical vacuum tube receivers. In 1918 he played phonograph records over the air, and it is reputed that the word *broadcast* was coined at this time. As a result of his work, station KDKA, one of the first commercial radio stations, made its initial scheduled broadcast from a small building on top of the East Pittsburgh plant in 1920—the returns of the Harding-Cox presidential election. *Location:* Wilkinsburg, 7750 Penn Avenue at Peebles Street.

G2. Lincoln Statue (copper) was erected in June 1916 by the schoolchildren of Wilkinsburg. It was purchased by pennies that the students collected and donated. Once stolen, it has been returned to the site. *Location:* Wilkinsburg, Penn Avenue at Belmont Street (bottom of the hill at light).

G3. Graham House (frame) was built at the forks of the road in 1830 by James Graham, pastor of Beulah Presbyterian Church (q.v.). His daughter Mary married Dr. Smith Agnew. She and her brother managed a tavern in this house at one time. *Location:* Wilkinsburg, 2015 Penn Avenue at Greensburg Pike.

G4. Singer House (stone), a Gothic structure, was built in 1865–69 by steel baron John F. Singer (1834–80), a partner in the firm of Singer, Hartman & Company, which later became Singer, Nimick & Company. In the 1860s Singer bought an estate of thirty acres near Wilkinsburg where he made a large ornamental lake. This structure, now apartments, was the home of artist William F. Singer. Near the house was a private chapel, now a garage. *Location:* Wilkinsburg, 1318 Singer Place.

Note: Wilkinsburg Pennsylvania Railroad Station (brick), built in 1916, was designed by Walter H. Cookson. It is located at the busway and railroad tracks off Penn Avenue, at Hay Street and Ross Avenue.

G5. Western Pennsylvania School for the Deaf (brick) was established in a public school building on Short Street in 1869 with fourteen pupils, the first day school for the instruction of the deaf in the United states. In 1870 James Kelly, Esq., donated land for the school in Edgewood and it was chartered the following year. Due to a legal controversy with a railroad company over the land, the school was held in temporary quarters (Turtle Creek Hotel) until resolved. In 1884 a school was built on the present site but it burned down in 1899. The present building was erected in 1901–02 and dedicated in 1903. Architects were Alden & Harlow; contractor George A. Cochrane Co. One of the school's benefactors and historians was Rev. John G. Brown, D.D. *Location:* Edgewood, Walnut Street and Swissvale Avenue.

G6. Edgewood Railroad Station (brick and frame) was built in 1905 by the Pennsylvania Railroad. The last train stopped here in 1964. Adjacent to this building is a small baggage house. In recent years antique shops have occupied both the station and the adjacent baggage house. *Hours:* Monday–Saturday, 11 A.M.–5 P.M. *Location:* Edgewood, 101 East Swissvale and Braddock avenues.

G7. Edgewood Club (stucco) was organized in 1903 as a recreational center for young people. In 1915 it purchased the old C. C. Mellor estate, setting up the present building with a grant from the Carnegie Foundation. Here on November 2, 1920, was held the first radio election party (see *Conrad's Radio Station),* with a makeshift loudspeaker and about thirty members present. It is now the home of the Edgewood (formerly the Wilkinsburg) Orchestra. *Location:* Edgewood, 1 Pennwood Avenue.

G8. Gardner-Bailey House (frame), a one-story Victorian building with a cupola in the center, was built in 1864. *Location:* Edgewood, 124 West Swissvale Avenue.

G9. Beulah Presbyterian Church (brick) was founded in the late 1700s. The early Georgian building, still standing, was erected in 1837. Although it was also called Pitt Township Presbyterian Church, its first name was Bullock Pens, since it was near the site of the commissary of Brig. Gen. John Forbes in his campaign of 1758. Beef cattle were kept here for pasture and slaughtering. At that time Charles Beatty served as chaplain for Forbes. The first recorded sermon was in 1784. Later Samuel Barr preached here, followed by the first regular pastor, James Graham. When he began to serve the congregation in 1804, the name of the church was changed to Beulah. An early cemetery is located around this structure, now used as a chapel, and the 1957 church nearby. *Location:* Churchill, on old US 22 about 3 miles west of Monroeville at Beulah and McCrady roads.

G10. Linhart House (double log) was erected in 1782 and 1794 by Christian Linhart, an early settler whose family owned a sawmill in the Turtle Creek Valley. His daughter, who married into the Metz family, lived in the newer section of the structure. When Indians attacked the area and burned the houses, the family fled to nearby Fort Braddock and their house was spared.

The Linharts' private cemetery is located near Harrison Street, and a memorial park in the area is named for this family. The R. M. Fisher family purchased the Linhart house and built additions to it in 1956, the same year the Century Club erected a historical marker in the front yard. *Location:* Wilkins Township, 221 Farnsworth Avenue, in a residential area.

G11. Riedl Building (brick) is the oldest building in Forest Hills. Built in the early 1900s, this structure was the first business house on Ardmore Boulevard. Originally known as the Bissel Store, it operated as a grocery and general store for many years. At one time the Forest Hills Public Library was housed here. *Location:* Forest Hills, Ardmore Boulevard between Lenox Avenue and Avenue L.

G12. The Westinghouse "Atom Smasher," decommissioned since 1958, was begun in the summer of 1937 and was operating in full by December 1939. At the time of its construction it was the world's largest unit for conducting experiments in the field of nuclear physics. Consisting of a large pear-shaped tank, thirty feet in diameter and forty-seven feet high, it housed an electrostatic tube through which particles were shot to bombard targets. The structure is sixty-five feet high. Its steel shell was constructed by the Chicago Bridge and Iron Company, with Dr. William H. Wells, head of the Westinghouse nuclear physics program at that time, being instrumental in its design. *Location:* Forest Hills, off US 30 at Westinghouse plant.

G13. McLaughlin House (log) is reputed to have been constructed in 1775 (deed dates back to 1784) by Edward McLaughlin, who came to America from Ireland at the age of twelve. After living at Fort Pitt, he and his wife Nancy (Wade) moved to this location, taking up a land grant of 236 acres called "Groton," where their nine children were born. The house was later owned by their son Edward, followed by their grandson J. W. McLaughlin, whose daughter married John W. Jackson. After the Jacksons lived here, their son A. Ivory Jackson owned it. He deeded it to the Girl Scouts but continues to reside in the neighboring frame house built in 1869. The log house, named "Tapawingo" by the scouts, is situated in a scenic meadow surrounded by trees and a stream. *Location:* Penn Hills, near Unity. From junction of Universal and Meadow avenues, follow Meadow to Pike Street and continue until road ends at barn. Cabin is nearby.

G14. Wilson House (painted brick) was built in 1860 by George Wilson. According to H. C. Bell (in Warner's history), Thomas Wilson resided in Penn Township in 1770 on Wilson's Mount, had a land patent in 1788, and moved to Fort Pitt in 1776. *Location:* Penn Hills, corner of Frankstown Road and Wilson Lane, house no. 11003.

G15. Schiller House (brick and log), with curtain chimneys, has been owned by the Bishops, the Owens, the Niesleins, and finally the Gerthoffers, who still occupy it. The log kitchen section was built about 1820, and the brick part around 1840. The original spring-house is in the basement. *Location:* Penn Hills, 123 Faybern Road.

G16. Penn Hebron Garden Club Barn was built in 1834 of hand-hewn oak constructed with pegs. The structure is situated on a land grant known as "The Flying Shuttle" on the H. S. Morrow farm. In 1928 it was purchased by the garden club. *Location:* Penn Hills, Jefferson Road.

Note: The 1819 Morrow log house is at 11401 Frankstown Road.

G17. Wyckoff-Mason House was built of chestnut logs in 1774–75. The land was originally part of a land grant to George Duffield and two others. Duffield deeded a portion of the land to Peter Wyckoff, who built the present house. In 1960 the Mason family purchased it. *Location:* Penn Hills, 6133 Verona Road.

Note: The Isaac Blackadore brick house was built about 1860 at 1235 Blackadore Avenue.

G18. Bartman House (log) was built in 1820 with random plank pegged floors and hand-hewn beams. *Location:* Penn Hills, 726 Hamill Road.

G19. Sri Venkateswara Temple (stuccoed masonry) was built in 1976–79 for $925,000. A Hindu cultural center and religious institution, it was modeled after the Tirupathi shrine in south India (seventh-century architecture) and built with the support and help of 6,000 Hindus from around the United States, most of them immigrants from India seeking ties with their mother culture. The temple is dedicated to Lord Venkateswara (known in India as Balaji, Govinda, Vishnu, or Krishna). One builder who continues to maintain the building is Ayyachamy S. Narayanan. Open for tours: Monday–Friday, 10:30 A.M.–12 noon and 4–5:30 P.M.; Saturday and Sunday, 4–5:30 P.M. *Location:* Penn Hills, South McCully Road which is off Thompson Run Road near its junction with Old William Penn Highway (McCrady Road); can be seen from Parkway (US 22–SR 0376).

G20. Lehner Livery Stable (stone) has name Joseph Lehner carved on a huge lintel above a double-hung front door. It was established in 1890 and is one of western Pennsylvania's few remaining liveries. It used to house horses and carriages for the river trade along the Allegheny. *Location:* Verona, next to 54 Penn Street, between the river and the railroad tracks.

G21. Second Presbyterian Church (brick), a one-story structure with a rubble stone foundation, was built in 1896. It still retains its wooden ceiling and one of its original windows. This architectural gem was fortunately saved from demolition when a former owner's plans to replace it with a car wash did not materialize. For the last sixteen years the building has been used for a furniture and design business, owned by Barbara Davis. *Location:* Verona, 625 Allegheny River Boulevard.

G22. Plum Creek Presbyterian Church (brick) was built in 1867–79. The congregation first worshiped at this site in 1791. About 1810 a log meetinghouse was erected, followed by a brick church in the 1850s. *Location:* Plum Borough, 550 New Texas Road.

Note: Logans Ferry Presbyterian Church (frame) was founded in 1854 and the present building was erected in 1856. First meetings were held in homes until the Logan family donated land for a church. Alexander Logan also purchased a tract nearby in 1803 and operated a ferry and an inn. *Location:* Logans Ferry, on Logans Ferry Road and SR 0909.

G23. Globe Powder Storage Building (stone), over eighty feet long, was built along Plum Creek about one hundred years ago. At one time there were five buildings here, one of which blew up. This property was owned by a coal company. (The Plum Creek branch of the Penn Central Railroad, established in 1872, ran alongside this structure. It hauled passengers and freight between Unity and Verona.) The building is now a residence and office of the Kirkpatrick trailer park. *Location:* Plum Borough, 1741 Hulton Road near East Oakmont.

Note: Nearby at 1831 Hulton Road is a restored early log house, partially burned in 1976.

G24. Laird Cemetery contains burials dating back to the early 1800s including Col. Hugh Davidson, a soldier and Indian trader. *Location:* Plum Borough, SR 0380 and New Texas Road.

G25. Rising Sun Stagecoach Tavern (frame) was the first stagecoach stop on the Northern Pike east of Pittsburgh. Across the road where a floral shop now stands is the site of the stable where horses were changed. The tavern was built in 1833 by Abraham Taylor, who operated an inn here. It was later occupied by the innkeeper's daughter and her husband, George Washington Warner.

There are fireplaces in every room and hand-hewn logs in the basement.

The community where the inn is located was named for Joel Monroe, the first postmaster in 1857. It was formerly called Patton Township and became a borough in 1951. *Location:* Monroeville, 3835 Northern Pike near junction with US 22.

Note: A stone earthen-bed bridge built about 1860 is just off old US 22 near Beatty Road.

G26. Cross Roads (Old Stone) Church, originally associated with Beulah Presbyterian Church (q.v.) in Churchill, was constructed in 1896–97 partly from stones of an earlier building. The congregation was organized in 1836 by Revs. Francis Laird and James Graham when a group of Beulah members left their church. The first regular pastor was S. M. McClung. The adjacent cemetery was donated by the Snodgrass and Monroe families. Andrew Mellon (the immigrant) and his family joined this church after breaking with an early Covenanter church near Export (see *Mellon House,* Westmoreland County). In 1969 T. M. Sylves purchased the church property and deeded it to the borough of Monroeville for their historical society and museum headquarters. *Location:* Monroeville, Center Road at Stroschein Road and Northern Pike.

G27. McGinley House (stone) was built in 1804 by James McGinley. This landmark, once owned by the Westinghouse Corporation, was turned over to the Monroeville Historical Society to be restored as a museum. *Location:* Monroeville, on McGinley Road off Greensburg Pike, next to Westinghouse Atomic Power headquarters.

Note: An oak tree nearly 300 years old is located close to an early log house in Monroeville, near the entrance to Beechwood Park on Northwestern Drive.

G28. Graham House (log), built between 1800 (reportedly 1805) and 1830, is a two-story log house preserved in an area in which most early buildings have been demolished. It retains its original stone arch fireplace. *Location:* Monroeville, Ramsey Road.

G29. Carpenter House (log), called Boyce Park House, was built in 1820. It was moved to this location in the 1980s and rebuilt by Brad Mooney of Heritage Restorations, Kittanning. Some of the logs are from the Dible log house that was originally in Murrysville. It is administered by the Foothills Historical Society. *Location:* Monroeville, Boyce Park, Pierson Run Road.

G30. Boyce House Site was the birthplace of William D. Boyce, born June 16, 1858. Inspired by the good turn of an English Scout, Boyce brought the scouting movement to the United States and helped make possible the incorporation of the Boy Scouts in Washington, D.C., on February 8, 1910. Although the house no longer exists, the visitor can see remains of a barn and other outbuildings near a deserted farmhouse. *Location:* 2 miles southeast of New Kensington, dirt road right off SR 0366. After a mile on this route, turn left at yellow brick house. At end of lane (0.25 mile) turn right off Old Leechburg Road. Continue about 200 yards on disused road. Foundation on left. Other old ruins are located in woods on right, near site of Boyce house.

Note: Nearby on Packsaddle Road off SR 0366 is a barn, 100 years old or more, adapted for a summer theater ("Sherwood Forest") more than twenty-five years ago by the De Simone family.

G31. Westinghouse Air Brake General Office Building and Museum (sandstone and brick) dates back to 1890, when its first section was built. Destroyed by fire in 1896, it was reconstructed in 1896–97. The new wing of early French Renaissance architecture was added in 1928. The older building is of Richardsonian Romanesque style. A clock is located in the tower overlooking the town. Known as "the Castle," this early building since 1985 has been the headquarters for the American Production & Inventory Control Society (APICS) which has opened a Westinghouse Museum in the building. Among the memorabilia are personal items from George Westinghouse's Homewood mansion. *Location:* Wilmerding, Station Street.

G32. George Westinghouse Memorial Bridge, built in 1930–32, is constructed entirely of reinforced concrete, and at the time of its erection the center span was the longest reinforced concrete arch in the country. It is a five-span bridge of the double-ribbed type. *Location:* North Versailles Township, over Turtle Creek on US 30.

G33. Wallace-Nasor House (quarried stone) was built after 1790 by James Irwin, who deeded 232 acres of his estates called "Vernon" and "Newry" to George Miller in 1805. The land was warranted in 1787, surveyed in 1789, patented in 1824, and later owned by James Michael, William Wallace,

Mary Lang, and Fred Nasor, in succession. The three-bay house contains six rooms and originally had double porches. Later called "Pickup Farm," the property also features a springhouse. The house overlooks Turtle Creek Valley. *Location:* Near Pitcairn, on Moss Side Boulevard (SR 0048), 1.9 mile south of SR 0130 (North Versailles Township).

H. McKeesport, White Oak

H1. Early Stone House was built around 1830 of temple-style Greek Revival, a small one-story residence. *Location:* 4232 Walnut Street at Versailles borough line.

H2. One-Room Schoolhouse (frame) was the first school in McKeesport. It was built in 1832 in the First Ward market area, prior to state public schools and moved to this park setting in the 1940s. Operated by McKeesport Heritage Center, a restoration project. Open by appointment. It is also open during holidays and for the Festival of Trees prior to Christmas. *Location:* Renziehausen Park, Tulip and Arboretum streets.

H3. McKeesport-Versailles Cemetery Gateway (stone) is a fine triple-arched structure, believed to have been dedicated in 1856 (possibly later). *Location:* 1608 Fifth Avenue.

H4. St. Sava Church (brick), originally built in 1904, was the first Serbian Orthodox church organized in the eastern part of the United States. The present church was erected in 1950. (See *Shadeland,* Crawford County.) *Location:* McKeesport, 901 Hartman Street.

H5. St. Mary's Russian Orthodox Greek Catholic Church (white brick), with colorful blue onion domes, was built in 1918. An outstanding ethnic church of the area. *Location:* Shaw Avenue and Locust Street.

H6. McKeesport National Bank (brick and stone), now Three Rivers Bank, was built in the 1890s. *Location:* Fifth and Sinclair streets.

H7. Carnegie Library (stone), in Richardsonian style including turret design, was built in 1902. William J. East was the architect. *Location:* Library and Union streets.

H8. Borland-Jones House (brick) was built in 1831. It has a signature stone bearing the inscription, "JA & NR 1831." *Location:* White Oak Borough, 2683 McClintock Road.

H9. Muse Homestead (stone), built around 1820 with additions in 1824 and 1910, is restored as a museum in White Oak Regional Park. A plaque at the entrance reads:

Original site of blockhouse built by an area settler as protection from Indians. The patent was acquired in 1788 by one of the builders, Adam Reburn, and became known as "Fort Reburn." Reburn's 218 and 3/4 acre homestead Galilee, was purchased in 1834 by John Jones Muse, Esq. in whose family it remained until it became part of the Allegheny Regional Parks System in 1967. Muse was a son of the American Revolution. Erected in 1972 by Queen Alliquippa Chap. D.A.R., McKeesport.

Location: McKeesport, White Oak Regional Park, 4222 Third Street.
Note: A nearby white oak tree nearly 300 years old marks Maj. Gen. Braddock's 1755 camp site. Franklin Street, in White Oak.

I. Munhall, Homestead, Braddock

I1. Hungarian Reformed Church (brick), with a date stone reading "Magyar Reformatus Templom 1904" is built in eclectic temple-style Greek Revival with a spire and Gothic windows. *Location:* Munhall, Dickson Street and Tenth Avenue.

I2. St. John's Greek Catholic Church (stone and brick), now a Ruthenian rite church, was built in 1903. *Location:* Munhall, Dickson Street and Tenth Avenue, across from Hungarian Church.

I3. Kostol St. Michael (brick), known as the Steelworkers' Church, was built in 1925 and dedicated two years later. The original Slovak church, erected in 1897 on Third and Dickson streets, was moved to this location in 1909 where it was reassembled. The present church, which replaced the original, is a large impressive building with a colorful tile and brick facade. The figure of St. Joseph the Worker which tops the campanile and looks over the steel mills of the valley was designed by Pittsburgh sculptor Frank Vittor. The statue depicts the patron saint as an ordinary worker with his sleeves rolled up and a hammer in his hand. Under his feet are sculptured flames rising from three crucibles (representing Pittsburgh's rivers) pouring molten steel into a globe which forms the vase. This aluminum (part stainless steel) monument was cast in Rome and blessed by Bishop Wright in St. Peter's Square, arriving via the SS *Paola Costa* from Naples, Italy. It was erected in

1966 and is lit up each night. *Location:* Munhall, Ninth Avenue and Library Place.
Note: Also in Munhall is the historic Bost Building, headquarters for the 1892 Homestead steel strike.

I4. Carnegie Library of Homestead (brick) was built in 1898, a gift of Andrew Carnegie. It includes a music hall (capacity 1,050) in its east wing and in its west wing an athletic center with a pool, gym, and club meeting rooms. *Location:* Munhall, 510 Tenth Avenue, at Homestead borough line.

I5. St. Markus Church (brick) was built in 1892. It is now owned by the adjacent United Presbyterian Church. This old German Evangelical Protestant Church is probably the last of the "rooster churches" in the Pittsburgh area. Years ago the early churches of this sect often placed a rooster at the top of their spire to taunt Roman Catholics with the fact that St. Peter, the first pope, had been reminded of his duty by the crowing of a rooster. *Location:* Homestead, Ninth Street near Ann Street.

I6. Railroad Station (brick) is a fine structure with a red tile roof. This building originally served the Pittsburgh, McKeesport, and Youghiogheny Railroad, a branch of the Pittsburgh & Lake Erie Railroad. *Location:* Homestead, Amity Street and East Sixth Avenue near Browns Hill Bridge.

I7. St. Mary Magdalene Roman Catholic Church (stone and brick) was built in 1895. Frederick C. Sauer was the architect. The building displays his imaginative use of patterned brick design. *Location:* Homestead, East Tenth Avenue and Amity Street.

I8. Mesta House (brick) was built at the turn of the century for George Mesta, founder of the Mesta Machine Company which manufactured steel mill machinery until 1983. *Location:* West Homestead, 540 Doyle Avenue.

I9. Braddock Carnegie Free Library (stone), in Richardsonian style, was the first of Carnegie's libraries in the United States. It was built in 1888−89 with William Halsey Wood as the architect. The community center annex was constructed in 1893 with Longfellow, Alden, & Harlow, architects. In later years it was adapted for use as a theater. *Location:* Braddock, 419 Library Street and Parker Avenue.

I10. Schwab House (stone), of Richardsonian Romanesque style, was built in 1890–93. From 1889 to 1892 Charles Schwab, superintendent of Andrew Carnegie's Edgar Thomson Works, lived here in this company house, built on a hill overlooking the Monongahela River and its mills. *Location:* North Braddock, 541 Jones Avenue.

I11. Kennywood Park, founded in 1898 with later additions, has a baroque carousel which was originally erected for the Philadelphia Sesquicentennial in 1926. This National Historic Landmark was originally Kenny's Grove at the end of the Monongahela Trolley Car Company line. The park setting continues its early tradition of beautiful gardens and walkways. *Location:* West Mifflin, 4800 Kennywood Boulevard.

J. Allegheny Suburban: West and Northwest

J1. Mansfield Brown House (stone), reputedly Carnegie's oldest home, was constructed in 1822 by Mansfield Brown. In 1842 James Brown and Col. M. B. Brown occupied the building. (The colonel's son Robert, who also lived here at one time, later moved to the mansion site now occupied by Carnegie Library on Beechwood Avenue.) The house has a cavelike structure in the rear, where a "moonshine" still operated during Prohibition days. In 1825 Rev. Joseph Kerr started one of the first seminaries here. In the early 1900s it was a girls' school, later it was made into apartments, and at present it is privately owned. *Location:* Carnegie, 602 Poplar Way.

J2. Andrew Carnegie Free Library (brick), built in 1899, contains a music hall and a Civil War memorial room. Struthers and Hannah were the architects. *Location:* Carnegie, 300 Beechwood Avenue.

J3. Obey House (frame) was built in 1823 by John Robinson. This old tavern on the Steubenville Pike was later remodeled with a larger addition. According to tradition, Henry Clay played a fiddle and danced here. Other famous guests included Andrew Jackson and Sam Houston. *Location:* Crafton, at Steuben and Obey streets.

J4. St. Philip's Roman Catholic Mass House (log with brick and weatherboarding) was built by a Mr. Flannigan and used for mass before the first church, named for Philip Smith who donated the land, was erected in 1839. (The site of this old church is near the crucifix in the St. Philip's cemetery at Crafton Avenue and Steuben Street, next to the present church.) The house, moved to its new location nearby, was where priests from St. Patrick's Church in Pittsburgh came to conduct mass. *Location:* Crafton, 37 Norma Street near St. Philip's Roman Catholic Church.

J5. Frew-Goran-McFall House (stone and brick) was built before 1800 by John Frew with an 1840 Greek Revival addition (brick). A springhouse on the property has been rebuilt. *Location:* Oakwood, 105 Sterret Place (off Poplar Street, which is off Noblestown Road).

J6. Dixmont State Hospital was the first institution for the mentally ill to be established in Pittsburgh and one of the first in America. Its oldest structure, the administration building, was completed in 1861, after the cornerstone was laid on July 19, 1859. It still contains some of the original furnishings and has an exterior iron-filigree balcony.

Dixmont was founded with the encouragement of Dorothea L. Dix, who selected the site overlooking the Ohio River, and the property was purchased through private and public funds. It began as the mental department of the Western Pennsylvania Hospital and after a series of name changes became Dixmont State Hospital on October 1, 1945. Among the notable people associated with the institution at its founding were Thomas Bakewell, John Bissell, F. R. Brunot, W. M. Darlington, John Herron, John Holmes, John Irwin, George W. Jackson, Governor William F. Johnston, James McCandless, E. W. H. Schenley, and J. H. Shoenberger. No longer a hospital, the property is now used for housing. Old Reed Hall is still standing. *Location:* Kilbuck Township, at Hazelwood Avenue.

K. Sewickley Area

K1. Alexander Hayes House (brick), Italianate and Second Empire style, was built around 1862 on land owned in 1805 by Henry Pratt. James Park, Osborn's first settler, owned this land in 1840. Alexander Hayes, one owner, was a descendant of Gen. Alexander Hayes who built the Baptist church in Leetsdale. *Location:* Osborne, 1440 Beaver Road, on Lantern Lane, on the Ohio River.

K2. Old Post Office (stone) is a regional cultural complex consisting of the Sweetwater Art Center and the Sewickley Valley Historical Society. The 1910 neoclassical building by

James Knox Taylor was renovated in 1987. *Location:* Sewickley, Broad and Bank streets.

K3. Garrison-Miller House (brick and stone) is one of the area's oldest Greek Revival houses. It is believed that local brickmaker John Garrison built it about 1858. *Location:* Sewickley, 503 Broad Street.

K4. "Fame" (marble and sandstone), a Civil War monument in Sewickley Cemetery, is the only statue in the Sewickley area. Created by sculptor Isaac Broome in 1866, it commands a prominent location on the hillside overlooking Sewickley and the Ohio River. *Location:* Sewickley, above Broad and Hopkins streets.

K5. Sewickley Municipal Building (brick), built in 1911 with an addition in 1984, was designed by Charles W. Bier in Beaux Arts, Georgian style. Its tower provides space for the fire department to dry its hoses. *Location:* Sewickley, Chestnut and Thorn streets.

K6. Sewickley Presbyterian Church (stone), of Gothic Revival design by J. W. Kerr, was built in 1859–61. Before the sanctuary could be dedicated it was taken over for the training of local troops during the Civil War. Rutan & Russell replaced the (1864) chapel in 1914 with a Tudor parish hall. J. Phillip Davis was the architect of the Chapel of the Resurrection (1953), incorporated into the main building. Another section, the Children's Chapel (1956), was given by the James Barr Haines family in memory of their son, Bruce McKinnon Haines. It contains a famous stained glass window which the Sunday school class of 1871 dedicated in an earlier chapel. It was purchased with funds from a play they produced starring Ethelbert Nevin, who became America's foremost composer at the turn of the century. Windows in other parts of the chapel and church are dedicated to members of his family as well as to many others. The window in the west transept was made by Howard G. Wilbert of the Pittsburgh Stained Glass Studios. *Location:* Sewickley, Beaver and Grant streets.

K7. Zorn-Miller House (brick and stone) was built around 1840–50. *Location:* Sewickley, 503 Broad Street.

K8. Flatiron Building (brick) was built around 1875, a fine commercial building with a mansard roof. Its unusual shape is the result of two early land surveys. *Location:* Sewickley, Beaver and Division streets.

K9. St. Stephen's Episcopal Church (stone), of Romanesque and Gothic design by Bartberger & East, was constructed in 1894 and enlarged in 1911 (Alden & Harlow, architects). The parish was organized in 1863 and chartered in 1864. In 1863–64 a small frame church designed by the rector, William F. Ten Boeck, was built by the congregation and later replaced with the present structure. The adjacent Christy House (1862) was built in Gothic Revival style for patent attorney George H. Christy. Today it is used by the church as a tea room (Frederick Avenue and Walnut Street). *Location:* Sewickley, Broad Street and Frederick Avenue.

K10. Frederick Way House (frame) is the home of the famous riverboat pilot and author, Capt. Frederick Way, Jr., whose great-grandfather was Abishai Way (see *Abishai Way House*). Frederick was the pilot of the *Betsy Ann* and the *Liberty,* the last two packet boats to run on the western rivers. He has written numerous books about riverboats and related subjects, and was editor of the *Inland River Record* for many years. *Location:* Sewickley, 121 River Avenue.

K11. Lees House (log), built between 1810 and 1830, is owned by Justin Lees. Nearby on Audubon Road is another log structure belonging to Lees. *Location:* Sewickley, Barberry Road off Blackburn Road.

K12. Ogden House (brick), of Greek Revival architecture with Georgian influence, was built around the 1820s. It is reported that the first lady of the house danced with Lafayette when he visited Pittsburgh and was welcomed by her father John Snowden, then Pittsburgh's mayor. Charles Stotz restored this house in the 1930s. Ralph Griswold designed the gardens. *Location:* Sewickley, 424 Beaver Road.

K13. German Evangelical Lutheran Church (brick), one story with an octagonal cupola, was built in 1868. *Location:* Near Sewickley in Franklin Park Borough, Brandt School Road.

K14. Thomas Leet Shields Homestead (brick), of Greek Revival style, was built in 1850–54 by Maj. Daniel Leet's grandson. Still in the Shields family, the house contains the signatures of several family members scratched by a diamond on the pane of a dining-room window. The architect was Joseph W. Kerr. *Location:* Edgeworth, 436 Beaver Road.

K15. Abishai Way House (brick), of Federal design with bull's-eye windows, was built in 1838 by Abishai Way, a successful Pittsburgh merchant and business agent for the Harmony Society (see also *Harmony,* Butler County). This house is sometimes mistakenly referred to as the Nicholas Way home (see *Way Tavern*). It was later purchased by W. L. Jones, followed by Campbell Hall. *Location:* Edgeworth, 108 Beaver Road.

K16. Way Tavern (painted brick) was built in 1810 by Squire John Way and enlarged in 1820. It was operated as an inn called the "Sewickley House." John's sons were Abishai, Nicholas, who later owned this house, and James, a riverboat captain. The Walker family purchased the property at a later date. It was rebuilt after a fire in 1841. *Location:* Edgeworth, Quaker and Beaver roads.

K17. Newington (brick), a large Greek Revival house in two sections, was constructed by David Shields in 1816–23 on depreciation land acquired by his father-in-law, Daniel Leet, a major in the Revolution. In 1825 the house became the post office of Sewickley Bottom and was modernized in 1959 by J. Judson Brooks, a descendant of Shields. In 1910 Bryant Fleming designed an addition. The gardens were designed by Samuel Parsons in the 1870s. The Shields brick schoolhouse dates back to 1826. *Location:* Edgeworth, Shields Lane and Beaver Road.

K18. Black-Morgan House (frame) was built around 1890. It was designed by Longfellow, Alden & Harlow for real estate broker Samuel Black. The house is an exact copy of the Thorp House in Cambridge, Mass., built in 1886 by architect Alexander Longfellow for his cousin Annie, the daughter of poet Henry Wadsworth Longfellow. *Location:* Edgeworth, 433 Maple Lane.

K19. "Old Edgeworth" (painted brick), of Greek Revival and Edwardian Georgian architecture, was built in 1835 on part of the former Shields estate. Mrs. Mary Olver had established the Edgeworth Female Seminary (which was named for novelist Maria Edgeworth) at Braddock's Field and moved it to East Pittsburgh in 1825. In 1836 she relocated her school in this house. At the time of Mrs. Olver's death in 1842 the seminary closed but reopened in 1846. The two frame wings of the house were destroyed by fire in 1865, thus closing the school permanently. The central section later became the residence of Mor-

K19. "Old Edgeworth"

rison Foster, brother of Stephen C. Foster; it was subsequently occupied by J. Wilkinson Elliott, an architect who enlarged and remodeled it with a large portico that faces Beaver Road. *Location:* Edgeworth, 420 Oliver Road (street name misspelled from Olver).

K20. Shields Presbyterian Church (stone), a fine one-story structure, was built in 1868–69 in Gothic style. *Location:* Edgeworth, Church Lane and Beaver Road.

Note: The Shields Family Mausoleum (stone), a one-story structure built in 1893–94 in Richardsonian Romanesque style, is a noteworthy landmark in western Pennsylvania. It is located to the left of the church.

K21. Vineacre (Nevin House) (brick), built in 1850 and remodeled in 1916, was the home of Pittsburgh editor Robert P. Nevin and the birthplace of Ethelbert W. Nevin (1862–1901), famous Pittsburgh composer of "Mighty Lak a Rose," "The Rosary," "Narcissus," and other well-known works. Ethelbert lived here for years, and thirty-seven years after his death, his widow insisted that his body be disinterred from its burial place in Sewickley, overlooking the Ohio River, and taken to Blue Hill, Maine. *Location:* Edgeworth, Beaver Road, off Ohio River Boulevard.

K22. "Braeburn" (frame), built in the late 1800s and designed by architect J. Wilkinson Elliott, was the home of the Slack family for years, and later belonged to a descendant, John C. Slack and his wife Margaret. Neighbors of the Nevin family, they often invited Ethelbert Nevin to play their grand piano for private concerts for their guests. This beautiful house retains its original wood paneling. The music room has an elevated stage where the Pittsburgh Orchestra, under the direction

K21. Vineacre

K27. Leet's Tavern

of Victor Herbert, used to play in the 1890s. *Location:* Edgeworth, 413 Woodland Avenue and Beaver Road.

K23. Andrew Bayne Memorial Library (brick), in Victorian Italianate style, was built around 1860. It was named for an Allegheny sheriff. Bayne's daughters, Jayne Bayne Teece and Amanda Bayne Balph, donated this family property to the borough. *Hours:* Monday–Thursday, 12 noon–8 P.M.; Friday and Saturday, 12 noon–6 P.M. Closed Saturdays in July and August. *Location:* Bellevue, South Balph Avenue and Bayne Street.

Note: Bayne Park, nearby, has one of the oldest elm trees in Pennsylvania.

K24. Mt. Nebo School (frame) is a one-room schoolhouse with a steeple. *Location:* Ohio Township, 701 Mt. Nebo Road, 1.5 miles west of Mt. Nebo Church.

K25. Railroad Station (brick), now a travel agency. *Location:* Leetsdale, T 65 at Ferry Street.

K26. D. T. Watson Home (brick) was owned by David T. Watson, one of Pittsburgh's greatest lawyers, who willed it at his death as a home for crippled children. It is an important rehabilitation center, which now includes several other buildings. *Location:* Leetsdale, Camp Meeting Road.

K27. Leet's Tavern (Lark Inn) (stone) was built about 1800 by Maj. Daniel Leet, brother of the William Leet who founded Leetsdale in 1796. In 1776 Daniel was commissioned deputy surveyor for Augusta County, Va., and after the Revolution, Pennsylvania authorized him to survey donation and depreciation lands in western Pennsylvania. *Location:*

Leetsdale, Leet Township, 634 Beaver Road (SR 0065) at Winding Road.

Note: Near this old tavern is a fine springhouse.

K28. Leetsdale Baptist Church (stone) was built between 1850 and 1860 by Gen. Alexander Hays, who was killed in the Civil War in 1863 at the battle of the Wilderness, while leading a group that included the Sixty-third Pennsylvania Regiment, which he had recruited at the opening of the war. *Location:* Beaver Avenue almost at Ambridge line.

L. Ohio River: Left Bank Area

L1. Shouse House (brick), an eight-bay house in Greek Revival style dating from around 1840 that is now the Gavlik Construction Company office, was built and occupied by Peter Shouse, founder of Shousetown (now Glenwillard) and the Shousetown boatyard. Here over eighty steamboats were built and launched into the Ohio River. Nearby is a two-ton Vermont granite monument bearing the likeness of the *Great Republic,* a sidewheel steamboat built in 1866. At the northern end of Main Street is the relocated Shousetown Cemetery surrounded by a stone wall. *Location:* Shousetown (Glenwillard), 451 Main Street off SR 0051 (McGovern Boulevard), which is intersected by Spring Run Road and Riverview Road.

L2. Sweeney House (dressed stone) was built in 1820. *Location:* Ohio Township, 480 Gene Drive (near Roosevelt Road).

L3. Hyeholde is a labor of love designed and built by William and Clara Kryskill during the Depression and completed in 1937. Operated as a restaurant by the Kryskills until 1974, this rustic, charming structure was constructed with materials from the old Stonesifer barn on the Steubenville Pike, which in turn had been fashioned from timbers cut in Westmoreland County and floated down the Monongahela and Ohio rivers on rafts. Scenes depicting Chaucer's *Canterbury Tales* were sketched by the innkeeper on the interior walls (later replaced by prints). A large walk-in fireplace is located in the main dining room, which also has unique stained glass windows. Directly in front of this building is another stone house that Kryskill constructed for one of his daughters. The book *Hyeholde*, written by the builder, gives a step-by-step account of the inn's construction and history. *Location:* Coraopolis, 0.5 mile north of Greater Pittsburgh Airport, 192 Hyeholde Drive off Coraopolis Heights Road.

L4. Pittsburgh & Lake Erie Railroad Station (brownstone and brick), in Richardsonian Romanesque style, was built in 1895. The architects were Rutan & Coolidge of Boston. *Location:* Coraopolis, Neville Avenue and Mill Street.

L5. Sharon Community Presbyterian Church (frame) was organized in 1817. Its first brick church was dedicated on October 7, 1828, in the village of Sharon, later called Carnot. Its first pastor was Andrew McDonald. In 1868–69 the present large frame building was erected with construction costs that amounted to $8,000, and services were held here until 1965 when a modern sanctuary was built next to it. The old structure is used for youth programs and a nursery school. *Location:* Moon Township, 522 Carnot Road off junction of SR 0051 and Beaver Grade Road.

L6. Beggs House (stone), one story, was built in 1835. It is the oldest house in the area. *Location:* Moon Township, SR 0051 at Pittsburgh & Lake Erie Railroad.

L7. Settler's Cabin Park, owned and maintained by the county, is the location of two notable early structures.

    a. Walker-Ewing House (log), the settler's cabin for which the park was named, has been restored. It was built in the late eigh-teenth century reportedly by John Henry. In 1785 Isaac and Gabriel Walker acquired the land. Isaac's daughter and son-in-law William Ewing owned the site in 1816. The Ewings' son, J. Nelson Ewing, lived here in 1843 with his wife. *Location:* North Fayette Township, on SR 3045 (Noblestown Road), northeast of Oakdale. Follow signs to settler's cabin.

    b. Ewing-Glass House (frame) was erected in 1855 by J. Nelson Ewing after he had moved from the log cabin. It was later occupied by his grandson, E. W. Glass. *Location:* North Fayette Township, Box 435, on SR 3045.

L8. Noblestown United Presbyterian Church (frame and shingle) was built in 1852–53 and was originally called the "Meeting House," the "Old Seceder," or the "Associate Presbyterian Church." *Location:* Noblestown, Mill Street off SR 3048.

Note: Noblestown was founded in the late 1700s by Col. Henry Noble, owner of a log mill near this site.

L9. Noble-DeVesse House (brick), built around 1840–50 by the Noble family, has five bays, double brackets at its eaves, and a Greek Revival doorway. It is situated high on a hill overlooking the town. *Location:* Noblestown, Mill Street just off Noblestown Road at the Presbyterian church.

L10. Dunlevy-Campbell House (stone) was built in 1814. An oval stone in one gable bears the date. An old barn and springhouse with a log loft above it are also on the property. A later owner, James E. Campbell, lived here all his life. *Location:* North Fayette Township, Box 162, on SR 0978 (on side of hill looking into valley, approached by winding dirt road and hidden from highway).

L11. North Star Hotel (brick), built about 1840, was once known as the Andrew W. Crooks farm. It was purchased by John Walker in 1857. In 1914 it became the property of the present owner, who has operated it ever since as a hotel-tavern. It is situated near the village of Santiago (named for a coal company), which was once called Tyre and also North Star (for a railroad station). *Location:* 2 miles east of Imperial, on old US 22, near Santiago.

L12. Mann's Hotel (frame), built in 1803 or before, is the oldest existing trading post in Western Pennsylvania still operating as a tavern. In the basement of this early relic is a jail, accessible through a trap door. The building

L12. Mann's Hotel

has been in the Bryan family, followed in more recent years by the Manns. *Location:* McKees Rocks, 23 Chartiers Street.

Note: This area, an old Delaware Indian town, was the site Christopher Gist selected for settlement for the Ohio Company, but George Washington chose the forks of the rivers instead. (The largest burial mound in Pennsylvania, dating from 1,000–300 B.C. the Early and Middle Woodland Period, used to be located at McKees Rocks.)

M. Allegheny Suburban: North

M1. St. Nicholas Church (brick), a Latin Rite Catholic church, was built in 1900 by a Croatian parish and remodeled with twin towers (after a fire) in 1922. The interior contains some interesting murals called *Life in the Old Country,* painted by Maximilian Vanka in 1937, along with a more recent group on American experiences. During the painting of the early series, Vanka claimed that he saw a ghost appear repeatedly in the church. *Location:* Millvale, 24 Maryland Avenue.

M2. Wilkins House (fieldstone) was erected before 1826 with a late Georgian fanlighted door and a subsequent frame addition. This property was part of a 230-acre tract of land marked "No. 1 of the Jones District Depreciation Land" granted to John Wilkins. A deed of 1826 confirms that two houses stood on the property at the time. *Location:* Millvale Borough, 144 Evergreen Street.

M3. Chalfant House (frame with aluminum siding), of Greek Revival design, belonged at one time to the Chalfant family and was moved to this location at an earlier date. The house at present is occupied by a women's club. *Location:* Etna Borough, 89 Locust Street.

M4. Shaw House (brick) was built in 1824–26 by Thomas Wilson Shaw, operator of a sickle factory on nearby Pine Creek. His father, John Shaw, who owned a blacksmith shop at the Point in Pittsburgh, had bought a 600-acre tract of land from John Wilkins, Jr., and in 1802 he built his five-bay, two-story frame house (recently well restored) south of the creek at 1021 Glenshaw Avenue, corner of Old Butler Plank Road. John Shaw and his sons operated an industrial complex, including the sickle factory, a gristmill, a coal mine, a sawmill, a brick factory, and others. The brick house was recently sold by members of the Shaw family. *Location:* Glenshaw, 1526 Old Butler Plank Road.

M5. Glenshaw Valley Presbyterian Church (frame), one story, with a tower and belfry, was built in 1885. A fine, picturesque church. *Location:* Glenshaw, Old Butler Plank Road.

M6. Kirk House (frame) was built in 1885 by James B. Kirk, general auditor of the Baltimore & Ohio Railroad. He made his headquarters at Glenshaw after being sent to the area by John W. Garrett, B&O president, who was financing Henry W. Oliver in the construction of the Pittsburgh & Western (which later merged with the parent road). Kirk, in order to induce his wife to bring their daughters to live in Glenshaw, built an exact replica of her girlhood home in Baltimore. His signature, written with a diamond, is still on a window pane, and some of those who have lived in the house since his death have reported seeing his ghost looking out a window toward the railroad. *Location:* Glenshaw, 1001 Glenshaw Avenue.

M7. Isaac Lightner House (brick) is a gem of Greek Revival architecture, built in 1833. One of its features is a cantilevered roof on a walkway to an outbuilding. *Location:* Glenshaw, 2407 Mount Royal Boulevard.

M8. Thompson-DeHaven-Leet House (brick in Flemish bond) was built in 1831 or 1836 by Robert Thompson. After Harmar DeHaven purchased it, the house was occupied for two generations by the DeHaven family. The next person to live here was Clifford S. Leet. *Location:* Glenshaw, 3201 Mount Royal Boulevard.

M9. McElheny House (rubble stone), with three bays, was one of the earliest in present Hampton Township. It was built in 1820 (date stone) by Samuel McElheny at a crossing of a former Indian trail and fording of Pine Creek where he also ran a mill, now gone. The building has had a checkered history. Located on the Mount Royal Pike (Etna to Butler), it was at one time a stagecoach stop and inn where horses were changed. (Lafayette stopped here in 1825.) At an early period one Mowery operated a sickle factory here. By the 1850s the house was known as the "Pine Grove House," at which time the old sawmill was still in operation. In 1862 Thomas Mellon owned the property; he sold it to Clement Tonner the following year. At the time of World War I it was a notorious house of prostitution, and from the 1920s to the 1940s it was a roadhouse known as the "Fountain Farm." In more recent years it became a restaurant under the ownership of Richard Miller. It now has the Gamma Building attached at the rear, next to Pine Creek. *Location:* Hampton Township, 4068 Mount Royal Boulevard (SR 4019) near Duncan Avenue.

M10. Sample House (brick). A fine five-bay house built in 1812 by Samuel Sample. *Location:* Vitullo Road, 1 mile from the intersection of Wildwood Road and SR 0008.

M11. Depreciation Lands Museum (brick), one story, in Greek Revival style, was built in 1860 as a sanctuary for the Reformed (Covenanter) Presbyterian Church on property acquired in the 1830s. The church was vacant from 1925 to 1948 when the Episcopal Church of St. Thomas in the Fields bought it. A Baptist congregation purchased it in 1963 after the St. Thomas members moved into their new building. At present it is a museum containing displays and memorabilia from the time when certificates for the depreciation of Continental currency paid to soldiers in the revolution could be used to buy certain lands in Pennsylvania.

The log house next to the museum was moved from Middle Road in Glenshaw. It was built in 1803 by James Armstrong, who paid for his land with depreciation certificates. (J. A. 1803/1839 on hearthstone.) *Hours:* Sunday, 1–4 P.M. Handicapped access. *Location:* Hampton Township, 4743 South Pioneer Road (SR 0008) Allison Park, south of Pennsylvania Turnpike.

M12. Ferguson-Early House (brick), a five-bay building with a Greek Revival doorway, was built in 1860–61 with an addition in 1890. *Location:* Hampton Township, Ferguson Road.

Note: Another five-bay brick landmark, built around 1825, is in Hampton Township at 4554 William Flynn Highway in Allison Park.

M13. "Plumb Springs"–Elkin House (brick) was built around 1850 by Thomas Richards. It was restored by the Samuel Elkin family. *Location:* Richland Township, Oak Hill Road.

Note: An oak tree nearly 300 years old stands near an early log house in Allison Park at 2841 McCully Road.

M14. Bakerstown Presbyterian Church (brick), of Greek Revival and Gothic detail, was built in 1838 and remodeled in 1888. It was built as a Methodist Protestant church. The slightly younger original Presbyterian church is nearby, built into a later structure, while the MP building still sits apart. *Location:* Bakerstown, Richland Township, on SR 0008, south of SR 4068.

M15. Deer Creek United Presbyterian Church (brick), in late Greek Revival style with Doric pilasters, was built in 1853. A replica of the outdoor pulpit from the 1811 "tent church" has been erected on the property. *Location:* Richland Township, Bairdsford Road.

M16. La Tourelle (brick), was built in 1924–25 for Edgar J. Kaufmann, Sr., founder of Kaufmann's Department Store. The medievalistic romantic design was by Benno Janssen. *Location:* Fox Chapel, La Tourelle Lane.

M17. Hill 'n Dale Mansion (brick with stone) was designed in 1936 by architect Brandon Smith as a country home for the Ernest Hillman family. Near the main house is "Long Meadow," a two-story log "cottage" on a tract of land which dates back to a 1786 grant. Three other mid-nineteenth-century log structures were joined to the original by architect Theodore Eicholtz. A smaller building was used as servants' quarters. *Location:* Fox Chapel, Squaw Run Road and Old Mill Road.

M18. F. Le Moyne Page House (log) was built in the early 1800s. A later owner named Boyle added another log house to the original structure. *Location:* Fox Chapel, 592 Squaw Run Road, past bridge cross over iron bridge.

M19. Shady Side Academy (brick), a boys' preparatory school, was founded in 1883 at 926 Aiken Avenue in Shadyside. The school was moved to the country soon after World War I, when Wallace H. Rowe, a trustee of the academy, purchased the Hanlin and Prager farms in O'Hara Township, a tract totaling 125 acres. Three buildings were erected here in October 1922. During the twenties two more dormitories, a dining hall, an infirmary, and a gymnasium were added. Memorial Hall was erected in 1954.

In 1940 the academy united with the Arnold School, thus making Shady Side the only boys' college preparatory school in the Pittsburgh area at that time. On the old Lewis estate nearby, overlooking this site and located on Squaw Run Road, is the middle school. The junior school is located on Braddock Avenue in Pittsburgh. *Location:* Fox Chapel, on Fox Chapel Road.

M20. Cross Keys Tavern (brick), built in 1850, first appeared on an Allegheny County property holders' map in 1851. It was known as the G. F. Thomas Tavern until 1876 and served as a halfway house on what was then the Kittanning Pike. In later years it was operated by a woman and her daughters. After a flourishing life it fell into disrepair, and restoration of this old inn was begun in 1972. The charming establishment now specializes in wild-game dinners. *Hours:* Tuesday–Friday, 12 noon–2:30 P.M., 6–10:30 P.M.; Saturday, 3–midnight. *Location:* Indiana Township, on Dorseyville Road south of Harts Run Road.

M21. Hartwood (stone), designed by Alfred Hopkins and built in 1929, was the home of John and Mary Flinn Lawrence, daughter of William Flinn, of the infamous Flinn-Magee ring that controlled Allegheny County politics from 1873 to 1909. In 1969 the Allegheny Department of Parks, Recreation, and Conservation acquired this 480-acre (now 629-acre) estate for $1 million, and since the death of Mrs. Lawrence in 1974, opened the home with its furnishing, paintings, rare china, and antiques as a cultural center, museum, and park for musical, dramatic, and art events. The Tudor Gothic mansion is situated high on a hill with a winding driveway leading up to it. The stables, with a medieval silo, were built in 1926. The property contains a great stand of native trees with understory growth typical of the early years of settlement in the county, as well as a variety of wildlife. It is maintained by Allegheny County. *Hours:* Tuesday–Saturday, 10 A.M.–3 P.M.; Sunday, 12 noon–4 P.M. Handicapped access with notice. *Location:* Indiana Township, north of Harts Run Road. Turn left on Saxonburg Boulevard and continue for 1.2 mile. 215 Saxonburg Boulevard. Gatehouse is just off road at left.

M22. Babcock House (frame) was built about 1900 by Edward Vose Babcock, Pittsburgh mayor, Allegheny County commissioner, lumberman, and early conservationist.

Babcock is remembered as the "father" of North and South parks, secretly buying up the land and transferring it to the county at no profit to himself. He also gave Pennsylvania the land for Babcock State Forest in Somerset County (see *Ashtola*) and West Virginia acreage for another state forest, as well as creating the Babcock National Forest in the far West. The house, in a parklike setting, is well maintained. *Location:* Near north end of Babcock Boulevard, across from Pine Junior High School.

Note: Howard Bowman Stewart (1913–82), county commissioner in 1956, continued Babcock's park acquisition program and developed seven regional parks.

M23. Evergreen Hamlet, the former farm property of Benjamin Davis, was an experimental commune (a romantic suburb and refuge from city industrial life) organized on May 16, 1851, and lasting until 1866. It was founded by William Shinn, a local lawyer. Its members, prominent Pittsburgh businessmen who wanted reasonable country-style homes, paid an initiation fee, a portion of the road assessment, and their share of the purchase price of the property, receiving in return "one building lot and one (undivided) sixteenth in the school lot, and that portion of the farm not laid off in lots." A schoolhouse was built and a community farmer employed. Only four English-type villas remain. Twenty were intended to be erected. In 1879 a later owner, J. J. Gillespie, built a narrow-gauge railroad from Millvale to the hamlet. Tours by reservation. *Location:* Evergreen, off Babcock Boulevard on Evergreen Hamlet Road (Ross Township).

M24. "Green Gables" (stucco) is an enlargement, much changed, of the Woods family's Tudor house dating from before 1876. About 1890 it was rebuilt into a typical Victorian mansion by one Johnston. Later it was owned by Harry Dipple. Now, renamed "Beverly Hills," it is a nightclub with dinner theater. It was severely damaged by fire in 1975, but is being repaired. *Location:* Ross Township, 3083 Evergreen Road and Babcock Boulevard, opposite end of Rochester Road.

M25. Russell's Pyramid commemorates Charles Taze Russell (founder of Jehovah's Witnesses) who died in October 1916. He was buried, by his own wish, in the United Cemeteries in Ross Township. There is only a small headstone, but beside it is a granite pyramid in which are copies of almost everything he wrote. *Location:* Ross Township, United Cemeteries, Cemetery Lane, off US 19 just above West View.

M26. Hilands Presbyterian Church (painted brick) was organized in 1797. The present church was built in 1836 (Darby & Evans, architects). An education building was added in 1914. In 1936 the church's interior was remodeled, and in 1940 its exterior was redone in the Georgian style. *Location:* Ross Township, 845 Perry Highway.

M27. Wallace-Richards House (stone) was built in 1830 on depreciation lands. The original patent was given to George Wallace in 1804. This 429-acre tract was called "Hookem Sneevy," from Old Saxon, loosely translated as "something acquired by deceit and treachery." At one time it belonged to an artist by the name of Peirsol. *Location:* Ross Township, 301 Jack's Run Road, Wexford.

M28. Stewart-Schlag House (brick), with five bays, has numerous outbuildings, reflecting a prosperous farm which began in 1834. One structure, moved from another site, is log *Location:* Ross Township, 537 Sangree Road, off Thompson Run Road.

M29. Graham House (brick), ivy-covered, having five bays, was built around 1840. It has a fine Georgian doorway. *Location:* Ross Township, 200 Twin Oaks Drive.

M30. Nelson House (brick), now the Maslanka House, has five bays with shutters. Once owned by the Howard Hill family, it was built in 1835. *Location:* Ross Township, 231 Nelson Run Road.

M31. Jordan House (brick), painted white, has five bays and a side-lighted Greek Revival door. It was built in 1826. *Location:* Ross Township, 3392 Evergreen Road.

M32. Flaig's "Old Lodge" (log), although not indigenous to the area, is one of the oldest structures in western Pennsylvania. The cabin was built in the 1850s and moved from the eastern foothills of the Allegheny Mountains east. It was erected at this site in 1927. Formerly a house, store, and school, today it is a gun shop. *Location:* Ross Township, junction of Thompson Run Road and Evergreen Road.
  Note: A 200-year old silver maple tree stands beside the home of Gov. David L. Lawrence at 3410 Evergreen Road in Ross Township.

M33. West View Borough Hall (brick), a two-story structure with a mansard roof, was built around 1870 in Italianate Second Empire style. *Location:* West View, Schwitter Street.

M34. North Hills Unitarian Church (frame) is a remarkable adaptation by John Schurko of a former dairy barn. The barn became the Unitarian Universalist Church in 1960. It is situated almost out of view from the road on a large tract planted in trees and gardens. *Location:* McCandless Township, on West Ingomar Road near borough line.

M35. Guyasuta Statue (Heinz Memorial) was a gift of Henry J. Heinz which he presented in 1896 (made by J. L. Mott Iron Works, New York) in memory of Seneca Indian Chief Guyasuta. Gen. James O'Hara had furnished a cabin for the old Indian leader on his estate at what is now Sharpsburg and provided necessities during his last years. When Guyasuta died about 1800, he was buried in an old mound near the north end of the Highland Park Bridge. His skeletal remains were taken to Carnegie Museum when the Pennsylvania Railroad received title to the ground in 1919. Guyasuta is also reported, with some believable evidence in each case, to be buried in two other places: one in Mercer County (see *Indian Burials*) and the other at an unknown spot on the Cornplanter Reservation in Warren County (see *Kinzua Dam*), Cornplanter having been his nephew. *Location:* Sharpsburg, corner of Main and North Canal streets.

M36. Aspinwall Railroad Station (brick and frame with shingle) used to serve the old Allegheny Valley Railroad (later the Pennsylvania Railroad). In 1922 this building was moved to its present site from along the nearby tracks. It is now an American Legion home. *Location:* Aspinwall, 131 Commercial Avenue at Eastern Avenue.

M37. Sauer Buildings (stone, brick, and terra cotta), seven in all, were built in 1900–40 by Frederick C. Sauer (1860–1942) who used his imagination and salvaged materials from other buildings for his fantasy creations. *Location:* Aspinwall, 613–25 Center Avenue.

M38. Harwick Disaster Graves and Monument are a grim reminder of the 1901 mine disaster that took 179 lives. The graves and monument are in the old Lutheran cemetery beside a road leading into the Colfax Power Station of Duquesne Light Company. One granite monument is a folk carving of the scene in the mine, with workers and mine mules falling dead from the explosion. *Location:* Cheswick, off SR 0028.

M39. Rachel Carson's Birthplace (frame), the former home of the author of *The Sea Around Us* and *Silent Spring,* has been restored by the Rachel Carson Homestead Association as a museum and a lending and research library. This structure was built in 1840. The original four-room section is on the right side. *Location:* Springdale, on top of Colfax Hill, 613 Marion Avenue.

M40. Allegheny-Kiski Valley Historical Society (stone), founded in 1964, is housed in the former American Legion Post No. 85 building, erected in 1931. The museum includes collections of glassware and pottery, military uniforms, models of regional industrial development, early lighting devices, Indian artifacts, early appliances, farm tools, photographs, and other memorabilia. *Hours:* Summer only, Wednesday and Sunday, 1:30–4:30 P.M. Tours by arrangement. *Location:* Tarentum, 224 East Seventh Avenue at Lock Street.

M41. Tarentum Railroad Station (brick), the third station on this site, was built in 1914 for passengers traveling on the Pennsylvania Railroad via the "Apollo Train." It is currently a restaurant owned by Rege Accetulla, open seven days a week. *Location:* Tarentum, 101 Station Drive.

M42. Highview United Presbyterian Church (brick) was built in 1869 by contractor George Dickey. It sits on a hillside overlooking the Allegheny River. *Location:* Tarentum, East Eighth Avenue and Dickey Street.

M43. Tarentum Methodist Church Camp consists of small Victorian frame cottages built at the turn of the century near an outdoor pavilion-type tabernacle. *Location:* Near Tarentum, close to junction of SR 0066 and SR 0356.

M44. Tour-Ed Mine, an educational museum which includes a 1785 log house, presents information on coal mining in the Allegheny Valley from about 1800 to the present. This enterprise, developed and owned by Ira Wood, includes a half-hour tour in man-trip cars through the half-acre mine, with views of displays depicting the various phases of coal-mining development, a series of rooms in a typical coal-mining community, and a mock-up of a company store. *Hours:* Memorial

Day–Labor Day: Daily, 1–3:30 P.M. Closed Tuesdays. *Admission fee. Location:* Burtner Road, 1 mile west of Tarentum, 7 miles from Oakmont interchange of Turnpike (no. 5), off SR 0028 on Bull Creek Road, across from Woodlawn Golf Course (northwest of Natrona Heights).

M45. Burtner House (stone) was built in 1821 by Philip Burtner and his wife Anna Negley, the first permanent white settlers in the area. This house, with large stone chimneys on the gable ends, was a polling place at the time of President Lincoln's election. The structure has remained in the possession of the same family until recent years. In the 1970s it was doomed for destruction by the expressway, but at the last minute was saved by public protest. Restored, it is now a museum. The Burtner private cemetery is on a hillside nearby. Tours: By appointment only. *Donation. Location:* Natrona Heights, on Burtner Road off SR 0028 along the Allegheny Valley Expressway (Harrison Township).

M46. Natrona Salt Works Buildings (brick), formerly occupied by the salt and soda works which gave the town its name, are now used in the production of chemicals from deposits shipped in from abroad. *Location:* Natrona Heights.

M47. Pennsalt Workers' Houses (brick and frame), with kitchen sheds and vegetable gardens, were built by Quakers in the 1850s at the Pennsylvania Salt Manufacturing Company. These Victorian Gothic Revival dwellings are fine rare relics of American industrial archeology. The plant, located in 1850 in East Tarentum, produced caustic soda for lye soap and marketed it as Natrona Refined Saponifer. East Tarentum was later called Natrona from the Greek *natron,* meaning soda. During an 1875 strike many Polish immigrants moved into these houses to replace the strikers. In 1981 two of the brick row houses on Blue Ridge Avenue were restored by the Pittsburgh History & Landmarks Foundation. *Location:* Natrona, Federal Street (oldest houses), Greenwich Street, Blue Ridge Avenue, and Wood Street.

M48. Bell Haven is the brain child and endeavor of J. Oliver Elliott, who started collecting bells after World War II. These bells sprawl over most of the acre of lawn which adjoins the Elliott family house, as well as much of the space within. The octogenarian's philosophy was that bringing joy to humanity is reward enough. The owners ring the bells

45

twice a year—on New Year's Eve and at 2 P.M. on July 4—when they include a two-hour tour of the grounds. Included are numerous bells from western Pennsylvania, such as the Avonmore and Parnassus school bells, the rare "nine muses and nymphs" bell cast in 1859 at Cincinnati, Ohio, and the (Chaplin) Fulton bells. There is also a large button collection. The present owner is the founder's daughter, Ida Mae Long. Tours by appointment. *Admission fee. Location:* West Deer Township. Take Bull Creek Road, off SR 0028 in Tarentum, and follow Red Belt for 5 miles.

M49. Old Bull Creek Presbyterian Church (brick) was erected in 1853. The first services of this congregation were held outdoors in 1796. The original church, made of logs, was built in 1801, followed by a smaller one in 1833 that was constructed because the first was too large to heat. The 1853 structure was replaced by a new church across the road and is now used as a recreation hall. *Location:* West Deer Township, Tarentum-Culmerville Road, 2 miles south of Red Belt.

Note: On the Bakerstown-Culmerville Road, two miles east of Bairdsford Road, is a five-bay fieldstone house built around 1860.

M50. Harmarville United Presbyterian Church (brick), one-story, of Greek Revival design, was built in 1851. Originally it was the Associate Reformed Church. *Location:* Harmar Township, 521 Indianola Road near SR 0028 interchange.

N. Allegheny Suburban: South

N1. Hugh Jackson House (stucco over stone), a massive and venerable home, narrowly missed destruction when it was almost inundated by an artificial lake that was built around it by the developers of Cedarhurst Manor at the beginning of World War II. Although some evidence seems to date its construction at 1808, the house was most likely built by 1794, because it was mentioned in reports of the Whiskey Rebellion. *Location:* Mt. Lebanon, just west of Lindendale Drive on lake bank.

N2. Mt. Lebanon Cemetery House (frame), with Victorian brackets at its eaves, was built around 1874 by the Bockstoce family, who started the Mt. Lebanon Nurseries here at that time. The cemetery was located at this site in later years; the present masonry pillars were built in 1902. The house has been occupied by caretakers and their families over the

years. *Location:* Mt. Lebanon, Washington Road, near Alfred Street and Shady Drive.

N3. Snyder-Bockstoce House (brick), a one-story structure built in 1845 of Greek Revival style, was originally owned by Henry Bockstoce, and later by the Snyder and Fulton families (Congressman James G. Fulton). Now owned by a development company, the house is to be moved to another site on this property formerly owned by the Mt. Lebanon Cemetery. *Location:* Mt. Lebanon, 3 Alfred Street, off Shady Drive near Washington Road.

N4. William Kennedy House (frame) was built in 1856. George Kennedy, father of William and George, Jr., came to this area in 1836 with his family. In later years William Kennedy's descendant, Kenneth Philip, became the owner. This two-bay house is the only remaining farmhouse in this residential area. *Location:* Mt. Lebanon, 709 Ridgefield Avenue.

N5. Dr. Joseph McCormick House (brick and stucco) was built around 1857. Dr. McCormick, who graduated from Jefferson Medical College in Philadelphia in 1838, practiced medicine in Upper St. Clair before moving here. In later years the Clarke Champion family bought the property. *Location:* Mt. Lebanon, 424 Kenmont Avenue.

N6. Peter Mink House (new siding) was built around 1860 near where an early log house once stood. The original owner, Peter Mink, operated a gristmill here. In later years the Robert E. Seymour family purchased the property. *Location:* Mt. Lebanon, 811 Rockwood Avenue.

N7. Mission Hills, laid out in the 1920s, includes many houses having medieval, colonial, and Gothic Revival designs. These houses, situated on high terraces, are characteristic of Frederick Olmsted's design in which landscaping was an important feature. *Location:* Mt. Lebanon, area bordered by Washington Road, Jefferson Drive, Orchard Drive, and Castle Shannon Boulevard.

N8. Early Jordan House (stone), built around 1800 and remodeled in more recent years, is the oldest house in the area. *Location:* Mt. Lebanon, 538 Becks Run Road.

N9. Arlington Park includes frame houses and summer cottages built in 1890–1920 with "gingerbread" ornamentation similar to those

N10. Lesnett Farm Octagonal Barn

in the town of Chautauqua, N.Y. Begun in 1892 by the Arlington Park Camp Meeting Association, this area still looks like a late-nineteenth-century "camp meeting" resort. *Location:* Mt. Lebanon, Arlington Park.

N10. Lesnett Farm Octagonal Barn (frame), apparently the last of its kind in the county, bears a date of 1897. It was copied from a barn on US 19 in Washington County. *Location:* Upper St. Clair, 2333 Lesnett Road.

Note: Lesnett House (log) was built over a spring between the barn and the main house by Christian Lesnett in 1774.

Tustin-Harrison, main house, was built of frame in 1840–41. *Location:* Upper St. Clair, 2333 Lesnett Road, off McLaughlin Run Road.

N11. Old Lesnett House (frame) was built in the middle 1800s by the Lesnett family and is still owned by them. *Location:* Upper St. Clair, 231 Old Lesnett Road.

N12. Gilfillan House (brick) was built in 1855–57 by John Gilfillan. This three-bay house has a transom doorway and a chimney at each gable end. The original glass windows have been preserved in the structure. Also on the property is a stone springhouse. This is the last piece of farmland in the area still held by the original family. The Gilfillans donated land for the Westminster Presbyterian Church located nearby. *Location:* Upper St. Clair Township, 1950 Washington Road near Orr Road on US 19.

N13. McMillan House (log and fieldstone) was built in 1840 or earlier by Andrew McMil-

lan. A stone and frame springhouse is next to the house. *Location:* Upper St. Clair, 1920 McMillan Road, off McLaughlin Road.

Note: Also off McMillan Road near Cook School Road is the Borland house, built in the 1850s.

N14. Gilfillan-Fulton House (log) was built in 1830 on the property of Alexander Gilfillan (1746–1836) by his son for hired hands and their families, according to tradition. Alexander, justice of the peace from 1799 to 1820, was married to Martha Boyd in 1781 by Rev. John McMillan. The house was purchased in 1923 by James E. and Emily Fulton (he was the founder of the St. Clair Country Club, chartered in 1916), and it was used for their summer home. Their son, Congressman James G. Fulton, served the 27th district of Pennsylvania, 1945–1971. He owned the house until his death (1971). (At one time Kindred McLeary, who painted murals in government buildings, lived here. One of his murals is in the Old Federal Building in Pittsburgh.) *Location:* Upper St. Clair, McLaughlin Run Road, SR 3004 off US 19, across from the Township Building.

N15. Phillips-Seeger Homestead (stone) was built by Joseph Phillips in 1806. It is the oldest stone house in the township and has been authentically restored by its present owners. A log springhouse sits to the left of the house which has a relocated log addition—an early log house moved to the site from Speers, Pa. *Location:* Upper St. Clair, 170 Seeger Road, off Fort Couch Road.

N16. Johnston-Cullen House (brick), with five bays, in Greek Revival style, was built in 1838 (datestone in gable) by William and Emily Caldwell Johnston and sold to Archibald Cullen in 1914. It still remains in the Cullen family. The bricks for the house were made on the property. *Location:* Upper St. Clair, 2430 Southvue Drive, off Johnston Road.

N17. James Fife House (frame) was built in 1870. This five-bay house has decorative carved window frames and has been restored inside and out. A frame kitchen house is nearby. *Location:* Upper St. Clair, 2535 Fife Drive, off Johnston Road.

N18. Will T. Fife House (brick, painted white), situated on a hillside, was built in 1840. It is Federal Colonial in style and has had additions. There is an underground railroad tradition associated with the house. *Lo-*

cation: Upper St. Clair, 2421 Old Washington Road, off US 19 (Washington Road).

Note: Another early house (frame) is at the corner of Johnston Road and Old Washington Road.

N19. John Williams House (frame) was built in 1845 by Hugh Scott, whose daughter, Nancy, married John Williams. Their daughter, born in the house in 1859, inherited the property. Congressman James G. Fulton purchased the house in 1952, and it became his home, private law library, and office. A huge eagle medallion was installed on the right wing of the house when Fulton owned it. *Location:* Upper St. Clair, 1630 North Highland Road, off US 19 (Washington Road).

N20. Boyce Railroad Station House (frame), an ell-shaped farmhouse built in 1885, formerly housed a grocery store and a post office. In more recent years it served as a B&O Railroad station. *Location:* Upper St. Clair, 1050 Boyce Road, beside tracks.

N21. Bethel Presbyterian Church (brick), the western division of Peters Creek Presbyterian Church (oldest congregation of this denomination in the county), was organized in 1796. (See *Lebanon Presbyterian Church.*) John Clark was the area's first regular pastor, serving from 1783 to 1794. A log meetinghouse was built in 1779 or 1780; a brick church in 1826; a third, also brick, in 1855; and the fourth and present structure in 1909–10. Bethel is the parent of five churches in the area. Housed in this building is a fine historical room containing memorabilia relating to the church. A cemetery adjoining the structure is one of the oldest in the area, containing the graves of early settlers and fourteen soldiers of the Revolution. *Location:* Bethel Park, junction of Bethel Church and Marshall roads.

Note: An early brick manse is at the corner of Marshall and Oakhurst roads. George Marshall, fourth pastor of Bethel Church (1833–72), lived here while he served the church.

N22. Joy House (brick) was built by Joseph Joy, who devised the first functional mine-loading machine, known today as the Joy Loader, and other mining machinery. Joy took an engineering course from a Scranton correspondence school, the only education beyond grade school that this farm boy had. The company became wealthy on his invention, which revolutionized the mining industry. This house had a specially built laboratory for his use. *Location:* Bethel Park, on southeast corner of Iroquois and Comanche roads (near South Hills Village Mall).

N23. Sheplar-Rowell House (stone) was built by John Sheplar in 1831. It is situated on the early land grant, Mullington, owned by Thomas McMillan (brother of Rev. John McMillan) in 1776. Before erecting the present house, Sheplar lived in a nearby log structure where his twelve children were born. *Location:* Library (Snowden area), 3914 Snowden Road off Ridge Road (South Park Township).

N24. Miller Homestead (stone) was built near Catfish Run (a branch of Peters Creek) in 1808 by James Miller, the son of Oliver Miller, Sr. James built a stone addition to the house in 1830. The building remained in the Miller family until the 1920s when it was purchased by the county. The homestead was built on the site of Oliver Miller's two-story log house where the first church service of Peters Creek (see *Bethel Presbyterian Church*) was conducted by Rev. John McMillan in 1776. The stone house was never a manse, though it has been referred to as such over the years.

In 1794 this area witnessed the first shots of the rebellion over a whiskey tax, fired as a response to federal officers' attempt to serve William Miller (James's brother) a warrant on his unregistered still. Their brother Oliver Miller, Jr., was killed at this time on Bower Hill. A newly erected log house serves as a reception center for visitors and represents the early log house replaced in 1808 by the stone dwelling. Hours: April–December: Sunday, 1–4 P.M. Tours by appointment. *Location:* South Park, on Stone Manse Drive off SR 0088 (South Park Township).

Note: At 3215 Kennebec Road in the Brookside Farms area is a stuccoed stone house built before 1790. It belonged to Sarah Couch Mannes, the daughter of Nathan Couch who built Fort Couch.

N25. St. Luke's Protestant Episcopal Church (stone), the first Episcopal church established west of the Allegheny Mountains, was first built of logs by Col. John Lea for services perhaps as early as 1770. Brig. Gen. John Neville (see *Woodville*) took the lead in building a frame structure and paid for the education of Francis Reno, the first regular Episcopal minister in the west. This second church rotted from neglect. The present Gothic stone one, intentionally archaic and rustic in appearance, was built by the diocese in 1851–53 as a memorial of its first congre-

N24. Miller Homestead

gation. It is one of the oldest churches in Allegheny County. *Location:* Scott Township, on old Washington Pike in Woodville section.

N26. Murray House (brick), in Greek Revival style, built around 1820–28 with a later addition, was used in part as a brick shop and later as a funeral home. *Location:* Bridgeville, 423 Washington Boulevard.

N27. Railroad Station Library, a former Pennsylvania Railroad station, was converted in recent years to a public library. A refurbished caboose next to it serves as a children's library. *Location:* Bridgeville, corner of Railroad and Station streets.

N28. High Tor (brick) was the home of Andrew W. Robertson, one of the founders of the Western Pennsylvania Conservancy and former chairman of the board of Westinghouse Electric Corporation, in which capacity he was a vital force especially during the Depression. A man dedicated to preservation of the nation's natural heritage, Robertson, with his wife Alice, formed the Pleasant Hills Arboretum Corporation in 1950 and donated eight acres of oak forest to the organization for public use. This was followed by another gift of eight acres in 1952, four of which were originally owned by John Shields, who obtained a patent in 1791. In 1953, Dr. O. E. Jennings headed a census of the plant and bird life here. In 1966, on the death of Robertson, the organization's name was changed to the

A. W. Robertson Arboretum of Pleasant Hills, in his honor. *Location:* Pleasant Hills, on Old Carton Road near Dutch Lane. Arboretum entrances are opposite 170 West Bruceton Road and 217 Oakcrest Lane.

N29. Torrence House (log and fieldstone) was built between 1782 and 1800 by Maj. James Torrence on land given to him for services during the Revolutionary War. His son David obtained the warrant for the land in 1827 and the following year paid $116.64 to the state and received the patent for the 237-acre tract. *Location:* Pleasant Hills, 121 Colson Drive.

N30. Large House (painted brick), of Greek Revival style, has a signature stone in one gable end which reads, "J. & E. Large 1838." This home, built by John Large, was later owned by Henry Large, John's grandson, who began operation of a distillery in 1863, engaging in the manufacture of Monongahela rye whiskey, the brand that his grandfather had established. This business was later bought by Abraham Overholt (see *Henry Clay Frick Birthplace,* Westmoreland County). Henry Large married Anna H. Greenly in 1861. *Location:* Large, on SR 0051 at Westinghouse atomic plant.

N31. St. Paulinus Roman Catholic Church (stone), an outstanding example of human resourcefulness, was erected in 1936 through the effort and determination of this congrega-

N25. St. Luke's Protestant Episcopal Church

tion. In 1935, when two existing church buildings could not accommodate the membership, an architect estimated the expense of a new building at $300,000, which was beyond the church's means. As a result, the congregation constructed this Norman French building, for the most part on its own. Men, women, and children, together with their neighbors, cleared the ground and collected cast-off stone. The steel-trussed roof was designed by a draftsman in a steel plant, and the architectural plan was copied from photographs of existing churches. Within eighteen months the volunteers had completed the edifice at a cost of only $37,000. *Location:* Clairton, corner of Carnegie and Delaware avenues and Fourth Street.

N32. Elizabeth Borough used to be a major American boat-building center on the Monongahela River. Here several boats for the Lewis and Clark expedition (1804) were built. During the town's heyday (1824–57) one steamboat per month, on average, was constructed in the Elizabeth yards. James G. Blaine, who ran for president three times, lived here when he was in the local coal business in the years following the boat-building era. Elizabeth is also the home of author Richard T. Wyley, who wrote *Sim Green*.

One particular landmark in Elizabeth Borough, St. Michael's Roman Catholic Church, now vacant after a new church was built in recent years, is worthy of preservation. Established in 1851, its original stained glass windows are preserved within the building.

N33. Red Lion Restaurant (stone), owned by the Rockwell family since 1980, originally

housed the First Bank of Elizabeth, which opened in 1906. It failed in 1913 and the building was eventually used as a drugstore. The present title perpetuates the history of the area, for an old Red Lion Tavern once operated nearby. *Location:* Elizabeth Borough, Plum Avenue and Second Street.

N34. Tollhouse (frame) used to function as a collection office for tolls taken at the West Elizabeth–Elizabeth bridge, built around 1900. This small structure is now a commercial building. *Location:* Elizabeth Borough, First Street and Plum Avenue.

N35. Train Station (frame) used to be the old Pittsburgh & Lake Erie Railroad Station. *Location:* Elizabeth Borough, Plum Avenue and First Street.

N36. Van Kirk House (brick), a one-story early Greek Revival house, was built around 1854 by the Van Kirk family. In view to the left is the Kosko house (brick), erected in 1875. *Location:* Elizabeth Borough, Round Hill Road (near Round Hill Farm), Scenery Drive at SR 0048.

N37. Round Hill Farm, consisting of 181 acres, is a modern working farm operated by the county, with a variety of barnyard animals. Located here is a brick farmhouse built in 1838 (with an 1870 addition) on an original land grant made to Elisha Peairs in 1790. It passed through six generations to Walter Scott. Marjorie Scott, of the seventh generation, lived on the farm with her parents until it was acquired by the county in 1958. The house now serves as the county park police headquarters. *Hours:* Year round: Daily, 9 A.M. to dusk. *Location:* Round Hill Regional Park, on Round Hill Road off SR 0048 near Elizabeth.

Note: Round Hill Park, a farm once owned by a relative of President William McKinley, has a 300-year-old white oak tree. A tree of similar age shelters an early log house at 916 Beaver Grade Road.

N38. Van Allen House (brick), of late Georgian style with a fanlight in the front entrance, was built between 1819 and 1823 by David Van Allen. This fine house with an interesting stairway and interior is situated on a high hill looking toward the Monongahela Valley. *Location:* Forward Township, on Mentor Road (SR 2011) about 1 mile off SR 0136 at Sunnyside.

Note: Also nearby on this road are the Sutton-Wunderlich House, painted brick with a double porch recessed at one end, built in 1860, and the brick King-Stracelsky House, with gable curtains between the chimneys, built about 1830–50.

N39. Experimental Mine (U.S. Bureau of Mines), a unique coal-mine testing laboratory founded by the U.S. Bureau of Mines in 1900, has been responsible for the creation of many mine-safety devices and the improvement of accident-prevention methods. *Location:* Bruceton, off Cochran Mill Road.

Note: The headquarters of the U.S. Bureau of Mines was at 4800 Forbes Avenue in Oakland (Pittsburgh), a building designed by Henry Hornbostel and erected in 1910.

N40. Lebanon Presbyterian Church (brick), known as the Lebanon Meetinghouse, was built in 1871–72, replacing a brick structure of 1823. The congregation was organized as the eastern division of Peters Creek Presbyterian Church on November 5, 1776, when Dr. John McMillan preached there (see *Bethel Presbyterian Church*). The building now houses administration offices, a learning center, a library, and student personnel services for a branch of Community College of Allegheny County. *Location:* West Mifflin, 2800 Old Elizabeth Road, near old Allegheny County Airport, 0.1 mile south of Lebanon Church Road, at junction of Lebanon School and Old Elizabeth roads.

N41. Jefferson Memorial Park, the county's largest cemetery of its kind, was founded in 1929–30 by Harry C. Neel and includes 325 acres on a tract originally called Beam Hill. The land patent, signed by Gov. Thomas Mifflin in 1798, went to Jacob Beam, who sold it to Aaron Work, the founder's great-great-grandfather. The Neel family has restored the 1782 Beam log cabin with eight of the original logs. The Aaron Work House (q.v.), built about 1800, also log with stone and frame additions, is nearby. Preserved on a hillside mausoleum are pillars from the Bank of Pittsburgh (1895) together with a bronze statue of Thomas Jefferson by sculptor Frank Vittor. A bronze replica of the statue of George Washington by Jean Antoine Houdon and the steps salvaged from the Henry W. Oliver estate are near another mausoleum. Future plans include the construction of a museum building to house memorabilia of the area collected by the Neel family. *Location:* Jefferson Borough, Jefferson Memorial Park.

N42. Payne House (painted brick), once a stagecoach stop halfway between Pittsburgh and Elizabeth, was built about 1802. John Payne, who married a daughter of Henry Large (see *Large House*), lived here. There is a porch on the side of the house, and a later rear patio is the site of an early springhouse. *Location:* Jefferson Borough, on Old Clairton Road at Pearson Road.

N43. Huffman Farm consists of a number of outbuildings from the early 1800s, including the remains of a one-story log cabin with a large stone chimney still standing. The clapboard farmhouse is over 100 years old. A stone springhouse is located between the house and log cabin. *Location:* Jefferson Borough, Castor Lane.

N44. Bedell Farmhouse (brick), Greek Revival in style, was built around 1820. A large frame distillery stood on the property at one time; now only the stone foundation remains. *Location:* Jefferson Borough, Cherry Road.

N45. John (Aaron) Work House (stone and log) was built in 1800, a fine pioneer house reflecting two types of early construction. *Location:* Jefferson Memorial Park, Curry Hollow Road.

N46. Gabriel Walker House (brick) was built in 1849. *Location:* Collier Township, Noblestown Road at Rennerdale.

N47. Walker-Ewing-Grace House (log), not to be confused with the above log house in Settler's Cabin Park, is said to have been built on a tomahawk claim by Isaac and Gabriel Walker. Although the date 1762 is inscribed on the chimney, the house was not finished until about 1787–95. Indians reputedly attacked Gabriel Walker's family at this site in 1782. The property was given by the Ewing family to the Pittsburgh History and Landmarks Foundation in 1973. Open by appointment. *Location:* Collier Township, on Noblestown Road near Robinson Run and Penn Central Railroad (across valley from Nike site, 3.4 miles from US 422).

N48. Woodville (Neville House) (frame), on the Avenue grant, was built in 1785 by Brig. Gen. John Neville (1731–1803), an officer in the French and Indian War and the Revolution, who was also inspector of taxes for the collection of the levy on whiskey. The nucleus of the house, now a kitchen, is an extremely early log cabin. Several years later the general built another house nearby (Bower Hill) on the Sidge Field grant which was burned by the insurgents during the Whiskey Rebellion

N48. Woodville

of 1794. His son Col. Presley Neville resided in Woodville at that time. The house was purchased about 1820 by John Wrenshall and is now owned by the Pittsburgh History and Landmarks Foundation. *Location:* Collier Township, 50 Washington Pike (SR 0050) at Thompson Run Road, south of Heidelberg.

Previous Sites Now Lost

Bellefield Presbyterian Church, demolished (bell tower still extant)
Elks Club, demolished
Forsythe Log Cabin, deteriorated
Granite Building, demolished
Holmes House, demolished
Jenkins Arcade, demolished
Pioneer Inn, demolished
Pollock-McGill House, demolished
St. Peter's Episcopal Church, demolished 1990
Thorn Hill School, demolished 1983
Voegtley Church, demolished

Covered Bridges

Although none of Allegheny County's original covered bridges have been preserved, a fine one in recent years was erected on SR 0366, about 1.2 miles west of SR 0380.

Pennsylvania Historical and Museum Commission Markers

Allegheny Arsenal Pittsburgh, opposite 257 Fortieth Street, Lawrenceville
Allegheny County Pittsburgh, at courthouse, 436 Grant Street
Avery College Pittsburgh, 619 East Ohio Street, North Side
Bethel Presbyterian Church Bethel Church Road between US 19 and SR 0088
Bouquet Camp SR 0380 east of Pittsburgh

Braddock's Crossing SR 0837 north of Duquesne at Kennywood Park
Braddock's Defeat US 30 southeast of Wilkinsburg
Chartier's Town Tarentum, SR 0028
David L. Lawrence Pittsburgh, Point State Park
Elizabeth Elizabeth, SR 0051
Ethelbert Nevin Edgeworth, SR 0065
Ferris Wheel Inventor Pittsburgh, West Commons, North Side
Forbes Road (Bouquet's Breastworks) Monroeville, SR 2066
Fort Duquesne Pittsburgh, Point State Park
Fort Lafayette Pittsburgh, Ninth Street just north of Penn Avenue
Fort Pitt Pittsburgh, Point State Park
Fort Pitt Blockhouse Pittsburgh, Point State Park
Fort Prince George Pittsburgh, Point State Park
George Westinghouse US 30 near Turtle Creek, east and west ends of bridge
Hand's Hospital Crafton, SR 0060
James Hay Reed Pittsburgh, at Buhl Planetarium, North Side
Jane Grey Swisshelm Pittsburgh, Braddock Avenue near Penn-Lincoln Parkway
John Scull Pittsburgh, Boulevard of the Allies just west of Market Street
Kier Refinery Pittsburgh, at parklet near Bigelow Square
Neville House SR 0050 south of Woodville
Pennsylvania Canal Pittsburgh, Liberty Avenue east of Eleventh Street, to the left of Union Station ramp
Pittsburgh On main highways leading into city
Polish Army Pittsburgh, 97 South Eighteenth Street, South Side
Shadyside Iron Furnace Pittsburgh, southeast corner of Bayard Street and Amberson Avenue, Oakland
Shannopin Town Pittsburgh, Fortieth Street at bridge, Lawrenceville
Station WQED Pittsburgh, 4802 Fifth Avenue, Oakland
Stephen C. Foster Memorial Pittsburgh, Forbes Avenue just east of Bigelow Boulevard, Oakland
V.F.W. Pittsburgh, Fifth Avenue and Bigelow Boulevard, Oakland
William D. Boyce SR 0366, two miles southeast of New Kensington
Yohogania Courthouse SR 0837 southwest of West Elizabeth

Armstrong County

Capsule History

Armstrong County, named for Maj. Gen. John Armstrong, an Indian fighter who served in the Continental Congress and the Revolutionary army, was formed on March 12, 1800, from parts of Allegheny, Westmoreland, and Lycoming counties. It has an area of 646 square miles and a population of 77,768.

Before 1740 Pennsylvania traders had established posts in the Indian villages of the area; and in 1749 Céloron de Blainville, a French army officer, was commissioned by the governor-general of France to claim the region for Louis XV by burying lead plates along the Allegheny River.

The county seat of Kittanning, whose name was derived from the Indian word for "at the great stream," was laid out on a famous Delaware and Shawnee Indian settlement which was claimed by the Six Nations by conquest. This Indian village is believed to have been one of the largest of its kind west of the Alleghenies. On September 8, 1756, during the French and Indian War, Armstrong's forces destroyed the settlement on account of atrocities the Indians committed against the English. (One of the earliest medals executed in America depicts this event, the die having been cast in Philadelphia in 1756 or 1757.) Among those killed was the Delaware Indian Captain Jacobs, who lived in a two-story log house in Kittanning (site at 313 Market Street).

Blanket Hill, east of Kittanning, was a stopping point for the troops en route to attack the Indians and the site of an army defeat when a returning party encountered a large Indian force. A monument marks the hill where the soldiers suffered severe losses and abandoned their blankets and other gear. Fort Appleby, built in 1776 at the site that later became Fort Armstrong, was the first United States fort west of the Alleghenies.

Kittanning, together with Ford City and Rosston, was included in Appleby Manor—surveyed in 1769 and one of the forty-four manors reserved by the Penns. The county seat was laid out about 1803–04 and incorporated in 1821. It was the terminal point of the old *Frankstown Path* (locally called the *Kittanning Path)*, which was used by both the Indians and the settlers for years and was part of a national system of trails, following much the same course from Shelocta to Kittanning as present-day US 422. Other principal Indian trails of the county included the *Great Shamokin Path,* which followed Cowanshannack Creek most of the way from Kittanning to about Nu Mine, thence turning northeast through Barnards, toward Smicksburg; the *Kuskusky Path,* running from Kittanning past Worthington, thence toward Herman; and the *Kiskiminetas Path,* a branch of the Frankstown Path, which cut off east of Shelocta, entered the county near West Lebanon, and followed a course similar to SR 0056 through South Bend and Spring Church, thence running directly to the Indian town of Kiskiminetas on the river northwest of Vandergrift. (The Baker Trail, a modern hiking path originally starting at Freeport and covering seventy-five miles to Cook Forest, was founded in 1950 by the Pittsburgh Council of the American Youth Hostels.)

Freeport, originally Todd's Town, was laid out by David Todd in 1796. It was traversed by the western division of the Pennsylvania Canal and is the oldest non-Indian town in the county. In the Freeport cemetery (junction of SR 0028 and SR 0356, north of Freeport) is the grave of Massa Harbison (see *Massa Harbison Log Cabin,* Westmoreland County).

Among other early settlers of the county were James Clark, William Green, James Kirkpatrick, Michael Mechling, James Claypool, Andrew Sharp, and Absalom Woodward. Others figuring prominently in the county's history were Edward Warren, who established a trading post near what is now Apollo (Conrad Weiser stopped there on his way to "kindle the first council fire with the Ohio Indians"); Capt. Samuel Brady, who was active in frontier campaigns against the Indians; Governor William Freame Johnston (see Westmoreland County); Nellie Bly (Elizabeth Cochrane), one of America's great reporters; Dr. David Alter, inventor of spectroscopy; and Margaret Shoemaker, an early feminist.

Natural resources in the area include bituminous coal, clay, salt, oil, gas, sand and gravel, and limestone. Among the principal industries are coal mining, brick-making, agriculture, lumbering, glass, and iron- and steel-sheet manufacture. Bradys Bend was the site at which the first iron rails west of the Alleghenies were manufactured. The county had fifteen early blast furnaces. In 1881 the first visible typewriter was invented in Kittanning by J. D. Daugherty and manufactured there for a number of years.

Two flood-control dams in the county form the Mahoning Creek and Crooked Creek reservoirs. The river park at Kittanning is one of the most beautiful waterfronts in western Pennsylvania. At Canal Street in Apollo are the remains of a canal lock.

Landmarks

1. Kittanning was incorporated as a borough April 2, 1821. The town was laid out by Judge George Ross around 1800.

1A. Courthouse (stone), erected in 1858–60 at a cost of $32,000, is a late Greek Revival structure with a Corinthian porticoed central pavilion and large domed cupola. The left wing was added in 1871. The first courthouse, of brick (Paul Morrow, brickmaker), was built in 1809 and remodeled in 1819. The present jail, beside it, with a ninety-six-foot battlemented tower, was built in 1873, at a cost of $252,000. Both the jail and the courthouse are of Clarion County sandstone. *Location:* Corner of Market and Jefferson streets.

1B. Armstrong County Historical Museum (painted brick), a Federal-style house, was built in 1842 by Thomas McConnell and occupied by his descendants for several generations. It was later known as the McCain house. About 1900 a spacious wing was added. Now a museum, it offers seasonal exhibits, a historical-genealogical library, and an educational classroom center. *Hours:* Wednesday and Saturday, 2–5 P.M. Special tours by appointment. *Location:* 300 North McKean Street at Vine Street.

1C. Early Bank Buildings on Market Street.
    a. Safe Deposit & Guaranty Company (stone), now Mellon Bank, was built in 1889. This fine Richardsonian Romanesque building once had a third-floor opera house and lodge halls. It seated 1,500 people. Unfortunately the upper floors were removed from this fortress of a building, thus destroying its historic integrity. Market Street.
    b. National Bank (granite front with brick). Market Street.
    c. Merchant's Bank (Gothic iron front). 222 Market Street.

1B. Armstrong County Historical Museum

    d. Farmers' National Bank (brick), chartered in 1884. Market Street.

1D. Grace Presbyterian Church (brownstone), called First Presbyterian Church of Kittanning until the late 1950s, was built in 1910–11 following a fire in 1909 that destroyed an 1890s stone building. An 1831 pewter communion service that survived the fire is still in use in the fourth church. In the nave of this Romanesque church are beautiful stained glass memorial windows designed by Louis C. Tiffany. In the late 1950s an educational annex was constructed and the sanctuary was remodeled. *Location:* 150 N. Jefferson Street.
    Note: The congregation's second church, built in 1857 after a wind storm damaged their first church (built 1830), is the present Hose Company No. 1 at the corner of South Jefferson and Jacobs streets. There is also an early brick Greek Revival church at 255 Jacobs Street. Several of the old manses are located nearby. These include Dr. Joseph Painter's house (brick) across from the church on North Jefferson Street and Dr. T. D. Ewing's house

1C. Merchant's Bank

5A. Old Stone Tavern

(brick) on the same street about half a block north of Arch Street.

1E. Kittanning Public Library (brick), Italianate with stone quoins and lintels, was built in 1860 by John A. Colwell. *Location:* 200 North Jefferson Street at Arch Street.

1F. Nulton House (brick) was built in Italianate style around 1855 by Barclay Nulton, an attorney who served in the Civil War. *Location:* 29 Market Street.

Note: Other noteworthy historic houses are located at 424 North McKean Street at Union Avenue (brick, Italianate) and at 216 North Jefferson Street (brick, five-bay Greek Revival).

2. Christ Evangelical Lutheran Church (brick) was built in 1894. Founded in 1796 as the county's first church, it was known as the German Meeting House, but was commonly called Rupp's after early settlers of the area. Originally, both German Lutheran and Reformed congregations worshiped here, but in 1815 the Reformed Church was absorbed by the Lutherans. The entrance bears the dates 1812, 1847, 1851, and 1894. *Location:* About 3 miles east of Kittanning, visible south of US 422. (Follow church sign.)

3. Holy Guardian Angel Church (brick and frame) was built in 1872. *Location:* Slate Lick, between old and new SR 0028.

4. Rhea House (stone) was built in 1817. *Location:* Slate Lick exit off SR 0028; follow road toward Worthington for 3–4 miles; turn left on T 314; cross Buffalo Creek bridge; turn right; house sits along the road.

5. Worthington

5A. Old Stone Tavern was once a stagecoach stop built by James Sample about 1820. It has been restored by the Kit-han-ne Questers. Worthington was originally called Mount Lorenzo and was founded in 1808 on Buffalo Creek. *Hours:* Wednesday–Saturday, 10 A.M.–4 P.M.; Friday, 10 A.M.–6 P.M.; Sunday, 1–5 P.M. *Admission charge. Location:* Main Street (off US 422 near corner of Bear Street).

5B. Graff House (painted brick) was built about 1840 by Peter Graff, who came to Worthington from Pittsburgh in the 1830s. In 1844 he purchased the Buffalo Iron Foundry in the village and in 1865 built the Buffalo Woolen Mill to help employ the widows of men killed in the Civil War. The old mill nearby is now an electric printery. The Lutheran chapel in Worthington was built in honor of Peter Graff by his widow. Private residence of a descendant. *Location:* West end of Buffalo Creek.

5C. Mushroom Mines, the site of the largest underground mushroom farms in the world. *Location:* Off US 422.

6. One-room Schoolhouse (frame) was built in 1861 and enlarged in 1880. *Location:* Perry Township, SR 4002.

7. Sedwick House (brick and frame) was built by Hiram J. Sedwick in 1860–79. *Location:* Millers Eddy Village.

13. St. Patrick's Sugar Creek Church

8. Frazer House (brick and frame) was built in 1889 (date stone) by the Frazer family. *Location:* Perry Township, Queenston Petrolia Road (SR 4002), 1.5 miles west of the MacIntyre School off a black-top road.

9. Indian Millstone, possibly eighteenth century, is marked by a sign along the highway. *Location:* Foster Mill Road off SR 0268.

10. Hart House (frame) was built in 1860 by William Hart and later owned by William Armstrong Wilson, a soldier in the Civil War. *Location:* Sugar Creek Township, on SR 4009, 1 mile north of SR 0268.

11. Victorian House (frame), one story with a slate roof. *Location:* Beltone, 425 North Main Street.

12. Hotel Sagamore (frame), with sixty rooms, was built by William Hays in 1904. *Location:* Sagamore, SR 0210 (Cowanshannock Township).

13. St. Patrick's Sugar Creek Roman Catholic Church (log), measuring 22 by 35 feet, was built on land owned by Rev. Sylvester Phelan in 1805–06. A brick church, constructed in 1842 at a new location, was burned by vandals in 1872. The congregation used the old log church as a place of worship for four years after the fire. The structure is now restored and preserved as the oldest

existing Catholic church in western Pennsylvania. *Location:* Northwest corner of county, off SR 0268, 6 miles northwest of Cowansville, take SR 4009 south to T 134; or from Worthington, take SR 3011, SR 4033, and SR 4011 to SR 4007 just north of site.

14. Bradys Bend, a loop in the Allegheny River (see Clarion County), is also the name of a community in Armstrong County along the bend of the river.

14A. Bradys Bend Furnaces were built by Philander Raymond in 1840–46. *Location:* Behind school on SR 0068, 1 mile from Allegheny River bridge.

14B. McKinney House (frame), built in 1848, was the first company house constructed by Bradys Bend Iron Company (1839–73). *Location:* SR 0068.

14C. Power House for Pittsburgh Limestone Mining Company (brick) was built in 1912. *Location:* SR 0068.

14D. St. Stephen's Protestant Episcopal Church (stone) was built in 1868; the adjacent frame parsonage in 1866. Both were designed by Joseph Minteer. The church is now the headquarters for the Bradys Bend Historical Society. *Location:* SR 0068, about 1 mile south of river bridge.

14E. Trinity United Church of Christ, in Greek Revival style, was built in 1868 and remodeled in 1952. *Location:* SR 0068.

14F. Dewey House, a magnificent mansion built in 1868 for the superintendent of Bradys Bend Iron Works, was purchased in 1894 by Edward Dewey, a cousin of Admiral George Dewey, "the hero of Manilla" (see *Gridley's Grave,* Erie County). *Location:* SR 0068.

15. Parker City, the smallest incorporated city in Pennsylvania (pop. 843), was founded by William Parker shortly before 1800.

15A. Parker House Hotel (frame), formerly the Parker City Hotel, is the oldest building in the city. Judge John Parker built this structure, which was used by Fullerton Parker in 1824 as a warehouse. With the oil and lumber boom in the 1870s it became a hotel and is still used as a tavern with little change in the original structure and decor. In 1933 the proprietor of the Parker House Hotel, Benjamin F. Faust, was issued the first liquor licence in Parker City, following the repeal of the Eighteenth Amendment. *Location:* Junction of SR 0368 and SR 0268, near Butler County border.

Note: At this location Ben Hogan's Floating Palace (gambling house and brothel) used to operate in mid-river between Clarion and Armstrong counties.

15B. Robinson House (brick and frame) was built in 1872 by Samuel K. Robinson, a descendant of Dr. Simion Hovey, a pioneer settler of Hovey Township. *Location:* T 350.

16. Round Barn (frame) was built on the Homer H. Shoemaker farm in 1912. This is a rare structure, worthy of preservation. *Location:* Deanville, Reedy Mill Road (T 634) and Deanville Road (T 632), 3 miles south of Distant (Madison Township).

17. Smith-Urban House (brick) is the oldest surviving post-colonial (Federal) house in northern Armstrong County, built for Joseph Yost (d. 1841) and Magdalena Smith in the late 1820s. The Smiths (whose German name was Schmidt) came with their nine children to Armstrong County around 1807, settling on a 465-acre tract which included the site of "Old Town," an Indian village commonly referred to as "Fish-basket." Smith was a farmer and operated a ferry across Redbank Creek as early as 1818. He also had a tavern and "keeping room" at his house. His daughter Catherine married Andrew G. Workman, who

16. Round Barn

was a partner with her brother Henry in the operation of Phoenix Iron Furnace in Redbank Township. In 1881 the property was sold to Frank Williams and Company, a coal company in Buffalo, N.Y., and the house became the superintendent's residence of the company town of Oak Ridge. That same year a plank-frame addition and an Italianate hip roof with cupola were added to the house. The company went bankrupt in 1914. After successive ownerships, the Thomas Urban family purchased the house (1975) and restored it. *Location:* Near Oak Ridge, on Redbank Creek (Redbank Township).

18. Furlong-Filson House (brick) is a five-bay modified Greek Revival structure with a central hall. The interior retains many of its early features. It was built around 1840 on an 1834 land grant (941 acres) to Wilhem Wilink "et al (known commonly as the Holland Land Co.)." In 1838, 133 acres were conveyed to Christopher Shannon who in turn sold to John Furlong in 1839. Furlong was justice of the peace in Redbank Township in 1860. After successive ownerships the property was sold to the present owners, Robert B. and Margaret deLourde Filson, in 1946. Mr. Filson became judge of the Court of Common Pleas of Clarion County in 1972. *Location:* About 2 miles east of Oak Ridge, on SR 0839 (Redbank Township).

19. Stone Bridge, built in 1895 and recently reopened to traffic, is a fine example of late-nineteenth-century masonry. *Location:* Mahoning Township, about 2 miles west of SR 0066–0028 from the intersection just north of bridge over Pittsburgh & Shawmut Railroad, on Hogback Hill.

20. Calhoun Schoolhouse (red frame), in its original condition, is a one-room country school with the date 1881 scratched into its foundation. It is maintained as a museum by a local group. *Hours:* Summer months: Sunday, 3–5 P.M. Tours arranged. *Location:* Wayne Township, on SR 1016. Leave SR 0066–0028 just north of Goheenville and proceed east toward Belknap (northeast of Kittanning). Building is located halfway between Goheenville and Belknap.

21. Dayton and area

21A. Baltimore & Ohio Railroad Station (brick and frame), built in 1896–98, was later purchased by the Douglas Coal Company for its offices. *Location:* Poplar Street.

21B. Marshall Building (frame), a one-story Greek Revival structure built in 1850, was operated as a general store by Robert Marshall. *Location:* East Main Street.

21C. Thomas Hindman Marshall House (frame) was built after 1850 by Robert Marshall's son. (This property was once owned by John Hays, son of Mary Hays, the legendary "Mollie Pitcher" of Revolutionary War fame.) A large wooden tank, which formerly had water pumped into it by a windmill, has been preserved in the attic. The home has been restored as a museum and meeting place. *Location:* State Street.

21D. Glade Run United Presbyterian Church was built in 1857 and in 1871, with extensive remodeling carried out in 1961. The old academy building erected in 1851 has been remodeled as an education unit. *Location:* SR 0839.

21E. Marshall House (brick) is reputed to have been built in 1801 by William Marshall, Sr., one of the first settlers in the area. (The unusual architecture shows alterations at a later date.) His sons Robert and William were among the founders of the Soldiers' Orphans Home and the Glade Run Academy. The house served as an underground railway station prior to the Civil War and is perhaps the oldest home in the county. *Location:* About 0.5 mile south of Dayton, just west of SR 0839 near Glade Run Church.

Note: William Marshall, Sr., was an elder and one of the founders of Glade Run Church. The Marshall family donated the Associate Presbyterian Church, built in 1863, to the congregation in Dayton.

21E. Marshall House

21F. Pennsylvania Railroad Station (brick), built in 1896–98, was a former B&O station. *Location:* Poplar Street.

21G. Mahoning Dam was completed in 1941. *Location:* North of Dayton.

22. Rural Valley Hotel (brick) was operated in 1876 by William Kirkpatrick. Its age is uncertain, but it was purchased from Peter Brown in 1856. *Location:* Rural Valley, 639 Gourley Avenue at SR 0085, across from bank.

23. Zions Valley Reformed Church (frame), 35 by 45 feet, was built in 1871–75 in Carpenter Gothic style at a cost of $2,747. The church was organized as a result of German Reformed members wishing for services in English, while the Lutherans objected. Originally it was a union church. *Location:* Near Rural Valley, about 4 miles west of South Bend, a short distance south of road leading to Apollo (SR 0028 and SR 0066).

24. St. Michael's Evangelical Lutheran Church (brick) was founded in 1806 by Michael Steck, Jr., and incorporated in 1850. The first church, built here in 1852, was blown down July 29, 1860, and rebuilt the same year. On the day it was demolished the congregation began reconstruction. An early minister was Daniel Earhart, great-great-grandfather of Amelia Earhart. The old church cemetery is about three quarters of a mile east of the church off SR 2005. *Location:* Brickchurch, at junction of SR 0359 and SR 2015, 4 miles north of Mateer near Crooked Creek Dam and north of Cochrans Mills.

25. Cochrans Mills House (frame) is the only remaining structure in the original village of Cochrans Mills. Foundation scars at the town are visible near Crooked Creek. *Location:* Turn east off SR 0359 at Cochrans Mills on SR 2026. It is last house on right before crossing steel bridge (north of Mateer).

Note: Two prominent feminists, Nellie Bly and Margaret Miller Shoemaker, lived in Cochrans Mills. Unfortunately their homes no longer exist. Nellie Bly (pen name for Elizabeth Cochrane Seaman) was a young aspiring reporter and advocate of women's liberation who made a record-breaking trip around the world in 1889–90, completing it in seventy-two days. Working for Joseph Pulitzer (editor and publisher of *The World* newspaper) and beating the record of Phileas Fogg, hero of Jules Verne's *Around the World in Eighty Days,* she was known for her colorful exposures of governmental and industrial fraud. Her birthplace was in Cochrans Mills. In 1979 a commemorative millstone was dedicated to Nellie Bly at Cochrans Mills United Methodist Church, SR 0359, 3 miles from alternate SR 0066.

Margaret Miller Shoemaker was an excellent businesswoman who astonished America in the early 1800s (and was much laughed at) by twice requiring prenuptial agreements to protect her children's inheritance before remarrying after being widowed. The agreements also protected the rights of the children of the widowers whom she married. They were legally drawn and scrupulously kept, and covered the separate use, occupation, and management of the respective properties. Following the death of her first husband, George, she married Barnard Davers and later George King. Her home was located on a tract of land called Monmouth on the north side of Crooked Creek near the mouth of Cherry Run. Only a house scar remains. *Location:* South of Cochrans Mills, off SR 2026, east of road about 200 yards before village.

26. Elderton (Plumcreek Township)

26A. One-room Schoolhouse (frame), built in 1848, was operated by John Ralston. A dormitory for this "select school" was adapted from a barn. *Location:* Cemetery Road and West Saltworks Street.

26B. Elderton School (brick), a three-story Romanesque building, was active around 1880–96. *Location:* East Saltworks Street.

26C. Ralston House (frame), built in 1844, was the home of David Ralston, Jr., brother of John Ralston (see *One-room Schoolhouse).* *Location:* SR 0422 and West Saltworks Street.

28A. Rogers Mansion

27. Myers House (partially log covered with siding) was built about 1810. Fanny Myers was one of the early owners. One room was added before 1850 and another in 1879. In 1970 it was remodeled and restored by the present owners. The house has unusual double sliding doors for the front entrance and a fireplace in every room. An old springhouse on the property is now an antique-furniture refinishing shop. *Location:* About 4 miles north of Leechburg, off SR 0066. At intersection of SR 0066 and SR 2063 turn east (at nursery sign) and continue about 1.5 mile. House is on right.

28. Leechburg, a canal town, was laid out by David Leech in 1828.

28A. Rogers Mansion (brick, stuccoed), now Sandy Kaye's Restaurant, was built in Second Empire style, with mansard roof, in 1866 by William Rogers. Rogers was a partner in Apollo Steel and established the Siberian Iron Works in Leechburg in 1872. In later years this was the home of a Dr. Armstrong. It has been a restaurant since 1936. *Location:* 85 First Street.

28B. Leech House (brick and stucco) was the home of David Leech, founder of Leechburg. The house, which originally faced Basin Street and now faces Market Street, was built in 1845, the golden age of the Pennsylvania Canal. It is now the Masonic Hall. *Location:* Corner of Market and Spring streets (between Hicks and Market streets).

28C. David Leech House (brick), with four bays, was erected in 1830 by David Leech (d. 1858), who built a canal lock and dam, mills, and a railroad from Kittanning to Pittsburgh. He also operated a packet boat company and boatyard. *Location:* 304 Main Street.

28D. Hiram McCreary House (frame) was built in 1886–87. It remained in the McCreary family until 1922. At one time half the house was rented and a piano was left in place of money owed. To the right of the house, at the corner, is an early store, built years before this house was constructed. *Location:* 69 Center Avenue.

28E. Parks Victorian House (brick), an old mansion belonging to Jacob H. Parks (b. 1847), a prominent druggist in Leechburg, has been adapted for use by the First National Bank, a fine preservation movement in a time when many banks demolish historic buildings in order to build anew. *Location:* Market Street.

29. Apollo

29A. Drake Log House, measuring 18 by 24 feet, was built in the south end of Apollo sometime between 1816 and 1848. The dwelling was purchased from Samuel Wilson of Conneaut Lake in recent years by the Apollo Area Historical Society and named for Mrs. Sarah Drake, who lived in it for about fifty years. The land for the structure was donated to the society by Robert Halstein, a California resident. The cabin was restored in 1971. *Hours:* By appointment and first Sunday of month, 2–4 P.M. *Donation. Location:* Off South Kiski Avenue, reached most conveniently from South Warren Avenue. (Look for log cabin signs after turning right off First Street.)

29B. Bible Church (frame), formerly a Baptist church, is a Carpenter Gothic structure built in 1896. It was heavily damaged in the St. Patrick's Day flood of 1936. The clock tower has been rebuilt. *Location:* Railroad Street at tracks.

29C. McCullough Log Cabin, one of only a few left in the county, was the home of Abraham Lincoln McCullough, a carriage manufacturer, in the 1870s. It was moved to this site from Dayton. *Location:* Jefferson and Atwood streets.

29D. Jackson House (frame), Italianate and Colonial Revival in style, was built in 1860–79. It was originally owned by Col. Samuel M. Jackson who served in Company G. 11th Pa. and was promoted to brigadier general in 1864. He was elected to the U.S. House of Representatives in 1869 and to the state house in 1874. *Location:* 411 Terrace Avenue.
　Note: At 565–67 Terrace Avenue is an outstanding ornate Colonial Revival house built around 1900–16.

30. Laurel Grange (frame) represents the many rural fraternal granges that were very active years ago. Known officially as Patrons of Husbandry, this national organization was formed in 1867 by Oliver Hudson Kelley (1826–1913). Local granges often built their own halls, such as this one, for recreational and educational programs and also for organized opposition to unfair practices. National headquarters were established at 1616 H Street, N.W., Washington, D.C. A number of granges still function and reflect the important farm communities in this region. *Location:* SR 0066, north of Apollo.

31. Dining and Keeping Room (brick), owned at one time by Elias Miller, was bought about 1830 by James and Robert Coulter. The house and property were assessed for the first time in 1844. The two-and-a-half-acre property was once the Pleasant Valley Stock Farm, where famous racehorses were bred. The house, restored in 1974 by its present owners, conforms with the original architecture. The eight-room structure has a new kitchen wing along with other additions, fireplaces in every room, and a roof of lead and wrought iron imported from Portugal. A brick springhouse is nearby. It was restored by the Gorelli family. *Location:* Gilpen Township, about 2.5 miles north of Leechburg on SR 0066.

32. Freeport (originally Todd's Town), laid out in 1796 by David Todd, is the oldest non-Indian town in the county. It was traversed by the western division of the Pennsylvania Canal.

32A. Massa Harbison Grave. See *Massa Harbison Log Cabin,* Westmoreland County. *Location:* Freeport Cemetery, junction of SR 0028 and SR 0356, north of Freeport.

32B. A. Guckenheimer & Brothers Distillery Kitchen (brick and frame) was built with other buildings in 1861–76. (The father, Asher, was born in Germany in 1825.) The most productive time for this business was in 1866. By 1913 it had become the largest rye whiskey distillery in the United States. During the Prohibition era of the 1920s it continued to operate illegally. *Location:* 512 Market Street.

32C. Truby House (frame) was built by a riverboat captain in colonial revival style about 1900–19. *Location:* 317 Fourth Street.

32D. Second Empire House (brick), built in 1875, is one of the best of its kind in the area. *Location:* 319 Fourth Street.

32E. Clothing Store (brick) was built in 1898 by J. H. Shoop. This was one of the earliest family-owned retail establishments for men's clothing in the region. *Location:* 201–05 Fifth Avenue.

32F. St. Mary's Roman Catholic Church (brick) was built in 1849 (date stone). The architecture is Gothic/folk vernacular. *Location:* 606 High Street.

32G. St. Mary's Parish Convent (brick), a five-bay structure built in 1822 as a residence (John Porter, Jacob Shoop), was a convent from 1858 to 1926. *Location:* 619 High Street.

32H. Trinity Episcopal Church (brick) was built in 1837. This one-story Vernacular Gothic church is the oldest existing church in Freeport. *Location:* Sixth and High streets.

33. Laneville Gristmill (frame), originally called the Valley Mill, is the third constructed on this site, about 1890. Mills have stood here for nearly two hundred years. The present structure, on the original foundation, is built of timber, some twenty-four feet long, floated down the Kiskiminetas River to Buffalo Creek. The mill used a stone burr, and from 1910 to 1968 had a massive gas engine and a vertical turbine (single shaft). Probably built by Levi Hill, it is now owned by the Freeport Community Park Association, which plans to remodel the structure with a running (not functional) wheel. *Location:* Near Freeport, off SR 0356. After heading northwest on SR 0356 beyond Freeport, cross Buffalo Creek and turn right to get to mill.

34. Transylvania Bible Institute (stone) was founded in 1938 by Rev. Henry Shilling. This nondenominational school was built by students, entirely on faith. Two later additions were also constructed by the student body. The school has fathered others of its type, one in Canada and another in Oregon. *Location:* Halfway between village of Slate Lick and Slate Lick exit off SR 0028.

35. Ross House (stone) was built about 1807–09 by George Ross (1777–1829), a judge and first permanent white settler in the Kittanning Manor. It is located on the site of Fort Green. *Location:* Rosston, 749 Ross Avenue. From Fourth Avenue in Ford City bear left before bridge and continue along Allegheny River to Rosston. Take left turn over railroad to first house on right.

Note: Fort Green was built by Judge Ross in 1807.

36. Crooked Creek Dam. *Location:* South of Ford City, off SR 0066.

37. Keystone Dam includes Keystone Generating Station on a 1,000-acre bend in Crooked Creek, one mile downstream from its Plum Creek branch. *Location:* Halfway between SR 0422 and SR 0156, off SR 0210.

38. Ford City Glass Factory, a plate-glass industry established by Capt. John B. Ford in 1887, was at one time the largest plant of its kind in the world. *Location:* Ford City, junction of SR 0066 and SR 0128 on Allegheny River.

Note: Ford's statue is in the Ford City Park, Fourth Avenue and Ninth Street.

Iron Furnaces
(originally fifteen)

McCrea (Olney) Furnace (1857), built by McCrea and Galbraith. About 0.7 miles north of Goheenville on SR 0028, turn right on SR 03080 for 3 miles, then left on SR 03075 for 1.3 miles to T 667. Turn right. Before crossing bridge, turn left on T 748 for 200 yards.

Mahoning (Colwell) Furnace (1845), built by John A. Colwell of Kittanning. Just east of SR 0028, across Red Bank Creek from village of Mahoning Furnace.

Ore Hill Furnace (1845). Turn west on SR 1034 just north of Mosgrove, to dam. Walk lane between railroad and river for 0.3 mile.

Stewardson Furnace (1851), built by Stewardson and Laughlin. Near Mahoning, go east on T 691 to sweeping uphill bend.

Pennsylvania Historical and Museum Commission Markers

Armstrong County Kittanning, at courthouse, Market and Jefferson streets

Blanket Hill US 422, 6.5 miles east of Kittanning

Bradys Bend Works Bradys Bend, SR 0068

Fort Armstrong SR 0066, 1.8 mile south of Kittanning

Kittanning Kittanning, US 422

St. Patrick's Church SR 0268, 6 miles northwest of Cowansville

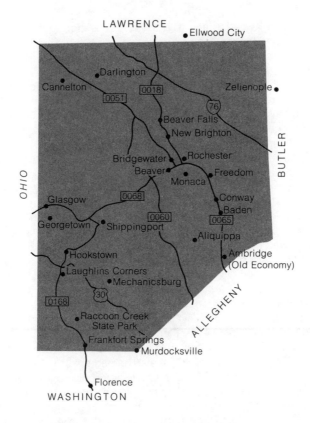

LAWRENCE

• Ellwood City

• Darlington

Cannelton •

[0051]   [0018]

Zelienople •

(76)

• Beaver Falls
• New Brighton

Bridgewater • • Rochester
Beaver •
Monaca • • Freedom

OHIO

Glasgow   [0068]
•
Georgetown • Shippingport
[0060]
Conway
• Baden
[0065]
• Aliquippa

BUTLER

Hookstown
Laughlins Corners
• Mechanicsburg

[0168]   (30)

Raccoon Creek
State Park
Frankfort Springs
• Murdocksville

• Ambridge
(Old Economy)

ALLEGHENY

• Florence

WASHINGTON

Beaver County

Capsule History

Beaver County (named for the Beaver River) was erected out of Washington and Allegheny counties on March 12, 1800. It decreased in size on March 20, 1849, when Lawrence County was formed, leaving it with 436 square miles. The county's population is 204,441.

Among the early settlers of the land that was to become Beaver County were John Bever, one of two first deputy surveyors appointed by Rufus Putnam, surveyor general of the United States in 1799, and Levi Dungan, who in 1772 lived near Frankfort Springs. Thomas White resided at Raccoon Creek about the same time and established the first gristmill in the county.

Logstown, an important trading settlement of the upper Ohio until 1758, was founded during the Delaware and Shawnee migrations of 1725–27. In 1749 Conrad

63

Weiser, a Pennsylvania Indian agent, brought a message to the Indians camped at Logstown proclaiming that the land belonged to the British. The same year the French claimed the area by placing lead plates along the Allegheny and Ohio rivers. This settlement was the scene of numerous Indian conferences, including the first one between the English and the tribes living along the Ohio River. Both the Delaware and the Six Nations Indians had other settlements near the mouth of the Big Beaver.

Gen. Anthony Wayne trained his army near Logstown (in 1792–93), renaming it Legionville. Montmorin (later Ambridge), above the site of Logstown, was a town projected by Col. Isaac Melcher in 1787. In 1824 the Harmony Society purchased the land and the following year laid out the village of Economy on the site.

Other towns played important parts in the history of the county. Beaver Falls, at the middle falls, was known as Brighton or Old Brighton until 1859, when the Harmony Society purchased the site. It was incorporated in 1868. Beaver, the county seat, was laid out September 28, 1791, and incorporated March 29, 1802. Until 1758 the settlement was known as Shingas Old Town, of the Shawnee and Delaware tribes. During the Revolution it was the site of Fort McIntosh. Monaca (Phillipsburg until 1892) was founded in 1822 by Stephen Phillips, a member of the Phillips and Graham boat-building firm. In ten years his company constructed thirty-two steamboats, including the *Mohawk,* at that time the longest boat on western waters. Other early villages included Darlington, Hookstown, Georgetown, Frankfort Springs, Enon Valley, Freedom, and Blackhawk.

Brodhead Road, built in 1778 by Gen. Daniel Brodhead for military purposes, ran from Fort Pitt to Fort McIntosh, following in part the route of present-day SR 0051. The Beaver and Erie Canal, built in the 1830s, also helped the area to develop. The Sandy and Beaver Canal left the Ohio River at the western edge of the county.

The Beaver River—which falls sixty-nine feet in five miles—and the Ohio River provided early industrial development and transportation. Shortly after 1800 manufacturing began at the falls of the Beaver River, and by 1835 there were four or five dams and sixteen to eighteen factories in operation. David Townsend erected a sawmill at the lower falls (Fallston) in 1799. Old Economy, final home of the Harmony Society, was a prosperous manufacturing and mercantile center. Boat-building was an important industry along the river for almost a century; and rich coal deposits, together with abundant supplies of building stone, helped promote industrial development. There was a shortage of iron, however, and Beaver County had only three stone blast furnaces in the early period. The Jones & Laughlin steel mill at Aliquippa was one of the largest in Pennsylvania. By 1987 most of the mills had closed.

Four important Indian trails crossed Beaver County. The *Great Path* followed the right bank of the Ohio, crossed the Beaver near its mouth, and turned west through Blackhawk into Ohio. The *Logstown Path* swung right off the Great Path at Conway and ran northward through Economy Township toward Zelienople. (George Washington and Christopher Gist took this course on their way to Fort LeBoeuf.) The *Mahoning Path* from Beaver followed the left bank of the Beaver River and then cut eastward near Slippery Rock. Finally, the *Kuskusky-Ohio Forks Path* cut across the northeast corner of Beaver County and ran northwest near Fombell toward Wurtemburg.

The county has been traditionally thought of as East, West, and South Beaver, divided by the Ohio and Beaver rivers.

Near Glasgow are Indian petroglyphs on the banks of the Ohio River.

Landmarks

1. Beaver, an early fort site and river town

1A. Courthouse (stone) was built in 1876–77. The first court of Beaver County had been held September 6, 1804, at Abner Lacock's tavern, and later courts met in the jail (on the northeast side of the square, fronting Third Street) until the original courthouse was built in 1810. The present building was erected west of this site; additions to it were made in 1906–07. Partly burned in 1932, it was remodeled in 1933 with a later addition in 1973–74. The architect of the present courthouse was David S. Geredel of Philadelphia and the contractor was John Schreiner of Pittsburgh. The stone jail is across from the courthouse. *Location:* Corner of Market and Third streets.

1B. Quay House (brick) was the home of Matthew Stanley Quay, who moved to Beaver with his family in 1840 and became prothonotary in 1856. During the Civil War he was military secretary to Gov. Andrew Curtin. He also served as an assemblyman, 1865–67; secretary of the commonwealth, 1872–82; treasurer of the commonwealth, 1885–89; and U.S. senator, 1889–1904. From 1867 to 1872 he was owner-editor of the *Beaver Radical*. A Republican, he was for decades the ultimate political "boss" of Pennsylvania and gained national prominence as manager of the presidential campaign of 1888. Quay died in 1904 and is buried in the Beaver Cemetery. His house is now a funeral home. *Location:* 205 College Avenue at Second Street.

1C. Johnston-McCreary House (weatherboarded log) is reputed to be the oldest house in Beaver. The original part was built in 1805 on a log foundation and cost seventy-one dollars. An early owner, David Johnston, was the first prothonotary of Beaver County. In 1815 he became the first teacher of the Beaver Academy. *Location:* Corner of Market Street and River Road, across from site of Fort McIntosh.

1D. Fort McIntosh (log) was the first U.S. military post north of the Ohio River and also served as a survey base. It was built in 1778 by Gen. Lachlan McIntosh (1725–1806), commander in chief of the western department during the Revolutionary War, and designed by Le Chevalier de Cambray, chief of artillery in McIntosh's army. This trapezoidal fort with four bastions was built on a 150-foot bluff as a base for launching attacks against the British and Indians in the West. In 1785 it was used as a meeting place for the U.S. treaty with the western Indians, the outcome of which enabled Congress to establish the Northwest Territory and made possible the sale of depreciation lands as payment to Revolutionary War soldiers. The fort was abandoned in 1788, and due to plundering the framework was completely gone by 1791.

Members of the Beaver County Chapter of the Society for Pennsylvania Archeology have excavated the site. Although the fort is not rebuilt, the Beaver Area Heritage Foundation has completely restored the site, with the original stone foundation preserved. A flag plaza is nearby. *Location:* River Road at end of Market Street on bluff overlooking Ohio River.

Note: A museum containing artifacts and information concerning Fort McIntosh is located in the Beaver Memorial Library, College Avenue at River Road (one block east of the fort site).

1E. Fort McIntosh Club was the home for Beaver College presidents. Rudyard Kipling was once a guest at this house. *Location:* College Avenue.

1F. Pittsburgh and Lake Erie Railroad Station (brick) moved to its present location in the 1920s. It serves as a county emergency service center. Inside is preserved its original brass hand rail, used by train passengers years ago. *Location:* River Road.

1G. Clark Square Cemetery, named for George Rogers Clark, has graves dating back to the 1790s (both whites and Indians). Many names of those buried here are recorded on a central monument in the square. *Location:* Fifth and Buffalo streets.

1H. Dravo House (brick) was built by John F. Dravo, steamboat operator, pioneer in coal-towing, and industrialist, who owned much of the land along River Road (formerly First or Front Street) in the late nineteenth century. The turreted house overlooks the Ohio River. *Location:* Corner of River and Dravo streets.

Note: Brewer School (frame), a one-room schoolhouse, was built in 1896. It closed in 1929. *Location:* SR 0068 in Daugherty Township, halfway between Rochester and New Brighton (about 3 miles from each town).

2. Rochester, once the hub of Beaver County, is on the Ohio River where the Big Beaver River joins it.

2C. *Bausman House* Photo: Beaver County Albums

3. *Dunlap House* Photo: Beaver County Albums

2A. Wharf was once busy with barges and riverboats unloading provisions here for surrounding towns. Later diminishing, river trade is again on the rise. The Pavilion Hotel was built in the area in its heyday. *Location:* Brighton Avenue (the first paved street in the county).

2B. Flag Tower was erected September 5, 1898, in honor of Company B, Tenth Regiment, Pennsylvania Infantry, U.S. Volunteers. The park was given to the community in 1834 by the Townsend family. *Location:* Third Avenue.

2C. Bausman House (frame), built around 1910, was the home of Rev. Joseph H. Bausman (1854–1927) who wrote a two-volume History of Beaver County (1904). *Location:* 439 Delaware Avenue.

2D. Royce Theater (brick), built in 1925, contains a scale composite of the great movie palaces of the 1930s (scaled one inch to the foot). It shows a stage and screen program that includes an organ prologue, newsreel, cartoons, and coming attractions as well as the main feature. Special education seminar available. Open by appointment only. *Admission fee.* The building used to be the Laclede-Christie company, manufacturers of glass melting pots for the glass trade. They used to furnish pots for Fry Glass, Phoenix Glass, and others. *Location:* 630 New York Avenue, in Frank E. Davis Associates Studios.

3. Dunlap House (brick) was built in the late 1800s by Samuel Dunlap. His son, Senator William Dunlap, also lived in the house. *Location:* Bridgewater, 1298 Market Street.

Note: The brick Presbyterian church near the bridge on Third Street was erected in 1845 and rebuilt in 1879–80.

4. Wray Homestead (cut stone) was built overlooking Beaner Hollow by Joseph Wray in 1835. An unusual signature stone is inscribed above the front entrance with the date and the builder's name in script instead of print. The original stone sink is still in use in the kitchen, and the windows throughout the house have the original glass. Many of the Wray family's furnishings, including a portrait of the first owner, remain in the home. The last of the Wray family to reside in this house, Joseph's granddaughter, Katherine Wray Peters, willed the property to its present owners. *Location:* Brighton Township, 1 mile north of Beaver, a quarter mile off Dutch Ridge Road (Market Street extension), 100 yards to left of Beaner Hollow Road (1020 Beaner Hollow Road).

5. Mount Pleasant (painted brick) was built in 1808 by John Wolf, Jr., who earlier had lived at Fort McIntosh. His son was Squire A. B. Wolf. The home has a double porch, and the property originally included 148 acres. *Location:* Brighton Township, 908 Western Avenue, 1 mile north of Beaver.

6. Small House (painted brick) is now a part of a housing plan, with the carriage house and greenhouse both remodeled as private dwellings. One of the early owners was in the oil business. A later owner was a Mr. Small, for whom the house is named. *Location:* At north edge of Beaver, on Dutch Ridge Road (Market Street extension).

7. Richmond Little Red Schoolhouse (brick) was in operation from 1844 to 1950. At present it is maintained as a one-room schoolhouse museum by the Richmond Little Red Schoolhouse Organization. *Hours:* Sundays in June, July, August, 2–5 P.M. Tours by appointment. *Location:* Park Road, Brighton Township, near entrance to Brady's Run Park

4. *Wray Homestead*

9. *Merrill Dam Lock House*

at Dutch Ridge Road (Market Street extension).

8. Sandy and Beaver Canal Lock No. 54 is located on the Little Beaver near the mouth of Island Run and, though in ruins, is the only early lock of this canal remaining in Pennsylvania. The canal basin near the Ohio River can be seen from SR 0068. *Location:* Glasgow. Just within state limits on SR 0068, drive 0.95 mile on unmarked cinder road; walk for about 2 miles over old railroad bed (right of way of Erie & Ohio Railroad). Lock is about 300 feet below tracks along Little Beaver.

9. Merrill Dam and U.S. Lock No. 6. At this site, two identical brick houses overlook the Ohio River. A large concrete step landing into the water is directly in front of the one that served as the lock house. The other was a residence/office building. The lock operated from 1905 to 1936. *Location:* SR 0068, 1.2 miles from west edge of Beaver, at SR 0060.

10. Potter-Barclay House (stone), a saltbox house, was built by James Potter and his five sons between 1820 and 1833. He and his family lived in a log cabin on this land (purchased in 1786 by Andrew Porter, appropriated for redemption of depreciation certificates given to Revolutionary War veterans) until their stone house was constructed. James's daughter, Hannah Christy (b. 1852), married Robert Hunter Barclay in 1871. The eight-room house, built of massive cut stones (some seven feet long), overlooks the Ohio River. James Potter died in 1861. Nearby is an Indian village site. *Location:*

Near Barclay's Crossing and Barclay Hill Road, on SR 0068 between Industry and Beaver (near Lock No. 6).

11. Point of Beginning Marker of the National Survey was erected in 1886 to mark the southern extremity of the Pennsylvania-Ohio border as resurveyed. About 112 feet south on the Ohio River bank was the point where Thomas Hutchins, first U.S. geographer, began the first survey of public lands in the United States, September 30, 1785. It was here that he began the system of quarters, sections, square townships, and ranges almost universally used since that time. *Location:* SR 0068 at Ohio-Pennsylvania line.

12. Pittsburgh & Lake Erie Railroad Bridge (1,787 feet long) was built about 1907–10 over the Ohio River. James M. Schoonmaker, head of the P&LE at that time, believed that the most important feature of a railroad bridge was strength. This structure for four tracks gantleted to two is one of the strongest ever built and has defied the ravages of time and changes in equipment. It was designed by Albert Lucius. *Location:* Over Ohio River between Monaca and Beaver.

13. Beaver Falls was incorporated in 1868 and chartered as a city in 1930.

13A. Beaver Falls Historical Museum (brick) was established in 1944 through the efforts of county commissioners, the Beaver County Research and Landmarks Foundation, and the Carnegie Library. The center is located on the lower level of the Carnegie

10. Potter-Barclay House

Free Library of Beaver Falls, which was built in 1902, the first public library in the county. A complete listing of Beaver County historical sites and landmarks published by the resource and research center for the county, too extensive to include here, is available at this library. *Hours:* Monday, 5–8 P.M.; Tuesday–Thursday, 11 A.M.–5 P.M.; Friday, 11 A.M.–4 P.M.. *Location:* 1301 Seventh Avenue at Thirteenth Street.

13B. Harmonist Houses, five stone structures built by the Harmony Society when Beaver Falls was founded, still remain in the town, mostly in good condition. (See *Old Economy* and also *Harmony,* Butler County.) All are private residences. Locations: 1314 Third Avenue, 1603 Fourth Avenue, 1618 Fifth Avenue, 1602 Sixth Avenue, and 1324 Tenth Avenue.

13C. Old Main Hall at Geneva College (stone, quarried on the campus) was built in 1880 at this liberal arts, coeducational college. The school was founded April 20, 1848, by the Reformed Presbyterian Church in Northwood, Ohio, and was moved to its present location when John Reeves, a representative of the Harmony Society, offered to give it ten acres of land. (Reeves Athletic Field is named in his honor.) The class of 1881 was the first to graduate at Beaver Falls. Geneva College is the only institution of higher learning of the Reformed Presbyterian Church (Covenanter) except for its theological seminary in Wilkinsburg. In 1945 the college awarded an honorary degree to John Duss (1860–1951), the last surviving member of the Harmony Society. *Location:* College Avenue (on College Hill).

13D. White Home (stone) was built about 1853 by Thomas White, son of John White,

one of the first settlers of Beaver Falls. *Location:* 3925 Thirty-ninth Street at Fourth Avenue (on College Hill).

13E. Greenway Farmhouse (painted brick), built about 1830, belonged to Joseph Swartz in 1876. The farm included 150 acres at that time. *Location:* 3186 Thirty-seventh Street extension.

13F. Mayfield Cottage Farmhouse (log and weatherboards with shingles) was built about 1825. The home has a belfry with the original bell, which was used for calling the farmhands to dinner or in times of distress. The barn, now a garage, once had a date of 1823 on it. Originally consisting of 200 acres, the property was named for Mayfield Station nearby. The Schutte family has owned this property for three generations. *Location:* 3181 Thirty-seventh Street extension at Clearview Street (across from Greenway Farm in West Mayfield).

13G. Theater (brick) was once used as an entertainment center in the golden days of the movies. It is now a multipurpose structure. *Location:* Seventh Avenue between Eleventh and Twelfth streets.

13H. Haley House (weatherboarded log) was built by John Haley about 1792, with subsequent additions. An early cupola on top of the house has been removed. *Location:* 191 Oakville Road.

14. Watt House (fieldstone), a long, primitive-looking structure, is composed of three sections, the first of which was built by the Watt family. Thomas, James, and their sister Mary, none of whom ever married, lived in this portion of the house, built in 1851–52. (Date on cornerstone is concealed underground.) The second section was added in 1866 (cornerstone by door), and the date of the third part is uncertain. *Location:* Daugherty Township, on Helbly Road, 0.2 mile from its intersection with Tulip Drive (which is off SR 0068). House sits 0.1 mile behind buff brick house on Helbly Road, near Beaver Falls.

15. Darlington

15A. Greersburg Academy (two sites—the older is stone, the newer is brick), under the auspices of the Presbytery of Erie, was chartered by the state of Pennsylvania on February 24, 1806, through the endeavors of Thomas E. Hughes, who was pastor of Mount Pleasant Presbyterian Church at Greersburg

15A. Brick Building at Greersburg Academy

(now Darlington) and New Salem Presbyterian Church at the village of Salem Church. He had built a log school near his home in 1802 and became the first head of the academy until its incorporation in 1806, when Daniel Hayden succeeded him. William Holmes McGuffey, editor of the famous *McGuffey's Readers,* attended this school. In 1833 the "stone academy" was sold to the Pittsburgh, Marion & Chicago Railroad Company to be used for a depot. For a while it was a private residence.

In 1883 the academy built a new two-story brick building on the corner of Second and Plum streets, which closed about 1910 and became a public school. Today it is the Little Beaver Museum. *Hours:* June–September: Saturday and Sunday, 1:30–5 P.M. Both academy buildings now belong to the Little Beaver Historical Society. *Locations:* SR 0168.

15B. Greersburg Free Presbyterian Church (brick) was founded by Arthur Bloomfield Bradford, an abolitionist leader and pastor of Mount Pleasant Presbyterian Church in Greersburg (now Darlington) from 1839 to 1847 (see *Bradford House*). In 1847 Bradford withdrew from the pastorate because of a disagreement with the synod on the question of slavery and organized the Free Presbyterian Church, becoming its first pastor. This house of worship, a charming structure, was erected in 1847. With the dissolution of the Free Presbyterian denomination after the Civil War, the congregation became affiliated with the Reformed Presbyterian Church. *Location:* South edge of Darlington, SR 0168.

15C. Wallace House (brick) was bought in 1839 by the Wallaces, and it has remained in this family ever since that time. *Location:* Wallace Drive off Market Street.

Note: "Sprott's Delight," another Wallace

house, built in the early 1800s, is in Darlington Township.

15D. Martin House (frame) was constructed with a double porch and a stone foundation about 1805. Much of its history is obscure. *Location:* Rohrmann Road, 1 block from Fourth Street.

15E. Alliance Brick Factory (brick) later housed the Federal Steel Corporation. Its two buildings are abandoned. Across the road is a brick house built in 1825. It was once owned by Rankin Martin, a Beaver lawyer. *Location:* Darlington Road near junction with Alliance Road.

16. Douthitt Farmhouse (brick) was built by Joseph Douthitt about 1832 and was a stagecoach stop on the Pittsburgh-Cleveland road. An old stile, or stepping stone, used for carriages stands in the front yard. This property is still owned by members of the Douthitt family. *Location:* 1 mile north of Darlington, on Hollow Road.

17. Veon House (stone) was built by a Mr. Veon and his son. The elder Veon had been a Hessian soldier who turned patriot during the Revolutionary War, making America his home. Local tradition dates this house from 1850, but its appearance and other factors would indicate a date nearer 1825. *Location:* 1.5 miles north of Darlington, on Hollow Road.

18. Bradford House (brick), called "Buttonwood," was built between 1837 and 1840 by Arthur Bloomfield Bradford, abolitionist and founder of the Greersburg Free Presbyterian Church (q.v.), who was once sent by President Lincoln to China as an ambassador. His home was one of the stops on the underground railroad. The small brick building behind the main house was a "prophet house" used for visiting parsons who could stay overnight and prepare their sermons. *Location:* About 2 miles north of Darlington, on Bradford Road off Hollow Road (Darlington Township).

Note: Clow-Schry House (frame) was built about 1820 by James Clow, a prominent abolitionist in the area. The house, documented as part of the underground railroad when Clow owned the property, is Greek Revival in style. Apprentice carpenters from England built the house, now owned by Frederick Schry. *Location:* Chapel Road, North Sewickley Township, near Darlington.

19. Morris House (brick) was built by Jonathan Morris. The signature stone on the chimney reads, "Jan. Morris 1837." Later John White (no relation to builder of White Home) bought the property. White incorporated the Darlington Coal Company in 1852 and was its president for the first eight years. A brick smokehouse stands near the home, and both are being restored by the present owners. The White cemetery is nearby on the same side of the road. *Location:* Cannelton, Cannelton Road, in industrial park area.

Note: Watt's Mill Bridge (iron) was built at the site of Watt's Mill, which was built around 1798. The stones from the mill foundation can still be seen. The bridge is still in use. *Location:* Cannelton.

20. Mansfield House (frame), built about 1840, was the birthplace and summer home of Ira F. Mansfield (who died in 1919 and is buried at Poland, Ohio), a prominent coal operator who bought out the Cannelton Mining Company interests in 1865. Mansfield was a Beaver County state representative in 1880–81. In 1887 he moved to Beaver, living in a home with turrets that was at times referred to as the Queen's Castle. This edifice was replaced by the new library building on the corner of College Avenue and River Road. *Location:* Northwest of Darlington, on Ridge Road, 0.3 mile from Cannelton Road near Ohio line.

21. Stone Face on Painter's Knob was created by Charles Jones, an eccentric who carved the face in a huge rock, with two round hollows for eyes, one for a mouth, and a square depression for a nose, so that water would collect for birds to drink. The rock, facing skyward, sits high on a steep knob, which has partially been stripped for coal. *Location:* 0.5 mile south of Cannelton, off Cannelton Road on unused road behind Morris house (q.v.). Hill where stone face is located is reached by crossing Little Beaver Creek over stringers of iron bridge with most of floorboards missing. Extremely difficult access, but rewarding climb.

22. New Brighton

22A. Merrick Free Art Gallery (brick) was founded in 1880 by Edward Dempster Merrick, an industrialist and philanthropist. The gallery contains French, German, English, and American paintings of the eighteenth and nineteenth centuries collected by its founder, himself an artist. Today it also houses the New Brighton Historical Society. Unfortunately all Merrick's own paintings were discarded about 1930. *Hours:* Tuesday–Saturday, 10

21. Stone Face

A.M.–5 P.M.; Sunday, 1–5 P.M. *Location:* Fifth Avenue and Eleventh Street.

Note: This building was a former railroad station, c. 1865.

22B. 1823 House (brick with frame addition in rear) has a marker on the front porch bearing the date of its construction. In the back is a stone well with a cement foundation that has Pennsylvania Dutch sayings inscribed on it at a later date. *Location:* 513 Third Avenue.

22C. White Cottage (frame) was the home of Sarah Clarke Lippincott, whose pen name was Grace Greenwood, an internationally known journalist who was ahead of her time. Born in 1823, she wrote a number of her books in this house in the 1850s. Some of her work was published in *McGuffey's Readers*. *Location:* 1221 Third Avenue (marker in front of house).

22D. Christ Episcopal Church (stone) was built in 1851 with stone buttresses added later. The first rector was J. P. Taylor. *Location:* Third Avenue next to White cottage.

23. Conway Railroad Yards, opened in 1880, are the largest push-button railroad yards in the United States. There are no tours, but operations of the yard can be viewed from streets overlooking the site. *Location:* Conway, Penn Central Railroad, running beside SR 0065 for 1 mile.

24. Vicary House (cut stone) was built in 1826–33 by William Vicary, a sea captain from Philadelphia. After living in Sewickley, where two of his eight children were born, Vicary purchased from the government about one thousand acres extending from Dutch Run in Freedom to Crows Run, where the stones for his three-story house were quarried. The home has eight rooms, each eighteen feet square, arranged around a wide hall and a winding staircase. The walls are two feet thick.

Vicary's last voyage was in 1803 as captain of the *Liberty,* a trading vessel which sailed from Philadelphia to the East Indies. His experiences at sea included a near-mutiny among his men, which he quelled, and a battle with Chinese pirates. A scar on his forehead was a permanent reminder of the latter encounter. In accordance with his wife's wishes, he finally gave up the life of the sea. In 1837 he laid out the village of Saint Clair, often referred to as "Vicary Extension," which has been part of Freedom Borough since 1896.

Recently a retaining wall was built to preserve this early landmark, located precariously close to the new Beaver Valley Expressway. The Beaver County Historical Research and Landmarks Foundation has preserved the house as a museum and headquarters for the organization. *Location:* Freedom, 1251 Fourth Street, on Harvey's Run Road above SR 0065, overlooking Conway Railroad Yards.

25. Legionville is the site of the encampment and training grounds for Gen. Anthony Wayne's "Legion of the United States" from November 9, 1792, to April 30, 1793. In 1794 he and his troops won victory over the Indians at the Battle of Fallen Timbers. The camp site was the first one established exclusively for the training of troops in the United States. This property overlaps with the Indian village site of Logstown where the county's first Roman Catholic mass was said in 1749. *Location:* Near Baden, between Duss Avenue and SR 0065 (Harmony Township).

26. Old Economy, a religious community founded in 1805 by George Rapp (1757–1847), was the third and last home (1825–1905) of the Harmony Society, builders of a large industrial empire. They adopted celibacy in 1807. (See *Harmony,* Butler County). There are five stone Economy houses nearby in the area. Now operated by the Pennsylvania Historical and Museum Commission. *Hours:* Daylight Saving Time: Weekdays, 8:30 A.M.–5 P.M.; Sunday, 1–5 P.M. Winter: Weekdays, 9 A.M.–4:30 P.M.; Sunday, 1–4:30 P.M. *Admission charge. Location:* Ambridge, Fourteenth and Church streets.

26A. Great House (brick), having thirty-five rooms, was the home of Father Rapp and some of his successors in office. Its hostess for many years was his granddaughter, Gertrude. The building is furnished in its original style.

26B. Feast Hall (brick), the society's cultural center, which included a school, museum, and printshop, was built about 1830. The tremendous single room upstairs was used for feasts, band concerts, and other events.

26C. Grotto (stone) is a small garden house that contains many symbolic decorations to encourage meditation. It is surrounded by a well-kept garden.

26D. Baker House (brick) was remodeled in 1847 at the time that Romelius Baker took over Father Rapp's position. Baker lived here until his death in 1868. It is on exhibit as a typical Harmonist house.

26E. Harmonie Associates House (brick), located outside the walled grounds of the original village, is now occupied by the Associates, a volunteer group that presents craft fairs, classes, and similar events.

26F. St. John's Lutheran Church (brick) was built by the society in 1827–31, replacing a wooden structure located on Fifteenth Street. It is not currently open to the public except for church services. A belfry clock with the mechanism for only one hand still keeps good time when in repair. In the front churchyard is a linden tree planted in 1917 in honor of the four hundredth anniversary of the Reformation. Encircling the tree is a large millstone.

26G. A granary, wine cellar, and other shops are also located on the property.

26H. Print shop.

27. Ambridge was named for Andrew Carnegie's American Bridge Company.

27A. Early structures and Harmonist houses in Ambridge include Mad Anthony's tavern on Fourteenth Street; Mulberry Lane Antiques; Nello's Tradin' Post on Merchant Avenue; Bill's Country Store on Duss Street; and Old Economy Village Bakery at Wagner and Merchant streets. On Thirteenth Street is a gift shop in a restored log house.

27B. American Bridge Company was the world's largest steel fabricating plant. Here

26A. Great House at Old Economy

the steel for the Empire State Building in New York City was produced.

27C. First Presbyterian Church (stone). Dr. William W. McKinney, the widely known church historian, was its pastor for many years. *Location:* Ninth and Maple streets.

28. Old Davis Schoolhouse (frame with fieldstone foundation) was probably built around 1890 and used for nearly forty years. Later it became the meeting place for Our Savior Lutheran Church, which was founded in this building. The first church of this congregation was built in 1931 and is located next to the school. *Location:* Near Ambridge, on Ridge Road extension.

29. Providence Baptist Church (brick), the first of that denomination in the county, was constituted November 14, 1801, by Henry Speer, an itinerant Baptist minister. The fourth and present church was built in 1856–57 and remodeled in 1957 and 1982. *Location:* North Sewickley Township, 4.5 miles south of Ellwood City, on SR 1005, 0.5 mile east of its junction with SR 0065.

30. Benvenue (cut stone, quarried on property) was built in 1814 by George Henry Mueller, who came from Baltimore. This twelve-room mansion, situated on a hill near the old Venango Path, was named Benvenue ("welcome here") by Mueller, and at times it was referred to as Mueller's Castle. It was in this home that St. Paul's Lutheran Church in Zelienople (q.v., Butler County) was organized. In 1902 the property was purchased by the Bethany Bible Society, founded by Mary Moorehead, with its original headquarters in Pittsburgh's North Side. On the same land is Sunrise Cottage, built in 1848 by Mueller for his niece, where the Bible Society operated a printing shop.

Benvenue has had exterior alterations, including the addition of a castlelike cistern, but the original interior has been preserved. The third and present owner of the property is Roger Hogan, who purchased it in 1963. *Location:* Marion Township, 1.3 miles west of Zelienople on SR 0068 (on Mueller Hill).

31. Bassenheim Iron Furnace was built in 1814 and operated until 1824. This structure (only a pile of stones from the stack still standing) was built by the German Baron Detmar Basse (Müller, a name he later gave himself), the founder of Zelienople and various business enterprises, and his partner John L. Glasser, a Philadelphia merchant. (See *Zelienople,* Butler County.) *Location:* Junction of Ellwood-Zelienople Road and Old Furnace Road (Franklin Township) on Connoquenessing Creek (SR 1009 and SR 0288).

32. Monaca, originally called Phillipsburg, was the headquarters of the bogus Count De Leon (Bernhard Müller) when, by claiming to be the new Messiah, he persuaded about 250 members (a third of the total) of the Harmony Society to join him. Thiel College was founded here, and the town has a branch campus of Pennsylvania State University.

32A. Oldest Harmonist House in Monaca (brick), with its high stone foundation, was built by Harmonists who separated from their society at Old Economy, partly because of their disagreement with the group's belief in celibacy. Some 250 members withdrew and moved to this section along the Ohio River in 1832. *Location:* Corner of Fifth and Atlantic streets.

32B. Baker-Dungan Museum, named for the first settlers of the county, includes artifacts of South Side Beaver County. Operated by the Mill Creek Valley Historical Society. *Hours:* By appointment, and one hour prior to performances at Broadhead Cultural Center. *Location:* On the Penn State campus.

33. Shippingport Power Plant is the world's first commercial electric-power generating unit to use nuclear energy as fuel. Construction began September 6, 1954, and the plant was in operation in 1957. Later a pit-mouth coal facility was added. One smokestack is 950 feet high. *Hours:* Open for tours Wednesday with advance reservations. *Location:* Shippingport, on south side of bridge.

Note: About a mile downstream from the plant is Duquesne Light's $250 million Beaver Valley Station, No. 1, which began operations in 1975.

34. Georgetown, a very early river town

34A. Georgetown Blockhouse (weatherboarded log) was built in 1796 by Benoni Dawson and until 1900 had two stories. John Bever, an immigrant from Ireland who built the first paper mill in Ohio, purchased and enlarged this house about 1800 and had a tavern and store here. George Henry Loskiel, an early Moravian traveler, visited here in 1803. *Location:* On Water Street overlooking Ohio River, near Old River Hotel.

34B. Old River Hotel (frame) was erected in 1802 by Thomas Foster. A structure with six columns, it is situated high on a hillside overlooking an old Ohio River landing. In 1805 Foster got a license to operate the building as a tavern; Samuel Lyon was a later owner. The house is located where the ferry used to operate, and no doubt this tavern had a thriving business during the era of the keelboat and

34B. Old River Hotel

steam packet boat. *Location:* Market and Water streets.

34C. Poe House (frame), of uncertain date, replaced the original log house on the property erected in 1820 by Thomas Poe, a raftsman. A Methodist church held its first services here. The present seven-bay house with four chimneys does not appear in a town map in an 1876 atlas, but a former owner and Poe descendant believes it is much older. The house is now open to the public as an antique shop. *Location:* Corner of Market and First streets.

34D. St. Luke's Protestant Episcopal Church (brick), founded about 1800, is the oldest of this faith in the county. Its first pastor was Francis Reno, a protégé of Gen. John Neville (see *St. Luke's Protestant Episcopal Church,* Allegheny County). Built in 1833, the present house of worship replaced an earlier log church. *Location:* Market Street.

35. Seceder Cemetery is the original site of Brush Run Seceder Church, chartered in 1798. James Duncan, the first pastor, held services in a tent, later replaced by a log cabin. The two-acre cemetery was founded in 1811. The church was relocated in 1848 as a United Presbyterian Church near Darlington. *Location:* South Beaver Township, Georgetown Road.

36. Service Associate Presbyterian Church (brick), now Presbyterian USA, is located in a beautiful scenic area overlooking the reservoir of the Ambridge Water Authority on Service Creek. Three wooden crosses were erected in 1963 on the bank in front of the church near the water's edge. The congregation was organized in 1790, and Rev. John Anderson served the church from 1792 until 1833. The first church, of log, was erected in 1793–94. The cornerstone of the existing church reads, "Service A.P. Church, Built 1800, rebuilt 1828, 1868, 1928. Dr. John Anderson first pastor." The present church was constructed with the bricks of the 1868 church, which had burned a few years before 1928.

Next to this house of worship is the John Anderson Memorial Cemetery, where numerous Revolutionary War soldiers are buried. Near the head of the reservoir is a stone marking the site of Service Theological Seminary, founded there by the Associate Presbytery of Philadelphia, April 21, 1794. It was the first such institution west of the Alleghenies and the first Protestant seminary in the United States not attached to a college or university. The seminary continued here with Dr. Anderson as head until 1821, when it was transferred to Canonsburg; in 1855 it relocated to Xenia, Ohio. It is the earliest forebear of the present Pittsburgh Theological Seminary (q.v., Allegheny County). *Location:* North of Mechanicsburg, on Service Church Road, 1.5 miles from SR 0018.

37. Frankfort Springs

37A. Frankfort Mineral Springs, now consisting of three springs of the original seven, located at a natural solid rock grotto, was at one time the most popular resort and health spa in western Pennsylvania. This scenic area, a 400-acre tract, once the site of wolf dens and steeped in Indian lore, was bought in 1784 by Isaac Stephens for less than ten dollars.

Later, Edward McGinnis, a ferryman and keelboatman, who found the mineral waters "healing to his ailment," bought twelve acres of the land. Sometime before 1800 he built a three-story hotel called the Frankfort House overlooking the glen where the springs are located. Originally the property also included a guesthouse, a carriage house, a dance pavilion (built in the 1800s), a livery stable, an icehouse, vegetable gardens, a ballfield, a dirt tennis court, and croquet greens. Except for the partly burned and rebuilt guest house, only the foundation scars remain. (Signs have been erected to mark these early sites.) The hotel itself was destroyed by fire.

The stone guesthouse, the only remaining building of the resort complex, was restored

37A. Frankfort Mineral Springs

in the 1960s by the Commonwealth of Pennsylvania and the Western Pennsylvania Conservancy. Originally it had three stories, but the fire in 1905 reduced it to one. It has been used as a guesthouse, a manager's residence, later a store, barber shop, and then a bottling works. In 1884 McGinnis's daughter, Eliza, sold the property to J. Moore Bigger, and in 1912 it was closed as a health spa, although mineral-water bottling operations continued for some time afterward. Today a scenic walkway leads to the spring grotto below the stone guesthouse. *Location:* North of Frankfort Springs (town), at Raccoon Creek State Park (a quarter mile south of park office on SR 0018).

Note: Raccoon Creek State Park is one of the oldest of its kind in Pennsylvania. Over two hundred thousand years ago it was part of an ancient sea bottom. The park also includes a wild flower preserve, where programs concerning conservation and early pioneer life are held. Dr. O. E. Jennings, well-known western Pennsylvania botanist, discovered over five hundred different species of plants here. The wild flower preserve is located along US 30, opposite east entrance of park's day-use area. Tours prearranged.

Across from the park entrance is the Cy Hungerford cabin (by appointment).

37B. Witherspoon Drovers' Tavern (stucco over brick) was the home of John Witherspoon, who was born in Ireland in 1785, came to America at the age of five, and settled with his family at Canonsburg, Washington County. Sometime between 1796 and 1809, they bought land on Travis Creek in Hanover Township. Witherspoon married Margaret Kennedy in 1813, built a house in Frankfort Springs, and operated a popular drovers' tavern here. The house is still occupied by his descendants. *Location:* SR 0018.

37C. King's Creek or Frankfort Springs Associate Presbyterian Church (brick) was organized in 1790 by Rev. John Anderson, who founded the Service Associate Presbyterian Church (q.v.) about the same time. The first house of worship was a log structure located two miles north of the present borough. The third and present church (now Presbyterian USA) was built in 1876. *Location:* SR 0018 near borough line.

38. Nelson House (stone and frame) was erected on land granted to Samuel Caughy in 1807. Matthew Nelson, the next owner, bought the property in 1810 and hired Cornelius Shane to build the house in 1817. Shane's name and the date are on an exterior signature stone. The frame addition was constructed at a later date. Nearby on the property is a stone springhouse. George Shields, a later owner, replaced the original windows with leaded glass in the 1930s. Private residence. *Location:* South side, near Hookstown on US 30, about 2 miles east of Laughlins Corners.

39. Church of Christ (frame), built about 1850, was originally an Associate Reformed Presbyterian Church. An old cemetery is located on the hillside behind the church. *Location:* Near Laughlins Corners and West Virginia line on Tomlinson Run Road.

40. Mill Creek Presbyterian Church (frame), organized in 1784, is the county's oldest religious institution and was attached to the Presbytery of Ohio in 1793. George M. Scott became its first regular pastor in 1799. Dr. John McMillan held one of his last services here in 1833. The congregation has had five church buildings, the first three located at the cemetery (marker on SR 3032, about 0.2 mile east of present church), and the last two on the site where the existing structure was built in 1882. In the cemetery is the grave of Andrew Poe, a celebrated Indian fighter who died in 1823. *Location:* Mill Creek, near Laughlins Corners (where SR 0168 crosses US 30), on SR 3026 (follow sign).

41. Locust Grove (Reed House) (cut stone) was built in 1820, costing $100 for labor. The stones for the house, which measures 24 by 40 feet, were hauled from the old Ernest Littell farm. In 1839 Samuel Reed bought the farm from Robert Wright, and it remained in his family until 1937. *Location:* 3 miles south of Laughlins Corners. Follow SR 0168 from Laughlins Corners to sign for Mill Creek Church; turn left on SR 3026 and continue

42. Reddick Grave

past church until first through crossroad (about 1 mile); turn right on T 368 and take first lane to left.

42. Reddick Grave is the spot where John Hoge Reddick, one of the first associate judges of Beaver County, is buried. The grave is enclosed by a sandstone wall several feet away from the West Virginia border. Reddick asked to be buried "with his face toward the east, his head in [West] Virginia and his feet in Pennsylvania," so that if the devil came for him on one side, he could quickly flee to the other. Ironically a resurvey in 1883 showed the grave to be entirely within Pennsylvania. Legend has it that Reddick feared the devil had heard him boast that a favorite horse could outrun "His Satanic Majesty" and would seek revenge. On his tombstone are written the words:

John Reddick
Pennsylvania
Ensign 5 Co. 2 Bn
Westmoreland County Militia
Revolutionary War
War of 1812
1756–1830

A survey boundary stone sits directly in front of the grave site. *Location:* South of Hookstown, go south for 3.5 miles on SR 0168 at intersection of US 30 (at Laughlins Corners); turn west for 2.8 miles on Harden Run Road (SR 3032) to Ross Road in West Virginia, thence left for three quarters of a mile to private lane leading to brick chalet in West Virginia. Grave is inside stone wall about 150 yards to rear of house, at edge of woods and state line.

43. White's Mill (ruin), once a focal point in establishing the Allegheny County boundary, was built by Thomas White before 1786. White had taken a 400-acre tract of land in this area in the early 1770s, and by 1786 there was a settlement around the mill, built on Raccoon Creek near the mouth of Potato Garden Run. The huge log mill operated until 1904, and it was razed in 1950. The stone foundation ruins and vestiges of the dam and race are discernible along the creek. *Location:* Northeast of Murdocksville on Raccoon Creek; on T 115 (1.6 miles south of junction with US 30 west of Clinton, Allegheny County).

44. Carnegie Library, Allegheny Regional (stone), built in 1890, was donated by Andrew Carnegie. *Location:* Aliquippa, Allegheny Square.

45. B. F. Jones Library (stone), built in 1929, was designed by Brandon Smith of Pittsburgh. It was named for Benjamin Franklin Jones of Jones & Laughlin Steel Company. *Location:* Aliquippa, 663 Franklin Avenue.

Previous Site Now Lost

Beaver Female College, demolished

Pennsylvania Historical and Museum Commission Markers

Beaver County Beaver, at courthouse, Market and Third streets
Fort McIntosh Beaver, SR 0068
Harmony Society Cemetery 1823–1951 Ambridge, Church Street, in center of cemetery
Harmony Society Church Ambridge, Church Street near Creese Street
King Beaver's Town Beaver, SR 0068
Legionville Duss Avenue north of Ambridge
Logstown Duss Avenue north of Ambridge
Matthew S. Quay Beaver, SR 0068, 205 College Avenue
Old Economy Ambridge, SR 0065
Old Economy Memorial Ambridge at Old Economy

There are over forty local historical markers in Beaver County.

Bedford County

Capsule History

Bedford County, named in honor of John Russell, fourth duke of Bedford, was formed out of Cumberland County March 9, 1771. It embraced almost all of western Pennsylvania. Today the county is 1,017 square miles in area with a population of 46,784.

The county's prehistoric wonders include the sinks of New Paris, where the bones of many animals—some now extinct—have been found, the only known underground coral reefs, at Manns Choice; and artifacts dating from the pre-Columbian period (A.D. 400–1500).

The first settlement of the county took place in what is now Southampton Township. Among the pioneers who arrived in the area in the 1750s were Bernard Dougherty, George Woods, Joseph Sheniwolf, and David Espy. Robert Ray, an Indian

77

trader, came to Bedford in 1750–51; Garrett Prendergast arrived in 1752 and was burned out by the Indians in 1755. The most fertile of the valleys, Morrisons Cove, was settled largely by Germans in the 1760s. From 1754 until the close of the Revolution, Indians made incursions into this region, which had been their hunting grounds. Here numerous massacres occurred.

The *Raystown Path* was the most important of the Indian trails of the county. The favorite of the fur traders en route to Kittanning, it followed much the course of US 30 in this area, passing through or near Breezewood, Everett, Raystown (now Bedford), Wolfsburg, and Shawnee Cabins. Another main route, the *Warrior's Path,* traversed the county in two and, farther south, three separate branches. One branch entered the county above King, following US 220 past Osterburg and Cessna where it forked, the western course going near SR 0096 past Manns Choice and Palo Alto, the eastern by Bedford, Bedford Springs, along US 220 to Centerville, and down Shaver Ridge. The other main branch entered the county southwest of Shy Beaver, ran down the Woodcock Valley toward Tatesville and Everett, then followed Black Valley toward Flintstone. Two minor paths ran from the eastern branch into Morrisons Cove, one taking off above King and running past Bakers Summit to Martinsburg, the other below King and going southeast to Salemville. The *Glades Path* left the eastern branch of Warrior's Path at Wolfsburg, going by Dry Ridge, West End, and Brotherton along the general course of the Turnpike and from about Somerset off SR 0031. The *Conemaugh Path,* from Bedford to Johnstown, ran north to Cessna and Reynoldsdale, turned northwest, and crossed the Allegheny Ridge near the head of South Fork.

In 1758 Brig. Gen. John Forbes cut a road along a route which was roughly the same as present-day US 30. One Forbes camp was located west of Schellsburg at Shawnee Cabins, a site now covered by Shawnee Cabin Dam.

Bedford, the county seat, was laid out in 1766. Bedford Manor had been surveyed by John Lukens in 1761 and the streets named for members of the Penn family. The town squares, set aside for public parks, still exist today. By 1806 there were wooden pipes supplying the town with spring water. There are at least 300 pre-1840 buildings still in use in the county, of which almost fifty are in the borough of Bedford. According to a 1983 survey, about forty-five hundred structures in the county predate 1901.

Included among the noteworthy residents of the county were Robert J. Walker, senator from Mississippi and governor of the Kansas Territory in 1857; Jeremiah S. Black, attorney general in Buchanan's cabinet; John Cessna, congressman and orator; and Maj. Gen. Arthur St. Clair, famed leader in the Revolutionary War. Thomas Bleistein, the beloved "Bozo Snyder" of vaudeville and burlesque, was born in Bedford in 1891. Friedrich Goeb (see Somerset County) lived for some years in Schellsburg and is buried there.

Important early industries of the county included farming and wool-growing. Numerous mills were operated by water power, while iron ore, coal, and limestone were plentiful natural resources. In 1791 William McDermott, pioneer steel manufacturer, built his establishment on the "Caledonia tract" near Bedford Springs. Hopewell Furnace and Lemnos Forge were the county's main iron producers. Altogether there were four early stone blast furnaces in the county. The Riddlesburg iron furnaces, operating from 1869 to 1943, were among the county's largest. In 1874 an iron industry was developed in Everett (once called Bloody Run).

Of forty-two covered bridges built in the county, fifteen remain. The largest was swept away by flood waters (see *Juniata Crossing Hotel* [Tavern]).

Bedford Village consists of restored and relocated early buildings. Also a covered bridge once over Dunning's Creek at Reynoldsdale has been relocated at the village. This seventy-two-acre tract is bordered by US 220 (Bedford North bypass), the Juniata River, and private lands, with access to the park over the covered bridge and at two other points.

Bedford County Home, scheduled for adaptive usage, is off US 30 on the County Home Road (SR 3021).

Landmarks

1. Bedford. The main section of town known as "The Squares" was set aside by William Penn's family for the town of Bedford during the Manor survey of 1761.

1A. Courthouse (brick) is the oldest existing courthouse in Pennsylvania. The first court of Bedford County was held April 16, 1771, in a log courthouse. Not until 1774 were a stone structure and a jail erected. In 1828–29 the present classic brick structure was built by Solomon Filler for $7,500; in 1876 it was enlarged. Its second-floor courtroom contains portraits of all the judges who have presided there. Among the early records preserved in its vaults is an Indian deed transferring title to a large area including Pittsburgh's Golden Triangle. The purchase was illegal and became void. The courthouse is open for tours. *Location:* Juliana and Penn streets.

1B. Early Bedford Buildings. The Bedford National Historic District includes a four-by-six-block area, about the same as the original survey ordered by the Penn proprietors in 1766. This area incorporates over two hundred structures that have historical, architectural, and cultural significance. Included among these buildings are the following.

On Pitt Street: Anthony Naugle House and tavern (1789), Union Hotel (1835), Steckman House (1835); on Thomas Street: Negro brick school (before 1860, now a residence); corner of Pitt and Thomas streets: Shuck brick house (ca. 1803, built by Thomas Vickroy, later owned by Dr. John Hofius and the Shuck family who operated a wagon-building shop here); on Juliana Street: Jacob Diehl House (ca. 1820), Solomon Filler Mansion (1825), Job Mann Law Office (1837), Reed Store (1850); at the Public Square: Lawyers Row (1870, an office complex), Market Building (1880), Soldiers Monument honoring civil War dead (1890).

On John Street: James Episcopal church (stone, 1865–66, built in the style of Sir Christopher Wren's church in London); Methodist Episcopal church (ca. 1870); John Arnold House (1825, Dutch style); Abraham Kerns House (1834, L-shaped brick with a summer kitchen); at Penn Street: Fort Bedford Inn (ca. 1832, where John L. Lewis often stayed).

Other noteworthy buildings are as follows.

1C. Bedford Hotel (brick) was erected in 1836 and now houses a modern hostelry. *Location:* 224 East Pitt Street.

1D. Lyon House (brick), Georgian style, was erected in 1833–34 by Solomon Filler as a private residence for the William Lyon family. This structure, flanked by two small buildings, one a former carriage house and the other an office, was later converted into the Timmins private hospital. Following this it was a residence once more, and at present is the courthouse annex. *Location:* 214 South Juliana Street.

1E. Russell House (brick), in Georgian style with an arched and gabled roof over the front entrance, was built in 1816 by Solomon Filler for James M. Russell, the first burgess of Bedford. Similar in appearance to the Anderson house (q.v.), the structure once served as a mortuary. Its old interior elevator is still operating. *Location:* 203 South Juliana Street.

1F. Bedford Presbyterian Church (brick), organized before 1783, was constructed in 1829 by Solomon Filler. It replaced a frame structure that had succeeded an 1810 church. The old Presbyterian burial ground (Bedford Memorial Park, South Juliana and East John streets) marks the site of the congregation's first church. It contains the graves of sixteen Revolutionary War soldiers. *Location:* On Penn Street, at the square.

Note: Next to the church is the Cessna building, erected in 1820. It is now an apartment house. The Presbyterian Manse (brick), built in 1862, is at the corner of Bedford and Penn streets.

1G. Union Common School (brick), built in 1859, replaced several one-room schools. Originally planned to house eight grades, this building was the county's first consolidated and graded school. In 1889 it was added to and became a high school. It is among the oldest school buildings in Pennsylvania still in operation. *Location:* South Juliana and Watson streets.

1H. St. Thomas Apostle Catholic Chapel (brick), the oldest Catholic church in the county, was erected in 1817. Though abandoned in 1833 when the congregation moved to another site, it was restored in 1958 as a memorial shrine. The church was first served by a missionary priest, Father Demetrius Gallitzin (see *Gallitzin Chapel and House,* Cambria County). Adjacent to the chapel is an early cemetery. *Location:* 225 East Street (between Penn and John streets).

1I. Jacob Krichbaum House (weatherboarded log) is a squat, one-story, gable-roofed structure built in 1816. It is now the Colonial Inn. *Location:* 113 West Pitt Street.

1J. Steckman House (brick), an early tavern known as the Sign of the Blazing Star in 1784, is today a discount store. *Location:* 114 West Pitt Street.

1K. Early Apothecary Shop (stone) was built in 1805 and now houses a commercial business. *Location:* 18 West Pitt Street.

1L. Fraser Tavern/Graystone Hotel (stone) was built in the mid 1800s partially on the site of an early log tavern and trading post operated by John and Jean Fraser. Their son William, the first recorded white child born in Bedford county, in 1759, died at age 85 and is buried near a monument on a farm he owned on Glade Pike west of Manns Choice. This hotel was the site of the first court in the county. *Location:* Northeast corner of East Pitt and Richard streets.

1M. Anderson House (brick) is a fine example of Georgian post-Colonial architecture, built by Solomon Filler in 1814 for Dr. John Anderson and his wife Mary Espy. This two-and-a-half-story structure, with a seven-bay facade and narrow one-story cast-iron porch

1M. Anderson House

added later, is more typical of the South than of Pennsylvania. It has a fanlight in the entrance and the original brass door knocker with the initials "J.A." on it. Anderson, who was a banker, doctor, and postmaster, operated the county's first bank, the Bedford branch of Allegheny Bank of Pennsylvania, from 1814 to 1832. Among Anderson's assets were the Bedford Springs Hotel (q.v.), gristmills, and coal lands. Since 1924 the property has belonged to the borough and now serves as headquarters for the Bedford County Heritage Commission, the Northern Appalachian Crafts Festival, and the Heritage Shoppe. *Hours:* Monday–Thursday, Saturday, 10 A.M.–5 P.M.; Friday, 10 A.M.–9 P.M. *Location:* 137 East Pitt Street.

1N. National House (brick), with an overhead porch, first operated as a hotel. It was built in 1800. Now site of Pioneer Historical Society and Library. *Hours:* Monday–Friday, 9 A.M.–4 P.M.; Saturday, 9 A.M.–12 noon. There is also an antique shop in the building. *Location:* 131 East Pitt Street, next to Anderson house.

1O. Espy House (stone), a three-bay structure built in 1770–71, housed the office of Arthur St. Clair, first prothonotary of the county, later succeeded by David Espy. During Espy's term in this office in 1794, President Washington made his headquarters here for two nights while inspecting the troops sent to quell the Whiskey Rebellion in western Pennsylvania. According to legend a soldier ran off with the roasted fowl that Mrs. Espy had prepared for a dinner in honor of the

1O. Espy House

president. The only major alteration to the structure has been a store window in front. It now houses the Washington Bakery. *Location:* 123 East Pitt Street.

1P. Old Mann Homestead (frame) was built in 1771 by David F. Mann and fronted on Mann Square. Contained in the basement of this long, narrow building are what are reputed to be the last remaining vestiges of Fort Bedford Powder Magazine, the main part of which was located about one hundred feet to the south. The homestead is now occupied by Pennell jewelry store. *Location:* South Juliana Street.

1Q. Fort Bedford, for which Raystown was renamed, was built by the British under the command of Brig. Gen. John Forbes in 1758. Col. James Burd was supervisor and Capt. Harry Gordon engineer. It served as the supply base from which Forbes's army advanced to Fort Duquesne with 7,580 men. George Washington was an unofficial adviser.

This stockaded fortress had five bastions which guarded the corners of the irregularly shaped structure and covered 7,000 square yards. It was the first British installation to fall to American forces, when Capt. James Smith's "Black Boys," masquerading with blackened faces, made a dawn raid to release friends who had been arrested for opposing official Indian policy. The fort withstood a siege during Pontiac's Rebellion and was later abandoned with little of the original structure remaining (see *Old Mann Homestead*).

In 1958 the present fort museum was constructed at the same location for the fort's bicentennial celebration, and in 1960 it was enlarged. Surrounded by a stockade, this structure contains numerous exhibits, including a model of the fort and one of the original Conestoga wagons which traveled on the old Forbes Road. The Fort Bedford Park and Museum were developed by the community in cooperation with the Pennsylvania Historical and Museum Commission. *Hours:* May 1–October 15: Daily, 9 A.M.–5 P.M. *Admission charge.* Special group rates. *Location:* Fort Bedford Drive at North Juliana Street, overlooking the Raystown Branch of the Juniata River.

1R. Grand Central Hotel (brick), built in 1840, in later years was renamed the Washington. It originally had a triple-deck porch which was removed along with one floor when it became a savings and loan office. It now houses a bank and a gas company. *Location:* Juliana and Pitt streets.

1S. The Groves (Barclay House) (stone) was built in 1794–96 and was the home of Hugh Barclay, who entertained Alexander Hamilton during the Whiskey Rebellion. It was enlarged in 1830. Another residence of Barclay is an 1810 brick house on the corner of Thomas and Pitt streets; the present public library was also a Barclay home. *Location:* Grove Lane and South Bedford Street.

Note: Another Barclay house (brick) is at 230 Juliana Street.

1T. Shuck Mansion, built in 1849, is one of Bedford's stately homes. *Location:* Juliana and John streets.

1U. Washabaugh-Hartley House (brick) and the stone distillery behind it were built about 1826 by Daniel Washabaugh, a major in the county militia between 1822 and 1842. He later served as postmaster of Bedford. *Location:* Pitt and East streets.

Note: Also nearby on Pitt Street are the Cramer Cottages, built around 1885 as private residences, later operating as apartment houses. The Hartley Mansion (stone), built in 1870 in Second Empire style, is now the "Victoria House" at Watson Avenue and Richard Street.

1V. Peter Shires House was built in 1826 by Peter Shires. Later this Federal-style building was known as the Blymyer House. Shires and John Jordan operated a foundry nearby. *Location:* Pitt and Bedford streets.

4. *Old Bedford Village Log House and Octagonal Schoolhouse*

1W. Coach Room Restaurant (frame and brick) was built around 1880 and has been operated by the Barnhart family since 1948. *Location:* 118 South Richard Street (old US 220).

2. Arundale Hotel (stone) later became the Elks Country Club. During the Whiskey Rebellion, President Washington's troops bivouacked on the plain around it. *Location:* South edge of Bedford, on old US 220 (on way to Bedford Springs).

3. Naugle Mill (stone) was built in 1797 by Frederick Naugle along Shovers Run. On the building is a protruding gable for a grain pulley. The miller's log house, dating back to 1798, is located across the road. *Location:* 2 miles south of Bedford, on Springs Road (old US 220), near Bedford Springs Hotel.

4. Old Bedford Village was inspired by Mr. and Mrs. Robert Sweet and constructed through the services of William Jordan and many others. It is located on land that belonged to Alexander Filson and his father-in-law, Walter Brown, in 1837. The village consists of over forty log (some frame and stone) buildings moved to this 72-acre park in the southern Allegheny Mountains and reconstructed to reflect the pioneer life style of Bed-

ford County from the 1750s to the 1850s. Costumed artisans demonstrate early American crafts and businesses. The oldest structure is the Riddle log house, erected in 1762—one of the oldest houses surviving in western Pennsylvania—by John Croyle, the county's first blacksmith, at "Dutch Corner." An octagonal schoolhouse (frame), called the "Eight Square School," erected in 1851 by Quakers and used until 1931 near Fishertown, is one of the most outstanding buildings. At the entranceway to the village is the Claycomb covered bridge. There is also a summer theater, constructed of logs in recent years. An interesting early stone house is situated across the road from this village. *Hours:* April–October, seven days a week, 9 A.M.–4:30 P.M. *Admission charge. Location:* 1.5 miles north of Bedford on old US 220, 1 mile south of Turnpike, exit 11.

5. Bedford Springs Hotel (brick and frame) was established soon after 1800 by Dr. John Anderson (see *Anderson House*) at a magnesia mineral spring. By 1848 the lodging rooms included adjoining buildings with a frontage of 557 feet.

The structure was known as the summer White House of Pennsylvania's only president, James Buchanan, who here received the first message over the Atlantic cable on August 17, 1858, from Queen Victoria: "Come let us talk together. American genius and English enterprise have this day joined to-

5. Bedford Springs Hotel

gether the Old and the New World. Let us hope that they may be as closely allied in bonds of peace, harmony and kindred feeling." President Buchanan's reply was, "New England accepts with gladness the hand of fellowship proffered by Old England." In 1859 Buchanan announced from Bedford Springs that he would not seek a second term.

Another event that took place here was the Passmore Williamson case, heard by the Supreme Court when it sat here in the summer of 1855—one of the legal actions leading to the Civil War. During World War II the hotel became a naval training center; soon after, personnel of Japanese embassies were incarcerated here.

The spacious structure with a large colonial portico in front adjoins a wooden bridge over the highway to the springs. It is situated on a 2,800-acre estate in the Allegheny Mountains. *Location:* 4 miles south of Bedford exit (no. 11) of Turnpike, on Springs Road (old US 220).

6. Mount Dallas (Hartley House) (stone and frame) was built by William Hartley in 1785 on land bought from Robert Morris, a Philadelphia statesman and financier of the Revolutionary War. The site was near that of the earlier log cabin inn and home of the adventurous widow Elizabeth Tussey, where it was reputed that the male traveler was offered more than food, drink, and a place to sleep. By 1803 the landlord of the Hartley house was Capt. William Graham, the second of three husbands of the former Mrs. Hartley. The large front room served as a tavern. In that year Thaddeus Mason Harris described this house as a "neat and commodius dwelling, principally built with limestone, laid in mortar. The rooms and chambers are snug, and handsomely furnished; and the accommodations and entertainment he provides are the best to be met with between Philadelphia and

Pittsburgh." In 1794 President Washington spent the night here on his way back after quelling the Whiskey Rebellion. Tradition reports that Mrs. Hartley and the president spent an evening playing backgammon. *Location:* 2 miles west of Everett on the north side of US 30.

7. Croyle House (stone and log) has a chimney on its eastern side on which is engraved: "I, Thomas Cruille built this house 1755." (Cruille was the German spelling for Croyle.) This home was built several perches (rods) from Snake Spring, by legend a Snake Indian camp, which has given its name to the valley to the north (originally Croyles Valley) and to the township. By legend, Croyle's wife was an Indian princess, accounting in part for the favorable treatment that the family received. The Indians would bring silver from a secret location not far distant for Croyle, a blacksmith, to fashion into ornaments for them. For many years a tavern, the house is the oldest stone structure standing in Bedford County. In later years the property was owned by J. G. Hartley and heirs. *Location:* 4 miles east of Bedford, on the old Forbes Road and Turnpike, today US 30, north side.

8. Thropp's Bridge for a broad-gauge railroad was built from the Earlston Furnace across the Raystown Branch of the Juniata River to Mt. Dallas. The furnace operated from 1884 to 1925 with capital stock of $860,000, of which $80,000 was provided by Joseph E. Thropp. Three of the original buildings are still in use, plus the Thropp Mansion and Earlston Thropp's home. Only an abutment of the bridge now remains, commonly referred to as "Thropp's Folly." *Location:* Just east of Everett, on north side of US 30.

9. Rainsburg Academy (brick), built in 1853–54, housed the Allegheny Male and Female Seminary chartered in 1853. It provided education equivalent to that given in high schools and junior colleges before such schools came into existence in the area. Samuel Williams, born in 1806 in Napier Township, acquired the old Friend tract in 1844 and founded the seminary, which operated until shortly before 1870. It was next bought by the Odd Fellows and later operated as a normal school until 1912. From 1912 to 1952 an elementary school was held here. In 1969 the building was purchased for a private home. *Location:* South edge of Rainsburg, in Colerain Township.

Note: Two old churches are near Rainsburg in Friends Cove: the "twin churches" (brick), the former Lutheran and Reformed (now Lutheran), built in 1833 with its galleries and high pulpit still intact; and the present Cove Reformed Church, erected in 1888.

10. Newry Manor and Mill (formerly Lutz Museum). The log section was built around 1780, the stone part around 1805, and the brick addition in 1858. Once owned by the founder of the Bedford County Historical Society, it is now a bed and breakfast inn. *Location:* Lutzville, Snake Spring Township, SR 2019, 1 mile south of US 30 near Everett (parallels Raystown Branch of the Juniata River).

Note: The Juniata Woolen Mill ruins are across the road from the manor.

11. Defibaugh Tavern (stone and log with stucco and frame), built about 1800, was one of the largest inns along the old Pennsylvania Road and for many years was known as the Willow Grove Tavern. It originally had seventeen rooms and a two-story drovers' porch. The stone section was built for Abraham Defibaugh by his brother-in-law, George Cruille (Croyle), and the five-room frame part was added by Joseph Mortimore. The barroom, unchanged since 1865, includes the original bar top, a single hand-hewn plank, thirty-six inches wide. Now renovated and owned by Willard G. Defibaugh, great-great-grandson of Abraham. *Location:* 1.8 miles east of Everett limits, on US 30.

Note: A log house built in the eighteenth century, now weatherboarded, and a large stone barn are across the highway.

12. Weaverling Tavern (stone) was operated before 1790 by Jacob Weaverling (see *J. P. Weaverling Inn*). *Location:* East of Everett, on old US 30, south of present highway and visible from it.

13. J. P. Weaverling Inn (stone), with a later two-story porch, was built by Jacob Weaverling's grandson John Peter on property purchased by the family in 1783. A signature stone in one gable reads, "J. W. 1843." The barn, now razed, bore the date 1837. In 1960 an addition was built on the house, at one time called the Old Stagecoach Inn. *Location:* 3.3 miles east of Everett, on US 30.

14. Everett, once known as Bloody Run, was the site of James Smith's attack on traders transporting guns and ammunition to the Indians. Patton House was built in 1738 by John Patton (or Paxton), an Indian agent, innkeeper, mapmaker, explorer on Hillside Street.

Note: Other historic buildings in Everett include a three-story brick school (ca. 1898), the railroad station (ca. 1870), a brick foundry (ca. 1860), and a gristmill (ca. 1866).

15. Juniata Crossing Hotel (Tavern) (stone) was built in the early 1800s. Early innkeepers at this site were a Mr. Householder, Abraham Martin, and Hugh Dennison (in 1818), followed by George McGraw in the 1840s. McGraw, who was a judge, died in 1872. There is much folklore associated with this building. One early tavern keeper was said to have been a horse thief; and the bandit Davy Lewis, arrested for counterfeiting in 1815, is supposed to have stopped here. At one time it was reputed to have been a center for illegal liquor during Prohibition days. A secret room with a door operated by a rope was discovered in the house. The building, now an antique shop, is situated between old and new US 30. Old US 30 ran directly in front of the house at one time, crossing the Juniata River where a famous old covered bridge was washed away by the St. Patrick's Day flood of 1936. Foundation stones east of the house show the location of this bridge, which had replaced General Forbes's old bridge built in 1758. The present bridge is between the sites of the two early ones. Forbes had built a small stockade, Fort Juniata, half a mile north of the crossing to protect his army. *Location:* 2 miles west of Breezewood, on US 30.

16. Maple Lawn Inn (brick), with fanlighted windows between gable chimneys, was built about 1815 by a member of the Rinard family and operated as a tavern for over 150 years. It has twenty-one rooms and eleven fireplaces; the kitchen fireplace could take nine-foot logs.

The inn is located at Breezewood, which was mostly farmland until 1940, when it mushroomed with tourist motels at the Turnpike interchange. The area has been nicknamed City of Motels. *Location:* West edge of Breezewood just beyond community sign, on US 30.

17. Crawford's Museum (frame) displays specimens of over three hundred game and wild birds collected by the museum's owners from around the world. *Hours:* April 16– December 30: Daily (except Wednesday and Sunday), 10 A.M.–6 P.M. *Admission charge. Location:* Breezewood, on US 30.

18. Old Schoolhouse (stone), the oldest in the county, was built in 1803–05 and used until 1879. The exterior has been repaired by the county's Pioneer Historical Society. *Loca-*

tion: About 4 miles north of Bedford, turn east from US 220 onto Belden Road and go 1.9 miles straight through Belden to iron bridge; 300 feet past bridge turn right on SR 1014 (unmarked); go about 1.6 miles to school.

Note: About halfway on SR 1014, near crossing of SR 1018, is the Messiah Lutheran Church built in 1906. A signature stone gives the names of the church officials and the bricklayer. The church was organized about 1790.

19. Chalybeate Springs Hotel (brick) was built as a tavern in 1786–87 by George Funk on land where Indians drank from springs having high iron content. In 1867 a new wing was added, at which time the resort became known by its present name. George H. Dauler bought the hotel in 1885 and added another wing in 1886–87. His son, George H. Dauler, Jr., became proprietor in 1898, built a ballroom in 1903, and continued to operate the summer resort until 1913. During the 1880s and 1890s the hotel prospered and became the summer "playground of presidents." Its register preserves the names of at least five incumbent presidents from Hayes to McKinley, along with cabinet members, political leaders, and famous people. A local contractor bought the property in 1947 and converted the hotel into apartments five years later. *Location:* At traffic light on US 220 just north of Bedford, turn east on Sunnyside Road. Go 1 mile to its junction with Chalybeate Road (can be seen from Turnpike).

20. Double Stone House is a massive but somewhat dilapidated structure with a front porch. The older portion of the house dates from around 1800. An early turnpike tollgate was nearby. *Location:* About 1 mile north of Bedford, on North Richard extension.

21. Chambersburg Raid Entrenchments (Gettysburg Campaign), still visible by the roadside, were prepared in June 1863 by militia under Col. J. C. Higgins against threatened Confederate attack toward the railroads at Altoona. *Location:* 5 miles south of Loysburg, on SR 0036 (Snake Spring Mountain Road) at Tussey Mountain near Morrisons Cove, on SR 1005.

22. Loysburg Gristmill (frame with stone foundation) was constructed by Martin Loy, who had a tannery here as early as 1818. This mill operated from 1836 to 1952, passing through several ownerships. *Location:* Loysburg, on SR 0036 on Yellow Creek.

Note: The large brick house across the road from the mill was built by Martin Loy, Jr., in 1822. Loysburg was called Pattonville from 1844 to 1884.

23. Snider House (stone) was completed in 1812 by John Snider, who built one of the first gristmills in Morrisons Cove about 1795. The present large building was erected near a mill, and its six stories were used as separate residences for Snider's sons and their families. This structure was known for a time as Snider's Folly. *Location:* About 2 miles north of Loysburg in Morrisons Cove, on SR 0036 at SR 0869.

24. Waterside Woolen Mill (frame) belonged to Joseph B. Noble, who in 1862 left his partner Jacob Furry and purchased this property. He tore down a building that had been erected on the property in 1830 and built the present mill in 1865–66. Its floors and machinery are supported by oak girders held together by locust pins. It continued in operation until a few years ago. *Location:* Waterside, on SR 0866 on Yellow Creek (South Woodbury Township).

25. Mowry-Way Mill (stone) was built on Bobs Creek in 1807 and was operated until 1931. Among millers who owned the structure were Mowry, Way, and Dubbs. The miller's log house, later painted, is located across from the mill. *Location:* Weyant (Mowrys Mills), junction of SR 0869 and SR 0096.

26. Riddlesburg Coke Ovens, eighty beehive ovens, were built around 1860 and restored in 1975. *Location:* Riddlesburg, 1.5 miles east off SR 0026 (Broad Top Township).

27. Bloomfield Iron Ore Mines, opened in 1845, are visible today as water hazards on the Iron Masters Golf Course. Ore from open pit mines in the area was of superior quality, and the iron from the local furnace was shipped to the U.S. arsenal at Pittsburgh during the Civil War for the manufacture of heavy artillery. *Location:* 5 miles south of Roaring Spring (Blair County), off SR 0867, east (Bloomfield Township).

28. Longenecker House (stone), once the home of John Longenecker, was built in 1811 over a spring. A frame addition was erected in 1846. *Location:* Maria (Bloomfield Township).

29. St. Paul's Barley Church (stone) was built in 1841, an exceptional structure in a rural setting. *Location:* Near Maria, SR 0868 (Bloomfield Township).

30. New Enterprise Elementary School (brick) was built in 1881. This two-story building (38 by 42 feet), erected at a cost of $1,625, is one of the few schools of western Pennsylvania to be included on the National Register of Historic Places. *Location:* New Enterprise (South Woodbury Township), off SR 0869 on SR 1015.

31. Globe (Keagy) Woolen Mill (log and frame), three-and-a-half stories, was built around 1865 by "Machine" Abe Keagy. *Location:* South of Woodbury (Woodbury Township).

32. Keagy House (stone) was built in 1813 by Michael Keagy. A house of similar stone construction, built before 1827 and possibly the home of the ironmaster of Elizabeth furnace, is in the heart of nearby Woodbury. *Location:* South edge of Woodbury, on SR 0866.

33. Lime Kiln (stone) is situated on the Charles Smith Farm. (See *Lime Kiln,* Indiana County; and *Seanor Lime Kiln,* Salem Township, Westmoreland County.) *Location:* Hickory Bottom (Woodbury Township).

34. Lost Children Monument marks the site where George, age seven, and Joseph, five and a half, sons of Samuel and Susanna Cox, were discovered after being lost in the wilderness near their home at Spruce Hollow close to the village of Lovely on April 24, 1856. Two thousand people searched the area for the children, and during this time Jacob Dibert, who lived at some distance, had a recurring dream in which he envisioned the spot where the boys were to be found. Dibert and his brother-in-law, Harrison Wysong, who recognized the area from Jacob's report of his dream, searched it and found the boys' bodies by a stream on May 8. A monument dedicated May 8, 1906, is at the site where the children died from exposure and starvation. Their graves are in the Mount Union Church cemetery at Lovely. *Location:* Near Pavia, north of Blue Knob State Park. From Pavia go 1 mile northwest on SR 0869; turn right on unimproved road at highway maintenance depot; thence 1.5 miles to clearing along the road. Cross two footbridges on left and follow visible path to monument in woods.

35. Fishertown, originally a Quaker community, aided fugitive slaves making their escape to the north and east. At Chaneysville,

fieldstones mark the burial sites of thirteen runaway slaves. According to legend these men, with their captors closing in on them, begged to be killed rather than return to the South. *Location:* East St. Clair Township.

36. Stone Creek Church (brick), built in 1877, is adjacent to an early cemetery. *Location:* About 1 mile west of Fishertown (East St. Clair Township).

37. J. W. Nelson House (log), two-story, was built in the mid 1880s. Hon. John Nelson, one owner, was an associate judge of Bedford County around 1878. He purchased the property in 1864. *Location:* At Bedford County line on US 220, about 10 miles north of Cessna (East St. Clair Township).

38. Old Moch Dunkard Church (log), a one-room structure built in 1877 (founded around 1843–44), is a rare survivor. Adjacent is an early cemetery. *Location:* West of Ryot, SR 0096, near Fishertown (West St. Clair Township).

39. Willis Gristmill, built around 1800, was the first mill in West St. Clair Township. *Location:* Southeast of Pleasantville.

40. Sears, Roebuck House, built around 1915 by Harry Oldham (whose ancestors came from England in 1768), is a good example of the early pre-cut house manufactured by Sears, Roebuck Company. They were usually shipped by rail. There are a number of these houses in Bedford County. *Location:* West St. Clair Township.

41. Miller's House (log and stone) is a very early structure probably built at the same time as a nearby mill, now gone. Currently this is the office of Friendly Village Campground. *Location:* 2 miles west of Bedford, on T 469, 0.5 mile north of US 30.

42. Bonnet's Tavern (also known as Old Forks Inn) (stone), reputed to have been built in 1762 by John (Jean) Bonnet, was an early inn at the forks of Forbes and Burd military roads. It was also the site of a former Indian village and military encampment. In 1763 Capt. John Stewart wrote a letter from this four-mile house, and in 1783 Dr. Johann Schoepf "breakfasted with a Bonnet" at this place. John Heckewelder, a Moravian missionary, stopped here in 1786, 1788, 1789, and 1792. Early western Pennsylvania farmers raised a liberty pole in 1794 at this site in defiance of the federal taxation of whiskey.

45. Coral Caverns

46. Mann's Choice Hotel

Location: At Milligans Cove, on Cove Road, 1 mile west of SR 0096, south of Manns Choice.

44. White Sulphur Springs Bowling Alley (frame), built in 1886, is the oldest of its kind west of the Alleghenies. It still retains its original alleys and equipment, ten and duck pins. Now owned by Christian Fellowship International. Location: On the grounds, next to White Sulphur Springs Hotel.

45. Coral Caverns, the only coral reef caverns in the world, date back to the time when the Appalachian Sea covered this area. The caverns, concealed for 300–400 million years, contain impressive stalactites and stalagmites. This natural phenomenon was discovered in 1928 and opened to the public in 1932. Vaughn E. Whisker is the first recorded person to explore the caves. The first owner was Robert Hillegast. A local train and tracks were added for tourists in 1967 by Ed McDivett and Hugo Frear. Present owner is Steve Hall. Hours: Memorial Day–Labor Day, 9 A.M.–6 P.M.; weekends in spring and fall. Location: Manns Choice area, SR 0031.

46. Manns Choice Hotel, "The Choice" (frame), was a railroad hotel built in 1850. It is still a public house (restaurant), and the early water trough spring in front of the building continues to serve passersby with fresh running water. Location: Manns Choice, SR 0031

Note: An early hardware store is located across the street; nearby is an 1881 Methodist church (frame), across from an early brick house.

47. Ryder-Bittner House (brick), once owned by the Ryder family, became the home of Leonard Bittner, justice of the peace born in Somerset County. In 1851 he moved to this 368-acre farm and built an addition to the

The house has been restored and is now a bed and breakfast inn. Location: 4 miles west of Bedford, at intersection of US 30 and SR 0031.

Note: A similar stone house, reportedly an old inn built in 1823, is within sight at the Cook farm on US 30 just east of the Forks. It has recently been substantially renovated.

43. White Sulphur Springs Inn (Harrison House Hotel) (frame) was built in 1884 by John Reed and George Lyon on land warranted to Samuel Barclay and William Lyon in 1847. In 1894 Ross and Michael Colvin bought the property, and between 1884 and 1914 it became known as a summer resort. A log tavern (razed), believed to have been built in 1771, operated on an earlier tract of this property warranted to Peter Wertz in 1844. It was a stopover for drovers on the Packers Trail close to the crest of Wills Mountain. Original logs from the first inn have been built into a sheep stable on the site. Both establishments were named for the famous mineral springs where various Indian tribes once met in peace because they believed it was hallowed ground.

In 1946 Paul and Patricia Cochran purchased the property and made extensive changes. The inn, located in a picturesque wooded setting, has been operated by Christian Fellowship International, an all-services retreat home, since 1978. Open year round.

51. Schellsburg Union Church

house in 1872. Windows throughout the house retain their original glass panes. Smokehouse and other outbuildings on farm, which was the site of an Indian village. *Location:* Junction of SR 0031 and SR 4036, 5.2 miles west of Manns Choice.

48. Hereline House (log) is an early structure owned by John Hereline at one time. *Location:* Near Manns Choice, on SR 4005, 7 miles west of Bedford. After crossing Hereline covered bridge, which is 0.5 mile north of US 30, turn east for 0.7 mile along Juniata River.

49. Sleepy Hollow Inn (Hi-De-Ho Tavern) (log) was built in 1775 as a stagecoach inn on the old Forbes Road. Early owners of this log tavern (before 1786) were one Taylor and later Charles Ruby. The structure was covered with siding after the 1820s and uncovered in 1969. It now serves as a camp store and recreation center for a modern public camping ground. *Location:* Just east of Schellsburg, on north side of US 30.

50. Schellsburg

50A. **Schell-Colvin House** (brick), with a fanlight entrance, was erected about 1820 and operated as a store by J. P. Schell. The Colvin family owned this building at a later date. *Location:* Junction of US 30 and SR 0096.

Note: Another brick Colvin house of 1855 is across the road.

50B. Danaker House (stone) was built in 1828 with a fanlight entrance. Another stone house having a similar doorway is on the same side of the street (US 30), across from the post office. The Thomas Taylor family owned both houses in later years. *Location:* US 30 and Peter Street.

50C. Clark House (stone) was built in 1780 by William A. B. Clark to replace the 1770 brick structure behind the main house. It has a fanlight entrance. Clark, an early settler, operated a steam tannery. His descendants retained ownership of this property until 1968, when the building was sold and became an antique shop. *Location:* On US 30.

50D. Schellsburg Academy (brick), with a portico, was built before 1877. In 1904 Edgar F. Johnson was principal. After closing about 1912, the building was used for a public school but now stands empty. *Location:* 2 blocks north of US 30 on SR 0096.

51. Schellsburg Union Church (log) was built in 1806 on land donated by John Schell. It is the county's oldest church building and the first Protestant church west of the Susquehanna River erected by the German Evangelical Reformed and Lutheran congregations. According to old records the structure was renovated in 1881, at which time it was probably weatherboarded. The church, with the logs again exposed, still contains the early balcony, the wine-glass pulpit, and high-backed wooden pews. Open to visitors. *Location:* 1 mile east of Schellsburg, on US 30 (in cemetery).

52. Black Lion Tavern (log), built in 1788, was operated by one Ryan (name often confused as "Lyon" because of sign) from an early period. John Heckewelder and Abraham Steiner stopped here on a western tour in 1789. Steiner noted that it was the only inn with a signboard between Bedford and Pittsburgh. "Nothing to be had here excepting a little whiskey, and no oats for the horses." Howell's map of 1792 shows it as the "Lyon." The tavern is in a settlement, later owned by Maj. James Burns, that included a gristmill he built about 1800, a blacksmith shop, a tannery, a store, a post office, and slave quarters. Some of the foundations can still be seen across the road from the house. *Location:* 4 miles west of Schellsburg, off US 30, 150 yards north over hillside at foot of Allegheny Mountain.

53. "Shot Factory" House (stone), across from Tollgate Spring at the foot of Allegheny Mountain (Grandview), is an old landmark situated on the sharp curve where Forbes's army built its road straight up the mountain. Gunshot used to be made on this property. Early owners were the Finleys. Traces of the old breastworks built by the British remain on top of the mountain. This house, later purchased by the Shaffer family, now operates as a candy shop. *Location:* West of Schellsburg, on US 30 just east of crest of Allegheny Mountain.

Note: Halfway between this site and the SS View Point Hotel (q.v.), on the north side of the road, is the site of an old tollgate on an early turnpike.

54. SS View Point Hotel, originally called the Grand View Point Hotel, was built in 1931–32 to give the impression of an ocean liner, since the owner, Herbert Paulson, from Holland, saw a resemblance between mists in the valley and ocean waves. He had opened a roadside hotdog stand here in 1927. Constructed of concrete and steel, with a top-deck promenade, it is known locally as the Ship, providing a view of seven counties and parts of Maryland and West Virginia. Metal from junk automobiles was used to cover the ship's exterior. Recently renovated, it is now owned (since 1987) and operated throughout the

year by the Ron Overly family. *Location:* 17 miles west of Bedford, on US 30 (old Lincoln Highway).

55. Fort Dewart, also known as McLean's redoubt or the breastworks, was established August 1758 as a temporary depot for work parties cutting through the military road for Brig. Gen. John Forbes's army. A monument erected in 1930 by the Pennsylvania Historical and Museum Commission is on the site where the outline of the breastworks can be seen. The site is on private property. *Location:* 3.6 miles east of Reels Corners (junction of US 30 and SR 0160); thence 0.6 mile north on private road off US 30 (about 400 yards from house on this site). (Partly in Somerset County.)

56. Stotler Tavern (brick) is a nineteenth-century, seven-bay structure worthy of preservation. Owned by George Gardill in 1865. *Location:* Glade Road, SR 0031, West End.

Note: Nearby on T 501, north of West End and SR 0031, is another early building (frame), possibly an early hotel.

57. Old Barn (frame), with a hand-carved hex sign, sits next to a white frame church and cemetery. *Location:* Glade Road, SR 0031.

58. Early Pioneer House (log and stone) was used, according to report, as a station on the underground railroad, The log portion of the house was built around 1750–58. A stone addition was made about ten years later. The house was purchased by the Heim family. *Location:* On US 220, 3 miles north of the Mason Dixon line in Cumberland Valley Township.

59. Williams Stagecoach Tavern (stone and brick) was built around 1799 when the owners, Thomas and Henry Williams, obtained a tavern licence. The inn was owned by the Bortz family at a later time. *Location:* About 1 mile north of Centerville on US 220 (Cumberland Valley Township).

Note: There are numerous old log and stone houses in this early settled area of Bedford County.

Jackson Mills (1839) and Covered Bridge (built by Karnes Rohm, 1889)

Previous Sites Now Lost

Algonkin Gap Indian Relic Museum, closed
Furry Gristmill, burned

Covered Bridges

Bowser (Osterburg) Bridge over Bobs Creek, T 575, northwest of Osterburg, East St. Clair Township

Claycomb Bridge (1886) at Reynoldsville, reconstructed at Bedford Village, 1975

Colvin (Calvin) Bridge (1880) over Shawnee Creek, southwest of Schellsburg, Napier Township

Cupperts (New Paris) Bridge over Dunning Creek, now on private land, near SR 0096, 1 mile north of New Paris, Napier Township

Dr. Knisley Bridge over Barefoot Run, near Pleasantville, West St. Clair Township)

Felton's Mill Bridge (1892) over Brush Creek, near SR 2029 at T 411 and T 386, East Providence Township

Fischtner (Palo Alto) Bridge (1880) over Gladdens Run, near Palo Alto, intersection of SR 0096 and SR 3002, Londonderry Township

Hall's Mill Bridge (1872) over Yellow Creek, southeast of Yellow Creek, T 528 near SR 1022, Hopewell Township

Heirline Bridge (1902) over Juniata River, SR 4005 across Turnpike from SR 0031, Harrison and Napier townships

Hewitt Bridge over Town Creek, T 305 at Hewitt, near Maryland line, Southampton Township

Jackson Mills Bridge (1889) over Brush Creek, T 412 at Jackson Mills, south of Breezewood, East Providence Township

McDaniel's Bridge (1873) over Brush Creek, T 419, East and West Providence townships

Raystown (Diehl's, Turner's) Bridge (1892) over Raystown Branch of Juniata River,

T 418 between SR 0031 and Turnpike, Harrison Township

Ryot Bridge over Dunnings Creek, T 559 east of Ryot, West St. Clair Township

Snooks Bridge over Dunnings Creek, T 578 north of Spring Meadow, East St. Clair Township

Pennsylvania Historical and Museum Commission Markers

Anderson House Bedford, East Pitt Street between Juliana and Richard Streets

Bedford County Bedford, at courthouse, Juliana and Penn streets

Bedford Springs Bedford Springs, old US 220

Bedford Village On main highways leading into Bedford

Capt. Phillips' Rangers Memorial At property on SR 0026 northwest of Saxton

Espy House Bedford, East Pitt Street between Juliana and Richard streets

Forbes Camp US 30 west of Schellsburg Forbes Road Junction of US 30 and SR 0031, 4 miles west of Bedford

Forbes Road (Fort Juniata) US 30, 6.2 miles east of Everett

Fort Bedford Bedford, US 30

Fraser Tavern Bedford, northeast corner of East Pitt and Richard streets

Gettysburg Campaign SR 0036, 5 miles south of Loysburg

"King's House" Bedford, East Pitt Street between Juliana and Richard streets

Old Log Church US 30 west of Schellsburg

Russell House Bedford, 203 South Juliana Street

Shawnee Cabins US 30 west of Schellsburg

The Squares Bedford, 203 South Juliana Street, southeast corner of square

Blair County

Capsule History

Blair is the only county in the state named in honor of a living native resident, John Blair, who served in the Pennsylvania legislature and was active in the development of turnpike and canal-boat transportation. It was erected out of Huntingdon and Bedford counties on February 26, 1846, and is 527 square miles in area with a population of 136,621.

The first European settlers who entered Blair County before the Revolutionary War were Germans who settled in Morrisons Cove and Scotch-Irish who located in the northern part of the county. Chief John Logan, one of the sons of Shikellamy, famous Indian vicegerent of the Six Nations, was a friend to the white people and lived at Logans Spring.

Numerous Indian trails ran through Blair County, the most important of which was the *Frankstown Path* (Kittanning Trail) running from near Harrisburg to the Allegheny River. It entered the county at Yellow Spring and crossed Canoe Mountain near the mouth of Canoe Creek. The trail ran along a ridge near present-day US 22 to Frankstown and followed the course of that highway to Hollidaysburg; thence it continued through El Dorado and on toward Ashville. The *Bald Eagle Creek Path* turned north from it at Hollidaysburg and ran through Altoona, Bellwood, and Tyrone. The *Frankstown-Burnt Cabins Path* ran by Shelleytown and above Marklesburg. The *Warrior Path* followed the course of US 22 from Water Street to Frankstown, thence south through McKee Gap, near Claysburg and Sproul. The *Raystown-Chinklacamoose Path* followed the same course in Blair County. The northern *Morrisons Cove Path* cut through a corner of Blair County northeast of King.

Situated strategically near the head of the Juniata River Valley and at the portals of mountain ranges (bounded by Tussey Mountain on the east and Allegheny Mountain on the other side), the county became a natural gateway to the West. Blair is noted for its transportation progress. The Indian trails became trader paths, which were superseded by turnpikes, the canal-portage railroad, railways, and modern highways. The Blair-Altoona Airport at Martinsburg was one of the earliest important fields in the state.

Hollidaysburg, the county seat, laid out in 1796 by Adam Holliday, whose brother William's three children were massacred by Indians, became the eastern junction of the Main Line Canal and the Portage Railroad. Altoona was founded by the Pennsylvania Railroad in 1849 and became a thriving village with the completion of the track over the Allegheny Ridge by the Horseshoe Curve in 1852. It became a borough two years later and a city in 1868, after the world's largest railroad shops of that era and a roundhouse were established there. Most of its streets were named for the sweethearts of the engineers.

Abundant ore, limestone, and timber made the Juniata Valley an important iron-producing area. In 1855 there were thirty-two charcoal furnaces, forges, and allied works in the county, including sixteen (possibly seventeen) stone blast (charcoal) furnaces. (One of Pennsylvania's foremost ironmasters, Dr. Peter Shoenberger, built his first furnace in Blair County in 1819.) Additional resources were coal and zinc. Lead-mining centered in Sinking Valley. Later, construction and repair of railroad cars provided major employment.

The county offers excellent views of scenic landscapes at such places as Homers, Riggles, Juniata, Blairs, and Bells Gaps, as well as at the top of Wopsononock Mountain.

Landmarks

1. Hollidaysburg, the county seat, was a transfer point between the Pennsylvania Main Line Canal (1832) and the Allegheny Portage Railroad (1834). This commercial center and gateway to the trans-Allegheny region became a borough in 1836. It contains 450 historic buildings, and 25 percent of the borough is a Historic District (mostly Walnut, Spruce, and Allegheny streets).

The Blair Foundation for Historic Hollidaysburg, at 516 Walnut Street (1872 brick house), offers walking tours which include a canal era tour; a commercial and residential tour; and a mansion tour. May–October, Saturday, 11 A.M. A self-guided tour is also available.

1A. Courthouse (stone) was erected in 1876. The first courthouse was put up by Daniel K. Ramey in 1846 and occupied by various county offices the following year. The present courthouse, dedicated in 1877, cost $103,000. It is a three-story structure of neo-Gothic style, with a high clock tower and spacious corridors, designed by David S. Gendell (contractor, John Shreiner). *Location:* Corner of Allegheny and Union streets.

1B. Stone Jail

1B. Stone Jail was built in 1868–69 by Jonathan Rhule (architect, Edward Havelan). The first keeper of the jail was Aden Baird. It is a spectacular structure. *Location:* Corner of Mulberry and Union streets.

1C. St. Mary's Roman Catholic Church was built in 1841 and dedicated three years later. *Location:* 700 block of Mulberry Street.

1D. Zion Evangelical Lutheran Church (painted brick) was founded in 1838 by members of the 1824 church at Frankstown. Jacob Garber was the first pastor. The cornerstone of the present church was laid in June 1853. It was remodeled between 1872 and 1883. *Location:* Corner of Allegheny and Union streets.

1E. Baldridge House (brick) was built around 1863 by William Hasty who had purchased the property (lot no. 281) in the early 1800s from Thomas Biddle. In 1887 the property was conveyed to H. M. Baldridge, Esq. (d. 1895). In 1906 Judge Thomas J. Baldridge acquired it from the heirs. He served as president judge of the Blair County courts from 1910 until 1927; as attorney-general of Pennsylvania; and in 1929 was appointed to the Pennsylvania superior court, resigning as president judge in 1947. *Location:* Southwest corner of Allegheny and Clark streets (620 Allegheny Street).

1F. Watson-McLanahan House (brick) was built around 1858 for David Watson. The style is Second Empire, and it has a bracketed cornice and a slate-covered mansard roof. Watson was a canal superintendent and a successful industrialist. The industrialist and inventor J. King McLanahan, Sr., lived here at a later date. *Location:* 703 Allegheny Street.

1G. Citizens National—Mellon Bank Building (brick), with terra cotta panels depicting the history of the town and large stone pillars, was built in 1902–03. Architects were M. Hawley McLanahan and William Prince. *Location:* 312 Allegheny Street.

1H. Methodist Church (brick) was built in Gothic Revival style in 1882. Daniel K. Ramey was the architect. *Location:* 400 Allegheny Street.

1I. Condron House (brick), with a cupola, was built in 1856 in Italianate style by James Condron. He also built the town's first opera house (first post office was located on the first floor). He was also a lumberman and a grain merchant. *Location:* 601 Allegheny Street.
Note: At 605 Allegheny Street is the 1860 Greek Revival house of the J. Lee Plummer and the Sen. Charles Mallery families. Plummer was a member of the Pennsylvania General Assembly, 1903–16.

1J. Holliday Marker: "Adam and William Holliday in 1768 stopped nearby and said: 'Whoever is alive 100 years from now will see a tolerable sized town here and this will be near the center of it.'" *Location:* 301 Allegheny Street, at Montgomery Street.

1K. Capitol Hotel (brick) was built in 1901 by Charles Brantlinger and in later years passed in ownership to the Campalong, Rossi, Trude, and Laratonda families. The hotel includes a restaurant, bar, and lobby. *Location:* Allegheny and Montgomery streets, southeast corner.

1L. Landis-Hoenstine House and Library (brick) was built in 1839 by Dr. Joseph Anderson Landis, one of the founders of the Blair County Medical Society. The office building on the property has been used over the years as a carriage house, a stable, a woodshed, and a loft, until it was converted to an office in 1946. In 1868 Dr. Irwin Crawford purchased the property. Floyd G. Hoenstine bought it in 1944. The Morrell family, previous owners, had made additions to the house. The smaller building next to the house, the doctor's office, is now a library. *Location:* 414–18 Montgomery Street at Cherry Alley.

1M. Calvin House (brick), built in Federal and Greek Revival style around 1840, was the home of Congressman Samuel Calvin from 1848 to 1851. Calvin, who read law under James Bell, died in 1890. *Location:* 421 Montgomery Street.

1N. Stewart-Elliot House (brick), of Second Empire architecture, was built in 1876. One owner, James E. Stewart, was a Blair County commissioner when the house was built. (Also owned by John B. Elliot.) *Location:* 515 Montgomery Street.
   Note: Second Empire brick townhouses built by the Elliot family are at 519–21 Montgomery Street.

1O. Presbyterian Church (brick), of Romanesque Revival style, was built in 1869–70 by building supervisor J. King McLanahan, Sr., and architect David S. Gendell. *Location:* 601 Walnut Street at Penn.

1P. Highland Hall (limestone), 1867–1911, was designed in Italianate style by Samuel Sloan (contractor, Daniel K. Reamey). It was originally Hollidaysburg Male and Female Seminary, founded in 1865 and first opened in the Town Hall since this building was not completed until 1869. The school was a female seminary between 1869 and 1910. In 1911 it became Miss Cowles School for Girls. The last commencement for the girls' school was in 1940, and from 1941 to 1945 it became Keystone Navy Training Center. In 1945 the Franciscan Fathers of Immaculate Conception purchased the building, and under their direction a boys' school was opened here, continuing until 1957. Since 1970 it has been the courthouse annex. *Location:* 509 Walnut Street.

1Q. Early Newry Street Houses, in Classical Revival style, were built around 1830. *Location:* Leamer House, 112 Newry Street; Mattern House, 316 Newry Street.

1R. U.S. Hotel (brick), with a mansard slate roof, was built on the site of an 1830s hotel, opposite the packet landing, by John Doherty. Englebert and Catherine Gromiller purchased the property in 1887 and rebuilt the hotel after it burned in 1886. The new hotel, containing nineteen "sleeping rooms" was, according to a newspaper account, "the best $1.50 a day house in the borough." In 1907 an adjoining barroom was added. *Loca-

1S. Manahath School of Theology

tion:* Northeast corner of Wayne and Juniata streets.

1S. Manahath School of Theology (stone), an impressive house with beams showing through the stone and a cupola, was built in 1854 by William Jack, an abolitionist leader who became a colonel in the Civil War. A tunnel connecting the basement and the river was closed in the 1940s. Jack also opened the first bank in the county and owned an iron furnace and other industries. Following his death in 1901, his wife and son and later a nephew owned the house. In 1953 it became a funeral home, and since 1964 it has housed an Evangelical Methodist school. The name is Hebrew for "God's resting place." *Location:* 1111 North Juniata Street at Cedar Boulevard.

2. Catfish House (frame), built before 1837, was owned by Robert Ullery from 1837 to the early 1860s when William and Mary Detrich bought it. They enlarged it for a public house called Huckster's Inn which accommodated merchants and farmers on their way to the Altoona Market House. Stables nearby housed horses used in pulling Conestoga wagons. The inn faced a large reservoir which was stocked with fish. The favorite among drovers and wagoners being catfish, the house (when it was later used as a boardinghouse) became known as "Catfish Manor." It is today a convalescent home. *Location:* South of Hollidaysburg on SR 0036.

3. Chimney Rocks, a 1,382-foot ridge, marks the spot where Indians reputedly held council meetings. This rock formation of limestone has been owned by the Blair County Historical Society since December 14, 1923. A bronze marker was placed on Pulpit Rock on October 17, 1924, to serve as a recognition of this gift of land to the society and to designate the property for public use. Similar rock formations can be seen at Fayetown on SR 0866. *Location:* Juniata Valley, south of Hollidaysburg near SR 0036.

4. Pennsylvania Railroad Museum is located in the restored Cove Station, formerly on the main line of the Pennsylvania Railroad about ten miles west of Harrisburg. This building and a caboose were moved to the property by Charles Hazlett, who owns the museum. *Hours:* April–October: Monday–Friday, 10 A.M.–5 P.M.; Saturday and Sunday, 1–6 P.M. *Location:* 1.5 miles south of Frankstown, on SR 2007 (off US 22 east of Hollidaysburg).

5. Hileman House (stone), built in 1795, first appeared on the tax list of 1820. After Hileman owned this property, it was purchased by Jacob Confer. It is situated in Frankstown, which was named for the early trader Frank Stevens, who established a trading post at the nearby village of Assanepachla. The villagers anticipated that this location would be the eastern terminus of the western section of the Pennsylvania Main Line Canal; but through the influence of John Blair, Hollidaysburg became the site instead. *Location:* Frankstown, on US 22 at corner hillside.

6. Lowry Homestead (stone) was built in 1785 by Lazarus Lowry, of the famous Lowry trading family, who came to the Frankstown region about 1768. In 1788 he owned 400 acres of land and was assessed for two horses, two head of cattle, and one Negro slave. A huge stone fireplace is in the kitchen, and additions, including porches, have been made to the original two-story structure. A stone springhouse, built at the same time as the house, is located nearby. *Location:* 1.1 miles east of Hollidaysburg, on old US 22 (0.1 mile west of Frankstown). House can be seen from US 22, where historical marker is located.

7. Royer House (quarried stone) was erected in 1815 for Daniel Royer, owner of the iron furnace nearby. This house, like many others in nearby Williamsburg, has ornate wrought-iron work. *Location:* 0.5 mile from village of Royer and 7 miles south of Williamsburg, on SR 0866.
   Note: William McAllister, the ironmaster, lived in the white frame house near the furnace. In the same vicinity is a frame Methodist Episcopal church built in 1872.

8. W. R. Metz House (brick), one of the first houses in Williamsburg, has typical architecture of this area. Many buildings have decorative porch railings made from wrought iron produced by the old charcoal furnaces nearby. *Location:* Williamsburg, 500 Second Street at Plum Street.

9. Presbyterian Church (brick), founded in 1816, was built in 1841. The structure is in good condition. *Location:* Williamsburg, on Second Street between Plum and Black streets.

10. Clover Paradise (frame and brick), with a first floor stone foundation, was built over 150 years ago. The Biddle family settled on this property in 1797. It is believed that the Ellsworth family (one member married a Biddle) built this house. In 1982 a descendant, Edward Biddle, converted this home into a public country vacation site. Nearby off Clover Creek Road is another historic house owned by the same family, the log home built by Capt. John Phillips in 1789. He was present at the 1780 massacre of settlers by the Indians. (Phillips' Rangers Memorial is in Bedford County, SR 0026 northwest of Saxton.) Also on the Biddle property near the log house is the gravestone of Eli Phillips, John's son. *Location:* Morrison's Cove, Woodbury Township, 20 miles southeast of Altoona, on T 454, near Williamsburg at Clover Creek.

11. Phillips House (log) was built in 1789 by Capt. John Phillips. It is situated near "Clover Paradise." *Location:* Morrison's Cove.

12. Octagonal Chapel (brick), now serving as a church, was formerly a schoolhouse. *Location:* Near Ganister, on Piney Creek Road (SR 0866), 3 miles from Juniata Run Bridge.
   Note: Nearby are several early stone houses worthy of study.

13. Patterson House (stone) was built about 1850 by George W. Patterson, who was on the tax list in Huntingdon County as early as 1846. A building next to the house, now used as a garage, was erected much earlier, perhaps 1820. *Location:* About 12 miles east of Hollidaysburg, on US 22 (1 mile west of Yellow Spring and 6 miles east of Canoe Creek).

14. Mount Etna Iron Furnace Plantation includes the first furnace built in Blair County; it was begun about 1807, put into blast in 1809, and went out of operation in 1870. Erected by Canan, Stewart & Moore, it passed through several ownerships before it was pur-

14. *Living Quarters at Mount Etna Iron Furnace Plantation*

18. *Isett House*

chased by Henry S. Spang in 1837. Spang built a huge stone mansion, a mill (in 1823 to replace a 1790 structure), a large store-office, and a new house twelve windows long. All the buildings are of stone. Later he sold the property to Samuel Isett and his son, descendants of Jacob Isett of Arch Spring (see *Isett House*). Samuel Isett developed the enterprise created by Spang, and the settlement became the Isett Post Office. *Location:* Turn southeast off US 22 at historical marker near dairy barn, about 2 miles west of Huntingdon County line. Follow 463 for 0.8 mile to site, which includes (in order) a large stone barn, twelve-windowed stone living quarters (four apartments), ruins of blacksmith shop, and furnace stack (one side fell in spring of 1975), all on left. On right are store-office and manager's stone residence. Continue 0.2 mile from furnace to river road and right 0.4 mile on SR 2017 to row of log cabins, built for workers and still occupied, and ironmaster's mansion erected by Spang.

15. Wilson Theater (brick), built in 1913, has been used principally for motion pictures since the end of the road-show era. *Location:* Tyrone, on SR 0350.

16. Home Electric Plant (brick) is a tremendous complex that includes a trolley-car barn dating from 1901. The power plant was built about 1892. *Location:* Tyrone, near "The Forks."

17. One-story Log Building, now used commercially, was built in 1824. *Location:* Bald Eagle, US 220 north of Indian Caverns at Spruce Creek (Huntingdon Township).

18. Isett House (limestone) is a magnificent seven-bay mansion built by Jacob Isett, who had come from Bucks County in 1785. A signature stone in the gable of the house reads, "Jacob-Elenor 1805," an unusual instance of a wife's name being included. Jagged stones projecting above the roof edge at the gables give an old-world flavor.

The house is almost the last trace of the former glory of the Sinking Spring Valley, which takes its name from the famed Arch Spring—a stream which sank into the earth and reappeared some distance away as a brook and which provided water enough to turn a mill. (It flows out of Tytoona Cave, q.v.) There are rebuilt weigh-scales on the property.

Isett also built a mill before 1788. Rebuilt in 1800, 1824, and 1869, it was torn down in 1943. Samuel Isett, Jacob's son, moved to Mount Etna about 1850 (see *Mount Etna Iron Furnace Plantation*). *Location:* Arch Spring, 2 miles west of SR 0350, on unmarked road. Turn just north of Fort Roberdeau marker, SR 1013 vicinity.

Note: Across the road is a large two-story limestone store building.

19. Sinking Valley Presbyterian Church (stone and brick) is an unusual structure with the lower part stone and the upper part wood and two peculiar round (bull's-eye) windows. The building dates from 1818, though the church was organized in 1790. The present church was built in 1885. *Location:* About 0.4 mile east of Isett house.

Note: Nearby is the old frame Arch Spring School, vintage 1850 to 1870 and St. John's Lutheran Church (brick, 1890s).

20. Fort Roberdeau (rebuilt stockade) was originally erected in 1778 by Brig. Gen. Daniel Roberdeau (b. 1727) at his expense. The fort was located near the Sinking Spring Valley

20. Fort Roberdeau

Lead Mines in order to protect the miners and settlers from Indian attack. (From 1778 until 1781 Roberdeau operated these mines which supplied lead for the Continental armies during the Revolution.) Although the fort itself was never attacked by Indians, settlers who did not seek shelter here were killed from time to time by the natives. In April 1779 a magazine and headquarters for a county militia were established here.

The present fort was reconstructed on the original site (excavated in 1939) in 1976. The palisade is copied from the original style—horizontal logs instead of vertical since a limestone strata was difficult to excavate. Surrounding the stockade is a forty-acre park containing fine nature trails. *Hours:* May 15–September 30: Tuesday–Saturday, 11 A.M.–5 P.M.; Sunday, 1–5 P.M. Non-season group tours by request. *Location:* Tyrone Township, south of Culp off US 220.

21. Tytoona Cave, a natural water cave whose source is half a mile away on private property, comes out at Arch Spring nearby. Years ago several Indians were seen entering this rock crevice but were never observed coming out. The cave, owned by the Western Pennsylvania Conservancy, is of the soda straw stalactite formation, the only one of its kind in North America. A similar one is in Australia. The site is beautiful but dangerous; it is not recommended to enter it. *Location:* Near Fort Roberdeau, SR 1013.

22. Cassidy Log House is reputed to have been built by Patrick Cassidy; he also founded the town of Newry in 1793, naming it for his birthplace in Ireland. This private residence has been well restored. A number of other early houses are in the vicinity. *Location:* Newry, corner of Allegheny and Cassidy streets (Blair Township).

23. Roaring Spring is Blair County's "Old Faithful," fed by an uncharted underground stream. The large stone castlelike building overlooking the lake houses the Blank Book Company, established in 1900 and still in business. The town, named in honor of this spring, contains many early houses. *Location:* Roaring Spring (Taylor Township).

Note: Spring Garden Farm (stone), a farmhouse built in 1824, is now a bed and breakfast inn. *Location:* Between Martinsburg and Roaring Spring on SR 0164 (Taylor Township).

24. Claysburg Library (log), the oldest house in this village, was built by John Ulrich Zeth in 1811. Arriving here in 1804, he was the first German settler. He built a sawmill in 1805 and a gristmill the following year. The house is now a public library, perhaps the state's only log library. *Location:* Claysburg, on Church Street near Bedford Street (Greenfield Township).

21. Tytoona Cave

25D. Baker Mansion

25. Altoona

25A. Mishler Theater (brick) was built by I. C. Mishler (called "Doc" after his father, a dispenser of herb medicines), whose dream was to have a "safe, perfect, and beautiful" playhouse for the people of Altoona. In 1893 he took over the management of the Eleventh Avenue Opera House, and on February 15, 1906, he realized his great ambition when his new Mishler Theater was opened.

Of French classic design and constructed of red brick in Flemish bond with Indiana limestone trim, the theater was built with the greatest attention to safety. A six-inch water main was run into it, a fire curtain installed, and extra-wide aisles planned. The interior was furnished lavishly with twelve dressing rooms and a 42-by-84-foot stage. The exterior entrance consists of four representations in color of the Muses, separated by Ionic columns and mounted on a stone balustrade. Above these are four circular windows, with carved stone garlands flanked by two life-size stone figures representing the Muse of Tragedy and the Muse of Dance. In October 1906 the building burned but was reopened on January 21, 1907.

Among the famous persons who played here were Ethel Barrymore and the John Philip Sousa Band. It was a legitimate theater from 1906 to 1919, after which it was a movie house and a dance studio until about 1950. In 1965 the building, though scheduled to be torn down, was rescued and bought by the Blair Arts Foundation and the Altoona Community Theater. In 1969, after being restored, it was opened as a legitimate theater and arts center. *Location:* 1208 Twelfth Avenue.

25B. Cathedral of the Blessed Sacrament (stone), built in 1926 as the seat of the Roman Catholic Diocese of Altoona, is one of the most beautiful of its kind in the United States. It is open for visitors during normal hours. *Location:* Thirteenth Avenue and Thirteenth Street.

25C. Pennsylvania Railroad Shops (brick) include erecting shops at Juniata, one of the largest car-wheel foundries in the world in South Altoona, and what was at one time reputedly the largest roundhouse in the world in East Altoona. Though the complex was very active at one time, much of it has been phased out in recent years. *Location:* Above south side of Tenth Avenue, from Sixteenth to Seventh streets, and from Seventh Street east to city line.

Note: The historic Central Trust Company buildings are at 1210–14 Eleventh Street.

25D. Baker Mansion (stone) was built in 1844–48 by Elias Baker, the county's wealthiest ironmaster and co-owner of the Allegheny Iron Furnace. The mansion is one of the finest examples of Greek Revival architecture in the United States, designed by Robert Cary Long, Jr., of Baltimore. The limestone of the building is set in sheets of lead. An impressive portico with six fluted Ionic columns two and one-half stories high is in the front, with a smaller one in the rear. The interior has black walnut woodwork and Italian marble trim. Among the furnishings are hand-carved pieces and an inlaid rosewood piano brought from Belgium by Elias Baker. This building now houses the Blair County Historical Society and Museum. In 1941 the society purchased this property from Charles Copeley and Louise Harding of London, England.

Hours: May 15–September 15: Tuesday–Sunday, 1–4:30 P.M. (weekends only through October 31). Other times by appointment. *Admission charge. Location:* 3500 Baker Boulevard (near Thirty-sixth Street).

25E. Allegheny Iron Furnace, built in 1811 by Robert Allison and Andrew Henderson and operated by them until 1818, was purchased by Elias Baker and Roland Diller in 1836. Originally fired by charcoal, the furnace was converted to coke in 1867. Following Baker's death in 1864 his son continued to operate the furnace until it went out of business in 1884. The large stone-furnace stack and the stone combination store and office building, erected in 1837, have been restored by the Women's Club of Altoona, which purchased the complex in 1939. *Location:* 3400 Crescent Road, at SR 0036 near Union Road.

25F. Dudley House (brick), built in the late 1800s, was owned by Charles B. Dudley, an 1874 Yale graduate. After working on a newspaper he was employed by the Pennsylvania Railroad (for 34 years) in the chemical department where he developed quality railroad products and better safety standards. *Location:* 802 Lexington Avenue.

26. Burns House (log covered with siding) was erected by the Cadwallader family. Although the house bears the date 1771 on its side, it was actually built in 1776. The daughter of the family married John Burns, for whom this area (Burns Crossing) is named. Antiques are now sold at the house. *Location:* Near Altoona, on SR 0764, house no. 7200.

27. Duncansville and area. At Duncansville are located the famous Wye Switches of the New Portage Railroad (successor to the Portage Canal and Incline Plane system). Andrew Carnegie once worked here at the tower.

27A. Duncansville Presbyterian Church (painted brick) was organized in 1846, with the present building erected in 1847. This structure, which now serves as the municipal building, is located in the village founded by Samuel Duncan, who flipped a coin with Jacob Walter to see whose name the town would honor. Prior to this time, about 1840, it was called Iron Town for the operations of the old forge here. *Location:* On US 22.

27B. Vipond's House (brick), now called "Olde Farm," is a two-and-a-half-story, L-shaped building in two sections, with a white wooden Doric portico. The older section was built in 1790. In 1914 Col. John Vipond lived here. On this estate is the Fort Fetter Monument (1777), 500 yards southwest of the fort site, where an Indian band met defeat. Seven skeletons were disinterred during the construction of the railroad that runs beside the monument. *Location:* Just east of junction of US 220 and US 22.

27C. Blair Homestead (weatherboarded log and stone) was built in 1785 by Capt. Thomas Blair on Blairs Gap Run; the stone part was a later addition. Blair's son John was president of the Huntingdon, Cambria, and Indiana Turnpike (Northern Pike) from 1819 to 1826. He served in the legislature from 1826 to 1830; and as a member of the Committee on Inland Navigation and Internal Improvements, he had much influence in locating the Pennsylvania Canal basin at Hollidaysburg. *Location:* 1.1 miles west of Duncansville, on old US 22, directly south of historical marker on new highway.

28. Horseshoe Curve, opened on February 15, 1854, and still operating, is a feat of engineering built when the westward expansion of the Pennsylvania Railroad demanded a main line connecting east and west. The roadbed was surveyed and the track, 2,375 feet in length, was laid out in 1847 by J. Edgar Thomson and his aides. At the outbreak of World War II, the railroad closed Horseshoe Curve to the public for fear of sabotage. In 1942, a Nazi submarine landed four highly trained saboteurs on the eastern coast of the United States in an unsuccessful attempt to blow up twelve key locations, one of which was this landmark.

In 1925 the Pennsylvania Railroad built a decorative stone horseshoe thirty-four feet long on the hillside. Also on display is a K-4 locomotive, no. 1361, at the curve beside the main line at an elevation of 1,623 feet. Before being made a memorial, this engine had rolled up 2,469,000 miles. A caboose, a 1916 version of the famed Pennsy "Mae West" cabin car, sits at the foot of the curve and is open to visitors. *Location:* 5.5 miles west of Altoona, on SR 4008 (Logan Township).

29. Glen White Coke Ovens, brick faced, are all that remain of a former bustling coke industry in this area: *Location:* Near Altoona, on SR 4008, 1.5 miles west of tunnel at Horseshoe Curve picnic area.

30. Skew Arch Bridge (stone) was built without mortar in 1832–33 to carry the

30. *Skew Arch Bridge*

Huntingdon-Blairsville section of the Northern Turnpike over the Allegheny Portage Railroad at the lower end of plane no. 6. It is one of the few arch stone bridges built on an oblique angle in Pennsylvania. Reputed to be the most famous masonry structure in America, it was abandoned in 1922 when US 22 was widened and straightened. Steps leading to the base of the arch are made of stones from the old Portage Railroad bed. A ten-foot monument near the bridge was erected in 1929. *Location:* East of summit at Cresson in Y of US 22.

31. Gallitzin Spring was a favorite stopping place of Father Demetrius Gallitzin, a Roman Catholic missionary who founded Loretto. In 1916 the Knights of Columbus, Knights of St. George Cadets, and other organizations landscaped the site and erected a stone springhouse. *Location:* About 1 mile east of Allegheny Portage Railroad monument (q.v.), on west side of US 22, east slope of summit at Cresson.

32. Allegheny Portage Railroad, plane no. 6, was a section of this amazing road which carried canal boats and other freight from the Pennsylvania Main Line Canal ending at Hollidaysburg to its resumption at Johnstown. This feat was accomplished by a series of levels and ten inclined planes, five east and five west of the summit. Construction was begun in 1831 and completed in 1834, when through rail and canal transport from Philadelphia to Pittsburgh was opened. At first cars were drawn up and let down by ropes, which wore out quickly, until John Roebling (see Saxonburg, Butler County) devised wire cables. Later, engines ran on some of the gentler inclines. The total cost of the railroad was $16.5 million. A section of plane no. 6 may be seen at the foot of the hill. This part of the Portage Railroad has been made a national historic site. *Location:* Just east of summit at Cresson, on US 22.

33. Rebecca Furnace, built in 1817 by Dr. Peter Shoenberger, is in ruins. The adjacent house was once owned by Mrs. Edward Lytle, Sr., the daughter of the ironmaster. Years ago it was described as being beautiful when it was in its prime. *Location:* Follow SR 0164 for Roaring Spring, east through Martinsburg to Clover Creek; turn north on first hard road (1.5 miles) to T 342 and continue for a quarter of a mile.

Other Iron Furnaces

(originally there were sixteen or seventeen)

Canoe (Soapfat) Furnace (date unknown), now Point View, northwest of Ganister. About 175 yards up along small stream from culvert, 0.3 mile from junction of US 22 and SR 0203 (round furnace).

Elizabeth Furnace (1832), near Pinecroft. About 100 yards from SR 4019 at bridge over Sandy Creek, 3.7 miles from SR 0764.

Springfield (Royer) Furnace (1815), built by John and Daniel Royer. From SR 0866 at Royer, drive southwest; take second road to right (T 392) to creek crossing. Little remains, but on the west side of SR 0866 a furlong (0.12 mile) before reaching T 392, you will see the ironmaster's house, worth the trip.

Pennsylvania Historical and Museum Commission Markers

Allegheny Furnace Altoona, SR 0036 south of Thirty-first Street

Altoona On main highways leading into city

Altoona Conference US 22 west of Hollidaysburg

Baker Mansion Altoona, SR 0036 at Mansion Boulevard

Blair County Courthouse, 423 Allegheny Street, Hollidaysburg

Blair Homestead Old US 22, 3.5 miles west of Hollidaysburg; and US 22, 3.3 miles west of Hollidaysburg

Canal Basin Hollidaysburg, US 22 at Canal Basin Park, western end of town

Etna Furnace US 22, 0.6 mile east of Yellow Spring

Fort Roberdeau SR 1013, 1 mile south of Culp; Altoona, US 220; and Altoona, Pleasant Valley Boulevard and Kettle Street

Frankstown US 22, 0.6 mile east of Hollidaysburg

Gallitzin Spring US 22 eastbound, 1 mile east of Cresson; and US 22 westbound, 1 mile east of Cresson

Juniata Iron US 22, 3.9 miles west of Hollidaysburg

Logan House Altoona, Eleventh Avenue at Thirteenth Street

Lowry Homestead US 22, 1.1 mile east of Hollidaysburg

Portage Railroad US 22, 7.9 miles west of Hollidaysburg

Butler County

Capsule History

Butler County, named for Gen. Richard Butler (lawyer, legislator, soldier, and Indian agent, killed in 1791 under the command of Maj. Gen. Arthur St. Clair), was erected out of Allegheny County, March 12, 1800. The land area, much of which lies in the plateau of the Connoquenessing Valley, is 789 square miles with a population of 147,912.

Pennsylvania set apart much of the section north of Pittsburgh and west of the Allegheny River for soldiers of the Revolution as reward for their services. A 1783 act of the legislature divided the territory by a line due west, surveyed under the direction of Surveyor General Daniel Brodhead. Land south of the line was known as "depreciation lands," given to compensate veterans for the depreciation in value of the Continental currency with which they had been paid; and north of it, as "donation lands," given as extra pay for their service. Butler County included both depreciation and donation lands.

Settlement of the county started in 1792 with David Studebaker, James Glover, Abraham Snyder, and one McKinney. Brady Township is named for the Indian fighter Samuel Brady.

Three principal Indian trails crossed the county. The *Kuskusky-Kittanning Path* ran from near Worthington to Butler, passing just north of Herman. It turned north of west through Portersville, and thence a little west of north through Allen's Mill, thence west near Rose Point. The *Logstown Path* entered the county below Zelienople, passing northward through Portersville and West Liberty, crossing Slippery Rock Creek at Crolls Mills, and continuing north through Harrisville. The *Venango Path* from Fort Pitt to Presque Isle followed much the course of US 19 at first and then ran near SR 0528 and SR 0008. It entered Butler County above Warrendale, passed through or near Evans City, Whitestown, Prospect, and Muddy Creek, crossing the Slippery Rock, at the mouth of Glade Run. It went through Keisters and Forestville and rejoined the Logstown Path at Harrisville.

Much has been written about Washington's course through the county en route to Fort LeBoeuf in 1753. The best evidence is that he followed the Logstown Path in this area, because more direct ways were blocked by high water. A monument in Forward Township marks the location where he narrowly escaped death when shot at by an Indian on his return by way of the Venango Path.

Butler, the county seat, was settled in 1793 and laid out in 1803, when John and Samuel Cunningham donated 250 acres to the county. It became a third-class city in 1918. Here, through the American Bantam Car Company, was pioneered the development of small, open, lightweight automobiles, the first jeep having been designed and built in Butler in 1940. Other cars designed and built in Butler County include: Huselton, 1912; Standard 8, 1916; Austin, 1930; and Bantam Car, 1939.

The world's largest builder of railroad rolling stock, Pullman-Standard, is in Butler City and Butler Township. The manufacturing of specialty steel (Armco) is supplemented by many smaller diversified industries throughout the county. Since the county embraces part of the rich oil fields of northern Pennsylvania, Petrolia became at one time the "oil capital of the world." Penreco, with an office in Butler and one in Karns City, is engaged in the processing of oil. Included among the county's numerous historic oil and gas sites were Bryon Center, oil-boom town of 1895; Six Points Oil Central Exchange of 1890; Parker Oil Pump Station of 1880; Daugherty Refinery; Spotty McBride Oil Wells; first 100-foot oil well at the Gelbach Farm; Portman gas well; and the Armstrong oil well. Ghost towns in Concord Township are Greece City (1872); Modoc City (1873); and Troutman (1873).

Mill site remains include Fletcher's Mill, built in 1819, Parker Township; and Daugherty's Mill, built by Dr. John Thompson in 1822, Slippery Rock Township. Two mills have continued to process buckwheat, one in Prospect and one in West Sunbury. Butler, known as the Buckwheat county, is also one of the leading agricultural counties in the state, noted especially for mushrooms. The county had seven stone blast furnaces.

Eau Claire, the highest spot in the county, has an elevation of 1550 feet.

Butler County Community College in Butler Township was the first to adopt the community college program in western Pennsylvania (1965).

Landmarks

1. Butler

1A. Courthouse (stone), Richardsonian, of mixed Gothic and French architecture, was built in 1886, costing $117,700. R. B. Taylor of Reynoldsville was the contractor and James P. Bailey of Pittsburgh the architect. It was enlarged and modernized in 1907–08 at a cost of $155,000 (J. C. Fulton, architect). This building contains a well-preserved clock 100 years old, which ran mechanically until 1940. A sixty-pound electric motor now operates the hands, though the original works remain in the tower. In 1958 the wood and slate tower shell was replaced by a stainless steel one.

The original log courthouse was located where the Mellon Bank now stands, until a brick one was built in 1807. The third building, erected across from the public square in 1855, was remodeled with a clock and bell tower in 1877, but it burned in 1883. *Location:* Main Street.

Note: Also at Diamond Street across from the courthouse is the stone Calvary Presbyterian Church, established in 1897 and built in 1902 in Richardsonian style. Behind Lafayette Building (site of Lafayette's visit) next to the courthouse is an exceptionally fine Second Empire (George III) house with a mansard roof, the Wiser-Kennedy-Robinson House.

1B. Little Red Schoolhouse Museum (brick) was built in 1838, the first brick school in Butler Borough. It has been restored as the headquarters for the Butler County Historical Society. *Hours:* May–October: Wednesday and Sunday, 1:30–4 P.M. Other times by appointment. *Location:* Corner of East Jefferson and South Cliff streets.

1C. Old Hospital (brick), incorporated in January 1897, was opened the following year at a construction cost of $25,000. This large building, now used for apartments, was the first Butler County General Hospital. *Location:* South end of Main Street bridge, at SR 0356.

1D. Yohe-Greenawalt House (brick), early Victorian with an Italianate tower, was built before the Civil War. The Yohe family owned it for 100 years. At a later date it served as a church with one room used for choir practice. In more recent times it was purchased by Roy Greenawalt. It is now a commercial building. *Location:* 350 North Main Street.

Note: There are numerous other fine old Victorian mansions on North Main Street, including the brick one at 529 Main Street at Polk Street.

1E. Potter House (frame), a one-story Victorian structure with an outstanding central barge board, is the present office of Dr. Leroy Potter. *Location:* 425 North Main Street.

1F. Troutman House (brick), Victorian, was built by the Miller family who had a merchant and carriage trade. Today the law office of George Atwell, it was part of the Troutman department store estate at one time. *Location:* 421 North Main Street.

1G. Troutman House (brick), built around 1867, was also part of the Troutman estate. A brick carriage house in the rear is now a little theater. *Location:* 417 North Main Street.

1H. Dougal-O'Brien House (log) was the homestead of David Dougal who laid out Butler (see *Gruenwald Cemetery*). In later years this building was altered extensively for the office of Martin O'Brien. It is now William D. Kemper's law office. *Location:* 209 West Diamond Street.

1I. Walter Lowrie House (brick) was built in 1828 for Amelia and Walter Lowrie, the parents of eight children (three sons and a grandson became foreign missionaries). Walter Lowrie was born in Edinburgh, Scotland, in 1784 and was one of the earliest settlers in Allegheny Township in 1797. Judge Lowrie served in the state house of representatives in 1811–12 and in the state senate from 1812 to 1819 when he resigned to enter the U.S. Senate. He was secretary of the Senate 1825–36 when he was elected secretary of the Western Foreign Missionary Society. This house is also known as the Sullivan and Shaw house, one of the first brick houses built in Butler. *Location:* West Diamond and Jackson streets.

1J. Elm Court (stone), a forty-room Tudor house, was built in 1929 by Benjamin Dwight Phillips, heir to the T. W. Phillips gas and oil fortune. Designed by Benno Janssen—designer of Pittsburgh's Mellon Institute, Athletic Association, and the (Westin) William Penn Hotel—Elm Court was in recent years sold to Mrs. Dean E. Burget, Jr. (granddaughter of Benjamin Phillips) and her husband, and later to Frederick R. Koch. *Location:* 500—600 blocks of Elm Street.

1K. Deshon Veterans Hospital (brick), was a tuberculosis hospital until the 1950s. *Location:* SR 0068, New Castle Road.

1L. North Cemetery, built in the late 1800s in the style of Frederick Law Olmsted, is known for its beautiful rhododendron bushes laid out at the site by Orlando Pride II, internationally known horticulturalist. *Location:* North Main Street, top of hill.

1M. Other noteworthy houses include: the Judge Greer House (frame, late 1880s, Queen Anne style) at 256 East Fulton Street; the house of W.H.H. Riddle, an attorney and champion for agriculture (brick, 1870s) at 224 East Fulton Street; the house of D. H. Wheeler, a Standard Plate Glass official (frame, 1890s) on Standard Avenue; the house of B. C. Huselton, known for building his own automobiles (brick, late 1800s) at 514 North Main Street; fine early brick houses at 510 North Main Street; and houses on the 500 block of McKean Street.

2. St. John's Roman Catholic Church (brick), measuring 90 by 42 feet, was erected of Gothic style in 1853, with a spire added in 1877. The bricks were kilned nearby. Beside the parking lot is the schoolhouse which now serves as a parish hall. The adjacent cemetery dates from the founding of the church. *Location:* Take Clearfield Road south off US 422, 9 miles east of Butler (6 miles west of Worthington). The spire of the church will soon come into view (Clearfield Township).

3. St. Fidelis College and Seminary was founded in 1877 by Capuchin Franciscan Fathers. In 1946 it became affiliated with the Catholic University of America and by 1948 was a four-year college. The college was closed in 1979 and the high school in 1980. Still operated by Capuchin Franciscan Fathers, the buildings are now used as a retreat center and are available for community use. Joe Kuhn built the Stations of the Cross in the grove across the street from the seminary buildings. *Location:* Herman, southeast of Butler, on SR 2002 (Summit Township).

4. Gruenwald Cemetery, the site of a German Lutheran church (many gravestones are inscribed in German), also contains the burial site of David Dougal (1778–1881) who surveyed and laid out the city of Butler in 1800. A trace of the Indian path which ran south to the Allegheny River at Freeport can be seen here. *Location:* East side of SR 1025 (Summit Township).

5. West Winfield, Winfield Township (SR 1019 and SR 2010), has been an industrial area since William Hazlett built a gristmill and sawmill on Rough Run in 1817.

5A. Winfield Furnace, which operated from 1847 to 1864, can still be seen from Winfield Road. Established by William Spear near where the Hazlett mill stood, it used the rich iron ore deposits of Long Run and Denny's Mill. The pig iron was hauled to Freeport where it was put on barges and shipped to Pittsburgh. In 1856 this industry passed into the hands of the Winfield Coal and Iron Company, then to William Stewart, who worked it until 1864 when the larger iron industries started making pig more cheaply. *Location:* In West Winfield, as you drive south on Winfield Road (SR 1019), on the right are the remains of some of the company houses; just after making a sharp left turn, the iron furnace can be seen on the left.

5B. Cement and Lime Industries began in 1893 with the Acme Lime Company quarry and the F. W. McKee mine, the world's first limestone mine. The worked-out mines are now used for various purposes. Still operating are Armstrong (opened in 1926 as West Penn Cement) and Winfield Lime and Stone, started in 1954. *Location:* All are near the iron furnace, and early Acme kilns may be seen on a hill.

5C. Moonlight Mushrooms, farmed in worked-out limestone mines, was started by Louis Lescobara, French chef at the Fort Pitt Hotel. The business was sold to the Yoder family in 1937. The McKee mine is now used as a research laboratory; the mushrooms are grown in a similar mine at Worthington (Armstrong County) which is among the world's largest mushroom farms. It has 100 miles of tunnels and 500 acres of rooms. *Locations:* Cabot-Winfield road, near Armstrong Cement plant; Worthington, off US 422.

6. Cooper Cabin (log) is the oldest house in Winfield Township and a project of the Butler County Historical Society. Four generations of the Cooper family lived in the cabin. Nancy Jane Cooper, the last, died in 1963 at the age of 101. On the grounds the spinning and spring houses have also been restored. *Hours:* May–October: Sundays, 1:30–4:30 P.M. and by appointment. *Location:* Near sign on Cooper Road, 1 mile from Cooper, or Pape, cemetery at Hannahstown, SR 0356.

6. *Cooper Cabin*

7. Cabot Academy (brick) was built in 1903 on land donated by Webster Keasey. Half the money for the construction of the building was donated by Godfrey L. Cabot and the other half by the community. The first principal was S. W. Frazier. In 1903 the school had sixty-five students. Later Winfield Township adapted the building for use as a high school. It is now a dwelling. *Location:* Cabot, off Helmbold Avenue, at top of hill (Winfield Township).

8. Old Stagecoach Stop Museum consists of restored buildings, including a barbershop, a country store, and the old Black Gold (railroad) Hotel (built in 1871), together with a kitchen house and stone well. Great Belt, where it is located, was at one time thought to be situated on or near an oil belt of the eastern part of the county, hence the name. The post office established in 1870 was also known as Coyle's Station, originally on the Gottlieb Wolf farm. *Hours:* By appointment only. *Admission charge. Location:* Great Belt (Jefferson Township), junction of T 578 and T 749, at railroad.

9. Hannahstown

9A. "Uncle Billy" Smith Monument was erected in memory of William "Uncle Billy" Smith (1812–90), driller of Edwin L. Drake's 69½-foot-deep oil well near Titusville (see *Drake Well,* Venango County). (In 1885 an oil well was drilled at Uncle Billy's home in Double Sales. It was called the "Midnight Mystery" since its flow soon disappeared.) The monument was erected by the petroleum

industry in 1959, the centennial of the Drake well. *Location:* Pape Cemetery, on SR 0356, 1.5 miles northeast of Saxonburg.

9B. Hannahstown Stagecoach Hotel (brick) was built in 1858. Nathan Skeer and Abraham Maxwell founded the town in 1829. Alphonse Kraus was an early proprietor of this hotel. *Location:* On SR 0356 (Jefferson Township).
   Note: Across the road, at 618 North Pike, is an old stagecoach tavern (Cabot area).

10. Gibben-Spurling House (log covered with shingles) was built in 1816 before Saxonburg was founded. It once belonged to an early settler, James Gibben, and later to one Spurling. An outstanding feature of the house is its huge stone chimney. *Location:* West Saxonburg (former railroad depot), on SR 2007 (Jefferson Township).

11. Saxonburg was founded by German immigrants in 1832 when Charles (Karl) and John Augustus Roebling (1806–69) were sent from Saxony to purchase a tract of 1,582 acres in Jefferson Township originally belonging to Robert Morris, financier of the Revolution. It was incorporated in 1846. About 1900, a mineral spring here became a popular health resort. Several original buildings remain.

11A. Roebling House (log covered with siding) was the home of John A. Roebling who laid out the town in 1832. He graduated from the Royal University of Germany and came to America in 1831. As the inventor of wire-cable suspended bridges, he improved the Allegheny Portage Railroad by introducing wire cable in place of rope. He was the designer of the Brooklyn Bridge in New York City. Roebling's son Washington, born in 1837, built the structure after his father's death. *Location:* Corner of Water and Main streets (SR 2011 and SR 2010).

11B. Roebling Workshop (frame), built in 1840, was John Roebling's rope factory. It was here he invented and made the first wire rope in the United States using hand-run machinery. The "rope walk" where the cable was wound was 2,500 feet long. The area around the shop was in recent years made into a park. The shop was moved back from the corner and is being restored by the Saxonburg Historical and Restoration Commission. *Location:* Corner of Water and Rebecca streets.

11B. Roebling Workshop

11C. Memorial Church (frame), originally German Evangelical Lutheran, dates back to 1832 when Rev. William Fuhrmann began preaching here. Built on land given by John Roebling, the present building was completed in 1857. The tower with its clock was added in 1863. At the equinox the sun rises behind the church and sets squarely before it. The church stands on the highest point of the watershed; water from the south side of the roof flows to Buffalo Creek and the Allegheny River and from the north side to Thorn Creek, into the Connoquenessing, the Beaver, and finally the Ohio River. The congregation became Presbyterian in 1955. *Location:* At the east end of Main Street.

11D. Steubgen House (frame). Christian Steubgen, a highly skilled locksmith, came to Saxonburg in 1840 and started a hotel in 1848. He was postmaster from 1845 to 1861. The present owner is a descendant of the Steubgen family. *Location:* 230 Main Street (north side), beside the Saxonburg Hotel.

11E. Saxonburg Hotel (frame) was built about 1852 with a later addition about 1863. It was known as the Union House from 1861 to 1865. Francis Laube, a musician born in Saxony in 1819, migrated to America in 1837. He rented this hotel in 1865 with E. F. Muder as a partner and called it the Laube House. Squire Laube also owned a brewery on the corner of Water Street and Old Butler Road.

Prior to Laube, George Vogeley and O. M. Raabe had run the hotel. Proprietors following Laube were Hedwig Helmbold, John E. Muder, Milton Newbert, Sam Bernstein, Dominick Gentile, and present owner Fred Gentile.

The house across from the hotel was a drugstore and doctor's office owned by E. B. Mershon about 1888. The property was originally owned by Vogeley and is now an antique shop. *Location:* North side of Main Street between 230 and 214. The sign still calls it the Saxonburg Hotel.

11F. Aderholt House, six bays, in Victorian style, was built in 1842 by H. F. Aderholt, who had arrived in Saxonburg in 1833. He kept the leading hotel, bakery, ballroom, and theater. He also managed the annual shooting matches. His enterprises were a mecca for Pittsburghers seeking entertainment. Aderholt, who died while baking bread, was from Bleicherode in the Harz, Germany. *Location:* 415 Main Street.

12. Todd Sanctuary, 160 acres, was founded in 1942 by W. E. Clyde Todd, author of *Birds of Western Pennsylvania*, for the Audubon Society on part of his grandfather's farm. Trails are open dawn to dusk the year round except during deer hunting season. *Location:* Kepple Road (Buffalo Township), about 1 mile from SR 0228 at Leasureville.

13. Knox Methodist Episcopal Church (brick), a one-story structure, was built in 1864. Beside the building is a stone having on it the date 1854, the period when the church was organized. The first pastor was John D. Knox. The building, with later-day etched windows preserved on the interior, has been adapted for use as a commercial business. At present it is a bakery-restaurant. The old cemetery is to the right of the church. *Location:* Knox Chapel, Winfield Road (SR 2010) and SR 0356 (Winfield Township).

14. Robins House (log) is an early structure, but its builder is unknown. It was sold at sheriff's sale in 1810. It was bought by Britnek Robins in 1819. Succeeding owners were James McGowan, the Kingan family, which owned it for nearly a century, Eli Eardly, Robert McGill, Helten T. Patterson, and Florie Lappan. A fine spring on the property was ruined by road construction. *Location:* SR 0228, 1.1 miles east of Glade Mills (Middlesex Township).

15. Middlesex (Bible) Presbyterian Church (brick) was organized in 1799, with Abraham Boyd as its first pastor. The present building, similar to the Beulah Presbyterian Church in Allegheny County (q.v.), was built in 1842 with later alterations to the interior. The oldest readable gravestone is of Mary Ann Boyd who died in 1813. *Location:* North of Cooperstown, 116 Church Road (T 492), just a short distance off SR 0008 (Penn Township).

16. Glade Mills House (brick) was built around 1830 by John Woodcock. On its front is a U.S. geological survey elevation marker stating it is 1087 feet above sea level. It was used as a stagecoach stop and the post office for Glade Mills. The present owners are the H. P. Starr heirs. In 1877 H. P.'s grandfather, William Starr, ran a frame sawmill and gristmill, which in 1878 he converted from waterpower to steam (now a lumber store). His sons, J. H. and J. W. Starr, inherited the business. The Glade Mills House is used for the office. *Location:* Southeast corner of SR 0008, SR 0228, and old PA 8.

Note: Below, at the corner of SR 0228 and old PA 8, is a large frame store building erected in 1883 by W. J. Marks during the oil excitement in the area. The Starrs now use it as a warehouse.

17. Cowan House (brick and frame) was built in vernacular Greek Revival style in 1838 by John Cowan II, on a land grant for service during the Revolutionary War. *Location:* East Franklin Township, SR 0268 and Pence Road.

18. Bowser Stauffer House (frame) was built around 1830 in Vernacular Greek Revival style by the Bowser Stauffer family in an area originally called Campbelltown. *Location:* Franklin Township, T 495, Dickey Road.

19. North Star Inn (brick), an old stagecoach tavern, was probably built about 1820 on the Pittsburgh Post Road (shown on David Dougal's map of 1817). It sits at about a hundred degree angle with the present highway, facing the old road scar still visible near the spot. Until a few years ago the early stagecoach barn and blacksmith shop were still standing. In 1876 the inn was owned by Simeon Nixon, who sold out in 1882 and built a hotel at Renfrew, where oil had just been struck. Three years later he moved to Butler and built the Central Hotel, relocated by his son, Simeon, Jr., in 1906 and renamed the Nixon. After Nixon's departure the North Star was operated by William Fisher. *Location:* South of Butler, east side of SR 0008, 0.2 mile north of Airport Road.

20. Phillips Mansion (brick), surrounded by a high iron fence, was the home of T. W. Phillips, Jr., congressman and member of a prominent oil and gas family. The palatial mansion and its appurtenant houses, built about 1922, have recently been converted into a restaurant and recreational club. *Location:* 6.5 miles south of Butler, at junction of Airport Road and SR 0008 (opposite Butler Graham Airport).

21. Evans City

21A. Miller Hotel No. 1 (brick) was built by J. N. Miller, a shoemaker, in 1872. This establishment was one of the finest hotels in the county at that time. In 1880 the roof was blown off the building, which had been converted into apartments. *Location:* Corner of East Main and Harrison streets.

21B. Miller Hotel No. 2 (painted brick) was built in 1876 as the successor to the Miller Hotel (see above). The Victorian-style structure is unoccupied and in danger. *Location:* Corner of South Washington Street and SR 0528.

21C. St. Peter's Lutheran Church (brick), at one time the union church of the German Reformed and Lutheran congregations, held its first services, conducted by Rev. John Esensee, in 1845. A frame church, now a residence on Pittsburgh (East Main) Street, was dedicated by Rev. Herman Manz in 1849 and was used for worship until 1869. Nearby this frame church site is a cemetery (between Petroleum Alley and Hill Street), with burial plots arranged according to the ages of the deceased. The second church, also of frame construction, was dedicated in 1869 by Rev. Frederick Wilhelm. It was later destroyed by fire.

The present house of worship, built in Gothic style in 1897 (designed by C. C. Thayer) and dedicated in 1898 by Rev. P. J. C. Glatzert, was erected on the former church cemetery grounds (used from 1869 to 1891). An addition was built in 1972. In 1915 an oil well was struck in the churchyard of this congregation. (There were about fifty wells in the area.) *Location:* Corner of Van Buren and South Washington streets.

22. Harmony, site of an Indian village, was settled by the Harmony Society, a religious community founded in 1804 (formally organized in 1805) by George Rapp and some five hundred German followers who came to America in 1803. The settlement under Father Rapp's direction chose celibacy as part of its lifestyle, in 1807, which inevitably led to its dying out. (In the fifteenth canto of *Don Juan,* Lord Byron refers to Rapp's approval of celibacy.) In 1814 the Harmonists decided to move to Indiana, where the next year they

22A. *Bentle House Museum*

22C. Drovers Inn and Barn, built in 1835, was used by cattlemen as a tavern stop on their way to the Pittsburgh market. The innkeeper was Aaron Schnatz. *Location:* Harmony.

22D. Wagner House (brick), originally a cooper shop built in 1809, is next to the Bentle House Museum and is part of the museum complex. *Location:* 222 Mercer Street.

22E. Stewart House (stucco) was erected in 1805 by the Harmony Society. It burned in 1856 and was rebuilt by Francis Colvert. *Location:* Main Street (across from Rapp's house, northwest corner of the Diamond).

founded New Harmony, finally settling at Old Economy (q.v.) in Beaver County in 1825. Abraham Ziegler, a Mennonite from Lehigh County, and five associates bought the Harmony property in 1815 for $100,000. The following are landmarks of this settlement.

22A. Bentle House Museum (brick) is administered by the Harmonist Historical and Memorial Association. This 46-by-36-foot warehouse, with a steeply pitched roof, was built in 1807. After Abraham Ziegler bought the property in 1815, this house was used as a female seminary. Above the entrance is the symbol of the Divine Wisdom, the Virgin Sophia (Angel of Peace), carved in relief by Frederick Reichert, Father Rapp's adopted son. Included in the museum's collection is the old tower clock works and one of three faces. This old timepiece was built to operate with one hand. *Hours:* June 1–October 1: Tuesday–Friday, 1–4 P.M.; Saturday and Sunday, 1–5 P.M. Other times by appointment. *Location:* Southeast corner of Mercer and Main streets (US 19).

22B. Harmony Inn (Pearce House) (brick) was erected by Alfred Pearce around 1875 when Harmony was expected to be the northern terminus of the narrow-gauge Pittsburgh, New Castle & Lake Erie Railroad, which was begun in 1877. Pearce was forced to sell this massive home after the railroad failed in 1879, and it passed to George Ramsey, Jr., who eventually found a way for the Wabash Railroad to run into Pittsburgh for George J. Gould. Later it was bought by the Zieglers and was operated as the Ziegler Hotel. Currently it continues under the name of Harmony Hilton. *Location:* Harmony, on old US 19, 1 block east of Bentle House Museum (off I-79).

22F. Shaffer House (brick), built between 1807 and 1809 with the same dimensions as the Bentle house, was used as a store and wine cellar. It is now the Harmony Fire Hall. *Location:* Northwest corner of Mercer and Main streets, on the Diamond.

22G. Frederic K. Reichert Rapp House (brick), the last house built here by the Harmony Society, has a "Philadelphia" doorway and bricks laid in Flemish bond. *Location:* Northeast corner of the Diamond on Mercer Street.

22H. Father Rapp's Chair was carved in the stone on Vineyard Hill and used as a place of meditation by Rapp. According to tradition it also was a lookout for him to watch his workers in the fields below. Originally reached by a stone staircase of about 120 steps, this lovers' rendezvous now has only a precarious dirt path leading to it. This "cell" is high above the Connoquenessing Creek. *Location:* On road northeast of bridge at outskirts of town.

22I. Log House is one of the few remaining early homes built between 1804 and 1814 at the first location in Harmony. There were originally forty-eight of these, measuring 18 by 26 feet. Traces of a mill race can still be seen near the property where a gristmill and barn once stood. (In recent years the house was moved upstream several hundred feet and is remodeled inside.) *Location:* North of Harmony just off US 19.
Note: Henry Zeigler House (log) was built in 1819 in Lancaster Township and moved to Harmony in recent years. It is now part of the Harmony Museum complex.

22J. Mueller House (brick) was constructed in the early 1800s with an angled corner to allow additional room for wagons to turn on the street. It was owned by Dr. Christopher Mueller, who raised his own herbs. *Location:* Corner of Mercer and Wood streets.

22K. Eidenau Stone Arch is all that remains of an elegant mill of hewn stone built by the Harmonists from 1809 to 1811. The mill arch can be seen along the highway at Minetta Spring, where Harry Etheridge built a monument in memory of his mother-in-law, Mrs. Minetta A. Walsh, which was dedicated October 31, 1932. *Location:* 2.8 miles east of Harmony, on SR 0068.

22L. Harmonist Church (brick) was built in 1807. A two-year supply of grain used to be stored in the attic of this building, as was the custom of the Harmonists. The former doorway through which they drove their wagons into the church is still discernible. A stone doorway dated 1809, once part of another building, is incorporated in the south entrance of the church. The town clock, now in the museum across the street, was originally located in the church tower and later in the public school nearby. *Location:* On south side of Mercer Street, midway between Main and Liberty streets, on the Diamond.

22M. Harmonist Cemetery is enclosed by a cut-stone wall built by Elias Ziegler in 1869, after the Harmonists had returned from New Harmony, Indiana, and had settled at Old Economy in Beaver County. A massive stone gate weighing more than a ton and revolving on a metal pin has inscribed over it, "Hier Ruhen 100 Mitsleiter der Harmonie Gesellschaft Gestorben von 1805, bis 1815" (Here rest 100 members of the Harmony Society who died from 1805 to 1815). All the graves within the burial grounds are unmarked, as was the society's custom, except that of John Rapp, son of Harmony's founder. His stone is attached to the south wall. *Location:* West edge of town, on SR 0068.

23. Mennonite Meeting House (cut stone) was built in 1825 under the direction of Abraham Ziegler. The first pastor was John Boyer. At that time the Harmonists and Mennonites worshiped here together. This church, with a later addition, and the cemetery are enclosed by a stone wall. *Location:* Just north of Harmony, 0.8 mile north of Zelienople off US 19. (Church is located between old and new US 19.)

24. Stouffer House (stone) was erected in 1825 by one of Abraham Ziegler's associates and was operated as a drovers' inn. *Location:* About 0.5 mile north of Harmony, on east side of US 19.

25. Lutheran Orphans Home (brick) was organized in Pittsburgh in 1852, and eight boys were moved to Zelienople two years later when Rev. William A. Passavant (see *Zelienople*) and Rev. Gottlieb Bassler bought twenty-five acres of land from Joseph Ziegler. In 1899 another similar institution in Rochester was merged with it. It now receives boys referred by the juvenile court. *Location:* Edge of Zelienople, on SR 0068 at South Green Lane.

Note: Another Passavant institution, the Passavant Retirement Community (US 19, south edge of Zelienople), includes a health center, nursing home, cottages, apartments, and condominiums. It is the largest employer in Zelienople.

26. Zelienople was founded by Baron Detmar Basse, later assuming the name Miller (Müller), who bought 10,000 acres of depreciation lands in 1802 and laid out the town in 1803. He built a wooden replica of a German castle which he called Bassenheim (destroyed by fire in 1842) and the Bassenheim iron furnace in 1814. His grandson, born in Zelienople, was Rev. William A. Passavant, editor, philanthropist, Lutheran clergyman, and founder of many hospitals and orphan homes throughout the United States. First called Zelie City, the town was named for Basse's daughter, Zelie.

26A. Passavant House (painted brick) was the home of Philip Louis Passavant. Philip married Zelie, daughter of Dr. Dettmar Basse. Their youngest son was Rev. William A. Passavant. This Georgian-style structure was built about 1810–14. Its present owner is the Zelienople Historical Society. *Location:* 243 South Main Street.

26B. St. Paul's Lutheran Church (stone) was built in 1826 on land donated by Philip Louis Passavant. The congregation was founded in 1821. In 1913 a tower and transept were added, with a new addition in 1960. The memorial stained glass windows were donated by Henry Buhl and Joseph S. Seaman. *Location:* 215 North Main Street at Grandview Avenue on the Diamond.

26C. Mollard House (brick) was constructed between 1800 and 1805 by an Englishman. The house was later used as a girls' finishing

29. John Irwin House

school and a fancy millinery shop. John Mollard was a later owner who sold antiques. *Location:* Main Street, US 19.

27. Mt. Nebo United Presbyterian Church (frame) was organized in 1805 by Reid Bracken, who was installed in 1808 as the first pastor. The original house of worship, a log structure built in 1808, was replaced by a stone church in 1827. The church cemetery off SR 0528, 1.5 miles south of Whitestown, marks the site of these two buildings. The third and present church was built in 1859. Mt. Nebo Cemetery was the first county burial ground. The first to be buried here was Barbara White in 1801. *Location:* Whitestown, at junction of SR 0528 and Harmony Road.

Note: Whitestown, settled in 1800 along the Venango Trail, contains two original buildings from the village and the foundation of the old White Horse Tavern, visited by Little Turtle, Chief of the Muncies.

28. St. John's (Old Stone) Lutheran Church (or Middle Lancaster) was organized in 1806. The present church was built in 1829–31. Near the pump in the churchyard are the remains of an old cut-stone lantern post erected in 1829. The first pastor was Gottlieb Schweitgenbarth. *Location:* Over a mile north of Harmony Road and 1.5 miles west of Whitestown on Stone Church Road, off SR 0528 (Lancaster Township).

29. John Irwin House (log), a two-story dwelling 25 by 30 feet with a log addition, built between 1796 and the middle 1800s, originally owned by John Irwin. The property is part of the depreciation lands along the Little Connoquenessing Creek where it intersects the Venango Indian Trail. The estate was called "Silvey" and was warranted in 1794 (434 acres). The property, surveyed by Jonathan Leet, includes a large barn built in later years by the Amish. In more recent times it was purchased by Harry Eigenrauch, followed by the present family who restored it. *Location:* 6 miles west of Butler at Welsh Bridge Road, off SR 0528 and T 360, which in turn is off SR 3032.

30. Old Clay Factory (brick) is now a glass factory. *Location:* Off SR 3077 between Renfrew and SR 0008.

31. Prospect is located on the old Venango Indian trail. Andrew McGowan, an early settler, lived here in 1796. Although the White Horse Tavern that once stood here is now gone, many old brick and covered log homes still exist. Among the original buildings that remain in and near the town are:

31A. Edmonson House (yellow frame), a former stagecoach tavern, was once owned by Caleb Edmonson. *Location:* 488 Main Street at Franklin Street.

30. *Old Clay Factory*

31B. Frazier House (brick), over 130 years old, was formerly owned by the Fraziers and later by the Hays family. *Location:* Franklin (Pittsburgh) Street.

31C. Allen House (painted brick) was a tavern owned by Robert Allen in 1845 and by Titus Boehm in 1895. *Location:* Junction of US 422 and SR 0528.

31D. McGowan House, built in the middle 1800s, was restored by the Clinton Mc-Gowans, descendants of the early settler, Andrew McGowan. *Location:* Franklin (Pittsburgh) Street.

31E. United Presbyterian Church (brick), or United Church of Prospect, was erected in 1859, a year after the union forming the United Presbyterian Church from the Associate and Associate Reformed churches. The special point of interest is the art metal sanctuary ceiling, copying the carved wood ceilings of Norman churches in England. The adjacent cemetery's most notable grave is that of Nathaniel Stephenson, a veteran of the Revolutionary War. *Location:* Church and Franklin streets (SR 0528).

31F. Emmanuel Lutheran Church (brick) was erected in 1849 after being organized in the Roth home. The adjacent cemetery has tablets memorializing the Roths who were part of the Moravian-Indian migration from Bethlehem, Pa., to Gnaddenhutten, Ohio. *Location:* Church Street.

Note: Here too is the grave of the Moravian missionary John Roth.

31G. Rube Waddell Tablet. Rube Waddell, once a Prospect resident, was a baseball pitcher of legendary ability. This tablet, on a pink granite stone of local glacial origin, was placed on the lawn in 1975 during Prospect's sesquicentennial celebration. *Location:* Prospect Library lawn.

31H. Site of Biddle Brothers' Capture. Jack and Ed Biddle, accused of murdering a grocer in a robbery, were caught in January 1902 after escaping from the Allegheny County jail in Pittsburgh with the assistance of the warden's wife, Kate Soffel. They were traveling in a horse-drawn sleigh stolen from a barn along the way. They changed horses nearby at Mt. Chestnut (Eagle Mill Road, North Road, and SR 0422). The Butler County sheriff and a posse killed the notorious brothers and wounded Mrs. Soffel, who lived until 1938 after serving a two-year term. The story was made into a movie, *Mrs. Soffel,* in 1984. (Not long after the events, a movie had been made but it was banned by local churches.) *Location:* 1 mile from Prospect, near junction of SR 0422 and SR 3029 on the George Dick farm.

31I. Dick Schoolhouse (frame), a one-room structure built around the turn of the century. It is now a private home. *Location:* 1 mile from Prospect near junction of SR 0422 and SR 2488.

31J. Mt. Zion Baptist Church (brick) was built in 1844. It is in a lovely setting overlooking Lake Arthur. *Location:* Near Prospect off SR 0528, south side of lake.

32. Washington Marker identifies the area where George Washington was shot at by an Indian as he was returning with Christopher Gist from his mission to the French. *Location:* Near Prospect (Forward Township), along the Venango Trail on the flats of Connoquenessing Creek, SR 0068.

33. Washington's Crossing marks the approximate site where George Washington crossed Slippery Rock Creek with Christopher Gist in 1753. *Location:* SR 4006, about half a mile east (upstream) from the bridge which crosses Slippery Rock Creek on SR 0008.

34. Mt. Chestnut Presbyterian Church (brick) was built in 1858. *Location:* Mt. Chestnut, US 422.

35. Moraine State Park, 15,767 acres, includes Lake Arthur, a 3,225-acre body of water. This terminal moraine was formed during Pennsylvania's Ice Age. A glacial lake covered the area 10,000 years ago. It is a fine

34. Mt. Chestnut Presbyterian Church

recreational area with a marina and 45 miles of shoreline. *Location:* 10 miles west of Butler, crossed north and south by I-79 and SR 0528, and east and west by US 422 (Brady, Worth, Franklin, Muddy Creek townships).

Note: North of Moraine State Park is Miller Esker, a thirty-two-acre serpentine mound of sand and gravel formed during the last Ice Age 16,000 years ago.

35A. Schneider Cemetery, an early grave-yard with a cut stone wall, dates back to 1803. *Location:* Brady Township.

Note: Other cemeteries within the park are the McCandless and Shafer cemeteries, both in Franklin Township.

35B. Bunker Hill Schoolhouse has been restored by the state. *Location:* Franklin Township.

35C. Davis Cabin was built in the 1790s (log) and 1830s (stone) and still remains in a wooded setting on what is now known as the Glacier Ridge Trail, a scenic hikers' path from Jennings Nature Reserve through McConnells Mill State Park past Lake Arthur. It was remodeled in the 1930s. The Davis family owned it when the state purchased the property for a park. *Location:* Near Lake Arthur at Davis Hollow (behind boat sales office at marina), Brady Township.

36. Muddy Creek United Presbyterian Church (brick) was organized in 1803, with John McPherrin as its first pastor. The present structure, succeeding log ones of 1804 and 1845, was built about 1854, with a new addition in 1954. Mrs. James Wigton and her five children are buried in the churchyard (see *Old Stone House Museum*). *Location:* On T 414, off SR 0008 opposite junction with SR 0138 north.

37. Old Stone House Museum perpetuates a tavern built by John K. Brown in 1822 on land he acquired from Stephen Lowery. Brown built a stagecoach and drovers' inn on the property, which was located at the crossroads of the first two public roads in the county, the Pittsburgh-Franklin and the Butler-Mercer pikes. Lafayette stopped here on his way from Pittsburgh to Erie in 1825. Due to financial difficulties, Brown's property reverted to the Lowerys, who retained control until the house was brought under public ownership.

In 1843 Sam Mohawk, a Seneca Indian, after becoming drunk at the tavern, went to a farmhouse north of the establishment and murdered Mrs. James Wigton and her five children, who are buried in the churchyard of the Muddy Creek United Presbyterian Church. The Wigton home site (unmarked) is on a nearby golf course.

About this period the first of several groups of counterfeiters, who went only by nicknames, began operations in the area under the leadership of Julius C. Holiday and for a while resided in the tavern. Also in the 1840s and 1850s a group of horse thieves, the "Stone House Gang," had their hideout about two miles southeast of the inn and ambushed many of the drovers going to and from the tavern along the pikes. During the Civil War, another band of counterfeiters led by a character known as "Old Man North Pole" had its headquarters nearby. By 1885, due to the advent of the railroad, which caused a decrease in wagon and coach trade, the tavern had become a farmhouse.

The two-story structure with a double front porch was rebuilt with much of the original stone through the efforts of the Western Pennsylvania Conservancy and the Old Stone House Restoration Committee in 1963–65. Nineteenth-century furnishings have been donated or lent by people in the area. The reconstructed tavern is administered by the Pennsylvania Historical and Museum Commission and is part of the Moraine State Park complex. *Hours:* Daylight Saving Time: Tuesday–Friday, 8:30 A.M.–5 P.M.; Sunday, 1–5 P.M. Winter: Tuesday–Friday, 9 A.M.–4:30 P.M.; Sunday. 1–4:30 P.M. *Admission charge. Location:* 12 miles north of Butler, on SR 0008 at junction with SR 0173 and SR 0528 in Brady Township.

38. Jennings Environmental Education Center, named for Dr. O. E. Jennings, beloved Pennsylvania botanist, is noted for its rare blazing star flowers which bloom in late July and early August. This relict prairie

113

began during the last ice age and is owned and operated by the Pennsylvania Bureau of State Parks as an environmental education center. *Hours:* Weekdays, 8 A.M.–4 P.M. Weekend programs are given as scheduled. *Location:* Near Old Stone House Museum, on SR 0528 at junction of SR 0008 and SR 0173.

39. Etna Mills House (Daugherty's Mills) (brick), a five-bay Georgian structure, was built in the early to mid 1800s. Dr. John Thompson established an iron forge here in 1822 which operated until 1841. Lafayette visited the forge and gave it a high rating. It was later moved to the present site of Etna near Pittsburgh. At the same time that the forge was built, a gristmill was erected at the site. The machinery, later taken to McConnell's Mill in Lawrence County (q.v.), was made in Philadelphia by Criscomb & McFeeley. The chief brand of flour was Fancy Roller. Other millers included David McJunkin, who operated the gristmill from 1829 to 1835, and owners by the names of Bingham, Rose, and McGowan. Zery Daugherty also ran the mill. His grandson, Joseph S. Daugherty (b. 1877), a graduate of Slippery Rock Normal School, was another owner of Etna Mills. The ruins of both the mill and forge can be seen near the millpond. Nearby is a very early keystone bridge, now under the main road. Present owners of the property are George and Chris Wilson. *Location:* 1 mile south of Slippery Rock, on SR 0173 at Slippery Rock Creek crossing, near Ralston Road, Box 44 (Slippery Rock Township, formerly called Etna).

40. Applebutter Inn (brick), with fine Victorian millwork, was built in 1844 by Michael Christley. The only other inhabitants of this house since then were the Plenty Wheaton Steele family. Restoration of the house began in 1987, with an addition, in keeping with the original architecture, to the rear. This lovely home, retaining its original chestnut and poplar floors and fireplaces, is now a bed and breakfast inn. *Location:* 152 Applewood Lane, 0.25 mile south of Slippery Rock on SR 0173 (between Etna Mills House and another early five-bay brick Georgian house).

Note: Wolf Creek Schoolhouse was moved to this property.

41. Slippery Rock University is a liberal arts college located on a campus of 410 acres. The first class of eleven members graduated in 1890. Its principal early building, Old Main, was completed in 1892. S. W. Foulk designed Old Main and the West Gymnasium (1900).

The institution was originally called Slippery Rock Normal School, dedicated in 1889. In 1960 it became Slippery Rock State College and in 1982 a university. In 1989 a one-room frame schoolhouse was moved to the campus for a museum. Donated by Joseph and Sara McCandless, it was originally built in 1891 at Hickory Corners. *Location:* Slippery Rock.

Note: The town was first known humorously as Ginger Hill, from an early tavern owner who specialized in Jamaica ginger. It was later called Centerville.

42. Christian Frederick Post Marker commemorates a treaty negotiated with the Indians by Post, a Moravian missionary from eastern Pennsylvania, in 1758. *Location:* Just west of the little bridge crossing Wolf Creek as you leave Slippery Rock on West Water Street (SR 4004).

43. National Storage Mine is a former limestone mine now worked out. It is now a unique underground storage center for historical documents, archives, government and corporate records, and various memorabilia. Visitation only through special arrangement. *Location:* Near Boyers (Annandale) (Marion Township).

44. Marion Furnace, a stone blast furnace now in ruins, was built around 1848–50 by Robert Breedon and James Kerr. It operated until 1862. Of the seven iron furnaces in Butler County, this one was preserved for the longest time. *Location:* Go to Harrisville on SR 0008. Turn east on SR 0058 for 3.3 miles to a bridge. Turn left at SR 4013 for about 0.25 mile. Furnace remains are in woods about 100 feet to the left of the road (Marion Township).

45. Oakland German Catholic Church, a frame structure with a steeple, was built about 1860 and is now a public health center. On the other side of the road is an English Catholic church, St. Joseph's, built in 1872 of brick and also having a spire. The German church resulted from a split of the St. Joseph's congregation. *Location:* Oakland, on SR 0068.

46. Turner House (stone), of unusual construction for its age, was built by H. R. Turner before 1875. On a hillside in view of the house and on the same side of the road is a brick house also erected by Turner somewhat earlier. The community here was first known as Martinsburg, surveyed by John Martin in 1837. *Location:* Bruin, on SR 0268 (South Parker Township).

47. Old Presbyterian Church was built in 1838 or before. *Location:* Hooker, SR 0038 (Concord Township).

48. Rocky Springs Cemetery, one of the oldest in the county, dates back as early as 1803. *Location:* Rocky Springs (Marion Township).

49. Karns City Oil Refineries are located in the city named for Gen. Stephen Duncan Karns of Antietam and Chancellorsville Civil War fame, who promoted the oil pipeline established by Van Syckel and in 1860 built one from Karns City to Harrisburg, to fight the United line. He also controlled the Parker & Karns City Railroad. (One of his oil wells, which happened to be unsuccessful, was drilled on the property of the Old Stone House Museum, q.v.) Today a modern industrial town and oil refineries have replaced the old Karns City of oil boom days. *Location:* Karns City, along SR 0268.

Note: A frame house built by Samuel Robinson, son of the first settler in the Hillville section (T 398) is on the site of an Indian encampment.

50. Chicora, in Donegal Township, was founded by James Hemphill of Westmoreland County in 1794. It was first known as Millers Town and later as Barnhart's Mills. When oil was discovered here in 1873, it had the third busiest telegraph office in the state. In its heyday the town had its own oil exchange, organized in 1882 (described in John J. McLaurin's *Sketches in Crude Oil*).

50A. Hays Hardware (frame), which still operates under the same name and with the original cash register, was built in 1892 on the site of the O'Brien House of the oil-boom days of the 1870s. In recent years the owner has installed a carillon which plays daily. *Location:* West Slippery Rock Road.

50B. Octagonal House (frame), a fascinating polygon with an interesting and efficient arrangement of interior walls and rooms, was once owned by Andrew Ford. Private residence. *Location:* Grove Avenue.

50C. Long Trestle Bridge, which spans Little Buffalo Creek and the town park, originally carried the Butler & Karns City Narrow Gauge Railroad. Built in 1876, it is one of three wooden trestle-type bridges at Chicora. *Location:* Near Chicora Cemetery, on SR 0068. (Cemetery has an interesting old chapel.)

53. Diviner Oil Well

51. Old Log School is the oldest one-room school in the county. *Location:* Donegal Township, near Chicora.

Note: Other Donegal Township landmarks include: Maloneys Corners, the site of an early cemetery dating to 1795–96; and St. Joe ghost town, founded in 1874 when the Mead oil well was struck. Here also was the Duffy gas well (1875), the largest in the country until the Haymaker well in Murrysville (q.v., Westmorland County).

52. Petrolia Store (frame) is one of the few remaining original structures in the former oil metropolis. It was originally a hardware store and now is once more in this trade. One former owner was William Stoughton.

Petrolia was settled in 1872 and chartered in 1873. The boom town grew up around the famed Fanny Jane oil well. Other wells in the area included the Daugherty, and the Taylor and Sutterfield "Boss" wells. This area was the center of the oil region for four years and doubled and quadrupled in size as new wells came in. Much of the town was destroyed by fire in 1889. It has been replaced by a new town of Petrolia. *Location:* Petrolia, in center of town across from post office and next to railroad tracks.

53. Diviner Oil Well, one of the world's oldest, has been producing since February 28, 1874, and still continues. *Location:* Southwest of Chicora. From SR 0068 turn northeast onto Medical Center Road (SR 1015); after 0.6 mile turn left on private dirt road. Well is 0.3 mile on left in wooded area (Donegal Township).

Previous Sites Now Lost

Central Hotel, Chicora, demolished
Evans City Station, demolished
Nixon Hotel, Butler, demolished (1977)
Willard Hotel, Butler, demolished

Other Iron Furnaces
(originally seven)

Beehive Iron Furnace, State Game Lands No. 95, Parker Township
Hickory Iron Furnace (1836–43), Slippery Rock Township
Marion Iron Furnace ruins (1850–62), Marion Township

Pennsylvania Historical and Museum Commission Markers

Butler County Butler, at courthouse, South Main Street (SR 0008)
George Washington SR 0068, 1.8 mile northeast of Evans City
Harmonist Cemetery Harmony, SR 0068
Harmony Harmony, SR 0068
Harmony Mennonites US 19 north of Zelienople
Old Stone House Stone House, at property, SR 0008 and SR 0173
The Roeblings Saxonburg, SR 2010
William A. Smith SR 0356, 9 miles southeast of Butler
Zelienople Zelienople, US 19

CLEARFIELD

Cherry Tree
Glasgow
Fallen Timber
St. Boniface

Patton

INDIANA

Carrolltown
Dysart

{219}

{422}

Loretto
Ebensburg
Gallitzin
BLAIR
Vintondale
{22} Cresson
Summit

{22} Mundys Corner
Lilly

Wesley Chapel
Wilmore
Mineral Point
Summerhill
South Fork
Johnstown
St. Michael
Westmont

WESTMORELAND

{219}

SOMERSET

BEDFORD

Cambria County

Capsule History

"Cambria" is an ancient name for Wales, so it is not surprising that the county was settled principally by the Welsh, along with the Irish and Germans. Cambria County was erected out of Huntingdon and Somerset counties March 26, 1804, and remained under the jurisdiction of the latter until January 26, 1807. Surveyors James Gwin and E. A. Vickroy adjusted the much-disputed east and west boundaries in 1849. The county is 691 square miles in area with a poulation of 183,263.

The first pioneers in the area were Samuel, Solomon, and Rachel Adams, who arrived prior to 1774. While the family was en route to Bedford in 1777, it was attacked by Indians. Samuel was killed and buried near the family home at Elton. Solomon became a county commissioner in 1787.

The first permanent white settlement of importance was at Beulah. This Welsh colony was laid out much like the plan of Philadelphia in 1797 by an agent of Dr. Benjamin Rush, Rev. Morgan John Rhys (Reese), who had taken a warrant for the land. This speculation failed because of poor soil and lack of roads. Beulah had a

117

library and a newspaper. The first post office and one of the earliest polling places in the county were located here, but today only the old cemetery and a monument mark the site.

The second community was at Ebensburg, the county's geographical center, settled by Welsh led there by Rev. Rhees Lloyd, a religious dissenter, about 1796–97. Lloyd acquired title to the land in 1804 from Thomas Martin, who had taken the original warrant in 1794. After Lloyd laid out the town in 1807, the site was moved to the top of the next hill on the west. Ebensburg officially became the county seat and the first borough in the same year, 1825.

The third settlement was at Loretto. According to tradition Capt. Michael Maguire came in 1768 as a hunter and established a camp about a mile from Loretto. In 1785 he purchased land in the name of Jacob and Adam Good. When Maguire patented the land, he secured an additional 400 acres for Bishop John Carroll of Maryland. Many Roman Catholics moved from that state and, through the help of Father Demetrius Gallitzin, established in 1799 the community named for a celebrated religious shrine in Italy near the Adriatic Sea. Loretto was laid out in 1816 and incorporated as a borough in 1845.

About the same time as Loretto's founding, Johnstown had its beginning. The earliest recorded patent was issued to William Barr in 1788. Though there were no large Indian settlements in the county, a small group of Shawnees migrated from the headwaters of the Potomac in the early 1700s when their chief died. One of their villages, Conemach Old Town, at the confluence of Stony Creek and the little Conemaugh River, later became Johnstown. It was named in 1834 in honor of Joseph Schantz (Johns), who laid it out in 1800; it is the county's only third-class city. Conemaugh Borough was organized in 1849. The great flood of 1889 almost destroyed both towns, as did one in 1936 which was followed by a gigantic flood-control project completed in 1943. However, on July 20, 1977, the area had another disastrous flood. The town of Cresson was known as the "summer capital" when President Benjamin Harrison spent his vacation there.

The county has had an interesting history of transportation. The old *Frankstown Path,* locally called *Kittanning Indian Trail,* crossed the county from a point near the village of Coupon, on top of the mountain on the east, to a point near Cherry Tree on the west. This path was used by Indians, traders, and settlers in moving from the headwaters of the Juniata River to the Allegheny River at Kittanning. The path entered the county near St. Joseph's Cemetery, running by Chest Springs, Eckenrode Mills, Baker Crossroads, and Plattsville, and exited 1.8 miles south of Cherry Tree and Pleasant Hill.

In 1820 the Huntingdon, Indiana, and Cambria Turnpike (Northern Pike) was completed, crossing the county from east to west through Ebensburg. Present-day US 22 follows this general direction. A tollhouse, whose site is marked by a tablet, stood from 1820 to 1943 at Lake Rowena.

The Allegheny Portage Railroad, linking the eastern and western sections of the Pennsylvania Main Line Canal between Pittsburgh and Philadelphia, was opened to Johnstown in 1834. The railroad-canal crossed the county from a point near Cresson on the east, through Lilly to Johnstown, and on down along the Conemaugh. It was fed by a reservoir above South Fork. In Johnstown the canal basin covered most of the section bounded by Clinton, Portage, Railroad, Five Points, and Canal (now Washington) streets. The canal system was abandoned in 1857, soon after the Pennsylvania

Railroad crossed the county along much the same course. Several important underground railroad stations were at Geistown, Johnstown, and Ebensburg.

The most important industries in the county are bituminous coal mining, begun in 1890, and the production of metal and metal products, with Johnstown the center of its iron-and-steel industry. Before the Civil War the county's iron production, with eleven stone blast furnaces, was one of the largest in America.

Lumbering was important in the days of charcoal furnaces. Oak grown in the county provided the raw material for the "shook" stave and shingle business after the Civil War, and many hogsheads used in New Orleans originated in the county. Other than around Ebensburg, agriculture was never important because of the terrain, but in recent years Cambria's potato growers have been among the foremost in the state.

Landmarks

1. Ebensburg (the county seat), at an elevation of 2,000 feet atop the Allegheny Mountains, was a famous resort town at the turn of the century.

1A. Courthouse (brick dressed with stone) was first built about 1808 from logs painted red. The jail was below the courtroom, but because of disturbances from inmates, there arose a need for two separate buildings. Rhees Lloyd donated the land, and his home was used for a temporary commissioners' office until the second courthouse was erected in 1828–30 on Lloyd Street. The third and present courthouse was built in 1880–82 in French Renaissance style at a cost of $109,962.44. The architect was M. E. Beebe and the contractor Henry Shenk. *Location:* Center Street.

1B. Stone Jail was built in 1870 of stones from buildings in Beulah. Contractor William Callan was in the middle of a controversy between Ebensburg and Johnstown over the location of the county seat. After much litigation the structure was finally erected in Ebensburg. *Location:* Corner of Center and Sample streets.

1C. Noon-Collins Inn (stone) was built as the Federal-style mansion of Philip Noon in 1834. He was later a judge of Cambria County. His daughter and son-in-law, Philip Collins, inherited the property in 1860 and added a Victorian flavor to their home. Philip Collins and his brothers received wide acclaim as builders of railroads. Then in 1905 the Park family purchased the property for $10,000, constructed a gymnasium for an

1C. Noon-Collins Inn

additional $10,000, and in 1907 donated it to the community as the Ebensburg YMCA. It served as the community center of Ebensburg until the mid 1970s. Lew and Jeanette Ripley acquired the property and spent three years completely restoring it to its original grandeur. Their Country Inn, which opened in the spring of 1986, has received an award for the best restoration of the year from the Pennsylvania Historical and Museum Commission. *Location:* 114 East High Street.

1D. Cambria Historical Society Headquarters, founded in 1924, contains numerous antiques, historical records, books, and other memorabilia. In this building is the oldest French piano in the county, brought over the Allegheny Mountains by a Conestoga wagon. *Location:* 521 West High Street.

1E. William Kittell House (brick) was built before 1830 by Jeremiah Ivory on land which had belonged to Rev. Rhees Lloyd and in

2A. *Stone Bridge (Johnstown Flood Landmark)*

1822 was sold to Stanislaus Wharton. *Location:* 301 Julian Street at High Street.

1F. Stone House (stone and log covered) is an early structure of uncertain date. This house warrants further research. *Location:* 412 East High Street.

1G. Webster Davis House (stone and plank) is an 1840 example of the Federal style of architecture. It was constructed without nails, using a time-honored method of notching wood and using wooden pins. The house features floors and ceiling beams made of hemlock, a one-piece spiral cherry bannister, and internal stone walls. The house is the birthplace of Webster Davis, a great orator who became assistant secretary of the interior under President McKinley. *Location:* 408 East High Street.

1H. Roberts-Davis House (log) was built in 1799 by Hugh Roberts who had three children: Elizabeth (b. 1799) and David (b. 1800) were the first children born within the Ebensburg town limits. The house was constructed with chestnut logs and includes an early board and batten ell addition of native yellow clapboard. Many of the original handmade window panes are still intact. This was the second house built in the county seat. A summer kitchen was erected on the property around 1900. The Richard Davis family pur-

chased this home in later years. *Location:* 415 East High Street.

1I. Fenwyck Hall (brick) was built by Johnston Moore about 1860 as the first house in Mooretown (an area now part of Ebensburg). In 1887 it was purchased by Emma McNamara who operated it as a guesthouse and a site for special events such as weddings. In 1904 the house was bought by T. Stanton Davis, who for a time leased it to Sarah and Ada Galagher for a new school, Hellesen Place. In 1910 an annex, built in 1894, was sold to F. C. Sharbaugh and moved to what had been the site of Fenwyck Hall tennis court. The house is still owned by descendants of the McNamara and Davis families. *Location:* 519 and 507 North Center Street.

Note: Another resort hotel, Castel Arms, built at about the same period, was later a boys' school and is now an apartment house. *Location:* Corner of Marian and Horner streets.

1J. Miton House, now a funeral home, was built by the architect Walter Miton. He designed many houses built in this area following the 1889 Johnstown flood. *Location:* Julian and Crawford streets.

1K. Educational Building (brick), now a multifamily residence, is of Second Empire architecture. *Location:* Horner Street.

1L. Old Denny Inn (brick), built in 1830, still retains one of its original sections. The house was later purchased by George Wright. *Location:* 605 West Horner Street.

2. Johnstown and the area of **Westmont** and **South Fork,** a major stop on the Pennsylvania Canal and, unhappily, famous for its many severe floods.

2A. Stone Bridge, a seven-arched structure which carried the Pennsylvania Railroad across the Conemaugh River, withstood the May 31, 1889, Johnstown flood when the South Fork Dam broke. The flood washed up a pile of debris thirty to forty feet high, which dammed the stream. Later this pile (covering thirty acres) took fire and its flaming houses have provided the subject matter for numerous artists depicting the holocaust. The Conemaugh River and Stony Creek meet at a point under the bridge. *Location:* Along SR 0056 next to Bethlehem Steel Company.

2B. Johnstown Flood Museum (brick), of French Gothic style, was built with Andrew Carnegie's aid in 1890–91, to replace the former Cambria Public Library building which was destroyed by the 1889 flood. It opened as a museum in 1973 through the efforts of the Johnstown Flood Museum Association, established in 1970 by a group of citizens concerned with preserving the history of Johnstown. The museum contains exhibits dating from 1800, other memorabilia of the area, and throughout the year various special displays. There is a mini-theater, and arts and crafts classes and seminars are offered. The museum was renovated for the centennial of the flood; for the celebration, the comedian Bob Hope appeared at the Cambria County War Memorial (built in 1949; 326 Napoleon Street). Tours: Tuesday–Saturday, 10:30 A.M.–4:30 P.M.; Sunday, 12:30–4:30 P.M. Group tours by reservation. *Admission charge.* Members free. *Location:* 304 Washington Street at Walnut Street.

Note: The First Methodist Episcopal Church that withstood the 1889 flood is still standing on Franklin Street at Locust Street. A former Presbyterian church that served as a morgue for the flood dead is partially rehabilitated on Main Street. It later became a theater, now part of Lincoln Center complex. Other buildings still standing on Main Street in downtown Johnstown from the time of the flood, when Central Park was under eighteen feet of water and debris, are: Griffith Drug Store, Alma Hall, Bantley Building, Horace Rose House (home

2B. *Johnstown Flood Museum* Photo: Johnstown Flood Museum

of the first mayor of Johnstown during the reconstruction), and John Ludwig House (where Clara Barton stayed during her Red Cross flood relief service). At Main and Market streets is an 1860s cast-iron statue of a dog which was recovered from the flood debris. It had stood in the yard of the Morley residence.

2C. Johnstown Corporation Steel Mill (brick and steel) began operating in 1884 as Johnstown Steel Rail Company which was largely reponsible for pioneering the street rail industry in the 1880s and 1890s. Later the plant became the U.S. Steel Johnstown Works. *Location:* Central Avenue and Village Street.

2D. St. Joseph's Church (stone) of High Gothic architecture, was built in 1857. The old cemetery for this church is the site of Hart's Sleeping Place, an early Indian cabin. Prince Gallitzin visited the church in 1830—the oldest original edifice in the Altoona diocese. Other noteworthy churches in the community include St. Stephen's Slovak Catholic Church (stone), built in Gothic style in 1909, and St. John Gaulbert Cathedral, 1845, Romanesque. *Location:* 731 Railroad Street.

Note: Cambria City (Johnstown) has many ethnic churches. In addition to the following, there are St. Emerich's, St. Rochus', Holy Cross Lutheran, Hungarian Reformed, St.

George's Serbian Orthodox, and St. Casimir's (Polish, with an octagonal dome).

a. Immaculate Conception Church of the Blessed Virgin (brick and brownstone) was established in 1859 by German immigrants. The present church was originally built in 1908 in Gothic style. *Location:* 308 Broad Street (SR 0056).

b. St. Columba's (brick) was built in 1913. On the interior are murals painted by Felix H. Leiflucher. *Location:* Broad Street (SR 0056) and Tenth Street.

c. St. Mary's Byzantine (Greek) Catholic Church (brick with mosaic tiles) was built by Ruthenians in 1920. Earlier churches included those erected in 1895 and 1900. *Location:* Power and Fourth streets.

2E. Inclined Plane, originally powered by steam and today by a 400-horsepower electric motor, was built in 1891 on Yoder Hill to permit settlement of the hilltop iron company suburb of Westmont after the 1889 flood. During the 1936 flood it became a vital emergency source of transportation. This funicular railway is the world's steepest passenger inclined plane, with a 71 percent grade linking Johnstown to Westmont. It has two counterbalanced cable cars, one of which moves up the 896-foot-long incline (to a height of 1,693 feet above sea level), as the other descends. The cable cars, designed to provide a level ride, accommodate people and (two) automobiles. An observation deck at the top offers a fine view. In recent years the incline was rebuilt with help from the original drawings of Samuel Diescher. *Hours:* Monday–Saturday, 7 A.M.–11:30 P.M.; Sundays and holidays, 9 A.M.–11 P.M. *Admission charge. Location:* Johns Street and Edgehill Drive; top level accessible from SR 0271 in Westmont Borough (Vine and Union streets).

2F. Johnstown Passenger Railway Station (yellow brick) was built in 1893. *Location:* Central Avenue.

2G. Cambria Iron Works was formed by King and Shoenberger in 1853. Here the first successful use in America of the Kelly steel converter—a pneumatic process for making steel—began in 1857–58, although it was first pioneered at the Eddyville forge in Kentucky. The hollow, pear-shaped iron vessel, developed by William Kelly and similar to that later used in the Bessemer process, once on display in the Bethlehem Steel Company office, is on permanent loan to the Smithsonian Institution.

The first steel rails produced commercially in America were manufactured at this site in 1867. The Cambria works were built expressly to roll "T" rails. Ore was brought here by canal and portage railway from Hollidaysburg. In 1889 portions of the buildings were damaged by the Johnstown flood. An 1850s blacksmith shop still stands on the property, as do the office and dispensary.

Bethlehem Steel Corporation, founded by Charles M. Schwab, acquired the Johnstown plant in 1923. (In 1904 the plant was owned by the Cambria Steel Company.) *Location:* Next to stone bridge (extending for 8 miles through city along Conemaugh River bank).

2H. Johns Log House Model is a small-scale replica of the home of Joseph Schantz (Johns) (memorial at Central Park). In 1793 he bought 249 acres at the site of Conemach, an early Indian town, the same year he built a log cabin which was at the site of present Vine and Levergood streets. In 1800 Johns laid out the town of Conemaugh (now Johnstown). He later moved to Somerset County (see *Johns House,* Somerset County). *Location:* On Valley Pike off Franklin Street.

2I. Johnstown Railroad Station (brick) has been renovated. *Location:* Walnut Street (formerly Iron Street).

2J. Grand Army of the Republic Building (brick) was rebuilt here after the 1889 flood destroyed a former GAR building. *Location:* 132 Park Place.

2K. Jupiter Building (brick, glazed terra cotta, limestone), previously known as Nathan's Department Store, was built in 1906 with alterations in 1932, 1936, and 1960 by the H. H. Kresge Company. The original structure was designed by Charles Bickel of Pittsburgh. This commercial building with Chicago-style windows and incised pilaster relief, was designated the Best Rehabilitation Project in Pennsylvania for 1981–82 by the Bureau of Historic Preservation. Today it houses an art gallery, offices, and shops. *Location:* 426–32 Main Street.

2L. Johnstown Bandstand and Shell (stone), a rare structure of its kind, is being restored. Built in 1939, it includes several storage and maintenance rooms, as well as the original masonry seats in semicircular positions in front of the shell. *Location:* Franklin and Plainfield streets.

2L. Johnstown Bandstand

2M. Grandview Cemetery has an "unknown plot" where 777 unidentified victims of the May 31, 1889, Johnstown flood are buried in unmarked graves. There are monuments to these and to many others whose names are known. *Location:* Westmont, on Millcreek Road, west of Johnstown.

2N. Stutzman House (log), or Log House Galleries, which now houses the Community Arts Center of Cambria County (established in 1968; purchased this property in 1975), was built in 1834 by Abram Stutzman, a circuit-riding Dunkard minister who followed the wilderness road between Johnstown and Ligonier. Here a pond was formed from a fresh-running spring around which the house was built. The Stutzman house was always known for its warm hospitality. Today this sole remaining log house in the area is open to the public without admission charge and offers art exhibits and a gift shop containing local arts and crafts. *Location:* 1217 Menoher Boulevard (SR 0271), Westmont.

2O. South Fork Dam was originally built in 1838–53 and enlarged by the state for a reservoir to supply the Johnstown canal basin and the western division of the Pennsylvania Main Line Canal during the dry summer months. The dam was 300 feet above the level of Johnstown. The reservoir and surrounding property were bought by a group of Pittsburghers in 1879 (see also *1889 Clubhouse*). The dam was raised to impound an area 2 miles long, with more than 540 million cubic feet of water and up to 65 feet deep. This edifice, 931 feet long and 72 feet high,

was one of the world's largest earth dams at that time. The faulty, neglected structure gave way May 31, 1889, between 2 and 3 P.M. during a period of heavy rain, contributing to the great Johnstown flood which killed more than twenty-two hundred people and caused property losses amounting to more than $17 million. This was one of the first important disasters aided by Clara Barton, founder of the Red Cross Society. Today one can see the breastwork remains at the edges of a 500-foot gap, a grim reminder of the devastation. A visitors' center is located here. *Location:* About 10 miles east of Johnstown, near Saint Michael and South Fork. From Johnstown go east on SR 0056, then north on US 219, and exit to right at sign one road before Sidman exit (junction with SR 0869).

Note: Johnstown Flood National Memorial marks the site where the South Fork Dam broke on May 31, 1889. A rainfall of six to eight inches in twenty-four hours and plugged fish screens on its spillway caused its destruction. *Location:* US 219 and SR 0869 near South Fork.

2P. 1889 Clubhouse (frame), with forty-seven rooms and a large porch, once overlooked the Conemaugh Lake at the South Fork Dam where two steam yachts provided excursion trips. It was originally built by a number of Pittsburgh businessmen and industrialists, including Andrew Carnegie, Henry Clay Frick, Henry Phipps, Jr., Robert Pitcairn, and Andrew Mellon, as a summer resort hotel for their South Fork Fishing and Hunting Club, organized May 19, 1879, when they acquired the land. The old building still contains hand-painted murals on cracked walls, depicting the area before and after the dam broke. The establishment, once called Cruikshank's Hotel, is now a tavern. *Location:* St. Michael, on Main Street (take Sidman exit from US 219).

Note: Nearby are some of the original twenty Queen Anne cottages built by club members prior to the flood. To reach these structures, continue on Main Street; just past the stone church, take a small road to the right.

3. Eliza Iron Furnace (stone), one of the best preserved of the county's original eleven blast furnaces, was built around 1846–47 by Ritter and Irvin. It was abandoned in 1849. Since 1963 it has been owned by the Cambria County Historical Society. It is interesting in still having at the top an iron heat exchanger, used to heat the blast with waste heat before

3. *Eliza Iron Furnace*

it entered the furnace. *Location:* On SR 3045 (in Indiana County, SR 2026) at bridge over Black Lick Creek, county line between SR 2013 and Vintondale (Jackson Township).

4. Heffley Spring, named after an early settler, continues to produce crystal-clear mountain water, flowing directly from its source above. From this location one can see an excellent view of the Conemaugh Gap. *Location:* 2 miles north of Johnstown, on SR 0056.

5. Staple Bend Tunnel, the first railroad tunnel in the United States, was a part of the Allegheny Portage Railroad, plane no. 1, between Hollidaysburg and Johnstown. Engineer Alonzo Livermore reported in 1827 that he had discovered a place where a bridge and the tunnel of 901 feet in length could be built. The structure was started in 1833, and on March 24, 1834, the first shipment of cargo by the portage railroad arrived in Pittsburgh from Philadelphia. The rails have been removed, but the masonry of the tunnel is intact. It is now owned by the Bethlehem Steel Company. *Location:* About 5 miles north of Johnstown. Go 4.4 miles south on SR 0271 from its junction with old US 22 at Mundys Corner to Wesley Chapel; thence 2.2 miles on SR 3043 to bridge over Conemaugh at Mineral Point. After crossing bridge and passing under railroad tracks, take first (extremely poor) road to right for about 2 miles to tunnel entrance. (This dirt road with numerous stone blocks is the original portage railroad bed.)

6. Carmelite Monastery of St. Therese of Lisieux (stone), constructed in Norman Gothic style around a quadrangle with a sunken garden, belongs to the discalced Carmelite nuns. The chapel on the property of this sequestered institution is open to the public. *Location:* On west edge of Loretto, near St. Francis College and Loretto Road.

7. St. Francis College, founded in 1847 as a boys' school by Franciscan friars, has a replica of the French shrine of Our Lady of Lourdes and a shrine to St. Joseph the Workman. The bell tower on the 600-acre campus is the only original structure from the early college. Much reconstruction followed two disastrous fires. *Location:* Loretto, on SR 0053 across from Gardens of Loretto.

Note: Southern Alleghenies Museum of Art (brick), a former gymnasium building, was remodeled in 1972. Its collections include works by Mary Cassatt and John Singer Sargent. Tours of the museum and nearby Charles Schwab Gardens begin here. (Branches of St. Francis College are in Johnstown and Hollidaysburg.) *Hours:* Monday–Friday, 9:30 A.M.–4:30 P.M.; Saturday and Sunday, 1:30–5 P.M. *Location:* On the Mall (campus) of St. Francis College.

8. Cresson Springs had a good reputation for its healing quality. Dr. Robert Montgomery Smith Jackson, a leading scientist and physician, built the Cresson Springs Sanitarium here before 1852. One of his patients was Senator Charles Sumner, who had been beaten unconscious with a cane by Senator Preston Brooks in a dispute over slavery. Here Jackson wrote *The Mountain.* Following his death during the Civil War, the property passed into the hands of Andrew Carnegie, who made his summer home in a small house here. He gave the commonwealth 500 acres, on which a tuberculosis sanitarium was built in 1912–13. It later became a school for retarded children. Grace Chapel (stone), built during the TB sanitarium period, is a charming structure well worth a visit. *Location:* Cresson, on west slope at south side of US 22 (west of Summit on old US 22).

Note: Unidentified graves with wooden markers are at a nearby site where 359 patients from the Cresson Springs tuberculosis sanitarium were buried. This cemetery is north of US 22. Take road next to Summit Hotel site to cemetery.

9. Lemon House (stone) was built by Samuel Lemon at the time the Allegheny Portage Railroad was constructed in 1834. In 1826 Samuel and his wife Jean had taken title to twenty-eight acres of land at Cresson Summit and

9. Lemon House

14. Alvernia Hall on Schwab Estate

built a two-story log tavern on the north side of the Huntingdon, Cambria, and Indiana Turnpike (Northern Pike). When the portage railroad came through, Lemon built the stone house as a residence and tavern at the junction of the ascending and descending planes. In addition to being innkeeper, Lemon also sold the coal on his land, which made him the wealthiest man in the county. Following the decline of the railroad, Lemon moved to Hollidaysburg, where he lived until his death in 1867, when his heirs used the house as a summer home. Later the property was operated as a farm. At present it is the headquarters and museum of the Portage National Railroad. Historic Site. *Location:* East of Cresson Summit, on old US 22.

10. Croyle House (stone), one of only four centenary stone houses remaining in the county at the time of the U.S. bicentennial survey, was built in 1804 by Thomas Croyle, Jr. An addition dates from 1835. (Thomas Croyle, Sr., 1705–1788, came to the area from Germany and married Judith or Stone King, daughter of Queen Alliquippa. Their original home can be seen in historic Bedford Village.) Thomas Croyle, Jr., and his wife Barbara settled here in 1794 and built a log house, later burned by Indians and replaced by the present stone structure. (Barbara, according to report, was the only doctor in the community until her death in 1864.) Thomas Croyle, Jr., also built a gristmill here in 1802. It operated well into the twentieth century. In 1807–08 a road was built from Ebensburg to Croyle's mill. *Location:* Summerhill, Marie Street.

11. St. Bartholomew's Church (stone), built in 1852 during the peak of the canal period, is a massive, impressive structure for this small rural community. *Location:* Wilmore, Munster Road.

12. Patton, at one time an active industrial town.

12A. Primble House (brick) was built in the 1890s by the owner of what at one time was the largest clay works in the world. Its products were used in building the Panama Canal. The American Legion Home nearby is now located at the site of this former company. *Location:* SR 0036.

12B. Miners' Rest (frame), at one time called "The Pig's Ear," according to tradition, was a popular hotel for local mine workers during the coal boom at the turn of the century. The old inn was built in 1892. *Location:* Fourth and Beech avenues.

13. Old Portage Railroad Tavern (frame) was built around 1835. *Location:* Lilly, 189–95 Grant Street.

14. Schwab Estate and Gardens of Loretto was the country retreat of millionaire steel magnate Charles Michael Schwab (1862–1939), first president of the United States Steel Company. This palatial estate, now the Mount Assisi Monastery of the Franciscan Order, is owned by St. Francis College. The industrialist called his country home Immergrun.

The first house built on the property is a three-story frame dwelling of fifteen rooms and is now called Bonaventure Hall. Schwab's second home, a limestone mansion now called Alvernia Hall, has twenty-six rooms and is surrounded by cascades, fountains, reflecting pools, and exquisite statuary. It was constructed by Jon Lowry, Inc. (builders of Rockefeller Center and Radio City Music Hall), and designed by architects Murphy and Dana of New York. On the grounds is a shrine to Our Lady of Fatima, which is open to visitors. The original property, of nearly 1,000 acres, included scores of buildings, special-purpose farms, greenhouses, stables, a nine-hole golf course, and an elaborate pumping system. *Location:* Loretto, on SR 0053.

Note: A nearby stone, castlelike water tower was built by Schwab for his estate. The tower stored his own private supply of water, while the adjacent flat section supplied the town and college. It is near Loretto, off SR 1007.

15. Klein Immergrun (brick) was the home of Robert Kimball. The Swiss-style villa was given this title by its owner to indicate "a small ever green estate" in comparison to Schwab's large estate nearby. *Location:* Loretto, 1 mile north of US 22 and a quarter mile east of Mt. Assisi.

16. St. Michael's Roman Catholic Church (gray stone), of Byzantine-Roman architecture, was built in 1899 on the site of a log chapel erected by Father Demetrius Gallitzin in 1800. The prince-priest's tomb and bronze statue are in front of the churchyard. The church, which has a red tile roof and steeple, was a gift of Charles M. Schwab (see *Schwab Estate*), whose boyhood was spent in Loretto. Schwab is buried in the adjacent cemetery and not, despite tradition, in New York City where he died. The church is open to visitors. *Location:* Southeast edge of Loretto, on SR 0053.

17. Gallitzin Chapel and House (covered with stucco) was built in 1832 and reconstructed in 1900. It was the residence and private chapel of Father Demetrius Augustine Gallitzin, who assumed the surname Schmet (Smith) on his naturalization papers. Upon a visit to America from Russia, he entered a Roman Catholic seminary at Baltimore, Md., and was ordained in 1795. Sent to Pennsylvania by the Baltimore Diocese, he helped lay out the colony of Loretto in 1799 and built a log chapel (14 by 16 feet) on the site of the present St. Michael's Church (q.v.) in 1800. After his father died, he refused to return to Russia in order to claim his inheritance. Father Gallitzin died May 6, 1840, and is buried in the churchyard next to the chapel. *Loca-*

tion: Southeast edge of Loretto, on SR 0053, next to St. Michael's Church.

18. Grange Hall (frame) is representative of the many rural granges (Patrons of Husbandry, national organization founded in 1867) that once served America's farm communities—some of which continue in this capacity today. *Location:* West of Cresson, junction of US 22 and SR 0164.

19. Peary Monument is a bronze statue of Rear Adm. Robert E. Peary, an arctic explorer who on April 6, 1909, became the first man to reach the North Pole, according to a somewhat questionable congressional decision. The monument, in a memorial park, portrays the hero in furs and parka, leading a husky. Peary was born on May 6, 1856, about 100 yards south of this tribute to him. *Location:* West of Cresson, on SR 1005 just north of its junction with US 22.

20. Wildwood Springs Hotel of the Alleghenies (ruin) was a summer resort built in 1850, destroyed by fire in 1860, and rebuilt in 1884. Overlooking Clearfield Creek at an altitude of 2,200 feet, the property at one time consisted of 200 acres with three log cabins in addition to the frame hotel. Today the only remaining structure is the log smoking house where guests were permitted to smoke. The site and buildings were converted to a state correctional institution in 1986. Prior approval is required for visitation. *Location:* About 4 miles north of Cresson, turn left off SR 0053 onto SR 1011 toward Loretto. Site is on wooded road off SR 1011 about 0.5 mile from highway.

21. Mt. Zion Evangelical Lutheran Church (frame), measuring 36 by 46 feet, was organized in 1853. This church, erected in 1859–60 about 150 feet east of the Old Donation Schoolhouse which also served as the congregation's first church, was originally called Christ Evangelical Lutheran Church of Glasgow. (The Lutheran cemetery was established between the church and the school.) The latter is the present location of the telephone exchange. Mt. Zion congregation, organized by Dr. Henry Baker, was at first undecided as to what denomination they were going to be, and were leaning toward the Presbyterians since they predominated over the Lutherans of the area. But a coin was tossed and the Lutherans won. In 1901 a new brick church was built across the road, with additions in 1960. The old frame church is now the parish hall. The adjacent parsonage was erected sometime before 1900. *Location:* Glasgow, SR 0253 (Reade Township).

22. Fiske Church (frame) was built in 1850. *Location:* Fiske, T 406 just south of Fallen Timber (White Township).

23. St. Joseph's Church (log) was built in 1830. A marker on the side of the building, now weatherboarded, relates the visit to this site by Prince Gallitzin. *Location:* Near Carrolltown, junction of T 532 and T 531, West Carroll Township near SR 4019.

24. Flick Birthplace (brick) was the boyhood home of Dr. Lawrence E. Flick (1856–1938) who in 1888 propounded the theory that tuberculosis is contagious and not hereditary. He studied medicine after curing himself of the disease and was the first to point out that sunshine, fresh air, good food, and bed rest were the best cures (before the discovery of penicillin). His idea was to construct screened-in porches for patients in tuberculosis sanitariums so they could get an ample amount of fresh air. Flick was a founder of the White Haven Sanitarium, the American Tuberculosis Society, and the American Catholic Historical Society. (His monument is in the front churchyard of St. Benedict Catholic Church [brick], built in 1850–60 in Carrolltown, which he attended as a boy.) *Location:* About 1 mile south of Carrolltown, turn east off US 219; thence about 0.25 mile. House is on left about 100 yards north of road on private drive.

25. Seldom Seen Valley Mine is a bituminous coal pit which provides an opportunity to see a simulated mining operation. Electric minicars transport visitors 2,200 feet to the working face. A related museum is also featured as well as a miner's home. *Hours:* Memorial Day–Labor Day: Daily, 9 A.M.–9 P.M.; May, September, and October: Weekends only. *Admission charge. Location:* About 1.4 miles north of St. Boniface, off SR 0036. Follow signs.

26. McGough's Sawmill, the first sawmill converted to a tourist attraction in Pennsylvania, provides demonstrations of how giant timber is transformed into usable lumber. Visits by appointment only. *Admission charge.* Special rates for community, church, and social groups. *Location:* Dysart, on SR 0053, 2 miles north of SR 0036.

27. Pennsylvania Purchase Monument stands at the junction of Cambria, Clearfield, and Indiana Counties (see *Canoe Place,* Clearfield County).

28. Historic Bridges include: Cassandra Bridge over Ben's Creek (SR 0053), and Lilly Bridge over Burgoon Run (SR 0053).

29. Meadowbrook School (brick and frame) was built in 1914. This former one-room schoolhouse has been readapted as a bed and breakfast inn by Andrew and Marylou Fedore. *Location:* 160 Engbert Road (Richland Township).

Previous Sites Now Lost

California House, demolished in 1987
Summit Hotel, demolished following fire in 1980

Pennsylvania Historical and Museum Commission Markers

Admiral Peary Park   On SR 1005 just north of junction with US 22 west of Cresson
Cambria County   Ebensburg, at courthouse, Center Street
Charles M. Schwab   Loretto, SR 0053
Demetrius Gallitzin   Loretto, SR 0276
Dr. Lawrence F. Flick   US 219, 1 mile south of Carrolltown
First Steel   Johnstown, SR 0056 opposite steelmill
First Steel Rails   Johnstown, SR 0056 opposite steelmill
Johnstown   On main highways leading into city
Johnstown Flood   SR 0053 at SR 0869, 1 mile south of South Fork
Lemon House   US 22 east of Cresson at county line
Loretto   Junction of US 22 and SR 0276 west of Cresson; and Loretto, SR 0053
Portage Railroad   US 22 east of Cresson
Robert E. Peary   US 22 west of Cresson
Sgt. Michael Strank   125 Main Street, Franklin Borough
Staple Bend Tunnel   SR 0271, 5 miles north of Johnstown

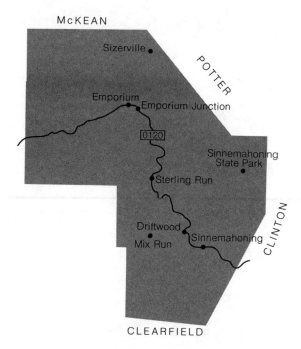

McKEAN

Sizerville

POTTER

Emporium
Emporium Junction

0120

Sinnemahoning
State Park

Sterling Run

Driftwood
Mix Run
Sinnemahoning

CLINTON

CLEARFIELD

Cameron County

Capsule History

Cameron County was named for Simon Cameron (1799–1887), U.S. senator, secretary of war under Lincoln, and ambassador to Russia. It was erected out of Potter, Clinton, McKean, and Elk counties March 29, 1860. This area was part of the "New Purchase" lands acquired through the 1784 treaty with the Indians at Fort Stanwix, N.Y. As part of Pennsylvania's last frontier, the region in 1782 was a portion of Connecticut's claim for Pennsylvania land which was settled by the Decree of Trenton.

The county has 398 square miles with a population of 6,674. It was first settled between 1809 and 1815 by Andrew Overdorf, Jacob Burge, Levi Hicks, and John Jordan. Many of the early landowners were veterans of the Revolution and the War of 1812.

Two important Indian trails crossed the county. The *Sinnemahoning Path* followed Portage Creek southward from Gardeau to Sizerville and Emporium and from there traced the Sinnemahoning Creek past Cameron, Sterling Run, Driftwood, and Sinnemahoning to the county line. The upper part of the path, from the "canoe place" (head of navigation) at Emporium to another on the Allegheny River at Port Allegany, was a very important route known as the *Big Portage*.

The main waterway, Sinnemahoning Creek, provided transportation for settlers as well as for timber, which at the time of early settlement covered the entire county. The town of Sinnemahoning, settled by Andrew Overdorf in 1808, was an important river landing in lumbering days.

Emporium, the largest town and county seat, was laid out in 1853 and was incorporated in 1864. It was originally known as Shippen, in honor of Edward Shippen, who owned the land. The first store was operated by Eli Felt in 1848 at Felt Block. Emporium is the hometown of World War II Gen. Joseph T. McNarney, who was deputy chief of staff of the United States Army and later was in command of American forces in the Mediterranean theater. It was for years the headquarters of the Sylvania Electric Products Company, one of the largest manufacturers of radio tubes and electronic equipment in the state, which still has a plant here. Emporium became known as the "powder city" after the Climax Powder Company began operations here in 1890. Dynamite for the building of the Panama Canal was manufactured in a number of powder plants, and ruins of the magazines where gunpowder and dynamite were stored may still be seen in the hills, now declared a wilderness area by the federal government.

Since the county was heavily timbered, its early industries were lumbering and tanning, out of which have risen numerous tales and folklore of this period. Wood manufacturing industries, sash-and-blind factories, and chemical plants have grown here. With the decline of lumbering, agriculture (especially dairying and livestock-raising) has become important. Naturally colored flagstone from the county's abundant supply was used at Arlington National Cemetery in the walks at the Tomb of the Unknown Soldier.

The major attractions of the county include hunting and fishing, with the rugged mountains bringing in numerous visitors. It is reputedly Pennsylvania's only county where fish are stocked via helicopter. Cameron boasts the largest elk herd east of the Mississippi in a natural habitat.

Cameron County was the birthplace of Katherine Mayo, a well-known reporter and author during the first third of this century.

Landmarks

1. Emporium is an industrial community and headquarters for the Elk State Forest.

1A. Courthouse (red brick with tower), completed in 1892, incorporates the 1861 courthouse, which was moved back from the street. The earlier one had cost $10,000, half provided by the citizens of Emporium and the remainder by the Philadelphia and Erie Land Company. *Location:* East Fifth Street.

1B. County Jail (frame and stone) was built in 1862 and rebuilt in 1885. Its first story was built of stone for security; the two upper stories are frame for economy. *Location:* Next to courthouse.

1C. First Sylvania Building (red brick), now deeply imbedded in a larger plant, was used by B. G. Erskine in 1924 when he began the Sylvania Electric Products Company, basing it on the old National Incandescent Lamp Company founded here in 1901. *Location:* GTE plant, near railroad.

1D. McNarney Birthplace

1D. McNarney Birthplace (frame) was the first home of Gen. Joseph T. McNarney. It is now used as a medical office. *Location:* Fourth and Maple streets (marked by small plaque).

1E. Emanuel Episcopal Church (frame and stone) was the first church built in Emporium. The original 1867 frame building may be seen directly behind the 1901 stone structure. *Location:* Fourth and Walnut streets.

1F. Henry Auchu Mansion (brick) was built in 1910 by a well-known local lumberman. It was later owned by the Sylvania Club and now serves a civic association. *Location:* West Fourth and Poplar streets.

1G. Dolan Hotel (brick), with a mansard roof and, at one time, a porch (as seen in an early photo), operated from 1902 until 1980. It was purchased by the Ostrum family at a later date. *Location:* Fourth Street between Chestnut and Cherry.

2. Sizerville Springs was the site of a large sanitarium and a hotel built in 1888, a few years after the public became convinced that mineral water from some of these springs could cure many ills. For many years people came from a wide area to drink the waters. Only the building foundations and the springs remain. *Location:* About 0.5 mile north of Sizerville on unmarked road northwest off SR

0155 near railroad crossing (Portage Township). Sizerville State Park is located nearby.

3. Memorial Spring, a wayside memorial, a strongly flowing fountain with a picnic grove, is dedicated to eight youths of the Civilian Conservation Corps who lost their lives fighting a forest fire October 19, 1938. They were Gilbert Mohney, Basil Bogush, Andrew Stephanic, John F. Boring, Howard E. May, Ross Hollobaugh, Stephen Jacofsky, and George W. Vogel. *Location:* 3 miles south of Emporium, on SR 0120.

4. Little Museum (frame), the former Sterling Run schoolhouse and now the museum of the Cameron County Historical Society, is a depression-days precut building ordered by mail from Sears, Roebuck & Company and used by several generations of students. It contains a treasury of early farming and lumbering tools, and houses the memorabilia of Gen. Joseph T. McNarney, who succeeded Gen. Dwight Eisenhower in the European theater of war, the youngest deputy chief of staff in the nation's history. (See also *McNarney Birthplace.*) In addition, the museum features many works of the famed pen artist Walter J. Filling, a Cameron native. It also contains a comprehensive chart of the area's natural history compiled by Charles Lloyd over a forty-seven-year period, including documentation of a meteor falling in Emporium in 1930. *Hours:* June–October: Wednesdays

4. *Little Museum*

5. *Bucktail Monument*

and Sundays, 1–4 P.M. Also by appointment. *Admission charge. Location:* Sterling Run, on SR 0120 (Lumber Township).

Note: Abandoned coke ovens can be seen beside the railroad tracks between Cameron and Emporium, SR 0120.

5. Bucktail Monument, a picturesque commemoration of a famous Civil War regiment, marks the place where companies from Elk, Cameron, and McKean counties, forming the nucleus of the famous Kane Rifles (Thirteenth Pennsylvania Reserve), started their raft trip to Harrisburg in April 1861. The woodsmen attached bucktails to their hats as a distinctive insignia. The oak tree to which the rafts were tied is gone, as is the old Commercial Hotel, whose fine cherry bar has been relocated in a later tavern at the site. The monument was erected by the state in 1908. *Location:* Driftwood.

6. Methodist Episcopal Church was built in 1890 and retains its original bell in the belfry. To the right of the church is a brick school dating to the early 1900s. *Location:* Sinnemahoning, Medical Center Street, near township line on SR 0120.

7. St. James Catholic Church was built about 1890. *Location:* Sinnemahoning, on hill across from post office on SR 0120.

8. Bucktail State Park was created in commemoration of the Bucktail Civil War regiment of area woodsmen, who acquired their name from the bucktail insignia they wore. *Location:* Southeast of Sinnemahoning, on US 120.

9. Mix Run is the birthplace (January 6, 1880) of Tom Mix, "the original King of the Cowboys," whose movies were popular during the thirties and forties. He spent his early years in Du Bois and performed in his last film in 1935. His father was a superintendent of the stables belonging to John E. Du Bois, a giant in the lumbering industry. As a result of this position, Tom Mix as a child became interested in horses, an interest which influenced his career as an actor in Western movies. Mix died in an automobile accident in 1940. Some of his films include: *Destry Rides Again, Tombstone Canyon,* and *Gun Ranger.* Much of his memorabilia can be seen in the Sterling Run Little Museum (q.v.). *Location:* Mix Run village on SR 0555 (Gibson Township).

10. Sinnemahoning State Park, with fine fishing, includes the impounding area of the George B. Stevenson Dam on the First Fork of Sinnemahoning Creek. *Location:* Along SR 0872 in Grove Township.

6. *Methodist Episcopal Church*

Previous Site Now Lost

Commercial Hotel, demolished

Pennsylvania Historical and Museum Commission Markers

Allegheny Portage Junction of SR 0120 and SR 0155 east of Emporium

Cameron County Emporium, at courthouse, East Fifth Street

Portage Path SR 0155, 5.5 miles north of Emporium Junction

Sinnemahoning Path SR 0120, 1.5 miles north of Driftwood; and SR 0120, 3.8 miles south of Emporium

"The Bucktails" Driftwood, junction of SR 0120 and SR 0555

Tom Mix SR 0555, 3 miles west of Driftwood

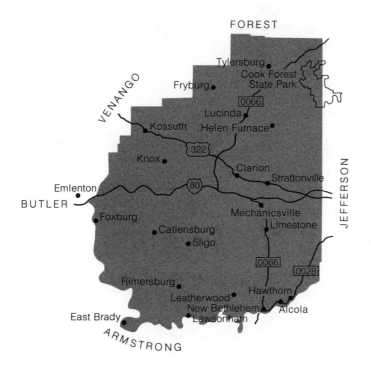

FOREST

Tylersburg
Cook Forest
State Park
Fryburg
0066
VENANGO
Lucinda
Kossuth
Helen Furnace
322
Knox
Clarion
Strattonville
JEFFERSON
Emlenton
80
BUTLER
Foxburg
Mechanicsville
Limestone
Callensburg
Sligo
0066
0028
Rimersburg
Leatherwood
Hawthorn
New Bethlehem
Alcola
East Brady
Lawsonham
ARMSTRONG

Clarion County

Capsule History

Clarion County was formed March 11, 1839, from parts of Armstrong and Venango counties and named for the Clarion River (which in turn was so called because of the "clear sound of the distant ripples") after the legislature had rejected the names "Stark" and "Jackson." The county seat, Clarion, was laid out and named later the same year, and courts were organized September 10, 1840, with first elections held October 13. Located on the Allegheny plateau, much cut by stream beds, the county covers an area of 607 square miles with a population of 43,362.

The county's pioneer settlers, predominantly Scotch-Irish, came from the older counties of the state. Absalom Travis, reputed to be one of the first pioneers, arrived in 1792, followed by permanent settlers from Westmoreland and Centre counties in the early 1800s. Many warrants for land included in the "New Purchase" obtained from the Indians at the Fort Stanwix and McIntosh conferences in 1784–85 were taken out by the Holland Land Company and prominent Philadelphians, including the Pickerings and the Binghams.

Gen. Daniel Brodhead's expedition passed through the area in its campaign against the Indians of the upper Allegheny during the Revolution. An Indian village was located at Fish Basket (SR 0028), west of Alcola in Redbank Township.

The *Goschgoschink Indian Path* nearly followed the course later taken by US 322 through Corsica and crossed the Clarion River at Clugh's Riffle, two miles east of Clarion. Thence it ran past Helen Furnace and north to Tylersburg and Nebraska. The *Venango-Chinklacamoose Path* followed the same course in the eastern part of the county but turned west at Helen Furnace, passing Lucinda, Fryburg, and Venus. River transportation was also important, especially before the days of the railroad, with the Allegheny and Clarion Rivers and Red Bank Creek providing the main waterways.

The county is notable for the numerous educational institutions that have flourished and declined during its history. These have included the Clarion Academy, 1840–45; Clarion Female Seminary, 1843–44; Carrier Seminary, built by the Erie Conference of the Methodist Episcopal Church in 1868 and later changed to what is now Clarion State University; Reid Institute at Reidsburg; Clarion Collegiate Institute, established in 1858 at Rimersburg; and Callensburg Institute. Of these only the state university remains.

Early industries included lumbering and pine-tar manufacturing. The major portion of Cook Forest State Park, with the largest stand of virgin white pine east of the Mississippi River, is within the county. The forest has an area of over 159,000 acres.

Clarion's growth was largely due to the rise of the iron, lumber, and oil industries. In 1846 its production of pig iron equaled the amount produced in 1831 by the entire state. There were thirty-one stone blast furnaces in the county, which in 1850 was known as the "iron county of the state." President James Buchanan was one of the owners of the Lucinda furnace. The iron industry collapsed following the rise of coke-smelting and the consequent removal of furnaces to cities, beginning shortly before the Civil War.

By 1876 nearly fifty oil wells were reported being drilled in the county. Natural gas and bituminous coal, together with oil, are still plentiful. Glass, clay, stone, and agricultural products are also important commodities.

Clarion is noted for its scenic forest lands and recreational areas. All the county's business has been considerably improved since the opening of the Keystone Shortway (Interstate 80), which traverses the county east and west near its center. The Susquehanna-Waterford Turnpike (later the Lakes to Sea Highway, now US 322), was an important route in the early days of settlement.

Landmarks

1. Clarion was incorporated as a borough in 1841.

1A. Courthouse (brick) was built in 1883–85. The first courthouse of brick cost $10,636.16 in 1841–43 and was replaced after a disastrous fire of March 10, 1859. The second, also of brick and costing $17,220, burned on September 12, 1882, the insurance paying $25,000. The present structure, of a variant Queen Anne style and with a 214-foot tower, was built at a cost to the county of $97,124.27, the contractors losing over $21,000. A milestone for the Bellefonte-Meadville Pike is located on the courthouse lawn. *Location:* US 322.

1B. Clarion County Prison (brick and stone) was built in 1873–74 and is an architecturally outstanding structure. *Location:* Fifth Avenue and Madison Street, behind courthouse.

1C. Clarion County Historical Society Museum and Library

1C. Clarion County Historical Society Museum and Library

1C. Clarion County Historical Society Museum and Library (brick) is a magnificent white-pillared mansion built in 1847–48 by Thomas Sutton, an attorney who had come from Indiana County and who died in 1853, leaving a wife and two children. The home was successively owned by William J. Reynolds, C. C. Brosius, and Nathan Myers. In 1897 it housed Keller's Academy. It was purchased in 1907 by John P. Reed and in the following year by John A. Ditz, who added a balcony and four Ionic columns in 1910. *Hours:* 2–4 P.M. every first and third Sunday; Tuesday and Friday: 1–4 P.M. *Location:* Across park from courthouse, 18 Grant Street.

Note: Some of the notable churches in the district include the old First Presbyterian Church, now H. Ray Pope, Jr.'s office in the Park; the First Methodist Church (now Lutheran) built in 1844 behind the courthouse; and the Baptist church on Main Street and Seventh Avenue. A Civil War monument stands in the park.

1D. Owens-Illinois Glass Plant. Tours start at the plant clubhouse from 1 to 3 P.M. (minimum age twelve years; flat, closed-toed shoes only). *Location:* 151 Grand Avenue.

1E. Judge Lyol F. Weaver House (brick) was built before 1865 by George Washington Arnold, who served as a cashier and director of the First National Bank of Clarion. He also was instrumental in purchasing land for

Carrier Seminary of Western Pennsylvania (Clarion University). The property was later owned by the Weaver family. *Location:* 720 Main Street.

1F. Kaufman Building was built in 1855. *Location:* Main Street and Sixth.

1G. Coulter House (brick) was built in 1876. Once a hotel, it later became a dry cleaning establishment. *Location:* Main Street and Sixth.

1H. Clarion State University was founded in 1867 as Carrier Seminary by the Erie Conference of the Methodist Episcopal Church. In 1886 it was sold to the state for $25,000 and became successively Clarion State Normal School, Clarion State Teachers College, in 1960 Clarion State College, and in 1982 a university. It has a ninety-nine-acre campus, twenty-five buildings, and one of the largest enrollments of any Pennsylvania university. Among its buildings are: Founder's Hall (stone), built in 1894 as the first additional classroom facility (it is the oldest on the campus, the old Seminary Hall having been razed in 1968) and Becht Hall (brick), one of the older buildings, which houses an interesting archeology and anthropology museum largely based on researches in the area.

2. Smith House (log), built in 1804 by Robert Smith, is one of the earliest houses in the county. *Location:* Troy Road, off SR 2014, Mechanicsville-Waterson Road.

3. Piney Dam (hydroelectric). *Location:* On the Clarion River south of Clarion, near SR 0066 and I-80.

4. Cook Forest State Park (see also Forest and Venango counties), of which more than half is in Clarion County, includes the following sites:

a. Fire Tower originally was built in 1929.

b. Seneca Spring, a mineral spring located on the Seneca Trail in the forest, was once a favorite of quacks. Mineral waters from this fountain were bottled and widely sold as a cure for arthritis.

c. Indian Rocks, visible at low water in the Clarion River some distance below the bridge, have on them pictures that include a tree and a rider on horseback. These have been authenticated as genuine Indian petroglyphs.

5. Helen Furnace, originally Highland Furnace, operating from 1845 to 1857, got its

135

7. The Country Store

9. Tylersburg Hotel

name from a misunderstanding of the Scottish pronunciation of "Hielan." A cold-blast furnace, it produced 756 tons of iron in twenty-six weeks during its last year, but failed because of low prices. It is being reconstructed. *Location:* On Clarion-Cooksburg Road (SR 1005). Furnace site is marked by Pennsylvania Historical and Museum Commission.

Note: Asbury Methodist Church (frame) was built about 1885 on a foundation of large cut stones from nearby Helen Furnace.

6. Fryburg

6A. Fryburg Hotel (brick) was built in 1879 by Ferdinand Ditz. Now called Washington House. *Location:* Junction of old state road and Shippenville-Fryburg Road; east side of SR 0208 at the Diamond (Washington Township).

6B. Lauer House (stone) was built in 1854 by John Kapp, an early settler in Fryburg. *Location:* SR 0208, west side of Shippensburg-Fryburg Road.

6C. St. Michaels Catholic Church was built in 1887. *Location:* SR 0208.

6D. Faller House (stone) was built in 1855–57 by Mathias Smerker. *Location:* SR 0208, midway on hill, east side of Shippensburg-Fryburg Road.

7. The Country Store (frame) occupies an early schoolhouse, now "a journey into yesteryear. Antique reproductions, pot-bellied stove, penny candy, pickle barrel," etc. Open seven days a week. *Location:* Leeper, SR 0036 and SR 0066.

8. St. Joseph Catholic Church (brick) was built in 1893. The adjacent convent, also brick, was constructed in 1877. On the same property are St. Joseph Hall (1950) and an early rectory. *Location:* Lucinda, SR 0066.

9. Tylersburg Hotel (brick), in Victorian style, has served for many years as an inn in this community. *Location:* Tylersburg, SR 0036 (Farmington Township).

10. Old Turnpike Tavern (stone), in later years the Van Meeter house, was built on the old Susquehanna-Waterford Turnpike in the middle 1800s, serving as a tavern from 1849 to 1876. From 1918 until 1944 it served as an inn on the Milesburg-Franklin segment of the Turnpike. *Location:* 1 mile southeast of Kossuth on US 322, junction with SR 4012 (Ashland Township).

11. Berlin House was a stagecoach house and meeting place for Civil War volunteers on their way to Meadville. *Location:* US 322 between Elmo and Kossuth.

12. Wolf's Den was built in 1831 by a Mr. Best, Philip Wentling, and Joel Wetzel for Nicholas Alt (Ault) who had purchased 117 acres of farmland in 1813. This barn, measuring 50 by 70 feet, partially burned in 1873 and was rebuilt. Philip Wentling, a cabinetmaker, had a shop at the end of the lane near the lake. His co-worker, Joel Wetzel, specialized in furniture and casket making. Between 1971 and 1972 the present owners, Carolyn and George Wolf, had the old barn reconstructed and adapted for use as a restaurant. *Location:* Wentling's Corners (near Knox), 500 feet north of I-80 (Exit 7).

18A. Fox Mansion

Note: Silver Fox Summer Playhouse near Emlenton is also located in an early barn.

13. Susannah Heeter House was built in 1855 by George Heeter. *Location:* Monroe, SR 0338 (Beaver Township).

14. Capt. Henry Neely House (stone, stuccoed) was built in 1814. Capt. Neely served in the War of 1812 and his sword is preserved in the Clarion County Historical Society. *Location:* Near SR 0338, on Heeter Road, off SR 0058 near Alum Rock.

15. Elias Ritts House (stone) was built in 1849 by an oil producer and river (flat) boat dealer and builder. *Location:* St. Petersburg, SR 0338.

16. Hovis Museum is a large private museum. *Location:* Near Emlenton on SR 0208.

17. Shortway Bridge (steel arch) on Interstate 80 over the Allegheny River at Emlenton is considered a masterpiece of engineering. Built in 1968 for $4.5 million, it stands 271 feet above the river, the third highest bridge in Pennsylvania. *Location:* Emlenton, on I-80 (partly in Venango County).

18. Foxburg was founded about 1870 by Samuel Mickle Fox II, son of Joseph Mickle Fox (1779–1845). The latter had purchased more than 13,000 acres in the area from the

estate of his father Samuel M. Fox, and came to live here in 1827, after marrying Hanna Emlen, for whose family the town of Emlenton (built on Fox land) was named. He, his son Samuel M. Fox II, and grandsons William L. and Joseph M. Fox II were all civically minded and active in industry and politics. In 1870 oil was struck on their land. President Rutherford B. Hayes and Dom Pedro II, emperor of Brazil, visited Foxburg in 1876.

18A. Fox Mansion (stone) was built in 1845 by Joseph M. Fox, who died before it was completed. A remarkable building, it was used by the family as a home (later as a summer home) until recent years, when it was sold to a group of investors as the nucleus of a recreational community. *Location:* Behind Allegheny Clarion Valley High School, overlooking the Allegheny River from a high hill.

18B. Memorial Church of Our Father (stone), an Episcopal church, was built by the Fox family as a memorial to Samuel M. Fox II and his son William. In 1882, before it was completed, Sarah Lindley Fox, William's sister, who had been active in its planning, also died and is buried here. *Location:* On SR 0058.

18C. American Golf Hall of Fame was established at the estate of Joseph M. Fox II, who first introduced the game of golf into America. Fox had learned it in England while

18D. Foxburg Library

traveling after graduation from college. He built a three-hole course on his estate about 1884, inviting his friends to play there. Later it was enlarged to five and in 1888 to nine holes. It is the oldest continuously operating golf course in the United States. Fox was first president of the Foxburg Golf Club, leasing the land at a nominal figure. In 1924 the club purchased the land and has enlarged it to eighteen holes. About thirty years ago it organized the Hall of Fame, with a museum that displays golf memorabilia, including some primitive clubs up to 300 years old. The club plans a new museum and golf course. *Location:* Across SR 0058 from Fox estate.

18D. Foxburg Public Library (stone), of unusual construction, is situated to the right of several other noteworthy brick buildings. *Location:* At bridge, overlooking Allegheny River.

Note: "Foxfire Studio" House, a fine brick nineteenth-century landmark, is at Railroad Street.

19. Episcopal Church (stone) was built in 1873. *Location:* SR 0338 near Foxburg (Richland Township).

20. J. Patton Lyon House is the site where Lyon Shorb & Co. operated an iron furnace from 1846 to 1871 (the company also owned Madison Furnace on Piney Creek). There are two Lyon houses here, one built in 1845–50. One served as a drilling company office. The earlier one was the first mansion in the county. *Location:* West of Sligo, on SR 0058, opposite school.

21. Clearview, Old County Home (brick buildings) has been converted to apartments. Across the road is Stoney Lonesome, a one-

room school. *Location:* Pine Township, east of Sligo.

Note: An early frame Presbyterian church is nearby at the junction of SR 2007 and SR 0068.

22. Last Seceder Church (stone and frame) was for many years the last Associate Presbyterian Church east of the Mississippi, until a recent merger with the Reformed Presbyterian (Covenanter). Once very strong in Pennsylvania, the church had been weakened when most congregations left the denomination to form unions establishing the Associate Reformed Church in 1782 and the United Presbyterian in 1858. The Rimersburg church was organized at Cherry Run in 1805 and moved to the village in 1858. The present church was built in 1912. An early cemetery is at this site. *Location:* North edge of Rimersburg, on SR 0068.

23. Flick House (stone) was built in 1844 by Charles Flick, a stonemason born in 1803 in Northampton County. Flick, who had eighteen children (eleven by his first wife, Catherine Reecer, and seven by his second wife, Mary Jane Mortimer), together with David Lawson built Franklin Furnace in 1843 on Wildcat Run, one mile southeast of Rimersburg. Charles Flick died in 1887 and is buried in Rimersburg Cemetery. His father, John Casper, and his grandfather, Gerlach Paul, were captains in the Revolutionary War. In 1895 the house was sold out of the Flick family to a series of owners, including the present residents, the Blair Walter family. *Location:* 1 mile south of Rimersburg on the east side of the Rimersburg-Lawsonham road, SR 2009.

24. Bradys Bend, a great scenic loop formed by the Allegheny River, takes its name from Capt. Sam Brady, an ardent Indian fighter who received a warrant for 502 acres in the bend in 1785 and gave it six years later to James Ross for defending him in a murder case. Although legend (perhaps growing out of this connection) says the bend was the site of a clash with Indians in June 1779, in which Brady killed a Muncy chief, wounded several other natives, and rescued two captives, better evidence would indicate that the clash occurred beside Red Bank Creek. The bend is a fine sight. *Location:* Viewed from hilltop along SR 0068 above East Brady.

25. East Brady

25A. Methodist Church (brick). This impressive Italianate structure was built in 1872 and has an addition from the 1900s. *Location:* Broad Street.

25B. Presbyterian Church (brick), another impressive church, was built in 1890–1910. *Location:* Fourth Street.

26. Lawsonham Church and School (frame), now an antique shop, was built in 1893. This was originally the Lawsonham Methodist Episcopal Church. *Location:* Lawsonham (Madison Township).

27. Corbett House was the birthplace of Dr. Hunter Corbett in 1835, a missionary to China from 1863 to 1920. The house was built in 1820. *Location:* Near Rockville, T 472 (Porter Township).

28. "Leatherwood Horse Thieves," as the Leatherwood Anti-Horse Thief Association was jestingly referred to, was a rural insurance group organized in 1868 to discourage horse theft and indemnify victims. It is known to have had at least two valid claims. For sixty years it has been a quasi-historical group meeting once every year in neighborhood churches or grange halls, and currently has more than one thousand members. A plaque about the group was set up on the grounds of the Leatherwood Presbyterian Church. *Location:* Now a mile west of the church at the corner of SR 2003 and T 472.

Note: Early Leatherwood Presbyterian and Baptist churches are at SR 2005 at Frosty Road (T 495).

29. Smithland Hotel, on the first post road in the county, was built in 1842 by George McWilliams. It served as a stage stop and halfway house in the 1840s. According to tradition, President James Buchanan stopped here in June 1843. *Location:* Smithland, south of SR 0861 past Leatherwood Presbyterian Church, near Frogtown church.

30. Baptist Church (frame), in Carpenter Gothic style, was established in 1848. The present structure, moved across the road to the present site, was originally built in 1891. *Location:* Limestone, SR 0066.

Note: Another large frame church is in disrepair nearby, concealed behind trees to the left on the descending hill leading to the above church.

31. Washington Craig House (frame). The Craig family came to Limestone in the late 1800s and here built a gristmill, sawmill, and woolen mill. *Location:* Limestone Township, SR 2016 on Piney Creek north of Frogtown.

32. St. Nicholas Church (frame) was built in 1838. *Location:* Village of Crates, SR 2016 (Limestone Township).

33. Samuel Sloan House (brick), in Federal style, was built in 1837 on Sloan Run by Samuel Sloan. Trees from this property (115 feet long) were shipped to England for the keel of a special boat that King Edward VII was building. The present owner is Leroy Kroh. *Location:* North of Brinkerton, Mahl Road, T 520 off SR 0066 (Limestone Township).

34. Clover House (stone) was built between 1818 and 1820 by Philip Clover, Jr. (1776–1840), a blacksmith. This house in the 1870s was a hideout for the notorious horse thief "Boss" Sebastian. In the 1920s it was a speakeasy. In more recent years it was purchased by H. Ray Pope, Jr. *Location:* Off SR 0066, at junction of SR 1007 and SR 1009 (Reidsburg and Strattanville Road).

35. Ion House was built in 1844. *Location:* Near Strattanville, on US 322.

36. New Bethlehem (formerly Gumtown) was incorporated in 1830.

36A. First National Bank (brick) is a fine twentieth-century building having a clock tower, cupola with bell, and weathervane. *Location:* Broad and Lafayette streets.

36B. Old Flour Mill (buff brick), now serving as a feed mill, was built in the early 1900s. Behind this structure is a small brick building which was originally the office for the mill. Henry "Gum" Nulph erected the first gristmill in the community in 1830. Fifteen years earlier he had established a sawmill there. Nulph was the son of Clarion County's first white settler, Henry Nulph, Sr., who had settled between present-day Strattansville and Clarion about 1792 but returned to Northampton County after his family was murdered by Indians. He remarried and returned in 1805, but finding his land taken, he settled near Hawthorn. *Location:* Along railroad tracks at Liberty Street.

37. Mohney House (stone) was built by Johannes (1774–1856) and Catherine Wagner Mohney in 1824 (date on west side chimney). Both are buried in Trinity Cemetery; the inscriptions on their gravestones are in German. According to tradition, Catherine, left alone one day, killed a bear that had invaded the pig pen. She tied a rope to a butcher knife and hurled it with accurate aim. *Location:* 3 miles east of New Bethlehem, on SR 0028, within 12 feet of the Pennsylvania Railroad.

Previous Sites Now Lost

Limestone Gristmill, burned
Nulph Stone House, demolished

Other Iron Furnaces
(originally thirty-one or thirty-two)

Buchanan Furnace (1844–58). Off SR 0368 east of Callensburg. About 0.1 mile north of Clarion River bridge turn left on private lane for a furlong. Furnace is on the right.

Eagle Furnace (1846–58), built by Curll, Kribbs and Co. northeast of Callensburg. About 0.7 mile north of Clarion River bridge on SR 3007 turn right (east) on T 385 for 0.3 mile. Furnace is on hill just before reaching Canoe Creek.

Lucinda Furnace (1833), bought in 1843 by James Buchanan (later president) and John Reynolds. On SR 4015 about 1.3 miles from Lucinda village, at roadside sign.

Mary Ann Furnace (1844–51). Near Shippenville, north of US 22, between SR 0066 and bridge over Paint Creek.

Pennsylvania Historical and Museum Commission Markers

Bradys Bend SR 0068, 1.3 miles east of East Brady, at lookout

Buchanan Furnace SR 0368 east of Callensburg

Clarion County Clarion, at courthouse, US 322

Foxburg Golf Course SR 0058 northeast of Foxburg

Helen Furnace SR 1005, 7 miles northeast of Clarion

Rural Electrification SR 0368, 1 mile east of Parker

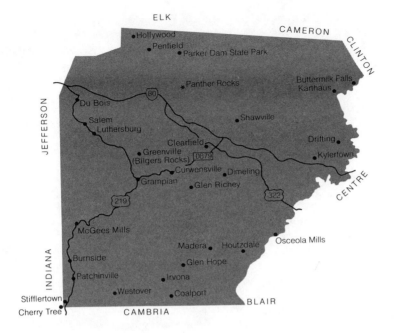

ELK

CAMERON

CLINTON

- Hollywood
- Penfield
  - Parker Dam State Park

* Panther Rocks

Buttermilk Falls
Karthaus

Du Bois

Shawville

Salem
Luthersburg

Drifting

Clearfield

Greenville
(Bilgers Rocks)

0879

Kylertown

Curwensville Dimeling

Grampian Glen Richey

CENTRE

219

322

JEFFERSON

McGees Mills

Madera Houtzdale Osceola Mills

INDIANA

Burnside

Glen Hope

Patchinville

Irvona

Stifflertown

Westover Coalport

BLAIR

Cherry Tree

CAMBRIA

Clearfield County

Capsule History

Clearfield County was named for Clearfield Creek, which in turn came from its large fields cleared of undergrowth by buffalo wallows. It was erected out of parts of Lycoming and Huntingdon counties on March 26, 1804, and was placed provisionally under the jurisdiction of Centre County. The area had been purchased from the Indians by the Penns in 1754, repurchased in 1768, and though later claimed by Connecticut was awarded to Pennsylvania in 1782. Although Clearfield elected its own commissioners from 1812, complete organization did not occur until January 29, 1822. The county occupies 1,149 square miles, the largest area in western Pennsylvania and the fourth largest in the state, with a population of 83,578.

Three main Indian trails crossed Clearfield County. The *Great Shamokin Path* traversed the county along the course of SR 0053 near Grassflat (with a short division going south of this course through that village to Kylertown), past Big Sand Spring to Clearfield, and thence by Curwensville, Chestnut Grove, Luthersburg, and Troutville. The *Goschgoschink Path* followed US 322 from Luthersburg past Salem toward Reynoldsville. The *Venango-Chinklacamoose Path* traced the Great Shamokin Path to

Luthersburg and thence the Goschgoschink Path. Marie le Roy and Barbara Leininger, two of the many captives of Indian raiders on the eastern Pennsylvania frontier during the French and Indian War, were taken through the county on these trails.

Among the earliest white visitors were Christian Frederick Post, David Zeisberger, and John Ettwein (Moravian missionaries). One of the first white settlers was Capt. Edward Ricketts, who arrived in 1783 at what is now Bigler Township. The first school and church were in a log cabin built in 1804 at the site of the present McClure cemetery, one of the oldest burial grounds in the county (on SR 0969 southwest of Curwensville).

Grampian, in Penn Township, was settled first by Quakers beginning in 1805. Dr. Samuel Coleman was one of its early settlers. In 1832 Frenchville, in Covington Township, was launched by pioneers from Normandy and Picardy in France. Luthersburg was founded in 1820 by Germans. John Curwen of Montgomery County founded Curwensville in 1812. William Irvin came to the county in 1818. Karthaus was established in 1814 on Allegheny Coal Company land and is the location of the only stone blast furnace in the county.

The early Indian village of Chinklacamoose, a name perhaps meaning "no one tarries here willingly," was selected by the French as a fort site but nothing was ever built. In 1757 the town was burned. This site later became Clearfield, the county seat, laid out in 1805 on land which had belonged to Abraham Whitmer of Lancaster. The village was part of the old township of Chinklacamoose until 1813, when it became a part of Lawrence Township. In 1840 Clearfield was incorporated as a borough.

Clearfield County's early industries were coal mining, iron manufacturing, and lumbering. At one time there were over 400 sawmills in the county. Coal, found mostly in the Moshannon area, is still plentiful, as are building stone, sand, and clay. Tanning, tile and brick manufacture, farming, and dairying are also important.

Landmarks

1. Clearfield

1A. Courthouse (brick) was built in 1860–62 at a cost of $16,500 to replace the original seat of justice erected in 1814–15. Owing to an architect's blunder, most of its high tower had to be rebuilt, and it was not finished for two years. The clock also proved defective and had to be replaced. This building, having Palladian windows, was remodeled and enlarged in 1882–84. The county jail, built in 1872, is now a health care facility. *Location:* East Market Street and North Second Street.

1B. Clearfield County Historical Museum (brick) was built in 1880 as the home of James Kerr, U.S. congressman, Clearfield coal operator, and railroad entrepreneur of the late 1890s. Kerr entertained William Jennings Bryan here in 1898. This home was later occupied by Brig. Gen. Frederick B. Kerr,

1A. Courthouse

adjutant general of Pennsylvania in the late 1930s. Now a museum, it contains over ten thousand items of historical interest, including an extensive genealogical library. Here, also, is a drift mine coal exhibit showing Clearfield's coal industry which began in 1862 with the excavation of the Moshannon vein. *Hours:* May–October: Thursday–Sunday, 1:30–4:30 P.M. Other days and winter months by appointment. *Location:* 104 East Pine Street.

Note: Artifacts from Goshen Township Indian Camp are at Shawville along the West Branch of the Susquehanna River.

1C. Raftsmen's Memorial Dam, 260 feet wide, dedicated in 1974, was named in honor of R. Dudley Tonkin (1880–1973). Born near Cherry Tree, he was a member of a famous West Branch lumbering family and a historian of the rafting and timbering era. *Location:* Lower end of Clearfield, off SR 0879.

1D. Old Clear Haven (brick), built in 1895 as the Clearfield County Home and later remodeled as a multipurpose center, is the birthplace of Zenos Leonard (March 19, 1809). This mountain man, explorer, and hunter wrote the *Narrative of the Adventures of Zenos Leonard,* published in 1839, one of the most accurate and complete accounts of explorations of the West. An original copy is said to bring $15,000. A monument was erected in Leonard's honor at this site in 1979. *Location:* Off US 322 on the outskirts of town.

1E. Clearfield Historic District consists of four blocks of Victorian houses built between the 1860s and the 1890s. They look out over the Susquehanna River. *Location:* Front Street.

2. Canoe Place, the upper limit of low-water canoe travel on the West Branch of the Susquehanna and the beginning of a portage to Kittanning, was a landmark for the Indians. By the treaty of 1768 at Fort Stanwix, N.Y., it was made the beginning of a line between the west branch and the Allegheny (at a fort at Kittanning) which marked the northern bounds for that area of land ceded to the whites for settlement. It is commonly referred to as the Purchase Line. (Land above "the purchase" was ceded at another Fort Stanwix treaty in 1784.)

This spot, where Cambria, Clearfield, and Indiana counties meet, was readily identified by an immense wild cherry tree which grew there until it was washed away in a flood in 1838. On June 16, 1893, the state appropri-

2. *Cherry Tree Monument at Canoe Place*

ated $1,500 for a monument on the site of the tree, at the mouth of Cush Cushion Creek. Erected the following year, the monument, 24.5 feet in height, bears the names of the three counties, a carving of a canoe, and a suitable inscription. It is surrounded by a small park at which the final meeting and dissolution of the Old Raftmen's Association was held in the fall of 1955. This spot should not be confused with other "canoe places" at Emporium and Port Allegany. *Location:* On US 219 near edge of village of Cherry Tree, Indiana County (Burnside Township).

3. Tonkin House (frame) was the home of Vincent Tonkin, pioneer lumberman of Cherry Tree, and his son R. Dudley Tonkin, author of *My Partner the River.* This house, built around the late 1800s, has a wrought iron fence and an 1885 log and shake playhouse. A fine large barn with louvered windows, a gazebo, and other outbuildings are also on the property. *Location:* US 219, at the Indiana County line at outskirts of Cherry Tree (Burnside Township).

4. Two-Room Schoolhouse (frame), originally one room, was expanded to two with a rear addition. This structure, painted red, has a cupola and is now used as a commercial

5. *John Patchin House*

business. *Location:* Between Patchinville and Cherry Tree (Indiana County) near Stifflertown, SR 3004 and US 219.

5. John Patchin House (frame), with five bays, was built in the 1860s by John Patchin, a lumberman and merchant and the father of eight children, who came to the area in 1836 from New York State. He died in 1863. Patchin introduced the rafting of timber on the West Branch of the Susquehanna River. This house replaced an 1847 home (also built by John Patchin) which burned down. It contains an attic room whose purpose remains a mystery; according to folklore, it concealed fugitive slaves. An early frame store, established by Patchin and later run by Aaron Patchin and his other sons, is located to the left of the house; to the left of the store is a frame sawmill used in John's lumber business. To the right of the house is a large barn. *Location:* Patchinville, US 219.

6. Horace Patchin House (brick), in Federal Italianate style, was built about 1860, possibly by William Irvin who erected a lumber mill across the road. (Irvin also built the first dam on the Susquehanna River.) In 1870 Horace Patchin (born in 1818 at Lake George, N.Y.) purchased this fourteen-room house. Horace, one of six sons of John Patchin, operated a store and a flour mill and was also one of the county's most successful lumbermen. Much of the timber was used for spars and masts for sailing ships. In 1880 this house was occupied by John Henry Patchin, a member of the General Assembly, who owned the Burnside rolling mill. The house originally had an iron fence (now brick) around it and a Victorian porch added in the late 1800s (now expanded), but no longer retains many of its early features such as the Tiffany leaded glass entranceway, carved oak stairway, and

five fireplaces. A cupola was added at a later date. Unfortunately this house, once worthy of the National Register, was gutted for no urgent reason and has had extensive additions made to it including an indoor swimming pool. For years owners such as the Frank Errigo and the Clifford Knect families cared for and appreciated this fine landmark. *Location:* Burnside, Main Street at Byers Road (US 219).

7. Camp Meeting Buildings (frame) were built near the turn of the century for a Bible conference center. Nearby (0.25 mile) on the same side of the road is an early railroad station that possibly served the southern branch of the New York Central Railroad. *Location:* 0.7 mile north of Mahaffey on US 219.

8. Thomas A. McGee House (frame) was the home of pioneer lumberman Thomas McGee. Built about 1835, it has fourteen rooms and was the first in the area to be made of planed lumber. The village had been founded about 1824 by his father James McGee, an itinerant Methodist preacher who held services mostly in schools. Shortly before beginning the house, Thomas (1813–91) built the sawmill from which the town took its name.

His wife, Isabel Holmes McGee (1816–99), had fled Ireland in the 1840s because of the potato famine. She and their daughters sometimes cooked for as many as 100 lumbermen daily in rafting time. She also ran the Chest, Pa., post office in her kitchen. The house is still in good condition and remains in the family. *Location:* McGees Mills, just off US 219.

9. McGee Mills Covered Bridge (white pine), one of the oldest of its type with Burr arch construction, was built in 1873 by Thomas A. McGee for $175. (The Burr arch truss was named for Theodore Burr, one of America's most outstanding early bridge builders.) Unchanged, this bridge (about 105 feet long), still crosses the West Branch of the Susquehanna and is used by hundreds of autos a day. It is probably the most photographed span in the state. *Location:* Southwest of McGees Mills, off US 219 and SR 0036.

10. Dr. Samuel Coleman Marker is at the gravesite of Grampian's first physician. He migrated here with a slave in 1809 and died in 1819. *Location:* Grampian, in a field north of the borough on private property, US 219 (Penn Township).

Note: Grampian's first Quaker meetinghouse (log) was built in 1811 at Friends'

Cemetery on Lumber City Road. The present building was erected in 1901. The Quaker settlement is in Penn Township and Grampian, US 219 and SR 0729.

11. Old Iron Truss Bridge, now a highway bridge, was formerly used by the Curry Run Railroad to haul logs to the Hall and Weiss Sawmill. *Location:* Curry Run, US 219 (Greenwood Township).

12. Bilgers Rocks is a natural formation of large sandstone boulders, many thirty feet thick, forming fissured walls thirty to forty feet high. Crevices lead to a 200-foot corridor where black birch trees have taken root in the rocks. Here can be seen a 500-ton boulder balanced upon a smaller rock. This formation, called "rock city" by geologists, is the result of the displacement of large blocks of rock from the parent ledge. The name is from an early landowner, not to be confused with Bigler. *Location:* 0.8 mile from Greenville, on unmarked road 0.5 mile east of SR 4005, near Bloom-Pike Township line.

13. Merchants Hotel (frame), now the Golden Yoke Restaurant, was built by William Moore in 1853. He was succeeded in its operation by Wallace and Shaw (a partnership), David Johnston, James Ziegler, and H. Wittenmyer. Greatly enlarged from time to time, it came under the management of Daniel Goodlander, who operated it as a "temperance house," although its trade was largely made up of lumbermen. In 1920 it was divided into apartments. In 1940 it became, and still is, a restaurant. *Location:* Luthersburg, Main and Olive streets.

Note: The famed Big Spring, at the western edge of the village, where Indians met for conference, has been covered and piped into a cistern, with no trace now visible.

At the junction of US 322 and SR 0410 in Luthersburg is a DAR monument in commemoration of the Susquehanna-Waterford Turnpike (1821–24) and the Snowshoe and Parkerville Turnpike (bas relief stagecoach in front of old Eagle Tavern pictured on memorial).

14. Old Brady Township School (brick), a one-room building, was one of the first built in Brady Township, perhaps as early as 1840. It was used until about fifteen years ago and is now a voting place. *Location:* Salem, on US 219.

15. John Du Bois Monument "Hope" marks the brick crypt of the founder of the city that

14. Old Brady Township School

bears his name. Du Bois (1809–86) was a multimillionaire lumberman who moved his business from DuBoistown, near Williamsport, to Clearfield County in 1871–76. In Du Bois a billion board feet of lumber were recorded before the operations were moved to Hicks Run in 1904. *Location:* Du Bois, at the top of a hill overlooking the Du Bois campus of the Pennsylvania State University and the site of Du Bois mansion; path leads up to site.

16. Henry Shaffer House was built on the farm of Henry Shaffer between 1870 and 1873. It is now the oldest building in the community. *Location:* Du Bois, corner of East Long Avenue and Stockdale Street.

17. Sabula Dam, a splash dam originally built with rock debris from the nearby 1873 railroad tunnel, was the largest of thirty used to float logs to the mills of John Du Bois. *Location:* 4.5 miles east of Du Bois (Sandy Township).

18. Lumber Ghost Town is the remains of two sawmills built on divided timberland in 1873–74 by men whose surnames were Craig and Blanchard. The stone foundations of Craig's sawmill can still be seen. Blanchard's, on the east side of Baker Run (South Branch), is gone, but the site is recognizable. Blanchard also had a logging railroad that ran eastward to the head of the valley. In later years the Wise Brothers from Bangor operated the sawmill and built another railroad into the Anderson Creek Valley. *Location:* 2 miles west of Penfield on an unpaved road, SR 0255 (Huston Township).

19. Tyler Hotel (red brick), sportsmen's, lumbermen's, and later miners' hotel, has been operated by three generations of the Tyler family. Gen. Ulysses S. Grant, who came to the area soon after being elected president in 1868, is reputed to have stayed here. *Location:* North edge of Hollywood, on SR 0255 near Elk County line.

Note: Nearby is the birthplace of Philip P. Bliss, noted hymn writer, who worked as a lumberman during his youth. Nothing of the building remains.

20. Parker Dam State Park. Tourist attractions at this fifty-year-old park include an extensive museum of memorabilia of the 1930s Civilian Conservation Corps (CCC) which operated camps here and at four other sites in Clearfield County. There is also an authentic reproduction of a log slide used by early lumbermen to transport logs to the nearest dam or waterway and a walk-through educational display on early lumbering, wildlife, etc. Park provides swimming, camping, hiking, fishing, and ice skating and skiing in winter. *Location:* SR 0153, north of Clearfield (Huston Township).

21. Panther Rocks. This natural landmark, over 300 million years old, is situated between S. B. Elliott Park and Parker Dam State Park. *Location:* Pine Township, State Game Lands, on McGeorge Road off SR 0153.

22. Curwensville is the site of many fine Victorian mansions from the lumber baron days. An outstanding cut-stone house sits on a knoll within the town limits. An early cemetery is believed to contain Indian graves. Also, there is a replica of Anderson Creek covered bridge in this area. *Location:* Curwensville, southwest of Clearfield, SR 0453 and SR 0969.

23. McClure Cemetery is the site of the county's first school (log), built in 1803–04, and its first Presbyterian meeting house (log), built in 1809 on land owned by Thomas McClure. Robert Cresswell was the first burial in the graveyard. *Location:* SR 0969, 2 miles southwest of Curwensville (Pike Township).

24. Turnpike Milestone (original) marks the road built in 1822 between Philadelphia and Erie. The old Erie Turnpike passed through Clearfield County from Blue Ball (West Decatur) to Jefferson County. *Location:* Near Clearfield Creek, SR 2024 at Dimeling, southwest of Clearfield.

25. Mitchell House (cut stone) was the home of John Mitchell, a prominent lumberman; a signature stone over the door reads, "J. M. 1840." A monument across the road marks the site of the first post office in the area, kept in 1815 by Alexander Read. *Location:* On Glen Richey Road, 1.6 miles north of SR 2024.

26. Read House (sun-baked brick), believed to have been the first brick residence in Clearfield County, was built by Thomas Read, son of Alexander (see *Mitchell House*). A signature stone in the gable reads, "T. R. 1833." Nearby is Read's barn, the first frame barn built in the county; it was constructed by George Leech, who probably also did the carpentry on the house. *Location:* On SR 2024, about 0.3 mile from Glen Richey Road.

Note: At this corner may be seen one of the old Erie Turnpike milestones.

27. St. Mary's Church and Cemetery. The church was built in 1873. *Location:* Covington Township, SR 0879.

28. Ames Airfield, consisting of forty acres, was built in 1924 as an emergency landing field by the Air Mail service. Taken over by Centre Airways in 1929, it was named for an air-mail pilot who was killed near Bellefonte. All United Airline planes were once required to land for passengers at this field, where a weather station was maintained. *Location:* Morris Township, I-80, Kylertown Exit, visible from highway.

29. Karthaus Furnace was erected in 1817 by Peter A. Karthaus, who was an associate of Dr. Frederick W. Geisenhainer and J. F. W. Schnars in the Allegheny Coal Company. Ore was brought four miles up the river from Buttermilk Falls; and about two hundred tons of pig iron a year were smelted from 1817 to 1822 and again from 1837 to 1839, when the business was closed because of transportation difficulties. The stack has partly fallen. This is the county's only stone blast furnace. *Location:* Karthaus, mouth of Mosquito Creek (Little Moshannon). Visible from SR 0879.

30. Old Raft Landing owned by Cataract Coal Company is at Buttermilk Falls, the terminus of dangerous rafting through the mountains from Clearfield. Here, at the lowest elevation in the county (1,006 feet), extra oarsmen were discharged and sent back on foot. *Location:* Buttermilk Falls.

31. St. Severin's Log Church was built in 1851 by Benedictine monks from St. Vincent

31. *St. Severin's Log Church*

32A. *Osceola Kilns*

Archabbey (q.v., Westmoreland County) and was used until 1891. Formerly in poor condition, it was restored in 1967. Its name came from Severin Nebel, an Alsatian immigrant who gave land for the church and cemetery. *Location:* Drifting, just off SR 0053.

32. Osceola Mills

32A. Osceola Kilns (buff brick) contains now abandoned kilns of Laclede Co. for the manufacture of bricks. This company went out of business in January 1976. *Location:* SR 0053 near mouth of Clearfield Creek.

32B. Hopfer House (brick) was built before 1879 by Samuel Hopfer. This Italianate house with eyebrow windows is believed (by the owner) to be the oldest building in the community. *Location:* 306 Coal Street.

32C. American Legion, built in 1876, is one of two oldest buildings in town. *Location:* Right of post office on Lingle Street.

33. Hotel St. Cloud (frame), with eight bays, was built in 1875 as a lumbermen's inn. *Location:* Houtzdale, Hannah and Good streets.

34. St. Mary's Orthodox Church (stone) was built in 1909 and features an onion tower. *Location:* Madera, Main Street off SR 0053.
Note: Capt. Edward Ricketts, a Revolutionary War veteran, and his sons settled in 1783 at the "oxbow" of Clearfield Creek (1 mile east of Glen Hope and 2 miles west of Madera).

35. Glen Hope Hotel (brick) is a commodious three-story structure built in the late 1800s. It retains its original facade and belvedere. *Location:* Glen Hope, SR 0053 and SR 0729.

Note: Nearby, Coalport was established around the 1870s home of coal operator James Haines who laid out the town. Within the same area is the town of Irvona, named for its founder Col. E. A. Irvin, which was the location of one of the largest tanneries in Pennsylvania. Both towns are on SR 0053.

36. Samuel Hegarty House (frame) was built in 1872 on a 358-acre estate. This Second Empire mansion, with a mansard roof and bracketed eaves, also has an impressive tower topped with wrought iron, eyebrow windows, and decorative millwork. Included on the property are associated buildings including a cantilevered barn with decorated eaves. Nearby is an early cemetery, the site of an 1832 Presbyterian church. Hegarty was a coal mine operator and president of a Coalport bank. *Location:* Hegarty's Crossroads, near Glen Hope, SR 0729 and SR 2002 (Beccaria Township).

37. American Tannery Inc. (brick buildings) was built in the late 1800s by William Mosser who also established a deer park on the property. The Mosser tannery was later owned by the Armour leather company before it became the American Tannery. This company was in business until recent years. *Location:* Westover, SR 0036 along Chest Run.

38. Westover Borough Building (frame) is a small one-room structure, the oldest in town. It was erected in the late 1880s and continues to serve the community as its borough building. The town once had a dam, sawmill, and creamery. *Location:* Westover, McEwen Street, at SR 0036 (Chest Township).

39. Westover Bridge (concrete) is a curved structure with decorative concrete end rails built in 1917 over Chest Creek. The contractors for this arched bridge were Whittaker & Diehl of Harrisburg. *Location:* Westover, SR 0036.

Previous Sites Now Lost

Du Bois Mansion, demolished
Ring Rock Hotel, burned down
Robison Tavern, burned down
William Bigler House, demolished

Pennsylvania Historical and Museum Commission Markers

"Canoe Place" US 219, 0.5 mile north of Stifflertown

Chinklacamoose Clearfield, old US 322, east and south

Clearfield County Clearfield, East Pine and Front streets, in front of Clearfield County Historical Museum

George Rosenkrans Penfield, SR 0025 (band and hymn music composer)

Karthaus Furnace Karthaus, SR 0879

Old State Road (Milesburg to Waterford) US 322, 6 miles northwest of Luthersburg

Philip P. Bliss SR 0255, 2.2 miles northeast of Penfield (song writer, 1838–76)

The Big Spring SR 0410, 0.5 mile southwest of Luthersburg (Indians camped here, as did Maj. McClelland's troops during War of 1812)

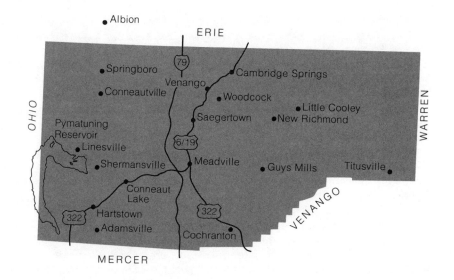

Crawford County

Capsule History

Crawford County was named for Col. William Crawford, friend and business agent of George Washington, who served in the French and Indian War, commanded an expedition into Ohio in 1782, and was burned at the stake in western Ohio by Indians. Originally the area was set aside as donation lands to be given or sold cheaply to Revolutionary War soldiers for their service (see Capsule History, Butler County). The county was erected out of Allegheny County March 12, 1800. It has 1,011 square miles with a population of 88,869.

The Holland and North American Land Companies and the Pennsylvania Population Company bought large tracts within the county. Harm Jan Huidekoper was a representative of the Holland Land Company, formed in 1789. He and his sons bought out the West Allegheny interests of the firm in 1836. Their home, built on Water Street in Meadville, was called Pomona Hall. On the same property was located the company office. The Huidekopers also owned a gristmill and sawmills in Fredericksburg. The county's first settlers in 1787–88 were John, Joseph, Darius, and David Mead, Thomas Martin, John Watson, James F. Randolph, Thomas Grant, Cornelius Van Horn, and Christopher Snyder.

The Delaware Indian town of Custaloga was on the west side of French Creek about four miles south of Meadville. Cussewago was a Six Nations town on the site of Meadville.

Meadville, the largest city and county seat, grew out of Mead's Settlement, started by David Mead in 1788 and laid out in 1793 (see *Mead House*). Mead himself had tried to name the town Lewisburgh and had in fact advertised lots for sale at "Lewisburgh" in the Pittsburgh paper. The plan for the town as it exists today was drawn by Roger Alden, first Holland Land Company agent, and Dr. Thomas Kennedy in 1795 when they bought out a large piece of Mead's holdings.

The *Venango Path* was Crawford County's most important Indian trail, entering near Carlton and running through Cochranton and up French Creek to Meadville. Then it divided, one course passing through Saegertown, crossing French Creek, and running through (present) Venango near Cambridge Springs and toward Indian Head; the other branch followed much the same route as SR 0086. On George Washington's trip to Fort LeBoeuf in 1753, he followed the Venango Path in this county almost to Cambridge Springs, but was forced by high water to detour to the Cussewago Path crossing of Muddy Creek near Little Cooley. He then followed a ridge north, near Ferris Corners, and rejoined the Venango Path near Mill village. The *Cussewago Path,* from Ohio to Warren, entered the county at Penn Line, running through or near Sandusky, Harmonsburg, and Cussewago (Meadville) and on through Blooming Valley, New Richmond, Little Cooley, and Spartansburg, toward West Spring Creek. The *Conneaut Path* ran north from Harmonsburg east of Conneaut Creek past Conneautville toward Albion.

The county's first highway was the old French military road from Fort LeBoeuf (Waterford) to Fort Machault (Franklin); and in 1809 the Waterford to Susquehanna Turnpike was completed.

In 1796 Titusville, the county's second city, was settled by Jonathan Titus, a surveyor for the Holland Land Company, who wished to call the town Edinburgh. Edwin L. Drake drilled the first oil well near there in 1859 (see *Drake Well,* Venango County), making it a boom town with the title "queen city of the oil region." Here along Oil Creek, Indians skimmed the surface oil off the water for domestic uses, and white settlers bottled it and called it Seneca Oil, for medicinal purposes. And this is where the first United States Oil Exchange was organized in 1871 and incorporated in 1880. The "Roberts torpedo," first successful device for increasing the flow of oil by setting off an explosion tamped by water in a well, was pioneered in Titusville.

About 1825 Linesville was laid out as a Quaker community by Amos Line, one-time miller, postmaster, and surveyor of the Pennsylvania Population Company in 1800.

Spartansburg is an early mill town, picturesque with its old order Amish community.

Numerous Greek Revival houses in the county suggest New England influence and migration.

Pioneer industries in the county were lumbering and agriculture. Today the most important products, in order of production value, are metals, food, and chemicals, and their allied goods. Meadville was once the world's largest producer of hookless slide fasteners, the invention of the talon (more popularly called Zipper—a trade name) having been backed by Col. Lewis Walker in 1893. He moved the talon factory from Hoboken, N.J., to Meadville in 1913. Other important industries include dairying; the manufacture of lubricants, tools, and machinery; and agriculture, with one of the largest county fairs in Pennsylvania held annually in Meadville. Among notable writers who have lived in the county are Ida M. Tarbell, Maxwell Anderson, and Wythe

Williams. Among the distinguished persons who attended Allegheny College over the years were President William McKinley, Ida Tarbell, Paul Siple (Antarctic explorer), and Pennsylvania Governor Ray Shaffer.

Landmarks

1. Meadville, originally called Cussewago or Meads Mills, is the national center of the tool and machining industries. The town was laid out by David Mead in 1793; it became a borough in 1823 and a city in 1866.

1A. Courthouse (red pressed brick, stone trim) was preceded by two earlier ones. The first was built of logs in 1804. A new one, of brick, was constructed in 1825. The present Renaissance-style courthouse was begun in 1867 and finished in October 1869. Complete with a dome, four clocks, marble floors, and an iron fence, it cost $249,000. A statue of Justice bearing scales was also erected, but the scales blew off during a storm in 1938. The fence and statue were later removed. The building was remodeled about 1950. *Location:* Public Square.

1B. Baldwin-Reynolds House (brick) was built by Henry Baldwin in 1841–43, based on a sketch of his son's mansion in Tennessee. Coming to Meadville from New England in 1800, Baldwin assisted in the organization of the first county seat, was the county's first district attorney, served in the U.S. Congress (1816–28), and was appointed a justice of the Supreme Court by President Andrew Jackson (1830–44). In addition, Baldwin was "the father of the American system of high protective tariff."

In 1847 William Reynolds, a nephew of Baldwin's wife, bought the property. The interior of the home includes black walnut woodwork, silver hinges and doorknobs, its own water system, a solarium, and twenty-five rooms on four floors. The Crawford County Historical Society purchased the property in 1963 from the estate of Katherine Shryock Reynolds and maintains the house as a museum. In 1976 a one-story rural physician's office (frame) was moved to the museum grounds from Little's Corners, a rural crossroads ten miles north of Meadville. Dr. J. Russell Mosier practiced in this office until his death in 1938. A museum in itself, this structure includes a waiting room, pharmacy, and office-examining room and memorabilia such

1B. Baldwin-Reynolds House

as a ledger indicating the price of an office call—fifty cents. Other additions include an ice house and a carriage house. *Hours:* Spring, summer, and fall: Wednesday, Saturday, and Sunday, afternoons. Also by appointment. *Admission charge.* School groups free. *Location:* 639 Terrace Street.

1C. Mead House (frame) was built in 1797 by David Mead, a one-time tavernkeeper at Sunbury. An ensign in the Revolutionary War, he later served as a major general in the War of 1812 and was an associate judge at the time of his death. Mead first acquired land on the west side of French Creek near the mouth of the Cussewago in 1788. Shortly after this he moved to Meadville on the east side and built a sawmill in 1789–90. He erected a blockhouse in 1791 overlooking French Creek. The second blockhouse served as a school between 1798 and 1800. A replica of Mead's cabin was scheduled for erection near the Mead Avenue bridge in 1988 for the bicentennial of the settling of Crawford County. Mead commenced to lay out the town and sell lots in 1793, calling the new town Lewisburgh. About 1805 its name was changed to Meadville.

Mead donated the land for the state arsenal, built in 1816–17 on the northeast corner of Main and Randolph streets (present school site). His house, a large, two-and-a-half-story building, now a private residence and apartments, has undergone many alterations, with little of the original structure remaining. The

1H. Market House

first blockhouse was part of the stockade around his original cabin on the bluff overlooking French Creek. The second one, used as a school, was at the corner of Steers and Water streets. *Location:* 263 Randolph Street.

1D. George Washington Bicentennial Oak was planted March 15, 1932, by the Women's Club of Meadville near a spot where Washington stopped on his trip to Fort LeBoeuf in 1753 (see *Washington Sentinel Tree,* Erie County). It is marked by a plaque. *Location:* 22 feet north of tablet at Mead house.

1E. Allegheny College, the oldest college in continuous existence under the same name west of the Alleghenies, was named for the Allegheny River basin where it is located. Founded by Timothy Alden in 1815, the college was granted a charter March 24, 1817. It was closed between the years 1831 and 1833 and reopened under sponsorship of the Methodist Episcopal church.

Ruter Hall was named for Martin Ruter, a missionary and educator. Bentley Hall (brick), one of the earlier buildings of the school, was begun in 1820 and completed in 1835. It was named in honor of William Bentley, pastor of East Church in Salem, Mass., who bequeathed his library to Allegheny College before his death in 1819. The building, designed by Timothy Alden (first president of the college), is a combination of New England and Greek Revival architecture. *Location:* Cam-

pus entrance is off SR 0086 (North Main Street).

1F. Meadville Theological Seminary was founded in 1844 by the Unitarian and Disciples of Christ churches as a nonsectarian school. It began its work in October of that year in Divinity Hall, a rebuilt Cumberland Presbyterian church on Center Street. Later the Disciples church withdrew. Dr. Rufus P. Stebbins became its first president in 1844. For most of its eighty-two years in Meadville, it averaged from twenty-five to forty students, including those of Jewish, Hindu, Buddhist, and other non-Christian religions. The second Divinity Hall was built on Chestnut Street in 1856, and Hunnewell Hall nearby in 1903. The school moved to Chicago in 1926. *Locations:* First Divinity House is gone; the second is now a rehabilitation center. Hunnewell Hall (now housing a redevelopment authority), is on Chestnut Street near Arch Street in upper Talon plant.

1G. Huidekoper Land Company Office (brick) is now the Christian Science building. In 1836 H. J. Huidekoper purchased the Holland Land Company where he had been working since 1805. *Location:* Chestnut and East streets, northeast corner.

1H. Market House (brick), oldest in continuous use in Pennsylvania, was built prior to 1880. This open-air market also houses the

Meadville Council on the Arts. It is a fine example of the early markets (few preserved) and a cultural hub of the community. *Hours:* Tuesday, Thursday, Friday, Saturday, 7 A.M.– 3:30 P.M. *Location:* 910 Market Street.

1I. First Baptist Church (frame), now used as the African Methodist Episcopal Church, was built in 1833, two years after fourteen original members met at the site to be baptized in a mill pond. This congregation, in 1861, erected a brick church on Center Street, later used by the IOOF (Independent Order of Odd Fellows, one of the largest benevolent fraternal orders in the United States, founded in America in 1819 in Baltimore, Maryland) and eventually razed. (For the present church see *Baptist Church*.) *Location:* Arch and Liberty streets.

1J. Baptist Church (brown stone) was built in 1905 as a new church whose congregation moved from Liberty and Arch streets to this site. In its bell tower is an original Paul Revere bell. *Location:* Diamond Park and Chestnut Street.

1K. Presbyterian Church (brick) is the oldest church in the community. Originally it was organized as a meeting house for all congregations. It was rebuilt after a fire. *Location:* Behind the courthouse on Public Square.

1L. Unitarian Church (brick), also called Independent Congregational, was begun in 1835 and dedicated the following year. Modeled after a Philadelphia Unitarian church (that was later destroyed by fire), this Greek Revival building was designed by Gen. George W. Cullum, architect of Fort Sumter, and built by Edwin Derby for $35,000. A chandelier of whale-oil lamps originally hung inside. In 1973 Carl Heeshen added the various world religious symbols on the facade. *Location:* Corner of Main and Chestnut streets.

1M. Christ Church (stone), built in 1884, houses the second oldest congregation in Meadville. It was organized in January 1825 by Rev. John Henry Hopkins of Pittsburgh, who later became a bishop. Its first rector was Charles Smith. *Location:* Public Square.

1N. United Methodist Church (stone), generally referred to as "the stone church," was built in 1868. After being gutted by fire on March 11, 1927, this massive building was restored, with its interior more in keeping with the Gothic exterior, and rededicated April 29, 1928. *Location:* Public Square.

1O. Atlantic & Great Western Railway Shops (brick) were built around 1862, an early constituent of the Erie Railroad. The shops are still in use by the Erie-Lackawanna as a testing lab. In the same vicinity is the Erie freight station. Buchanan Junction's railroad building, listed on the Historic American Engineers Record, can be seen from US 322 south of Meadville (Clark Road and South Main Street). *Location:* On a dirt road off Mead Avenue, cross all tracks from center of Meadville (Park Avenue and Chestnut Street), go west on Chestnut 3 blocks, then left 1 block to Mead Avenue.

1P. Double-Intersection Whipple Truss Bridge, listed on the Historic American Engineers Record, was built in 1871 over French Creek. *Location:* On Mead Avenue, 4 blocks west of Atlantic & Great Western Railway Shops.

1Q. Greendale Cemetery, incorporated in 1852, is noteworthy for its architecture, lay out, and array of rhododendrons. There are over three hundred cemeteries in the county. *Location:* Northeastern Meadville, head of Randolph Street.

2. Saegertown (Woodcock Township) was known as Aldens Mills before 1800. Daniel Saeger migrated here in the eighteenth century with other German settlers.

2A. Patrick McGill House (log), the oldest in the county, was erected about 1805 by the area's first settler who had arrived ten years earlier. It is the oldest house in the county. *Location:* 649 Main Street.

2B. Daniel Saeger House (gold frame) is of Greek Revival style, with white pillars and a fanlight. A remarkably well-preserved structure, built by the man who laid out Saegertown in 1824, it is one of the first houses in the village. In 1829 he erected a general store in the town. *Location:* 373 Main Street.

3. Venango Borough, along French Creek, retains a number of early tourist cabins, a type of building fast disappearing from the American scene.

3A. Venango Valley Inn (brick), with five bays, is reminiscent of the fine early landmarks of this area. It now is part of a golf course. *Location:* SR 0019.

4A. The Inn at Cambridge Springs

3B. Venango Railroad Station (brick) was later adapted as a Veteran of Foreign Wars post. *Location:* SR 0019 and SR 1002.

3C. Methodist Church (frame) is a picturesque Carpenter Gothic building worth preserving. *Location:* SR 0019.

4. Cambridge Springs (until 1877, Cambridgeboro) became widely known in the 1890s when the mineral spa craze swept the country. Dozens of hotels, boardinghouses, and sanatoriums sprang up around the mineral rich springs of this area. A beautiful octagonal building which formerly housed a magnesia spring is still in place nearby.

4A. The Inn at Cambridge Springs, formerly the Riverside Hotel (frame), originally 34 by 100 feet, is an enormous building erected in 1885–86 by Gray's Mineral Fountain Company. Dr. John H. Gray, a local oil prospector had in 1860 accidentally discovered a mineral spring while walking along French Creek. In later years he found other such "fountains" and the area became known as Fountain Valley. Here he erected a springhouse (1884) and began selling mineral water. (The springhouse, which was rebuilt after a 1941 fire, was approached by a long boardwalk in later years—the concrete supports can still be seen.) In 1895 a retired bridge builder, William Baird, purchased the hotel from Rider & Company and also acquired the Gray Mineral

Springs Company. In addition, he operated a bottling plant and a therapy department until 1946. The inn, in recent years bought by the Halliday family, is being renovated, with plans for the restoration of the mineral springs. *Location:* Overlooking French Creek, off SR 0019, north edge of Cambridge Springs.

4B. Alliance College, founded in 1912 by the Polish National Alliance to provide low-cost education for youths of Polish extraction, was the only one of its kind. It closed in 1988. *Location:* SR 1006.

5. Millers Station Octagonal Barn (frame). *Location:* Millers Station, just east of Cambridge Springs, north of SR 1016.

6. Woodcock, originally Rockville, was incorporated as a borough in 1844.

6A. Woodcock Methodist Church (brick) was organized in 1810 by Rev. Joshua Monroe. The building, the church's third, dates from 1839. *Location:* Woodcock.

6B. McPheeter House (brick) was built in the 1830s. *Location:* SR 0086, north of Gravel Run Road.

6C. Gravel Run Presbyterian Church (organized 1809, built 1854) and Woodcock Academy Building, together with other fine buildings of early architectural interest are in

5. Millers Station Octagonal Barn

6C. Woodcock Academy Building

the same part of town. *Location:* SR 0086, just north of Gravel Run Road.

7. Titusville, birthplace of the oil industry in 1859. Many mansions from the oil baron days are still preserved here. One area has been designated a historic district. Walking tours are available.

7A. Edwin L. Drake Monument, erected by Henry H. Rogers of the Standard Oil Company, marks the burial site of the pioneer in the petroleum industry. The famous sculptor Charles H. Neihaus created the bronze figure, called *The Driller,* which was exhibited by the National Sculpture Society in New York before its erection in 1902. The cut-stone monument has two Ionic columns around the statue. On each side is a curved high-backed bench. Drake's body, brought here from Bethlehem, Pa., in 1902, lies with that of his wife in a vault in front of the monument. *Location:* Near entrance of Woodlawn Cemetery.

7B. Oil Creek & Titusville Railroad runs through the oil-boom country of the 1860s. Trains leave from Perry Street Station, Drake Well Park, and Rynd Farm. *Hours:* Weekends and holidays. *Location:* Oil Creek State Park.

7C. Ida Tarbell Home (frame) was once the residence of Ida Minerva Tarbell (1857–1944), eminent American journalist and one of the most powerful women of her time in America. Born in Erie County, she graduated from Titusville High School and from Allegheny College in 1880. She was associate editor of the *Chautauquan* in Meadville from 1883 to

1891. Her books include noteworthy biographies of Abraham Lincoln and Napoleon, and the *History of the Standard Oil Company,* an expose that led the Supreme Court to break up that monopoly. In her time people called Tarbell a "muckraker"—today she would be called an investigative reporter. *Location:* 324 East Main Street.

7D. Mather Home (frame) belonged to John A. Mather (1829–1915), a native of England who devoted his life to photographing the oil industry from 1860 on. Most of his surviving work is in the Drake Well Museum (q.v., Venango County). *Location:* 407 East Main Street.

7E. McKinney Hall (brick) was built in the 1860s by D. H. Cady, a refiner. It was later owned by John D. Archbold of the Standard Oil Company in the 1870s and subsequently by Col. John J. Carter. This Victorian home was remodeled in 1929 as a French chateau by L. C. McKinney, who was in the oil business. The stables were converted into a laboratory. The house is now a classroom. *Location:* On University of Pittsburgh branch campus.

7F. Titusville City Hall, in Greek Revival architecture, was originally constructed as a private residence in 1865. It later became the Bush Hotel and then the city hall, which it has been for the last hundred years. *Location:* 107 North Franklin Street.

8. Drake Store and Residence (frame), now in poor condition, is an early nineteenth-

9. John Brown's Tannery

century structure first designed as a store and residence. It was later lengthened to serve as a hotel and dance hall. *Location:* Little Cooley.

9. John Brown's Tannery was built in 1825–27 by the famous abolitionist of Osawatomie and Harpers Ferry, and operated by him until 1835. The stone foundation ruins, on a half-acre site, are in the John Brown Memorial Park, enclosed within an ornamental stone wall. Brown's homestead (frame) is located opposite the tannery. The John Brown's Association offers guides to interpret this site. The tannery was a stop on the underground railway during the Civil War. *Location:* New Richmond, on SR 1033 just off SR 0077 (Richmond Township).

Note: Nearby sites include the Erie National Wildlife Refuge, home for thousands of shorebirds, waterfowl, and songbirds; and Townville, where John Brown's son Owen hid following his escape from Harpers Ferry.

10. Stone Schoolhouse, dating from about 1835, is believed to be the oldest public schoolhouse in Crawford County. It was later used by Dr. W. J. Burgwin to house machinery that provided the village with its first electric power about the time of World War I. *Location:* Guys Mills.

11. Octagonal Barn (frame) displays a type of construction popular in some areas around 1840. *Location:* On SR 0027, 0.5 mile west of Venango County line, east of Guys Mills.

12. Atlantic & Great Western Railroad Station (frame, board and batten), built in 1862,

has been moved to this location and restored. *Location:* Cochranton, fairgrounds, corner of Walnut and River streets.

13. Conneaut Lake, founded as Evansburg, changed its name as the area developed as a summer tourist destination for the Bessemer and Lake Erie Railroad. It still has the turn-of-the-century Exposition Park founded in the 1890s by Frank Mantor to be a new Chautauqua on the largest natural lake in Pennsylvania (929 acres). A country store and Indian museum have been landmarks here for years. *Location:* Junction of US 322 and US 6.

14. Erie Extension Canal, part of the Beaver and Lake Erie Canal system connecting the Ohio River and Lake Erie, ran through the western part of Crawford County and was in operation from 1842 to 1871. The feeder canal began at the dam built by Dr. Daniel Bemus at Bemustown north of Meadville on French creek, continued south to Shaw's Landing, crossed French Creek on an aqueduct and continued to Conneaut Lake which was dammed to contain the water, raising it an additional twelve feet, then continued west to supply the Beaver and Lake Erie main canal with sufficient water to lift it over the Summit divide between the Lake Erie basin and the Ohio River basin. The necessary water came from French Creek through the Conneaut Reservoir. Evidences of the feeder may still be seen. *Locations of feeder:* About 5.5 miles west of village of Conneaut Lake, between US 6 and SR 0285. (Can be seen from Towpath Road which connects with US 19 at the northern edge of Conneaut Marsh.)

15. Conneautville Camp (Old Fairgrounds, owned by the Peniel Holiness Association) traces its origins to the National Camp Meeting for the Promotion of Holiness, formed in 1867 at Philadelphia and Vineland, N.J., with Rev. John Inskip as the first president. First and second tent camps were held in Greenville in 1896–97, then the camp moved to Springboro the following year. In 1900 a permanent campground was acquired at Conneautville, the old fairgrounds. Here the Crawford County Agricultural Association buildings became the tabernacle (originally Floral Hall); the dining hall and kitchen (cattle display building); the women's dormitory (Agricultural Hall); a cottage for evangelists (the judges' stand); a prayer room, called the "Power House" (a barn), etc., all interesting adaptive usages. Here at the turn of the century revivalists came by horse and buggy to camp and sang revival songs, many from the song book *The Cleansing Fountain* by Rev. J. R. Burchfield. *Location:* Conneautville, about 2 miles from Springboro.

16. Pymatuning Reservoir, the largest man-made lake in Pennsylvania and one of its most visited areas, was formed in 1932 when the state dammed Pymatuning Swamp, a pre-glacial lake, forming a body of water fifteen miles long, with a seventy-mile shoreline, and regulating the flow of the Shenango and Beaver rivers. Pymatuning State Park, surrounding it, has a total of 17,000 acres. Three pairs of bald eagles nest here and can be seen from the Waterfowl Museum. The fourth of the state's four pairs nests at nearby Conneaut Marsh. The University of Pittsburgh's field biology laboratory is located here. The lake is a major resting point on the Atlantic flyway and hosts hundreds of thousands of birds each fall. *Location:* Accessible from SR 0006, SR 3018, SR 3011, SR 3010, SR 0285, and other roads.

17. Waterfowl Museum and Fish Hatchery, maintained by the Pennsylvania Game Commission, are on the northeast end of Pymatuning Lake, which is part of the wild waterfowl sanctuary. The state fish hatchery is the largest inland fish hatchery in the world. At the dam spillway ducks literally walk on the backs of the carp when bread is thrown into the water. *Museum hours:* July–September: Daily, 10 A.M.–7 P.M. May, June, October, and November: Daily, 10 A.M.–5 P.M. Closed December–April. *Locations:* Museum, Linesville. Hatchery, sanctuary area at lake.

18. Shadeland was the Powell Brothers Stock Farm, famous for breeding horses and cattle, including the Hambletonian Roadster—a fast, aristocratic carriage horse—and for improving the strains of the Clydesdale and French Percheron. Queen Victoria is reputed to have purchased a pair of their horses. They also raised a fine strain of Holstein cows, one of which produced 103 pounds of milk in a day.

In 1816 Watkin Powell settled here on a 1,500-acre tract, and his grandsons James, William, and Watkin Powell made this stud farm a success. In a nearby field are several boulders marking the graves of their horses. The sixteen barns have been razed, and the main house became the St. Sava Home for elderly Serbian men, under the direction of St. Sava's Serbian Orthodox Church in McKeesport (q. v., Allegheny County). Now privately owned. *Location:* Springboro, 8 miles south of Albion, on SR 0018.

18. Shadeland

19. Adamsville Associate Reformed Church (white frame) has unusual peaked, Carpenter Gothic entry and windows and an open belfry. It was built in 1851 and became United Presbyterian in the union at Pittsburgh in 1858. *Location:* Adamsville.

Previous Sites Now Lost

Crawford County Pioneer Village, demolished
First Divinity Hall (Meadville Theological Seminary), demolished
White House, demolished

Pennsylvania Historical and Museum Commission Markers

Allegheny College Meadville, US 6 and US 19 (Park and Baldwin streets)
Baldwin-Reynolds House Meadville, US 6 and US 19 (Baldwin Street and Reynolds Avenue)
Bishop James M. Thoburn Meadville, SR 0077
Conneaut Reservoir US 6 and US 322 east of Conneaut Lake
Crawford County Meadville, at courthouse, Public Square
Early Refinery Titusville, East Main Street on SR 0027
Edwin L. Drake Titusville, SR 0008 near Woodlawn Cemetery
Erie Extension Canal SR 0018 north of Conneautville; US 6 west of Shermansville; SR 0618 south of Conneaut Lake Park; US 6 and US 322 east of Conneaut Lake; US 322 east of Hartstown; and SR 0018 south of Adamsville
First Oil Exchange Titusville, West Spring Street on SR 0008 eastbound
French Creek US 6 and US 19 south of Venango; and US 322 southeast of Meadville

French Creek Feeder US 322 south of Meadville; and US 19 south of Meadville

Ida M. Tarbell Titusville, 324 East Main Street on SR 0027

John A. Mather Titusville, 407 East Main Street

John Brown Tannery New Richmond, SR 1033 south of SR 0077, and New Richmond, SR 0077

Meadville On main highways leading into city

Oil Creek Titusville, Smock Boulevard on SR 0008

Oil-producing Salt Well SR 0198 at Lawrence Corners

Richard Henderson Meadville, at Liberty and Arch streets

Roberts Torpedo Titusville, Smock Boulevard on SR 0008

Rural Electrification SR 0198 near Woodcock Dam

Unitarian Church Meadville, Main and Chestnut streets

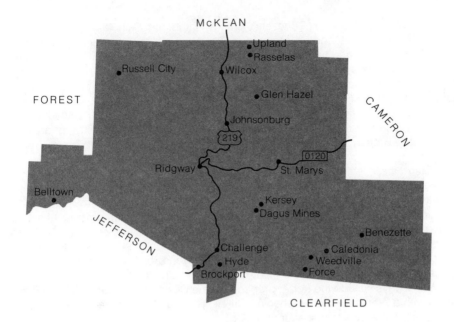

McKEAN

Upland
Rasselas
Russell City
Wilcox

FOREST

Glen Hazel

CAMERON

Johnsonburg

219

0120

Ridgway
St. Marys

Belltown

Kersey
Dagus Mines

JEFFERSON

Benezette

Challenge
Caledonia
Hyde
Weedville
Brockport
Force

CLEARFIELD

Elk County

Capsule History

Elk County, named for the herds that once roamed the area, was erected out of Clearfield, Jefferson, and McKean counties on April 18, 1843. It has an area of 830 square miles and a population of 38,338.

Among the first settlers were John Bennett, near Caledonia, in 1787, and Gen. John Wade, who arrived at the mouth of Little Toby Creek in present Ridgway Township in 1798.

A year before the formation of the county, Col. Mathias Benzinger of Philadelphia purchased 35,000 acres (later increased to 66,000) in the Saint Marys area to be settled by Catholics from Philadelphia and Baltimore through German Union Bond Societies. He divided the land into twenty-five-, fifty-, and one-hundred-acre parcels, and gave each colonist twenty-five acres and a town lot free. The first group arrived on the Feast of the Immaculate Conception, hence the town's name. Their descendants and those of Irish railroad workers of the 1860s have made the area predominantly Catholic.

Ridgway was named for wealthy merchants Jacob and John J. Ridgway of Philadelphia, who owned over 40,000 acres in the territory; and although it became the county seat in 1845, Wilcox, Benezette, Brandy Camp, and Saint Marys contended for the honor, with the first court being held at Caledonia. An early settler at Ridgway was Enos Gillis in 1822, and he and James Gallagher established the first tannery there in 1830. The town was laid out in 1833. William Pearl "Bunker" Rhines (1869–1922), from Ridgway, played major league baseball at Cincinnati and Pittsburgh and was famous for perfecting the underhand pitch.

Johnsonburg, first known as Coopersburg and then Quay, was settled in 1810 and was named for the pioneer David Johnson. It is the gateway to sixty square miles of the East Branch Valley of the Clarion River, where numerous trout streams are located.

Glen Hazel, settled by Belgian glass workers under the leadership of Count DeHamm, was known as New Flanders and today maintains a summer camp colony. An Indian cemetery was located near New Flanders.

Jones Township was the site of an ancient Indian village, and remains of another have been found near Russell City. The only principal Indian trail crossing Elk County in historic times was the *Catawba Path*. It entered the county near James City, passing near Highland Corners, Sackett, and the eastern "teardrop" of Forest County, finally crossing the Clarion River at the mouth of Millstone Creek.

Waterways include the upper branches of the Clarion River and Driftwood Creek, along with a branch of Sinnemahoning Creek. The old Buffalo Swamp extended into the county as far as Daguscahonda.

The county's principal natural resources are fire clay, bituminous coal, oil, gas, silica sand, and lumber. Its earliest industries were lumbering and tanning. Elk Tannery once had branches as far away as Bedford and Warren counties. Located in Wilcox (on US 219), it once was the largest in the world. Established in 1865, it turned out more than one million tanned buffalo hides between 1866 and 1876.

Today, the county also manufactures paper, metals, leather, and rubber goods. Coal mining began in the 1860s with the opening of the Shawmut mines. The scars of five switchbacks of the Shawmut Railroad, built from Ridgway, may still be seen west of US 219 near Bootjack and on SR 0120 between Ridgway and Saint Marys. Saint Marys is the metropolis of carbon products; Ridgway was long the center of the leather industry, and Johnsonburg is the paper city.

Allegheny National Forest occupies a large portion of the county. It provides lumber (mostly oak and hemlock) and related products; it is also a sportsman's paradise. Stands of virgin timber are still in existence there. The first state game lands in Pennsylvania, 6,288 acres bought in 1920 by the Game Commission with money from hunting license fees, are located a short distance north of Glen Hazel.

Landmarks

1. Ridgway

1A. Courthouse (brick), replacing an earlier 1845 structure, was erected in 1879–80 and was modeled after the Warren County courthouse of that day. It cost $63,543, with an additional $700 for the clock. An 1846 stone jail was replaced in 1884 by the present brick one, costing $37,000. In 1890 the first courthouse was moved down Main Street and became the nucleus of the Bogert House, later operated as a tavern; it burned in 1990. The Elk County Historical Society, very active, is located in the present courthouse. *Location:* Main Street.

1B. Elk County Historical Society Museum, owned and operated by the Elk County Historical Society, is the official depository for records and information on the county. *Hours:* Monday–Friday, 1:30–4 P.M. Other times by appointment. *Location:* 109 Center Street.

1C. Old Opera House (brick), later the Strand Theater and now a commercial building, opened in 1891. *Location:* 416 Main Street.

1D. Harry R. Hyde House (stone) was built by the Hyde family in 1900–08. *Location:* 344 Main Street.

1E. McCloskey House (frame) was the home of S. L. McCloskey, a painter and writer. Private residence, Kotts family. *Location:* 403 Oak Street.

1F. Ridgway Library (brick), of Georgian style with a beautiful leaded glass doorway, was built in 1902–04, the home of Senator J.K.P. Hall. His wife, Kate Maria Hyde, described as the "greatest benefactress in Ridgway," established the library in 1922 and also was instrumental in founding the Elk County Hospital in 1901. *Location:* Center Street.

1G. J. S. Hyde House (frame) was the first town home of this self-made millionaire lumberman and land dealer, who moved into the borough about 1846 from his original base of operations to the south (see *Early J. S. Hyde House*). In his old age he lived on Hyde Avenue. *Location:* 21 East Street.

1H. James Knox Polk Hall (frame), a typical mid-Victorian millionaire's residence, was built about 1890 by J. S. Hyde's son-in-law, a lawyer, banker, lumberman, and land dealer. It is now the American Legion home. *Location:* Main Street.

1I. George Dickinson House (frame), in Greek Revival style, a tastefully designed house built by a prominent lumberman in 1855, is now a private home. *Location:* 106 West Main Street.

1J. Ridgway Academy (frame) was erected in 1834 for the county's first classical school, which continued in operation until after 1850. Later the building was used as a residence, a church, and a hotel, and is now an apartment house, its original appearance largely disguised by siding and alterations. Originally located on the east side of the street, it was moved to its present site about 1883 to make room for the Buffalo, Rochester, & Pittsburgh Railroad depot. *Location:* 231 West Main Street.

Note: Two of the town's railroad stations (both brick) have been preserved (the only ones remaining in Elk County). The B&O, now a commercial building (restaurant), is at West Main and Montmorenci streets, and the Pennsylvania is at the junction of US 219 (North Broad Street) at the bridge and railroad. The latter is owned by the Hammer Mill Paper Company in Erie.

2. Bonifels (stone) was the mansion of attorney and coal-lands dealer Norman T. Arnold. This great granite structure was erected in 1898–99, but its owner lived only a short time to enjoy it, dying in 1906. Now surrounded by the Elk County Country Club, it is privately owned. *Location:* 1.1 miles northwest of SR 0949 in Ridgway, on Laurel Mill Road.

Note: A massive red sandstone structure at the northwest edge of town (0.6 mile from the highway) is its former gatehouse. It is also a private home.

3. Johnsonburg, originally Coopersport, named for Benjamin Cooper, an early landowner.

3A. Armstrong House was built in the late 1800s by Samuel K. Armstrong, superintendent and later vice-president of the New York and Pennsylvania Company. The residence was later owned by Richard Stutz (mill superintendent), and then became the Penn Club. It is now the Anthony Ferragine Funeral Home. *Location:* 410 Chestnut Street.

3B. E. L. Myers House. Myers, general superintendent of the paper mill, built this pretentious home known as "The Mansion" in the late 1800s on the former site of the John A. Craig house. It later became the R. Neal Jones residence and then the Holy Rosary Convent. It is now the residence of C. H. Wu, M.D. *Location:* 701 Penn Street.

3C. The Brick Block was built by Meylert M. Armstrong, Sr., and the Armstrong Real Estate and Land Improvement Company. It is an elongated brick and stone structure, with commercial enterprises on the first floor and apartments on the second. The Brick Block is considered the first shopping mall or plaza in Elk County and the surrounding area. *Location:* North side of Market Street.

2. *Bonifels*

3D. Hotel Johnsonburg (brick) is the only remaining hotel in the town. Built at the end of the last century by either L. C. Horton or John Foley, it is a four-story structure that once was a favorite place for summer tourists and business people. The hotel is owned by Mr. and Mrs. Frank Marlara. *Location:* 617 Center Street.

4. East Branch Dam (rolled earth fill structure) has a total length of 1,725 feet; maximum height above stream bed, 184 feet; maximum width about 1,115 feet; top width, 20 feet. It was built by the U.S. Army Corps of Engineers in 1947–52. *Location:* On Clarion River about 7 miles above junction with West Branch of river.

5. Colonel Alonzo I. Wilcox House (frame) was built by the colonel in the mid 1800s and is now the American Legion Club House. The town, named for the colonel, was settled in 1858. *Location:* Wilcox (Jones Township).

6. Upland, a famous stagecoach and wagon stop on the turnpike, includes two houses (both frame). The older one was in turn the home of W. P. Wilcox, Thomas L. Kane, and Capt. Anthony A. Clay. Kane was the founder of Kane, Pa. This modest home to which Kane brought his bride, Elizabeth, in 1857 had been built by Wilcox about 1842. Kane sold it to Captain Clay in 1866. It was moved back from the highway in 1880 by Clay when he built the mansion that stands on the former site. Ulysses S. Grant and Simon Cameron visited Upland in 1868, and Theodore Roosevelt was at Upland about 1906. Unfortunately, both houses are unpainted and badly run down. *Location:* North of Wilcox, on Wilcox-Clermont Road (SR 1001), 0.7 mile from McKean County line.

7. Holy Cross Catholic Church (stone) was built during the years 1884–85. *Location:* Rasselas (Jones Township).

8. Highland Hotel (red frame) was an early lumbermen's hotel. *Location:* Russell City, near Warren County line, SR 0948.
Note: North of Russell City are the ruins of an Indian "fort."

9. Early J. S. Hyde House (frame), a very old structure built over a long period, was occupied for a short time by this pioneer lumberman. The central portion, probably weatherboard over log, was reputed to date from 1801 (now torn down). The two-story newest part was built about 1850. About 1890 it became a hotel. The house is somewhat neglected and may soon be lost. *Location:* Hyde, west side of US 219, 0.3 mile south of Challenge.
Note: The store and home of W. H. Hyde, a son, dating from about 1865, stands 0.1 mile to the north and is now a private home.

6. Mansion at Upland

10E. Old St. Benedict's Academy

10. Saint Marys

10A. Bell Tower (brick), built in 1935, replaced two former towers (the first was erected in 1875; the second in 1897 at which time a 900-pound brass bell was acquired). This 65-foot-high structure with a 15-foot square base, functions as a fire tower where an alarm bell is sounded. Hoses are dried by hanging them from the top of the tower. *Location:* Market Street, in municipal parking lot.

10B. Saint Marys Catholic Church (stone) was built in 1852–53. Men, women, and children trundled earth and carried stone for the new church. The first church, of wooden frame construction and built in 1845, was destroyed by fire in 1851. *Location:* Corner of Maurus and Church streets.

10C. George Weiss House (stone) is a two-door 1845 house and harness shop, requiring three years to build. It was one of the first businesses in Saint Marys. Twenty years later Weiss moved his business into the 1865 stone house next door. *Location:* 45 Saint Marys Street.

10D. Historical Society of Saint Marys and Benzinger Township Museum specializes in material concerning the eastern half of Elk County. *Hours:* Tuesdays, 1–4 P.M.; Thursdays, 7–9 P.M. *Location:* 319 Erie Avenue, in municipal building.

10E. Old St. Benedict's Academy (frame) housed the first girls' school in Elk County, begun in 1854. Later the school moved into the gray (painted) brick building next door. Both are on the grounds of St. Joseph's Convent, the first house of the Benedictine Sisters in America, which took over an old

Redemptorist monastery in 1852. *Location:* 303 Church Street.

Note: Saint Marys Convent, dedicated to St. Walburga (see *St. Walburga Wayside Chapel,* Westmoreland County), is also located in the town.

10F. Straub's Brewery, one of the smallest breweries still in existence in the United States, was built by Capt. Volk in 1870. Peter Straub, Sr. (wife Sabina) and his sons bought it in 1872. Peter had left Wurtemburg, Germany, in 1850 for a position at the Eberhart and Ober Brewery in Allegheny City (q.v., Allegheny County). Over the years the entire plant has been rebuilt by descendants. A 1901 copper kettle is still in use at this family owned business. *Visiting hours:* Monday–Friday, 9 A.M. and 12 noon. *Location:* 303 Sorg Street, just off SR 0120.

11. Decker's Chapel (frame), a 12-by-18-foot white pine church, sometimes incorrectly called the smallest in America, was built in 1856 as a thank-offering by Michael Decker, father of Msgr. M. J. Decker (1839–1914), who preached in the area for many years. In addition to a shrine and pews, it includes a fine collection of historical photographs and other local memorabilia. The building has recently been renovated. Always open. *Location:* 1.6 miles south of Saint Marys, on west side of SR 0255 (Benzinger Township).

12. Dagus Mines Post Office (frame), built in 1880, is probably the oldest post office in Elk county still in use. *Location:* Dagus Mines (Fox Township).

13. St. Boniface Cemetery Cross is located behind the Catholic church of this name. The imposing twenty-foot marble cross was do-

11. Decker's Chapel

nated by the Urmann family. *Location:* Kersey, Main Street (Fox Township).

14. Old Company Store (frame) is now a Country Cupboard gift store. *Location:* Force, SR 0255.

15. Benezette House (frame) was a lumbermen's hotel and store built by Henry Blesh in 1864. It was retained in the family for more than a century. *Location:* Benezette, on Water Street.

16. Elk Herd, the only one in Pennsylvania, roams freely over the area bounded by Elk and Cameron counties. It descended from the herd imported into Pennsylvania in 1913 from Montana and Wyoming. *Location:* Benzinger and Benezette Townships. (A buffalo herd is in the Johnsonburg area.)

17. United Methodist Church (frame). The cornerstone was laid on July 4, 1879, and the church was dedicated on October 26, 1881. *Location:* Brockport (Horton Township), US 219.

18. Brockway House (frame) was built in the mid 1800s by Chauncey Brockway, Jr., son of one of the first Elk County commissioners. A farmer and lumberman, he gained statewide recognition as a gunsmith, inventor, and master mechanic. He was buried at Brandy Camp, north of Brockport. This house is now owned by Raymond Youngdahl. *Location:* Brockport.

19. Old Belltown Hotel (frame), now disguised with a porch and other changes, was built about 1865 in Elk County's gas-boom days, as a drillers' boardinghouse. After the dream of riches for Millstone Township faded, it became a lumberjacks' tavern. In more recent years it has been used as a hunting and fishing lodge. *Location:* Belltown, on SR 3001, 0.4 mile east of store.

Previous Sites Now Lost

Bogert House, burned February 1990
Mt. Zion Church, burned 1976 (cemetery preserved)
Wilcox House, burned 1980s

Pennsylvania Historical and Museum Commission Markers

Elk County Ridgway, at courthouse, Main Street
First State Game Lands SR 1001 southeast of Glen Hazel
Iroquois "Main Road" SR 0948 east of SR 0066, Highland Township
Saint Marys Saint Marys, near the Diamond

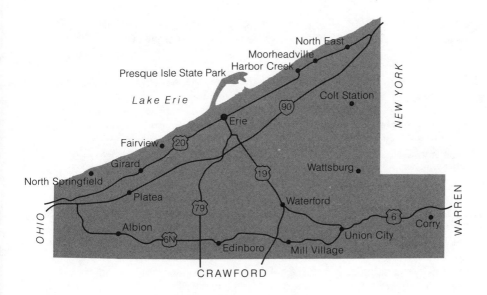

Erie County

Capsule History

Erie County, erected March 12, 1800, and organized April 2, 1803, was originally called Erie Township, then a part of Allegheny County. Named for Lake Erie, which in turn was named for the Erie Indian tribe, the county has 804 square miles with a population of 279,780.

The French claimed the area by discovery under the treaties of Utrecht and Aix-la-Chapelle. They built forts at Presque Isle and LeBoeuf (Waterford) in 1753. In 1758–59 the British captured Fort Pitt and Fort Niagara, and the French abandoned the Erie County forts, which the English rebuilt. Although the Indians recaptured these forts in 1763, Col. Henry Bouquet's victory at Bushy Run that year and the peace treaty with the Six Nations the following one gave Pennsylvania the right to all of this territory except the Erie Triangle, which at different times was claimed by Massachusetts, Virginia, Connecticut, and New York. In 1792 the Triangle was ceded to Pennsylvania by the United States for seventy-five cents an acre, or a total of $151,640.25 for 202,187 acres—more than William Penn had originally paid for all the rest of the state. This gave Pennsylvania a lake shoreline of forty-six miles.

Following the sale the Indians under Mohawk Chief Joseph Brant resisted white settlement. Finally, following Anthony Wayne's 1794 victory over the western Indians at Fallen Timbers and the Treaty of Greenville, Ohio, the danger lessened and settlement began shortly afterward. The first permanent white settler was Seth Reed. Gen. John

Phillips, founder of Phillipsville (near Wattsburg), was paymaster general of the U.S. Army during the War of 1812 and later became canal commissioner of Pennsylvania. He is buried in the Wattsburg cemetery. Another early settler was Aaron Himrod, an Indian fighter.

The Holland Land Company and the Pennsylvania Population Company purchased large tracts of land in Erie County for settlement.

Mill Village, on US 6 west of Union City (once the chair capital of the world), is built on part of a tract granted to the Moravians by the Commonwealth in 1791. However, the land was sold to individuals in 1850. Waterford, formerly LeBoeuf, was laid out in 1794 and was an important shipping point on the route from the Great Lakes to Pittsburgh. The liquefied petroleum gas industry originated in this area in 1912.

Five Indian trails traversed the county. Branches of the *Venango Path,* running past Indian Head and Mill Village, joined at Waterford and followed much the course of SR 0097 to Erie. This was also the course of the Presque Isle Portage from French Creek to the lake. The *Lake Shore Path,* from Sandusky to Buffalo, ran near the lake all the way through Erie County. The *Brokenstraw Path,* from the Allegheny River at Irvine to Waterford, came up Brokenstraw Creek through Spring Creek and Corry; thence it ran down the right bank of the South Branch, crossing the main French Creek west of Union City and joining the Venango Trail a little south of Waterford. The *Conneaut Path* entered Erie County south of Albion, crossed Conneaut Creek at or near that town, and made a fairly straight course toward Conneaut, Ohio.

On the old French Road (which begins on Parade Street in Erie), where French soldiers traveled in 1753 on their way between Fort LeBoeuf and Fort Presque Isle, was the Cold Spring well, now capped, in a tavern lot in Erie at Twenty-eighth and Parade streets. The first turnpike in the county was the Erie-Waterford Road, completed in 1821. The building of the railroads resulted in a war over the gauge of track to be used. It was finally settled after several years of conflict in the 1850s.

The Erie extension of the Pennsylvania Canal provided a main artery for transportation from the Ohio to the Great Lakes. Remains of this waterway can be seen along US 20 at Asbury Chapel and followed through Lockport, now Platea. Silas Pratt, contractor for the locks, erected the first buildings of Lockport in 1840. In 1870 the collapse of the aqueduct over Walnut Creek ended the real use of the canal.

Erie, the county seat, was laid out in 1795 by Gen. William Irvine and Andrew Ellicott, the first U.S. surveyor-general; it became a borough in 1805 and a city in 1851. It has grown considerably since World War I and is now Pennsylvania's third largest city and the state's only lake port. Erie has one of the best harbors on the lake, and the county still remains an important transportation center, both for rail and waterborne commerce. In 1813 Oliver Hazard Perry defeated the British during the battle of Lake Erie and gave the United States control over the Great Lakes, making possible the recovery of the Northwest Territory. His fleet was built mainly at Erie.

Among the county's residents have been Henry Thacker Burleigh (1866–1949), eminent singer, composer, and arranger of spirituals including "Deep River" and "Swing Low, Sweet Chariot"; Ida M. Tarbell (1857–1944) (see *Ida Tarbell Home,* Crawford County), biographer of Lincoln and historian of Standard Oil, born at Hatch Hollow; Denman Thompson, actor and playwright born near Girard in 1833; Dan Rice (1823–1900), the famous circus owner and clown; magician Harry Keller; and Paul Weitz, astronaut.

In the early days the county's main trade was in salt. It also had two iron furnaces, the first built in 1833. Now it is known for its diversified industries, including metal and related products, paper and printing, electrical machinery, iron and steel forgings, hardware, aircraft, toys and games, plastics, and rubber goods. Presque Isle Foundry, established in 1840, later became the Erie City Iron Works. The Hammermill Paper Company, founded in 1898, is one of the world's best-known makers of fine paper. The General Electric Company built its first plant here in 1911. The county is important for agriculture, especially truck farming, ranking first in the state for the production of grapes and cherries. At North East, a rich fruit-growing area, are some of the largest chrysanthemum gardens in the world.

Presque Isle State Park attracts thousands of vacationers every summer. Outstanding natural phenomena include Six Mile Creek Falls, six miles east of Erie, where an abundance of fossils have been discovered; Howard's Falls, five-and-a-half miles south of Fairview; and Oxbow at Elk Creek, a beautiful scenic area steeped in folklore. Four covered bridges remain in the county. Walnut and Elk Creek aqueducts for the Erie Canal are now occupied by railroad trestles.

There are only half a dozen log houses, or even fewer, left in Erie County.

Landmarks

1. Erie

1A. County Courthouse (stone) has been in use for court sessions ever since May 7, 1855. The cornerstone of the west wing was laid in 1852, and the building was enlarged in 1889–90, with the east wing added in 1929. The original structure was modeled after plans drawn by Thomas U. Walter and is similar to the courthouse in Chester County. The later matching section was planned by Walter Monahan of Erie. Another addition has been constructed. *Location:* North side of West Sixth Street, between West Park and Sassafras streets.

Note: The old Pennsylvania Railroad freight house is at Fourteenth and Sassafras streets.

1B. Hoskinson House (brick), a double dwelling built in 1840 in Greek Revival style with a twin Doric doorway, was the home of the Hoskinson brothers, James and William. The latter was the general contractor for the west wing of the courthouse. *Location:* 127 West Sixth Street, across from courthouse.

1C. St. Paul's Protestant Episcopal Cathedral (stone), of Gothic architecture, was completed in 1866 and consecrated in 1869. *Location:* 133 West Sixth Street, across from courthouse.

Note: Also on West Sixth Street near Myrtle Street is the Church of the Covenant (Presbyterian), built in 1931. The stained glass windows are by Connick and Ascenzo.

1D. Reed House (brick) was built in 1849 by Gen. Charles M. Reed, grandson of Erie's first settler Dr. Seth Reed, who built the first inn at Erie in 1795 and served in the Revolution. It is now the Erie Club. *Location:* West Sixth and Peach streets.

1E. Strong Mansion (brick) was built in the late 1880s and early 1890s by William L. Scott (died 1891) for his daughter Annie Wainwright Scott, who married Charles Hamot Strong. It is now the administration building of Gannon University, originally known as Cathedral College. The first classes were held in 1941, with a two-year, arts-and-science term, and in 1944 it became a four-year college. *Location:* 109 West Sixth Street at Perry Square.

1F. Colt House (aluminum siding) was the second Erie home of Judah Colt, agent for the Pennsylvania Population Company, who settled at Colt Station in 1797. Colt read the first Protestant service the same year in Erie County. He moved to Erie in 1804 and lived in this house until his death in 1832. Lafayette was entertained here in 1825. The home originally was located at the southwest corner of Fourth and French streets until it was moved to its present site. *Location:* 343 East Front Street.

Note: The old Colt Station burial ground is at the junction of SR 0089 and Station Road.

1G. Wood-Morrison House (brick) was constructed by Dr. William Maxwell Wood, first U.S. surgeon general and a noted author. His son Charles Erskine Scott Wood (1852–1944) became a soldier, explorer, and nationally known lawyer and poet. This pre–Civil War home stands about twenty yards from the site of the old Erie-Beaver Canal, which ran into the basin at Erie harbor. The building is distinguished by a ship's house cupola. Capt. William Morrison and his wife were the last to reside in the house. Following their deaths, their daughter Mrs. Eric Brooke of Ohio sold it to the Art Club in the 1950s. It is being used as law offices. Capt. Morrison and Dr. Wood both served on the USS *Michigan* (see USS *Wolverine*). Morrison was associated with the early development of Presque Isle State Park. *Location:* 338 West Sixth Street.

1H. Erie Historical Museum and Planetarium (stone) are housed in this thirty-five-room Richardsonian Romanesque mansion, built in 1891–92 for the industrialist Harrison F. Watson, a gift to the Erie School District. It formerly was the Frederick F. Curtze home and became a museum in 1942. The planetarium was founded in 1960. *Hours:* September–May: Tuesday–Sunday, 1–5 P.M.; June–August: Tuesday–Friday, 10 A.M.–5 P.M.; Saturday and Sunday, 1–5 P.M. *Location:* 356 West Sixth Street at Chestnut Street.

1I. Erie County Library (brick and granite) was built in 1897–99. Designed by Alden & Harlow of Pittsburgh in classic Italian Renaissance style, it is located on the site of the first Methodist log church in Erie. *Location:* Southwest corner of South Park Row and French Street.

1J. St. Peter's Roman Catholic Cathedral (limestone) took twenty years to build. The ground was broken in 1873 and the cornerstone laid August 1, 1875, on St. Peter's Day. The structure was completed and dedicated in 1893. The four-faced clock on this Gothic edifice is surmounted with an eleven-foot copper cross. Every quarter hour it plays the melody "Chimes of Erie" written by Bishop John Mark Gannon. *Location:* Northwest corner of West Tenth and Sassafras streets.

1K. Joseph M. Sterrett House (brick with aluminum siding) was once the home of Horace Greeley, founder and editor of the *New York Tribune,* whose famous words were, "Go west, young man, and grow up with the country." He resided here while working for Sterrett as a printer in 1830–31. In 1936 a

1I. Erie County Library

tablet in his memory was placed on the building by the Erie Typographical Union. The house has been altered in recent years. *Location:* 414 State Street (directly across from Custom House and Cashier's House).

Note: Also on State Street, at Twenty-sixth Street, is the Erie Stadium, built in 1924 as a memorial to World War I veterans.

1L. Cashier's House (stone) was authorized to be built as a residence for the cashier of the branch Bank of the United States in 1837–39. Peter Benson, the first resident and cashier, lived here at that time. In later years Samuel Goodwin ran a boardinghouse in the building, and at another time Calista and Louisa Ingersoll operated a select boarding school for girls here. The Samuel Woodruff family occupied the house from 1872 to 1913, when it was purchased by the Ashby Printing Company. From 1920 to 1963 it was the home of the Erie Drug Company. Restored in 1974, this structure, owned by the state, became the headquarters of the Erie County Historical Society the same year. (The society was incorporated in 1903.) A dining room in the building is named the Reed Room, in honor of an early pioneer family. *Hours:* Tuesday–Friday, 9 A.M.–4 P.M.; Saturday, 1–4 P.M.; Sunday, 2–5 P.M. (seasonal). *Location:* 417 State Street, next to Custom House.

1M. Old Custom House or United States Bank Building (stone), now home of the Erie Art Museum, was designed by William Kelly of Philadelphia and built between 1837 and 1839. It was planned for the Erie branch office of the Bank of Pennsylvania, which suc-

1M. Old Custom House

ceeded that of the United States. This structure, the first building of the county constructed with native marble, hauled from Vermont via the old Erie Canal, is an example of Greek Revival architecture of classical Doric design, modeled after the Parthenon. (Its parent branch in Philadelphia was also known as the bank of Nicholas Biddle, its president.) Peter Benson was the first cashier. The building was used as a bank until 1840 and was sold to the government for $29,000 in 1849. From 1849 to 1888 it was a custom house. From 1853 to 1867 it also included a post office, and from the early 1890s to 1932 it was the headquarters of the Grand Army of the Republic. In 1932 it was leased to the Erie County Historical Society, which moved to the Cashier's House (q.v.) in 1974. *Hours:* Tuesday–Saturday, 11 A.M.–5 P.M.; Sunday, 1–5 P.M. *Location:* 407 State Street.

1N. Firefighters Historical Museum (brick), housed in the two-story No. 4 Erie firehouse, contains firefighting memorabilia, displays, and early equipment. *Hours:* May–August: Saturday, 10 A.M.–5 P.M.; Sunday, 1–5 P.M.; September–October: Saturday and Sunday, 1–5 P.M. (sometimes by appointment only). *Location:* 428 Chestnut Street.

1O. Studebacker Laboratory (brick) was founded by Latimer O. Studebacker and operated for over fifty years. *Location:* Eleventh and German streets.

1P. USS Wolverine (bow mounted on a base), the first iron-hulled warship of the U.S. Navy, designed for lake patrol, was assembled in 1842–43 at the foot of Peach Street, where Capt. Daniel Dobbins had built some of Commodore Oliver Hazard Perry's fleet in 1813. This ship, first named the Michigan, launched itself on December 5, 1843, after

an unsuccessful attempt the previous night by the builder Samuel Hart. It was limited to one gun due to a previous agreement with Canada in 1817.

The ship was the only U.S. war vessel on active duty patrolling the lakes for eighty years, a symbol of peace. During the Civil War the *Michigan* guarded a camp of Confederate prisoners near Sandusky, Ohio. In 1910 it was under its last command, that of Lt. Comdr. William Leverett Morrison (see *Wood-Morrison House*). After the ship was renamed the *Wolverine*, it pulled the restored USS *Niagara* (q.v.) across the Great Lakes for the 1913 centennial celebration of Perry's victory. It continued to be a training ship until 1923. (Charles Gridley began his naval career on its decks, and Stephen Champlin, commander of Perry's *Scorpion,* ended his career on the same ship.) In 1924 one of the *Wolverine's* piston rods failed while the ship cruised on Lake Huron, but Capt. Morrison managed to get it back to the dock at Erie, where it was maintained until 1927 when the iron steamer was moved to Misery Bay. In 1949 it was sold for scrap. The prow was later brought to the present site. *Location:* In Niagara Park, foot of State Street near public dock.

1Q. USS Niagara, built in 1813 with a 110-foot keel by Capt. Daniel Dobbins, was Commodore Oliver Hazard Perry's second flagship in the battle of Lake Erie during the War of 1812. During the three-hour battle on September 10, 1813, when Perry and his fleet found the British ships at Put-in-Bay near Sandusky, Ohio, the *Lawrence,* Perry's first flagship, was damaged. He left it and boarded its twin, the *Niagara,* with his battle flag bearing the motto Don't Give Up the Ship. These words, originally those of Capt. James Lawrence, in command of the USS *Chesapeake,* were adopted by Perry. After Perry defeated the British, he reported to Gen. William Henry Harrison, "We have met the enemy and they are ours." It was the only time that an entire British squadron surrendered to anyone: two ships, two brigs, one schooner and one sloop. Perry, who was master commandant at this time, received a promotion to the rank of captain. The *Niagara* was later sunk in Misery Bay upon government orders but was lifted in 1913 and rebuilt for the Perry centennial. Since 1939 the ship has been administered by the Pennsylvania Historical and Museum Commission. In 1963 it was restored again, this time for the sesquicentennial of Perry's victory. The major original portion of the ship remaining is a seventy-eight-foot section of the black oak keel.

169

1Q. USS Niagara

1R. Perry Memorial House

The ship sits on a bank beside the historic canal basin, the northern terminus of the Erie extension of the Pennsylvania Canal system, now used for small harbor craft. The ship, containing 100 pieces of the original timbers, has been restored for sailing on the Great Lakes under its own power for the first time since 1814. (The adjacent dock, Erie's public steamboat landing, was built in 1909 and extends 538 feet into Presque Isle Bay.) *Hours:* Tuesday–Saturday, 9 A.M.–5 P.M.; Sunday, 12 noon–5 P.M. *Location:* In Niagara Park, foot of State Street.

Note: In 1989 the compass used by Commodore Perry during the Battle of Lake Erie was donated by heirs to the restoration project.

1R. Perry Memorial House (frame) was built by William Himrod after peace was established following the War of 1812. (It is reputed that Oliver Hazard Perry visited this inn.) John Dickson printed Erie's first newspaper here. The Dickson Tavern was one of the leading hostelries in the area for over thirty years, during which time it was also known as the Steamboat House and the Washington Hotel. In 1825 innkeeper Dickson prepared a banquet here for General Lafayette, but due to lack of space tables were arranged on the Second Street Bridge (between State and French streets) for a banquet hall. The building has the original plank floors, small-paned windows with imported French glass, and handwrought door locks and keys. The walls are honeycombed with narrow stone passages that were used during the pre–Civil War era of the underground railroad. (One of

these, now closed, led to the waterfront.) In 1826 the tavern was sold to Josiah Kellogg, in 1841 to the Rogers family, and later to the Stantons. In 1923 the city of Erie purchased it and restored it in 1928. It is administered by the Erie Historical Museum and Planetarium. *Hours:* Memorial Day–Labor Day: Tuesday–Friday, 10 A.M.–5 P.M.; Saturday and Sunday, 1–5 P.M. *Location:* Second and French streets, across from Hamot Medical Center.

1S. Soldiers and Sailors Home (brick) was established in 1885 and opened in 1886 on a 133-acre tract that includes the Anthony Wayne Memorial Blockhouse (q.v.). Behind the home is a cemetery with a memorial to servicemen. A greenhouse on the property is another landmark. *Location:* 560 East Third Street at Ash.

1T. Anthony Wayne Memorial Blockhouse (log), built in 1879–80, is a replica of the structure which stood on the site of the (northwest) American fortification, Fort Presque Isle, in which Gen. Wayne died December 15, 1796. The French and English forts at Presque Isle were located between Parade Street and the mouth of Mill Creek. Wayne, who defeated the Indians in 1794 at the battle of Fallen Timbers, was buried here and later his bones reinterred in 1809 at St. David's Episcopal churchyard in Radnor, near Philadelphia.

Built in 1795 on Garrison Hill by 200 federal troops from Gen. Wayne's army under the command of Capt. John Grubb, the first blockhouse was part of a defense system being reestablished due to Indian uprisings. Later it was used during the War of 1812. (Other fortifications at this time were located at the mouth of Lees Run, the mouth of Cascade Creek, and on the peninsula, where Perry's monolith stands. There were five

1T. Anthony Wayne Memorial Blockhouse

1V. Peninsula Lighthouse

blockhouses built at various times in the vicinity.) *Hours:* Memorial Day–Labor Day: Tuesday–Sunday, 1–4 P.M. *Location:* 560 East Third Street (foot of Ash Street), north of Soldiers and Sailors Home, overlooking harbor entrance.

1U. Asbury Woods is a forty-acre outdoor laboratory with over a mile of all-weather nature trails. *Location:* Asbury Road, south of West Thirty-eighth Street.

1V. Peninsula Lighthouse (brick and frame) was constructed in 1872 and started to operate the following year, its revolving lenses being visible sixteen to eighteen miles out in Lake Erie. The light is now run automatically by a time-clock system. No lighthouse keeper has lived here since 1941, when the Coast Guard took it over. *Location:* On peninsula between beaches nos. 8 and 9.

1W. Old Land Lighthouse (stone) stands on the approximate site of the first U.S. land lighthouse on the Great Lakes. The original building was erected in 1818 and rebuilt in 1858. The third and present structure was built in 1866–67, originally with an imported $7,000 lens which cast a light seventeen miles out into Lake Erie. The focal point of the lens is 67 feet above lake level; the top, 127 feet. The lighthouse has been out of use since 1885. A later one is in operation today at the channel entrance on Presque Isle. *Location:* Foot of

Lighthouse Street or Dunne Boulevard in Land Lighthouse Park (east side).

Note: Near the old stone lighthouse is the site of a War of 1812 redoubt, which stood until 1829.

1X. Perry Victory Monument is a memorial to Commodore Oliver Hazard Perry, who defeated the British fleet at Put-in-Bay near Sandusky, Ohio, September 10, 1813, during the battle of Lake Erie (War of 1812). The monolith, rising 101 feet above water level, was built by the state in 1926. Made of reinforced concrete faced with limestone and surmounted by an eight-foot bronze tripod, it stands on the peninsula's Crystal Point, overlooking Misery Bay. *Location:* In Presque Isle State Park.

1Y. Old Villa Maria College and Academy (brick), founded in 1891 by the Sisters of St. Joseph, was established as a college in 1925. This institution, providing elementary, high school, and college training for girls, has been moved to another location (2403 and 2551 West Eighth Street). The old academy building still stands on the original campus. *Location:* West Eighth Street from Liberty to Plum Street where elementary school is now located.

1Z. Gridley's Grave is the burial site of Captain Charles Vernon Gridley, commander of the flagship *Olympia* in the Battle of Manila,

Philippine Islands, May 1, 1898. This combat, in which the Spanish were defeated, started when Adm. George Dewey gave his order, "You may fire when you are ready, Captain Gridley." Four bronze eighteenth-century Spanish cannon captured in this battle surround his grave. *Location:* 1715 East Lake Road (Gridley Circle, in Lakeside Cemetery).

Note: A granite monument in his honor erected in 1913 is in the middle of Gridley Park (West Sixth Street).

2. Glacial Kame, resembling an Indian burial mound, was deposited by the glacier about sixteen thousand years ago. *Location:* East of Erie, on Twelve Mile Creek between SR 0005 and US 20.

3. Wintergreen Gorge is a beautiful natural chasm best viewed from Wintergreen Gorge Cemetery. The chapel here was built in the 1930s in memory of the son of the Behrend family who died accidentally. *Location:* Southeast of Erie in Belle Valley off SR 0008 and SR 4030.

4. Douglas Moorhead House (brick) was built in 1832 by five Moorhead brothers, who came here from Lancaster County between 1801 and 1805. A fine natural-gas well, the first in the county, has provided light and heat for this house for years. In 1906, when US 20 was improved, this house was moved back fifty feet. *Location:* Moorheadville (near North East), about 10 miles east of Erie on US 20.

5. North East, the home of St. Mary's Seminary (College), now closed.

5A. Lake Shore Railway Historical Society Museum (frame), the largest of its type in the tristate area, is located in the original Lake Shore & Michigan Southern Railroad station built in 1899. The station was last used as the depot for the New York Central Railroad. *Hours:* Mid-May–Labor Day: Wednesday–Sunday, 1–5 P.M. *Location:* Wall and Robinson streets.

5B. Franklin Paper Mill (stone remains) was erected in 1833 and operated until 1883. The miller's house is across the street from the mill site, in Paper Mill Hollow. Once owned by the Snyder family, it was later purchased by the Thompsons. *Location:* On North Mill Road off SR 0005 (Lake Road).

5C. Scouller Gristmill (stone remains), built in 1844 by John Scouller, was the largest gristmill in the county. *Location:* On North Mill

5E. Brown's Village Inn

Road. Remains of mill and spillway are best seen on left just before junction of North Mill Road and Sunset Drive.

Note: Also on Sixteen Mile Creek, within one mile of the center of North East, were a turning works, a table factory, a sawmill, a paper mill (see *Franklin Paper Mill*), a brewery, a cider and vinegar mill, and a tannery, among others.

5D. Robinson-Hampson House (brick) was built in 1834 by an architect, Royce Tuttle. Later it was sold to W. A. Robinson. In 1893–94 the Hampson family purchased it and lived there until 1967. It is now the property of an insurance agency. *Location:* 55 East Main Street.

5E. Brown's Village Inn (brick), a stagecoach stop which once served as a station on the underground railroad, was built in 1832 (Federal style) by Dyer Loomis, father-in-law of Bester C. Town, a prominent North East merchant who owned a number of general stores in the 1840s. Other early owners included Britton and Olson. It is now a bed and breakfast inn. Several other houses nearby were also constructed by Loomis. *Location:* 51 East Main Street.

6. Hornby School Museum (frame) is a restored one-room schoolhouse built in 1873. *Hours:* May–October: Saturday and Sunday, 1–5 P.M. *Location:* 2 miles west of Colt Station Road (SR 0430 and 10,000 Colt Station Road).

7. Middlebrook Church Site and Burying Ground, where an 1801 Protestant log church once stood, is still occupied by early nineteenth-century gravestones and a bronze marker. *Location:* 5 miles south of Colt Station, SR 0089.

8. Glass-Sprague House (brick) was built by John Glass, who erected the first iron foundry in the county at the mouth of Sixteen Mile Creek and was active in the underground railroad. Although the H. Churchill family occupied the house in 1865, it is again owned by the Sprague family. *Location:* Freeport, on SR 0089 (north of SR 0005) at junction of Old Lake Road.

Note: Spragues Beach, on SR 0089 near North East, was once a fishing village and is now a summer resort. It was at one time the last stop for Canada-bound slaves. Other interesting early buildings in the area include the Mary Stone house on SR 0089 and the Old Wine Cellar, now South Shore Inn, on SR 0089 (about halfway between US 20 and SR 0005).

9. Grimshaw Woolen Mill (stone remains) was built in 1845 by William Grimshaw, an expert weaver from Leeds, England. During the Civil War many blankets were made here for the federal government. Later the mill was converted to a winery, supplied first by water power, then by steam, and finally by gasoline. The Grimshaw family lived here for years. *Location:* 1 mile north of North East, on Curtis Road, close to SR 0005.

10. Dill House (brick) is a long Greek Revival structure, a former summer boardinghouse. The original section is the east end. The Victorian trim and porch have been removed. *Location:* 2 miles northeast of North East, at end of Dill Park Road.

11. Butt's Octagonal Barn (brick) was built by Alonzo Butt, who was born in 1827. His father, Wendell, a native of Virginia, settled here in 1817, buying 300 acres from the Holland Land Company. The structure is eighty feet in diameter, and has black walnut and black oak timbers eighteen inches square. A signature stone reads, "A. W. Butt 1879." *Location:* 2 miles northeast of North East, on Middle Road, between SR 0005 and US 20.

Note: Nearby on the property is a brick house constructed in the early nineteenth century.

12. Frog Pond Schoolhouse (frame) was built about 1820 on the farm of B. P. Spooner and used until 1955. The name was derived from the fact that when the fields became flooded in winter the children could skate up to the door. The school is now a private home. *Location:* 3 miles south of North East, on SR 0089 just south of Town Line Road.

11. Butt's Octagonal Barn

13. Corry Area Historical Museum includes among other items a restored Climax locomotive. *Hours:* Memorial Day–Labor Day: Saturday and Sunday, 1–5 P.M. *Location:* Corry, on Mead Avenue in Mead Park.

14. Mennonite Church (stone) is an early structure worthy of preservation. *Location:* West of Corry, east side of SR 0089 at Beaver Dam just north of where SR 0006 intersects SR 0089.

15. Union City

15A. Union City Historical Museum is a 100-year-old building housing collections that reflect the local history from frontier days to the space age. It is owned by the borough and maintained in cooperation with the Union City Historical Society. *Hours:* May–August: Tuesday–Saturday, 9:30 A.M.–4:30 P.M.; September–April: Tuesday–Saturday, 1–4:30 P.M. *Location:* 11 South Main Street.

15B. Humphrey-Rockwell House (frame) was built about 1840 by Dr. Jonas Humphrey, who came to Union Mills (now Union City) from New Hampshire. This Greek Revival home was later occupied by the Rockwell family. *Location:* 38 East High Street (SR 0006).

16. Waterford

16A. United States Fort LeBoeuf was built in 1794 by Maj. Ebenezer Denny under orders from Gov. Mifflin to protect from Indian attacks the state commissioners who were laying out Waterford and Erie. In 1796 Gen. Anthony Wayne further strengthened the defense already there by erecting another blockhouse, making a total of four. The last blockhouse at this site later operated as the

Fort LeBoeuf Hotel until it was destroyed by fire (see *Eagle Hotel*). Most of its foundation was filled in during 1973. This area is unique, for it was under three different flags at various times (see *Judson House*).

The George Washington Monument, dedicated in 1922 and originally erected on US 19, nearby, now overlooks the location of this fort. It is the only memorial of Washington as a young man in British uniform, as he delivered the message of the Virginia governor to the French.

Permanent exhibits on the colonial history of the area are at the Fort LeBoeuf Museum, administered by Edinboro University of Pennsylvania on behalf of the Pennsylvania Historical and Museum Commission. By appointment only. *Location:* On US 19 (High and First streets).

16B. Washington Sentinel Tree was the hemlock that, according to legend, Gen. George Washington climbed to reconnoiter the French Fort LeBoeuf in 1753 when Governor Dinwiddie of Virginia sent him to the French commander to deliver a message claiming the area for the British and demanding withdrawal of the French forces. As a result Washington was able to observe the fort and write a description of it. Though the tree, over 300 years old, is still standing, its top is missing after being struck by lightning. *Location:* On US 19, a quarter mile from Eagle Hotel (on private property behind supermarket).

16C. Eagle Hotel (stone) was built in 1826–27 (date on signature stone) by Thomas King. Its cut sandstone was quarried on Dr. Vere Worster's property. A stone opposite the signature bears the stonemason's name "E. [Ebenezer] Evans." Evans was a Welshman who built other stone structures in Erie. This fine example of Georgian architecture is the only stone house in Waterford and the oldest hotel that is still operating as an inn in the county. A large dance hall was constructed on the third floor. In 1868 a demented woman started a fire inside; it spread and destroyed Fort LeBoeuf Hotel (see also *United States Fort LeBoeuf*) along with other structures in town.

A wooden eagle, which identified the Eagle Hotel for years, used to be above the door and once stood on a pole near the road. According to legend, it was carved from a single block of wood by a vagabond in gratitude for having been allowed free accommodations. The eagle is now on display at the state museum in Harrisburg. In 1848 President Zachary Taylor was a guest at the hotel.

The Eagle Hotel has undergone restoration for a hotel/restaurant/museum. *Hours:* Eagle Hotel special events and third Sunday of month, 1–4 P.M. *Location:* On US 19, corner of High and First streets.

16D. Judson House (frame), of Greek Revival style, was built in 1820 by Amos Judson, who migrated from Connecticut in 1795. Judson was the first burgess of the town and a successful salt merchant. He was employed by Holmes and Herriott of Pittsburgh but later opened a store in this house, which was on the sites of French Fort LeBoeuf, built in 1753, and later of English Fort LeBoeuf, built in 1760, and near that of U.S. Fort LeBoeuf (q.v.) built in 1794. It is administered by the Fort LeBoeuf Historical Society. *Location:* On US 19 (31 High Street at First Street).

16E. Grave of Michael Hare, under a 300-year-old maple tree, has a burial stone that reads:

Michael Hare, born in Armagh County, Ireland, June 10, 1727, was in the French war at Braddock's defeat, served through the Revolutionary War, was with [Gen. Arthur] St. Clair and was scalped at his defeat by the Indians. Died March 3, 1843 AE 115 years, 8 months 13 days. Elizabeth, his wife, died March 3, 1813, AE 90 years.

Recovering from the scalping, he volunteered for service during the War of 1812 at the age of eighty-five. *Location:* Waterford Cemetery.

16F. Lindsley House (frame) was built in 1816 by Moses Himrod, who never lived in the building. It was first occupied by Jesse Lindsley, and for at least six generations this family lived in the home. To the north of it on the same side of the street is a structure covered with siding which formerly was a store with a blacksmith shop in the back. Both houses are private. *Location:* 660 High Street.

16G. St. Peter's Episcopal Church (brick) was built in 1832. The Old Waterford Academy, now gone, stood across an alley from it until 1954. *Location:* East Park.

16H. Brotherton House (frame), once a tavern, belonged to some early settlers, the Brothertons, an enterprising family that owned various mills in the area. This house was constructed in the mid nineteenth century. *Location:* On east side of Cherry Street above First Street.

174

16D. Judson House

17. Edinboro

17A. The Old Academy (frame) of the Northwestern Normal School founded in 1857, was originally built in 1856 at a cost of $3,200. It was used as an academy until 1859. On January 26, 1861, the state recognized the institution as a state normal school. By this time several other buildings had been constructed. The Commonwealth acquired the school in 1915. In 1926 it became Edinboro State Teachers' College, in 1960 Edinboro State College, and in 1984 Edinboro University of Pennsylvania. It is the oldest institution of higher education in Erie County and the second oldest state-owned college in Pennsylvania. *Location:* On Normal Street at Edinboro University.

17B. Eagle House (frame), once an active stagecoach tavern, was built in 1843 on the site of an earlier hostelry which had burned. In 1896 it became the Robinson house, and later was owned by an auto company. It later became a commercial business and barbershop. *Location:* 119 Erie Street.

Note: The frame Biggers house, once a hotel, was built in 1850 and is at 148 Meadville Street at West Normal Street. Also of interest is the frame Goodell house built in 1841 at 109 Waterford Street.

17C. Vunk House (frame) was built in the mid nineteenth century by Francis C. Vunk

and later owned by the Hencke family. A diner has been attached to it in later years. *Location:* On US 6 opposite restaurant (west of junction of US 6 and Edinboro road).

17D. Edinboro Pharmacy (brick) of Second Empire design with a two-dormer mansard type roof, was built for Dr. Sidney Hotchkiss in 1876. It was originally known as the Brick Drugstore. Two Erie County doctors developed well-known patent medicines: Dr. John S. Carter, known for Carter's Little Liver Pills, and Dr. Peter Hall, who developed Dr. Hall's Cough Remedy in 1848. *Location:* 107 Erie Street.

18. Juliet Mill Pond and a dam are the only reminders of Amos King's gristmill built in 1828. In 1840 W. H. Gray built a woolen mill here. Thomas and William Thornton later owned the property. *Location:* Albion, Main Street (north).

19. Old Country Store, formerly Amy's General Store, has been in business since it was built in 1872. *Location:* McKean Township, corner of West Road and Sterretania Road, SR 0832.

20. Girard

20A. Dan Rice Soldiers' and Sailors' Monument, a twenty-five-foot cylindrical marble shaft, was dedicated in 1865 to the memory of

Erie County Civil War servicemen who died in action. Dan Rice, America's most famous comic of the nineteenth century and a native of Girard, donated this monument, which is the earliest Civil War memorial in the county. *Location:* On US 20 in public square.

20B. Universalist Church (frame), of Greek Revival design, was organized a few years before 1850, and the building was erected in 1852. Rev. Charles L. Shipman, who was a leader in the underground railroad during the Civil War and organized the route from the Ohio River to Lake Erie, served this church for over twenty years. *Location:* Main Street.

20C. Methodist Church (brick), built in 1868, has a tower clock presented to the congregation in 1904 by the Battles family. *Location:* Main Street.

20D. Iron Front Building (brick), built in 1862, is now a jewelry store. *Location:* 223–25 West Main Street.

20E. Hazel Kibler Museum is operated by the West County Historical Society. It contains memorabilia of Dan Rice, a local circus owner and famous humorist of the 1850s. *Hours:* By appointment only. *Location:* 522 East Main Street.

20F. Battles Bank Farm Museum (brick complex) depicts rural life in northwest Pennsylvania from 1840 to the present. Rush Battles and his brother-in-law Henry Webster opened their banking business here in 1859. Around 1890, Rush Battles, then the sole owner, built the Battles Bank, which was not only fire proof but had an effective security system as well, due to its complicated safe. When President Franklin D. Roosevelt declared a moratorium during the Great Depression, this bank was one of the few that stayed open for business. Battles's daughter, Charlotte Elizabeth, owned the bank following her father's death. It later became the Girard Battles National Bank, followed by the Security Peoples Trust and Penn Bank before the historical society acquired it for a museum. Nearby on Tannery Road are several middle 1800s houses belonging to the Battles family and now part of this complex which is administered by the Erie County Historical Society. *Location:* 12 East Main Street.

20G. Hutchinson House (brick) was built in 1830 by Judge Myron Hutchinson. It has parapet walls and a later Georgian doorway with fan- and sidelights and a raised keystone. *Location:* 155 Main Street.

21. Fairview Township is located in the Erie Triangle. The Fairview Bicentennial Steering Committee of 1976 had published a tour guide of all the early noteworthy buildings in the community.

21A. Cemetery Chapel (brick), one story, built in 1902 by T. Woods Sterrett, a prominent area builder, has been chosen for restoration as a museum and depository. *Location:* Maple Avenue.

21B. Oriental Mills (frame), built by Thomas McCreary in 1869, operated as a gristmill until 1937. Another member of the McCreary family, Samuel, lived nearby in a Greek Revival frame house belonging to John Caughey around 1841. *Location:* Both mill and house are on Hathaway Drive before intersection of SR 0098 and SR 0005, near bridge.

21C. Schoolhouse (brick), built in 1878, was the first township building to have two rooms. *Location:* Intersection of Hathaway Drive and Avonia Road.

21D. Helen Weeks House (brick), originally owned by the Pettit family, was later occupied by Dr. Weeks who had her office and home here in 1898. Her husband, Welcome J. Weeks (also called Dr. Weeks) operated a store. Helen Weeks also practiced and owned property in Girard. *Location:* Avonia Road, near railroad station.

21E. Avonia Railroad Depot was built in 1852 when the first tracks were laid here. *Location:* Avonia, Avonia Road.

21F. Baptist Church (frame) was built in 1842 and has served four different congregations. It has been adapted for use as a factory as well. *Location:* Garwood Street (SR 0098) and Water Street.

21G. Rusterholz House (frame, Victorian vertical clapboard) was built around 1871 by the John Rusterholz family. *Location:* Intersection of Heidler and Millfair roads.

21H. Coach Tavern (frame and shingle) is reputed to have been built around 1818. *Location:* Swanville Road (US 20), east of Kahkwa Road.

21I. Remains of Erie Extension Canal, a canal bed still filled with water where the canal was in operation between 1844 and 1871. Here can be seen a viaduct across Walnut Creek (site of canal viaduct), a 700-foot span. A frame house nearby was a way station that accommodated canal travelers and bargemen and was the turnaround point for the animals. *Location:* Eaton Road, across first railroad tracks, evidence of canal trench.

Note: Another way station house is near the end of Tow Road (unpaved), across Dutch Road to second (southern end) of set of tracks.

21J. Wallace-Grossholz House (frame), a saltbox, is located on land once owned by William and Eleanor Wallace, who had purchased it from Col. Thomas Forster in 1815. In 1897 Adolph Grossholz owned the house and used the adjacent house (north side) as a loom house. An Indian burial mound in this area dates back to A.D. 600. "Mayside," Manchester area. *Location:* Dutch Road near SR 0005 intersection.

21K. Stone House (brick) was built in 1856 by George Stone who came to the area from Iowa. He was a merchant and postmaster of Avonia. His house was adapted as an orphanage by the B'nai B'rith prior to 1927. It later became an egg market. A large barn theater operated here in the 1930s and 1940s. Nearby is Lake Manchester, once the location of numerous mills. *Location:* Avonia, SR 0098.

21L. Presley Heidler House (frame, clapboard) was built around 1851. Nearby is a cemetery that dates back to the 1840s. A one-room schoolhouse, known as Kreider's, is also nearby on Kreider Road. *Location:* Ruhl Road (unpaved) and Kreider Road.

21M. Presbyterian Church was built in 1874. *Location:* Sturgeonville, northwest corner of West Water Street, across from Sturgeon House (historical society), SR 0098.

21N. Temple House (frame), a saltbox, was, according to tradition, the home of Dr. Frank Temple, grandfather of the actress Shirley Temple. Dr. Temple, it is believed, established a practice in Fairview about 1884. *Location:* Maple Avenue.

21O. Sturgeon House (frame), a saltbox, was built between 1820 and 1838, probably by Jeremiah Sturgeon. It was restored by the Fairview Area Historical Society as a museum, meeting room, and depository. By ap-

21M. Presbyterian Church

pointment only. *Location:* Sturgeonville, 4302 Garwood Street.

21P. Howard's Falls, a high, rocky gorge. *Location:* 5.5 miles south of Fairview, beyond Ryan's Hill on Mischler Road, just west of SR 0098.

Note: According to tradition Gudgeonville was named for a mill at the site where gudgeons (parts of cogwheels) were made. The Oxbow here at Elk Creek is a beautiful natural gorge.

22. Frances Miles House (brick) was built in 1832 on property which had two miles of lake frontage, adjoining the Holliday farm. Frances Miles's nephew, William B. Holliday, later occupied the house. A natural-gas well nearby has provided the energy for this house and others in the neighborhood ever since it was drilled in 1898. *Location:* North Springfield, on Miles Road.

23. Holliday House (frame), a saltbox, was built in 1806 by Capt. Samuel Holliday, who in 1796 had purchased 700 acres of land on Crooked Creek. This house replaced a log cabin where Holliday, his wife, and their six children had lived. Descendants of the family for at least six generations lived on the property. *Location:* Just north of North Springfield, on Miles Road just south of Miles house.

24. Triangle Marker designates the former (1786–87) northern boundary of Pennsylvania before the purchase of the Erie Triangle, acquired in 1792. Each of the stone's four sides displays a bronze plaque. The monument was erected in 1907. *Location:* 2 miles west of North Springfield and 2 miles east of Ohio line. Go north for 0.5 mile on dirt road from old Lake Road.

Previous Sites Now Lost

Cunningham House
Sacred Heart Mission House, demolished

Covered Bridges

Carman Bridge (ca. 1870) over Conneaut Creek, T 338 between Conneaut and Springfield townships
Gudgeonville Bridge (ca. 1868) over Elk Creek, T 460, Girard Township
Harrington Bridge (ca. 1870) over the West Branch of Conneaut Creek, SR 3003 between Conneaut and Springfield townships
Waterford Bridge (ca. 1875) over LeBoeuf Creek T 459, Waterford Township

Pennsylvania Historical and Museum Commission Markers

Anthony Wayne Erie, SR 0005 at Sixth and Ash streets
Canal Basin Erie, north end of State Street
Captain C. V. Gridley Erie, SR 0005 at East Lake Road
Cashier's House Erie, 417 State Street
Circus History Girard, US 20 at the Diamond
Climax Locomotives SR 0077 at south end of Corry
Colt's Station Colt Station, SR 0089 at SR 0430
Dobbins Landing End of Peach Street
Drake Well Park Union City, SR 0008

Edinboro State College Edinboro, US 6 and SR 0099 at College
Erie On main highways leading into city
Erie County Erie, at courthouse, West Sixth Street
Erie Extension Canal Asbury Chapel, US 20; and Platea, SR 0018
First Prebyterian Church Upper Greenfield, SR 0089 about 1.5 miles north of Lowville
Flagship Niagara Erie, at property on State Street
Fort LeBoeuf Waterford, US 19
Fort LeBoeuf Memorial Waterford, at property on US 19
Fort Presque Isle Erie, SR 0005 at Sixth and Parade streets
French Creek US 19 south of Waterford
George Washington Waterford, US 19
Harry T. Burleigh Erie, East Sixth Street
Ida M. Tarbell SR 0008 southwest of Wattsburg
LP-Gas Industry Waterford, US 19 at square
Old Custom House Erie, 407 State Street
Old French Road SR 0097 south of Erie
Old State Line Wattsburg, SR 0008; Strongs Corner, US 19; Middleboro, SR 0099; US 20 west of Girard; and SR 0005 east of North Springfield
Perry's Shipyards Erie, SR 0005 at Sixth and Cascade streets
Platea Environs SR 0018
Presque Isle Portage US 19 north of Waterford
U.S.S. Wolverine Erie, north end of State Street

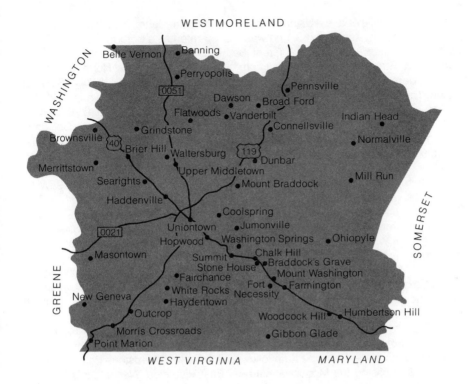

WESTMORELAND

WASHINGTON

Belle Vernon • Banning

• Perryopolis

0051

Dawson • Broad Ford

Flatwoods • Vanderbilt

• Grindstone

Brownsville

40 Brier Hill Waltersburg 119

Merrittstown

Searights •

Upper Middletown

Haddenville

Pennsville

Connellsville

Indian Head

Normalville

Dunbar

Mill Run

Mount Braddock

Coolspring

Uniontown • Jumonville

Hopwood Washington Springs • Ohiopyle

0021

• Masontown

Summit Chalk Hill

Stone House • Braddock's Grave

• Fairchance Mount Washington

• White Rocks Fort • Farmington

New Geneva Necessity

• Haydentown

• Outcrop

Woodcock Hill • Humbertson Hill

Morris Crossroads

• Gibbon Glade

Point Marion

SOMERSET

GREENE

WEST VIRGINIA   MARYLAND

Fayette County

Capsule History

Fayette County was named for the Marquis de Lafayette, a friend of the colonies in their effort to secure independence. It was erected out of Westmoreland County on September 26, 1783, and has an area of 794 square miles with a population of 159,417.

The county's early development was begun by the Ohio Company of Virginia, whose storehouse, The Hangard, was burned by the French after Washington's defeat at Fort Necessity. Christopher Gist, the first settler, arriving in 1754, was a friend of George Washington, who later owned land at Perryopolis. Pioneers started to migrate to the area from the South and from eastern Pennsylvania in 1758. In 1767 Henry and Thomas Beeson came to the area; they built a mill on Redstone Creek in 1772 and erected a blockhouse nearby in 1774. This area was first called Beeson's Mills, then

Beeson Town, followed by Union, and Uniontown; the latter was laid out in 1776, became the county seat in 1783, and was incorporated as a borough in 1795. Several old burial grounds, such as the Great Bethel Regular Baptist cemetery on South Morgantown Street and the Methodist cemetery at West Peter and North Arch streets, are reminders of early Uniontown churches. Fort Mason was built in 1774–78 by John Mason. The blockhouse was later moved to Main Street in Masontown in 1823.

Brownsville, founded by Thomas Brown who settled there before 1770, was near Redstone Old Fort. It was an early boat-building center. Fort Burd, built by Col. James Burd in 1759, was fifty yards from the Monongahela River at the mouth of Dunlaps Creek, one and a quarter miles above the mouth of Redstone Creek. In 1793 Zachariah Connell laid out Connellsville at the site of Stewarts Crossing on the Youghiogheny River, where Braddock's army had crossed en route to Fort Duquesne in 1755. William McCormick was the first settler in Connellsville in 1770. Perryopolis, named for Oliver Hazard Perry, was laid out in 1814.

Others prominent in the county's history were Albert Gallatin; Col. William Crawford, friend of Washington and owner of a plantation at the site of Connellsville; Dr. John Brashear; Philander Chase Knox (see *Knox House*); and Gen. George Catlett Marshall, U.S. army chief of staff.

Various Indian paths were located in the county. The *Catawba Path* entered Fayette near Laurelville, passing Prittstown and Connellsville; it followed much the course of US 119 past Uniontown, swinging southwest through Smithfield, Outcrop, and Gans and entering West Virginia near Point Marion. The *Warrior's Path* left the Catawba at Smithfield, running through New Geneva on the way to Moundsville, W.Va. Another branch of the Catawba Path followed the northern Redstone Path (see below) to Brier Hill, crossing the Monongahela near East Riverside. *Nemacolin's Path,* from Cumberland, Md., to the forks of the Ohio, followed much the course of the Braddock Road and US 40 to the top of Chestnut Ridge; there it turned through Jumonville to Mount Braddock and followed the Catawba Path to a point outside the county, near Mount Pleasant. The *Redstone Path,* to present-day Brownsville, had two branches, one following US 40 from Nemacolin's Path through Uniontown, the other leaving the Nemacolin's at Mount Braddock and running through Bute and Vances Mill to a junction near Brier Hill.

The Mason-Dixon Boy Scout Trail, dedicated in 1967, follows the original survey completed in 1767 by the English astronomers-surveyors. The old portage path cut by the Delaware Indian Nemacolin, later Braddock's military road, became the general course of the Great Cumberland National Road, built between 1811 and 1818 through the efforts of Albert Gallatin and Henry Clay. In the 1920s it became US 40. It extended from Cumberland, Md., to Wheeling, W.Va., passing through Uniontown and Brownsville in Fayette County.

The Monongahela River made possible the transportation of coal, and after the Civil War spur railroads were built into the county in order to tap natural resources. The Youghiogheny River was an important commercial waterway. In Connellsville flatboats were built for transporting salt, pig metal, hollow ironware, whiskey, and flour. Here the Connellsville Basin, containing the world's finest coking coal, was an early center of the coal and coke industry. At Perryopolis along SR 0051 are the remains of the world's largest single bank of coke ovens. The first beehive oven in America was designed and built in Connellsville in 1833. The county had twenty early stone blast furnaces.

Glass was an important early industry. On September 20, 1797, Albert Gallatin and Company established the first factory to produce glass in western Pennsylvania, and actual production started at the New Geneva works the following year. (The first glass factory built was O'Hara's in Pittsburgh, but glass was not produced there until 1799.) The New Geneva glass works, about a mile away on Georges Creek, moved to Greene County near Greensboro in 1807 because coal was more available there. The old American Window Glass Factory, which closed almost half a century ago, may be seen at the south end of Belle Vernon, between SR 0906 and Monongahela City.

Landmarks

1. Uniontown, founded at a sale of lots July 4, 1776, was laid out by Henry Beeson.

1A. Courthouse (stone), showing the influence of Richardson's courthouse at Pittsburgh (q.v.), was built in 1891–92 at a cost of $250,000. The first courts were held in a schoolhouse. An early courthouse of uncertain date and construction was sold at auction January 1, 1796, for £15 12s. 6d. The second, of brick, was built in 1797 at a cost of $1,362.53. It burned on February 4, 1845. A brick replacement, built the same year, cost $16,000. The adjacent stone sheriff's house and jail are located at the site of Henry Beeson's blockhouse. A statue of Lafayette is on display in the courthouse. It was carved out of poplar planks, pinned together, at the old West Schoolhouse (q.v.) in 1847 by David Gilmour Blythe, an important genre painter of western Pennsylvania. *Location:* Main Street.

1B. West Schoolhouse (log) was built about 1839 by a carpenter, Enos West. George Brown and Noble McCormick were early teachers. The school was restored for the area Girl Scouts and is owned by the Uniontown Service League. *Location:* 75 South Street.

1C. Beeson House (brick) was built in 1847 by Col. Isaac Beeson, a local merchant who owned a hammer and scythe factory. A historical plaque is on the side of this structure, which now serves as apartments. *Location:* Near corner of Union and West Fayette streets (on same side of street as Great Bethel Baptist Church).

1D. Mount Vernon Inn (brick) was built in 1785–86 by Jacob Beeson on a tract of land called Mount Vernon. The house remained in the Beeson family until 1831, when it was sold

1A. Statue of Lafayette at Courthouse

to Daniel Moore, who gave the house to his daughter Mrs. Lucius Stockton. Stockton, the manager of the National Stage Lines (Good Intent Lines) named the house Ben Lomond and added to it. In 1855 Judge Samuel A. Gilmore purchased the property. It became known as Bliss House (or Hill) after his daughter Mrs. Lida Bliss inherited it. Her family resided there until 1946 when it was established as an inn. *Location:* Junction of US 40 (Main Street), Fayette Street, and Mount Vernon Avenue.

Note: The apartment building on the corner across from the inn is the site of the log house built by Henry Beeson and later the home site of Princess Lida (née Nichols) of Thurn and Taxis, a niece of J. V. Thompson (see *Oak Hill*).

1E. Playford House (brick) was the home of Robert W. Playford, heir to a coal fortune, who killed his wife and five children and himself in this home, due to financial losses during the

1B. West Schoolhouse

Depression. The mansion, with a widow's walk on top, is now St. Anthony's Friary of the Franciscan order. *Location:* 115 Oakland Avenue.

1F. Frank M. Seaman Mansion (painted brick), with a large front one-story portico, was originally owned by Frank M. Seaman, one of J. V. Thompson's partners, who escaped the coal baron's ruin by withdrawing his personal holdings just before the crash in 1915. The house, formerly facing Ben Lomond Street, was the scene of fabulous parties. The owner once hired the New York Metropolitan Opera Company to entertain on the lawn in a circle lighted by auto headlights. *Location:* 30 Mont View Street.

1G. Highland House Hotel (brick), a four-story building measuring 50 by 150 feet, was founded in 1900 by George F. Titlow and was originally called the Titlow. During Prohibition days the old hotel was run by a Dr. Reagan. In 1970 Charles May purchased it from the Reagan family and restored it. *Location:* 92 West Main Street.

1H. Douglas House (brick) was built in 1901 by John S. Douglas (1856–1902), a director of the National Bank of Uniontown. In 1887 he established a real estate and insurance business in the community. This house is now a funeral home owned by Thomas M. Dolfi. *Location:* Walnut Street and North Gallatin Avenue.

1I. Theophilus Bowie House (brick) was the home of a local tin- and coppersmith who built

this five-bay house around 1840. *Location:* 44–46 Union Street.

Note: The old Conn family mansion is at 84 Ben Lomond Street. This street has many early homes of coal operators and entrepreneurs.

1J. General George C. Marshall's Birthplace, is the present site of the VFW Home. Marshall, a five-star general during World War II, was secretary of state and defense under President Harry S. Truman, author of the Marshall Plan, and a winner of the Nobel Peace Prize. (The George C. Marshall Library and Museum honor this hero in Lexington, Va.). *Location:* 142 West Main Street.

1K. Old Settlers' Cemetery, on ground donated by Henry Beeson, founder of Uniontown, in 1795, contains the graves of many pioneers and original settlers. Neglected for many years, it was renovated by the Uniontown Area Historical Society and is now maintained by the city. *Location:* On hill overlooking the courthouse, at corner of Penn Street and Bailey Avenue.

2. Oak Hill (Mt. St. Macrina) (brick) was built in the early 1900s by multimillionaire coal baron, financier, and banker Josiah Van Kirk Thompson, who died a pauper. Today this palatial estate is owned by the Sisters of St. Basil, a Byzantine Rite (Greek Catholic) order. It serves as a sanctuary for the devout, aged, and ill and is visited each fall by 100,000 worshipers from all over the United States and Canada who attend the pilgrimage to the Shrine of our Lady of Perpetual Help. A newer mansion, Fox Hill, also part of the complex, was owned by Thompson's son Andrew. *Location:* About 1 mile west of Uniontown, on US 40.

3. Jasper Thompson House (brick) was erected about 1850. Thompson was collector of internal revenue and commutation funds under Lincoln, serving two terms. J. V. Thompson (see *Oak Hill*) was born here in 1855. *Location:* 2.5 miles south of Uniontown, off SR 0021.

4. Searight's Tollhouse (brick) is one of two remaining National Road tollhouses. Originally there were six on the Pennsylvania section of the road (see *Petersburg National Road Tollhouse,* Somerset County). This hexagonal structure was built in 1835, after the road was returned to the state, and was used until 1905. The building has been restored (1966) and is operated by the Uniontown Area Historical Society under the direction of the Pennsylvania Historical and Museum Commission. *Hours:* Daylight Saving Time: Weekdays except Monday, 8:30 A.M.– 5 P.M.; Sunday, 1–5 P.M.; Winter: Weekdays except Monday, 9 A.M.–4:30 P.M.; Sunday, 1–4:30 P.M. *Location:* Near Searights, 4 miles northwest of Uniontown, on US 40.

Note: The Annual National Pike Festival, the longest festival in the United States (in mileage), spans an 89-mile stretch of US 40, the nation's first federally financed highway. Events of the festival are planned and presented by various communities along the highway from Cumberland, Md., to Wheeling, W. Va., late in May. The original section of the road, built from 1811 to 1818, connected Cumberland with Wheeling. The federal government turned the road over to the states in 1839 when it could no longer maintain it. The states erected tollhouses and the National Pike became the nation's first interstate toll road, later US 40.

5. Searight's Tavern (remains) was built about 1819 by Josiah Frost. John Gray managed it for a time. He held a memorable political gathering, known as "Gray's meeting," here in 1828. Prior to 1840 many Democratic county meetings and conventions were conducted here. William Searight took over the management in 1821 and his family maintained it at least until 1894. Searight, one of the wealthiest men in Menallen Township at that time, also owned a wagon shop, a blacksmith shop, a large livery stable, and a general store, and operated the post office. He was appointed road commissioner from 1842 to 1852. Other owners were John Risler, Matthias Fry, Joseph Gray (John's son), and two men both having the name of William Shaw but not related. This house, halfway between Uniontown and Brownsville, served as a drovers' stop. It was destroyed by fire in 1944, and the ruins can be seen along the road. The property surrounding the foundation has been excavated by archeology students from California State College. *Location:* Searights Crossroads, on US 40, north side of road.

6. Grace Episcopal Church (brick), built in 1840, is now used as a barn for storing hay. Nearby is the old cemetery, which contains a 1799 stone. The first church (log) was built before 1793. In 1794 Robert Jackson, who had come to the area in 1790, donated the land and most of the money for the construction of the brick church. *Location:* 5 miles west of Uniontown, on US 40.

7. St. Maximilian Kolbe Shrine. This shrine, in St. Thomas Roman Catholic Church, honors a Polish priest who gave his life to save others in the German concentration camps of World War II. A museum here has pictures and maps of the Holocaust. It also honors the American soldiers who liberated the camps and lists the names of those from Fayette County. *Location:* Footedale, SR 3023 (German Township).

8. Johnston-Hatfield Tavern (stone) was built in 1816–17 by Randolph Dearth for Robert Johnston, who kept a tavern here until 1841. William Hatfield operated the inn from 1852 to 1855. He began his career as a blacksmith and formed the iron barrier gates for tollhouses along the pike. *Location:* About 2 miles west of Searights, on US 40.

9. Peter Colley Tavern (stone), one of the oldest inns still standing on the National Road, has a signature stone which reads "P. & H. Colley, 1796." The original bar, complete with a wooden grill, is intact in the interior. Peter Colley, an early settler and father of Abel, who also owned a tavern (see *Abel Colley Stand*), was reputed to have been the first innkeeper on the National Road to have literally made and displayed a barrel of money. He was born aboard a ship near Philadelphia in 1757 and ran this tavern from two decades before the National Road was built until his death in 1838. Later owners were his son George, Solomon Crumrine, D. Ramsey Woodward, and the Brier Hill Coal Company. The land was excavated by archeology students from California State University, who discovered that the original road was ten feet in front of the tavern doorway, not built to established standards. They also uncovered sites of a granary and a bake oven. An early barn is included with this inn on the National Register. *Location:* Brier Hill, on old US 40.

Note: Brier Hill has one of the smallest post offices in the country, 12 by 12 feet.

10. Wallace Tavern (stucco over stone) was first kept by Arthur Wallace prior to 1840. Later Isaac Baily operated it, before he became postmaster of Brownsville and a lawyer. Then George Craft owned the house, but he was not a regular tavern keeper. At one time the eccentric "Jackey" Craft owned it. He was known for "starting out over the road in a sleigh with bells, when there was no snow on the ground." *Location:* Brier Hill, on north side of US 40 west of the Peter Colley Tavern.

11. Abel Colley Stand (stone) was run successfully as a favorite tavern by Abel Colley, though it had been kept by several earlier owners. Abel built a brick house across the road where he retired. His wife Nancy is remembered as a large, amiable woman who habitually wore a Queen-Anne-style cap. Their son W. Searight Colley later lived in the brick farmhouse. Abel's father Peter also operated a tavern east of here (see *Peter Colley Tavern*). *Location:* 1 mile west of Brier Hill, on the north side of US 40.

12. Sharpless House (stone), built by Jonathan Sharpless, who settled here sometime after 1793, is located across from the site of the first paper mill west of the Allegheny Mountains. The mill was built by Sharpless and Samuel Jackson on Redstone Creek at the mouth of Washington Run in 1794–97 and destroyed by fire in 1842. *Location:* East of Grindstone, on SR 4028. House is situated next to railroad tracks at Jefferson Township line.

13. Wilkes Brown Tavern (stone) was built in 1805 by the son of Basil Brown and operated until 1830. A signature stone on an addition at the back is dated 1817, the year before the National Road opened. This was a drovers' tavern, and from its immense size it must have had a good trade. *Location:* South side of US 40, 0.7 mile east of US 40–SR 0166 Brownsville bypass.

14. Brubaker Tavern (brick) was sold by David Auld in 1826 to a Somerset County "Dutchman" who kept it until his death except for a brief time when it was operated by Alexander R. Watson, who ran an omnibus line between Uniontown and Brownsville. It was later called the White Pillars Hotel, after pillars were added. *Location:* Near Brownsville, on US 40, almost at bypass at top of Brownsville Hill (0.6 mile west of Wilkes Brown tavern).

15. Brownsville, the site of Redstone Old Fort (an early Indian fortification) and an early boat-building center and river town, was laid out in 1785.

15A. Nemacolin (Bowman's) "Castle" (brick) was begun in the 1700s and incorporates the original stone trading post constructed by Jacob Bowman in 1787–89 (another section in 1850). Containing twenty-two rooms, hallways as long as seventy feet, marble-mantled fireplaces, fine glass chandeliers, and an open circular stairway, this Tudor-style edifice, sometimes known as Nemacolin Tower in honor of an Indian chief, overlooks the Monongahela River. About 1795 President Washington had appointed Bowman the first postmaster of Brownsville, and he served till 1829. Bowman founded the Monongahela Bank in 1812 and served as its president until 1843. This castlelike structure is operated by the Brownsville Historical Society. *Hours:* Closed Mondays except holidays. *Tours:* 1–4:30 P.M. *Admission charge. Location:* Facing Front Street.

15B. Black Horse Tavern (stone) was the location of a meeting, "the first public act in the Whiskey Insurrection," held July 27, 1791. Here David Bradford and others looted mailbags taken by force. The last meeting of the local insurgents was also conducted here August 28 and 29, 1794. Amos Wilson was an early innkeeper. The house has been completely altered and modernized. Private residence. *Location:* On Front Street next to Nemacolin's Castle.

15C. Brownsville Academy (stone) was built as a private residence by George Boyd about 1812. It was later leased by the Episcopal church for a women's seminary, established in 1866 by Charlotte Smyth. In the 1880s it housed a free-lance publishing company. At another time O. K. Taylor, the president of the Brownsville National Bank, owned the property. *Location:* Front Street.

15D. Knox House (stucco and brick) was the birthplace of Philander C. Knox in 1853. Knox served as U.S. senator and secretary of state under President William Howard Taft. *Location:* Junction of Fourth Avenue and Front Street.

15E. Shreve House (brick) was the home of Henry Shreve, a boat builder who in 1814 constructed the *Enterprise,* the first steamboat to return to Pittsburgh after going to New Orleans. Shreve also invented a method of removing tree stumps from rivers which kept boats from being snagged and sunk. Shreveport, La., was named for him. *Location:* Junction of Front and Third streets (below Brownsville Academy).

15F. Brashear Tavern (stone) was built about 1796 by Basil Brashear. When Lafayette visited Brownsville in 1825, he addressed the citizens from the door of this house. Basil's grandson John A. Brashear, astronomer and educator, was born here in 1840. The tavern was later owned by James Searight and by Westley Frost. It is now a beer distributor's shop, and the front door has been altered as an access to a garage. *Location:* 519 Market Street (old US 40).

15G. Christ Protestant Episcopal Church (stone) was organized in 1785 and at first was served by missionaries. Robert Davis was rector from 1795 to 1805. The congregation purchased property from Charles Wheeler in 1796 and in 1815–23 erected the first building. The present church was built in 1856. Thomas Brown, the founder of Brownsville, is buried near the church door. The brick manse built about 1825 has been restored nearby. *Location:* Church Street and Fourth Avenue.

15H. St. Peter's Roman Catholic Church (stone), patterned after a village church in Ireland, was dedicated April 6, 1845. A fine example of provincial Gothic architecture, it overlooks the Monongahela River and is reached by a long flight of steps. This church was built on the site of an earlier brick house of worship, erected by Father Patrick Rafferty in 1827 and destroyed by fire in 1842. *Location:* 300 Shaffner Avenue at Church Street.

15I. Bar House (brick), now the Barr Hotel, stands at the site of the old Kimber house. The present structure was operated as a tavern for many years by Ephraim H. Bar. Other proprietors were Robert Carter (an old wagoner), Thornton Young, George Garrard, Matthew Story, Eli Bar, and W. F. Higinbotham. *Location:* Bridgeport section of Brownsville, on Water Street at bridge.

15J. Old River Captain's House (brick and stone), of unusual construction, looks out over the Monongahela from a hillside. It was built about 1855 and has a front portico. *Location:* 322 Catherina Avenue.

15K. Early Fieldstone House is located next to the Grable blockhouse site. The blockhouse was built in 1788 at the corner of Lewis and Woodward streets. *Location:* 710 Lewis Street.

Note: Another early stone house, located behind St. Andrew's Church, next to the parking lot at High and Angle streets, was originally servants' quarters for the T. S. Wright family.

15L. First Cast Iron Bridge west of the Allegheny Mountains, a National Historic Civil Engineering landmark, was built in 1836–38 (dedicated 1839) at a cost of $39,901.63. It was designed by U.S. Army engineer Capt. Richard Delafield and constructed by iron-

15L. First Cast Iron Bridge

master John Snowden (Brownsville foundry). This eighty-foot single-arch structure spanning Dunlaps Creek is still in use as an integral part of the Brownsville business section. It was nicknamed the "neck" because its thirty-foot width used to cause a bottleneck on US 40. It remains a relic of a period when it provided means for immigrants to continue their trek south and west on the Monongahela and Ohio rivers—from Cumberland (Wills Creek), Md., to Brownstone (Redstone), Pa. William Searight did the stone work for this structure. *Location:* Market Street (old US 40).

Note: The first iron-chain suspension bridge in the United States was also in Fayette County, built by James Finley in 1801 over Jacobs Creek on the Connellsville–Mt. Pleasant Road. This structure has been replaced by the present bridge at the site. A marker commemorating it is located in the Connellsville quadrangle on SR 1027. Another county landmark bridge is the steel Pratt truss style one at Redstone Creek north of Uniontown.

15M. Union Station Building (brick), five stories, reflects the growth of rail transportation during the early twentieth century. *Location:* Market Street.

15N. Stone Arched Railroad Bridge was erected about 1920 by the Monongahela Railway Company. *Location:* Brownsville Avenue.

15O. Plaza Theater (brick and stone), of Beaux Arts style, was built about 1920. It reflects the peak period of the town during the coal and coke boom. *Location:* Brownsville Avenue.

15P. Central Presbyterian Church (brick) was adapted in recent years as a Masonic Lodge. *Location:* High Street.

Note: Other historic buildings in the area include the former Monongahela National Bank, the former post office building, and the former Arcade Theater.

16. Jackson House (stone covered with stucco) was built in 1785 by Maj. Samuel Jackson, a Quaker. He was a banker, farmer, miller, and boat builder who bought property here in 1777 adjoining land belonging to Thomas Brown and Andrew Linn. More than five generations of heirs have lived in the house. Nearby was the site of the Ohio Company's warehouse, The Hangard. The old brick Forsythe house is a short way north on the same road. *Location:* Jefferson Township, at mouth of Redstone Creek near Brownsville on SR 4003.

17. Maxwell Locks and Dam, completed in 1965 and operated by the U.S. Army Corps of Engineers. This five-gate high-lift dam creates an elevation of 1915 feet. The twin chambers locks on the right bank are 84 feet wide and 720 feet long. *Location:* On Monongahela River at Maxwell, on SR 4022, 5 miles southwest of Brownsville.

18. Penncraft, a self-help village from the Depression days, was launched when the American Friends Service Committee bought 200 acres on Bull Run Road on June 1, 1937, and settled ten unemployed miner families here. Houses, mostly of stone, were built on a traded-work basis; and a knitting mill and cooperative store were launched with thirty-one members and a capital of $165. Within ten years seventeen families had built homes, 165 acres were added, and the store had 550 members and a capital of $22,000. *Location:* 4 miles south of Brownsville, on Bull Run Road (Luzerne Township).

19. Hopewell Presbyterian Church (brick) was organized as Cumberland Presbyterian in 1832, and the present structure was built forty years later. *Location:* Between Merrittstown and Penncraft on SR 4020.
Note: Just south of this road, about a half mile west, is West Bend United Methodist Church, organized in 1830 and built about twenty years later.

20. Merrittstown and area. North of Merrittstown at SR 0166 are the remains of the Allison Coal and Coke Works which include 283 ovens, a tipple, and a company store, originally owned by W. J. Rainey, Inc. South of Merrittstown at Newboro is a frame flour and feed mill which served the mines of the area.

20A. Dunlaps Creek Presbyterian Church (stone) was organized by Rev. James Power in 1774. (About this time Laurel Hill Presbyterian Church on SR 4010 at T 656 near Waltersburg, q.v., and Tyrone Presbyterian Church off SR 0819 on SR 1061, q.v., were also founded by Power.) Rev. James Dunlap was installed in 1782 as the first regular pastor. The present church was completed in 1814 with extensive remodeling done in 1887. In 1962 the panes in all the windows were replaced with stained glass. About 0.2 mile east of this structure just off SR 4020 is the cemetery, partially enclosed by a stone wall. The site of the first log meetinghouse was half a mile away near the creek. *Location:* At junction of SR 4024 and SR 4020.

20B. Dunlaps Creek Presbyterian Academy (brick) was founded in 1848 and completed in 1849, during the pastorate of Samuel Wilson. It ceased to exist as a school in 1896, and in 1908 the academy trustees turned it over to the church. The restored building (remodeled 1969–73), used for many purposes over a period of years, continues to serve the recreational needs of the church and community. *Location:* 0.2 mile west of Merrittstown crossroads, on SR 4020.

20C. Old Manse (stone) was probably built before 1800 by Jacob Jennings, lifetime physician and pastor of Dunlaps Creek Church from 1792 until 1811. It continued to be used as a manse for more than sixty years after his death in 1813. *Location:* Between crossroads and post office.

20D. Darnell House (frame and stone) was begun by Caleb Darnell. A log section, replaced by a frame one after a fire, was built before 1790. The stone part was constructed no later than 1810. It has been owned by the Moore family for more than 160 years. *Location:* Across from post office.
Note: The Moore blacksmith and wood shop (brick) south of Merrittstown (west of SR 0166) is a fine representative of an early nineteenth-century industry.

20E. Coleman House (stone) was built by Elijah Coleman, who ran a tannery nearby. A frame portion was added later. The Conwell family has owned it since about 1820. *Location:* Just south of post office.

20F. Hibbs House (stone) is an early building worth preservation. *Location:* Between crossroads and post office.

21. Fredericktown Ferry (see *Fredericktown Ferry,* Washington County) is the last inland river ferry in Pennsylvania. Since 1972 it has been jointly owned by Fayette and Washington counties. For many years there were six such crossings in eleven miles of river just above Brownsville. They were, in order, Jacobs', Davidson's (later called Arensberg's), Rices Landing, Millsboro, Fredericktown, and Crawford's. *Ferry hours:* Monday–Friday, 6 A.M.–10 P.M.; Saturdays and Sundays on request to Fayette County commissioners. *Ferry toll. Location:* East Fredericktown (near LaBelle) on T 300, off SR 4020 at SR 4022 junction (Luzerne Township).

Note: In the early years of the telegraph there was a line from Brownsville to offices at Jacobs' and Davidson's ferries.

The brick house at the Davidson site (T 306 and T 307 at Arensberg) was built by Samuel Davidson in 1852. It and the ferry were bought in 1890 by Louis F. Arensberg and operated by him until 1915. For almost half a century the house was heated with gas from a nearby coal mine.

22. Old Mennonite Church (brick). *Location:* Near Masontown, off SR 0166 (German Township).

23. Jacobs Lutheran Church (brick). Services here are said to date from 1773, in a log church built at an uncertain date. This church was organized about 1793 by Rev. John Stough. Like many others, it was used by both Lutheran and Reformed congregations until 1854. The present brick building, according to a signature stone, was built in 1846. A small replica of the original log church has been erected in the adjoining cemetery. *Location:* 0.5 mile east of intersection of Shoaf and High House roads, 2 miles from Masontown.

Note: An early log house is at the intersection of Shoaf and High House.

24. Old Stone House. *Location:* SR 3002 near Gans and Lake Lynn, off SR 0857 at Springhill Furnace Church.

25. New Geneva was founded by Albert Gallatin, who became secretary of the treasury under Thomas Jefferson.

25A. Harmony House (stone) was built by Col. George Wilson in 1773 as a wedding present for his son John, who married Drucilla Swearingen in 1775. (Swearingen's Fort was in Springhill Township near the Cheat River.) Wilson was the founder of Wilson Port, later renamed New Geneva by Albert Gallatin. This home was later operated by the Harmony family as a tavern called the Harmony House. Succeeding owners have been the Gans family, George Hager, and Harry Riffle. As a tavern the Harmony House prospered when New Geneva was an important river port. *Location:* 65 Ferry Street.

25B. Stone Inn, in disrepair, has a double wooden front porch and may have been owned by the Wilson family. *Location:* Junction of SR 0166 and SR 3003.

Note: Across the street is a brick house built about 1856 with a fine doorway, and next to it is the old Davenport general store, built earlier.

25C. Old Stone Church was erected in 1810–11. Adjoining it is a walled-in cemetery. Soldiers from the Revolution, the War of 1812, the Mexican War, and the Civil War are buried here. The building has been used by the Methodists, Baptists, and Presbyterians as a place of worship. *Location:* Near SR 0166 on hill above main section of New Geneva.

Note: Hunter's mill, a large stone structure, was built by Andrew Oliphant and later operated by Samuel Hunter. It was originally part of the Sylvan Mills industry. The complex included a sawmill, an iron forge, and an oil well. *Location:* On Georges Creek, southeast of New Geneva, west of US 119.

26. Friendship Hill (brick, frame, and stone), a national historic site, was built above the Monongahela River between 1789 and 1823 (last section built in 1902) by Albert Gallatin (1761–1849), who had migrated from Switzerland and joined the side of the colonies during the Revolution. At Wilson Port, which he renamed New Geneva, he built a log store and with his company laid out the town in 1797, after purchasing two tracts of land in 1786 (Friendship Hill) and in 1795 (New Geneva) from Nicholas Blake. In 1789 he and his bride Sophia Allegre moved into their new home, which he called Friendship Hill. Due to his wife's death five months later and his dedication to public service, Gallatin spent little time here until he retired. He owned the property from 1786 to 1832.

Gallatin served as representative to the State Constitutional Convention, was a member of the U.S. House of Representatives, was secretary of the treasury under Jefferson and Madison, served as chief U.S. diplomat for the promulgation of the Treaty of Ghent ending the War of 1812, and was minister to France and Great Britain. Between 1831 and 1839 he was president of the National Bank of

26. *Friendship Hill*

New York. In addition, he established the American Ethnological Society and was one of the founders of New York University. He operated a gun factory (established in 1799 and operated until 1801) and also a glass works founded in 1797.

A new wing of stone was added to the house by his son Albert Rolaz Gallatin in 1823. Lafayette addressed 1,000 guests from the building's second-story balcony in 1825. In 1832 Albert, Sr., sold Friendship Hill, and it passed through several ownerships including those of Albin Mellier, Representative John L. Dawson, and coal baron J. V. Thompson (see *Oak Hill*).

Gallatin and his second wife, Hannah Nicholson, whom he married in 1793, are buried in Trinity Churchyard in New York City. His first wife's unmarked grave is surrounded by a stone wall in the woods at Friendship Hill. This landmark is now operated by the National Park Service. *Park hours:* Memorial Day–Labor Day: Daily, 9:30 A.M.–5 P.M.; other months, weekends only. *Location:* 1 mile south of New Geneva and 4 miles north of Point Marion, on SR 0166.

27. St. John's Evangelical Lutheran Church (brick) was built in 1854 by "Col. Alex. Crow" (according to the signature stone above the door). The building now serves the Pentecostal Apostolic church. A cemetery is across the road from the church. *Location:* At

Morris Crossroads turn off US 119 and go east 0.5 mile on SR 3002.

Note: Nearby at Morris Crossroads is an old hotel that has been a landmark for many years.

28. Oak Grove Church of Christ (brick), one-story, was built in 1861–63. The organization of the church stemmed from the "New Lights" movement which originated in Springhill Township about 1820 with converts of Peter T. Lashley, a minister. At that time William Gans and his cousin George Gans and their families worshiped in their homes and became some of the first members to support this church. *Location:* Morris Crossroads, US 119.

29. Hayden House (stone) was built before 1836 by John Hayden (1749–1836), the ironmaster at the Haydentown furnace. Hayden, who served in the Revolution, came to the area in 1784 and was the father of twenty-four children. He donated the land for the cemetery at Little Whiterock Methodist Church. Nearby Haydentown was named for him. In Hopwood (q.v.) is another Hayden house. An old stone dwelling, possibly his work, is situated at the Mountain Road Bridge in Fairchance, behind the site of the log Nixon Tavern, torn down about 1940. *Location:* On Mountain Road, 0.2 mile south of Little Whiterock Methodist Church.

30. Polly Williams Grave

32. Fort Gaddis

Note: Nearby is the small stone H. C. Frick Company building, a survivor of the Fairchance coal mine. The company controlled the town during the mine's heyday. This industrial landmark is located in the Kyle housing development in Fairchance. Also in this area, at Outcrop, is an early double stone house that is worthy of preservation.

30. Polly Williams Grave is the burial site of Polly (Mary) Williams, who was thrown to her death in 1810 from a sixty-foot cliff, now called White Rocks. Her unfaithful lover Philip Rogers was brought to trial and acquitted. The legend has been perpetuated by ballads and prose tales. A stranger traveling through the area heard the story and carved the following on a stone:

Polly Williams
1792–1810
Behold with pity you that pass by,
here does the bones of Polly Williams lie,
who was cut off in her tender bloom,
by a vile wretch, her pretended groom.

(The original stone was chipped away by souvenir hunters and replaced with another in 1910.) A historical novel entitled *White Rocks,* written in 1865, relates this story. Both Polly and Philip lived near New Salem. *Location:* Village of White Rocks, south of US 40 near Hopwood, in Little Whiterock Methodist Churchyard. (White Rocks can be reached by trail going up mountain from fishing lodge near small lake at northeast end of Fairchance.)

31. Tent Presbyterian Church (brick) acquired its name from its first services which

were held in an arbor, along what was then the old Catawba Indian Trail. In 1791–92 a log structure was erected. It was replaced by the present church in 1878. *Location:* 4 miles south of Uniontown, on US 119.

32. Fort Gaddis (log) was erected on the Catawba Trail in 1774 by Thomas Gaddis, one of the founders of Great Bethel Baptist Church in Uniontown and third in command under Col. William Crawford in the fatal campaign against the Indians in 1782. The stockade around the cabin is no longer standing. Within it were three springs. Basil Brownfield, a relative of Gaddis, built an addition to the dwelling and lived there for many years, as did his descendants. This fort is the only one remaining in the county. It is reputed to have been attacked by Indians several times. In recent years students from California State University have excavated the site. *Location:* 2 miles south of Uniontown, 300 yards east of US 119, at historical marker.

33. Hopwood, originally Woodstock and later called Monroe after President James Monroe visited here in 1816, was founded by John Hopwood (an aide-de-camp to George Washington) in 1791. This mining and coke-producing center at the base of Chestnut Ridge consists of six original stone houses and other early dwellings along the National Road, in addition to modern structures. A signature stone on one of these stone houses reads, "Wm. Morris September the 7th 1818." (The Morris family also operated a brick tavern—the Morris Hotel, built in 1874—in the community.) The stone structure, an inn, was later run by Joseph Noble, Andrew McMasters, and German D. Hair. Another stone building bears the inscription, "Hayden 1839"; at one time Benjamin Hayden operated a store here. The stone post office—fire department building was an early inn. John Fair was the carpenter for many of the early Hopwood houses, and Gabriel Gretadamzer was the principal stonemason. *Location:* East of Uniontown, on US 40.

34. James Barnes Estate (frame) was built in 1906–07 for $1 million by Barnes, one of J. V. Thompson's partners who, like Thompson, went bankrupt as a result of a business deal. A stone gazebo, now in disrepair, is situated by a stream running through the once beautifully landscaped grounds. *Location:* East end of Hopwood, south of US 40.

Note: South of this property on Mountain Road are other interesting log, brick, and stone houses.

35. Watering Trough is located at a well-known spring where travelers still stop to refresh themselves with mountain water, as they have since the early pike days. Here William Downard lived in a stone house (now gone) against the hillside, but did not keep it as a tavern because of lack of land for a wagon yard. He maintained the water trough, although Thomas B. Searight in his book *The Old Pike* states that Downard was eccentric and begrudged use of the water by those he disliked. *Location:* East of Uniontown, on US 40, two-thirds of way up Summit Mountain.

Note: A later tavern is in the area of Downard's homesite and next to the watering trough. Remains of the old Turkey's Nest Tavern are visible south of US 40, one-third of the way up Summit Mountain (Chestnut Ridge) east of Uniontown, before reaching the watering trough. Once a fine tavern, it was destroyed by fire about 1940. It derived its name from a wild turkey's nest found by road workmen constructing the original pike.

36. Mount Summit Inn (masonry and frame) is located on the site of two previous buildings. One of them, the old Summit House, had been an early popular summer resort which formerly belonged to Col. Samuel Evans. He was followed by Ephraim McClean, Henry Clay Rush, Brown Hadden, Stephen Snyder, John Snyder, William Boyd, Leo Heyn, and Webb Barnet. Mount Summit Inn was built about 1900 as another summer resort. In 1936 the eight-foot-square bed of John Gilbert, idol of the silent movies, was purchased and brought here for the honeymoon room.

Location: 6 miles east of Uniontown, at summit of Chestnut Ridge on US 40.

37. Laurel Caverns, visited as early as 1800, are the largest natural formation of their kind above the Mason and Dixon line. Called Dulaneys Cave prior to 1940, the caverns were developed extensively in 1962. Located on top of Chestnut Ridge, they contain unusual limestone formations, and their entranceway provides an excellent view of seven counties. Open all year. *Admission charge. Location:* 5 miles south of Mount Summit Inn, on SR 2001.

38. Fayette Springs Hotel (stone), now called the Stone House, was built in 1822 for Congressman Andrew Stewart by masons who had erected the bridges along the National Road. After Stewart's death the property was sold to Capt. John Messmore, followed by Cuthbert Wiggins, John Risler, B. W. Earl, Samuel Lewis, William Snyder, William Darlington, John Rush, Major Swearingen, Redding Bunting, Cuthbert Downer, and others. It was a favorite resort of visitors to the Fayette Springs, about three-quarters of a mile away, and many parties of young people from Uniontown visited the hotel during its halcyon days. Marah Ellis Ryan wrote *A Pagan of the Alleghenies* while staying here. *Location:* Midway between Summit and Chalkhill, on US 40.

39. Downer House (brick) was begun in 1823 by Jonathan Downer, taking seventeen years to build. The Downers had been on their way to Kentucky from Philadelphia when winter set in. After the father had helped his five sons build a log house, he went to Kentucky but was never heard of again. Later, about 1790, the boys erected a small stone house on the Braddock Road near Orchard Camp. After Jonathan built the brick house, he moved the stone one across the road next to it. (This village was named for white clay found when the National Road was built in 1818.) *Location:* Chalkhill, on US 40.

40. Braddock's Grave is marked by a granite monument surrounded by an iron fence and a grove of evergreens. A footpath north of this site leads to the spot where Maj. Gen. Edward Braddock was buried beneath a tree, later called "Braddock's oak," located in the twenty-three-acre Braddock Memorial Park. Here on the west side of the Great Meadows was Braddock's Orchard Camp where his army stayed June 25, 1755, and where he was brought (July 13) after being fatally wounded in the battle of the Monongahela. His body was buried in the roadbed, traces of which can still be seen, and wagons were driven over the grave to keep the Indians from finding it. In 1804 a party of road workers led by Andrew Stewart (later a congressman) removed Braddock's remains and placed them at the present site, south of the original grave. Some of the bones were later sent to Philadelphia. The Braddock Park Association was formed in 1909, and the twelve-foot-high monument at the second grave was unveiled in 1913. *Location:* About 10 miles east of Uniontown, on US 40 (about 1 mile west of Fort Necessity Museum).

41. Mount Washington Tavern Museum (brick) was built by Judge Nathaniel Ewing in 1827–28 on a 134-acre tract which George Washington owned from 1770 to 1799 and recommended as "an exceeding good stand on Braddock's road, from Ft. Cumberland to Pittsburg, and besides a fertile soil, possesses a large quantity of natural meadow, fit for the scythe." The tavern was a popular stagecoach stop for the Good Intent Line. Subsequent proprietors were James Sampey (1833–44), John Foster, and James Moore. It was owned by Godfrey Fazenbaker in 1855. After the business closed, Ellis Beggs purchased the property, followed by Godfrey Fazenbaker. In 1932 the state bought it, and in 1962 the National Park Service acquired it as part of Fort Necessity National Battlefield. On the grounds is a Conestoga wagon, and inside the building (restored to 1830–50 period) are displays of artifacts and other memorabilia. *Hours:* Winter: Weekends only; remaining months: Daily, 10:30 A.M.–5 P.M. *Location:* On US 40, just west of Fort Necessity park entrance.

42. Fort Necessity National Battlefield was begun in May 1754 by the Virginia militia commanded by Lt. Col. George Washington. The stockade was quickly finished at the Great Meadows natural clearing, which Washington later bought. On May 28 Washington and his troops had killed or captured a party of ten French soldiers, whose leader Coulon de Jumonville (see *Jumonville Glen*) was among the slain. On July 3, Washington and his men suffered a retaliatory attack by the French and Indians led by Jumonville's half brother, Capt. Louis Coulon de Villiers. After Washington evacuated the fort on July 4, the French burned it. This battle was a prelude to the opening of the French and Indian War, which ended in 1763 with the expulsion of French power from North America.

In 1933 the Fort Necessity National Battlefield was established under the National Park Service. Excavations were carried out under the direction of Jean C. Harrington in 1953, and it was discovered that a circular stockade about fifty-three feet in diameter had been built here instead of a rectangular one as previously surmised. A replica of the original was later built on the site. It is believed that within the battlegrounds are buried the unknown soldiers killed in the action. A modern round structure on the property provides a visitors' center where visual aids depict the events of the battle. *Park, fort, and visitors' center hours:* Daily, 10:30 A.M.–5 P.M. *Admission fee. Location:* 11 miles east of Uniontown, just south of US 40.

43. Rush Tavern (stone), once a stand for the Stockton Mail Line and later covered with a brick facade, was built on the National Road in 1837 by Judge Nathaniel Ewing. Soon after its completion Sebastian "Boss" Rush moved in as a lessee of Ewing's, ran the stagecoach establishment, and later purchased it, operating it until his death in 1878. Rush was appointed superintendent of the road and was township constable. He entertained many distinguished and interesting persons, including P. T. Barnum and the Swedish singer Jenny Lind. Before this tavern was built there had been a frame inn on the site operated by "the widow Tantlinger."

The house, privately owned and closed to the public, contains the reconstructed bar, and old graffiti were found on the wall under the layers of wallpaper. The 1841 ledger of the National Road Stage Company and the 1858 hotel license of the Rush Tavern are preserved in the Mt. Washington Tavern. *Location:* Farmington, at junction of US 40 and SR 0381.

44. Canaan School Museum (frame) is a one-room schoolhouse built in 1878. The building also served as a church until 1943 and was closed in 1955. Maintained as a museum, it is operated by the Retired Teachers' Association of Fayette County. The structure was restored in 1971, and its original bell is still intact in the belfry. A fine spring is located across the road. *Hours:* May 30–September 30: Weekends, 1–4 P.M. *Donation. Location:* East of Uniontown, south of US 40 on SR 2007, 0.6 mile south of Gibbon Glade Post Office.

45. Gorley's Lake Hotel (masonry and frame), erected in the 1920s, was a famous landmark for years. Now called Oak Lake, although the lake has been drained, it houses the Society of Brothers, which maintains a toy factory and a publishing company here. *Location:* 0.5 mile east of Farmington, on US 40.

46. John Stone Tavern (stone), built on the John E. Stone farm, was an early National Road house first kept by William Shaw, followed by William Griffin, Charles Kemp, Isaac Denny, and William A. Stone. It was later operated by Job Clark. At one time a large carriage house and stables were located across from the house. *Location:* 3.5 miles southeast of Farmington, on south side of US 40 at crest of western slope of Woodcock Hill (near Braddock Road "Twelve Springs Camp" marker).

47. Brown Tavern (stone) was built in 1826 by Thomas Brown, who operated it until the time of his death. Brown, a good fiddler, entertained prominent guests who came here on sleighing excursions. After the Brown family owned the property, Jacob Umberson bought it. The elections of Henry Clay Township were held in this house. *Location:* About 7 miles southeast of Farmington, on south side of US 40 just west of its junction with SR 0281.

48. Ohiopyle Falls in the Youghiogheny River was a site reconnoitered by George Washington on his first military expedition in May 1754, while looking for a clear-water passage for ordnance and supplies from his Great Meadows Camp. Washington's party was forced ashore at these falls, where the river drops sixty feet within a mile. Today this beautiful historic site is part of the nature reserve of the Western Pennsylvania Conservancy. Ohiopyle State Park (18,463 acres) offers rafting, hiking, biking, and nature trails. More than 100 acres known as the Ohiopyle Peninsula are located within the loop of the Youghiogheny at the falls. *Location:* Ohiopyle.

Note: Other natural landmarks in the area include Ferncliff Park, also operated by the conservancy, on SR 0381, and Keister Park at Cucumber Falls, on SR 2019, 0.5 mile southwest of Ohiopyle Falls.

49. Bear Run includes a 1,500-acre environmental center run by the Western Pennsylvania Conservancy which offers guided tours and lectures. Founded in 1931, the conservancy acquires and preserves land and presents educational programs to teach the importance of conserving water, land, and life systems. Ohiopyle is one of its land acquisition programs. A large modern building contains the library, offices, and assembly/display rooms. *Hours:* Daily, year round. *Location:* 0.5 mile north of Fallingwater on SR 0381.

50. Conservancy Farmhouse (frame) was built about 1871 by Ross Tissue. In 1940 Edgar J. Kaufmann bought the property, where the tenants ran a dairy business for him. In 1963 the late Edgar Kaufmann, Jr., gave the farmhouse to the Western Pennsylvania Conservancy, and when that agency started tours of Kaufmann's famous Fallingwater (q.v. below), the farmhouse was used by college students who worked as tour guides. In 1968 the farmhouse was remodeled by the conservancy for the director of the nature reserve. The headquarters for the Bear Run Nature Reserve are in a restored barn. *Location:* Between Mill Run and Ohiopyle, next to Bear Run Nature Reserve on SR 0381.

51. Fallingwater (sandstone and concrete) at Bear Run Valley, "the most successful example of American architectural design" (Forum of American Institute of Architects, 1986). It was designed and built by Frank Lloyd Wright in 1936 for Edgar J. Kaufmann, Pittsburgh department-store owner. This impressive building, architecturally ahead of its time, features bold cantilevered construction. Perched on gigantic boulders over a rushing waterfall, it blends with the mountainous terrain. It was completed with a guest and service wing in 1939. One of Wright's most widely acclaimed works, this masterpiece was the weekend retreat of the Kaufmann family until 1963. At that time Edgar J. Kaufmann, Jr., donated the property and an endowment was provided by the Kaufmann Charitable and Education Foundation to the Western Pennsylvania Conservancy as a memorial to Edgar and Liliane Kaufmann. Opened to the public in 1964, it is maintained as a cultural center. *Hours:* April–November: Tuesday–Sunday, 10 A.M.–4 P.M. Reservations required. *Admission charge.* A child-care center is provided for visitors' children under twelve. A visitors' pavilion presents the history and early graphics of the site. *Location:* 3 miles north of Ohiopyle State Park, off SR 0381 (Mill Run address), on Bear Run.

52. Indian Head Railroad Station, once a coal company store, in later years was and continues to be operated by the Resh family as a general supply store. *Location:* Indian Head, near Seven Springs Resort.

51. Fallingwater

53. Mill Run, near Indian Creek Valley Railroad and historic Killarney Park.

53A. Ora May House (log), once owned by Samuel and Catherine (Enfield) Nicholson, was built in 1856. Ora May and her family moved here in 1915. The hand-hewn structure is held together with wooden pins. *Location:* About 2 miles from Mill Run, on Hampton Road.

53B. Stickel House (frame), commonly referred to as the "big house," was probably erected during the 1860s by a Dr. Gallagher who operated a tannery. This ownership was followed by those of William Dull, Meade Hutchison, A. C. Stickel, and Glenn Work. *Location:* Mill Run, on SR 0381 across from old post office (now a store).

53C. Indian Creek Stone Bridge was built near the early logging town of Indian Creek by Fred Dahl, a stonemason. Although the bridge is still in use by the B&O Railroad, nothing remains of the nearby lumbering village along Indian Creek except a few foundation stones where the Stickel general store and the McFarland Lumber Company were located. The lumber mill's floating pond for logs can still be seen along the creek and the railroad tracks. *Location:* 1,000 feet down a private road where the Youghiogheny meets Indian Creek (about 2 miles from a church camp).

53D. Livingston Store (frame) is the oldest continuously operating store in the community. It was built in 1880 by August and Fred Stickel and called A. C. Stickel and Company. Purchased by Frank Livingston in 1912, it continued to serve as a general mercantile store. It is now an antique shop. *Location:* Main section of town, SR 0381.

53E. Indian Creek Valley (ICV) Scenic Railway was conceived in 1982 to provide a four-mile trip through the Laurel Highlands on a motorized train using the old railroad bed of a 1908 coal and lumber railroad. The engine was built locally. The frame B&O station was moved from its original location in Confluence and is now a restaurant station. The dining room section is an 1890s general store moved from Mill Run. It is operated through the cooperation of the Westmoreland Water Authority and the Western Pennsylvania Conservancy. *Hours:* May–October (closed Mondays, except holidays). *Train schedule:* 11, 12:30, 2, 3:30, 5. *Location:* Runs between Mill Run and Normalville, both on SR 0381.

54. Dunbar is a town with most of its fine buildings still preserved. It has high potential for a historic district.

54A. Dunbar Railroad Station (brick), built with a curved facade to conform with the angle of the road, is of unusual design and should be preserved. It is situated on Dunbar

Creek. *Location:* East Railroad Street beside the tracks at Connellsville Street.

Note: Nearby is a fine brick flatiron building.

54B. R. W. Clark Building (brick) is a four-story Italianate structure built in 1881 along the railroad tracks. *Location:* East Railroad Street.

54C. Methodist Episcopal Church, now Wesley Methodist Church, was built in 1902. *Location:* Connellsville Street.

54D. Second Empire Building (brick), in George III style with Italianate eyebrow windows and a slate mansard roof, is a fine five-bay building worth preserving. *Location:* Behind Methodist church on Church Street.

54E. Early Stone House, three-bay, built in the late 1700s or early 1800s, is an important landmark in this historic town. The type of construction and facade is similar to the Peter Colley Tavern, q.v., built in 1796. *Location:* Across from Presbyterian church on Connellsville Street.

54F. Presbyterian Church (frame) is a picturesque Carpenter Gothic church, important to the town's character. *Location:* Connellsville Street.

54G. School (stone) is an early one-story building, a landmark worthy of preservation. It is now owned by the Boy Scouts of America. *Location:* SR 1053 and SR 1055 at Dunbar Creek.

54H. Rose House (stone), across from the schoolhouse, is an early double house with sections built at two different times. *Location:* At Dunbar Creek, SR 1055 and SR 1053.

55. Connellsville, named for Zachariah Connell.

55A. Crawford House (log), constructed in 1975 by the Connellsville Historical Society and Fayette County Manpower program, is a reproduction of Col. William Crawford's home on his plantation, called Spring Garden. Crawford, who settled here in 1769, was a lifelong friend and adviser of George Washington and was Virginia's licensed surveyor for the West. He was an outstanding officer in Dunmore's War of 1774 and in the Revolutionary War. On the Allegheny River he built Fort Crawford, which was named for him by Gen. Lachlan McIntosh. Crawford took an active part in the 1778 campaign against the western Indians, helped defend Westmoreland County in 1781, and was burned at the stake in the Sandusky expedition of 1782. His son, John, sold the original tract of land in 1787 to Edward Cook, who later transferred it to Isaac Meason. *Hours:* Memorial Day–October: Sundays, 2–5 P.M. *Location:* North Seventh Street and US 119, at old Youghiogheny River fording path.

Note: A statue of Crawford stands on the lawn of Carnegie Free Library.

55B. Carnegie Free Library was built during the peak years of the coal and coke industry in the town. The building, in Italian Renaissance style, was financed through Andrew Carnegie and was completed in 1903. *Location:* South Pittsburgh Street.

55C. PL&E Railroad Stations, one used for freight and the other for passengers, are located on SR 0711 (West Crawford Avenue). The frame station, at the junction of SR 0711 and US 119 south, was built in 1913 with a slate roof. It is now used as a produce market. The brick station, with a tower that is connected to the high-level railroad tracks, has a green tile roof and today functions as a motor shop. It is located at the junction of SR 0711 with North Seventh Street.

Note: Between the two stations at SR 0711 and US 119 north, is St. John's Roman Catholic Church (brick), in Romanesque style, built in 1899.

55D. United Presbyterian Church (stone), in Gothic style, was built in 1915. The congregation was organized in 1831. The building contains six stained glass windows which were produced in Germany by the Von Gerichten firm in the early days of World War I. The ship transporting the windows at that time was escorted by a German submarine. They were assembled at the company's studio in Columbus, Ohio. *Location:* South Pittsburgh and Green streets.

55E. Colonial National Bank (stone) was built near the turn of the century. It is an outstanding Greek Revival building. *Location:* SR 1037 and SR 0711 (Pittsburgh Street at Crawford).

Note: Other noteworthy early buildings in this section of the town include an 1893 brick three-story building; an 1892 brick building at the bridge (date stones on both).

55F. First National Bank (brick), six stories, organized in 1876, was built in French Renaissance style in 1900–03. Constructed of

55H. David P. Cummings Monument

pink Milford granite, white marble, and brick, it was designed by Mowbray & Uffingen of New York. The facade is surmounted by a copper cornice. In 1903 an Italian bank and a steamship agency were located here. In 1913 the Wright-Metzler department store also operated in the building. In later years it became the Troutman Store. *Location:* 125 West Crawford Street (SR 0711).

55G. Zachariah Connell Grave, a memorial marker for the founder of Connellsville, laid out March 21, 1793. *Location:* East Francis Avenue near East Crawford, on the outskirts of town.

55H. David P. Cummings Monument was dedicated by the Cummings family to commemorate the young hero who died at the Alamo in March 1836. David Cummings graduated from Jefferson College in Canonsburg, Pa., during the early stages of the Texas War for Independence. At the earliest opportunity, he went to the scene of the activity and was one of the 172 men garrisoned at the fort known as the Alamo. These men held off the 4,000 men of Gen. Santa Anna for eleven days. On March 6, 1836, the fort was captured and not a soul escaped alive. *Location:* Hill Grove Cemetery, lot no. A43, on Snyder Street 1 block from US 119 north (Crawford Avenue).

55I. Hughie Cannon Grave is the burial site of a songwriter born in Detroit in 1875. His most famous song was "Bill Bailey Won't You Please Come Home?" which he wrote at age sixteen. His mother, Mary Smith Robbins, was an actress who moved to Connellsville in 1902 where she managed several theaters. Hughie died in 1912. *Location:* Hill Grove Cemetery, lot no. E305, on Snyder Street 1 block from US 119 north (Crawford Avenue).

55J. Olympic Oak. This oak tree is one of only six English oaks *(Quercus robur)* surviving of the twenty-six seedlings brought to the United States and presented by the German Olympic Committee to the athletes who participated in the 1936 Berlin games. This seedling was presented to John Y. Woodruff, an African-American and a Connellsville native, who won a gold medal in the 880-yard dash. The tree was permanently planted at the north end of the stadium close to the track where John Woodruff ran as a high-school athlete. *Location:* Campbell Field (built in 1938) at Falcon Stadium on Arch Street.

55K. CSX (Chesapeake, Seaboard) Railroad Yard. This is an active yard where one can see freight trains being assembled, an operating turn table, and remnants of an older round house. *Location:* Falcon Stadium, near Arch Street.

56. Leisenring, a coal and coke "patch," or town, was established about 1881 by the Connellsville Coke and Iron Company. The duplex houses have unique saltbox style roofs. *Location:* Dunbar Township, southwest of Connellsville.

57. Thomas Graham House (stone), in Greek Revival style, was built about 1820. *Location:* SR 1051 and SR 1047, between Leisenring and Monarch.

58. Tyrone Presbyterian Church (brick), built in 1871, was dedicated May 4, 1873. The original log church was built on land patented in 1787 by John Stewart and known as Pleasant Garden. The second meetinghouse was also built of logs, before 1800. The church is one of the four founded by Rev. James Power in 1774, the other three being Laurel Hill, Dunlaps Creek, and Middle Church (the last is in Mt. Pleasant, Westmoreland County). Next to the church cemetery is a one-room schoolhouse. *Location:* Near Dawson, off SR 0819 on SR 1061.

59. Strickler House (stone), now restored, was built about 1798–1810 by Jacob Strickler on a tract originally consisting of 394 acres. The patent was issued in 1787 as "Plantation Tinian." Strickler purchased the land in 1769 and constructed the house on the site of a log cabin. Over the years this dwelling has been used as a farm building, workshop, and partly as a smokehouse. It is now owned by the Oliver family. *Location:* South of Scottdale, on Primrose Path, off SR 0819, north of Tyrone Presbyterian Church.

60. 1803 Stone House includes the date stone in its construction. It was once owned by the Keister family. *Location.* Dry Hill, SR 1038 and T 785.

61. Keister House (brick), built by Solomon Keister and later owned by the Rush family, was named Creekline Farms. This dairy farm, owned by Alfred Rush, was part of the original Keister property and site of Jacobs Creek Post Office in 1843. The old Keister gristmill, built in 1842, once stood near the bridge into Scottdale. *Location:* Scottdale-Dawson Road, SR 0819.

62. Peter Newmyer Farm, settled by German immigrant Peter Newmyer, is an early nineteenth-century farm complex which includes a stone barn, rarely found in western Pennsylvania, and an early five-bay brick house. *Location:* Pennsville, SR 1027 and SR 1066.

63. Brotherhood House (brick) is reputed to have been the meeting place of the Pennsville Mennonite congregation before and during the time when its brick church was being constructed in 1852. This house, later owned by the Albright family, is located on what was known as the "Moreland place" and also the "Ganier place." *Location:* Pennsville, 1 mile south of Mennonite cemetery.

64. Pennsylvania Railroad Station (frame) has a later addition, the Henry Clay Frick laboratory, but both are early buildings. Twelve crews used to pull out of this station at one time. *Location:* Everson, near railroad tracks, Graff Street.

65. Rist House (brick) was built in 1852 by Peter Rist. His father, John, was a Mennonite pioneer who settled in the area around 1790. According to tradition, Peter's wife Sally carried stones in her apron to help construct the wall surrounding this farm, which was later purchased by the Benzio family. *Location:*

About 2 miles north of Connellsville and about 1.5 miles northeast of Broad Ford, on Narrows Road (Bullskin Township).

66. Smith House (brick) was built in 1795 by Jacob and Catherine Galley Smith, a Mennonite couple who raised eleven children on this farm. A small stone structure built earlier than the brick house now serves as a storage building on the property. *Location:* 0.5 mile south of Rist house, on Narrows Road (Connellsville Township).

67. Abraham Overholt and Company Distillery (brick) was established before 1834 by Abraham Overholt, son of Henry, who came here in 1800. Abraham improved his father's stills and built a grain mill in 1834. The present buildings were erected in 1899. *Location:* Broad Ford, near Connellsville.

68. Brick House, built in 1832, was the residence of Abraham Overholt's grandson Henry Clay Frick while he worked at the distillery. The smaller red brick house next to it was the former post office. (See also *Henry Clay Frick Birthplace,* Westmoreland County.) *Location:* Broad Ford, near Overholt Distillery.

69. Meason House on Christopher Gist's Plantation (cut sandstone), an outstanding Georgian home at Mount Braddock, was built in 1802 by the English architect Adam Wilson for Isaac Meason, the leading ironmaster in the region. Meason owned the Plumsock Iron Works on Redstone Creek in 1815. The main house, with a center hall flanked by one-story servants' quarters on one side and an office wing on the opposite, is one of the finest examples of early post-Colonial architecture still standing in western Pennsylvania. In 1803 it won high acclaim from Francis Asbury, bishop of the Methodist Episcopal church.

The land originally belonged to Christopher Gist, who built a log house there in 1753. Gist and the Ohio Company intended this area to be the first permanent English settlement west of the Allegheny Mountains, but French occupation of the Ohio in 1754–58 prevented this. This estate, called Mount Braddock, is the site of Maj. Gen. Edward Braddock's encampment on June 27, 1755, while en route to Fort Duquesne. He died at Orchard Camp on July 9. Call for tour. *Location:* About 6 miles northwest of Uniontown, off US 119.

Note: On January 6, 1816, in the *Pittsburgh Gazette,* Isaac Meason of Mount Braddock advertised for sale his iron works to which was attached "an excellent Stone Coal Bank," probably the first captive coal mine in the country. (About one-quarter mile north of Mount Braddock are the Fayette County Fairgrounds.)

70. Shady Grove Park contains an early dance pavilion, one of the largest swimming pools in the state, concessions, and rides. This landmark was established in the early 1900s. *Location:* Northeast of Uniontown, 0.5 mile east of US 119 on SR 1055 via SR 1020.

71. Millstone Quarry, "Zebley Flats," is one of southwestern Pennsylvania's few remaining millstone quarries. Abandoned for over 150 years, this mountain acreage rock outcrop is now covered by mountain laurel and oak. Some of the millstones are still attached to the virgin rock, from two to four feet in diameter, of conglomerate rock (sandstone and limestone) left from the glacial period. A millstone sometimes took a week to complete, after which it would be transported by oxcart to a gristmill. *Location:* Zebley Flats, between headwaters of Dunbar and Limestone creeks. This may be reached up Dunbar Creek (dirt road to right above seventh fording, near gamelands maintenance building) or from Jumonville Glen. Area is large and quarry may be hard to find.

72. Jumonville Glen, sometimes referred to as Jumonville's Rocks, was the site of George Washington's first combat (May 28, 1754) in which one of his Indian allies killed the French commander Coulon de Jumonville (see *Fort Necessity*). Jumonville's grave is in a glen in the area. Here also is a plaque in memory of the only man whom Washington lost in the skirmish.

The area near the glen later became the site of a Civil War orphans' home, at which time the present stone buildings were erected. It operated here from 1875 to 1880, subsidized by the U.S. government. It had previously been organized in 1866 at Madison College in Uniontown. The property is now a training center and camp owned by the Western Pennsylvania Conference of the United Methodist church and encompasses 275 acres and forty buildings. (The glen is administered by the National Park Service.) *Hours:* Mid-April–October: 10 A.M.–5 P.M. *Location:* On SR 2021, 3 miles north of US 40 at Summit. A private road leads to some of the sites.

72A. Great Cross, a 60-foot steel cross (which replaced a wooden one) weighing 35 tons, was erected on Dunbar's Knob in 1950, on a 183-ton, 8-foot-high base. Three states

can be seen from this point. The road leading to the cross is scattered with fossils which attest to the area's having been under the sea at one time.

72B. Whyel Chapel (stone), built in 1882, was formerly a Lutheran Evangelical church. Now a chapel, it was dedicated to the memory of Florence Williams Whyel, the wife of Harry Whyel who donated the campsite in 1941.

72C. Faculty Lodge (frame) was one of the original buildings from the orphans' school.

72D. Various stone buildings are classic examples of post–Civil War architecture. (As late as 1939 the YMCA operated a summer hotel called Washington Lodge in one. In 1939 it became a Works Progress Administration training school for young women.)

72E. Dunbar's Campsite was used during June and July of 1755 by Col. Thomas Dunbar, who was in charge of artillery for General Braddock's army. At Braddock's defeat, Dunbar destroyed the supplies and retreated. A small cannon was cast from metal artifacts discovered here, and it was used for morning and evening signals when the orphans' home operated. The site is a few hundred yards off Jumonville Glen.

72F. Half King's Rocks is the spot where Tanacharison, Delaware Indian chief and friend of the English, met with Washington at the Jumonville victory.

72G. Washington Spring, once a landmark, is now in disrepair.

73. Coolspring Stone House was possibly erected by Thompson McKean, who built the Coolspring Iron Furnace before 1820 on Shute's Run. The cut stone from the exterior of the furnace stack was used to build a water reservoir for Uniontown. The furnace was near Coolspring, off SR 2021 at the reservoir. *Location:* Coolspring, off SR 2021.

74. Three Gaddis Houses, all located near Upper Middletown, were built between 1790 and 1820. The Gaddis family were among the first settlers in Fayette County (see *Fort Gaddis*).

   a. John Gaddis House (fieldstone with quarried-stone corners) is a very early structure with an outside fireplace and lintels above the doors and windows. There are large stone chimneys at both gable ends of the house. It was erected by John Gaddis (1741–1827) who had bought 295 acres of land he called Gaddistown. A log house nearby dates back to 1856. *Location:* Near Upper Middletown, on SR 4010 west.

b. Thomas Martin Gaddis House (quarried stone) is a later house built by T. M. Gaddis. It is a two-bay structure with a stone porch added later. An old stone smokehouse is in the rear. This house was purchased by the Kelley family. *Location:* Near Upper Middletown, on old PA 51, 0.6 mile north of SR 0051.

c. Thomas Martin Gaddis House (stone) is another early Gaddis home that has stone keystone lintels above the windows and doors and is a two-bay structure. *Location:* Near Upper Middletown, 0.2 mile south of other T. M. Gaddis house (0.3 mile off SR 0051, on old PA 51, turn west for 0.7 mile to house on left side of road).

75. Sickle House (cut stone) was built at an uncertain date near the bridge over Redstone Creek. A stone wall is in front of this house, and a porch was added about 1940 on one side. Peter Sickle owned the property at one time, followed by H. W. Hamilton. *Location:* North of Waltersburg, on old PA 51 at Redstone Creek bridge.

76. Laurel Hill Presbyterian Church (brick) was built in 1892. First founded in 1774, the church earlier had buildings at this site dating from 1782 and 1852. In an adjacent cemetery is buried Col. James Paull (1760–1841), a Revolutionary War soldier. *Location:* SR 4010 at T 656, Franklin Township, near Upper Middletown.

77. Associate Reformed Church site and cemetery are behind Laurel Hill Church. *Location:* T 656 just north of T 615.

78. Osborne Log House (covered with aluminum and modern stone) was built in 1790 by Abraham Osborne, Sr. This house, with a central chimney, was built over a spring. Abraham is buried at the Grace Episcopal Church cemetery. The home was later owned by the Holloways, Todds, and McGinnesses, in succession. In 1886 the property was sold to James Vail, followed by Porter Ewing. *Location:* Near Upper Middletown, on SR 4010.

79. Wetzel-Shanefelter House (fieldstone) was covered with stucco in 1913 and scored to resemble cut stone. There are single-stone lintels above the windows and solid interior walls. It was owned by A. J. Wetzel in 1872. A nearby stone house, later owned by the Duff family, belonged to G. W. Wetzel. *Location:* About 9 miles north of Uniontown, 0.4 mile off SR 0051 on SR 4030.

80. Hazen House (cut stone) was built in 1847. The date stone, now obliterated, was found on the chimney. Large stone lintels are above the windows. The family of Abraham and Jacob Hazen owned this property from 1847 to 1941. In 1939 one of their tenants murdered his wife and stepdaughter here with a knife and then shot himself. *Location:* Spillway Lake, on SR 0051 south of Perryopolis.

81. Patterson-Blaney House (stone) was constructed on a tract of land called Reservation. It was granted to James Patterson in 1785, with a patent two years later. Once called the Old Shotwell Mansion, it was built between 1775 and 1785, with a porch added in 1937. The home was later purchased by Harold and Kate Blaney. *Location:* Just south of Perryopolis, on west side of SR 0051.

82. Three Harris Houses still remain from an early period. *Location:* All northwest of Perryopolis, on Fairhope Road, a short distance off old PA 51.

a. Original House (log) was built by Jacob Harris, who came to Fayette County about 1798. It is of log construction, covered with aluminum siding, and has been added onto through the years. Here, about 1940, social workers found a five-year-old girl who had been tied in an attic chair and fed only on a bottle all her life at the behest of her grandfather, Isaac Harris, because she was her mother's second illegitimate child. This "second-sin-baby" case created worldwide attention. Placed first in a foster home and then in Polk State School, the girl appeared to be developing well but died of pneumonia after about two years. *Location:* At top of hill to right, about 0.5 mile from road junction.

b. Large Brick House was built by Jacob Harris about 1823. Its interior has been considerably altered, and its exterior has been given a modern appearance with tall white pillars. *Location:* On left just before road starts up hill (second house to right, west of 1798 house).

c. Another Brick House, built for a son James about 1840, is not far away on same road.

83. Perryopolis Historical Sites. Perryopolis, named for Commodore Perry, the naval hero of the Battle of Lake Erie, was incorporated in 1814. Ever since it received an inheritance from the estate of Mary Fuller Frazier (see *Fuller House*), the town has been very active in historical restoration. Unfortunately, this activity has dwindled in recent years. However, America's Industrial Heritage Project plans to restore the area's important industrial sites.

83A. Country Store (weatherboarded log) was formerly the Gue house and is now owned by the borough. It is used by the Boy Scouts. *Location:* Circle and Independence streets.

83B. Snyder House (frame) once belonged to J. Buell Snyder, congressman during Franklin D. Roosevelt's administration. As chairman of War Department appropriations, he did more than any other person to prepare the nation for World War II. *Location:* On Liberty Street across from post office.

83C. Fuller House (frame), originally the Becky Bishop house built in the 1860s, was formerly owned by Alfred M. Fuller. He and his brother were among the largest owners in the stockyards of New York, Philadelphia, St. Louis, and Boston, and first in the field as exporters of American livestock to Europe, initiating the shipment of frozen meat. Fuller, a millionaire, was the largest landowner in Fayette County in 1912. Although not a member of any church, he bequeathed funds impartially to various churches in the area. In 1882 Fuller married Margaret Coleman (whose sister Lucy married Andrew Carnegie's brother Thomas). Mary Fuller Frazier, daughter of Alfred, was born in this house. She willed over $1.5 million to Perryopolis and its schools. *Location:* On Circle Street between South Liberty and East Independence streets.

83D. Old Stone Bank housed one of the oldest banks west of the Allegheny Mountains and one of the few state banks. In 1816 the Youghiogheny Bank of Pennsylvania was established here. Following a bankruptcy in 1820 the building was established as a school, but during Andrew Jackson's administration it was again used as a bank (1829–37). It was later used again as a school, and as a Methodist church, a store, a poolroom, a fruit store, a doctor's office, an insurance office, and a restaurant. In recent years it became a private residence. *Location:* On South Liberty Street.

83E. Early Schoolhouse (frame), built in 1865, is now the VFW *Location:* Washington Street near blacksmith shop.

Note: Next to the shop is an early cemetery with Revolutionary War graves.

83F. Sisley Blacksmith Shop (frame), one of the few surviving structures of its kind, is located near an old Revolutionary War cemetery and the old Malta Hall schoolhouse. *Location:* Washington Street near Union Street.

83G. Providence Meetinghouse (stone) was founded in 1789 by the Society of Friends as a "preparative meeting of Redstone monthly Meeting." The first log structure was built in 1789 by John Cope. It was followed in 1793 by a stone building that was used until 1872. In 1893 Mary Binns, a descendant of an early Friend, had the present one-story house constructed according to the specifications of the original stone structure, using the stones from the former building. It is located next to a cemetery. The building is operated by the historical society. *Location:* On SR 4038 west of SR 0051.

83H. Washington Gristmill (stone remains) was built for and owned by George Washington. The land deal was made through Washington's friend William Crawford. Construction began on the mill about 1774 and after delays caused by Indian uprisings and the approach of the Revolution, it was completed in 1776. Washington sold the property in 1789. It was leased to Col. Israel Shreve, father of Henry Shreve (see *Shreve House*). The stone foundation of this frame structure, which operated till 1917, is all that remains today. The historical society plans to restore it. A scale model of this mill is on display at the borough building. *Location:* On East Independence Street.

83I. Stone Distillery was active during the Whiskey Rebellion days. Plans are being made to restore this structure, which is located next to the Washington gristmill. *Location:* On East Independence Street.

83J. Old Stone Bakeshop and Stone House date from the nineteenth century. Only the lower part of the bakeshop remains, with its original stone stove. The second floor was burned. It was restored in the early 1970s and will be open to the public in the future. Nearby on a hillside is the stone house, which at one time belonged to a Smith family, the third owners of the property. *Location:* Within view of Washington gristmill and stone distillery.

83I. Stone Distillery

83K. Old Stone Fulling Mill was erected by William Searight about 1810. The operation of fulling cloth was carried on in the basement of the building. The first floor contained equipment for carding, and a restored carding machine is on this level. The mill machinery was originally powered by water. In 1968 the historical society purchased the mill, which houses artifacts together with implements relating to the wool and flax industries. *Location:* On Strawn Road, off East Independence Street.

83L. Beehive Coke Ovens can still be seen on SR 0051 south of Perryopolis.
Note: Northwest of Perryopolis, west of SR 0051, is a double-pen barn, one of the few left representing early rural architecture of the area.

84. Linden Hall Estate includes a stone mansion built in 1911–13 by Sarah Boyd Moore Cochran, widow of Philip Galley Cochran, coal baron of the county. It was named for the linden trees that Mrs. Cochran imported from Germany. This palatial thirty-five-room mansion, set on a hill 600 feet above the Youghiogheny River, features signed Tiffany windows, bowling alleys, and an Aeolian pipe organ, and is decorated with gold leaf, sterling and Wedgwood inserts, and marble fireplaces. It is now owned by the United Steel Workers and is open for tours by reservation. *Admission charge.*

Philip Cochran, born in Lower Tyrone Township in 1849, was the president of the Washington Coal and Coke Company, Brown and Cochran Coke Company, Cochran Coal and Coke Mining, Dawson Bridge Company, and the First National Bank of Dawson. In 1879 he married Sarah, and they had a son Philip who died at the age of twenty-one. Philip, Sr., died in 1899.

85B. Cochran House

The Cochran's original frame house, built in the late 1890s, is now a golf-course clubhouse. A 200-year-old log house on the property is used as a guest house. This estate, where European royalty and financial tycoons were entertained, was later owned by St. James Church. *Location:* 3 miles northwest of Dawson, on T 662 off SR 0201, 5 miles east of Perryopolis.

85. Dawson

85A. Dawson Fairgrounds and Racetrack were financed through H. T. Cochran, a prominent coal and coke entrepreneur. The fairgrounds operated from about 1900 to 1933. Many of the original buildings are still standing on the property. *Location:* SR 1002 at SR 0819 just north of town.

85B. Cochran House (frame), in Queen Anne–Victorian style was built in 1890 by James Cochran who was responsible for large-scale coke manufacturing in the county. *Location:* SR 0819 at Railroad Street.

85C. National Bank of Dawson (brick), now the Gallatin National Bank, was built in 1897 by the James Cochran family during the coal and coke boom. *Location:* Railroad Street across from Cochran house.

87. Round Barn

85D. St. James Memorial Church (stone), a Methodist Episcopal church, was built in 1900 by Philip Cochran in memory of his son who died at age twenty-one. It was rebuilt in 1927. *Location:* Howell and Griscom streets.

85E. Bethel Church House (brick), a five-bay early house, now restored, is located near the marker for the site of Bethel Church, built of stone in 1845 and torn down in 1928. *Location:* North of Dawson, off SR 0819.

86. Vanderbilt Distillery started out as a flour and feed mill until about 1917 when it was adapted for use as a distillery. Few of these small-scale industrial buildings have been preserved in Pennsylvania. *Location:* Vanderbilt.

87. Round Barn (frame), with sixteen sides, is a rare structure and an important rural landmark. Built about 1860–88, it is the only round barn in the county. *Location:* SR 1043, between SR 1016 and SR 1014, near Buena Vista.

88. Curfew Grange No. 1052 (frame) was built in 1934 (organized in 1892). In view is an early country store, across the intersection. *Location:* Flatwoods, junction of SR 1012 and SR 0201.

89. Townsend Country Store (frame) was built about 1880–1900, in Victorian style. *Location:* Flatwoods.

90. Frick Company Colonial Coal Belt was built by the H. C. Frick Coke Company and was in operation until 1956. The remains of the tipple can be seen on the Monongahela River bank. This company was the first to move coal by conveyor belt from inland mines to a river loading dock. *Location:* South of Fayette City (between Gillespie and Brownsville). Go on SR 4003 for 0.4 mile north of its junction with SR 4036 to unmarked road; thence west on this road for about 1 mile across P&LE Railroad tracks to site.

Note: On the way to this site is a very early fieldstone house, later stuccoed. Now badly damaged by undermining, this house was reportedly built in 1775 by the Goe family. It has three chimneys and is built in two sections. *Location:* On SR 4003, 0.2 mile north of its junction with SR 4036.

91. Opera House (brick), with seven bays, was built in 1885. This three-story landmark is now a community center. *Location:* Fayette City, 225 Main Street.

Note: Fayette City, originally Cookstown, was founded by Col. Edward Cook.

92. Cook Mansion (limestone) was built in Rehoboth Valley in 1774–76 by Col. Edward Cook, who came here in 1770. Former slave quarters have been converted into a parlor, and the sheet-iron ceiling is reputed to be the first rolled in this part of the country. The smokehouse and kitchen washhouse are still standing. This property has been in the Cook family for at least five generations. Edward Cook was a member of both the Provincial Congress (1776) and the State Constitutional Convention (1776). In addition, he was lieutenant of the Westmoreland County Militia (1777–82) and one of the founders of the Rehoboth Presbyterian Church (q.v., Westmoreland County) where he is buried. He was also active in the 1794 Whiskey Rebellion. The large brick house on the same side of the road on the next farm was also a Cook house. *Location:* Near Belle Vernon. Follow SR 0201 north from Fayette City, turn right on Perry Avenue and left on Cook Road. House is 0.7 mile on left, near Westmoreland County line and Rehoboth Church.

93. Alliance Iron Furnace (stone) was the first of its kind west of the Alleghenies. It was so named because of its alliance with other business holdings, and was built on Jacobs Creek in 1789 by William Turnbull, Col. John Holker, and Peter Marmie. According to legend, Peter Marmie, an avid hunter, drove his faithful hounds into the fiery furnace and followed them after financial failure. However, this tale actually started at another furnace in the eastern part of the state. In 1792 the furnace provided shot for six-pounders at the Fort Pitt arsenal and in 1794 supplied ammunition for Gen. Anthony Wayne's expedition against the Ohio Indians. It went out of blast in

93. *Alliance Iron Furnace*

1802. It was also known as Jacobs Creek Furnace, Alliance Iron Works, Turnbull's Iron Works, and Colonel Holker's Iron Works. Peter Marmie's unmarked grave site is in the First Baptist Church cemetery at Jacobs Creek village. *Location:* From village of Banning, go 2.6 miles on SR 1002 to Rough farm on left, across from sawmill; thence to dirt road behind house and continue for over 0.5 mile under railroad to furnace. Or go 1.5 miles east of Perryopolis on SR 4038; turn left at Alliance Furnace marker for 0.5 mile on SR 1002; turn right on t. 568; thence to railroad track, and proceed on foot under bridge. Furnace is about 100 feet from creek.

94. Layton Bridge, of metal truss construction, was built in 1899. *Location:* Perry Township, across the Youghiogheny River.

Previous Sites Now Lost

Kline Gristmill
Meason House (West Side Hotel), Connellsville, demolished
Steam Locomotive, moved away
Stillwagon's Rock Museum, moved away
Uniontown Country Clubhouse, burned down

Other Iron Furnaces
(originally twenty)

Coolspring Furnace (ca. 1820–60), built by Thomas McKean. From SR 2021 at foot of mountain east of Coolspring, take road to right, past reservoir, to its end. Furnace is in woods, near Shutes run.
Fayette Furnace (Bucks Run) (1815–27). Northeast of Normalville, inquire for T 685. Furnace sits where this road crosses Bucks Run.

Mount Vernon Furnace (ca. 1800–30), built by Isaac Meason. From Wooddale on SR 0982, go east on SR 1044 about 1.5 miles, then left on SR 0819 for 0.3 mile.
Wharton Furnace (1839–73), built by Congressman Andrew Stewart. About 2 miles south of US 40 on SR 2003, east of Summit Hotel, to marker and small park. In fine shape and easily found.

Pennsylvania Historical and Museum Commission Markers

Albert Gallatin Junction of US 119 and SR 0166 north of Point Marion; and SR 0166 north of New Geneva
Alliance Furnace SR 0819, 1 mile north of Dawson; and SR 1002, approximately 6 miles northwest of SR 0819
Braddock Park US 40, 2.5 miles northwest of Farmington.
Braddock Road (Dunbar's Camp) SR 2021, approximately 3 miles north of US 40 at Jumonville
Braddock Road (Rock Fort Camp) US 40, approximately 6 miles southeast of Uniontown at Summit
Braddock Road (Stewart's Crossing) US 119, 0.2 mile south of Connellsville
Braddock Road (Twelve Springs Camp) US 40, 3.5 miles southeast of Farmington
Brashear House Brownsville, US 40, at Market, Sixth, and Union streets
Brownsville Brownsville, US 40
Coke Ovens Perryopolis, SR 0051
Col. William Crawford US 119, 0.2 mile south of Connellsville
Dunbar's Camp US 40, approximately 6 miles southeast of Uniontown, at Summit
Fayette County Uniontown, at courthouse, Main Street
Fort Gaddis US 119, 2 miles south of Uniontown
Fort Mason Masontown, SR 0166
Fort Necessity US 40, 1 mile northwest of Farmington
George C. Marshall Uniontown, 142 West Main Street
George Washington Perryopolis, SR 0051
Gist's Plantation US 119, 4.5 miles southwest of Connellsville
Jumonville Defeat US 40, approximately 6 miles southeast of Uniontown at Summit
Meason House US 119, 4.5 miles southwest of Connellsville
Mt. Washington Tavern US 40, 1.2 miles northwest of Farmington

National Road   US 40, 1.7 miles northwest of Farmington; and US 40 northwest of Brier Hill

Old Glassworks (Albert Gallatin's)   New Geneva, SR 0166

Philander Knox   Brownsville, US 40 at Market, Sixth, and Union Steets

Searight's Tavern   US 40, southeast of Brier Hill

Searights Tollhouse   US 40, 5 miles northwest of Uniontown; and at property on US 40, 5 miles west of Uniontown

Uniontown   On main highways leading into city

Washington Mill   Perryopolis, East Independence Street

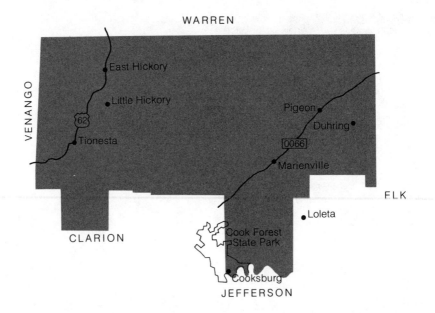

WARREN

VENANGO

East Hickory

Little Hickory

62

Tionesta

Pigeon

Duhring

0066

Marienville

ELK

Loleta

CLARION

Cook Forest
State Park

Cooksburg

JEFFERSON

Forest County

Capsule History

Forest County, named for its heavy timberlands, was erected out of Jefferson County on April 11, 1848, by joint resolution of both houses of the legislature, the only county in the state that was established in this way—a safety device designed to prevent defeat. In 1866 it received additional territory from Venango. This county, the most sparsely populated in the state, has an area of 428 square miles and a population of 5,072.

As early as 1749 the French, led by Céloron de Blainville, visited the western section of the county. The Munsees (Delawares) inhabited the area when Moravian missionaries, under the leadership of David Zeisberger, came to convert the refugee tribes. These Indians had fled their villages at the time of John Penn's proclamation in 1764 offering huge bounties for Indian scalps and had settled in the villages of Goschgoschink. (The upper town was possibly near Hunter in Forest County, while the middle and lower towns were probably in Venango County.) These Indians were later driven out of the area.

Cuscushing Indian town was located somewhere between the Tionesta and Little Tionesta creeks; and Lawunakhannek Indian town was possibly at Tionesta where the first Protestant church west of the Alleghenies was built by Zeisberger in 1769.

Among the earliest white settlers were the Valentine family, who came to Jamieson's (Jamison's) Flats about 1797; John Middleton, the county's first teacher, who arrived in 1802; Eli Holeman, who operated a ferry in 1800 across the Allegheny and later worked for the Waterford and Milesburg Turnpike or Bald Eagle Road; George Siggins, who settled in the West Hickory area in 1818; Poland Hunter in 1805; and George Tubbs. Others came in small numbers between 1815 and 1840, including John Range.

Cyrus Blood, a surveyor and founder of the county, who had been principal of the Chambersburg Academy, the Hagerstown Academy, and a member of the faculty of Dickinson College, established Blood's Station and later laid out the town of Marienville (see *Cyrus Blood House*). This town was the first county seat, where courts were held from 1857 until 1866, when five townships from Venango County were annexed to Forest. Tionesta, the county's only borough, became the next and present county seat. It derived its name from Tionesta Creek (*Tionesta* being an Iroquois word meaning "it penetrates the land"). The area was acquired by Lt. John Range, Sr., a Revolutionary War officer, who was granted a land warrant, taken out in the name of his oldest son Tehollas Range, in 1785 and settled here in 1815–16. His monument is located at the Tionesta courthouse.

Cobbtown village remains are along Toms Run. William Armstrong was the founder of Armstrongs Mills (now Clarington), and the German settlement in Green Township was settled in 1842 by Herman Blume. Guitonville was named for Robert Guiton, a noted hunter, trapper, and woodsman.

The *Catawba Path* touched corners of Forest County at Spring Creek and again near the mouth of Millstone Creek. The *Goschgoschink Path* from West Hickory to Clearfield crossed Tionesta Creek at about Nebraska and ran south to Tylersburg. The Allegheny River is the county's chief waterway.

The county contains vast timberlands, amounting to more than two hundred thousand acres, almost three-fourths of its entire area, including part of both Cook Forest State Park and Allegheny National Forest. The firm of Wheeler & Dusenbury built a sawmill near Newtown in 1837 and one in the Endeavor area about 1853. Lumbering was an important early industry, reaching its peak in 1900. Timber still provides a major source of income, and the county has the richest history of lumbering and related folklore in the state. Large stands of hemlock have encouraged the development of chemical industries and tanneries. The county's leading industry is recreation.

Other natural resources include petroleum and natural gas. Harmony Township figured prominently during the oil rush; and Balltown, northeast of Tionesta between Mayburg and Porkey, was the center of the county's oil boom of 1882–83. Forest County had one stone blast furnace. Today important products include gravel, concrete, glass containers, and plastics. With its forests, mountains, and streams, it is an outdoor paradise.

The county's school system claims to have been the first in Pennsylvania to have drivers' training at all its high schools, to close all one-room schools, and to complete joint organization among all its districts.

The Forest County library system has two units, one at Marienville and the other at Tionesta. The library at Tionesta contains a collection of antique tools used in the logging and boat-building era.

The county has one newspaper, the *Forest Press,* which covers the entire county. There are twenty-two churches in the county, five in Tionesta, four in Marienville, and the rest one to a town.

1A. Courthouse

1E. Masonic Hall

Landmarks

1. Tionesta, named for Tionesta Creek, was incorporated as a borough in 1856.

1A. Courthouse (brick), built in 1868–69 and still in use, is the county's second. The first, a frame structure erected in 1848 when the county seat was at Marienville, was put on ox wagons and hauled across the county when the courts were transferred to Tionesta in 1867. (Site is across from Marienville Presbyterian Church.) For many decades it sat not far from its successor but was torn down some years ago. *Location:* Elm Street.

Note: Most of the Forest County Historical Society's materials are in storage, but local Indian artifacts are on display on the first floor of the courthouse.

1B. County Jail (brick), which also contains offices, looks much older than the courthouse but was actually built in 1895. *Location:* Beside courthouse.

1C. Tionesta Library (Sarah Stewart Bovard Memorial). There is a museum in the basement of the building. *Location:* Elm Street.

1D. Lawrence Tavern (frame), built in 1872 by William Lawrence, was an early river-town hotel with sample rooms, billiard parlor, and barbershop. The proprietor kept six horses and a number of carriages for the use of the guests. About 1930 it was called the Weaver House, and the barroom featured a blood-curdling mural of settlers being massacred by Indians. It may still exist under subsequent layers of paint and paper. Today it is an apartment building called the Towne House. *Location:* 171 Elm Street.

Note: A fine Second Empire house is nearby on the same side of the street.

1E. Masonic Hall (frame) was built in the late 1800s. The unusual siding is bevelled to resemble masonry. To the right is another early frame building, once a store, and now an antique shop. *Location:* Elm Street (SR 0036) and SR 4004.

1F. Stone Arch Bridge was built over Tionesta Creek in 1919 and is now covered by concrete. *Location:* Elm Street Extention.

2. Tionesta Flood Control Dam, a beautifully landscaped recreational site, completed in 1941, is operated by the U.S. Army Corps of Engineers. This structure impounds the waters of Tionesta Creek. *Location:* South of Tionesta, near Allegheny River on SR 0036.

3. Tionesta Fish Hatchery was opened in 1930. The hatchery building contains interesting exhibits, and the entire complex is an attraction with its ponds and landscaped grounds. *Location:* North of Tionesta on US 62.

4. Cook Homestead (frame) was constructed about 1868–70 by Andrew Cook, a judge. His father John Cook, the founder of Cooksburg, came to the Clarion River Valley in 1825–26, built a log cabin and sawmill on this property along Toms Run, and brought his family two years later. His wives bore him a total of seventeen children. John Cook died in 1858 and is buried in the Cooksburg cemetery. The Cook family used to float huge rafts of lumber with temporary dwellings on them to Pittsburgh. The Cook house is now used as a service building and as apartments for the Cook Forest State Park employees. *Location:*

4. Cook Homestead

Cooksburg, at junction of River Drive and SR 0036.

5. Cook Forest State Park (also in Jefferson and Clarion counties) has one of the largest stands of virgin white pine in eastern America, the largest in Pennsylvania. Although its office and more than half of its area are in Clarion County, it really "belongs" to Forest County.

Anthony W. Cook, grandson of John Cook, whose family had cut thousands of acres of timber, had long planned to preserve the section of forest near his Cooksburg home. On an August day in 1910 he and Maj. M. I. McCreight of Du Bois sat on a log and pledged themselves to save the great trees, some of which had stood there since the disastrous drought and fire of 1644. Four times the Pennsylvania legislature turned down bills to buy the tract at a nominal price. Finally, in 1923 the Cook Forest Association was formed, with S. Y. Ramage of Oil City as president and Taylor Allderdice of Pittsburgh as vice-president.

Thomas Liggett, a Pittsburgh lumber dealer, led a campaign which raised $200,000—part of it from contributions made by school children. The Commonwealth contributed $450,000 and purchased the 6,055-acre tract (later increased to 8,200 acres) on December 28, 1925, exactly 100 years after John Cook had erected his first sawmill in the area. This park was created by an act of the Assembly in 1927.

Although the cyclone of August 18, 1956, destroyed some of the finest trees, there are still many in the forest over 200 feet in height and four feet in diameter. A survey taken about 1960 showed the existence of 600,000 trees with trunk diameters of eight inches or more. *Location:* Cooksburg, on SR 0036 at Forest-Clarion County line, Allegheny National Forest.

5A. Shelter No. 1 (frame) was built by the Civilian Conservation Corps in Depression days, about 1935. It includes a fine cut sandstone fireplace.

5B. Saw Mill Buildings (frame) were constructed about 1940, when timber was still being cut in the forest. Currently one of them is being used as an exhibition building for lumbering and sawmill tools and models.

5C. Memorial Fountain was built in 1950 on the Longfellow Trail in memory of the Cook Forest Association's founders.

6. Cook Mansion (frame) was built by Anthony W. Cook, a wealthy lumberman, about 1880. It is still occupied by his descendants. *Location:* Cooksburg, on River Drive.

Note: Nearby is the Cooksburg frame schoolhouse built about 1890.

7. Cook Mausoleum, a marble vault built in 1916 following the death of Andrew Cook, son

10. Cyrus Blood House

11. Pigeon, a village named for the extinct passenger pigeon. For years pigeons nested in the area's beech groves, and the trees grew according to the weight on the branches. It is believed that the Seneca Indians used to take the spring nestlings for food. (A passenger pigeon net is exhibited at the Clarion County Historical Society.) *Location:* 5 miles northeast of Marienville, on SR 0066.

12. Cornplanter State Forest, mostly in Harmony Township in the northwest, is accessible via SR 4002. Kittanning State Forest, in Barnett Township in the southeast, is crossed by T 311.

13. Forest Furnace, small in size, is much dilapidated, but some of the stack still remains. It was built in 1853 of unique design. *Location:* About 1 mile northeast of Little Hickory between Furnace Run and Little Hickory Run. From SR 3004 take T 347 to end (Hickory Township). Extremely difficult to reach.

Pennsylvania Historical and Museum Commission Markers

Damascus Tionesta, US 62
Forest County Tionesta, at courthouse, Elm Street
Goschgoschink US 62, 0.9 mile south of East Hickory
Hickory Town US 62, 2 miles south of East Hickory
Holeman Ferry US 62, 3 miles southwest of Tionesta
Indian Paths US 62, 2.3 miles south of East Hickory
Lawunakhannek US 62, 0.2 mile north of East Hickory
Pigeon SR 0066, 5 miles northeast of Marienville
Refugee Towns US 62, 0.5 mile south of East Hickory; and US 62, 1.5 miles south of Tionesta Station

of John Cook, has spaces for twenty bodies. His was the first to be entombed within. On its back wall is a stained glass window depicting a log drive out of the mouth of Toms Run, which enters the Clarion River at Cooksburg. *Location:* Cooksburg, at top of village cemetery.

8. Buzzard Swamp on Muddy Fork is the site of a wild animal refuge, a natural haven for a variety of wildlife including bear, turkey, deer, rattlesnakes, and snowshoe rabbits, as well as waterfowl and pond species. Millet, sorghum, and other grasses are planted to provide food for the animals. The propagation area includes about eighty acres. Group tours are available through the U.S. Forest Service and the State Game Commission. It is accessible by automobile to within one mile, and the remainder of the distance can be covered by foot. *Location:* 4 miles southeast of Marienville, near Loleta.

9. CCC Campsite, originally a Civilian Conservation Corps camp in the 1930s, was converted into a prisoner-of-war camp during World War II. Later it became a 4-H camp, but today it is privately owned and is the location for nationally attended horse trail rides. *Location:* Duhring, 12 miles east of Marienville.

10. Cyrus Blood House (frame) belonged to Cyrus Blood, one of the first land and lumber merchants in Forest County, who named his town Marienville for his daughter. The house was built about 1843 and still contains many of the original furnishings. Blood planted the stately hemlocks that form a lane in front. Fortunately, the house was located far enough from the town to escape the disastrous fires of 1902 and 1913. *Location:* Marienville, off Hemlock Street, at Marienville School.

WASHINGTON

Ruff Creek

Rice's Landing

Jefferson
Dry Tavern

Wind Ridge

WEST VIRGINIA

Ryerson
Station

Waynesburg

Carmichaels

FAYETTE

0021

Morrisville
Rogersville

79

Garards Fort

Kirby

Greensboro

19

Ned

Mount Morris

WEST VIRGINIA

Greene County

Capsule History

Greene County, named for Maj. Gen. Nathaniel Greene, military strategist of the Revolution, was erected out of Washington County on February 9, 1796. It has an area of 577 square miles and a population of 40,476. This southwest corner of Pennsylvania was the scene of both Indian warfare and constant jurisdictional dispute between Virginia and Pennsylvania in the 1700s. Finally, in 1784 the first U.S. scientific survey completed the extension of the Mason and Dixon line and later established the western boundary of the county and the state.

Among the stations or outposts of early settlement were Fort Jackson of 1774 in Waynesburg, Fort Swan of 1774 near Carmichaels, Garard's Fort of 1777 at the town of that name, and Ryerson's blockhouse of 1792 near Wind Ridge. Among the county's pioneers were Creaux Bozarth, first settler on Whiteley Creek (about 1747); Augustine Dilliner in Dunkard Township (about 1754); and Rev. John Corbly. John Spicer, his wife, and five children were attacked by Indians on Dunkard Creek in 1774.

The county was the birthplace of Pennsylvania Governor and U.S. Senator Edward Martin, who also was a major general in World War II, as well as serving in the Spanish American War, Mexican border campaign, and during World War I. (His home is preserved in Washington, Pa.) Native son Albert B. Cummings, U.S. senator and governor of Iowa, acted as vice-president when President Harding died. Arthur Inghram Boreman was elected first governor of West Virginia. Col. Reese Hill served the county twenty years in the state legislature and seven as speaker of the house. He also was active in securing pensions for widows of the War of 1812 and veterans of the Revolution. Dr. Jesse William Lazear, of Johns Hopkins University, served on the Yellow Fever Commission with Dr. Walter Reed at the time of the building of the Panama Canal and during the Spanish American War. William Thompson Hays began the county's first newspaper, the *Waynesburg Messenger,* in 1813.

A branch of the *Catawba Path* ran south in the county from about East Riverside to Mount Morris, with a fork near Garard's Fort leading to the main path near Point Marion. *Catfish's Path* ran north from Brant Summit through Waynesburg and Ruff Creek, following much the course of US 19. *Warrior's Branch Path* ran west from about Greensboro through Luke, Camp, Brant Summit, Bluff, and Nettle Hill to Morford, where it forked, the northern route leading past Rocklick, the southern to Cameron, W.Va. (The latter, a sixty-seven-mile path, is now used as a cross-country hikers' trail and is unique in that it crosses several ridges but not a single waterway. The trail scars were discovered in the 1940s, and the Warrior Trail Association, Inc., created in 1965, is studying the path and Indian artifacts found along the way. The association has also erected trail markers and shelters for hikers, and has located many of the original Mason and Dixon survey stones.)

In 1836 the Monongahela Navigation Company began improving that river for navigation, and the first railroad in the county was constructed in 1877. The county has preserved fourteen covered bridges.

Waynesburg, the county seat, was laid out in 1796 at the south fork of Ten Mile Creek and named for Gen. Anthony Wayne. It now has a district listed on the National Register of Historic Sites.

The bituminous coal industry is the most important in the county, which contains some of the richest coal lands in the state, with the Robena mine one of the largest in the Commonwealth. The county had one stone blast furnace. Oil and natural gas production are other main enterprises. The Great Tanner Well, drilled in 1866, flowed for fifty years. In addition, Greene is the largest sheep-raising county in the state.

Greensboro was the early glass center of the county, as well as a key shipping point. The first glass factory (New Geneva) west of the Monongahela River, and second in western Pennsylvania, was moved about 1810 to Greene County (on SR 2014 east of Greensboro) where it was operated by James W. Nicholson, Albert Gallatin's brother-in-law and former partner, until 1849. Only the foundation scars remain. The county is also famous for its clay pottery.

Landmarks

1. Waynesburg, named for "Mad" Anthony Wayne.

1A. Courthouse (brick) originally was constructed of logs in 1796. The second one, built of brick in 1800, was used for exactly fifty years. Prior to the first building, courts were held in the home of Isaac Kline on Muddy Creek.

The present structure, erected in 1850, is a classic example of Colonial and Greek Revival architecture; its portico has columns with cast-iron capitals. Samuel and John Bryan, builders of the Fayette County courthouse, were the contractors, receiving $16,000 for their work. Within a copper box in the cornerstone, laid by the Freemasons on June 24, 1850, are memorabilia of the era, including copies of the *Waynesburg Messenger* and *Greene County Democrat* newspapers. The

1B. Old County Courthouse

The college was chartered in 1850 under the auspices of the Cumberland Presbyterian Church, and classes were held in that church. The same year the female seminary of the college met in the Baptist church. In 1851 Hanna Hall (brick), the first college building, was erected on the campus. It and Miller Hall are now listed on the National Register of Historic Places.

The first piano used by the college is on display in the Greene County Historical Society Museum, east of Waynesburg. In Paul R. Stewart Science Hall is one of the finest mineralogy and archeology museums in the county. *Location:* On College Street (US 19).

1D. Waynesburg Historic District, a Victorian-style downtown, encompasses sixty-one acres, almost 15 percent of the entire borough, including the Waynesburg College campus. The town has become known for its July 29 rain day—it has rained in Waynesburg on that date in 95 of the past 114 years. A walking tour of the buildings in this district is available through the Greene County Historical Society and the chamber of commerce.

1E. Brock House (brick) was the home of Dr. R. E. Brock, a Morgantown doctor who came to Waynesburg in 1879. This house and numerous other brick houses in the town were built by Clement Brooks. *Location:* High and Morgan streets.

1F. St. Ann's Church was built in 1871 on a lot purchased in 1796 by Fr. Patrick Lonergan. *Location:* High and Cumberland streets.

1G. Ganiear Building, erected in 1899, was the first furniture store in Waynesburg. It has a fine floral frieze on its facade. *Location:* High Street, between Morgan and Cumberland streets.

1H. Green House. The Female Seminary of Waynesburg College was formed on the second floor of this hotel in 1850. This was a popular public house years ago when cattle drovers came to the town from Baltimore and other cities. *Location:* High Street, between Washington and Morgan streets.

1I. Allison Building was erected in the early 1820s and is one of the oldest structures in Waynesburg. There used to be a footbridge leading from this building to Monument Park, site of the Cumberland Presbyterian Church. *Location:* High Street, between Washington

original bell, remolded in 1926, is now inside the building. Bradley Mohanna carved the first statue of Gen. Nathaniel Greene that surmounted the clock tower. A new statue (made by Albert Wise) and dome were created following a 1925 fire. In 1952–53 the building was completely restored, at which time the white paint, applied in 1935, was removed from the bricks; and in 1968 it was redecorated. *Location:* Corner of High and Washington streets.

1B. Old County Courthouse (log, covered) is the county's first courthouse, a unique landmark since most of these pioneer structures have been lost to time and demolition in western Pennsylvania. Erected in 1796, the building is now used for auto parts storage. It is to be hoped that this treasure will be restored and preserved. *Location:* 144 East Greene Street, next to fire department.

1C. Waynesburg College was founded in 1849, and in 1853 it was one of the first two institutions of higher learning to award degrees to women. (See *Westminster College,* Lawrence County.) It is the successor of Greene Academy (q.v.) and Madison College (Fayette County). Rev. Joshua Loughran of Greene Academy was the first president, followed by Rev. J. P. Wethee, former president of Madison. In 1849 the Pennsylvania Synod of the Cumberland Presbyterian Church requested proposals from various towns for contributions toward erecting buildings and endowing professorships for a college. Waynesburg won by volunteering to subscribe $5,000 to build a three-story brick building on a 50-by-70-foot lot on College Street.

First classes were held in 1849 in the Hayes Building, the site now designated by a plaque at the corner of Main and Washington streets.

and Morgan streets, across from Old County Office Building (Peoples Bank), built in 1906.

1J. Opera House, originally the Town Hall, opened as a theater in 1889. William Jennings Bryan and Will Rogers were among the notables who appeared here. *Location:* High Street, between Morris and Washington streets.

1K. Denny House was built in the 1850s with an addition in 1907. This is the home of Miss Josephine Denny, a prominent member and official of the Greene County Historical Museum. The house still retains its wrought-iron fence, a common feature of the period. *Location:* High Street, between Richhill and Morris streets.

1L. Lindsey-Rinehart House was the home of Sarah and James Lindsey. James Lindsey was the presiding judge for the district in 1863 and 1864. Surrounding the house is a wrought-iron fence and a city garden. *Location:* High Street, between Richhill and Morris streets, across from Denny house.

1M. Messenger Building (brick) was built in 1851, the home of the *Messenger*. Waynesburg College was founded on the second floor of the Hayes building which formerly occupied this site. *Location:* Northeast corner of High and Washington streets.

1N. Wise House (brick) was built in 1834 by Morgan Ringland Wise (1836–1902), twice a member of the state house of representatives for three Pennsylvania counties, and twice a state senator. He laid out lots in East Waynesburg, known as the Wise Addition. In 1882, in order to go into the cattle business out west, he sold his house to Timothy Ross. After leaving the area, Wise served as U.S. consul to Mexico. He became one of the "forty-niners" seeking gold in California. *Location:* East High Street.

Note: William Jennings Bryan was once a guest in this house when the Rosses owned it.

1O. Glass House (brick) was built in 1860 and is being restored. *Location:* Southeast corner of Monument Park.

1P. Old Station Inn. *Location:* Near Waynesburg, Mt. Morris Star Route.

2. Rick Kelsey House (brick ell) has a plaque which reads "1794." *Location:* West of Waynesburg, SR 0021.

Note: Nearby on the same road is the old one-room Hill Schoolhouse. Between the house and the school, on a side road and in view of both, is another early brick farmhouse (Keener-Glenn Arnold).

3. Triangle Tavern (stuccoed brick) was built in 1860. An addition was built in 1923. *Location:* Morrisville, SR 0188.

Note: The Buckeye Coal Company (brick), which includes the Nemacolin Mines, is nearby in Paisley, SR 0021 just west of SR 0188.

4. Mt. Pleasant Methodist Church (brick) was built in 1872, the congregation having been organized before 1820. *Location:* Near Waynesburg, about 2.5 miles south of junction of Gordon Hill Road and US 19.

5. Ganiear House (cut stone and fieldstone) was once owned by the Inghrams, John T. Hook, and later by Hiram Wood. At least three generations of the Hiram Wood Ganiear family have lived here. *Location:* Smith Creek, on SR 0218, 1 mile south of Waynesburg.

6. J. B. Gordon House (cut stone) was built in 1843 by John Brice Gordon. This unique home of adapted Greek Revival architecture has two columns in front approached by impressive curved-stone steps. A stone stile is in the front yard.

Gordon, who owned much land in the area, sold his coal to J. V. Thompson (see *Oak Hill*, Fayette County). He married Delilah Inghram, who one day noticed that the red-brick house on the hill across the valley was on fire. She rode over on horseback and offered to rebuild the home for the family in need. The same house can be seen from this property.

The present owner, George W. Gordon, is a grandson of the original builder. The family cemetery is on a hill nearby. *Location:* East of Waynesburg. Turn off US 19 onto Gordon Hill Road (old brick); thence 0.6 mile to house on right.

7. George Gordon House (brick) was built about 1860 by George Gordon, son of John Brice Gordon. A stone stile is located in front of the house. *Location:* Near Waynesburg, on side road, 0.3 mile south of Gordon Hill Road, 1 mile west of J. B. Gordon house.

8. Greene County Historical Society Museum and Library (brick) is owned by the county and operated by the historical society, founded in 1925. This fifty-two-room mansion built about 1860 as the County Home (the

8. *Green County Historical Society Museum and Library*

original section an earlier private residence) was opened to the public in 1971 as a mid-Victorian mansion and museum. This outstanding endeavor includes a large collection of Indian artifacts, hand tools, and spinning wheels; rooms furnished as a country store, schoolhouse, and an old-time kitchen; a railroad room; and collections of glass and pottery. Located on the nineteen-acre property is the old Waynesburg and Washington narrow-gauge steam locomotive (formerly situated at the Waynesburg fairgrounds). There is also a carriage house which contains antique printing equipment. The library contains extensive genealogical records. A nature trail leads to a family cemetery dating from 1811. *Hours:* 1–4:30 P.M. *Library hours:* Wednesday–Saturday, 1–4:30 P.M. *Admission charge. Location:* 3 miles east of Waynesburg, on SR 0021 (follow signs).

9. Harry House (stone) was built by Jacob Harry before 1831. The present owner is a fourth-generation descendant of the original family. *Location:* East of Waynesburg, on SR 0188, 3.5 miles from SR 0021.

Note: Other old stone houses along the same side of the road include the Crayne and Madlock houses. The latter has a stone porch. An early log house is nearby at a bridge.

10. Old Stone House, a primitive fieldstone structure with a porch added later, has been remodeled. It was probably built by David Wise around 1805. *Location:* Just south of Ruff Creek, on US 19.

11. Jefferson

11A. Jefferson Presbyterian Church (brick), erected in 1845, is typical of many early churches having separate entrances for men and women. A new church building is located in front of the old one. *Location:* Pine Street.

Note: Near the corner of Green and Pine streets is the site of Monongahela College, the first Baptist college in western Pennsylvania. It was established in 1867 and operated at different times during the years 1869 and 1894.

11B. Hughes House (stone) was built in 1814 with slave labor. The earliest owner of the house was Thomas Hughes, whose homestead later served as a way station for the underground railroad, helping slaves escape to Canada. The house has been restored for public visit. Hughes, who laid out the borough of Jefferson, was the county's first Catholic, and visiting priests occasionally held services at his house. *Location:* SR 0188, Hatfield Street.

Note: The William Cree House, built in two sections—log and stone—has several walk-in fireplaces. A stone springhouse is located on the property. The house was built in 1790

13A. W. A. Young & Sons Foundry

13C. Old Jail

with an 1840 addition. *Location:* Off I-79, 5 miles east of Waynesburg on SR 0021, about 1 mile south of Jefferson.

12. Fort Swan House (brick), on land which possibly once belonged to Col. Charles Swan, is an early structure that has a large wooden porch extending across two sides. The Fort Swan site is 1.3 miles east of the historical marker across from the house. The fort was built in 1774 for protection against Indian raids. In 1767 the first settlers—Swan, Van Meter, Hughes, and Hupp—had crossed the Monongahela River into this area. *Location:* South of Dry Tavern, on SR 0088, north of Carmichaels.

Note: Across the road are the ruins of a brick one-room schoolhouse built in 1893.

13. Rice's Landing

13A. W. A. Young & Sons Foundry (frame), now a museum, was built about 1900 from lumber cut from the Young family farm nearby. The building was expanded in 1908–10. This business, which specialized in repairing boilers and river steamboats, first operated by steam, but the shop was electrified in 1928. All equipment dates from 1870 to 1920, a remarkable and authentic representation of America's industrial revolution. During certain times of the year, blacksmithing is scheduled at this museum. *Hours:* Saturday, 10 A.M.–4 P.M. *Location:* Water Street, SR 1020 near Pumpkin Park.

13B. Hewitt Pottery (frame) is a large early stoneware pottery company. Here Isaac Hewitt made pottery as early as 1870 to 1885. *Location:* Near Monongahela River and borough school.

13C. Old Jail (brick). This one-room structure along Hollow Run was built in the 1850s. It is complete with bars and bunks. *Location:* Water and Main streets, at underpass.

14. Dowlin House (brick) is a Victorian structure with a cut-stone foundation. A smokehouse is also on the property. A date stone over the door reads: "1861 J & E. Dowlin." *Location:* SR 0188, just west of Dry Tavern.

15. Carmichaels

15A. Murdock House (fieldstone) was constructed in 1824 by the father of Mrs. Emma Syphers Murdock. *Location:* 303 Old Town Road and Market Street.

Note: Next to the house is a covered bridge spanning Muddy Creek. A mill, converted into a shingle-covered residence, is located on the other side of the bridge. There are many old brick and log-covered houses in this section, called Old Town, which is situated partly on a peninsula formed by a curve in Muddy Creek.

15B. Hathaway House (brick) was built in 1844 (date above door) by the Hathaway family and was later used as a store. The home, with the rear entrance surrounded by a courtyard, is still owned by the Hathaways. *Location:* Old Town, 110 Market Street at Greene Street.

15C. Greene Academy (native fieldstone and brick). The original section was built in 1791 as an Episcopal church. In 1810 the church trustees offered their building as a

15C. Greene Academy

school and the brick addition was constructed. As a pioneer in coeducation, the Greene Academy had a Female Department as early as 1837. It continued to serve as the educational center of the county until the founding of Waynesburg College in 1849. It continued as an academy until 1860.

Through the efforts of many volunteers, the academy was restored and is now listed on the National Register. *Location:* 310, 312, and 314 Market Street, in Old Town.

15D. Hartley Inn (brick), built in 1848, was originally a stagecoach stop called the Davidson House. The Jennings family bought the property in the late 1800s. Later owners were John Riley and the Hartley family. *Location:* Corner of Market and George streets.

16. Biddle House (brick) was erected by Isaac Biddle in 1842 on a farm purchased in 1839. The construction date is above the front door. A large cut-stone and brick fireplace has been restored in the interior of the house. Also, a custom-made ceiling-to-floor cabinet, made exclusively for hat storage at the time one of the Biddle daughters married, has been preserved inside the house, which is still owned by the descendants of the original Biddle family. This property is on the site of Hughes' Fort (1768), which was once attacked by Indians. *Location:* 1 mile east of Carmichaels, on Jacob's Ferry Road.

17. Harper House (painted brick) was built about 1800 by Samuel Harper, who constructed a stone springhouse at about the

same time. *Location:* 1.2 miles south of Carmichaels, on SR 0088, at bottom of Glade Hill.

18. Greensboro and area

18A. Blackshere Homestead (frame) originally consisted of 450 acres of land that was a wedding gift from William Gray of Grays Landing to his daughter Eliza in 1859. Eliza married James Edgar Blackshere, who built the house. The foundation is made from hand-cut stone, and the lumber came from pine and hemlock trees on the farm. It is still owned by descendants of this family. *Location:* 3 miles north of Greensboro, on SR 0088.

18B. Flenniken House (frame) was a hotel owned by Elias A. Flenniken, born in 1824. He had operated a livery stable in Greensboro and later was captain of a steamer on the Monongahela for several years. His wife was Mary Kerr. After leaving the river in the 1850s, he built the hotel and was still running it as late as 1888. *Location:* Corner of Main and County streets.

18C. Monon Center (stone) was built as a grade school in 1904. The architect was James Perricho of Italy. In 1965 the school district abandoned the building and deeded it to the borough which in turn transferred it to the Monon Center Society in 1974. Exhibits at this site include a pioneer heritage room with Greensboro–New Geneva pottery, Gallatin glassware, Indian artifacts, and coal-mining exhibits. *Location:* On Second Street.

19. Goshen Baptist Church (brick), the first recorded religious congregation in the county, was organized before April 1771. It is now the John Corbly Memorial Baptist Church, named for its first pastor. The church was constituted by Rev. Isaac Sutton and Daniel Frisbee of the North Ten Mile Baptist Church. Corbly served this church until his death in 1803. The present edifice was built in 1862.

In the churchyard is a monument commemorating the site of Fort Garard, possibly built in 1777. The fort's first settler was Jacob Van Meter who arrived at Muddy Creek in 1769. The land on which the fort was built was warranted to John Garard in 1785.

Corbly's wife Elizabeth, son, and two daughters were killed by Indians on their way to church on May 10, 1782. Two other daughters were scalped but lived for at least three years. Elizabeth's grave is located in this church cemetery; the epitaph reads:

> Beneath the Indian tommy hawk
> Me and my babe we fell,
> Was hurried suddenly away,
> With Jesus for to dwell.

(See also *North Ten Mile Baptist Church,* Washington County, and *Turkeyfoot Regular Baptist Church,* Somerset County.) *Location:* Garard's Fort, on SR 0218.

20. Western Terminus of Mason and Dixon Survey, a National Historic Civil Engineering Landmark, is the point at which Indians of the Six Nations stopped Charles Mason and Jeremiah Dixon while they were surveying the boundary line between Maryland and Pennsylvania on June 22, 1767. At this spot, where the Warrior Path met the line, slightly east of what was known as the "second crossing" of Dunkard Creek, the Indians said they could not guarantee the party's safety if they went farther, for their understanding had been that the line should not extend beyond the "War Path." More than fifteen years later the Pennsylvania-Virginia line was completed (see *Pennsylvania Southwest Corner Monument*). A monument marks the Sinclair resurvey (1883) of the Pennsylvania–West Virginia boundary on the spot where the commissioners were stopped by the Indians. During the survey no corrections were made in the original line, but monuments were placed in the original molds. *Location:* Travel southwest of Mount Morris on SR 2003 to West Virginia line and continue on this road along Dunkard Creek to old Spencer Fetty Farm (3.3 miles from small bridge in Mount Morris to farm). A lane leads about 1.5 miles farther to marker on ridge.

21. Mount Morris Log Cabin, a one-story restored house, was built in 1790 according to tax record estimation. Peter Vox, whose great-grandfather (according to tradition) married a Delaware Indian princess, was the first owner of this site, then called "Fox Coon Chase." It is said that Peter's brother, John, gave George Washington a white stallion. *Location:* Just north of the Mason-Dixon line, in the valley of Mount Morris.

22. Robena (Cumberland) Mine is the largest underground coal mine of its type in the world. *Location:* Near Kirby.

23. Willow Inn (frame), reputedly built in 1816, this restored farmhouse is now a country inn. *Location:* Oak Forest, 6 miles from

25A. Jacktown Fairgrounds

Waynesburg. Take SR 0018 south for 3 miles to village of East View; about one-eighth mile south of East View, turn left on Oak Forest Road (SR 3013), about 3 miles to Oak Forest.

24. Little Red Schoolhouse (brick), built in 1900 with a belfry and front porch, has been preserved as a memorial to the one-room schoolhouses of the past. The Crouse Schoolhouse Association has authentically re-created the original interior. *Location:* Between Waynesburg and Rogersville, on SR 0021.

25. Wind Ridge, in Richhill Township

25A. Jacktown Fair was organized July 6, 1866, by the Richhill Agricultural, Horticultural, and Mechanical Society. It is the second oldest fair with an unbroken record of exhibitions in the United States. (Jacktown, shortened from Jacksonville, was the original name for the present village of Wind Ridge.) The fair, still sponsored by the agricultural society, is held annually in August as a nonprofit project for the improvement of the community. According to tradition, "You'll never die happy unless you've been to the Jacktown Fair." *Location:* Wind Ridge, on SR 0021 at the southwest edge of village.

25B. Wind Ridge Post Office (frame) has been a wagon shed, a church, and a GAR hall, and at present it is the post office. *Location:* SR 0021.

Note: There are many old houses, some covered log, in this community. The main road through town was once a drovers' path. Two early frame hotels still exist here on opposite sides of the street.

26. Ryerson Station State Park contains 1,104 acres and a 61-acre lake. It is the site of Fort Ryerson, built by Virginia authorities as a

216

refuge from Indian raids. The property includes nine miles of walking trails. *Location:* Richhill Township off SR 0021 between Bristoria and Wind Ridge, near Hatfield Power Station.

27. Old Drovers' Tavern (brick) was built in the 1840s. Later it was operated as the Ryerson Station Inn by one Supler. *Location:* Near entrance of Ryerson Station State Park, on SR 0021.

Note: Also in this area were three blockhouses erected by Capt. James Paul's company in 1792, the same year that soldiers carrying supplies from Thomas Ryerson's mill clashed with Indians. At Ryerson State Park is an early brick house, now occupied by the park's caretaker.

28. Crow Rock, a large boulder along the side of the road, which has fallen from its original position, bears the inscription, "May 1, 1791 Sus. and Cath. Eliz.—Tina." This was the site where the Crow sisters were massacred by Indians. Two were killed outright, one lived for a few days after being scalped, and the fourth escaped. The Crow house was situated a little way down the road, along Crow Creek. *Location:* On Crow Creek Road, 1 mile from village of Crabapple (which is 3 miles on SR 3001 from SR 0021, west of Wind Ridge).

Note: About 1.5 miles away is the site of an Indian burial ground, excavated by Carnegie Institute of Pittsburgh.

29. Pennsylvania Southwest Corner Monument marks the completion of the state's southern boundary by the Mason and Dixon line on November 18, 1784. Prior to this time only a temporary line marked the border between Pennsylvania and Virginia. On August 31, 1779, the states' commissioners agreed that the Mason and Dixon line would be extended to its full length, with Virginia ratifying on June 23, 1780, and Pennsylvania on September 23. (The commissioners for Pennsylvania were John Lukens and Archibald McClean, with James Madison and Robert Andrews for Virginia.) Joseph Reed, president of Pennsylvania, agreed with Thomas Jefferson's "proposal for astronomical determination" of the line. On April 23, 1781, the Pennsylvania commissioners and party were directed to cut a swath fifteen feet wide and mark the large trees. Due to threat of attack by the British, the work was delayed until May 1, 1782, and the line was finally completed in 1784. In 1883 the western extension of the line was resurveyed, and dilapidated and

missing monuments were replaced. This square sandstone monument reads, "1883 P WV, WV, WV," and "P WV" on its north, west, south, and east sides, respectively. *Location:* Near Ned. Go west from Garrison on SR 3004 to its intersection with SR 3001; thence on this ridge road (SR 3001) through Ned and directly west on poor township road (T 301) which is intersected by SR 3001. Monument is about 1 mile west on this road.

30. Cole's Log Cabin Bed and Breakfast (log) consists of two log houses dating from the 1820s. It is owned and operated by Jerry and Jane Cole. *Location:* Pine Bank (Gilmore Township).

31. New Sites on the National Register include: John Corbly farm north of Garards Fort; Fisher site in Richhill Township; Richard T. Foley site, Holbrook area; Greene Hills farm east of Waynesburg; and Sugar Grove petroglyph site in Monongahela Township.

Previous Site Now Lost

Monongahela House, demolished

Covered Bridges

Barneys Run (Bryan) Bridge over Wheeling Creek, Richhill Township

Carmichaels Bridge (1889) over Muddy Creek, Carmichaels, SR 1006

Davis Bridge (1889) over Ten Mile Creek, T 325, Morgan Township to West Bethlehem Township, Washington County

Grimes Bridge (1888) over Ruff Creek, T 546, Washington Township

Hawkins (Rainey) Bridge (ca. 1900) over Ten Mile Creek, Morgan Township, to Deemston, Washington County

Hero Bridge over Dunkard Creek, Gilmore Township

King Bridge (ca. 1880) over Hoover Run, T 371, Wayne Township

Lippincott Bridge (1943) over Ruff Creek, T 568, Morgan Township

Neddie Woods Bridge (1882) over Pursley Creek, T 487 just north of Oak Forest

Red (Neils) Bridge (ca. 1900) over Whiteley Creek, SR 2015, Greene Township

Scott Bridge (1885) over Ten Mile Creek, T 424, Center Township

Shriver Bridge (1900) over Hargus Creek, T 454, Center Township

White Bridge (1919) over Whiteley Creek, SR 2015, Greene Township

Willow Tree Bridge (ca. 1875) over Whiteley Creek, Greene Township

Note: A concrete bridge built in 1919 spans Ten Mile Creek in Franklin Township, near Morrisville (on the National Register)

Pennsylvania Historical and Museum Commission Markers

Fort Jackson   Waynesburg, East High Street at Woodland Avenue

Fort Swan   SR 008 south of Dry Tavern

Garard's Fort   T 616, 0.6 mile east of Garard's Fort

Greene Academy   Carmichaels, on SR 0088 near intersection of Greene and Vine streets

Greene County   Waynesburg, at courthouse, High and Washington streets

Monongahela College   Jefferson, SR 0188 at Greene and Pine Streets

Old Glassworks   SR 2014 east of Greensboro

Ryerson's Blockhouse   Wind Ridge, SR 0021

Waynesburg College   Waynesburg, US 19

Indiana County

Capsule History

Indiana County, named for its original inhabitants, the Indians, was organized March 12, 1803, out of portions of Westmoreland and Lycoming counties, although it remained under the jurisdiction of the former until 1806. It now has an area of 829 square miles with a population of 92,281.

About 1727 James Le Tort established a trading post near present-day Shelocta. At Cherry Tree was "Canoe Place," the head of canoe navigation on the West Branch of the Susquehanna River. One of the first white settlers to clear a "tomahawk" claim in the county was George Findley in the late 1760s. In 1772 Fergus, Samuel, and Joseph Moorhead, James Kelly, and James Thompson moved to the county west of Indiana. The majority of early migrants were Scotch-Irish, coming from the Cumberland Valley. Rev. John Jamison, of the Associate Reformed Presbyterian faith, was the first resident minister in the county, arriving in 1796. German Lutherans, many coming from Virginia, began to settle in the area by 1795.

The county seat, Indiana, was laid out in 1805 on land given by George Clymer, a Philadelphia landholder and signer of the Declaration of Independence. Blairsville, laid out in 1818, became a borough in 1825. (In 1786 James Campbell was granted warrants for a tract of land called "Lisbon" in this area.) Blairsville was important as the western terminus of the Huntingdon, Cambria, and Indiana Turnpike, better known as the Northern Pike. From 1829 to 1860 it was a main depot on the Pennsylvania Canal.

Four principal Indian trails, two of the most important in the area, crossed Indiana County. Most traveled were the *Catawba Path,* the main north-south route, and the *Frankstown Path,* variously called the Kittanning or Armstrong-Kittanning Trail, used more than any other across the mountains. The Catawba Path, running from near Olean, N.Y., to the Carolinas, entered Indiana County below Hamilton, passing through or near Trade City, Georgeville, and Home. It crossed Crooked Creek and intersected the Kittanning (Frankstown) Trail at Shaver's Spring west of the Indiana University campus. Thence it ran through Penoland's Town (Homer City), crossed Black Lick Creek near Palmerton, and forded the Conemaugh close to New Florence. The Frankstown Path entered the county near Emeigh, followed much the course of SR 0240 to Cookport, forded Two Lick Creek at Shawnee Bottom, and ran thence to Diamondville and Penn Run. From there it went west to Two Licks, passed through what is now the Indiana University campus and near Moorhead's Fort, and followed the general route of US 422 to Shelocta. The *Cherry Tree Portage* ran from the famed tree south for about two miles, then followed the Frankstown Path. The *Frankstown-Venango Path* branched off the main trail east of Cherry Tree and ran through Purchase Line, Marion Center, Frantz, and Smicksburg, thence through the northwest corner of Indiana County.

The county's first gristmill was built on a run flowing into Black Lick Creek in 1773. Agriculture, salt-refining, iron-smelting, coal-mining, grinding of grain, distilling of alcohol, hide-tanning, and lumbering were the main industries before 1850. Salt wells were located along the Conemaugh and Kiskiminetas rivers. Saltsburg (laid out in 1816 by Andrew Boggs and incorporated as a borough in 1838) derived its name from salt discovered in the vicinity in 1812. The first salt well was drilled in 1813 by William Johnson near Saltsburg and resulted in the Great Conemaugh Salt Works. Coal mining and agriculture are still thriving industries. The county has had four stone blast furnaces. The dense virgin pine forests of former years have given way to field-grown evergreens, and today the county is known as the Christmas tree capital of the world.

Landmarks

1. Indiana Borough, laid out in 1806. A historic walking tour, including Philadelphia and Sixth streets, is available through the Historical and Genealogical Society.

1A. Old Courthouse (brick and stone), designed by James W. Drum in Second Empire style, was the second Indiana County courthouse, built in 1871 at a cost of $186,000.

This structure, with a clock tower, replaced an earlier one dating from 1809. Courts had first been held in the upper story of a stone jail constructed in 1807. The 1871 building was restored by the National Bank of the Commonwealth. A new courthouse was dedicated in 1970 to replace the old one, which is now occupied by offices. *Location:* 601 Philadelphia Street at Sixth Street.

1A. *Old Courthouse*

1A. *Statue of Jimmy Stewart at Courthouse*

1B. Houston House (First National Bank Building) (brick), built about 1838, housed Indiana's first banking house, opened in 1857 by John T. Hogg and managed by William C. Boyle. In 1864 the First National Bank was organized here with James Sutton as president (see also *Sutton-Elkin House*). The title to the lot can be traced back to June 15, 1808, when it was sold to William Wrigley of Greensburg. Succeeding owners included William Clark in 1809, William Houston in 1822, George Christy's shoe store in 1865, Henry Hall's news agency and book store in 1870, Houk Drug Store, and James S. Blair in 1920. The rear of the building houses an authentically researched half-timbered English pub, Coventry Inn. *Location:* Philadelphia and Sixth streets.

1C. Black Horse Inn, now American Legion (brick) was also known as the Detwiler, Sweeney, and Central Hotel. Built about 1820, this Federal-style building with seven bays now has a third story added in the late 1800s. John Huey first owned the property, which was sold to William Caldwell in 1819 and to Philip Gallagher in 1837. The American Legion bought the building in 1943. It was remodeled in 1983. *Location:* 532 Philadelphia Street.

1D. A. W. Taylor House (stuccoed stone with quoins) was built by John Lucas between 1807 and 1831; according to some, in 1817. It is believed to be the oldest structure in Indiana County. In 1846 Alexander W. Taylor, a lawyer and congressman, purchased it for $700 from the Johnston estate. It was sold

from the Taylor family in 1950, to the Charles Hawk family. A wooden addition housed the library. *Location:* 530 Philadelphia Street.

1E. H. P. Griffith House (brick) was built in 1892. This Queen Anne house was later purchased by Robert Marcus, Esq. The front gable is quite decorative. *Location:* 555 Philadelphia Street.

1F. Barr House (brick), with fanlighted doorways, was built around 1904. This five-bay house was built on a lot first bought by Hon. John Young, first president judge of Indiana County. The property, once supporting a tavern, has other significance, for here in 1772 Fergus Moorhead camped by a spring, which is now walled in at the rear of the property. Moorhead's stone house at the old fort site has been demolished in recent years, making this site the only remaining link to this early settler. *Location:* 429 Philadelphia Street.

1G. A. W. Wilson Building (pressed brick) was erected in 1880 by Andrew W. Wilson and John Sutton on land purchased in 1858 from Ephraim Carpenter. This store, designed by James Drum, had the borough's first large display windows. In later years it became a furniture store (Sutton family), and in 1907 a hardware store purchased by A. T. Taylor and Son, followed by numerous hardware dealers. *Location:* 636 Philadelphia Street.

1H. Wissel House (brick), in Greek Revival style, was built about 1870 by John Adam Wissel, a German immigrant who sold bark to local tanners. In 1867 Wissel had purchased this property from John Sutor. Now a law office, the building was purchased in 1977 and then restored by an attorney, Robert Douglass. *Location:* 917 Philadelphia Street.

1I. Buffalo, Rochester, & Pittsburgh Railroad Station (frame) was built in 1904 of typical railroad architecture with bracketed overhanging roof eaves. An adjacent gasoline station has been renovated to match this style and contains offices, while the station has been converted to a restaurant by the same owner. *Location:* 1125 Philadelphia Street.

1J. County Sheriff's House and Jail (brick, with cut-stone quoins) includes the sheriff's office and eleven other rooms. This is the fourth county jail, designed by C. H. Sparks and built by John Hastings. Years ago executions took place in the courtyard between this house and the old courthouse. The last hanging occurred in 1913. *Location:* North Sixth Street near Nixon.

1K. Gov. Fisher House (frame), which included a ballroom, was built by the Edward Rowe family in 1902 and copied from a house in Warren, Pa. It was the home of Gov. John S. Fisher prior to his election and until his death. In 1927 the Queen-Anne-style Georgian house was occupied by Robert M. Fisher. (See also *Gov. John Fisher Birthplace.*) *Location:* 220 North Sixth Street.

Note: The Brown Hotel (brick) is a late Victorian landmark at North and Water streets. It has been adapted for use as a restaurant in recent years.

1L. Vogel Brothers Building (brick) was built in 1830–40. This Federal-style structure became the Vogel brothers' tailor and harness shop in 1849. *Location:* 11 North Sixth Street.

1M. Messenger Building (brick), having ornate cast-iron window heads, was built about 1840. Once used as a post office, it is the home of the *Indiana Messenger*, an independent local journal established about 1856. *Location:* 15 North Sixth Street.

Note: Graff's Market, listed on the National Register of Historic Places, is also on this street.

1N. Woolen Mill (frame) was moved to this location after it was no longer used as a blanket outlet at the turn of the century. In recent years it has been converted into an apartment building. *Location:* Near railroad station (behind gasoline station) on Philadelphia Street at North Eleventh Street.

1O. "Marion Center Creamery" (brick)—the old name is on the building—was built in the early 1900s. It represents a type of business that was once common. Over the years buildings such as these have either been torn down or converted to other uses. *Location:* Foundry Avenue at 1075 Water Street.

Note: In view, to the rear of this building, is a five-story brick structure of similar Romanesque style, part of the creamery complex. Located on North Eleventh and Oak streets.

1P. David Ralston House (brick) was built by David Ralston when he moved to Indiana from Shelocta to serve as sheriff (1842–45). Bennet Whissel purchased this house and ran the "Mansion House" inn here. The house, built in 1843, has an addition erected about 1850. It is now used for offices and apartments. *Location:* 33–41 South Sixth Street.

1Q. Clark House (brick) houses the Historical and Genealogical Society of Indiana County, founded in 1938 by Frances Strong Helman. It was built by John Sutton and was later the residence of Silas M. Clark, associate justice of the Pennsylvania Supreme Court. It was built in 1869–70 on the site of Indiana County's first academy building, opened in 1816. The county bought the home from the Clark heirs in 1917 for $20,000. After World War I the American Legion removed the partitions between several rooms to increase meeting space. In 1951 the Indiana County Historical and Genealogical Society moved its headquarters into the building, where it also maintains a library and museum.

On the front lawn is the signature stone from the Alexander Stewart hardware store, which was established in 1853 and stood on the site of the Savings and Trust Company, corner of Philadelphia and Eighth streets. (See *Stewart House.*) Tours and visits by arrangement. *Location:* Wayne Avenue and Sixth Street.

Note: Nearby is the first community cemetery, known as Memorial Park, which was in use before the town was laid out.

1R. Indiana Female Seminary (brick, stuccoed) is the last remaining building constructed by Adam Rowe, in 1840. This old seminary in later years became the home of J. Blair Sutton. Hickory pins were used in construction and a well on the property was used by the town's fire company in the days of bucket brigades. *Location:* 56 South Sixth Street.

1S. James Mitchell House (brick) was built in 1849 by James Mitchell, a local merchant and borough councilman. This Georgian- and Federal-style house has two front doors since it served both as a private residence and as a general merchandising store. A frame addition dates from about 1873. Later occupants included Hugh Weir and Dr. Howard B. Buterbaugh, a well-known Indiana physician. Land was originally owned by George Clymer, one of the signers of the Declaration of Independence. *Location:* 57 South Sixth Street.

1T. Zion Lutheran Manse (frame) was built in 1885–90. This Queen-Anne-style mansion is situated near the 1923 stone Gothic church of the same denomination. *Location:* 114 South Sixth Street.

1U. John W. Sutton House (brick) was built about 1882–83 by John W. Sutton, an Indiana merchant and son of John Sutton. The building served as the Calvary United Presbyterian manse from 1920 until 1963. This Second Empire house later became the law offices of Mack and Bonya. *Location:* 134 South Sixth Street.

1V. Nixon House (brick) was built in 1843–44 by Edward Nixon on the site of the old 1841 jail. Stones in the foundation came from the early structure. It was once the post office for Indiana, when Nixon's daughter was the postmistress. At one time Judge Silas Clark practiced law here. *Location:* 595 School Street (299 Sixth Street).

1W. Carter-Sutton House (brick), having a combined style of Second Empire (mansard roof) and Italian villa, once had a large square tower which was removed in the 1970s. J. P. Carter built this mansion for $30,000 in 1870 to retaliate for neighbor Silas Clark's hiring the architect Carter had wanted. In 1879 Thomas Sutton, son of John Sutton, bought the house. Today it is an apartment building. *Location:* 209 South Sixth Street at School Street.

1X. Old Borough Hall (brick) was built in 1912. This eclectic Beaux Arts structure was designed by the architect H. King Conklin of Newark, N.J. The contractor was Fred Herlinger. It has been restored in recent years. *Location:* 39 North Seventh Street.

1X. Old Borough Hall

1Y. Stewart House (brick and stucco) was the home of Alexander Stewart, a prominent citizen and the father of motion-picture star James Stewart. (See *Clark House.*) *Location:* 104 North Seventh Street.

1Z. White's Woods Nature Center is on land originally owned by Thomas White and his son, Harry White, both well-known judges of Indiana County. An English-style estate was planned here but never completed. The foundation of the gatekeeper's house is all that remains on the property, which has been developed with marked trails for nature study. *Location:* At end of North Twelfth Street.

1AA. Indiana University began in 1875 as a state normal school for the training of teachers. The Student Union Building is on the site of Shaver's spring and is marked by a fountain plaque. The school, noted for its department of music, was the first university in the Commonwealth to be completely state owned.

    a. Indian Springs Marker over a spring site in the cafeteria on the first floor of the Student Union building reads: "Troops camped here Sept. 6, 1756, led by Lt. Col. John Armstrong."

    b. John Sutton Hall (brick), built in 1875, is the original college building and one of the finest of its kind at that time.

5. *McCormick House*

c. University Museum contains watercolors done by an alumnus, James Drake; a nineteenth-century dormitory room; etc.

d. Sutton-Elkin House (brick), known as Breezedale, is the oldest structure on the campus. George Cedric, first passenger agent for the Pennsylvania Railroad in Indiana, sold the property to James Sutton, brother of John Sutton (see *Clark House*) and first president of the First National Bank in Indiana. Sutton married Sarah Stansbury, a teacher in Blairsville. This Victorian house was built by 1868. When the Suttons owned it, the estate included a driveway gate that closed automatically. Sutton died in 1870, and the home was sold in 1899 to John P. Elkin, state supreme court justice. Elkin added a law library and a Turkish room, which has a hexagonal tile fireplace. A cupola on top of the third story provides a fine view. The structure became part of the campus in 1947 and was first used as a men's dormitory. It later housed the music, foreign language, and art departments. Since a recent remodeling and restoration, it houses alumni offices, guest rooms, a library, and other rooms. *Location:* School Street between Seventh and Oakland streets.

2. Cumming's Dam was built in 1908 by the Buffalo, Rochester & Pittsburgh Railroad to provide a water supply for its steam locomotives. The dam has a span of 455 feet and is maintained to provide fishing and other recreation. *Location:* Near Ernest, off SR 0110 (in Rayne Township at Blue Spruce Park).

3. Creekside Station (frame) is a beautiful example of one of the few remaining railroad stations once common along the Buffalo, Rochester & Pittsburgh route, now the Baltimore & Ohio. *Location:* Creekside.

4. Gov. John Fisher Birthplace (frame) was the birthplace of John S. Fisher (1867–1940), whose family still owns the house after more than 120 years. Fisher won the Pennsylvania governorship in 1926 by the largest majority given any man for this office in the state's history. He supported an extensive state road-building program, revised the state fiscal system, and promoted conservation of natural resources. *Location:* From Plumville go north for 0.9 mile on SR 0210; turn right 0.2 mile on Fisher Road, SR 0085 (South Mahoning Township).

5. McCormick House (stone) was the home of John B. McCormick (1834–1924), musician, painter, and inventor of the water turbine used in early hydroelectric plants, including those in Niagara Falls and St. Petersburg, Russia (Leningrad). He also published several musical works. One of his turbines operates at Ewing's Mill (q.v.). Inside the house is a model of the 1876 steam Hercules turbine, the design of which is basic to all the hydroelectric plants in the world. This structure was partly built by Judge Joshua Lewis in 1817, and the medieval-style tower was added by McCormick. The home was later owned by John Kerr Stewart, great-grandfather of actor Jimmy Stewart. *Location:* 3 miles northeast of Smicksburg, off SR 0954 on McCormick Road.

6. Mahoning United Presbyterian Church (frame) was organized about 1825. This handsome building was constructed of adzed timbers and round joists with the bark left on. It is now in poor condition and is used as a voting place for East Mahoning Township. *Location:* 0.7 mile west of Gilgal, on SR 0210.

7. Gilgal Presbyterian Church (brick) was organized in 1808 under Redstone Presbytery with James Galbreath installed as the first regular pastor. He served until 1817. The first church of 1810 was of log construction; the second, built in 1838, was brick. The third and present church, with a tower, was erected in 1887. *Location:* North of Hamill. From US 119 turn west 0.1 mile on SR 4016 to Gilgal Road; thence 0.6 mile to church.

Note: In the Gilgal cemetery is the grave of Samuel Brady, uncle of the famous Indian scout and one of those who took part in the 1756 Armstrong expedition.

8. Old Mill (frame), once a gristmill, now serves as a feed mill. *Location:* Marion Center, SR 0403 near US 119.

9. Lewis House (stone), with three bays, is an early landmark. It was once the home of Joshua Lewis. *Location:* North of SR 4018, 1 mile west of SR 0210 (South Mahoning Township).

10. Lockard Octagonal Barn (frame), built between 1860 and 1880 with a cupola, is a one-story structure now used for storage. This building is a rare type and should be preserved. *Location:* Between Trade City and Plumville (South Mahoning Township).

11. Smicksburg, a tiny borough founded in 1827 by Rev. J. George Schmick, a Lutheran minister from Huntingdon County, is worthy of preserving. Half of this community was destroyed during the flood control project of 1938–40. Today the town is known for its Amish farmhouses, quilts, and hickory chairs. *Location:* SR 0954, northwest part of county.

12. Lime Kiln (stone), built in 1897 (date on top stone), is a treasured landmark in western Pennsylvania. Very few of these early struc-

tures have been preserved. (Another of this type is in Salem Township in Westmoreland County.) Years ago farmers brought limestone from an area now known as Groundhog Park on US 119 to this site and dumped their loads into the top of this kiln. They then loaded the ashes from the stone onto wagons for spreading on their farms in order to neutralize the soil. This kiln was built by George Gourley, who owned all the land from this site to the town of Covode, as well as the limestone quarry. It operated until the 1930s. Its present owner is Donald Gourley, grandson of George. *Location:* East of US 119 across from Harrick's service station and store, on Gourley Road which bears to the left off the highway (opposite a green gas tank) next to Jefferson County line north of Covode.

13. Commodore Coal Town is composed of over eighty concrete coal patch houses, most in shotgun style. (Some of the buildings are of bricklike tile construction.) A large company store (concrete) and a school (brick, partially stuccoed) also remain. *Location:* Commodore, off SR 0286, northeast of Clymer (Green Township).

14. Gipsy, a coal mine town, has a timbered coal tipple, brick mine buildings, and frame company houses. Few tipples of this type from the bituminous coal mining era are still standing. *Location:* On SR 1056 off SR 0289 near Hooverhurst (Montgomery Township).

15. Old Mill Antique Shop (unpainted vertical frame) was built prior to the Civil War as a gristmill by Martin Wissell. It was said that "no one could shoe a horse or turn a piece of wood like Mart Wissell." He operated his gristmill, a blacksmith shop, and a wood shop in this rustic building. On the property are the stone burrs from the mill. Across the road is the old frame house which used to be known as Owens' Hotel. The Owens family had the house and property before the Wissells. It is also reported that counterfeit money used to be made at this place in the evening hours in the late 1800s. On display are several large paintings on tin, once belonging to Alexander Stewart, actor Jimmy Stewart's father. Pictures of Alexander's race horses were painted by Lester Patterson. Nearby are several small red brick buildings once operated by the Clearfield Bituminous Coal Company. Present owners of the gristmill property are Samuel and Mary Kemp. Open weekdays. *Location:* Past Faith Road on road to Tanoma (SR 1005) off SR 0286 (2 miles south of Clymer) in Rayne Township 6 miles east of Indiana.

17C. Presbyterian Church

16. Moorhead House (stone) was built about 1835. In recent years it was owned by the File family, followed by Dr. Michael Cavoto. *Location:* Clymer, 480 South Benjamin Franklin Street.

17. Cherry Tree has many fine Greek Revival buildings constructed in the 1840s and later.

17A. Cherry Tree Joe McCreery Grave is the burial site of Joseph McCreery (1805– 95). Much folklore has grown up around this famous Pennsylvania lumberman; and many of the tales that first evolved about him were later told about Paul Bunyan. McCreery, who served in the Eleventh Pennsylvania Cavalry Regiment of the Civil War, lived in Cherry Tree, an important corner of the 1768 Pennsylvania purchase. *Location:* Cherry Tree Cemetery.

17B. Pennsylvania Purchase Monument is at the junction of Indiana, Cambria, and Clearfield counties (see *Canoe Place,* Clearfield County).

Note: Purchase Line Academy, a boarding school established in 1873 and operated until 1913, is off SR 0286 near the village of Purchase Line (Green Township).

17C. Presbyterian Church (frame), an altered Greek Revival structure, was built in 1859. *Location:* SR 1026 at SR 0580.

17D. National Bank of the Commonwealth (brick) is an impressive three-story building with Richardsonian arched windows. It also has a rusticated stone foundation and parapeted gables. *Location:* Junction of SR 1026 and SR 0580.

18. Jacksonville Passenger Station (frame) was built in 1913 and serviced the Buffalo,

Rochester & Pittsburgh Railroad. In 1945 it was adapted as a tavern/restaurant. *Location:* Jacksonville, Black Lick Township, SR 0286.

19. Ross House (limestone), with a frontdoor fanlight, was built in 1823 by John Ross who had purchased the land in 1811. The land was first settled by James Wilkins who, according to legend, planted an apple orchard here in 1769 and was later driven away by Indians. It is also stated that the Caldwell family lived here around that time. Robert McGee moved to this homestead in 1852. Alex Bennett erected the barn; and a fine stone springhouse, built with the house, has been preserved. In more recent years the property was bought by the Chillingworth family. (Also known as the N. C. Mather property.) *Location:* Homer City, north of Jacksonville Road at end of Liberty Street at Two-Lick Creek (Center Township).

20. Church of God (frame), dating from the late 1800s, is a two-story Carpenter Gothic building with Victorian S-brackets under the eaves. This fine rural church has marbled stained glass (orchid) windows, a box steeple, and radial decor. *Location:* West Lebanon, SR 3027 (Young Township), near Armstrong County.

21. Horner Houses (stone), built by stonemason John Horner, both have arched entrances. It is believed that the construction was paid for with whiskey. One house, later purchased by the Cameron family, is north of Shelocta Road; the other, built for Judge Thomas White, is just north of Indiana. *Location:* Armstrong Township.

22. Shelocta Passenger Station (frame), built between 1903 and 1910, formerly served the Buffalo, Rochester & Pittsburgh Railroad. It was converted into a church in recent years. *Location:* US 422 about 1 mile east of intersection with SR 0156 in Shelocta, adjacent to B&O crossing (Armstrong Township).

23. Martin Smith House (log), later owned by John Smith, Martin's son, is one of the few log cabins (one story) still remaining in Indiana County. *Location:* Between West Lebanon and Elder's Ridge (Young Township).

24. Penn Run Roller Mills (frame) are housed in a three-story, 4,500-square-foot gristmill built in 1885–86, replacing an earlier grain-grinding mill destroyed by fire. The present one was built by James C. Rugh, Frederick Cameron, and William McFeaters.

24. Penn Run Roller Mills

29. Stone House Stagecoach Stop

The mill pond was drained after the drowning of Elder Fyock in the late 1800s. In later years the original burr stones were replaced by three stands of Knowlton & Dolan Roller Mills. A (B. D. Hess) gasoline pump stand is preserved inside. The millers and their approximate time periods were: James Barr, 1874; James and Samuel Rugh, 1886; James Rugh (bought out Samuel), 1912; John Lytle, 1925; D. G. Strong, 1937; Jake and Roy Bash, 1950; and Grant Cramer, to 1980. The present owner, Charles Shultz, researched the history of this old industrial site. All the original machinery is still intact in the mill. *Location:* Penn Run, SR 0553 (Cherryhill Township).

25. Deal (Diehl) House (log) was built in 1800–06 by the Lamburgs; it was later owned by the George Deal family. *Location:* Near Penn Run, on T 633 (Springfield Road) near Clymer and crossroads of T 752 and T 868 (Cherryhill Township).

26. Martin House (stone), with three bays, was built by Joseph Askins in 1808. In later years it was owned by Allen and John Martin. More recently the Larry Buterbaugh family purchased the property. *Location:* Between Penn Run and Heilwood, just north of Penns Manor High School off SR 0553 (Cherryhill Township).

27. Diamondville Cut is a man-made gorge for the passage of a branch of the Penn Central Railroad. It was opened about 1901 by the D. F. Keenan Company, which lost money on the project and went bankrupt. Its purpose was to eliminate six very crooked miles of railroad. The cut is about one-fourth mile long

and one hundred feet deep below the trestle, which is now closed to automobile traffic. *Location:* Diamondville (Cherryhill Township).

28. Ewing's Mill (frame with stone foundation) was built in the 1820s and put in operation about 1824 by Christian Keller. It was purchased by John Ewing in 1913. It is one of the few early American flour mills still in existence in this area. The structure contains a McCormick turbine, built in 1869, and an Oliver Evans hoist. The original records have been preserved inside the building. The old mill, containing a country store, an 1880 saloon, and a museum, has been restored by Ray Rodkey and William Rodgers as a tourist attraction and in more recent years has been operated by the William Rodgers family. There is an early stone house near the mill. Tours by appointment. *Location:* Strongstown, 10 miles east of Indiana on US 422 near Nolo, next to Yellow Creek State Park.

29. Stone House Stagecoach Stop (stone), a three-bay house, originally had holes beneath the windows and according to legend was an underground railroad station. The property was owned by Thomas Monahan from 1821 to 1825 and by Henry Kinter from 1825 to 1829. It served as the Nolo post office from 1836 to 1923. The first postmaster was Josiah Lydick. In more recent years it was purchased by the Jonathan Mack family. There is a springhouse behind the house. *Location:* Nolo Summit (once known as Stone House), just south of US 422 at SR 1011 (Pine Township).

30. McCrory Home Site, now owned by a Christian retreat center, was the homestead of John B. McCrory, founder of the McCrory store chain. The house, which burned in 1986, was used as his summer home until

1931 when he retired, at which time he and his wife made this their permanent residence until his death in 1943. His widow then sold the estate to a worldwide West Indian mission for a rest home and headquarters. *Location:* South of Brush Valley, SR 0259.

31. Old Home Manor was the mansion of John M. Mack, founder of the Murphy chain store. Below the new Mack family residence are the foundation stones and remains of the old Mack farmhouse and outbuildings. *Location:* 2 miles south of Brush Valley, off SR 0259.

32. Brush Valley

32A. Truby House (brick) was built in 1858 by Simeon Truby, who kept a store in this community. The Nesbitt family occupied the home at a later date. In more recent years it was purchased and restored by the Thomas Harley family. *Location:* Main Street, SR 0056.

32B. Victorian Doctor's Office and Maternity Hospital (frame) was built in the late 1800s. It was originally a residence. *Location:* Across from Truby house.

32C. Mack-Murphy Family Memorial (stone), situated over a spring, has the following inscription: "A cup of cold water given in my name." It is a memorial to Sarah Ellen Murphy, wife of John M. Mack. She was the daughter of George Murphy, and granddaughter of John Murphy (son of Sir John Murphy) who left his home "Irish Lands" in Ireland in 1801 to settle in Brush Valley. Here he married Mary Armitage and together they established an early educational system. *Location:* Across from Truby house.

32D. Campbell House (brick) was built in 1855. Formerly it was known as the "old Campbell Hotel." This five-bay house has been restored in recent years. *Location:* SR 0259 and SR 0056 (Main Street).

33. St. Patrick's Roman Catholic Church (frame) was erected in 1872 on land purchased on July 2, 1776, by Joseph Cauffman and another merchant by the name of Cottringer from Philadelphia. Although Cauffman and Cottringer wanted to establish a Catholic settlement here, nothing much was done until 1806 to 1815. In 1806 Cauffman transferred the tract to Mark Wilcox and Rev. Matthew Carr with the proviso it should be held for a house of worship. In 1810 it was transferred to the bishop of Philadelphia. There is evidence

that the parish is an offshoot of the Loretto colony of Father Demetrius Gallitzin. A log church was completed about 1821–22. Between 1827 and 1832 a stone church was built, and the Franciscan brothers later maintained an orphanage here until it was moved to Pittsburgh. They conducted the first seminary for the Diocese of Pittsburgh until Bishop O'Connor transferred it to Pittsburgh. Only traces of the second church's foundation remain in the woods adjacent to the cemetery. The third church was erected in 1852 and, according to tradition, burned in 1869. In 1870–72 the fourth and present building was constructed. Among the many priests who served this congregation were Terence McGirr, Bonaventure Maguire, William Lambert, Richard Phelan (fourth bishop of Pittsburgh), and Augustine Marzhauser. *Location:* Camerons Bottom, 2.5 miles north of old Benjamin Franklin Pike (now US 422), in Pine Township (near Yellow Creek).

34. Power Stations
a. Keystone Generating Station, built in the late 1960s, is one of the first and one of the largest mine-mouth, electric-generating stations in the world. Using five million tons of coal annually, the plant is designed to supply power for thirty to forty years. Its twin smokestacks are 800 feet high. It can best be viewed from the Power Vista, an overlook off SR 0156 near the site that provides information about the plant. *Hours:* May 30–September 15: Daily, 1–7 P.M. *Location:* 1 mile south of Shelocta, off SR 0156.

b. Penelec Generating Station (brick, original buildings), owned by the Pennsylvania Electric Company, is a component of the billion dollar Chestnut Ridge Energy Center. A 600-foot chimney towers over the complex, which was built in 1919 and opened in 1921, the first pit mouth station in the region. A new industrial waste treatment system was added in 1979. Penelec, increasing from 18 megawatts to 200, operates and owns eight coal-fired stations, including Homer City's, and two hydroelectric stations. *Location:* Near Seward, on the northwestern bank of the Conemaugh River in East Wheatfield Township, near SR 0711 on SR 2009 at Westmoreland County line.

c. Homer City Electric Generating Station has the tallest smokestack in the United States (over 2,000 feet high) and is located at a mine mouth. *Location:* US 119 at Coral, 1 mile south of Homer City.

35. Sutton House (stone), with three bays, is one of the early rare stone houses of the county. *Location:* Just north of SR 2013 at T 882 (East Wheatfield Township).

36. J. S. Wagoner Spring House (stone) is built of rubble stone with quoin cut stones. The second story of this structure once served as a schoolhouse. The building was erected in 1818. *Location:* T 726, 1 mile south of Clyde (West Wheatfield Township).

Note: One of the few early coal tipples left in the county is 1 mile south of SR 0259 on SR 2008, 2 miles north of Bolivar.

37. Buena Vista Iron Furnace (cut stone) was erected in 1847 by McClelland & Company during the Mexican War. In 1853 it was absorbed by Cambria Ironworks, and was later owned by Warren Delano, uncle of Franklin D. Roosevelt. In 1957 the Delano Coal Company donated the blast furnace to the Historical and Genealogical Society of Indiana. It is now in deteriorating condition. *Location:* Between Brush Valley and Armagh, off SR 0056 at Black Lick Creek. Follow US 22 to Armagh and SR 0056 north 2.25 miles to north end of bridge over Black Lick Creek. Turn left and continue on dirt road 200 to 300 feet. Furnace is below bank on south side of railroad tracks.

Note: An old blacktop road is within seventy-five feet of the furnace. It was the highway before the bridge was built.

38. Liggett House (brick) is a one-and-a-half-story cottage style house built in 1818 by William Liggett, whose father came from Glasgow, Scotland. *Location:* Centerville (West Weatfield Township).

39. Mount Park (brick), a five-bay house built about 1820–30, once known as the Meaner Tavern, is now a private home. *Location:* On US 22, West Wheatfield Township, 1 mile east of Burrell Township line.

40. John Leard House (brick), a five-bay house constructed of bricks made on the property, was first occupied by the Fergus Moorhead family. *Location:* Black Lick, across Conemaugh River (Black Lick Township).

41. Black Lick Greek Orthodox Church (buff brick) has a fine set of gold onion towers. *Location:* Black Lick, US 119, above Strangford near Catalpa Drive.

42. Luther Chapel (brick) was built on a lot purchased in 1850 for five dollars. It cost $2,500 to construct and was dedicated in 1852. Services had been started in 1828 in the Black Lick School by Rev. Peter Sahm. *Location:* Coral, off US 119 on Power Plant Road.

Note: Grove Chapel, a frame Lutheran church, is on US 119, 5 miles south of the village of Home.

43. John S. Agey House (brick, stuccoed) was owned by one of the first settlers in the area, later by William Bigler Hill. A woolen mill once operated at this site. *Location:* North of Two Lick, near US 119, above Homer City (White Township).

44. White Township Stone House is one of the county's early surviving stone houses. *Location:* Just east of old US 119, 0.5 mile south of new US 119.

45. Ferguson House (stone) was built in 1823 by the Ferguson family and occupied by S. Ferguson in 1855–56. An addition was built in 1950. The stones for both sections came from a quarry near Two Lick Creek. In recent years the house was purchased by Thomas D. Goodrich. A stone springhouse is also on the property. *Location:* Northwest of the intersection of SR 0954 and Lucerne Road, on Indiana–Brush Road at the forks between Two Lick and Yellow Creek (White Township).

46. Packsaddle Gap was believed in the canal and portage railroad days to be haunted by a man who accidentally shot his girlfriend, mistaking her for a deer. A widely known landmark, it was utilized by the Frankstown Path, Northern Pike, Pennsylvania Canal, Pennsylvania Railroad, and William Penn Highway as an access route to the west. *Location:* From Blairsville go east for 2 miles on Old William Penn Highway; turn south past golf course and through village of Strangford; continue 1.5 miles to open coal field on SR 2002 at lower end of village for fine view through gap.

47. Blairsville Bridge Abutments (stone) are all that remain of the first bridge at this location, built in 1821–22 for $15,000. This 300-foot structure, of Wernwag style, was the largest single-arch bridge in the United States at that time. James Moore was the contractor. The bridge fell in 1874 and was replaced by another in 1875. A third structure was erected in 1889 following the Johnstown Flood, which destroyed the second bridge. The fourth and present bridge, built in 1934–35, is adjacent to the abutments of the original one. *Location:*

Blairsville, spanning the Conemaugh River between Indiana and Westmoreland counties.

48. The Conemaugh River Reservoir, the "dry" type (capable of absorbing a large quantity of runoff when needed), is adjacent to a concrete gravity dam 137 feet high, 128 feet wide, and 1,265 feet long. *Location:* North of New Alexandria, take T 939 east to its intersection with T 912; follow T 912 north (left) to its intersection with T 312; turn off to the east (right) and follow T 312 to the dam.

Note: The Conemaugh Dam was completed September 1953 and is one of the largest flood-control dams in western Pennsylvania; it has 14 crest gates. The maximum pool extends twenty-one miles up the Conemaugh and Blacklick valleys and can impound 11.76 billion cubic feet of water. Below the dam are the remains of two old railroad tunnels and bridges built in 1883 and 1905.

49. Pennsylvania Main Line Canal is partly in Indiana County—when it runs on the north side of the Conemaugh River. The Kiskiminetas-Conemaugh line opened in 1829. Every effort should be made to preserve the noteworthy vestiges of this famous canal.

50. Blairsville

50A. Marshall House (brick) was built by James Campbell about 1820. Early owners were a blacksmith named Thomas, Sarah Lindsey, Alexander Nesbett, and Samuel Baird. In 1840 Baird sold the property to Dr. Robert Johnson Marshall. The property originally included a granary and stables. Private residence. *Location:* 125 Market Street, between Spring and Main streets.

50B. St. Peter's Episcopal Church (brick stuccoed), the oldest surviving church structure in Indiana County, was built in 1830, a gift of William G. Davis who was on the building committee. Its contractor was Robert Gregory. Church meetings had begun August 17, 1828, before the church was erected. The first rector was David C. Page, and S. K. Brunot conducted the first service. Alonzo Livermore, one of the promoters of the Pennsylvania Canal, was influential in establishing the church. Unfortunately the earliest records of this church have been lost. The adjacent rectory was built in 1889. *Location:* On West Campbell Street between North Walnut and Spring streets.

50C. Antes Snyder House (brick) was the home of the grandson of Pennsylvania's third governor, Simon Snyder. In 1864 Antes Snyder moved to Blairsville and engineered the right of way for the Pennsylvania Railroad. *Location:* 36 East Campbell Street.

50D. Cunningham House (log, completely concealed) was one of the first three homes erected when Blairsville was laid out in 1818. At this time a contest was held in which a free lot was given to the person who built his house first. Among the men who participated—John Cunningham, Isaac Green, and James Rankin—the winner was Green. It is now adjacent to a large brick market and is behind the old Lintner house. *Location:* Near corner of West Market and Spring streets. (Structure in front of log house is brick with stucco and faces Market Street.)

Note: Another early house built about the same year is located at 146 South Walnut Street.

50E. Artley House (frame) was built in the manner of an early railroad station in 1852 by Daniel Artley, master carpenter for the Pennsylvania Railroad, which ran past the house down old Main Street to the wharf at the river. After Artley's death the house was sold to Samuel Miller, an attorney. It is reputed that President Taft visited the Millers in this house. The Biesingers purchased the property in 1947. *Location:* 304 South Walnut Street.

50F. Railroad Station House (frame), converted into a beautiful residence, was built as a station in 1851 when the Pennsylvania Railroad was completed to Blairsville. It later became the home of the Zimmer family, early residents. *Location:* 152 Old Main Street at Liberty Street.

50G. Graff House (brick) was owned by Henry Graff in 1837 and was sold to his brother John in 1851. This L-shaped home formerly had four porches and has nine fireplaces. Bricks from an outside oven were used to build an adjacent garage. On the property near the house is a smaller red brick building, originally a stable but later used as a hiding place for escaped slaves. (John Graff was an agent of the underground railroad.) In 1847 John bought the warehouse business belonging to his brothers Henry and Peter. *Location:* 195 South Liberty Street.

Note: John's son Alexander lived in the Graff house at 216 South Liberty in 1857. It was purchased by Charles Graff in 1969.

50H. Blairsville Railroad Station (brick) is restored and now serves as a bank, a fine example of adaptive use for an early building of consequence. *Location:* 190 East Market Street at railroad.

Note: Nearby at 138 East Market Street is a fine Italianate brick commercial building.

51. Smith Station House (brick) was built as a summer home by Robert Smith, a broker and coal operator. His grandfather settled in the area in 1797. Robert purchased the property from Moss Stewart in 1825. It is reputed that "Buffalo Bill" Cody visited here while traveling with his show, which performed at the Old Town Hall (now gone) in Blairsville. The house was later purchased by William Torrance. *Location:* About 1.5 miles north of Blairsville, on Socialville Road off US 22.

Note: The old Brainard-Earhart brick farmhouse nearby, built in 1833, has been completely surrounded by strip-mining.

52. Marshall House (stone), on Black Legs Creek, was built about 1790 by Christian Miller. A spring below the house runs into Black Lick Creek. The owner in recent years is Fred Kunkle. This five-bay house is reputed to be the oldest in the county. *Location:* Clarksburg, east of SR 0286, at end of town on SR 3007, 200 feet across bridge. Sits back from road just beyond a fine early five-bay brick house.

53. Hart House (stone), with four bays, is an early house, worthy of preservation. *Location:* West of SR 3003, 0.5 mile west of SR 3002 (Conemaugh Township, between Tunnelton and SR 0286).

54. Saltsburg, an early salt industry town, later a stop on the Pennsylvania Canal, was laid out in 1821 by Andrew Boggs and incorporated in 1838. Three stone canal markers remain on Point Street at the canal site.

54A. Stonehouse Museum, home of the merchant Robert McIlvain, was built about 1840. It was purchased in 1968 by the Saltsburg area branch of the Indiana County Historical and Genealogical Society. It is furnished with interesting early memorabilia. *Hours:* April 15–October 15: Saturdays, 2–5 P.M. Group tours by appointment. *Donation. Location:* 105 Point Street.

Note: Another stone house at 214 Washington Street (SR 0286) is a canal rowhouse, once a drygoods store run by the brothers Robert and William McIlvain until 1831. Robert continued to own the property until 1875.

54A. Stonehouse Museum

54B. McIlvain House (stone), built by John White around 1835, was also the home of the Presbyterian minister, Rev. W. W. Woodend from 1847 to 1873. The Greek Revival portico was added in 1910. This house is next to the library. *Location:* 519 Salt Street.

Note: The Presbyterian church next to this house was built of brick in 1874.

54C. Altman's Mill (frame), formerly owned by George Altman, was built in the late 1800s. This early flour mill is an important link to the area's industrial past. All the original equipment is still intact. *Location:* Across from Stonehouse Museum.

54D. Saltsburg Bank (brick), later First National, and now Savings and Trust, was built in 1875. An earlier, smaller building was the predecessor of this bank. This long structure built in 1836 across the street (211 Point Street) belonged to Robert Taylor, a canal boatman and saddler. *Location:* 214 Point Street.

Note: Next to the bank on Point Street is the house of Samuel S. Moore, a tinner. It has a deed dating back to 1827 and a pre–Civil War addition. Doomed for destruction, the bank later saved it for the community. Also in this downtown area is the Salt Tavern, a former 1890s frame and door shop.

54E. Saltsburg Academy (brick) was built in 1851 and opened the following year. This co-educational school originally cost $3,300 with an additional $300 for the cupola. At first a civic venture (although W. W. Woodend, a Presbyterian, was its principal until 1859), it was purchased by the Presbyterian church in 1870 and renamed Memorial Institute. It was in operation after 1880, and probably at least for a decade more. The building was used as

54C. Altman's Mill

a public school until 1912. *Location:* High and Point streets.

54F. St. Matthew's Roman Catholic Church (brick) was built in 1847 and is adjacent to an early cemetery. It is now used for storage. A Catholic church erected in 1960 stands next to it. *Location:* Cathedral and Washington streets.

54G. John Martin House (frame), built around 1854, was the home of a stonemason employed by the Western Pennsylvania Railroad who built the 1855 railroad bridge (remains near Plum and Washington streets); the contractor was S. S. Jamison and the chief engineer S. H. Kneas. Martin is also credited with some of the stone houses in Saltsburg. *Location:* 502 High Street.

55. Ebenezer Church (brick) was organized about 1790. Joseph Henderson, its first regular pastor, served from 1799 to 1824. The congregation has erected four churches, two log and two brick. The present and fourth structure was built in 1870–71. *Location:* Lewisville, on SR 3009 northeast of Saltsburg (Conemaugh Township).

Note: In a nearby cemetery is the grave of John Montgomery, who died November 11, 1840, at age eighty-one. He was born in County Antrim, Ireland, came to America in 1774, and enlisted in 1776, serving as Washington's bodyguard all through the Revolution. His monument is signed, "Littell, S.C. [probably the stonecutter] Blairsville."

56. Baker Furnace (Indiana Iron Works) was built about 1850 by Elias Baker. (See *Baker Mansion,* Blair County.) *Location:* SR 0403, just north of SR 0711, 1.25 miles east of Armagh, near Cramer (ask permission at house).

Previous Sites Now Lost

Covode Academy, demolished
Josephine Furnace, demolished
Log House Museum, demolished (after it was moved to Clark House property)
Fergus Moorhead House, demolished
Proposed (Blairsville) Museum, not completed
Stump Fence, removed

Covered Bridges
(originally fifty)

Harmon's Bridge (1910) over Plum Creek, T 488 between Willet and Davis, Washington Township
Dice's (Trusal) Bridge (1870) SR 4006 over Plum Creek, between Willet and Davis, Washington Township
Kintersburg Bridge (1877) over Crooked Creek, T 612 near Kintersburg, Rayne Township
Thomas Fording Bridge (1879) over Crooked Creek, T 414, northeast of Shelocta, Armstrong Township

Note: The bridge over Richards Run in West Wheatfield Township is on the National Register of Historic Places.

Pennsylvania Historical and Museum Commission Markers

Indiana County Indiana, at courthouse, Philadelphia and Eighth streets
John B. McCormick US 22 west of Armagh
John S. Fisher SR 0085 east of Plumville
Moorhead's Fort Old US 422, 0.6 mile west of Indiana
Purchase of 1768 Cherry Tree, US 219
Rural Electrification Airport Road, off SR 0286, east end of Indiana
Saltsburg SR 0286 at Washington Street, Saltsburg

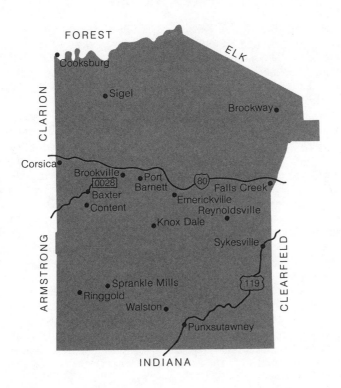

FOREST

ELK

CLARION

• Cooksburg

• Sigel

Brockway •

Corsica •

ARMSTRONG

Brookville •
[0028]
• Baxter
• Content

• Port
Barnett

Knox Dale

• Sprankle Mills

• Ringgold

Walston •

(80)

Falls Creek •

• Emerickville

• Reynoldsville

Sykesville •

(119)

CLEARFIELD

• Punxsutawney

INDIANA

Jefferson County

Capsule History

Jefferson County was named for Thomas Jefferson, who was president at the time of the county's founding on March 26, 1804. The county was erected out of Lycoming, and by the same act attached to Westmoreland. This political jurisdiction was transferred to Indiana County in 1806 and lasted until 1830, when Jefferson became independent. In 1824 the county began to vote for its own officers, with John Jenks, Andrew Barnett, and John Lucas elected as commissioners.

The county was diminished in size in 1843 when a part of Elk County was taken from Jefferson and again in 1848 when Forest County was derived solely from Jefferson. Then in 1868 its acreage was increased by a small section of Clearfield County. Today it has 656 square miles with a population of 48,303.

The first pioneers were Joseph and Andrew Barnett, who came from central Pennsylvania in the 1790s and settled on Sandy Lick Creek. Here, at the village known as Port Barnett, was the site of a sawmill built in 1795 by the Barnett brothers and Samuel Scott. Joseph Barnett became the first postmaster and owner of a hotel and store there. Near this site is a roadside park developed by an industrial firm. Many early settlers in the county were Revolutionary War soldiers who sought land and had come by way of the Susquehanna and Waterford Turnpike or on the Susquehanna and Allegheny rivers.

Several Indian trails crossed the county. The *Catawba Path* entered near Clarington and followed much the course of SR 0036 past Sigel, Brookville, and Stanton, then turning toward Worthville and Hamilton. The early Olean Road to Kittanning followed this path. The *Goschgoschink Path* followed the general course of US 322 by Corsica and Brookville and north of Rathmel. The *Great Shamokin Path* (over which Marie Le Roy, Barbara Leininger, and other captives were led on their way to Kittanning in 1755) entered near Troutville, running through or near Big Run, Punxsutawney, and Trade City. The *Punxsutawney-Venango Path* ran past Frostburg and Ringgold, toward Hawthorn. The *Venango-Chinklacamoose Path* followed the Goschgoschink through Brookville, thence by or near Emerickville, Sandy Valley, and on to West Liberty.

In 1814 soldiers under command of Maj. William McClelland encamped at Soldiers Run near Reynoldsville and at Port Barnett on their way to Erie on the old State Road.

Brookville, due to its location on the Erie Turnpike and the confluence of the Sandy Lick and North Fork creeks, was chosen for the county seat and laid out in 1830. It is reputed that Moses Knapp, a settler who came to Port Barnett in 1796 and operated a gristmill, built a log house here in 1801. Col. A. A. McKnight of Brookville organized the famous Wild Cat Regiment of the Civil War in 1861.

The county's oldest and largest town is Punxsutawney, settled in 1814 by John Jacob Fisher and in 1816 by Abraham Weaver, Dr. John Jenks, and Rev. David Barclay. It was laid out in 1819–21 by Barclay at an old Indian village. The name is derived from the Indian words *Ponks-utennick,* meaning "the town of the Ponkies" or "gnat-town." According to legend, the Indians told a Moravian missionary, John Heckewelder, that an old Indian sorcerer, Chinklacamoose, frightened people by appearing in grotesque forms. The sorcerer was finally killed and his ashes burned and scattered in the air. The ashes turned into "punkies." This area was mentioned in diaries of Moravian missionaries Christian Frederick Post, who visited here in 1758, and John Ettwein, who passed through in 1772.

Many stories have been told concerning wolves, bears, and panthers in the county, along with hunting expeditions, especially those of hunter Bill Long, who died in 1880. Other tales have been related about the halcyon lumbering days.

The log railroad era began here, with the first such railroad operating in 1874 in Jefferson County and Pennsylvania's last in 1948 in Elk County. The rich timberlands brought from New York and New England numerous individuals and companies making heavy investments at the headwaters of the Clarion River. After much of the forest land was depleted, coal, natural gas, and building stone provided resources for mineral industries. Coal was first discovered in the county at Pine Creek Township by a man named Douglass.

Today mine and quarry products are the main industries, followed by glass and clay products. The county has a varied economy, with slightly more invested in agriculture than in manufacturing. Part of Cook Forest State Park is in Jefferson County.

Landmarks

1. Brookville

1A. Courthouse (brick), the county's second, was built in 1868 at a cost of $78,742, not counting $668 for a bell and $725 for a clock. It was extensively altered in 1927. The first courthouse, a brick structure, was built in 1832 at a cost of $3,000 and was two stories high, with a one-story wing. An addition was made about 1850. It was torn down in 1866. *Location:* Main Street.

1B. Jefferson County Historical and Genealogical Society Museum (brick) is located in the Brady Craig house, built about 1840. This headquarters also houses a library and displays antiques and artifacts of the area. This is one of the first brick houses built in the area and is currently painted buff. *Hours:* Wednesday, 1–4 P.M.; Sunday, 2–4 P.M. Closed October 1–April 1. *Location:* About 236 Jefferson Street, above and behind courthouse.

1C. Brookville Historic District was designated the "Outstanding Pennsylvania Community for 1986" by the Pennsylvania Chamber of Business and Industry. It is an award-winning national model for the successful revitalization and restoration of Victorian buildings. At Christmastime a special program of Victorian entertainment, with costumed carollers, is performed by local merchants. *Location:* Main Street.

1D. Clark House (brick), Italianate in style, was built for Elizah Heath Clark, a local judge born in the 1830s (d. 1909). *Location:* 306 Main Street.

1E. McKnight House (white brick, painted gray), a typical Victorian house dating from shortly after the Civil War, was the home of Dr. W. J. McKnight, civic leader, historian, and physician. During the early years of his practice, he and other young physicians dug up the body of a man who had died of fever and began dissecting it. Discovery of this act shocked the town but helped to promote the 1867 legislation permitting dissection for scientific purposes. The home is still in the McKnight family. *Location:* 105 West Main Street.

1F. Marlin's Opera House (brick) when built in 1883 was one of the finest in northwestern Pennsylvania. Now the Marlin Building, it

1J. Hall House

houses a clothing store and offices. *Location:* 233 West Main Street.

1G. The Victoria House (brick) was originally Dr. W. J. McKnight's office and pharmacy, later a furniture store, and currently a restaurant. Now restored with a fine tin ceiling, it was built in 1873. The door with Dr. McKnight's name on it is preserved inside. *Location:* 209 Main Street.

1H. McCracken Hall (brick), with five bays and a large cupola, was built in 1868 by William McCracken. It later became the Union Hotel, then the McKinley Hotel. A music hall used to be on the third floor. The original painted ceiling is still intact. *Location:* 895 Main Street at Valley Street (Landmark Square).

Note: The owner of this building and several other historic structures in the area is the Dr. Martin McKinley family whose 1921 house (built by Frank Burnham), with a fine gazebo as an entranceway, sits on a hill across from this building.

1I. McKinley Hotel (brick) is a Victorian landmark in its original condition. It was built in two sections: one with five bays, and to the right, one with three bays. *Location:* 407 Main Street at Valley Street.

1J. Hall House (frame), a Greek Revival building with symmetrical wings, was built by Joseph E. Hall in 1848. It is described as "Brookville's oldest quality building." The Shaffer Mining Corporation is now located at this site. *Location:* 419 Main Street at Valley Street.

1K. Presbyterian Manse (brick), in George III style with a mansard roof, was built in 1886.

A twentieth-century stone church is next to it. *Location:* 120 White Street at Valley and Main streets.

1L. Litch Mansion and Art Gallery (frame), a Victorian mansion with a large cupola situated high on a hill, was built in 1850 (remodeled in the 1890s) by lumber baron T. K. Litch for his son Edward, a playboy and later an eccentric recluse. A big and remarkably well built home, it has survived five fires, has been struck by lightning, and was abandoned for fifteen years, during which it was stripped of its fireplaces, stained glass windows, and most of its doors. About 1920, as the mansion was being torn down, it was rescued and made into apartments. *Location:* 16 Taylor Street.

Note: The Litch summer cottage, behind the ball field up the hill, is occupied and in reasonably good condition.

1M. Sandt Homestead (frame), built about 1888, was the boyhood home of Earl Sandt, an early aviator of the Wright brothers' era. He is reputed to have been the first person to fly over Pittsburgh. *Location:* 42 South Pickering Street.

1N. Railroad Station (frame), built in 1913, in later years was used as a glove factory. *Location:* Railroad Street and Western Avenue.

1O. Cemetery, the first in Brookville, contains many tombstones of the 1830s. *Location:* Behind Free Methodist Church.

Note: The Historical Society library contains a two-volume book listing all the cemeteries (including private ones) in Jefferson County.

1P. Brookville Locomotive Works (brick), almost the last in America making narrow gauge as well as standard gauge locomotives, was founded at Brookville in 1919. It has occupied its present plant, the old Brookville Foundry, since 1936. *Location:* Pickering Street, at railroad.

1Q. White Elephant, a tremendous, white brick theater, was built in 1915 to provide a place for Chautauqua troupes and other traveling shows. After motion pictures killed off road shows, it was used for boxing matches and other entertainment. It now houses an industrial plant. *Location:* Sylvania and Mabon streets, on flat across North Fork from business district.

1R. Old County Home (brick), built in the late 1800s, now houses the county planning

2. Biblical Carvings

department. *Location:* Northeast of Brookville, off SR 0028 on Manor Drive which is off Jefferson Road.

2. Biblical Carvings were the work of Douglas Stahlman, a teacher in 1890 at Clear Run School who became fanatical following a head injury received during a controversy with a lumberman. Stahlman wore a steel plate in his head, and about 1900 came under the influence of Dr. John A. Dowie, Chicago faith healer and founder of Zion, Ill. With hammer and chisel Stahlman carved over 500 biblical passages—still legible—with references on beech trees and stones (mostly along or near streams) between 1907 and about 1914. Before 1920 he was committed to Dixmont Hospital at Pittsburgh, where he became an inmate librarian. He died about 1937 and is buried in Temple Cemetery. *Locations of carvings:* All in Brookville–Port Barnett area. (1) Old Brookville Park, along Sugarcamp Run, between North Fork and junction of two township roads near SR 0968 (on rocks); (2) on US 322, south side of road in wooded lot just east of and across from the Pinecreek Fire Hall (large beech tree just east of stucco bungalow); (3) south of SR 0028, 0.5 mile from junction with US 322, just east of McCullough farm (area of rock carvings

3. Memorial Smokestack

equivalent to two city blocks); (4) at Port Barnett east and south of Humphrey Charcoal office, which stands where pioneer Joseph Barnett had his inn and store (on rocks); (5) along Pennsylvania Railroad at deserted lumbering village of Bells, near Sandy Lick Creek and south of Pinecreek School (rock carvings cover area of possibly two miles on hillside).

Note: Near Temple Cemetery at Cat Rocks on the Hazen-Brockway Road are rocks with potholes believed by many to have been Indian gristmills.

3. Memorial Smokestack (brick) is at the site of the sawmill and lumber business of Joseph and Andrew Barnett and Samuel Scott. Established in the 1790s, the complex later had a gristmill added to the site. In 1905 the Humphrey family operated gas wells and brickyards here, the last vestige being the angular smokestack. Humphrey's charcoal corporation office is located across from the stack. *Location:* Port Barnett, US 322 at SR 2023 on outskirts of Brookville.

4. Old Tavern (frame) was the inn of Isaac Packer years ago. *Location:* Emerickville.

5. Knox Dale Octagonal Barn (frame) is in poor condition. This two-story structure, built between 1850 and 1880, is rare and worthy of preservation. *Location:* Pleasant Hill Road between Knox Dale and Emerickville.

6. Bee House (frame) was built in 1903 by Alonzo M. Applegate, a beekeeper. A quintuple hexagon, this house is made up of modules patterned after the cells of a honeycomb.

Reynoldsville, where the house is located, was named in 1873 for its founders, David and Albert Reynolds, sons of Woodward Reynolds who came here with his bride from Kittanning in 1838 to occupy a farm of 300 acres given him as a wedding gift by his father. *Location:* Reynoldsville, 820 East Main Street.

Note: The Soldier Run mine nearby, now exhausted, was at one time the most productive bituminous coal mine in the world, with a daily output of 8,000 tons.

7. Beechwoods Church (frame) was organized in 1832. The second building, an early 1850s structure, is incorporated in the present one, which was erected in the 1880s. *Location:* 4 miles west of Falls Creek on SR 0830, turn north 0.8 mile on SR 1009 (Washington Township).

8. James Smith House (frame), dating back nearly a century and a half, was built by Smith, an early Irish settler who helped scores of later arrivals from his homeland find homes in Pennsylvania. The house originally faced away from the present road. An 1820s log and stone springhouse is in the original front yard of the house. *Location:* Northwest of Falls Creek and 1.9 miles from Beechwoods Church, on SR 1009.

9. Brockway area

9A. Historical Museum (brick) is operated by a young but active organization with a good collection of materials on area history. *Hours:* Sundays and holidays, 2–5 P.M. *Location:* Memorial Park.

9B. Clarke House (frame) was built about 1860 by A. M. Clarke, miller, teacher, and surveyor, who laid out the town in 1836, naming it for Alonzo and Chauncey Brockway, lumbermen, who settled here in 1822. *Location:* 900 Ninth Avenue.

9C. N. B. Lane Mansion (frame) is a typical lumber baron's home, with six white pillars probably added later. It is occupied by Lane descendants, who have retained the original lumbering records. *Location:* 1 mile southeast of Brockway, on Broad Street extension (visible from US 219 east of town).

9C. N. B. Lane Mansion

10. Sigel

10A. Gable Tavern (frame) was a lumbermen's tavern built about 1850 by Hiram Gable. It was sold about 1860 to Andy Slike, who operated it for many years in a Prohibition township. It is now a residence. *Location:* At crossroads (SR 0036 and SR 0949).

10B. Truman General Store (frame) was built by Henry Truman, who came here as an orphan from Nottingham, England, in 1848 at the age of twelve. He fought in the Civil War and in 1865 opened a store in a log cabin until the present store, also a residence, could be finished. He became an associate judge and, in 1881, a postmaster. The building has been in his family ever since. On the second floor the present Henry Truman maintains for his friends an interesting museum of early life in the area. *Location:* At crossroads.

11. Fiscus House is a 140-year-old former hotel where it is reported that President Abraham Lincoln once stayed overnight. *Location:* Near Sigel.

12. Wolford School (frame), an early one-room rural school. *Location:* About 3 miles from Sigel. At SR 0899 turn onto SR 0036.

13. Three Wilderness Wonders should be visited together, preferably in good weather, as much of the road is unpaved.
　　a. Beartown Rocks, a large group of gigantic boulders deep in the forest, are located on the crest of a hill, providing an excellent view of a mountainous area along the Clarion River. *Location:* From SR 0949 about 1 mile northeast of Sigel, take Gilbert Road (marked) east 1.1 miles to Spring Creek Road (T 438); follow this northeast 1.4 miles to Cor-

bett Road; turn north 0.3 mile to sign for rocks, a short walk (Warsaw Township).
　　b. Laurel Fields, on the old Tillotson farm, is now owned and maintained as a tourist attraction by National Fuel Gas Company. It is the site of the Northwestern Pennsylvania Laurel Queen crowning, in connection with the annual Laurel Festival in Brookville the second full week of June. *Location:* Near Sigel. At Corbett Road, continue on Spring Creek Road 1.8 miles to sign for Laurel Fields (Heath Township).
　　c. Slyhoff's Grave is the burial place of Richard Slyhoff. According to a legend traceable back to a 1936 picnic program, Slyhoff, who died on January 2, 1867, at age forty-three, had been such a wicked man that he had asked to be buried beneath a giant leaning boulder, in the belief that at the last trump it would fall on him, putting him out of reach of the Devil. With passing years the rock has gradually moved nearer to a vertical position instead of falling on him. Unfortunately for the legend, close inspection of the marble tombstone indicates that it gives the age as thirteen, not forty-three. That Richard was a boy and not a man is confirmed by the length of the grave—less than four feet—but the spot is an interesting one. *Location:* From Laurel Fields, continue on Spring Creek Road 1.9 miles to Munderf Road; turn right 0.9 mile on T 484 to house. Ask permission to follow path about a furlong to grave (Polk Township).

14. Buffalo-Susquehanna Coal Company Buildings (brick) are visual reminders of the earlier coal era. *Location:* US 119, south edge of Sykesville close to highway.

15. Punxsutawney

15A. Gobblers Knob is the home of Punxsutawney Phil, the weather groundhog since 1887. Each February 2 it is the weather capital of the world as devotees and newsmen gather to see if Phil will see his shadow and delay spring for six weeks. *Location:* South on SR 3012, 1.9 miles east of US 119 and 0.8 mile east of crossroads.

15B. David Brown House (variety stone) was erected by Brown, an eccentric widower, oilman, and lumber tycoon, who traveled twice around the world collecting stones from many countries and almost every state, receiving many as gifts. From 1914 to 1916 he had these built into a singular but livable house with ornate fireplaces faced with stones and shells. The dining-room fireplace

238

15B. David Brown House

has his name and picture worked into it. *Location:* 906 East Mahoning Street.

15C. Clawson House (frame), built in 1825 by Mathias Clawson, sits far back from the street. Its east wing was once used as a school. *Location:* 808 East Mahoning Street.

15D. McKibben House (brick and frame), with square white decorated columns, was built by Stanford White in 1903 for Edwin McKibben, last manager of the Punxsutawney Iron Works. Bought in 1918 by a retired hotel owner, Thomas E. Bennis, it is now the Punxsutawney Historical Society Museum. *Location:* 401 West Mahoning Street.

15E. Fisher House (stone) is a big, shapeless structure built about 1890 by Jacob Fisher, and for years it was the home of photographer and journalist Florence Fisher Parry. It was later a public library. *Location:* 219 West Mahoning Street.

Note: The restored Pantall Hotel (1882) is at 135 East Mahoning Street.

15F. Winslow House (brick) was the home of Reuben Winslow, a prominent attorney, coal-mine operator, and railroad promoter, who was involved in a famous railroad right-of-way suit. He began this fantastic Victorian house before the Civil War and finished it after the conflict ended. The plate glass in the downstairs windows came from France to New Orleans, then up the Mississippi, Ohio, and Allegheny to Kittanning. The house was the first in town to have electric lights. Now apartments, it is rather run down. *Location:* East Gilpin and Pine streets.

Note: A previous Winslow house (frame), said to date from 1850, is a charming Carpenter Gothic structure, with board and batten and three arched front doors in one. Later

15F. Winslow House

a summer home, it is located at 95 Cherry Street, on the hill overlooking the other house.

15G. Jenks House (frame), built in 1819 by Dr. John W. Jenks, is still in the same family. It is the oldest house in town and an original two-story Greek Revival structure. *Location:* 100 Jenks Avenue.

15H. Punxsutawney School (brick), built in 1891, was later used as a high school for Clayville and Lindsey as well as Punxsutawney. In the 1950s this building was used as an elementary school and since 1962 has been a branch of Indiana University. *Location:* 1010 Winslow Street.

16. Mount Hope "Plantation" (brick), with five bays, was built by William Long in 1856. William, born in 1816, was the son of Joseph Long from Wurttemberg, Germany. William married Susannah Miller in 1841. In the early 1900s Dr. W. S. Blaisdell purchased the property and remodeled the house, which contains fifteen rooms, eight bathrooms, and five fireplaces. The 129-acre property was sold to Dr. F. D. Pringle in 1920 and ten years later to John Wargo. In 1959 the Frank J. Basile family purchased this site, renaming it "The Plantation." The bank between the highway and the house is landscaped with the Basile family collection of historic stones. *Location:* US 119, 3 miles south of Punxsutawney, near Indiana County line.

21. Meade Chapel

Previous Site Now Omitted

Game Commission Training School, closed

Pennsylvania Historical and Museum Commission Markers

Cooksburg SR 0036 near the Clarion River Bridge

Great Shamokin Path US 119, 4 miles northeast of Punxsutawney

Iroquois "Main Road" SR 0949, 3.8 miles north of Corsica

Jefferson County Brookville, at courthouse, Main Street

Olean Road Corsica, US 322

17. Walston Coke Ovens were built in 1883 and were reputed to be the largest continuous line of ovens in the world. *Location:* Walston, SR 3021 (Young Township).

Note: An early stone house is a few miles north of Punxsutawney on US 119.

18. Sprankle Viaduct, constructed in 1911, carries the Pittsburgh & Shawmut Railroad over Little Sandy Creek at Sprankle Mills. It is 142 feet high, 1,430 feet long, and is constructed of 1,467 tons of steel. The railway hauls three million tons of coal from Jefferson County over the bridge each year. *Location:* Sprankle Mills, on SR 3014 (Oliver Township).

19. Content Octagonal Barn (frame), two stories, erected between 1860 and 1880, is one of two of its type in the county. Barns of this kind were built for economy of lumber and as a status symbol. Said to be the best-preserved octagonal barn in the state, it is on reclaimed land stripped by the R. D. Baughman Coal Company. *Location:* On SR 3003, 0.7 mile from SR 3022 at Content, 3 miles off SR 0028 at Baxter (Clover Township).

20. Ringgold Mill (frame) was built in 1870 and was used as a flour mill. *Location:* Ringgold, SR 3303 and T 317 (Ringgold Township).

21. Meade Chapel (frame, board and batten), with decorative vergeboard, was built in 1872 (established 1871) as a German Reformed church. The present Carpenter Gothic church replaced a log house of worship constructed about 1847. An adjacent house on the property was built with similar architecture between 1900 and 1924. The chapel now serves the United Church of Christ congregation. *Location:* Clover Township, T 345 and SR 2023.

Lawrence County

Capsule History

Lawrence County was organized March 20, 1849, and named for Capt. James Lawrence of the U.S. Navy. His famous command, "Don't give up the ship," aptly applied to the county's struggle to become organized in the face of strong political opposition. Taken from parts of Mercer County to the north and Beaver County to the south, it now has an area of 363 square miles, the smallest county in western Pennsylvania. Its population is 107,150.

Situated around the confluence of three rivers, the Shenango, Mahoning, and Beaver, this area was a favorite location for Indians since it was accessible from many directions by canoe. According to legend the Delawares named Neshannock Creek, and the Senecas first called the Shenango River by its name.

A network of Indian trails radiated from Kuskuskies (present-day New Castle). The *Kuskusky-Chartiers Path, Kuskusky-Kittanning Path,* and *Kuskusky–Ohio Forks Path* ran together down the east bank of the Beaver past Chewton and Wurtemburg. The *Kuskusky-Cussewago Path* ran up the east side of the Shenango River past Pulaski. The *Kuskusky-Venango Path* followed much the course of US 422 past Rose Point and McConnell's Mill and then turned northeast to join the Venango Path near Harrisville. The *Mahoning Path* came up the west side of the Beaver River to New Castle, thence up the north side of the Mahoning toward Youngstown, Ohio.

Following Col. John Armstrong's expedition of 1756, which destroyed the Delaware village of Kittanning, Indians living there moved to Kuskuskies and made it their capital until it was abandoned in 1773. Gen. Edward Hand's campaign of 1778 against the British near Cleveland, Ohio, ended here when an old man and a woman, the only remaining Indians at Kuskuskies, were killed. This fiasco acquired the name "squaw campaign." A monument in the Y at US 224 and SR 0551 marks the farthest point reached by Hand.

Following Christian Frederick Post's visit in 1758, two other Moravian missionaries—David Zeisberger and Gottfried Senseman—ministered in 1770 to the Indian village of Friedensstadt (meaning "city of peace"), which was established through the influence of a convert by the name of Glikkikan. A year later a mission chapel was built there. (In 1834 the town of Moravia, halfway between New Castle and Ellwood City, was laid out near this site.) In 1773, due to internal disturbances, the missionaries, including John Heckewelder, and their converts left and went to the villages of Gnadenhütten and Schoenbrunn on the Muskingum River in Ohio, where some of them were massacred in 1782.

After Gen. Anthony Wayne's victory over the Indians of the northwest in the battle of Fallen Timbers in 1794, white settlers, including Edward Wright, began to make permanent homes in this area. Among the early arrivals in 1798 were John Carlyle Stewart (who built a small iron forge on Neshannock Creek and his first log cabin at Falls Spring on North Mill Street in front of the present Trinity Episcopal Church parish house of New Castle), his brothers-in-law John and Hugh Wood, John McWhorter, and Joseph Townsend, Jr., all from New Castle, Del. In the early 1800s the Sankey family moved to the area. David Sankey was a leader in the movement to erect Lawrence County, a state senator in 1847, and the contractor for Harbor Bridge, completed in 1853. He was also president of the Bank of New Castle and publisher of the *Lawrence Journal.* His son Ira D. Sankey (1840–1908) was a famous hymn writer and singer, a fellow worker with Dwight L. Moody. Ira, who was born in Edinburg, donated the YMCA building (replaced in 1911 by a new one) to the city of New Castle in 1885. In later years the county was settled by many Amish.

New Castle, the geographical center of the former Indian town of Kuskuskies (one of four such villages), became the county seat in 1849. The only city in Lawrence County, it was laid out on fifty acres in 1802 by John C. Stewart, who had discovered this tract of land overlooked in any survey and without private ownership. It was named for Stewart's home in New Castle, Del., and Stewart became the first justice of the peace. In 1825 it was incorporated as a borough and became a city in 1869.

The construction of canals from Pittsburgh to Erie and Youngstown, Ohio, supplemented the natural waterways of this region. The Beaver and Erie Canal traversed the county south to north through New Castle, and the Pennsylvania and Ohio Canal, or "Cross-Cut" Canal (1838–72), bisected the former at Lawrence Junction. Western Reserve Harbor, established in 1833 on the Beaver and Erie Canal, was the shipping point for freight for the Western Reserve in Ohio. (Many of the early settlers of Lawrence, Crawford, Erie, and Mercer counties were from Connecticut, and these areas are often referred to by the same term as Ohio's Western Reserve area.) Harbor Creek was the northern terminus of the Beaver division of the Pennsylvania canal system, which was completed to this point in 1834. The *Isaphena,* launched in 1840, was the first steamboat to operate on the canal. It was built by Daniel Frisbie in New Castle for Dr. Joseph Pollock and named for the doctor's daughter.

Natural resources in the area include coal, iron ore, clay, and limestone. The iron industry, employing charcoal furnaces, flourished from 1840 until after the Civil War. The county had ten stone blast furnaces. New Castle is one of the largest manufacturers of chinaware in the United States, and once was known as "the tinplate capital of the world." Other products of local industries include chemicals and allied products, leather goods, lumber, and dairy and agricultural goods. The Neshannock (also Mercer and Gilkey) potato, a choice variety once widely known, originated on the farm of John Gilkey. (Gilkey's orphan sister, Peggy, after growing up in Washington County, was caught in a blizzard December 24, 1804, on her way to find relatives whose address she did not know. She stopped at a cabin for shelter and found it was the home of her brother James.) One of the largest greenhouses in the world under a single span is located two miles from New Castle.

Landmarks

1. New Castle was once an important port on the Beaver and Lake Erie Canal.

1A. Courthouse (brick) has a signature stone that reads "1851." The structure was completed in 1852 at a cost of $32,000. Another wing was added in 1885. Of Greek Revival design, the building has two stories and an Ionic portico with six columns. The first court was held in the First Methodist Episcopal Church on South Jefferson Street in 1850. *Location:* Court Street.

1B. Hoyt Institute of Fine Arts (brick), a cultural complex, is located in the former residence of coal heiress May Emma Hoyt, built in 1914–17 at a cost of about one quarter of a million dollars. Plans for the structure were started by Charles Owsley of Youngstown, Ohio, and finished by Frank Foulke, an architect from New Castle. There are twenty-two rooms, several of which are concealed, with a ballroom on the third floor. The dining room is paneled in French Provincial walnut, the living room in Italian Provincial walnut, and the hand-carved stairway, hall, and office are of English oak. The home, built on one-and-a-half acres, was donated to the Lawrence County Cultural Association in January 1965 by Mr. and Mrs. Alex Crawford Hoyt. In 1968 the center was incorporated as the Hoyt Institute of Fine Arts, which provides a permanent art gallery for the works of local artists; an arts and crafts shop of institute work; adult and childrens' classes; and lectures, recitals, film showings, and art exhibits. *Hours:* Tuesday–Saturday, 9 A.M.–4 P.M. Guided tours by appointment. *Location:* 124 East Leasure Avenue.

1C. Scottish Rite Cathedral (brick and Indiana limestone trimmed with terra cotta) was opened in 1926 and was built at a cost of over $2 million. The Greer memorial organ was donated the same year by George and Charles H. Greer. The building, of Renaissance style, has a ballroom and banquet room that accommodates over 1,000, together with a large auditorium. *Location:* Corner of Highland and Lincoln avenues.

1D. Kennedy Square was first named the Diamond, later Central Square, and then Pershing Square after World War I. After John F. Kennedy was assassinated, the area was renamed. A Civil War monument, completed December 15, 1897, by the Lawrence County Veterans Association, is located here. Charles Andrews, a resident, posed for the soldier statue. *Location:* Central area.

1E. First Christian Church (Disciples of Christ) (brick) was organized in White Hall. The main structure, including the sanctuary and spire, was built in 1864. Later additions were made in 1911 and 1962. The sanctuary once had a domed ceiling, which has since been lowered. The old pipe organ at one time was one of the largest in this part of the country. *Location:* Next to Kennedy Square.

1F. Shenango Ceramics, Inc., one of the nation's largest producers of chinaware, started with the organization of the New Castle Pottery Company in 1862. Founded by Harmon and Hill, the original company continued in

1B. *Hoyt Institute of Fine Arts*

operation for two decades. In 1901 the New Castle China Company, a six-kiln plant, was founded in this area and lasted about four years. Then in 1905 the Shenango China Company was organized. Due to financial difficulties it became the Shenango Pottery Company. This company had similar problems, and in 1908 James M. Smith, Sr., reorganized the business and became its first president. In 1912 it purchased the old defunct New Castle China Company. After Smith's death, his son James, Jr., took over the management, followed upon his early demise by Bowman and Long, who bought the plant and renamed it Shenango Ceramics, Inc. In 1968 the company and its subsidiaries were purchased by International Pipe and Ceramics Company of Parsippany, N.J. For many years the seventeen-acre plant manufactured all of the Haviland china sold in the United States. It was also a large producer of Castleton china. *Tours:* 10 A.M.–1:30 P.M. (no children under twelve). *Location:* West edge of town, on US 224 near railroad tracks.

1G. Lawrence County Historical Society is a Colonial Revival building erected in 1904–05 by industrialist George Greer. It is the former home of Joseph A. Clavelli, for whom it is named. A museum and sports hall of fame are housed in this restored home overlooking the town. *Hours:* Wednesday and Sunday, 1–4 P.M. *Location:* 408 North Jefferson Street.

1H. Raney House (stone), in Queen Anne style, was built about 1891 for Leonden Raney, a local industrialist. It was later bought by David Jamison, a philanthropist, for Jamison Memorial Hospital. *Location:* 330 North Jefferson Street.

1I. Ohl House (brick), in Queen Anne style, was built in 1899 for Edwin Newton Ohl (1850–1922), president of the United Iron and Steel Company, established in 1906. *Location:* 208 East Lincoln Avenue.

1J. Crawford House (brick) was built in Second Empire style for James H. Crawford, the founder of the Crawford Iron Works. *Location:* 715 Harbor Street.

1K. George House (brick), a three-bay house, was built before 1855 for James Rigby George. *Location:* 101 North Mill Street.

1L. Cascade Park was built as a turn-of-the-century amusement park in an area noted for its waterfalls and scenic beauty. In 1892 it was called Brinton Park. Six years later a dance pavilion was built here. This community center became Cascade Park in 1897. *Location:* East Washington Street, along Big Run.

1M. Disciples of Christ Church, in Gothic Revival style, was built in 1864–65. G. H.

1Q. Meehan Funeral Home

4. Amish School

McKelvey was the architect. *Location:* 23 West Washington Street.

1N. Patterson House (brick) is a Second Empire house with a mansard roof. It was built before 1886 for the industrialist William Patterson (1824–1905). *Location:* 315 North Mercer Street.

1O. Reinolt Block (brick), two stories, is the only commercial building remaining from the canal era in this community. It was built in 1850. *Location:* 1 North Mercer Street.

1P. New Castle Post Office (stone) was built in 1904 in neoclassic style. Between 1934 and 1980 it served the community as a library. In recent years it has been converted to a restaurant whose theme is a library, the Olde Library Inn. *Location:* North and Mercer streets.

1Q. Meehan Funeral Home (brick) is a fine example of a turn-of-the-century mansion still retaining its original carriage house on the property. It was built in 1897 by Mathias Henderson, a banker and vice-president of the Pennsylvania Railroad. *Location:* Across from Hoyt Institute at Blaine, Lincoln, and Highland streets.

2. Country House Christmas Shop (frame) was built in the middle 1800s. Its earliest known deed dates to 1878 and involved Solomon Kaufmann and the parties of Reed and Clinefelter. The farmhouse has been converted to a holiday gift shop. *Hours:* Monday–Saturday, 10 A.M.–5 P.M. *Location:* Near New Castle and New Wilmington, on Old Mercer Road (SR 1005) north of Cunningham Lane.

3. Amish Tour Farm is an authentic working 150-acre farm complete with an Amish house,

a barn with animals and machinery, and an educational program for teaching the customs, beliefs, and ways of the Amish, especially the Old World Amish of the New Wilmington area. *Tours:* Tuesday–Saturday, 10 A.M.–4 P.M.; Sunday, 12 noon–4 P.M. *Location:* Near New Wilmington, turn left (from SR 0018) on Mercer-Pulaski Road toward Mercer; at second crossroad (Bend Road) turn right; first farm on right.

4. Amish School (brick) is in a picturesque setting in the heart of the Amish country. Across the road is a stone house. *Location:* Between Volant and New Wilmington, SR 0208 and SR 1005 (at Cunningham Lane).

5. Volant Mills (frame) was originally built of oak in the early 1800s on Neshannock Creek. It is said that farmers first brought their feed here in 1812. In the 1890s J. P. Locke operated the mill, which was enlarged to include grain bins in the 1920s. It closed in 1963 due to the high cost of operation. In 1984 William and Susan Kingery bought the site from William Clark and restored the 6,000-square-foot structure, which now has a moving water wheel and turbine generated power to operate the original grinding stone and machinery. The mill is now a three-story business selling Amish and country furniture, antique wicker items, and gifts. The first floor houses the mill's original machinery. A large porch was added in recent years to the loading dock area. The restoration and business success of this mill has brought life back to the town of Volant which now has numerous readapted early buildings around the mill, now used for boutiques. The entire village (formerly Lockesville) is now a historic attraction. *Hours:* April–December: Weekdays, 9 A.M.–5 P.M.; Sunday, 12 noon–5 P.M. Closed holidays. *Location:* Volant, Main Street, SR 0208.

6. New Wilmington, the home of Westminster College, in recent years has become a historic attraction for the readapted early buildings in the town center (many now housing boutiques). Early settler families included James and John Waugh (the latter laid out the town in 1824), John McCrumb, and Hugh Means, who established a gristmill here in 1802. The town, which became a half borough in 1863 and a full borough in 1873, was once part of the underground railroad. It is situated in the heart of Amish country.

6A. Campbell House (frame), built in 1880, is Victorian in style with stained glass windows. In the 1920s it was used as a fraternity house. It is now Gabriel's Bed and Breakfast. *Location:* 174 Waugh Avenue.

6B. Westminster College was chartered in 1852 by the Associate (now United) Presbyterian church. It was one of the first two colleges in Pennsylvania to grant degrees to women and the first to grant them the A.B. degree, in 1857 (see *Waynesburg College,* Greene County). Some of the brown sandstone buildings are of Collegiate Gothic design. Hillside, a dormitory, is the oldest building. Another early structure is "Old 77," the gymnasium, where the home basketball team was undefeated in seventy-seven consecutive games. Old Main was erected in the late 1920s on the site of an earlier building which was destroyed by fire. *Location:* Market Street (SR 0956).

6C. The Tavern (frame) was built in 1850 by Dr. Seth Poppino, a physician who served as a surgeon in the Civil War. It is believed that he sheltered runaway slaves. An underground tunnel connects his house with his office, which is now a gift shop. Ernst and Cora Durrast opened a restaurant here in 1931. In 1964 Mrs. Durrast developed the Tavern-Lodge guesthouse across the street. Known as the Lawrence House, it predates the Civil War. Closed Tuesdays. *Location:* On the square, SR 0158.

Note: The original New Wilmington Tavern was in an early 1900s house located on SR 0158, now the John Kehoe residence.

6D. Thompson House (frame) is a fine Victorian stick style structure of the 1880s. It is believed to have been built by Professor Samuel R. Thompson about 1887. In 1884 he returned to Westminster College, his alma mater, where he became professor of physics and a leading developer of the science department. The house was acquired by the col-

9. *Ten-sided House*

lege in 1945, having always been in the Thompson family. It has been adapted as a sorority house and an administration building over the years. *Location:* Westminster College Campus.

6E. Means-Lehman House (stone) was built in 1842 on a 1794 land grant by the Hugh and Ralph Means family. It is now owned by the Michael Lehmans. *Location:* Means Road off SR 0208.

7. Ligo Springhouse (frame and stone) was adapted in 1918 for use as a house with numerous levels. In recent years it was purchased by the Ron Ligo family. *Location:* West edge of borough, off ST 0208 on lane across from Dutch Isle.

8. Ohio Division "Cross Cut" Canal, Erie Extension, built between 1838 and 1844, was part of the Beaver–Lake Erie Canal connecting New Castle to Youngstown. These remains are the last vestiges of the structure. *Location:* Just south of Pulaski on US 224 north of Edinburg at bridge.

9. Ten-sided House (brick), two stories, was built by William Walker (b. 1819). He married Anna Jane Bailey in 1848, erected the house not long afterward, and lived here until 1903. William's father James was a leader in the Free Presbyterian Church (q.v.) and an abolitionist. Another early owner of this home was Frank Phillis. It was later purchased by Thomas Rupnick. *Location:* Near Pulaski, on old US 422, 1.2 miles from SR 0208 at New Bedford.

10. Brown House (brick) was built by George Brown. James Brown, of the same family, was an early settler here. A log house foundation is nearby. *Location:* 2 miles west of Pulaski, on SR 0208.

11. Twelve-sided House (brick) was built about 1860 by Joseph Brown, a stonemason. The two-story polygon has five rooms on each floor. *Location:* Near Pulaski, on SR 0208.

12. Free Presbyterian Church (frame) was organized before 1850 as a protest against slavery. Services were held here until 1871. The motto of the congregation was, "Anyone can worship here." James Walker (see *Ten-sided House*) was active in this church, which was one of the first of its kind organized in the United States. This building was later a town hall, which "anyone desiring to discuss a public question" could use. *Location:* New Bedford, on SR 0208.

13. General Store (brick), built in canal days, was at one time owned by Thomas Murray. In later years the building was used for a market. *Location:* Edinburg, junction of SR 0551 and US 224.

14. Slippery Rock is visible only when the creek is low in the fall. This rock, steeped in folklore, has given rise to the name of a township, a town, and a university in Butler County, as well as a creek, an oil field, an oil sand, and a favorite football team. It appears on J. P. Lesley's Slippery Rock Creek map of 1874. The Moravian missionary John Heckewelder wrote that the Delaware Indians called the creek "Wescha-cha-cha-polka," meaning "slippery rock." *Location:* Near Wurtemburg, on Slippery Rock Creek on John Eicholtz's property. It can be seen from Glasser bridge on east bank of creek or from southern tip of Camp Allegheny, looking across downstream, on west bank.

15. McConnell's Mill (frame) is located in Slippery Rock Gorge, which was carved out in the glacial period. The scenic gorge is seven miles long and from 300 to 500 feet deep. Johnson Knight built the first mill here in 1824–25, and Alexander McConnell the second in 1857. Following a fire in 1867, the third and present mill was erected in 1868 by Thomas McConnell whose son, James, acquired it in 1875 and operated it until 1928. His employee Mose Wharton kept it open as a tourist attraction until 1953 when the Western Pennsylvania Conservancy purchased the original 2,000 acres and turned it over to the Commonwealth. The park was dedicated in 1957, and the mill was restored in 1964 along with the reconstruction of the dam (see *Etna Mills House,* Butler County, for the mill works). A picturesque covered bridge is near the mill. *Hours:* Summer until September 1: Weekdays, 12:30–4:30 P.M.; Mondays by appointment. Tours conducted every half hour from 10 A.M.–6 P.M. on weekends and holidays during summer. *Location:* In McConnells Mill State Park, just south of US 422, between New Castle and US 422 interchange of I-79.

16. Moore House (stone), a one-story, three-bay stone house, was built before 1830 on the Moore family farm. Across the road is an even earlier frame house on the same property (in Butler County). *Location:* At county line, 4 miles south of Harlansburg, US 19 and US 422 (Rock Springs Road).

17. McCracken House (stone), with five bays, was built in the early 1840s by the McCracken family; it is still owned by the same family. Originally a mother and her three sons from Ireland lived here. An artesian well site is between the house and the creek. *Location:* US 19, 1 mile south of Harlansburg.

18. Harlansburg, an interesting town easily missed by travelers on US 19 (also on SR 0108).

18A. The Village Inn (brick) was erected around 1845 in the village founded in 1800 by Jonathan Harlan, who built the community's first dwelling, a log house on a 400-acre tract. Years ago this building was Jordan's Country Store where people would arrive in buggies on Saturday nights to purchase supplies and exchange local news. About 1935 the Jordan family sold the building and it was converted to an inn. For years it was known for its smorgasbord. It continues to operate as a restaurant. *Location:* Intersection of SR 0108 and old US 19 (Pittsburgh Street).

18B. Old Hotel (brick), built at about the same time and in similar style to the Village Inn, has served as a hotel at this crossroads for years. A tavern operated here until the evangelist Billy Sunday visited the community. In more recent years this house was converted to an antique shop. *Location:* Across from Village Inn, SR 0108 and old US 19 (Pittsburgh Street).

19. One-Room Schoolhouse (brick, with ashlar stone foundation) is now a private home. It was built in the 1860s. A date stone

20. Liberty Grange

in the rear reads, "L. Partan" (name not clear). Across the road is an early stuccoed brick house. *Location:* Harlansburg area, within view of SR 0108 and T 494 junction.

20. Liberty Grange (brick, with ashlar stone foundation). This rural grange (no. 1780) is reminiscent of the numerous early farm centers that once graced the area. *Location:* Grange Hall Road and SR 0108.

21. Eastbrook Presbyterian Church (frame) was built in 1841 and rebuilt in 1884. It contains beautiful solid panels of stained glass in its windows. The church was originally Reformed Presbyterian. *Location:* Eastbrook, SR 0388 near SR 1010 (Hickory Township).

22. Rich Hill Presbyterian Church (frame), one story, was built in 1842, remodeled in 1879. *Location:* SR 0168 north of SR 0956 (Washington Township).

Covered Bridges

Banks Bridge, T 476, built 1889 over Neshannock Creek, Wilmington Township
McConnell's Mills Bridge, T 415, built 1874 over Slippery Rock Creek, Slippery Rock Creek Township (in McConnell's Mills State Park)

Iron Furnaces
(originally ten)

Lawrence Furnace (1846–75), built by Emory, Culbertson and Brackenridge. Unusual in that it is built like a well in a cliff, with an opening at the top and a hole cut into the cliff face at the bottom. From Energy, take T 395 about 1.4 miles to a creek.

Walk downstream to the furnace site, near a fine waterfall.
Wilroy Furnace (ca. 1854), built by Stewart and Foltz. Near T 791 (turns right from US 322 about a mile from US 19) at old bridge over Slippery Rock Creek.

Pennsylvania Historical and Museum Commission Markers

C. Frederick Post SR 0018 and SR 0108 south of New Castle
"Cross-cut Canal" US 224 north of Edinburg at bridge
Friedensstadt SR 0018 north of Moravia (2 markers)
Harbor Creek US 422 northwest of New Castle
Ira D. Sankey Edinburg, junction of US 224 and SR 0551
Kuskuskies Towns Junction of SR 0018 and SR 0108 south of New Castle; and Edinburg, junction of US 224 and SR 0551
Lawrence County New Castle, 408 North Jefferson Street
Neshannock Potato US 19 south of Leesburg
"Squaw Campaign" SR 3007 south of New Castle
Westminster College Intersection of SR 0018 and SR 0208 west of New Wilmington; and New Wilmington, SR 0208 at Market and Neshannock streets.

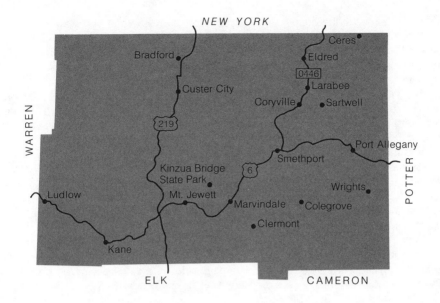

McKean County

Capsule History

McKean, the "governor's county," was named for Thomas McKean (1735–1817), chief justice of the state supreme court, president (governor) of Delaware, and a signer of the Declaration of Independence. McKean was governor of this state when the county was erected out of Lycoming on March 26, 1804, with judicial authority remaining temporarily with the parent county. In 1814 McKean and Potter counties were given common commissioners, and in 1826 McKean became independent. It has 979 square miles with a population of 50,635.

Although few Indians lived in this county, the area was known as "Seneca Land" and provided excellent hunting grounds for the Iroquois. There were three main Indian trails crossing the county. The *Catawba Path* entered McKean below Knapp Creek, passing six miles east of Bradford, crossing Kinzua Creek at Tallyho, and running through Cartwrights and East Kane. The *Forbidden Path,* a route to Olean, N.Y., long off limits to any white man, cut the northeast corner of the county from near Shinglehouse to Ceres. The *Oswayo Path* followed the same route at this point. One of the Iroquois paths used in pigeon-hunting touched the county near Ludlow.

Early settlers in the county came mostly from New England and New York, often along the Allegheny River Valley or up the Susquehanna. Others came from southeastern Pennsylvania. In 1861 Thomas Leiper Kane (later a major general) recruited the famous Bucktail Regiment (Forty-second Pennsylvania) from McKean and adjacent counties.

The first school was opened in 1809 at Old Instanter, and Smethport Academy was chartered in 1837. The county seat, Smethport, was laid out in 1807 by Francis King, land agent and surveyor, and named for Theodore de Smeth, who was a member of a Dutch banking firm with investments in the Ceres, Susquehanna of Connecticut, and the United States Land companies.

Bradford was named for the former New England home of John F. Melvin, who arrived in 1827. Dr. W. M. Bennett built the first log cabin there the same year. In 1875 the county's first oil well was drilled in this area by Jackson, Walker, and Urquart. Two years later the first oil exchange was established in 1877 in Bradford. The world's first monorail was operated there.

Teutonia (now Clermont area), laid out in 1843, and Ginalsburg were founded by Henry Ginal, agent of the German Cooperative Society of Industry, founded about 1840. No vestiges of either settlement remain today. Ceres was founded by Francis King and Quaker friends in 1797 on John Keating's property. King's house was a stopping place for Quaker missionaries.

The county was a leader in the oil industry and today is the largest single producer of world-renowned Pennsylvania crude oil, as well as much natural gas. Chief products are lubricating oils and greases, gasolines, and oil-well supplies. Other outstanding industrial products include wooden toys, chemicals, powder and explosives, and glass and clay products. Beef and dairy cattle provide most of the county's agricultural income.

Lumbering was the first important industry. The county is among those having the largest wooded acreage in the state (500,000 acres), most of which is included in the Allegheny National Forest—the only national forest in Pennsylvania.

Port Allegany, known to the Indians and pioneers as a "canoe place," was an important rafting center at one time. Early settlers in this area, Samuel Stanton, his son Daniel, and Daniel Webber, established the first sawmill at the site in 1824.

Landmarks

1. Smethport is said to have been a way station for escaping slaves during the Civil War. Many fine old mansions remain on West Main Street from its days as an oil boom town.

1A. Courthouse (brick and stone) is an expansion and remodeling of the county's second. The first one was built of brick in 1827–31, with Solomon Sartwell as contractor, at a cost of about $5,000. In 1850 it was enlarged to almost three times its original size, at a cost of $20,000. It was torn down and a new one erected of brick and stone, begun in 1879 and dedicated September 12, 1881, at a cost of about $75,000. The east wing was added in 1914 and the west In 1938. The front part of this structure was destroyed by fire February 12, 1940, and the present courthouse, incorporating the back and two wings of the former one, was built at a cost of $400,000 and dedicated June 15, 1942. It was paid for in cash.

The sheriff's house and jail, in the rear, dates from 1870. The stone part is not older, as might appear, but was built for strength. Many years ago a convicted murderer, who was about to be hanged in the dungeon below the jail, announced to his witnesses that he would come back to haunt the jail. According to tradition, his ghost did return.

1A. Courthouse

The McKean County Historical Society, with headquarters in the courthouse, is open to the public Tuesday–Friday, 1–4 P.M. (closed January and February) and contains many old-time tools and other types of furniture and equipment used by the pioneers of the area. *Location:* Main Street.

Note: Several later and more pretentious mansions built by heirs of the Hamlin family are to be found in Smethport.

1B. United Methodist Church (brick), the only building left from the original Courthouse Square, was built in 1839 by Solomon Sartwell. Perhaps the first house of worship in the county, it served as a courthouse until one could be built. Over the years the architecture has been modified. *Location:* Church and King streets.

1C. McKean Manor (frame), a tremendous structure with tall Doric pillars, was built in 1905 by Charles McKean, a lumber baron perhaps distantly related to the governor. The rooms are finished in a variety of woods from a wide area. It is now an apartment building. *Location:* West Main and Mechanic streets.

Note: An early stagecoach tavern, completely disguised by a modern brick face, is on a nearby corner.

1D. Benjamin Lamphier House (frame) was built in 1837. *Location:* West Eldred Road.

1E. Medbury House (frame), L-shaped, was built in the middle 1800s. *Location:* 604 East Main Street at Nelson Street.

1F. Bachus House (frame) was built between 1825 and 1840 and was listed on the Historic American Building Survey. *Location:* Green and State streets.

2. Port Allegany, incorporated in 1882, was settled in 1816 by New Englanders led by Samuel Stanton who died on his way to the site at the junction of the Allegheny River and Allegheny Portage Creek. Lodowick Lillibridge, Stanton's son-in-law, replaced him as leader, and the group established this community originally called "Canoe Place" by one of William Bingham's surveyors. Here, prior to white settlement, Indian war parties were equipped with white pine canoes. By making a portage between the two streams at this location, a canoe could travel from the Chesapeake Bay to the Gulf of Mexico. Here logs were rafted down the river to mills as far as Cincinnati and Pittsburgh. The lumber era lasted until the railroad arrived in 1873. Other industries which followed were natural gas (1883), four large glass manufacturers (1895, two still operating), two tanneries, and a nationally known doll manufacturer.

2A. Canoe Place Inn (frame), built at the turn of the century as a home for the Lay family, carries the tradition of the area's history. One of its proprietors, Catherine E. Lay, in 1928 advertised that it was on the Roosevelt Highway with "quiet restful surroundings, pure water, plenty of shade, a large porch and easy chairs." It is still a restaurant. *Location:* US 6, 101 Main Street.

2B. Presbyterian Church (frame) retains its original bell donated by Aaron S. Arnold, a McKean County associate judge and a local lumber pioneer. The building was the original Union Church which served several denominations around 1870. *Location:* Church Street.

Note: Another noteworthy landmark is the Methodist church (old Evangelical United Brethren Church, frame) on Pine Street. An early cemetery is located at the Grimes District Church, 6 miles west of Port Allegany; turn right across river bridge.

2C. Holden House (frame), typical of the area's Victorian houses dating from the turn of the century, was the home of the lumber baron E. L. Holden. It once had an early elevator, and it retains the original woodwork and a reed organ. It was later purchased by the Eiswerth family. *Location:* Church at 109 Chestnut Street (the original center of town, across from the library).

2D. Benton Mansion (frame), with twenty rooms, was built in 1859 by A. M. Benton, a lumberman, politician, and railroad promoter. It is a striking house with a square tower and

251

wide overhanging eaves. Later a hotel, it was the scene of a still-unsolved murder in 1924 when E. J. Fetterly, who was operating it as Maple Shade Inn, was shot while playing cards with a group of friends, one of whom was wounded by a stray bullet. *Location:* 500 West Main Street.

3. Mt. Equity Plantation is a 299-acre tract purchased in 1805 by Gov. Thomas McKean in order to give Pennsylvania equity in lands settled and claimed by Connecticut. *Location:* 3 miles northwest of Port Allegany on SR 0155.

4. St. Mary's Catholic Church (frame), of Carpenter Gothic style, was built between 1869 and 1872, replacing an earlier structure built in 1848. It is the oldest Catholic church in the area and looked upon as the mother church of those at Bradford, Eldred, Smethport, Port Allegany, Duke Center, and Austin. Missionary priests from Elk County held services here soon after the first seven Irish families settled on Newell Creek in 1842. The parish was organized in 1847. Inside the church are paintings of the stations of the cross formerly at St. Bernard's Church in Bradford. An early cemetery is nearby. *Location:* Sartwell (Annin Township). On SR 0155, 1.4 miles northwest of Turtlepoint, watch for St. Mary's Catholic Church sign. Turn east on Newell Creek Road (black top); go 0.5 mile to intersecting black top road; stay right and go 0.4 mile to the Driscoll Hollow dirt road. Turn left, continuing on black top 0.5 mile to the church.

5. Tidewater Pipe Company is the site of a pumping station on the first pipeline to carry oil across the Alleghenies. The pipeline ran 109 miles to Williamsport. *Location:* 13 miles southwest of Coryville, SR 0446.

6. Eldred

6A. Gold Eagle House (frame painted gold) was built about 1893 by Harry Oglevee. It was a typical "railroad house," complete with bar, poolroom, barbershop, rental rooms, and ladies' parlor. Oglevee gave it the name because of his opposition to the "free silver" policies of William Jennings Bryan. Frank Slavin bought the hotel in 1908, and it was in his family for many years. *Location:* Railroad Street at railroad.

6B. St. Raphael Church (frame) was built in the late 1800s. *Location:* 22 First Street.

7. Ceres, the first permanent white settlement in present McKean County, was established in 1798 by Francis King, a surveyor for a Philadelphia land company. *Location:* 1 mile south of Ceres, SR 0044.

8. Crook Farm includes a farmhouse (frame) that is believed to be the oldest existing structure in the Bradford area, dating from 1856. It was continuously occupied by the Crook family until it was deeded to the Bradford Landmark Society in 1974. It is based on a post-and-beam skeleton, with thin board curtain walls. It has the original shingles and most of the original trim and hardware. The Crook farm is the site of the famous Olmsted oil well, first large producer in the Bradford field. The society plans to construct a replica oil-field village with early drilling rig and pumping equipment. There will also be nature walks and cycling paths. *Location:* Foster Township, on Seaward Avenue extension, about 3 miles north of Bradford. Watch for sign.

Note: An early cemetery is at Lafayette Church several miles south of Bradford on SR 0059. An old frame country store (Singer's) is in this area on US 219 and SR 0770 near Custer City.

9. Penn-Brad Oil Well Park, a museum of the history of oil in McKean County, is sponsored by the Bradford District Oil Producers Association and the Desk and Derrick Club. It displays early drilling and shop equipment set up for operation, as well as photos, curios, and other memorabilia of the county's early oil days. *Hours:* June 1–October 1: Weekdays, 10 A.M.–4 P.M.; Sunday, 12 noon–5 P.M. *Location:* Just north of Custer City, on US 219.

10. Bradford, an important oil town.

10A. Bradford Landmark Museum (frame) was earlier Gus Herbig's French bakery, which he opened here in 1876. His granddaughter, Mrs. Virginia Loveland Miles, gave the building (second oldest in Bradford) to the Bradford Landmark Society ninety years later for a headquarters. It includes a museum store, the original bakery (except for ovens, restored after a fire), upstairs living quarters, and an extensive collection of early women's clothes. In the rear is a restoration of Frances A. Crook's candy store, with its original equipment. A display room has been added. *Hours:* Monday–Friday, 1:30–4:30 P.M. *Location:* 45 East Corydon Street, back of public library.

10A. Bradford Landmark Museum

15. Nebo Lutheran Chapel

10B. Historic Bradford. The district, located primarily within the area bounded by High Street, Elm Street, South Avenue, and Washington Street, is designed to protect those portions of the city with a rich architectural and cultural heritage.

10C. Bradford City Hall (brick), with a prominent ornate wooden interior staircase, high Victorian ceilings, and four large steeple clocks, was built in 1897. It is under the auspices of the Bradford Preservation Committee. *Location:* Kennedy and Boyleston streets.

11. Colegrove

11A. Colegrove Chapel (frame), always a union church, was built in 1885–86 as a nonsectarian place of worship. The structure, having a cut-stone foundation, was built by Jonathan Colgrove, among others. At the site is an early cemetery containing the graves of Revolutionary War veterans. *Location:* West Valley Road (Norwich Township).

11B. Redhouse is one of the oldest homes in the county. Stones in the foundation, hewn and shaped by hand, are perfectly matched. *Location:* SR 0046 (Norwich Township).

12. Old Kilns still show the great size of an early clay plant that began about 1890 as the Clermont Sewer Pipe Company, later becoming the Clermont Clay Products Company. About 1900 it was bought by the Kaul Clay Products Company and principally made tiles. It was unique in that the same strip operation which provided coal as fuel also gave the clay which was the company's raw material. It was closed after a disastrous fire in 1963 destroyed much of the plant. *Location:*

Clermont, on SR 2001, about 0.5 mile from SR 0146.

13. Free Methodist Church (brick), built in the late 1800s, is in the vicinity of an old round barn that burned. *Location:* Village of Wrights, SR 0155

14. Kinzua Viaduct over Kinzua Creek was the old Erie-Lackawanna Railroad bridge, once among the biggest in the world. This famous viaduct, built of iron in only ninety-four days in 1882 by the Bradford, Bordell & Kinzua Railroad, is 301 feet high and 2,053 feet in length. It has 20 lower spans of 38.5 feet in length and 21 intermediate spans of 61 feet each. It was designed by Mason R. Strong and Octave Chanute (an aviation pioneer) who were engineers for the Erie Railroad. The bridge was rebuilt of steel and reinforced with steel girders in 1900. It is an impressive sight, and the more courageous visitors may walk across it. In 1974 the area was made into Kinzua Bridge State Park, with picnic grounds and sanitary facilities. *Location:* North of Mt. Jewett. From US 6 take SR 3011 past Kushequa and follow it to park (total of about 2 miles, and there are signs).

15. Nebo Lutheran Chapel (frame), two stories, is a unique octagonal church built at this site in 1887 and patterned after Ersta Kyrka at Danviken (near Stockholm), Sweden. This Swedish Evangelical Lutheran congregation was organized in 1886 (the first Lutheran membership in the Mt. Jewett area) and served in this capacity until 1919 when Zion Evangelical Lutheran Church was organized. In 1950 Nebo (named for the mountain where Moses stood when first viewing the Promised Land) and Zion congregations merged and formed the present St. Matthew's Evangelical Lutheran Church (Main Street, Mt. Jewett).

Services are still held at the chapel on Easter Sunday (6 A.M.), Ascension Day (7:30 P.M.), and Swedish Festival Sunday (10:30 A.M.), and it is open for weddings and funerals. An early cemetery is next to the church. *Location:* Mt. Jewett, US 6, east end, north side of road.

Note: A beautiful roadside spring and rest area is on US 6, 0.6 mile east of Mt. Jewett borough line.

16. Kane

16A. Kane Manor (buff brick with columns) was the former estate of the town's founder, Gen. Thomas L. Kane, who died December 26, 1883 (see *Old Presbyterian Church*). Built in 1870, this house was reconstructed after a fire in 1896. Inside the Victorian, two-and-a-half story building, with numerous wings, chimneys, and a side portico with tall white columns, is a fine exhibition of Arctic paintings by Elisha Kent Kane (Thomas's brother, who went in search of Sir John Franklin, the Englishman who was never found after pioneering an expedition to the Arctic). Also included are many Civil War relics. On a front step is the inscription, "Dure la vida que con ella todo se alcanza" ("Let life last, because with it all can be accomplished"). Over a fireplace a descendant of the builder has put a plaque that reads, "Life is like iron. Use it, it wears away. Use it not, it rusts away." The manor is now a restaurant with rooms for overnight guests. *Location:* 230 Clay Street.

16B. Old Presbyterian Church (stone), of Gothic design, now the Kane Memorial, was organized November 15, 1874, and built soon afterward by Ann Gray Thomas from Philadelphia, aunt of General Kane (see *Kane Manor*), as a memorial to her father Thomas Leiper. General Kane, his grandfather's namesake, laid the cornerstone. The Mormon church bought the building in 1970 as a memorial to General Kane, who had helped its members in many ways, especially on their westward migration about 1850. He was buried just in front of the church. *Location:* Chestnut Street near Edgar Street.

Note: An early cemetery is at the Kanesholm Church, US 6, about 10 miles east of Kane.

16C. General Kane Statue (bronze) is a replica of one standing in the Utah State Capitol building in Salt Lake City. Thomas Leiper Kane was thus honored by grateful members of The Church of Jesus Christ of Latter-Day Saints whom he befriended. He is also known for being the first Pennsylvania volunteer for the Union Army. When Fort Sumter was fired upon in 1861, he offered his services to Gov. Andrew Curtin in response to President Lincoln's call for militia. At that time he recruited the Bucktail Regiment from McKean and Elk counties, one of the most honored fighting units during the Civil War. *Location:* Old Presbyterian Church.

17. Seneca Indian Spring was a stopping place on the Indian trail which crossed the Big Level on the way south, once the main route from Onondaga, the Iroquois capital, to the Ohio and the Carolinas. It still sends a fine flow of water into a rather poorly kept pool. *Location:* From old US 219 on southeast edge of Kane, take SR 0321 south about 100 yards to Wetmore Township line marker. Walk another 100 yards to right on old road, swampy in places, to spring.

18. Olmstead Manor (wood and stone), built by George Welsh Olmstead of Ludlow, was finished in 1917. Olmstead came to the town as the young secretary at the tannery built here in 1872 by John J. Curtis, associate of Thomas L. Kane and Samuel M. and William L. Fox (see *Foxburg,* Clarion County) in railroad and other industrial ventures. Olmstead took over the plant after Curtis died around 1904. Later he was president of the Long Island (N.Y.) Lighting Company. He died in 1940, and the tannery closed in 1956.

After Olmstead's wife died, the family gave the manor to the Methodist church in 1969. It is now a retreat center open to all faiths. Another part of the estate, given to the village of Ludlow, has become Wildcat Park, a community recreation area. *Location:* Southeast edge of Ludlow, on US 6.

Note: Under the small bridge on the street to the south, almost across from the manor, may be seen well-preserved timbers of the tannery's dam, under the waters of Two-Mile Run.

Previous Sites Now Lost

Hamlin House, demolished 1986
Port Allegany Hotel, demolished

Pennsylvania Historical and Museum Commission Markers

Allegheny Portage Port Allegany, at junction of US 6 and SR 0155
"The Bucktails" Smethport, US 6 at courthouse
Ceres SR 0044 near Ceres at bridge

Kinzua Viaduct   Kinzua Bridge State Park
McKean County   Smethport, at courthouse,
   Main Street (US 6)
Mount Equity Plantation   SR 0155, 3 miles
   northwest of Port Allegany
Port Allegany   US 6, 0.2 mile west of Port Al-
   legany; and Port Allegany, at square
St. Mary's Church   Northeast of Turtle Point,
   Newell Creek Road, off SR 0155
Seneca Spring   SR 0321 south of Kane
Smethport   Smethport, US 6 at courthouse
Thomas L. Kane   Kane, 50 Chestnut Street
Tidewater Pipe Company   SR 0446, 13 miles
   southwest of Coryville

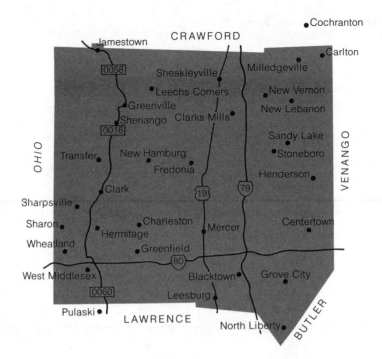

Mercer County

Capsule History

Mercer County, named for Brig. Gen. Hugh Mercer, a Scottish surgeon and commander during the Revolution, was formed March 12, 1800, from Allegheny County and organized in February 1804. The county encompasses 672 square miles, bordering the Ohio line for 32 miles, and has a population of 128,299.

Indian trails that traversed the county included the *Cayahaga Path* from Franklin to Akron, which entered the county near Sandy Lake, followed its north shore to Pymatuning (now flooded by the Shenango Reservoir), one-and-a-half miles west of Big Bend, and turned southwest to West Middletown, following SR 0368 to the state line. The *Kuskusky-Cussewago Path* ran by Pulaski, West Middlesex, Clark, and Greenville, thence northwest to the county line.

The Wyandot and Delaware Indian village, Shenango Town, was situated on the river bank (marker on SR 0018 near West Middlesex) in 1750–85 and was under the control of the Seneca Indians, of whom a few remained in the area until 1812. Pymatuning Delaware Indian Town, at Big Bend, was located in 1764 to 1785 on the Shenango River at about Clark (marker on SR 0258 east of Clark).

The Beaver and Erie Canal traversed the county, following the course of the Shenango River north to Greenville and thence to the Crawford County line via Little Crooked Creek Valley.

The county had "depreciaton lands" and "donation lands" (see Capsule History for Butler County). Benjamin Stokely, deputy surveyor for the county, surveyed some of these lands in 1785. The Holland Land Company and the Pennsylvania Population Company, among others, were active in the region. The county had few settlements until after 1795, when Anthony Wayne signed the Treaty of Greenville with the Indians.

Many of the first settlers were Scottish Presbyterians. Others came from Washington County and introduced sheep-raising, with the county ranking third in the state in wool-growing as late as 1868. William McMillan, one of three trustees appointed to conserve the assets of the new county and son of Rev. John McMillan, erected a blockhouse in Coolspring Township and several area churches. In 1885 a large number of Italians settled in Sharon and Farrell when a pipeline was laid from the Butler and Venango County oil fields through Sharon to Youngstown, Ohio.

Among the prominent residents were James Pierce, of Hickory Township, who helped develop the bituminous coal industry in the mid 1800s; Jonathan Dunham, who settled in Sharpsville in 1798; and James Sharp, an original landowner of the area. Alfred Landon, governor of Kansas and Republican candidate for president, was born in West Middlesex. The Bigler family, whose two sons became governors on the same day, lived near Greenville (see *Bigler Graves*).

The borough of Mercer, in the area of a former important Indian village and centrally located, was laid out August 24, 1803, by John Hoge, who donated 200 acres for the county seat. In 1805 the Junkins family built the first mill here. The Harthegig health springs were well known in the area for years. In 1825 General Lafayette was entertained in Mercer on his visit to the United States.

The county's two third-class cities are Sharon and Farrell, with Greenville, Grove City, and Sharpsville its larger boroughs. Sharon, first settled in 1803 by Benjamin Bentley, was laid out by William Budd in 1819. Farrell, a company town originally incorporated as South Sharon, was renamed in 1911 for James A. Farrell, a noted steel manufacturer. Greenville, formerly West Greenville, honors Gen. Nathaniel Greene. Wheatland, first settled by the Henry Shilling family prior to 1797, was laid out by James Wood in 1865 and named in honor of the Lancaster estate owned by President James Buchanan. West Middlesex was settled in 1821 and laid out in 1836. Hickory Township was created in 1832, and Shenango Township, originally plotted in 1866 as Atlantic City—derived from the Atlantic and Great Western Railroad—had much land set aside for railroad terminals.

The iron and steel industries, largely in Sharon and Farrell along the Shenango River, have promoted county growth. There were once fifteen stone blast furnaces in the area. Among the important products of the county's industries are iron and steel ingots and bars, railroad cars, gas and gasoline engines, and electric machinery. The 300-ton transformers for Boulder Dam in Colorado were built at one of Sharon's electrical manufacturing plants. Mercer County once ranked high in bituminous coal-mining, paper and printing products, and agriculture.

Landmarks

1. Mercer was incorporated as a borough in 1814.

1A. Courthouse (brick and stone) was built in 1909. The first court was held in the home of Joseph Hunter of Mercer in 1804, and the original courthouse was built in 1807–08. It was replaced by a second building in 1866–67, which was destroyed by fire in 1907. The third structure is in use today. It was designed by Owsley, Boucherie, and Owsley of Youngstown, Ohio. *Location:* On square.

1B. Bingham House (brick), built about 1805, was the birthplace of John A. Bingham (1815–1900). He presided as judge advocate at the trial of Mary Eugenia Surratt and other alleged conspirators in the assassination of Abraham Lincoln. Bingham, a Republican, was also U.S. minister to Japan and was counsel in the impeachment of President Andrew Johnson in 1868. This house is now the county Republican headquarters. *Location:* South side of Courthouse Square on South Diamond Street.

1C. Old Stone Jail, a square two-story building with narrow windows and a hip roof, was built about 1810 by Thomas Templeton. It served the county until about 1868 when a man by the name of Lafferty bought it for a hotel. At present it houses commercial offices. The second jail, built of brick in 1868, is near the courthouse on Diamond Street. A new one has recently been built. *Location:* 107 West Venango Street.

1D. Magoffin House (frame), of Georgian style, was built in 1821. It is the former home of James Magoffin, Jr., who with his father and Dr. Beriah Magoffin operated a doctor's office here. The south wing is the older section, and the rooms in the back were added after the Civil War. This house, constructed on the old Butler-Erie Pike, was donated by Mrs. Henrietta Magoffin to the county and dedicated in 1951 as the headquarters for the Henderson Historical Center (Mercer County Historical Society), which includes a museum, print shop, memorial chapel, historical library, county records, Indian artifacts, pioneer displays, and other memorabilia. *Hours:* Summer months: Tuesday–Saturday, 10 A.M.–4:30 P.M.; Friday, 7–9 P.M.; Sunday, 1–4:30 P.M. *Location:* 119 South Pitt Street.

1E. Magoffin Guest House (brick) is Victorian in style with a wrap-around porch. De-

1D. Magoffin House

signed by Owsley, Boucherie, and Owsley, it was built in 1884 as the home of Dr. Montrose B. Magoffin and Henrietta Magoffin. Dr. James Magoffin, the grandfather, came to America from Ireland in 1821. Two generations of this family occupied the house. It was restored as an inn in 1985 by Gene and Gala Slagle and includes seven guest rooms furnished with antiques. *Location:* 129 South Pitt Street.

1F. McClain Print Shop (frame), which once set ads for the *Saturday Evening Post,* was owned by Squire T. W. McClain and later by his son T. W. McClain, Jr., until his death in 1965. The building, donated to the Mercer County Historical Society in 1973 by the McClain family, was moved from its location on South Diamond Street to its present site and dedicated in 1974. Hours on request. *Location:* South Pitt Street, at Henderson Historical Center.

1G. Helen Black Miller Memorial Chapel (frame), formerly Grace Episcopal and later St. Edmund Martyr Episcopal Church, is now nondenominational. It was dedicated in 1973 as a memorial to Mrs. Miller, a local musician and vocalist. The church was originally located on Venango Street on property donated by Charles W. Whistler (see *Whistler House*). The restored church, built about 1884 and purchased by the county historical society, contains the original pews with doors and is now part of the Henderson Historical Center, dedicated in 1973. (The land was a gift from Mr. and Mrs. George M. Henderson. Restoration funds for the church were donated by William W. Miller of Mercer.) The church is used for weddings and other special services. Hours on request. *Location:* South Pitt Street.

1H. Stewart-McLaughry House (frame), of New England Greek Revival architecture, was built in 1853 by William Stewart, a lawyer and state senator. The Stewart family later rented the house to Judge James McLaughry who bought it in 1911. In 1953 the Beringer family restored the building. *Location:* 237 West Market Street, at corner of North Maple Street.

1I. Congregational Church (frame) was originally built by this congregation in 1852. From 1887 to 1960 the Reformed Presbyterian church owned the building. Later a Baptist church sold it as a private residence. In recent years the Cooper Evans family restored the interior and exterior historical features including stained glass windows. *Location:* West Market Street.

1J. Hanna-Small-White House (brick) was constructed in 1839 by Robert Hanna. This house and the Hanna one next to it (built about 1818) are both made of locally fired bricks. Later Edward Small, an abolitionist minister of the United Presbyterian church who married Mary, the daughter of Robert Hanna, lived in the house with his family and operated an underground railroad station for escaping slaves. Years later a secret room hidden under the kitchen was revealed when a loose stone was discovered in the foundation. During the Civil War a ten-foot addition was constructed. Scratched on a first-floor window is the inscription, "F. H. S. 1870." This residence, later purchased by the Yeager White family, is described by Anna Pierpont Siviter in her 1861–68 *Recollections of War and Peace. Location:* 245 South Pitt Street.
Note: Another house (frame) which was used as an underground railroad station is the Kilgore home located on South Erie and Beaver streets. A Mrs. Mary Hanna owned the house at 301 Pitt Street in 1840. Twenty years later it was sold to William and Rachel Turner.

1K. Herrington House (glacial stone) was erected in 1812 by Jacob Herrington and operated as a stagecoach stop. It was in the attic of this home that the Masons of the county held their secret meetings during the anti-Masonic excitement. The Robinsons restored the house in 1962. *Location:* 208 North Pitt Street.

1L. Whistler House (frame), of Greek Revival style, was built in 1840 by Samuel and Fred Hays. Several years later it was sold to David W. Findley, a Mercer merchant, county prothonotary, clerk, and associate judge. David Grier, a Presbyterian clergyman, bought it next, followed in 1890 by Capt. Charles W. Whistler, hotel owner, captain in the Civil War, and editor of the *Western Press* (Mercer's Democratic party newspaper). The house later became the home of Whistler's great-grandson. *Location:* 317 North Pitt Street.

1M. Garrett Cenotaph, a family monument resembling a small pyramid and dating back to the 1830s, is over eight feet in height. Its unusual construction, of the Greek Revival mode, is noteworthy. The family is buried elsewhere. *Location:* At junction of US 62, US 19, and SR 0058 in old Presbyterian cemetery.

1N. Logan-Johnson House (frame), over 100 years old, formerly was a summer mansion for the Logan family. The house cost the original builder so much to erect that he went bankrupt before it was finished. It was bought at a later date by the Virgil Johnson family. *Location:* 235 North Shenango Street.

1O. Bell-Miller House (frame), built about 1856, once was a post office and also doctors' offices. *Location:* 200 North Pitt Street.

1P. Kilgore-Harrington House (frame), built prior to the Civil War, reputedly once served the underground railroad. *Location:* 246 Erie Street at Beaver Street.

1Q. McDonald-Mason House (brick) is the oldest brick house in the borough. Between 1777 and 1785 Theophilus McDonald built this house, later occupied by the Mason family. The early lantern (painted in 1805) is in the front yard. *Location:* 340 East Market Street.

2. Boston Tavern (brick) was built in 1833 by John Crill. With a distillery on his farm, Crill supplied spirits for the St. Cloud Hotel in Mercer, which he ran. In 1845 Crill's daughter Christeena inherited the farm, and she, with her husband Adam Boston, son of an innkeeper of Delaware Township, converted the farmhouse into a tavern.

Sometime in the 1850s a peddler with a carpet bag containing valuables stayed overnight at the inn. According to legend, he mysteriously disappeared early the next morning before the arrival of the stagecoach, leaving blood stains on the floorboards (a familiar bit of tavern folklore). Following this occurrence, bricks began to fall periodically from the wall above where the peddler stayed. Claude Eckman, who restored the inn, removed the paint which a former owner had applied over the stains, replaced the bricks, and was never haunted by the peddler ghost. The home, still owned by the Eckman family, is now called Candlewood. *Location:* 2.7 miles south of Mercer, on Mercer–Slippery Rock Pike (South Pitt Street extension, Findley Township).

Note: Another early brick house on the same road is the old David Gilson property, originally called Green Knoll Farm. The house was built prior to 1850 (a bay window was added) on land patented in 1794. *Location:* Blacktown, on SR 0258 north of London at northeast corner of intersection with SR 2006 (Springfield Township).

3. Big Bend Canal Ghost Town was a bustling port during the canal era of the middle 1800s. At that time it had numerous hotels, shops, and iron furnaces. Located seven miles from Mercer, it served as the shipping port for the county seat. With the advent of the railroad the town nearly disappeared, with only sixteen houses remaining today. *Location:* SR 3022 near New Hamburg.

4. Howard House (brick) was built in 1848 by William Howard, a stonemason for the Erie Canal. This one-story home has H-chimneys which enabled it to include four fireplaces. *Location:* Scrubgrass Road (SR 2014), east of Crill's School Road (T 728), an extension of East Market Street in Mercer (Findley Township).

5. Pew Estate belonged to Joseph Newton Pew, founder of the Sun Oil Company and president of the board of trustees of Grove City College (q.v.). For about forty years the buildings had remained unoccupied but well maintained. The landmark house has been razed and now only the frame tenant house, barn, and a few outbuildings remain. *Location:* Southeast of Mercer, on SR 0058 across from Pew Road.

6. Clay Furnace House (brick), once owned by the Grandy family, could have been the residence of one of the ironmasters—Vincent and Himrod—who built Clay furnace (named for Henry Clay) in 1845. Raw bituminous coal instead of charcoal was first used successfully in 1846 at this site near the house. *Location:* From Mercer travel 8 miles west on US 62 to historical marker on right side of road (west of Charleston); turn north on T 496 for 2.2 miles. House and furnace ruins are against hillside in pasture on right.

7. Old Timber Farm, now Timber Village Center, was originally called the Little Apple

Farm, once owned by William W. Miller. The barn, built in 1872, has been adapted for a restaurant and country stores. It was renovated in 1982. There are massive forty-foot oak beams in the interior, and the barn retains its original siding. The adjoining farmhouse is over 100 years old. *Hours:* Monday–Friday, 10 A.M.–5 P.M.; Saturday, 10 A.M.–3 P.M.; Sunday, 12 noon–4 P.M. *Location:* 1 mile west of Mercer on US 62, 3 miles from I-80 exit 2, and 5 miles from I-79 exit 33.

8. Octagonal Barn (frame) was built by Jason and Robert Coleman in the late 1800s. A two-story springhouse that served as a post office was across the road from this structure. *Location:* 0.25 mile west of Centertown, on south side of SR 2014 (Scrubgrass Road).

Note: Another early octagonal barn was on SR 1028 off SR 1015 south of Carlton. It was burned in recent years by an arsonist, but a smaller barn of this type still remains across the road from the site on the Heydrick farm.

9. Grove City, earlier Pine Grove and Slab Town—two villages connected by Wolf Creek, became a borough in 1883.

9A. Fleming House (frame), built before 1850 by the first postmaster of Grove City, William Fleming, served as his home and was also used as a tannery and harness shop, as well as a select school (1858 to 1876), with Richard M. Thompson the first teacher. Classes were held on the third floor. Later the school was moved to its present location and renamed Pine Grove Normal Academy, forerunner of Grove City College (q.v.). The house is now owned by Young's Dairy. *Location:* 455 Liberty Street.

9B. Grove City College began in 1876 (chartered in 1879) as Pine Grove Normal Academy, a teacher-training institution under the auspices of the Presbyterian church. In 1884 the academy became Grove City College. It was founded by Dr. Isaac Conrad Ketler, former principal of the Select School (see *Fleming House*). Ketler was president of the college from 1876 to 1913, and his son Weir Ketler was president from 1916 to 1956. WSAJ radio station, owned by the college, started broadcasting in 1920 and was one of the first established in the United States.

The institution has been generously supported by Joseph Newton Pew (see *Pew Estate*) and his son John Howard Pew, both presidents of the board of trustees. (Joseph Newton Pew had taught school in a one-room brick building at London, junction of SR 0208 and SR 0258, and one of his students was Isaac Ketler. The school is now used as a garage.)

Cunningham Hall (brick), of Greek Revival style, is the oldest building on the Grove City campus. It was built in 1854 by Squire James Glenn Cunningham and replaced a frame house of 1840. James's parents, Valentine and Margaret Glenn Cunningham, came to this area from Huntingdon County, built a log cabin on land taken up by squatter's rights, and ran a grist- and sawmill. Their sons James and Charles laid out the town of Pine Grove in 1844 (changed to Grove City in 1883). The college purchased the property in 1888. This ivy-covered home, once used as a dormitory, is now a faculty residence. *Location:* Main Street.

9C. Cunningham Memorial Park, dedicated in 1982, is part of the original 400-acre Cunningham grant settled in 1798 and the site of Grove City's first gristmill. In 1908 the mill became the first electric plant in the community. A millstone at the site is from this early industry on Wolf Creek. *Location:* Main Street (SR 0058), at Greenwood Drive.

9D. Filer Homestead (frame) was the home of William H. Filer, father of five brothers who in 1922–23 started an awning business which during World War II manufactured tents, gun holsters, Air Force tool kits, jungle first-aid kits, and diesel engine covers for Westinghouse Electric Company. After the war the company started a new line of baby car seats and swings. In 1971 the line changed to four-poster-canopy frames and utility bags. William (father of Clarence, Sherman, Arthur, Grant, and Clifford) was originally in a building material business and worked with Edwin J. Fithian in the invention of the gasoline power engine which gave rise to the Bessemer Gas Engine Company. Next to the house is a smaller Filer house moved to this site. *Location:* Kinder Avenue.

9E. Cooper-Bessemer Corporation (brick and steel), incorporated in 1899, began the previous year when Dr. E. J. Fithian and John Carruthers started a factory to make a gas engine with a new friction clutch. The first building was a small frame structure known as J. C. Brandon's tile works. The company expanded, covering many acres, and has become world-renowned for diesel-powered machines and equipment. The Bessemer Gas Engine Corporation (1900–29) merged with the C. and G. Cooper Company in 1929 and became Cooper-Bessemer Corporation. To-

day it is known as Cooper Industries. *Location:* Bessemer Avenue.

9F. Wendell August Forge, Glassworks, and Museum (cement block), built in 1932, is one of the few remaining forges in America that makes aluminum, bronze, pewter, and sterling silver products—no two alike—entirely by hand, using no production machinery. The forge was begun in 1923 in Brockway, Pa., by Wendell August, a coal baron of the early 1900s. In 1929 while producing wrought iron decorative gates for the Aluminum Company of America, he conceived the idea of making them out of aluminum. As a producer of architectural aluminum products, Mr. August used to present each customer with a little aluminum hand-hammered gift, which later developed into a giftware line of products sold at the forge—the first aluminum giftware business in America. The showroom and museum were opened in 1979 and include a unique collection of hand-cut glass and crystal. *Hours:* Monday–Saturday, 8 A.M.–5 P.M. (Friday to 9 P.M.); Sunday, 11 A.M.–5 P.M. Free tours by arrangement. *Location:* Grove City, 620 Madison Avenue.

Note: Another specialty industry in Grove City, and a local landmark, is Palmer Smith Linens. *Hours:* Saturday, 9 A.M.–4 P.M. *Location:* 2 miles north of Grove City on SR 0173.

9G. George Junior Republic is one of three institutions endowed by William R. George of Freeville, N.Y., to involve delinquent boys in a situation where they are given responsibility and the opportunity to direct their own rehabilitation. The other two are in New York and California. The Pennsylvania George Junior Republic, founded in 1909, is one of the most successful efforts of its kind in America, with boys sent by juvenile courts of many states and a nationwide reputation. One of its prominent supporters was Dr. Morgan Barnes. The small square flat-roofed brick jail became the printing school in 1950. In 1914 the brick chapel beside the jail and close to the road was dedicated to the memory of Jeremiah Sturgeon. The Donald Lobaugh Auditorium resulted from the bequest of an alumnus killed in action in Korea, who had made out his insurance to the Republic as "next of kin." *Location:* Grove City, on SR 0058 (Mercer Road).

10. North Liberty (Liberty Township) was laid out around 1821 by James Foster on the Mercer and Butler Turnpike.

11. Johnston Tavern

10A. Courtney-Lindley House (shingle siding), of Georgian architecture with a double front porch the length of the house, was built by David Courtney about 1819. It is overshadowed by huge pines that match the house in age. Courtney, who came from Franklin County, erected Courtney's Mill on Wolf Creek in 1803. In 1953 the house was bought from Courtney's great-grandson by John W. Lindley, who restored it in 1959. *Location:* Junction of Lindley Lake Road and SR 2028 off SR 0258. Lindley Lake is nearby.

10B. Cowden & Christy General Store (frame) was the site of a stagecoach stop along the early turnpike. The building is the first general store in the town, lately owned by a Mrs. Sankey. *Location:* SR 0208, west side of road.

10C. Old School (brick), a two-story structure, was built in 1869 and in later years converted to a municipal and community building. *Location:* SR 0208, east side of road, north of Cowden & Christy General Store.

11. Johnston Tavern (stone) was built on the Pittsburgh-Mercer Road in 1831 by Arthur Johnston, who had come from Ireland. He no doubt had operated a log tavern prior to this one, for he was issued a license in 1827. Johnston managed the stone tavern until 1842, calling it the New Lodge Inn. It served workmen from the Springfield iron furnace

nearby. In 1836 the Springfield post office was opened in the building, with the innkeeper as postmaster. (The post office was moved to Leesburg in 1845.)

Restored by Charles M. Stotz under the direction of the Western Pennsylvania Conservancy, the building is administered by the Pennsylvania Historical and Museum Commission. The front entrance, with a fanlight above the door, has been reconstructed as it appeared originally, and the furnishings are from the Andrew Jackson period. *Hours:* Tuesday–Saturday, 10 A.M.–8 P.M.; Sunday, 12 noon–5 P.M. *Location:* 3 miles south of Mercer, on US 19 (Perry Highway) about 1 mile north of Leesburg.

12. Schollard House (frame) was built in 1840–50 by William Schollard, the first Springfield furnace operator. At one time some of the iron furnace operators lived in the house. It is believed that it once served as a station on the underground railway. The Schollard family lived here until 1944. Now an antique shop, it was restored by the Thompson family. *Location:* On US 19 just north of Leesburg, Schollard Road (Springfield Township).

13. Iron Furnace, the first in Mercer County, was built in 1836–37 on Neshannock Creek by Seth and Hill. William Schollard became manager of the furnace in 1846. The outline of the old furnace, which went out of blast in

1862, can be seen at the foot of Springfield Falls, which made possible an unusual feature of the furnace—a waterwheel thirty-eight feet in diameter. The iron from this furnace went into the production of hollow ware. *Location:* From Springfield go north on US 19 through Leesburg to its intersection with SR 2002; thence continue on T 335 to Springfield Falls (near Schollard House).

14. Schoolhouse (brick), with two stories, now has gift shops in former classrooms. *Location:* On US 19 just north of Leesburg, near SR 0208 and Schollard Road (east of Volant).

Note: Two miles north of Leesburg on US 19 is an early iron bridge over Slippery Rock Creek (at Creek Road).

15. McFarland House (brick) was built in 1860 by Ebenezer McFarland at a crossing named for him. Constructed on Western Reserve land, the home has original black walnut and chestnut woodwork in its interior. A hidden room is underneath the stairway. A large cupola on top of the house provides a fine view of the countryside. *Location:* 3 miles northeast of Pulaski and 4 miles southeast of West Middlesex, at junction of SR 3007 and SR 0018.

16. Bell House (brick), with five gables, was built in 1882 by a former legislator, John Bell. His son William S. Bell lived in the house, which was subsequently purchased by the Hopkins family. A bull's-eye window, also called a "wedding-ring light," is above the date stone over the front entrance. The house is situated at what used to be called Battle Row, in a schoolhouse area named for its typical school-yard squabbles. *Location:* South edge of West Middlesex, on Mitchell Road (T 412) near its junction with Gilkey Road.

17. Wheatland School (frame) was built in 1871, the second school erected in the borough. It replaced an 1817 log structure. It is now a private residence. *Location:* Wheatland Borough, second street on north side just east of Church Street.

18. Byers-Bartholomew House (brick), a large structure built in 1855 by the A. M. Byers family, was formerly a general store. When it was operating commercially, one half of the building was also used as a post office. *Location:* Greenfield, on SR 0318 (at Bartholomew Orchard) southwest of Mercer, Greenfield-Charleston Road (Lackawannock Township).

19. Charleston Hotel, now a residence, was one of the first hotels in the township. It was built by Levi Buchanan in the middle or late 1800s. *Location:* Charleston, southeast corner of US 62 and Greenfield-Charleston Road (Jefferson Township).

20. Plank Road School was used until 1942. In later years it was adapted for Jefferson Grange. *Location:* Jefferson Township, South Lake Road (SR 0258), 0.25 mile east of Skyline Drive.

21. Stranahan House (stone) is situated on donation land issued to James O. Kane in 1789. He sold the land in 1828 to Thomas Newcomb, who built the house. In 1851 Newcomb transferred the property to Andrew Stranahan, who retained it as a farm for over half a century. *Location:* 3 miles west of Mercer, off US 62 (first road to left) in Hells Hollow School area (East Lackawannock Township).

22. Hermitage, near Sharon (Hickory area)

22A. 444 Flags Monument and Museum is a tribute to fifty-three Americans held hostage in Iran for 444 days in 1979–81. The citizens of Scranton and Hermitage donated funds for the eagle-topped monument surrounded by an avenue of flags within the park. Here an eternal flame also is a memorial to those who died trying to free the hostages. *Hours:* Daily, 9 A.M.–dusk. *Location:* Hillcrest Memorial Park, 2619 East State Street (near Sharon).

22B. Mt. Hickory Farm, or Thompson House, was the original homestead of Gen. James Pierce, an industrialist who had large holdings and iron mills in Sharpsville. The house was built in the late 1800s. *Location:* 1202 North Keel Ridge Road.

23. Sharon was an early canal town. It is now the county's largest city and industrial town.

23A. Raisch House (log) was built nearby in 1800 and moved to this site in 1978. *Hours:* Memorial Day–Labor Day: Holidays and Sundays, 2–5 P.M., or by appointment. *Location:* Buhl Park at Tenth Street.

23B. The Springhouse was built over 100 years ago as a residence and now houses five shops. *Hours:* Tuesday–Saturday, 10 A.M.–4 P.M. *Location:* 1427 East State Street.

23C. Stevenson Mansion (sandstone) was erected in 1898–99 by John Stevenson, who had come to Pittsburgh from Glasgow, Scotland, in 1872. The sandstone was first cut in 1891 by Stevenson for a house in New Castle on East Lincoln Avenue. Seven years later, seeking more land, the industrialist had the stone hauled by rail to Sharon and rebuilt into a house with twenty-two rooms on the west hill, which originally belonged to an early settler, Isaac Patterson. Andrew Carnegie and President Taft were entertained in this mansion. The building was later used as a kindergarten and nursery. It was damaged by fire in 1961. Again plans were made to move the house owned by Sacred Heart Church, this time to St. Mary's Cemetery, but it remains at its second site. *Location:* 109 North Irvine Avenue.

23D. Boyce House (painted brick) was built in 1866 for $15,000 by George Boyce, a construction engineer on the Erie Extension Canal. He operated the Sharon furnace, built in 1846, at the present Westinghouse plant site and the Shenango furnace near Sharpsville. The house was described as "tall, square, and butter-colored, with a hipped roof, iron brackets, eight uneven rooms, and black marble mantels." Boyce maintained numerous greenhouses on the property. *Location:* Silver Street (formerly Boyce Street) at Second Avenue behind Buhl Club.

23E. Old Express (frame) is a former Erie & Pennsylvania Railroad station that was opened in 1972 as a restaurant. Included on the property are a Pullman car complete with baggage, a locomotive, and a freight station. *Hours:* Monday–Saturday, 11 A.M.–2 A.M.; Sunday, 5 P.M.–2 A.M. *Location:* 110 Connelly Boulevard, at Depot Street.

Note: Also near Old Express is an old gasoline station that has been converted into a restaurant containing automobile memorabilia and antique autos.

23F. Sharon Iron Company, later Sharon Steel, was organized and built in 1850. In 1851 it bought the controlling interest (640 acres) in Iron Mountain, Jackson County, Mich., and also controlled sixty acres of land at Iron Bay and the firm's harbor on Lake Superior. In 1853 the company brought seventy tons of Lake Superior ore to the Clay and Sharpsville furnaces, before the Sault Ste. Marie Canal was completed. In 1861 Gen. Joel B. Curtis, the president, bought the business and four years later sold it to the Westerman Iron Company. Following additional ownerships, National Steel Company purchased it in 1899. South Sharon resulted from

the establishment of Sharon Steel. *Location:* Sharpsville Avenue.

23G. Buhl Mansion (gray sandstone) was built in 1896 for $60,000 by Frank H. Buhl, steel maker and public benefactor who heavily endowed the Sharon Valley. Styled like a French castle, the fourteen-room mansion was designed by Charles Owsley of Youngstown and decorated with furnishings from a castle in France. While the many-turreted landmark was being built, the Buhls stayed in the ten-room house on the property, now the caretaker's residence. In 1936, following the death of Mrs. Buhl, the mansion became the home of Henry B. Forker, Jr., Mrs. Buhl's nephew. The Forkers converted the building into apartments. *Location:* 422 East State Street.

23H. J. M. Willson House (brick), now the Sample-O'Donnell Funeral Home, was built in 1845 by J. M. Willson, a furniture manufacturer. His store is still operating under the same name. *Location:* East Street at corner of North Oakland Avenue.

23I. Sharon Commercial Printing Company was the site of the town's first newspaper, the *Sharon Weekly Herald,* in 1864. At that time the publishers were the brothers R. C. and James Frey. The building now houses the Commercial Printing Company—a spinoff business from the *Herald's* job printing shop in 1973. *Location:* Southeast corner of East State and Railroad streets.

24. Whispering Pines (brick), with fourteen rooms and a tower originally having a cupola, was built in 1855 by Robert Stewart, who gave it its name. Stewart, a dealer in sheep and lumber, gradually increased the size of the property. The structure has been a residence since its construction except from 1922 to 1935, when the front section was operated as a tea house by the Jesse Wilsons. Included on the property are the servants' quarters and a garage once used as a carriage house. *Location:* Near Sharon, in Hickory Township, 5465 East State Street (US 62).

25. Sharpsville was founded by James Sharp, who erected a log gristmill at this site in 1820.

25A. Sharpsville Schoolhouse (frame) was built in 1847 by Vincent, Hemrod & McClure, three ironmakers. Later it was purchased by Gen. James Pierce, who donated several lots

25C. Pierce Lock

for a new school at a new location. *Location:* Northwest corner of Mercer and High streets.

25B. Iron Bank (brick), now Geddes, Pierce, & Co., is a large building with shutters, built in 1871. Later the McDowell Bank, it became the First National Bank in 1907. A historic iron plaque is on the facade. *Location:* 517 Mercer Avenue at Shenango Street.

Note: Nearby on Mercer Avenue is a fine white frame Italianate mansion with a mansard roof and belvedere. At Canal Street and Mercer Avenue is an early feed mill.

25C. Pierce Lock (no. 10) of the Erie Extension Canal (numbered from New Castle to Erie) is the only well-preserved lock of the Beaver-Erie system. The canal operated from 1844 to 1871 between Pittsburgh and the Great Lakes. The lock, adjoining dam no. 1 and made of huge, hand-chipped, fitted stones, was built in 1835–38. It is the only extant lock masonry of the canal in northwestern Pennsylvania and was important to the western Pennsylvania iron industry before the rise of railroads. In the 1880s, James and Frank Pierce, sons of Gen. James Pierce, a coal and iron tycoon, bought the lock and towpath for a spur of the Pittsburgh, Shenango & Lake Erie Railroad, but it never materialized. Today the towpath is used for the Bessemer & Lake Erie Railroad bed. The Shenango Trail (an eight-mile hiking path from Kidds Mills Bridge to Big Bend in Jefferson Township) follows another section of the towpath. *Location:* Sharpsville, on Bridge Street just south of Shenango Reservoir dam. At

bridge take dirt path for about 150 yards into wooded area along Shenango River.

Note: See the list of historical markers for locations where the canal is visible.

26. "Tara" (brick), the present name inspired by the movie *Gone with the Wind,* is a Greek Revival mansion built in 1854 by Charles Koonce, a coal and real estate dealer, on the property of his parents who came to the area in 1808. Charles Koonce, Jr., a Youngstown lawyer, extended the porch and added Georgian columns in 1923. The building at one time housed a television station. Today it is a luxurious country inn and tour home with three restaurants and a gift shop. It is furnished with period furniture, including President James Buchanan's table (once at the White House), Strauss Austrian crystal chandeliers, and a Gourmet Room with murals depicting the antebellum South painted by Earl C. Martz in 1986. The inn was restored by James and Donna Winnep, the present owners. *Location:* 3665 Valley View Road at SR 0018, Clark, overlooking Lake Shenango.

Note: Since 1963 the village of Clark (formerly Clarksville, settled by Samuel Clark in 1804) has been almost completely submerged by the Shenango Reservoir developed in 1960. Albert Bushnell Hart, distinguished scholar, historian, and Harvard professor, was born nearby in 1854.

27. Duncan House (frame), also referred to as the Tidewater Manor, on the crest of Prospect Hill, was built by James Duncan, who followed an architectural style popular in South Carolina, where he lived after he had served in the Revolution. The structure, with log beams in the basement, has five marble fireplaces. Duncan, who died in 1835, is buried across the road from the house near a barn in a private cemetery with an iron fence around it. *Location:* West of Transfer, on Rutledge Road, 0.2 mile from its junction with SR 0846 (Greenville-Sharon Road) (Pymatuning Township).

28. Bortz Farm (brick house and barn) was owned by Levi and Eliza Bortz, who were married in 1853. A date stone on the barn reads, "L & E. Bortz, H. S. & wife, builders 1870." Levi was a shoemaker and prominent farmer. *Location:* Shenango, south of Greenville, SR 0018.

29. Kidds Mills Covered Bridge, built in 1868, is the county's only remaining early covered bridge and the only Smith-Cross truss bridge east of Ohio. It spans the She-

26. "Tara"

nango River. The Shenango Conservancy has restored this bridge. *Location:* South of Shenango on T 653, just off SR 4012, between SR 0058 and SR 0018. (It can be seen from historical marker on SR 0058.)

Note: A more recent covered bridge stands near I-80 and SR 0018 north of West Middlesex. There are two metal truss bridges in the county, both built in 1898: one over French Creek on SR 1015 near Carleton (French Creek Township); and the Quaker Bridge over Little Shenango River near Greenville.

30. Greenville, on part of the Donation Lands (fifth district) in the late 1700s—parcels of land given as pay to Revolutionary War soldiers, was laid out around 1798 by Probst, Lodge, and Walker.

30A. Mann-Stewart House (frame), built in 1854 of Greek Revival style with a pedimented front portico and a fanlight window, was the home of Robert Mann. The property was purchased by Vance Stewart at another time. *Location:* 115 Columbia Avenue at Vance Street.

30B. Thiel College opened its Greenville campus in 1871 in the old Greenville Academy building. Prior to this, Thiel College, of the Evangelical Lutheran church, the oldest institution of higher education of this sect west of the Allegheny Mountains, was located in Phillipsburg (now Monaca, Beaver County). It had been opened as a "classical school" in 1866 at a former summer resort purchased by Rev. William A. Passavant, acting for the Lutheran Synod. A. L. Thiel, a member of the Second Lutheran Church of Pittsburgh, donated the money for this endeavor, and the school was incorporated as Thiel Hall in 1870, the year it was opened as a college. At that time the city of Greenville, through a gift of seven acres and $20,000, induced the Pittsburgh Synod to move the school to Greenville. The oldest remaining structure on campus is Greenville Hall (brick), erected in 1872–74. *Location:* College Hill.

30C. Goodwin House was built about 1831 by Samuel Goodwin who owned the Goodwin gristmill. He was an original stockholder and officer of the First National Bank of Greenville, organized in 1864. *Location:* 36 South Mercer Street.

30D. Hillside United Presbyterian Church (brick) was built in 1867. *Location:* North High and West Main streets.

30E. Greek Revival House (brick) has pillars and a carved eagle surrounded by twenty-six stars on the facade. *Location:* 41 Mercer Street at Harrison Street.

30F. Irvin Mansion (brick), of Greek Revival and New England style, was built in 1846 by

29. *Kidds Mills Covered Bridge*

Himrod and Woodworth and purchased by William Irvin, whose brother Lot became the ironmaster in the family business. When their concern went under in 1851, the original owners bought back the property; and Lot Irvin, despondent over the failure, hanged himself in the bridge house of the deserted furnace. It was said that this lavish house, not his furnace, led to his downfall. The grave of Lot, a thirty-year-old bachelor, is in Shenango Valley Cemetery. In the 1860s George Bittenbanner bought the house and built twin wings at the rear and a thirty-five-foot, three-story turret on the south side. Later the twenty-room house was divided into apartments. The furnace was fifty feet from the house over the bluff. *Location:* On bluff, North Front Street.

30G. Waugh House (brick), a large structure with chimneys built in steplike fashion at the gable ends, was the home of Judge William Waugh, who was one of the first graduates of the University of Pittsburgh, one of the founders of the National Bank in Greenville, and editor and proprietor of the *Mercer Whig* from 1845 to 1848. His house was built in 1843. *Location:* Corner of Second and Main streets.

30H. River and Canal Museum (pole construction) is a structure measuring 48 by 96 feet built on approximately two acres (boundary line has traces of Erie Extension Canal). It contains exhibits and memorabilia on river and canal travel in the Lakeland area. The canal once followed what is now the Besse-

mer & Lake Erie Railroad tracks, formerly a canal towpath. Plans include construction of a canal packet boat. The project, inspired by James Kerr, is directed by the Greenville Area Leisure Services Association. Underprivileged young adults from the area performed most of the labor, as well as local contractors. *Location:* Landfill between Alan Avenue and the Bessemer & Lake Erie Railroad, Riverside Park.

30I. Railroad Memorial Park includes the 604 Engine (a steam switch, the last of its kind) and the 1912 Empire automobile, both part of the Greenville legacy. A newly built railroad station and dispatcher's office are recent additions to the park. All the work on the train and park has been volunteer, and all the memorabilia were donated. Area businesses also helped. The park became the Shenango-Pymatuning chapter of the National Railroad Historical Society in recent years. *Location:* Just east of the Conrail tracks, near the old Erie Lackawanna depot.

Note: Greenville over the years has been an important railroad town. The Greenville Steel Car Company, originally the Metal Products Company (1910), manufactured railroad cars.

30J. Ghost House (frame), built around 1850, is a Greek Revival house with a two-story Ionic facade. Once known as the Mann-Stewart house, it is now owned by the William Ghost family, who restored it and also created a "Kindred Spirits Shop." *Hours:* By appointment. *Location:* Columbia Avenue.

31. Bigler Graves are the burial sites of Jacob (d. 1827) and Susan (d. 1851) Bigler. They were the first parents in America to have reared two sons who became governors of two different states during the same year. William Bigler was governor of Pennsylvania from 1852 to 1855, and John Bigler was governor of California from 1852 to 1856. Shortly after moving to Fredonia in 1814, the family was swindled in a land deal and lived for some time nearly in poverty. Their frame house is still standing nearby in Delaware Township. *Location:* 3 miles southeast of Greenville, in Bigler Cemetery, on SR 0058 at Mercer and Salem roads (near historical marker).

32. Caldwell One-Room Schoolhouse, now the Historical Society Museum, was built in 1880 of brick fired on the Ball farm, four miles southeast of the site. The building, donated by Delaware Township, was dedicated in 1962 by the Mercer County Historical Society

32. Caldwell One-Room Schoolhouse

34B. Jamestown Opera House

in commemoration of the more than 225 former public one-room schools which operated in the county from 1800 to 1900. It is furnished with the original desks, an iron stove, a pipe organ, and other memorabilia. A reconstructed well and bake oven are also on the property. *Hours:* June–September: Sundays and holidays, 1–5 P.,M. and by appointment. *Location:* 5 miles south of Greenville, on SR 0058.

Note: Another early brick one-room schoolhouse, built in 1888, is near Greenville at the junction of Porter and East James streets (SR 0058).

33. St. Paul's Home (brick) includes a building complex on 627 acres of woodlands, originally incorporated in 1868. Historically affiliated with the United Church of Christ, it offers retirement living and professional care for the aging. *Location:* Near Greenville.

34. Jamestown was laid out as a village in 1832 by John Keck and named for the original settler, James Campbell.

34A. Gibson House (brick), built in 1855–56, was the residence of a local physician, Dr. William Gibson (1813–87) and his wife Susan. This mansion was built in 1855. Gibson was a stockholder in the Pittsburgh & Lake Erie and the Franklin & Jamestown railroads, an officer of a Stoneboro coal company, treasurer of a metallic and lumber company, president of the Jamestown Banking Company, and operator of a drugstore across from his house. The Gibsons met Mark Twain on a round-the-world tour in 1867 and became the focus of ridicule in Twain's book *Innocents Abroad*. The author is reputed to have been a guest in the Gibson home after a speaking engagement in Sharon in 1869.

The doctor and his wife erected an enormous ninety-foot monument for their grave sites in 1884 at the Jamestown Cemetery, on a knoll south of SR 0058. It cost the Gibsons between $95,000 and $100,000 to build, with a special railroad spur constructed to transport the materials to the cemetery. The monument and tracks are still at the cemetery.

Their house later became an inn known as Mark Twain Manor, now a restaurant. A brick carriage house on the property is now a commercial business. *Location:* 210 Liberty Street at Main (SR 0058).

34B. Jamestown Opera House (brick) was built about 1860 by Dr. William Gibson. *Location:* Water and Liberty streets.

34C. Jamestown Historical Society (brick) is housed in a small Victorian doctor's office established by Dr. M. A. Bailey. It was built by James Campbell, Jr.—the second oldest house in the borough. *Location:* 314 Liberty Street, next to Victorian house.

34D. Moats House (brick), a Victorian house built in the middle to late 1800s, is now a photography studio. *Location:* Liberty Street, next to Historical Society.

34E. Campbell-Hodgson House (frame), the oldest house in Jamestown, is a one-story structure built in 1840 by James Campbell, Jr., whose father came to the area in 1798 and lived in a cave (Seminary Hill) until he could build a log cabin. In later years it was bought by a geologist, Robert Hodgson. *Location:* 316 Liberty Street, at Depot Street.

35. Hunter's Choice (log), reputed to be the oldest house in the county, was built on a 500-acre tract in 1786 by Dr. Absalom Baird, a surgeon who had received the land as a

Revolutionary War grant October 8, 1785. The property was patented in 1807 to Jacob Stroud as Hunter's Choice. In 1913 it was purchased by George C. Hinckley, one of the engineers who designed the Roosevelt Dam, and nicknamed Yellow Breeches Farm. The Hinckleys had offers from the Ford Foundation to purchase the log cabin and move it to Dearborn, Mich., but they decided to preserve it at its historical location. Later it was sold to Donald and Valeria Dukelow. The house, of oak and poplar logs, had a loft which was converted to bedrooms; a porch and a kitchen were added at another date. *Location:* Near Fredonia. At Mercer greenhouse on US 19, turn east onto SR 1008 (District Road) and continue 1.7 miles to Furnace Road; thence west 0.1 mile to lane on right, where Dukelow farm is located (Fairview Township).

36. Harry-of-the-West Furnace, was built in 1838 by J. G. Butler and William McKinley, father of the president. Originally called Temperance Furnace as a compliment to Butler's wife, it acquired its later name in tribute to Henry Clay. *Location:* Near Hunter's Choice.

37. Sellers House (frame) was built in 1860 by an Englishman named Sellers, exactly halfway between Pittsburgh and Erie. The family lived in a smaller saltbox house on the property while this home was being constructed. A brass pike marker north of the farmhouse was placed by the side of the road (now under the highway) in 1812, presumably to mark Commodore Perry's route to Lake Erie or the exact midway point between the two towns. In 1915 the location was resurveyed by the U.S. government, using the bull's-eye window of the house and by consulting century-old notes to help calculate where the marker was situated. The house was later purchased by the Owen Clair Neal family and has large additions in the rear. *Location:* North of Fredonia and Mercer, on US 19 just past Mercer greenhouse on right side of road (Delaware Township).

38. Old Salem Methodist Church (frame) was built in 1850 and retains its original style. It replaced a church erected about 1798. *Location:* North of Leechs Corners at junction of SR 4019 and SR 4020.

39. Byerly House (frame) was built between 1832 and 1838 by the Byerly family, early German settlers of South Pymatuning Township. Andrew Byerly, a son of Joseph and Mary Smith Byerly, lived at the house for years. *Location:* Byerlys Corners, southeast corner of Buckeye Drive and Saranac Drive.

40. Echo Dell Whistle Stop consists of two vintage railroad cars that have been converted into an art studio and a gift shop with railroad memorabilia. *Hours:* Daily, 12 noon–5 P.M. Closed Wednesdays. *Location:* Clarks Mills, Carpenters Corners Road, 2 miles northwest off I-79 at exit 34.

41. Clark's Gristmill (frame) was built in 1852. Giles Clark established the first mill here in 1838. Originally run by waterpower, the present structure continues to operate as a mill powered by electricity. *Location:* Clarks Mills, on Mill Road off SR 0258.

42. Sheakley Halfway House (frame), once a tavern built in 1820 by Moses Sheakley, where General Lafayette was entertained in 1825, was the home of James Sheakley (1829–1917), fourth territorial governor of Alaska in 1893–97. He also served as U.S. commissioner of schools for Alaska in 1887–92. *Location:* Sheakleyville, on US 19 in center of town near bridge.

43. Country Studio is an art gallery and gift shop in a turn-of-the-century house. *Hours:* Daily, 1–9 P.M. Closed Wednesdays. *Location:* Williams Corners, 2 miles east of Sheakleyville near Goddard State Park.

44. Fairfield Presbyterian Church (frame) was the first church established in the county, with its first service held in 1799 by Rev. Joseph Stockton and Rev. Elisha McCurdy. The congregation adopted the name Fairfield in 1800. William Wiley from the Ten Mile settlement in Washington County was the first pastor, installed in 1802. At that time New Vernon was called the community of "Ten Milers" for the settlers who came here in 1798 from a creek by that name. The present church, built before 1876 adjacent to the cemetery, is on the site of the original structure. *Location:* New Vernon, New Vernon Township.

45. New Lebanon Institute (brick), a large Victorian structure with five gables and bull's-eye windows, was erected in 1880 at a cost of $7,000. It was incorporated as McElwain Institute in 1883, honoring its most liberal supporter, John McElwain. An academic school for both men and women, it continued until shortly after 1909. It now serves as a nondenominational church. *Location:* New Lebanon, on SR 0173 (Mill Creek Township).

46. Indian Burials contains a monument to Chief Guyasuta that bears the following inscription:

Guyasuta, a Chief of the Delaware Indians, had his town here known as Custaloga "he was buried here before 1810."
Erected by descendants of Charles H. Heydrick. History of Venango County, Page 28.

A burial stone nearby with an outline of a hatchet reads, "Guy a sooter—1810 H.S." Another stone simply has written on it, "Boy." The Indian buried here and thought to be Guyasuta is more likely Custaloga, whose town was about twelve miles northwest of here, south of Meadville. Guyasuta, who was actually chief of the Senecas, is more widely believed to have been buried near Sharpsburg (Allegheny County) where his cabin was located. The bones of an old man, believed to have been his, were dug up in 1919 at Sharpsburg and are now preserved in Carnegie Museum in the Oakland section of Pittsburgh. *Location:* Halfway between Milledgeville and Carlton, turn east off SR 0173 and go 1.7 miles on SR 1028 to Scout reservation on Heydrick farm.

Note: Nearby is the brick Heydrick house, built in 1871 on donation land given to Charles H. Heydrick in 1787 for service in the Revolution.

47. Carnahan House (brick) was built in 1836 for Gen. James M. Carnahan by John Hawthorn, John Henderson, and John McKean from bricks made on the property. It was the first brick house in the area, then known as Kerrtown. In later years this house was purchased by the Crawford family. *Location:* Mill Creek Township. About 3 miles north of Sandy Lake toward Cochranton, take first dirt road to left off SR 0173. House is on right at crossroads.

48. Freedom Road Cemetery contains the graves of a number of slaves who escaped from the South by the underground railroad and settled near here about 1825 and later. After 1855 most of the rest moved on to Canada. Their cemetery lies a short distance south of the road. As a result of this settlement, nearby Stoneboro, on the south side of Sandy Lake, was once called Liberia. *Location:* Southwest of Sandy Lake, on US 62 (Sandy Lake–Grove City Road) across from Stoneboro fairgrounds.

49. Sandy Lake Church of Christ (frame) was purchased about 1880 from an oil lease and brought to this site along Sandy Creek. Originally known as Brownsville, Sandy Lake was the home of Dr. John Goodsell, a scientist and physician who accompanied Peary on his trip to the North Pole in 1909. The church has been adapted for use as a commercial business. *Location:* Sandy Lake, east end of lake (Sandy Lake Township).

50. Stoneboro, situated on the south side of Sandy Lake, was established as a post office in 1868. The Mercer Iron and Coal Company, responsible for the origin of the town, began operating there in 1864 (Lake Township).

50A. Stoneboro Fairgrounds originally were operated by the Mercer County Agricultural and Manufacturing Society in 1867. The organization became the Mercer County Agricultural Society in 1876 when it moved to its present location. The site has been in continuous use as a fairgrounds from its early beginning. The fair is held annually from the last Wednesday in August through Labor Day. *Location:* North of US 62.

50B. Stoneboro Hotel (frame) was built about 1866 as Hotel Clarence, later known as the Homer Hotel. It is now a restaurant. *Location:* Southwest corner of Maple and Lake streets.

51. Methodist Campground, covering twelve acres, was built in 1900 by the Allegheny Wesleyan Connection, a group of churches with headquarters in Salem, Ohio (Rev. P. B. Campbell, president). Tents were used until the 1950s, when fifty frame cottages and twenty dormitories replaced them. Other buildings include three tabernacles, a dining hall, and offices. The Allegheny Wesleyan Connection resulted from a merger of the Wesleyan Church of America, an antislavery group that broke with the Methodist Episcopal Church at the time of the Civil War, and the Pilgrim Wesleyan Connection. *Location:* Fredonia Road, near Stoneboro (SR 1004 near SR 1006).

52. Henderson General Store (cut stone) was built in 1859 and is now an antique shop. Mathias H. Henderson, for whom the town was named, was vice-president of the Pennsylvania Railroad in 1897 and vice-president of the Sharon National Bank. *Location:* Henderson, southwest corner of SR 0965 and Bradley Road at SR 2021 (Worth Township).

Pennsylvania Historical and Museum Commission Markers

Albert Bushell Hart   Clark, SR 0258
Bigler Graves   SR 0058 southeast of Greenville
Bigler Home   SR 0058 southeast of Greenville
Clay Furnace   US 62 west of Charleston
Erie Extension Canal   Wasser Bridge Road 0.3 mile east of SR 0018, south of Greenville; and junction of SR 0018 and SR 0518 east of Sharpsville
"Freedom Road"   US 62 southwest of Sandy Lake
James Sheakley   Sheakleyville, US 19
Johnston Tavern   US 19 north of Leesburg
Mercer County   Mercer, at courthouse, on square
Pymatuning   SR 0258 east of Clark
Shenango Town   SR 008 southeast of West Middlesex

The map shows Somerset County with the following locations labeled:

Surrounding areas: CAMBRIA, WESTMORELAND, FAYETTE, BEDFORD, MARYLAND

Towns: Davidsville, Windber, Ashtola, Jennerstown, Gray, Hooversville, Stoystown, Champion, Buckstown, Reels Corners, Seven Springs, Somerset, New Baltimore, New Centerville, Brotherton, Berlin, Ursina, Confluence, Meyersdale, St. Pauls, Addison, Salisbury, Springs

Routes: 70, 76, 30, 219, 40

Somerset County

Capsule History

Somerset County was named for Somerset in western England. It was erected out of Bedford County, April 17, 1795, and was reduced in size in 1804 when Cambria was organized in part from Somerset. It now has 1,073 square miles with a population of 81,243.

The earliest land surveys were made in 1767; and the first settlers, who were German of the Reformed and Lutheran faiths, came to the vicinity of Berlin about 1769. In 1780 a number of Mennonites migrated to the county. John Yoder, nicknamed "Axie" Yoder, was an early resident who made and signed more than 5,000 axes. The first permanent settler at the village of Somerset was Harmon Husband, a Quaker from North Carolina. Jeremiah Sullivan Black (1810–83) was born in the county near Brotherton. He served as chief justice of the Pennsylvania Supreme Court and under President James Buchanan as U.S. attorney general and secretary of state. The Black family cemetery and a memorial park named in their honor are located on SR 0031. Friedrich Goeb, who built a log cabin at the site of 151 West Main Street in Somerset, printed the first Bible west of the Allegheny Mountains in 1813 in German. Abner McKinley, President William McKinley's brother, lived in Somerset (129 East Main Street) from 1892 to 1904.

Five principal Indian trails traversed the county. The *Raystown Path* ran completely across it, following much the course later taken by US 30. *The Conemaugh Path* cut the northeastern corner of the county from Pleasantville, above Ogletown and Windber, toward Johnstown. The *Fort Hill Path* ran from Salisbury to Fort Hill through still wild country over Negro Mountain. The *Turkeyfoot Path* entered the southeastern corner of the county near Pocahontas, running by Engles Mill, Salisbury, south of the highest peak of Mt. Davis, and north of Listonburg to Dumas and Harnedsville. *Nemacolin's Path* cut across the southwest corner near Addison.

Braddock's, Burd's, and Forbes's early military roads traversed sections of the county; and several military camps along the last-named highway later became the villages of Stoystown, Buckstown, and Jennerstown. (Near Stoystown, now under the present Quemahoning Reservoir, was the site of Delaware Chief Kickeney-Paulin's cabin, a sleeping place on an early traders' path.) The Great Cumberland National Road (now US 40) passed through the southwest tip of the county.

Somerset County has preserved ten of its covered bridges as well as numerous log houses. At Fort Hill, three miles northeast of Ursina, two palisaded Indian villages dating from the Discovery Period have been excavated.

Lumbering was an important early industry in the county, later succeeded by agriculture. Limestone was another natural resource. The county has had five stone blast furnaces. Today the leading industries include coal mining, dairying, and farming. Oats, buckwheat, and maple syrup are among the leading products.

Landmarks

1. Somerset, at 2,190 feet, has the highest elevation of any county seat in Pennsylvania. A self-guided walking tour of the town is available through the Somerset Historical Society or the Chamber of Commerce.

1A. Courthouse (limestone) was erected in 1904 in classical Renaissance style with a dome patterned after St. Paul's Cathedral in London, England (J. C. Fulton, architect). The earliest court in the county was held on December 21, 1795, in a room in the Webster Tavern in Somerset. The first courthouse was built in 1798. Construction of the second building began in 1851 and was completed in 1852. The third and present structure is on the site of the second. *Location:* East Union Street and North Center Avenue.

1B. Coffee Spring Farmhouse (frame), once an inn, was the home of Harmon Hus-

1A. Courthouse

band, a leader of North Carolina's revolt against the British shortly after the Stamp Act was passed in 1765. Husband wrote the resolutions adopted by the Regulators who hoped to solve public grievances. In 1771 under an assumed name, Toscape Death, he fled to

273

1B. Coffee Spring Farmhouse

Pennsylvania. As the town of Somerset's first settler, he built the farmhouse in 1773. During the Whiskey Rebellion, Husband became a pamphleteer and was Bedford County's delegate to the Parkinson Ferry meeting. In 1794 he was one of thirteen insurrectionists who were taken from Bedford to Philadelphia where they were imprisoned for about eight months. He died in 1795, shortly after being released.

Husband's farm acquired its name from the fact that Indians used to dig wild chicory roots near the spring which still flows on the property. Inside this house is preserved an oil painting portraying the natives gathering their "coffee" to dry for a beverage. Above the fireplace is a mural depicting the life of Harmon Husband. Open for tours. *Location:* 555 East Main Street (junction of SR 0031 and US 219).

1C. Old Jail and Sheriff's Residence (brick), now business offices, were built about 1856 by John Mong. The jail was noted for its double gallows and numerous escape attempts. In 1890 it was equipped with iron cell blocks. According to tradition the sheriff's wife prepared meals for the prisoners. *Location:* East Union Street beside courthouse.

1D. Printing House Row (brick), an Italianate style commercial building, was erected in 1872 by F. H. Riley and Jacob Walker. It housed the presses of the *Somerset Herald* newspaper and the law offices of William

H. Koontz (1830–1911), a lawyer, orator, and legislator elected to the U.S. Congress (1864–66). The newspaper business was operated by Edward Scull (1818–1900), the grandson of John Scull, publisher of the first newspaper printed west of the Alleghenies. Scull also was elected to Congress (1886, 1888, and 1890). The building now houses law offices. *Location:* 110 East Union Street.

1E. "Manor Hill" (brick), a Georgian Revival structure designed by Horace Trunbauer, was the home of Daniel B. Zimmerman, a coal operator and cattle dealer, between 1915 and 1918. *Location:* North Center Avenue.

1F. Koontz-Lansberry House (brick), Italianate in style, was built by William H. Koontz in 1869. Here President McKinley as well as various governors and prominent people were guests. In later years Judge and Mrs. Thomas F. Lansberry were the owners and entertained Vice-President Richard Nixon here (1954) among other notables. *Location:* 139 East Union Street.

1G. "Heart of Somerset" (frame), now a bed and breakfast inn, was purchased in recent years by Kenneth and Rita Halverson. The house, owned by a previous family for 109 years, was built about 1839. *Location:* 130 West Union Street.

1H. *Philip Dressler Center for the Arts*

1H. Philip Dressler Center for the Arts (brick). This five-bay structure, built in 1832, has over the years served as an inn and as the Edgewood Summer Resort. It is now the site of Laurel Arts, Inc., the only rural Pennsylvania arts center of its kind. It is located on the farm of Philip Dressler, a Pittsburgh industrialist who invented the tunnel kiln. *Location:* 214 South Harrison Avenue.

1I. Historical Murals in the reading room of the Mary S. Biesecker Public Library were painted by three artists who were associated at Carnegie Institute of Technology in Pittsburgh and who all had summer homes in Somerset County around 1930: (1) Kindred McLeary (from Texas), whose murals are also on display in the Federal Building in Pittsburgh, the new War Department Building in Washington, D.C., and the Post Office Building in New York, among others; (2) Esther Topp (Mrs. Edmonds), born of Norwegian parents, who studied in Paris, painted in Norway, and exhibited extensively; and (3) Alexander J. Kostellow, who was born in Persia of French parents and later became director of the Department of Design at Pratt Institute in Brooklyn. The murals depict historical events in Somerset County, including the lives of such notables as Friedrich Goeb, Harmon Husband, and Judge Jeremiah S. Black. *Location:* Somerset Library.

2. Hillcroft Farmhouse was built in Georgian style by John Kosser in 1829. It is situated on land originally surveyed in 1774, once known as Woodchuck's Bottom. In 1979 Hayes Lorene Ling restored the house, which had been purchased by the owner's father in 1917. *Location:* SR 0281 about 5 miles southwest of Somerset.

3. *Log House at Somerset Historical Center*

Note: Two other Georgian houses built by John Kosser for his children are to the left and right of the Ling house.

3. Somerset Historical Center is an indoor-outdoor museum exhibit pertaining to mid-eighteenth-century rural life on the Laurel Highlands frontier. It is administered by the Pennsylvania Historical and Museum Commission. It also serves as headquarters for the county historical society. In the late 1960s Dr. and Mrs. Earl O. Haupt sold sixteen acres of property adjacent to their home to the state; included, among other structures, was an 1804 log house they had bought after it had been used in the 1954 county sesquicentennial celebration. The center also displays a bridge originally built in 1859 at Walters Mill, ten miles to the south and relocated at the site in 1961; a maple-sugar camp of 1840; and a lean-to barn, all from the unique Haupt collection. In 1969–70 the modern stone exhibit building and board and batten administrative offices were opened to the public, along with nature trails. *Hours:* Tuesday–Saturday, 9 A.M.–5 P.M.; Sunday, 12 noon–5 P.M. Closed Mondays and holidays except Memorial Day, July 4, and Labor Day. *Admission charge.* Annual Mountain Craft Days in September. *Location:* 4 miles north of Somerset, on SR 0985.

4. Herb's Old Tavern (frame) was a stage-coach stop, and in later years, a general store. A blacksmith shop once operated at one end of the building. It is reputed to have the oldest horseshoe bar in Pennsylvania. More recently the building was purchased by

Herb and Pearl Siperek, and it is now an oyster house. *Location:* Jenners Crossroads, US 30.

5. Rauch House (painted brick), built in 1806, was once an inn and is now a gift shop. It was formerly the home of Squire Henry Rauch, who conducted a hearing here on charges against Joseph and David Nicely, who posed as constables and killed Herman Umberger, after finding $16,000 in his house in February 1889. The two brothers were convicted and hanged in 1891, after escaping and being captured twice. After the hanging the noose was taken to the courthouse for preservation. During the War of 1812 the "Allegheny Blues," part of the 109th Pennsylvania Regiment dined here. *Location:* Jennerstown, on US 30.

6. Mountain Playhouse (log) and **Green Gables Restaurant** (stone) had their beginning in 1927 when James, Robert, and Louise Stoughton, then in their teens, built a roadside restaurant on the old homestead farm belonging to the family since 1795. Their Green Gables establishment won a $3,000 prize in a highway beautification contest sponsored by the Rockefeller Foundation, and the prize launched them on a lifetime career. In 1938 James and his sister Louise Stoughton Maust purchased the Cronin-Grover log gristmill, built in 1805 and in use until 1918 at Roxbury, near Berlin, thirty miles away. (It is similar in construction to the 1806 Simon Hay's mill, now destroyed, which was erected on Blue Lick Creek near Meyersdale.) After it was rebuilt on their property it became a summer theater, opened in 1939, and the Jenner Art Gallery. This is one of the oldest summer-stock theaters west of the Alleghenies. The 2,500-acre recreation complex was enlarged in 1950 to include a lake built by Robert Stoughton, an additional dining room, and an old barn converted into apartments and guest rooms. The theater is open from late May to mid October, and the restaurant daily, year round. *Location:* On old US 219, 0.5 mile north of Jennerstown.

7. Seese's Museum (partly frame) is a primitive building in a rustic setting. Privately owned. Visits by appointment. *Admission charge. Location:* About 3 miles north of Jennerstown on Thomas Mills-Jennerstown Road.

8. Johns House (frame) was the last home of Joseph Schantz (Johns), a Swiss Mennonite who came to America in 1769 at the age of twenty. (See *Johns Log House Model,* Cambria County.) He moved in 1806 to this site, the Stock Farm, north of Davidsville, which had been laid out by David Stetzman. Behind the house is a Johns family cemetery enclosed by a picket fence. *Location:* Just north of Davidsville, turn off Main Street onto East Campus Street. House is a quarter mile on left.

9. Lohr Barn (frame) has interesting Pennsylvania Dutch round louvres decorated with cut-out hearts and stars on both sides, and is reminiscent of the barns of the early German settlers in this area. J. W. Lohr built the structure about 1875. *Location:* Near Davidsville. Turn west off Main Street onto West Campus Street and continue for almost 0.5 mile to barn on right.

10. Conemaugh Township Area Historical Society (frame) is located in the former home of Dr. P. L. Swank. Built in 1888, the house also included a doctor's office. In 1984 the historical society bought it from the Naugle family. *Location:* Davidsville, 104 South Main Street.

11. Thomas Mill (frame) was built in 1836 and today functions as a commercial building. *Location:* Thomas Mills, SR 0985.

12. Soap Hollow is noted for its craftsmen from successive generations of Mennonite (German and Swiss) families in the furniture-making business. A sign at this location relates the names and dates of the artisans, such as Sala, Stahl, Thomas, and Livingston, who signed their distinctive furniture. The earliest of these settlers were Jacob and Anne Blauch who migrated here in 1790. The greatest productive time for this Federal-style furniture was between 1850 and 1882 (see *Made in Western Pennsylvania: Early Decorative Arts* [Pittsburgh: Historical Society of Western Pennsylvania, 1982]). *Location:* Soap Hollow, Miller Road, off SR 4041, about 7 miles southeast of Johnstown (Conemaugh Township).

Note: Soap Hollow log house was built from logs which were originally part of the old Mennonite church near Davidsville.

13. Saylor School (frame), a one-room school, was built in 1887 to replace the smaller log structure across the road. It closed in 1938. Five-year reunions are held here by former classmates. A booklet on the history of the Conemaugh Township schools

11. *Thomas Mill*

is available. *Location:* Saylor (Conemaugh Township).

14. Windber Museum (frame), which opened in 1972, occupies a house with a double front porch, the oldest house in the borough, which owns the structure. It was built by David J. and Rachel Holsopple Shaffer in 1869. The Shaffers at one time owned most of the area which is present-day Windber. Johnny Weissmuller, champion swimmer and movie actor (his greatest role was Tarzan), was born in Windber. *Hours:* Tuesday– Sunday, 1–4 P.M. *Donations accepted. Location:* Windber, 601 Fifteenth Street.

Note: The *Christ of Gethsemane*, a painting by Lawrence L. Whitaker, is in the United Brethren Church in this borough. Whitaker, a member of the church, donated it in memory of the congregation's founders.

15. Ashtola (frame, remodeled, partly covered with original hemlock slabs) was built as a summer vacation home by E. V. Babcock (see *Babcock House,* Allegheny County). (The town of Ashtola was named by Mrs. H. L. Baer at the time of her wedding. She was impressed by the abundance of ash trees in this region. Her son married into President McKinley's family.) *Location:* Ashtola (Ogle Township), on SR 1033, 3.5 miles northeast of SR 0160 near Hagevo, or 3.5 miles southeast of SR 0160 at Windber.

16. St. Paul's German Reformed and Lutheran Church (frame), now the Hooversville Museum, was built in 1849 on land donated by John Weigle for $1,000. Its bell tower was erected in 1929. The church, bought by the borough in 1950, is surrounded by Pleasantdale Cemetery. In 1886 the two denominations split, and the Lutherans built a brick church at the corner of Clark and Church streets. *Location:* Hooversville, Clark Street.

17. Shade Church (frame) housed congregations of Lutheran and Reformed faiths, later Reformed only. The first church organization was in 1835, but there had been preaching at an earlier date. The building was erected in 1822–23, but looks more modern, having been completely renovated and repaired in 1884. *Location:* 1 mile west of Reels Corners turn north off US 30 at church sign, and follow Shade Church Road for 1.7 miles.

Note: Nearby an army oven has been reconstructed at the site of Fort Bellaire near Kantner. It is off SR 1010.

18. Berlin was laid out on a tract called Pious Springs, owned by the Lutheran and Reformed congregations of Brothers Valley Township. In 1784 the members established the town with the stipulation that the parishioners build their houses with frontages of at least twenty-two feet and with stone chimneys "so that there will be no danger of fire." Those who did not abide by this order were to forfeit their land or lot to the village for the use of the church and school. The manufacture of hats for southern markets was the town's largest industry until the Civil War. The existence of two market squares is a result of an early dispute among the settlers. Today the principal activity is maple-sugar production and farming.

18A. Trinity Reformed Church (brick), now the United Church of Christ, was built in 1883. In 1777 the congregations of the Trinity Reformed and Lutheran churches agreed to worship in the village schoolhouse until each could erect a house of worship. Rev. John W. Weber was the first regular pastor of the Trinity Reformed congregation (see *Milliron Church,* Westmoreland County). In 1794 Rev. Cyriacus Spangenberg, pastor of Trinity, fatally stabbed an elder, Jacob Glessner, in a church dispute. Despite the statement often made that he was hanged, Spangenberg received a pardon and moved to the northwestern part of the state. *Location:* Corner of Vine and Main streets.

18B. Holy Trinity Evangelical Lutheran Church (brick) was built in 1889, replacing the first two-story log structure, erected in 1800. *Location:* Corner of Fifth and Main streets.

18C. Hunter's Inn (brick) is an early hotel. *Location:* Main section of town.

19. Meyersdale, a maple sugar center, formerly (1803) Meyers Mills.

19A. Meyersdale Railroad Station (brick) is a landmark worthy of preservation. *Location:* Near center of town.

19B. Maple Manor (log, 1805–17; frame, 1830) is the oldest house in Meyersdale, which was laid out in 1844 and named for Peter Meyers, son of Jacob, an owner of the house. Andrew Berdreger (Borntrager), prior owner, had built a mill nearby. The house is the headquarters of Festival Park. It has a fine collection of antiques. Here also is a cobbler's shop, a typical doctor's office, and a country store in addition to a sugar camp. Each year in March the state maple festival is held here, the maple capital of Pennsylvania. *Hours:* Weekdays, 8 A.M.–4:30 P.M.; Saturday–Sunday, 1 P.M.–5 P.M. *Location:* 124 Meyers Avenue.
Note: A stone over the fireplace in one of the craft buildings has a face and the date

19B. Maple Manor

1818 inscribed on it. It came from a barn nearby. The brick Italianate house adjacent to the craft buildings was built by Dr. William Meyers (Peter's son), after 1870.

20. Warren Truss Bridge was built by Wendel Bollman in 1871. It was originally in the Baltimore & Ohio Railroad main line as Bridge No. 6 north of Cumberland on the route to Pittsburgh, most likely over Wills Creek. It is now used as an automobile bridge over a railroad. Notable is the use of decorative cast-iron sway bracings which have added to the height of the truss. *Location:* On T 516 off US 219, 1.25 miles north of Meyersdale (Summit Township).

21. Hillcrest Grange No. 1674, "Patrons of Industry" (frame), is a Victorian building with decorative millwork. *Location:* North of Hays Mill, SR 2025 and SR 2024 (Brothers Valley Township).
Note: Nearby is a brick United Church of Christ, built in 1898.

22. Homer Boger House (stone), built in 1796, is the only stone house remaining in Brothers Valley Township. Hays Mill, the site, was named for Simon Hay, a native of Germany and the mill operator. Blue Lick Creek was the source of power for this mill which is now in ruins on the property. The mill was said to have been "the most remarkable log mill ever constructed in western Pennsylvania" (Charles Stotz). *Location:* Hays Mill, near Meyersdale, T 415 and T 658.

23. Blue Lick Schoolhouse, one room, was built across the road from the historic Hays Mill. *Location:* About 2 miles northeast of Meyersdale on Blue Lick Creek, T 415 and T 658.

24. Salisbury (founded in 1796 by Joseph Markley and incorporated in 1862) and West Salisbury.

24A. Keagey House (stone), once a tavern, was built in 1815–20 by John Keagey, postmaster and son-in-law of John Markley, founder of Salisbury. Keagey died in mysterious circumstances and is buried near the house. The Haselbarth family later owned the house. *Location:* SR 0669 (Ord and Smith streets), across from *Early Salisbury House.*

24B. Early Salisbury House (frame) is easily recognized by the date 1795 written across one gable end by one of its recent owners. Names associated with the house are Peter Short, Michael Miller, and Christian Livengood. It was later purchased by Samuel S. Garlitz. *Location:* On SR 0669.

Note: Old Reformed Church (brick) is across the street from this house.

25. St. Michael the Archangel Roman Catholic Church (frame), Gothic, was built in 1887 and retains its original interior. Church services were first held in Michael Knecht's home and in a schoolhouse. At the time of construction, the work was done despite dissension due to prejudice against Roman Catholics. Crosses were burned in protest. *Location:* 0.5 mile north of West Salisbury on SR 2003.

26. Compton's Grain Mill (frame) was operated by Samuel Compton (b. 1827), who purchased the Hostetter mill in 1868. In 1872 Compton and Israel Schrock erected the present structure, which was a "burr" flouring mill, and added a sawmill to the plant. Compton also served as justice of the peace. His father Phineas invented the first meat grinder in the county. The mill operated until 1941. *Location:* Near St. Pauls, about 2 miles on SR 2001; halfway between St. Pauls and SR 0669.

27. Beachy House (frame) was erected by Peter Beachy (originally Bitsche, 1793–1854), a dairy farmer. Known as "River Pete," he was the only son of Abraham (d. 1833) and Barbara Beachy. Abraham had migrated from Switzerland by way of Philadelphia. At least six generations of the family have lived in this

25. St. Michael the Archangel Church

house. *Location:* On SR 0669, 0.5 mile south of West Salisbury (Elk Lick Township).

28. Springs Museum (cement-block) houses collections of thousands of items depicting early life in the Casselman Valley. It was founded in 1957 and established here on an abandoned poultry farm in 1964. The museum is operated by the Springs Historical Society. The adjoining grounds are the site of an annual folk-art festival held the first Friday and Saturday in October. The community of Springs, settled between 1760 and 1775, is the state's highest unincorporated village, lying at the foot of Negro Mountain at Mt. Davis. *Hours:* Memorial Day–October: Wednesday–Saturday, 1–5 P.M., and by appointment. Closed Sunday. *Admission charge. Location:* Springs, on SR 0669 halfway between Salisbury and Grantsville, Md.

29. Mt. Davis is the highest point in the state, with an altitude of 3,213 feet. It is marked by a column of rocks with a brass plate indicating the landmark. Negro Mountain, at its base, was reportedly named by a Maryland hunting party in honor of a black member who was killed during an Indian attack. A forty-five-foot observation tower provides a view of the countryside. *Location:* At Mt. Davis Recreation Park, near Salisbury. Take SR 2004 from Meyersdale to Summit Mills; continue on this road and watch for signs to rock. Nearby is large picnic area on south edge of road, connected to tower site via High Point Trail, a mile-long footpath.

30. Petersburg National Road Tollhouse (stone), a two-story, seven-sided structure joined to a one-story wing, was built in 1835 when the state took control of this section of the National Road (US 40). It ceased operation in 1888. (The only other existing tollhouse of the original six built on this road in Pennsylvania is Searights in Fayette County, q.v.) This well-preserved structure with its old toll rates still posted on the exterior was restored and is maintained by the Great Crossing Chapter of the DAR. Iron tollgate posts removed from the building were taken to a cemetery to be used for an entranceway. Visits by appointment. *Location:* Addison, on old US 40 (Main Street).

Note: The Turkeyfoot (confluence of the Youghiogheny and Casselman rivers and Laurel Hill Creek at Confluence) was a famous landmark in pioneer days.

31. "Great Crossings" Bridge (stone), once spanning the Youghiogheny River at Somerfield (formerly Smithfield) and leading into Somerset County, was built in 1817–18 by Kinkead, Beck & Evans. It was dedicated July 4, 1818, by President James Monroe, followed by much celebration in conjunction with the holiday. The structure, 375 feet in length with three arches, has since been covered, along with the village, by the waters of an artificial lake and replaced by another bridge south of the site. The old bridge is visible during dry seasons when the water is low. A marker located at the Petersburgh National Road Tollhouse (q.v.) reads:

About one-half mile above this point is the "Great Crossings" of the Youghiogheny River, where George Washington crossed Nov. 18, 1753, when sent as envoy by Governor Dinwiddie of Virginia, to the French Commander at Fort LeBoeuf. Washington, on his military expedition to the Ohio, encamped there with his forces May 18 to 24, 1754, and from that point explored the Youghiogheny. There, also Major General Braddock, with his army crossed June 24, 1755, on his march against Fort Duquesne. [Tablet placed by Great Crossing Chapter, DAR, May 18, 1912]

Location: Somerfield, on US 40, 0.5 mile west of Addison.

32. Turkeyfoot Regular Baptist Church (frame), the oldest of its sect in the county, was also known as the Jersey Baptist Church,

since a group of Baptist settlers from New Jersey organized it June 14, 1775. At that time Rev. Isaac Sutton and John Corbly met with the congregation gathered at Moses Hall's house and formed the Turkeyfoot and Sandy Creek Glades Union Church. The first house of worship was built in 1788, the second in 1838, and the present one in 1877. Nearby are several covered bridges. *Location:* 1.7 miles on SR 3003 from its junction with SR 0281 in Ursina (on Jersey Road to Ohiopyle).

33. Fort Hill is a flat-topped mound, the site of a large palisaded Indian village dating from the prehistoric Woodland period. *Location:* 2 miles north of Ursina. Spectacular view from SR 0281.

34. Farm Equipment Museum has a fine collection of steam traction engines, threshers, and other nineteenth- and early twentieth-century farm machinery. A regional display is held here each summer. *Location:* New Centerville (Milford Township).

35. Seven Springs Resort was built after World War II by Helen and Adolph Dupre and is still owned by this family. It now has the largest ski lodge in the United States, a glass enclosed ski-side swimming pool, and accommodations for 800 overnight guests. *Location:* 8 miles east of Champion.

Note: Helen's Restaurant (stone), one story, was the home of Helen and Adolph Dupre, founders of Seven Springs Farm. It originally had one room (now the dining room) and two lofts, the small one their bedroom and the larger one the bedroom of their children, Philip, Herman, and Luitgarde. To the right of the main fireplace is the original stone sink, hand-hewn by Adolph. A natural spring furnished water for the house. Next to the house is a spring-fed fish pond. *Location:* On hillside above conference and hotel buildings.

36. Hidden Valley Historic Trails offers guided tours, mountain biking, and skiing along logging and tram roads built in the late 1800s. *Location:* Hidden Valley Resort Community & Conference Center, Gordon Craighead Memorial Drive, 8 miles east of Donegal, 12 miles west of Somerset on SR 0031.

37. Glades Pike Inn (brick) was established as a stagecoach stop in 1842 on the old Glades Pike in the Laurel Mountains. In 1987 the present owners remodeled this landmark which now serves as a bed and breakfast inn. *Location:* SR 0031, 6 miles west of the Somerset exit (no. 10) of the Pennsylvania Turnpike and 13 miles east of the Donegal exit (no. 9), 5 miles east of the entrance to Hidden Valley Resort.

38. Old Barn, with hand-hewn beams, has been adapted for commercial use (shops) by George and Helen Parke. *Location:* Near Hidden Valley.

39. Lumber Railroad Tunnel dates back to 1883 when Andrew Carnegie and William H. Vanderbilt planned the South Pennsylvania Railroad through Cumberland, Franklin, Fulton, Bedford, Somerset, and Westmoreland counties to break the Pennsylvania Railroad's stranglehold on Pittsburgh freight rates. But while Carnegie was in Europe, Vanderbilt sold the railroad to the opposition, and it was only half-built. Later, six of its nine tunnels were used by the Pennsylvania Turnpike (one through Laurel Hill, now unused, was in Somerset County). This is the only one of the nine ever used by a railroad—the Pittsburgh, Westmoreland & Somerset, principally a lumber railroad developed by Andrew and Richard B. Mellon in 1906. *Location:* About 3 miles west of Somerset, on north side of Pennsylvania Turnpike halfway between 106- and 107-mile markers.

40. St. John the Baptist Catholic Church (brick), in Romanesque style, served by the Carmelite Monastery of the Franciscan Order of Monks, was organized in 1824, and the present edifice, built on land originally warranted to Harmon Husband, was dedicated August 15, 1890. Its interior, including the ceiling of the sanctuary, is constructed mostly of wood by local craftsmen, including Henry Engbert. The friary, built in 1895, connects the church and the rectory. This picturesque church sits high on a hill overlooking the German village of New Baltimore and the turnpike. (From 1890 to 1915 New Baltimore was the novitiate for the Carmelite Order in the United States.) *Location:* On the Pennsylvania Turnpike at New Baltimore, about 25 miles east of Somerset. It can be reached from turnpike by long flight of steps or from Bedford exit (no. 11) by SR 0031 (Findley Street).

41. Zimmerman Mansion (brick), built in 1915–18, was the home of Daniel B. Zimmerman, a coal baron, cattle dealer, and agriculturalist. It is now restored, the center building of the Georgian Place Outlet. *Location:* SR 0601, off the Somerset exit (no. 10) of the Pennsylvania Turnpike.

Previous Sites Now Lost

Beam's Reformed Church, burned
Kline Gristmill, burned
Tunnel Spring, now underground

Covered Bridges

Barronvale Bridge (1930) over Laurel Hill Creek at the village of Barronvale, about a mile north of SR 0653

Burkholder (Beechdale) Bridge (1870) over Buffalo Creek about 250 feet west of US 219; about 5 miles southwest of Berlin; and about 2 miles northeast of Garrett

Glessner Bridge (1881) over Stonycreek on dirt road turning west about 0.5 mile north of Shanksville off SR 1001 on T 565

King's Bridge (1802) over Laurel Hill Creek, restored 1906, 30 feet south of SR 0653, about halfway between New Lexington and Scullton

Lower Humbert Bridge (1830) over Laurel Hill Creek about 50 feet east of SR 3007, 2 miles north of Ursina, T 393

New Baltimore Bridge (1879) over Raystown Branch of Juniata River, north of New Baltimore, T 812

Packsaddle (Doc Miller) Bridge (1870) over Brush Creek, 2 miles northwest of Fairhope, 3 miles southwest of Glen Savage, off SR 2019 on T 407

Shaffer's Bridge (1877) over Bens Creek. Visible from SR 0985 about 5 miles north of Thomas Mills, T 634

Trostleton Bridge (1845) over Stonycreek some 500 feet south of, but visible from, US 30, 0.5 mile east of Kantner, T 647

Walters Mill Bridge (1859) over Coxes Creek (now spans Haupts Run at Somerset Historical Center)

Note: *Bollman Bridge* (1871) is a metal truss bridge crossing the old B&O Railroad tracks on US 219, north of Meyersdale (Summit Township) over Wills Creek (see *Warren Truss Bridge*).

Iron Furnaces
(originally five)

Jackson Furnace (ca. 1825–33). Workers at nearby Lutheran Camp Sequanota welcome groups to visit the remains. Camp is about 1.25 miles north of US 30 on SR 4027, 1 mile west of Jennerstown.

Wellersburg Furnace (1856–66). The lining is now used as a chicken coop. Near Maryland line, on SR 0160, south of village. Make enquiries there.

Pennsylvania Historical and Museum Commission Markers

Adam Schneider Somerset, northwest corner of square

Ankeny Square Somerset, Patriot Street at cemetery

Braddock Road Addison, US 40

Early Bible Somerset, 151 West Main Street

Forbes Road (Edmunds Swamp) Buckstown, US 30

Forbes Road (Fort Dewart) US 30 near Bedford County line

Forbes Road (Stony Creek Encampment) US 30 east of Stoystown

Forbes Road (The Clear Fields) US 30, 1.3 mile west of Jennerstown

Fort Hill SR 0281, 3 miles northeast of Ursina

Great Crossings US 40 at the Youghiogheny River

Harmon Husband US 219 east of Somerset

Jeremiah S. Black SR 0031, 6.5 miles east of Somerset

Log Gristmill US 219, 0.5 mile north of Jennerstown

National Road US 40 southeast of Addison near state line

Somerset County Somerset, at courthouse, East Union Street and North Center Avenue

Toll House Addison, US 40

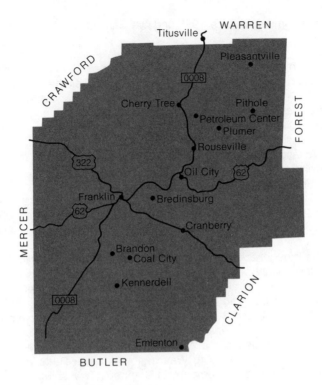

Venango County

Capsule History

Venango County, named for the old Indian town at the mouth of French Creek, was erected out of Allegheny and Lycoming counties, March 12, 1800. Although Franklin was chosen as the county seat at that time, Crawford County had jurisdictional authority over Venango until 1805. The county has 679 square miles with a population of 64,444. The formation of other counties from Venango has reduced its original 1,390 acres by about half.

George Washington in 1753 was sent here by the governor of Virginia to reconnoiter the French forts and to order the French out of northwestern Pennsylvania, a territory claimed by Pennsylvania, Virginia, and the French. The forts of the county, all within Franklin, included Machault, at Sixth and Elk streets (French, 1753–59), Venango, at Eighth and Elk (English, 1760–63), Franklin, at Franklin Avenue near

Thirteenth Street (American, 1787–96), and Old Garrison, east of Tenth Street (American, 1796–99).

The county's most famous Indian road was the *Venango Path,* which came up the route now taken by SR 0008 from Harrisville by Wesley, Springville, and Mays Mills, then cut over Gurney Hill to Franklin; crossing French Creek there, it followed the east bank toward Cochranton. The *Kuskusky-Venango Path* followed the same course in this area. The *Frankstown-Venango Path, Punxsutawney-Venango Path, Venango-Chinklacamoose Path,* and *Venango-Kittanning Path* all came up along what is now US 322 from Kossuth. The *Cayahaga Path* followed US 62 to the county line. The *Cornplanter-Venango Path* followed SR 0417 to Titusville, thence ran along a ridge east of Caldwell Creek. The *Venango-Conewango Path* ran up the Allegheny River all the way past President.

In 1785 Gen. William Irvine and Andrew Ellicott surveyed donation lands in the county set aside for Revolutionary War soldiers (see Capsule History, Butler County). Also the Seneca leader Chief Cornplanter was granted land on the east bank of Oil Creek for his service during the treaty talks with the Indians in 1784–89. During the War of 1812 he brought 200 Indian volunteers to serve in the conflict.

Franklin, the county seat, named for Benjamin Franklin, was once the Indian village of Venango, where an early settler, John Fraser, lived from 1742 to 1753. Joncaire, a French officer, had his headquarters at Fraser's cabin when Washington visited the site in 1753, and it is believed that this structure was embodied in the French fort. Another pioneer was George Power who settled here in 1790. In 1864 John Wilkes Booth boarded at the Webber house (corner of Buffalo and Thirteenth streets) in Franklin before going to Washington to assassinate President Lincoln. Booth owned the Dramatic Oil Company in Cranberry Township.

The world's first well drilled specifically for oil was established in Venango County just south of Titusville (Crawford County) in 1859 by Edwin L. Drake. Oil City, the county's largest city once a rafting center, became an important oil exchange, but a great fire on May 26, 1866, destroyed most of the original structures of this town. Two other oil-boom communities were Pithole and Petroleum Center; the latter was also a famous gambling place where $64,000 was bet on one throw of the dice.

The Van Sykle Pipe Line was the first in the world to successfully carry crude oil. It ran from Pithole to the Miller Farm, where Andrew Carnegie purchased property and first invested in oil. The line, built in 1865 by Samuel Van Sykle, followed a straight course for about five and a half miles and revolutionized the transportation of petroleum. Definite traces of the original trenches can still be seen along the course of the old pipeline.

The county is still an important oil industrial center. Natural gas, limestone, glass and molding sand, and gravel are also abundant resources. It has had twenty-five stone blast furnaces and was once known as "the iron county."

Landmarks

1. Franklin, incorporated as a city in 1868, offers a walking tour of a restored district (thirty-five blocks) that includes many fine old homes and varied examples of nineteenth- and twentieth-century styles of architecture from the days of the oil industry fortunes. Tour brochures may be obtained through the Rotary Club and the Chamber of Commerce.

1A. Courthouse (brick), the county's third, was built in 1867−69 by J. W. Brady with an addition in 1931−32 by Samuel Brady. The architects were Sloan and Hutton. Col. James S. Meyers and John S. McCalmont were the orators for the ceremony at the laying of the cornerstone July 15, 1868. The Italianate structure has double towers, one taller than the other. The first courthouse was erected in 1811; the second, in 1847. *Location:* Twelfth and Liberty streets.

1B. Venango County Jail (stone) was designed in Romanesque style in 1910 by the Stewart Jail Works of Cincinnati and built the following year. It is reported that years ago the tower was equipped with a scaffold and noose for hangings. *Location:* Beside courthouse.

Note: Bandstand is located in one of two parks flanking the courthouse on property surveyed and laid out by Gen. William Irvine and Andrew Ellicott in 1789−95. The Franklin Silver Cornet Band, which has played at this site over the years, was founded in 1856 and is one of the oldest musical organizations of this type still in existence in America.

1C. Civil War Monument was erected July 4, 1866. Its dedication in September of that year consisted of an elaborate military parade with orations in the park given by Col. J. S. McCalmont and Galusha A. Grow. This memorial with over four hundred names of Venango County men killed in the war is believed to be the oldest Civil War monument in the state. *Location:* South Park in courthouse square.

1D. Hoge-Osmer House (brick), headquarters of the Venango County Historical Society, was built by Senator Thomas Hoge, an oil and iron furnace pioneer, in 1864−65. In later years the Osmer family (prominent lawyers) owned the building; it was bought by the historical society in 1981. Museum collections include permanent and rotating exhibits. There is also a research library. *Hours:* May−October: Tuesday−Thursday, 11 A.M.−3 P.M.;

1A. Courthouse

Saturday, 10 A.M.−2 P.M. Winter hours vary. *Location:* 301 South Park Street.

1E. First Church of Christ Scientist (stone) became a private home in 1986. Once an inn, this country Federal-style structure was built about 1828 by Edward Pearce, a wheelwright. The church congregation, organized in 1894, acquired this house for a church home in 1903. It is believed to be the oldest building in Franklin. *Location:* 1142 Elk Street at South Park Street.

1F. Grossman Brewery and Icehouse (brick). The smaller building was erected about 1868; the larger, the brewery, about 1880. In 1861 John Minich established the first brewery here and also built a cavelike structure for the storage of beer across French Creek. He drowned making the crossing four years later. One story coming from the oil bonanza tells of an oil company accidentally drilling into a beer-filled storage tank, striking beer instead of oil. The driller paid for the damaged cask and continued his work, finding an oil well that yielded thirty barrels a day. *Location:* Behind First Church of Christ, Scientist.

1G. South Park House (brick) was built by Raymond and Prentice in 1865. This elegant Italianate house retains the curb carriage step, a stone stile from the past. *Location:* 307 South Park Street.

1E. First Church of Christ Scientist

1S. Franklin Depot

1H. Egbert Memorial Fountain was erected in 1896 in memory of Dr. A. G. Egbert, an oil magnate who (according to a 1919 county history) "sold one-twelfth of the Coquette well for $250,000.00, cleared at least $1,500,000.00 from the Davidson investment, pitched his tent in Franklin, served capably in Congress, and died in 1895." *Location:* West Park.

1I. Grace Lutheran Church (frame), with a square bell tower, was built in 1887. This Queen Anne, stick-style structure is now Faith Holiness Church. *Location:* 1101 Buffalo Street.

1J. St. Patrick's Catholic Church, of Gothic Revival design, was built between 1879 and 1882 by May and Osborne of Franklin at a cost of $30,000. It was designed by P. C. Kelly of Brooklyn, N.Y. *Location:* Liberty Street.

1K. Old United Presbyterian Church (brick) was built in 1875 in four-room-over-four construction, a style originated in eastern Pennsylvania by German and English settlers. *Location:* 1033–35 Elk Street.

1L. McGough House (frame) was built in 1858 by Peter McGough, a local merchant. This Carpenter Gothic house is constructed of board and batten with gingerbread detail. *Location:* 917 Elk Street.

1M. Heydrick House was built in 1864 by Christopher Heydrick, a prominent Franklin attorney. An illustration of this Italian villa style house, with a fine square tower, appeared in the 1865 issue of the *Atlas of the Oil Regions.* *Location:* 927 Elk Street.

1N. Dale House (brick) was built in 1875 by Samuel F. Dale. It is in Second Empire style,

with three bays and pressed tin window hoods. *Location:* 1409 Elk Street.

1O. Myers House (frame) was built in Greek Revival style in 1845 by James Myers, an attorney. *Location:* 1242 Elk Street.

1P. Gillett House, in Greek Revival style, was built in 1841 by Dr. Buckland Gillett, one of Franklin's early physicians. *Location:* 1224 Elk Street.

1Q. Duffield House, in Italian villa style, was built in 1874 by John Duffield (1818–79), whose family had moved to the county in the 1790s. Duffield operated a general store and gristmill, also investing heavily in the oil business. *Location:* 116 Elk Street.

1R. Twin Gables (frame) was built in 1900 as a stable and carriage house for the Miller Park residents. Now a private home. *Location:* Miller Park.

1S. Franklin Depot (brick) was the station for the New York Central railroad, built in 1866 when rail service from Chicago to New York was brought here to handle passengers and the shipment of oil. (The rail service soon phased out the riverboat service.) Originally the station had two waiting rooms, "the dining room for men and the lounge for the ladies." It was readapted for use as a restaurant in 1984 by Ken and Ellen Martin who purchased seventeen acres of abandoned tracks from Conrail. The original clock and other local memorabilia are on exhibit inside. Nearby are other early buildings, including a mill and freight house. Here also are two 1898 Erie railroad dining cars which became troop trains during World War II and later served as living quarters for railroad section gangs. *Location:* 1515 Depot Street at railroad.

1U. Franklin Public Library

1T. Hancock Building was built in the late 1800s. *Location:* Twelfth and Liberty streets.

1U. Franklin Public Library (brick), a Greek Revival structure built in 1847 by Judge Alexander McCalmont, was remodeled in the 1880s in Second Empire style. It became a library in 1921–22. The smaller building to its left was the law office of John S. McCalmont, born in 1822 and admitted to the Venango County bar in 1844. He served as a colonel in the Civil War. *Location:* Twelfth Street (adjacent law office, 417 Twelfth Street).

1V. Shugart House was built in 1845 by a printer, John Shugart, who published the *Democratic Arch. Location:* 1402 Liberty Street.

1W. Brady House (frame) was the boyhood home of Samuel Brady who contributed much to the area's architecture. After graduating from the University of Pennsylvania in 1906 he worked with the architect Stanford White in New York City for two years. Brady lived in the Italianate house until his death in 1966 (age 90). His father, James Brady, contractor for the courthouse, built this home. *Location:* 1110 Buffalo Street.

1X. Fort Franklin Park is the site of the city's four forts and of a Johnny Appleseed historical marker. Reconstruction of Fort Franklin is proposed. *Location:* Franklin Avenue and Thirteenth Street.

1Y. Franklin Club (brick) was built in 1866 by Dr. J. W. Stillman, who later sold the house to a Mr. Troller, succeeded by the White family. In 1889 the Nursery Club purchased the property from the George H. White family for $8,000. (Early histories of the county refer to the town of Franklin as the "nursery of great men.") This social organization, which had 100 members, had been established in the Hancock Building in 1877 and now is known as the Franklin Club. Before the structure was occupied by this group, a ballroom had been added to the house. In 1910 other alterations were made by Corrin and Wilt. *Location:* Liberty Street (SR 0008) one block from its junction with US 322.

1Z. Franklin Pioneer Cemetery was set aside as a burial site at the time the town of Franklin was laid out in 1795. Buried here is one of the first settlers of the county, George Power (1762–1845), who had helped build Fort Franklin in 1787. Also at this location is the grave of an old soldier of Napoleon's army who came by stagecoach to Franklin and died at George Power's inn before anyone learned his name. The cemetery was restored in 1952 by the Venango Chapter of the DAR. *Location:* Otter and Fifteenth streets.

3. River Ridge

2. Duncan McIntosh Mansion (stone) is a typical oil millionaire's home of the post—Civil War era. In 1954 the White Sisters of Africa bought this estate for their order. At present it houses the Venango County Human Services, operated by the Department of Welfare. *Location:* 1 mile from bridge at Franklin, on US 322 east.

3. River Ridge (stone), previously the Argeon Farm, was the estate of Joseph Crocker Sibley, who was an agent of the Galena Oil Works at Chicago. In 1873 he lived in Franklin, developed the Signal Oil Works, and later was elected mayor of Franklin. He was director of the American Jersey Cattle Club, president of the Franklin Opera House Company, and a director of both the Railway Speed Recorder Company and the First National Bank of Franklin. He also served as a U.S. congressman and was once a presidential contender. This huge structure with angled wings looks out over the Allegheny River. In 1948 the property was converted into a seminary by the Roman Catholic Society of the Missionaries of Africa. At present it is operated by a conservative religious group as a Bible school. *Location:* 5.5 miles north of Franklin. From Franklin turn left across bridge on US 322 toward Oil City. Just north of Bredinsburg, proceed west on golf course road for 0.2 mile; thence 1.8 mile on unimproved road (Cranberry Township).

Note: A stone carriage house with an attached portico over the driveway is nearby. All along the dirt road to the estate, in the wooded area, can be seen evidences of secondary oil recovery from early rich oil fields.

4. De Bence's Antique Music Museum and Old Country Store are both located in an old barn which has been remodeled and includes a fine collection of musical instruments and

memorabilia. *Hours:* Summer months by appointment. *Admission charge for museum.* *Location:* About 2 miles south of Franklin on SR 0008 (Pittsburgh Road) in Sandy Creek Township.

5. Indian God Rock on the left bank of the Allegheny River is a twenty-two-foot-high sandstone with prehistoric petroglyphs on its surface. It was first recorded in the annals of western Pennsylvania history by the French army officer, Céloron de Blainville, who in 1749 arrived in the Upper Ohio River Basin and claimed it for Louis XV, king of France. Father Joseph Pierre de Bonnecamps, who accompanied Céloron on his mission, wrote in his journal:

> In the evening after we disembarked, we buried a 2nd plate of lead under a great rock, upon which were to be seen several figures roughly graven. . . . Our officers tried to persuade me that this was the work of Europeans; but, in truth, I may say that in the style and workmanship of these engravings, one cannot fail to recognize the unskillfulness of savages.

The lead plates have never been recorded as found, and the rock has been disfigured by erosion, vandalism, and graffiti. A sketch from this rock made by Capt. S. Eastman in 1853 has been preserved in Archives of Aboriginal Knowledge, vol. 55. It represents one of the oldest written records of man in western Pennsylvania. It is said that George Washington stopped here on his way to Fort LeBoeuf. *Location:* Several miles south of Franklin. Go 6.5 miles south on SR 0257 from its junction with US 322. Turn right onto SR 3020 and continue through Coal City to Brandon, 6.4 miles, where road ends at railroad tracks. From here walk about 2 miles up (to right) Pennsylvania Railroad tracks to 115-mile stone. Rock is at river's edge directly below and is best seen from boat.

6. Oil City, incorporated in 1871, is the site of the Seneca Indian tribe under Chief Cornplanter.

6A. Venango Museum of Art, Science, and Industry (stone), built in Beaux Arts style between 1905 and 1913, was originally the federal post office building. In 1981 it was offered to the county and four years later it opened as a museum. The original construction of the building was the result of the rapid commercial growth following the oil boom of the late 1800s. Exhibits include Venango County fort models and industrial machinery. *Hours:* Tuesday—Saturday, 10 A.M.—4 P.M.;

Sunday, 1–4 P.M. Tours available upon request. *Location:* 270 Seneca Street.

6B. Oil Creek and Titusville Railroad is known as the local Ride-a-Railroad "Trail of History" sponsored by the Oil Creek Railway Historical Society. Sights along the thirteen-mile, two-hour trip include the Drake Well and Museum and historic oil-boom towns such as Petroleum Centre, which is now a recreational park featuring a museum. Locations: Boarding sites include (1) Rynd Farm (where Jonathan Watson became the world's first oil millionaire from the wells he drilled here), 4 miles north of Oil City off SR 0008; (2) Drake Well Museum, near SR 0008, Titusville; (3) Perry Street Station (a former freight station which houses a small railroad museum), SR 0008, Titusville. *Advance tickets* may be purchased from the railroad, P.O. Box 68, Oil City, Pa., 16301.

6C. Blood Farmhouse (frame), in Carpenter Gothic style, was sold for $550,000 by John Blood in 1864, the highest price paid for oil property up to that time. The house now serves as the park office. *Location:* Oil Creek Valley Historical Park.

6D. National Transit Building (brick), in Romanesque style with a large rock-faced stone foundation, is attached by an arch to a buff brick building in the rear (Chamber of Commerce). *Location:* Seneca and Center streets.

6E. First High School (cut-stone foundation), with its original foundation, has been rebuilt with a flat roof and adapted for use by the fire department. It is considered historic property since John Dewey, the famed philosopher and advocate of progressive education, attended school here. *Location:* West Fourth Street and Central Avenue.

6F. Innis Mansion (frame), in Queen Anne Victorian style typical of the area's oil baron homes, was built by the Innis family in the late 1800s. Innis made his fortune with the invention of the sucker rod joint used in the oil-drilling business. He was also the originator of an engine used during the oil boom. *Location:* West Fourth and Innis streets, south side of Allegheny River (once called Venango City).

Note: Other fine early buildings in the city include: St. Joseph's Catholic Church (brick with twin spires), built in 1890 on Pearl Street; an art deco theater at Central Avenue and First Street; and an Edwardian style (stone) public library at Central Avenue and Orchard Street.

7. *McClintock Oil Well*

7. McClintock Oil Well (no. 1), the world's oldest producing oil well, was drilled in August 1861. The well is across the railroad tracks west of the historical marker on the highway. *Location:* Rouseville, on SR 0008 south of bridge.

Note: Also on SR 0008 north of Rouseville is the old frame Rynd Farm schoolhouse, a two-story structure with a bell and belfry.

8. "Coal Oil Johnny" Steele House (frame), on the old Culbertson McClintock oil farm, was inherited in 1864 by John Washington Steele from his aunt after she was burned to death while lighting her kitchen stove with kerosene. Steele acquired his nickname from a Philadelphia newspaper, and he sported a bright red carriage decorated with flowing oil derricks and tanks on its sides. Long after he had squandered his fortune (he had an income of $2,000 per day), all within a year, he admitted, "I spent my money foolishly, recklessly, wickedly, gave it away without excuse; threw dollars to street urchins to see them scramble"—a reflection of the early opulent waste of the oil industry. He became a respected railroad stationmaster in Nebraska. This house was given to the Venango County Historical Society in 1984. *Location:* North of Rouseville, across Oil Creek from SR 0008.

9. The Great Petroleum Shaft was built in the early oil days above the best wells of Oil Creek Valley. This shaft was constructed down to the level of the oil-bearing strata so that oil could be collected in a large pool and then pumped out. Welsh coal miners from Pennsylvania's anthracite region started the work. Huge foundation stones were set around the top of the shaft for ventilating machinery, and threaded steel rods were inserted in these stones to hold the machinery in place. The money ran out after 150 feet of digging and the project was abandoned. The stones and shaft (partly filled up to keep out stray cows and horses) can be seen in the woods. *Location:* Southeast of Petroleum Center, 0.5 mile south of SR 1004 on hillside.

10. Cherrytree Presbyterian Church (frame), now a Bible church, was organized in 1837 with thirteen members. This early structure originally had a belfry which was destroyed in recent years when it was struck by lightning. *Location:* 0.3 mile north of Cherrytree and 0.25 mile off SR 0008.

11. Drake Well was the world's first well drilled specifically for oil, sunk and operated by "Colonel" Edwin L. Drake (see *Edwin L. Drake Monument,* Crawford County), general agent of the Seneca Oil Company, which was organized March 23, 1858. Drake, who later lost his oil fortune in speculation, came to western Pennsylvania to observe salt-well operations and to drill for oil. On August 27, 1859, his driller William A. Smith (see *"Uncle Billy" Smith Monument,* Butler County) struck oil here at sixty-nine and a half feet. This well, whose derrick was designed and built by Smith, yielded eight to ten barrels of petroleum a day. Its success ushered in a new industry which provided an efficient illuminating and lubricating oil. A replica of Drake's original derrick and engine house occupies the exact site of the well.

Nearby in the 229-acre Drake Well Memorial Park is a museum-library, the largest single depository for historical records and relics of the oil industry (collected since 1934). It is operated by the Pennsylvania Historical and Museum Commission. Available here is a narrated auto tour of historic sites along Oil Creek from Titusville to Oil City. *Hours:* Tuesday–Saturday, 9 A.M.–5 P.M.; Sunday, 12 noon–5 P.M. Closed Mondays and holidays except Memorial Day, July 4, and Labor Day. *Admission charge. Location:* 1.5 miles south of Titusville, along Oil Creek. Go 0.5 mile south on SR 0008; thence 1.25 miles southeast on SR 1011.

12. Free Methodist Church (frame) with a spire is a fine example of mid-nineteenth-century design. It was built in 1848. *Location:* Pleasantville, end of Main Street (Oil Creek Township).

13. Pithole, sometimes spelled Pit Hole, was created in 1865 by the discovery of oil when the United States or Frazier oil well started producing 250 barrels per day on Thomas Holmden's property. The town site was laid out May 24 and by the summer of that year had a population of 15,000. It at that time was reputed to have the third largest post office in the state and had two banks, countless saloons, about fifty-seven hotels, three churches, the county's first daily newspaper, a water system, and a railroad. The oil wells began to go dry in less than a year, and decreased oil production along with numerous fires caused the inhabitants to move away. Today the only remains of this ghost town are street grades, foundation scars, and signs which were placed in recent years to locate the original streets. The last building to be torn down was the Methodist church in 1939.

In 1957 James B. Stevenson, publisher of the *Titusville Herald,* purchased the Holmden farm and opened the main streets to visitors. Stevenson deeded the site to the state in 1963. It now has a modern museum and one producing oil well administered by the Pennsylvania Historical and Museum Commission. *Hours:* By appointment. *Admission charge. Location:* North of Plumer. Go 1.8 miles on SR 0227 to SR 1006, thence 2 miles to site (10 miles north of Oil City).

Note: Pithole Schoolhouse (frame) was built several years after the decline of Pithole. A few stone foundation ruins of the ghost town can be seen up the road from this school. *Location:* At Pithole site, off SR 0227.

14. Kennerdell Area Recreational and Cultural Center is located in the town of Kennerdell, known as "the little Switzerland of Pennsylvania." A gift of twelve acres by W. B. Wilson who died in 1970, this natural wooded setting provides the background for an annual music and art festival that commenced in 1955. The Memorial Art Center and native stone monument were erected in honor of Harry Hickman, Sr., who was the art director from 1955 to 1964. For over thirty years Eugene Reichenfeld, the founder of the musical program, has conducted orchestra concerts here in the woodlands. *Location:* Kennerdell, at Wilson Park near Allegheny River.

Note: A picturesque waterfall known as "Little Niagara" is next to the Rockland Kennerdell Road near a famous lookout point.

15. McMurdy House (stone) was built in 1797 by Isaac McMurdy and his son George who came here from Northumberland County. *Location:* On SR 0008, Irwin Township at Butler county line.

Note: Irwin Township has at least three brick nineteenth-century one-room schoolhouses on SR 0008 near Barkeyville.

16. Irwin United Presbyterian Church (brick), one story, was built in 1868. Nearby is an early stone house. *Location:* SR 3002 off SR 0008 at Mercer County line (Irwin Township).

17. Polk State School and Hospital (brick), in Queen Anne style, was created by an act of the Pennsylvania legislature in 1893 and opened in 1897 as the Western Pennsylvania Institute for the emotionally ill, the second and largest institution of its kind in the state. Dr. James Murdoch was the first superintendent. The first 157 residents were transferred from the Elwyn Training School in eastern Pennsylvania. The original tract of land in this area, called Waterloo Valley, consisted of 773 acres, increasing to 2,094 and falling in 1982 to less than 800 acres with the closing of the dairy farm. The original buildings were constructed with bricks manufactured on the property and stone brought in on a narrow-gauge railroad from a nearby quarry. At one time there were 102 buildings; 90 remain. This complex serves fourteen northwestern counties in Pennsylvania. It has undergone many progressive changes and improvements, including the cessation of seclusion for problem behavior in 1975. The administration building was erected by C. A. Balph in 1896 (F. J. Osterling, architect). *Location:* Outskirts of Polk Borough, US 62, west of Franklin.

18. Cranberry Country Store (frame), with five bays, was built in the middle 1800s and once served as a hotel. Today it is an antique and gift shop with ten display rooms. *Location:* Cranberry, SR 0257 and US 322 (Cranberry Township).

19. Emlenton, laid out in 1820 on the Andrew McCaslin and Joseph Fox property, was named for Fox's wife, Hannah Emlen.

19A. Shortway Bridge. See Clarion County.

19B. Old Emlenton Mill (frame), built about 1875 as a gristmill by George Fox, was steam operated by natural gas, followed in succession by gasoline, diesel, and electric motors. The lumber for the original rear section of the structure was brought down the river from northern communities on rafts for $2.50 per 1000 board feet. The building, converted to a shopping complex by William Stump and Eugene Terwilliger (the last miller), now includes a hardware store and canoe sales. *Hours:* Monday–Saturday, 10 A.M.–5 P.M.; Sunday, 1–5 P.M. *Location:* On Allegheny River, Main Street, at bridge (I-80 exits 5 and 6).

18. Cranberry Country Store

19C. Emlenton United Presbyterian Church (brick) was established in 1852. *Location:* Main Street.

Note: On Main Street between Fifth and Sixth streets is another Presbyterian church (brick), organized in 1858 and built in 1874.

19D. H. H. Porterfield House, now the Emil Long Furniture Store, was built in the 1870s by a prominent iron magnate. *Location:* Main Street near Fifth Avenue.

19E. Roschy Carriage Shop, now a garage, was owned by a German-born craftsman who made carriages and wagons here. *Location:* Main and Third streets.

19F. James Bennett House (called Daubenspeck House), built by a founder of the First National Bank, was later occupied by T. B. Gregory, an oil and gas baron. *Location:* Main and Second streets.

19G. Methodist Church (frame), situated picturesquely on a hillside, has a noteworthy interior. It was built in 1872. *Location:* Hill Street.

19H. St. John's Reformed Church was organized in 1869. The Lutheran and Reformed congregations shared this building until 1885 when the Lutherans built a separate church at Kerr Avenue and Hill Street. *Location:* Main and Fourth streets.

19I. St. Michael's Catholic Church was built in 1871 in an area called Irish Town. *Location:* Hill Street.

19J. Valley House, originally Otto's Tavern, was built in 1840 as a hotel with a livery and barber shop. *Location:* River Avenue near Sixth Street.

Iron Furnaces
(originally twenty-five)

Bullion Furnace (1840), now in bad condition. Take T 349 for 1.7 miles east of Bullion and inquire. Requires much walking.

Castle Rock (Lytle) Furnace (1836), built by William Cross and Thomas Hoge. Closed 1860. South of US 62 off SR 0965, take T 399 east about 0.75 mile and park. Requires much walking in rough terrain.

Horse Creek (Clay) Furnace (1836–56). Inquire for road to Oil City Boat Club and watch for furnace at creek crossing near river.

Jackson Furnace (1833–56). About half a mile north of Van on T 391 take lane going straight ahead at sharp left curve for 0.75 mile to path going to creek at right.

Porterfield (Glen, Mill Creek) Furnace (1838–52). About 0.25 mile on old road turning off T 522, about 5 miles north of Emlenton.

Reno (North Bend) Furnace (1844). On US 62, 3.5 miles west of Polk, cross creek on railroad bridge and follow rails back east a furlong, near cut.

Rockland Furnace (1832–54). Near waterfall on creek 0.25 mile north of Rockland Station, end of T 480, off SR 0257 at Freedom.

Stapely (Shippen) Furnace (1840). To left of SR 0038 about 1.75 miles north of Mariasville.

Valley (Orleans) Furnace (1848). Near curve on SR 0427, 0.25 mile east of US 322.

Van Buren Furnace (1836). On right of SR 6077, about 1.4 miles from US 322, near Franklin.

Webster Furnace (1838). On lane at turn near bridge off T 381, about 1.5 miles from SR 0038.

Pennsylvania Historical and Museum Commission Markers

Drake Well Park Cranberry, US 322; and on property in Venango County southeast of Titusville

First Oil Pipeline SR 0227, 4 miles southwest of Pleasantville

Fort Machault Franklin, Eighth and Elk streets

Fort Venango Franklin, Eighth and Elk streets

Johnny Appleseed Franklin, Fort Franklin Park

John Dewey Oil City, Central Avenue and West Fourth Street

Oldest Producing Oil Well SR 0008 just south of Rouseville

Old Garrison Franklin, US 322, South Park and Elk streets

Pithole SR 1006 on hill

Pithole City At property off SR 0027 on SR 1006 at Pithole, southeast of Titusville

Pithole Fabulous Ghost Town Intersection of SR 0227 and SR 1006, 5.6 miles southwest of Pleasantville

Venango County Franklin, at courthouse, Twelfth and Liberty streets

Venango Path Wesley, 0.25 mile north on SR 3013

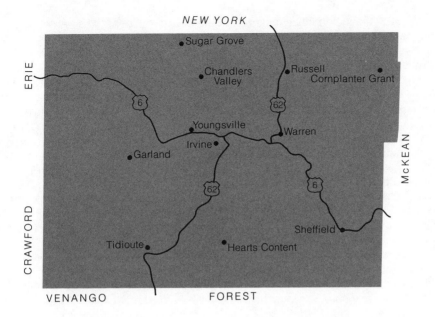

Warren County

Capsule History

Warren County, named in honor of Maj. Gen. Joseph Warren, a doctor killed at the battle of Bunker Hill in 1775, was erected out of Lycoming and Allegheny counties on March 12, 1800. Separate judicial arrangements were finally made in 1805 when the county was attached first to Crawford and then to Venango. In 1819 Warren acquired its own judicial authority with the community of Warren selected as the county seat. Warren County is 885 square miles in area with a population of 47,449.

The first to arrive here were French explorers who came from Canada to the mouth of the Conewango by way of Lake Erie and Lake Chautauqua. They were succeeded by many Scotch-Irish settlers after the Revolution.

Baron de Longueuil's expedition through this area was in 1739. This led to the one by Céloron de Blainville in 1749 at the mouth of Conewango Creek, where he buried lead plates claiming the region for France. However, Pierre Paul de Marin, commander of the French military expedition to the Ohio the following year, rejected Céloron's route and forbade the erection of a fort due to the shallow water of the Conewango.

Most of the Indian inhabitants were Senecas from the Iroquois nation and Munsees, a subtribe of the Delawares. In 1779 Gen. John Sullivan drove the Indians northward after the so-called "Wyoming massacre"—actually a regular military action in which British and Indian troops fought against American garrisons. Gen. Daniel Brodhead made a similar expedition into the county in the same year and had a skirmish with the Indians at Thompson's Island, the only Revolutionary battle in northwestern Pennsylvania. He destroyed the remains of the Buckaloons Indian town (Irvine) and burned the deserted village of Conewango, where in recent years burial mounds have been excavated. (This area later became Warren, the county seat which was laid out in 1795 and became a borough in 1832.) Sugar Run Mounds at Cornplanter have also been excavated, revealing another village site.

Four Indian trails traversed Warren County. The *Brokenstraw Path* entered just east of Corry, followed Hare Creek to a crossing at its mouth, thence down the left bank of Brokenstraw to Youngsville and the right bank to its mouth at Irvine. The *Cornplanter Path* from Warren went up Conewango Creek and Hatch Run, turned along Quaker Ridge to Scandia, and passed down Hodge Run and up the Allegheny River to the mouth of Cornplanter Run. The *Cornplanter-Venango Path* entered northeast of Titusville, following a ridge east of the East Branch of Caldwell Creek to Pittsfield, thence down the left bank of Brokenstraw to Irvine and up the Allegheny River to Warren, finally following the Cornplanter Path. The *Venango-Conewango Path* followed the Allegheny River from below Tionesta to Irvine and Warren.

Early industries in the county were lumbering and tanning, together with oil production after 1859. That year in August at an oil spring north of Tidioute, J. L. Grandin began the second well (which was dry) drilled specifically for oil, after Col. Edwin Drake's discovery. Succeeding wells nearby proved successful. Triumph Hill, above Tidioute, was producing oil in the 1870s, and Cherry Grove had a boom in 1882 and 1883, where the famous "646" well was located (SR 2001 nine miles southwest of Weldbank). During the oil boom the Harmony Society (see *Old Economy,* Beaver County, and *Harmony,* Butler County) made $6 million in this county when oil was struck in 1860 on their timber tract in Limestone Township. Their Economy Oil Company and village enterprise was liquidated in 1895. A monument at the site of the world's first flowing oil well (1860) is across the river from Tidioute just below the bridge.

Today natural gas, petroleum, wood and metal products, and glass are important. In agriculture, potatoes, poultry, cereal grains, and dairy products are noteworthy. In addition, the county is a hunting and fishing paradise.

A recent study has been made on a number of early existing structures in this county. Further information can be obtained in a series of books entitled *Historic Buildings in Warren County,* published by the county historical society.

Landmarks

1. Warren

1A. Courthouse (brick and stone) is an Italian Renaissance building (replacing an 1828 structure). Begun in 1875, it was completed two years later at a cost of $97,434.59, with furnishings costing $6,000 more. It has a large dome with four clocks and a 1,600-pound bell. A statue of Justice stands 125 feet above the sidewalk. Additions were made in 1916 and 1925. *Location:* Fourth Avenue and Market Street.

1B. New Mansion House (cut stone), built in 1833 by Ebenezer Jackson, is a fine building which opened as the Warren Hotel in March 1834. A year later it became the Lumberman's Bank, and after that institution's failure in the Panic of 1837, it became, successively, the Tanner House and the Diamond House. After the closing of an earlier Mansion House (1814–56), the newer building adopted its name. For a time it was also the Temperance Hotel. It has served as a women's club and a music club, and its upper story was once a ballroom. *Location:* 215 Fourth Avenue.

1C. Wetmore House (brick, wood trim) was built in 1870–73 by Thomas Struthers as a wedding gift for his daughter Anna, wife of George R. Wetmore. She died in 1880, her husband in 1890, and their only child, Thomas Struthers Wetmore, in 1896. Struthers died in 1892. The house was occupied by the Charles Schimmelfeng family from 1893 to 1950, when it was sold to Warren County for offices. It has been occupied by the Warren County Historical Society—a most active organization—since 1964. *Location:* 210 Fourth Avenue.

1D. Struthers Library Building (brick) was a gift to the Warren community in 1882 from Thomas Struthers, lawyer, land baron, railroad promoter, politician, banker, and foundry operator. The cost was over $80,000, besides the $7,050 raised by public subscription to buy the ground. The building was designed to include store and office spaces, a Masonic hall, and an opera house to provide income for maintenance and improvement to the library. In 1983 the 1919 Library Theatre, which had replaced the old opera house within the same space, was fully renovated, and the library room was restored in 1984. *Location:* Third Avenue and Liberty Street.

1E. Charles W. Stone House (brick), a 1905 Greek Revival structure with Ionic columns, was the home of Charles Warren Stone, attorney, legislator, lieutenant governor from 1879 to 1882, and member of Congress from 1890 to 1899. In 1974–75 it was completely restored by J. H. DeFrees. *Location:* 505 Liberty Street.

1F. Hazeltine House (frame), perhaps the oldest house in Warren, was built about 1823 by Dr. Abraham Hazeltine, who in 1834 sold it to the Summerton family. From 1925 until it was bought in 1934 by Dr. Hugh Robertson, it belonged to the Moose Club and was leased to Ora and Oleta Brown, who operated a tearoom there. *Location:* 412 Third Avenue.

1G. Roscoe Hall (brick) is one of the few remaining theaters that blossomed all over the oil region of Pennsylvania during the boom of about a century ago. It was built by Orris Hall and named for his son, a sergeant in the Bucktails (Forty-second Pennsylvania Infantry) who was killed August 30, 1862, at Second Bull Run. The hall occupied the third floor of the Keystone Block. Blind Tom played here, as did local and many touring theatrical troupes. Bret Harte lectured here March 1, 1873. Following the opening of the Struthers Library Building (q.v.) in December 1883, Roscoe Hall faded from the theatrical scene. For a while it was a National Guard armory, a roller rink, and an Eagles Club home. Currently it houses the Sons of Italy in America. *Location:* Pennsylvania Avenue near Hickory Street.

1H. Revere House (brick and frame), a thirty-three-room, three-story structure erected in 1872, was a typical railroad hotel in the palmy days of rail passenger traffic. Built by Frank Metzgar, who first intended to call it the Allegheny House, it was named the Revere House until 1951 when it became the Riverside Hotel. Under almost a score of owners, it has been continuously operated for more than a century. *Location:* 914 Pennsylvania Avenue, West.

1I. The Honorable Charles Warren Stone Museum (brick), built as a residence by a Warren banker, A. J. Hazeltine, in 1905, this Jacobean-style mansion is operated by the Warren County Historical Society as a museum of local and county history. Extensive exhibits feature photographs, archives, and artifacts from the museum's collections. *Hours:* Tuesday and Friday, 1–5 P.M.;

1C. Wetmore House

Wednesday and Thursday, 9 A.M.–5 P.M. *Location:* 710 Pennsylvania Avenue.

1J. Heritage Point. Four flags—representing sovereignty over the land by the Seneca Indians, the British, the French, and the Americans—are flown here annually from Memorial Day to November. Included in the complex are a memorial recognizing Céloron's visit in 1749 and a handsome, stylized birdstone monument created by a Seneca artist honoring Chief Cornplanter and the Seneca Nation of Indians. *Location:* Crescent Park, south bank of the Allegheny River at the Hickory Street Bridge.

Note: The early Oakland Cemetery is located at 37 Mohawk Avenue.

1K. Allegheny River Bridge (concrete) was built in 1918 to replace the suspension bridge constructed in 1871–72 by the Pleasant Bridge Company. A three-foot-long timber from the older bridge is preserved at the Warren County Historical Society. Other timbers from the early bridge were incorporated in Walker's plant on Union Street in 1919 and in 1920 when the building was enlarged.

2. Kinzua Dam (masonry), completed in 1966 at a cost of $114 million, is 2,000 feet long and 80 feet high; it impounds a lake 27 miles long, holding 61 billion gallons of water. It provides a defense both against low water from drouth and against floods. The lake al-

most completely inundated the Chief Cornplanter grant of 779 acres, one of three made to him in 1791 by the Commonwealth. Cornplanter (John O'Bail, son of a Seneca woman and a Dutch trader) died on the grant in 1836, probably at about the age of eighty-five, though his chronology is much confused. His half brother, Handsome Lake, initiated the Seneca "Good Message" religion here. After much litigation, Cornplanter's descendants were removed to the Seneca reservation in New York. His body and others, and the monument erected to him in 1866 by the state, were moved to the Riverview-Corydon Cemetery at the New York state line. *Location:* East of Warren, on SR 0059, 6.7 miles east of US 6.

3. Rimrock Overlook is a natural rock overlooking the Kinzua Creek arm of the Allegheny Reservoir, the largest branch of the largest man-made body of water in the East. At the base of the rocks is a flowing spring. The surrounding recreation facility was completed in 1964 by the U.S. Forest Service. *Location:* East of Warren in Allegheny National Forest through a 3-mile black top road from east of Warren on SR 0059 west side of Allegheny River across river from Jakes Rocks Lookout SR 0059.

4. Allegheny River Hotel (brick) was built in 1885 by C. B. Willey on the site of the Glade Run House, where a slab tavern had been

1I. The Honorable Charles Warren Stone Museum

1J. Indian Monument at Heritage Point

operated by Solomon Hudson from 1844 until Orren Hook built a more modern house in 1850, which burned in 1875. This hotel was enlarged some time previous to 1905 and has been run by various hosts. (The Jacob Johnson family operated it the longest, from 1911 to 1969.) It was much used by raftmen and traveling salesmen, and for a time it housed a ticket office for the railroad and electric cars. It is still a popular tavern. *Location:* East of Warren, on Hemlock Street and Pennsylvania Avenue, at river and Mead Township line.

5. Cobham Castle (frame) was built by George Ashworth Cobham, who came to America in 1834 and was called Lord Cobham, having descended from a nobleman. An attorney, he planned a castle, which he built with the help of two stepsons, cutting the timbers and lumber for the house and barn at a sawmill they operated for the purpose. Begun in 1856, it was completed seven years later. Cobham died in 1870, and the "castle" passed from his family in 1912. Visitors are not permitted. *Location:* Northeast of Warren, 3.5 miles north of US 6, on Park Avenue at Cobham Road.

6. Warren State Hospital (brick and stone). Begun in 1874, the original sandstone building (still occupied), 1200 feet long and a model of early asylum construction, was completed in 1880. Although an extensive farming operation has been discontinued, another large complex of architecturally interesting buildings still remains in active use for the

treatment of mental illness. *Location:* North Warren, 2 miles north of Warren, on US 62.

7. The Pines (stone) was erected in 1839 by Lansing Wetmore, Warren County prothonotary, as a magnificent summer home. It was originally a square structure of four rooms. On his death in 1858 it passed to his son Lansing D. Wetmore, who remodeled and enlarged it in 1900. It is now the Barley Nursing Home. *Location:* North Warren, South State and Weatherbee streets.

8. The Locusts (brick) was begun in 1831 by Guy C. Irvine, the "Napoleon of the lumber business," and his brother-in-law Rufus Weatherby. Weatherby's death in 1833 delayed its completion until 1835. Clay was dug nearby, and bricks burned by William and John Thompson, who, with John Voverse, made all the woodwork by hand. The trees surrounding the house were planted at the time it was built. *Location:* 1.5 miles south of Russell City, on US 62 (Pine Grove Township).

9. Robert Russell House (brick) was built about 1825 by Robert Russell, who had operated a sawmill in the area since 1806. He died in 1847. The property was purchased in 1875 by Erastus Weatherby, whose family has occupied it for a century. *Location:* Russell, old US 62.

10. Old Lutheran (Swedes) Church (brick), the Hessel Valley Lutheran Church, which held services in Swedish until 1933, was organized in 1853 and built in 1883–85. It has a hand-carved pulpit showing the ascension of Christ and a mural behind the altar. *Location:* Swedes Church, Chandlers Valley (Sugar Grove Township).

11. Miller Home (frame) was erected originally as a saltbox about 1821 by Richard and Cynthia Miller to replace an 1814 log cabin. In 1828 they had it enlarged, paying Orrin and Morgan Hancock $190 ($50 in cash and the rest in leather, livestock, and grain) to hew timbers and frame the house. Miller agreed to lay the foundation; haul the timber; provide the boards, nails, and glass; board the hands; and "find whiskey for the raising." Miller, an agent for the Holland Land Company, died of fever in Maysville, Ky., June 10, 1832, aged forty-one, while on a lumber-selling trip. Cynthia, with five children, lived more than half a century and kept the family together. Miller descendants owned the home until 1944. *Location:* Sugar Grove (Sugar Grove Township).

12. Irvine Presbyterian Church (buff stone), a charming structure with a fanlight, was built in 1838–39 by Dr. William Armstrong Irvine (1803–86) for his wife Sarah, who died after childbirth before it was quite finished and whose funeral was the first held here. Regular services have been conducted here ever since, but it continued in the possession of the Irvine family until 1963, when (under a 1916 will) it passed to the Presbytery of Lake Erie. *Location:* Irvine (Brokenstraw Township).

13. Miller's House (stone) is a very early structure, the two-story central portion probably dating from 1840, the two one-story wings at either side added somewhat later. *Location:* Across Brokenstraw Creek from Irvine, on US 62.

14. Rouse Farm was named in honor of Henry R. Rouse of Enterprise, who lost his life in the first great oil fire of April 17, 1861, in Venango County. He left his fortune to Warren County, half for the benefit of the poor and half to improve the roads. The farm is now a home for aged, indigent men and women and is operated by the county. *Location:* East end of Youngsville, just off US 6 (Brokenstraw Township).

15. Indian Paint Hill contained large deposits of red ochre which, along with adjacent petroleum springs, provided the Indians with materials for face and body paint. *Location:* 3 miles northeast of Tidioute, on US 62.

16. Tidioute

16A. Courson Home (frame) was erected by Anthony Courson, farmer, lumberman, and tavern keeper, who came from Centre County in 1825. He built this home immediately after his first house burned. It is still occupied by his descendants. *Location:* 333 Main Street.

16B. Tidioute Presbyterian Church (frame) is an interesting Carpenter Gothic structure dating from about the time of the oil boom of 1870. *Location:* 200 Main Street.

16C. Tidioute Overlook provides a good view of Tidioute (location of Pennsylvania State Fishing Championship) and islands on the Allegheny River. *Location:* Allegheny River, T 337.

17. Angus Gillis House (frame), an early settler's home, dates from about 1840. It was once Gillis post office. *Location:* SR 3005, set far back across road from junction with SR 3020, just north of Old Plank Road School (Watson Township).

18. Heart's Content is one of the two remaining stands of virgin timber in Pennsylvania with evergreens over 160 feet high. One tree is believed to be over five hundred years old. The Wheeler and Dusenbury Lumber Company, a pioneer concern, sold about two-thirds of its last timberlands to the United States in 1922, together with a gift of twenty acres of virgin pine, hemlock, and hardwood "as a memorial to three generations of the families connected with the company." In 1929 the government augmented the gift with the purchase of 100 more acres of virgin timber from this company. The purchases and the gift are a part of 500,000 acres comprising the Allegheny National Forest (see also *Cook Forest State Park*, Clarion County). *Location:* Halfway between Warren and Tidioute, on SR 2002, 3.6 miles east of SR 3005 (Watson Township).

Note: A fine spring is on the east side of SR 3005, a short way below its intersection with SR 2002.

19. Wagon Wheel Inn (frame covered with siding) was a roadside tavern built in 1885 by the Salmon family. The community is named Slater for John and Robert Slater, lumbermen, who later operated this place and were the only two postmasters. The Slater post office was discontinued in 1887. *Location:* 10 miles south of Warren, on SR 3005 (Watson Township).

20A. Ruth M. Smith Center

20C. Industrial Boarding House

20. Sheffield (Sheffield Township)

20A. Ruth M. Smith Center is a large Victorian mansion built in 1885 by the George Horton family. In 1901 it was purchased by the C. H. Smith family. The house and acreage were given to the predecessor organization of the United Methodist Women of Western Pennsylvania in 1922 in order to serve as a children's home in memory of Ruth Margaret, the daughter of the Smith family. The following year the first thirty-two children moved into this home. New additions in 1932, donated by the Olmsted family of Ludlow, included dining and kitchen facilities, laundry, and gymnasium. Two new dormitories were built in 1972. Fifteen boys from the home served in World War II and another, John Gertsch, a hero of the Vietnam War, was the first Warren County resident to receive the Congressional Medal of Honor. By 1982 the buildings were no longer used for a children's home and were converted to a community service facility, still operated by the United Methodist Women of Western Pennsylvania. *Location:* South Main Street and Horton Avenue (nearly across street from George Horton House).

20B. George Horton House (stone and frame). This Victorian home, built in the late 1800s, has scalloped shingles on the frame second floor and a stone structure on the first. *Location:* 416 Main Street.

20C. Industrial Boarding House (frame with siding) has sixteen rooms and a large attic; it was once the Elk Tanning Company boarding house. Mrs. Ida Miller operated the house from about 1900 to 1932. She and her daughters fed and washed clothing for almost 250 men, who slept two to three to a bed, four beds to a room, with many beds in the attic

during rush times. It went out of business with the closing of the tannery during the depression. *Location:* 219–21 Horton Avenue.

Previous Sites Now Lost

Grandin Opera House, demolished
Philadelphia and Erie Depot, demolished
Village Inn, burned

Pennsylvania Historical and Museum Commission Markers

Buckaloons In Buckaloons Park near US 6 and US 62 east of Irvine
Céloron's Expedition Warren, US 6 at Pennsylvania Avenue and Hickory Street
Conewango Warren, US 6 at Pennsylvania Avenue and Conewango Creek bridge
Gen. William Irvine Irvine, old US 6 west of US 62
The Grandin Well US 62, 0.4 mile south of Allegheny River bridge near Tidioute; and SR 0127 north, 0.6 mile northwest of Tidioute
Indian Paint Hill US 62, 3 miles northeast of Tidioute
Thompson's Island US 62, 9 miles southwest of Warren
Warren County Warren, at Courthouse, Fourth Avenue and Market Street

BEAVER

Murdocksville

Florence

Paris

Candor

22

0018

Cross Creek

ALLEGHENY

WEST VIRGINIA

Venice

Bishop

Hickory

79

Pattersons Mill

Avella

Independence

West Middletown

Buffalo

Canonsburg

Houston

Strabane

Morganza

Venetia

WESTMORELAND

Gastonville

Elrama

Finleyville

Hill Church

Wolfdale

Meadow Lands

Mingo Creek Park

Monongahela

Eighty Four

Budaville

Taylorstown

Washington

Donora

Gabby Heights

Laboratory

East Buffalo

Lagonda

Charleroi

Claysville

70

Glyde

Bentleyville

70

West Alexander

Chambers

40

Ellsworth

Speers

79

Scenery Hill

Baker Station

Lone Pine

Prosperity

Amity

Beallsville

California

Daisytown

Centerville

Malden Inn

Dunns Station

Marianna

West Brownsville

Old Concord

Zollarsville

Fredericktown

Millsboro

FAYETTE

GREENE

Washington County

Capsule History

Washington County, organized during the Revolution, was named in honor of George Washington, commander in chief of the Continental Army, and was at first claimed by both Virginia and Pennsylvania. Erected out of Westmoreland County on March 28, 1781, it originally included all of Greene and Beaver counties, together with a large portion of Allegheny. It now has an area of 858 square miles with a population of 217,074.

Most of the early settlers came from Virginia by way of the Monongahela River and up Ten Mile and Big Whiteley creeks. Abraham Teagarden established a ferry across.

the Monongahela at the mouth of Ten Mile (now Millsboro). Prior to 1781 John Canon, militia officer and member of the state assembly, operated a gristmill (called Canonsburg Milling Company since 1802) and laid out the town of Canonsburg in 1787. In 1774 George Washington purchased 2,813 acres in Washington County. When Pennsylvania erected the county, Virginians countered with an attempt to set up the disputed territory as a new state, which would have been called Westsylvania. The dispute between Pennsylvania and Virginia over territorial claims was settled in 1779 and a temporary border survey run in 1782.

Washington, the county seat often referred to as "Little Washington" to avoid confusion with the national capital, was laid out by David Hoge in 1781, incorporated as a borough in 1810, and chartered as a city in 1923. Originally called Bassett Town, it was settled at the Indian village known in the 1770s as Catfish's Camp, since the Delaware chief Catfish lived there. The first (Virginia) county court west of the Monongahela River was held at Augusta Town, a few miles southwest of Washington at present-day Gabby Heights.

The western section of the county was the scene of many Indian uprisings, including one by Mingo Chief James Logan who attacked settlers in 1774 during Dunmore's War after the murder of his brother and sister. Jacob Wolfe erected a stockaded house southwest of Washington in 1780. At Jacob Miller's blockhouse (site east side of Dutch Fork Fishing Dam), there was a retaliatory attack by Indians whose fellow tribesmen had been massacred at Gnadenhütten in 1782. The Miller family burial plot includes the memorial stone of Ann Hupp, who led a heroic defense here. One of the last battles of the Revolutionary War took place at Rice's Fort in 1782.

Monongahela is the site of several Indian burial mounds which have been excavated in recent years. Once known as Williamsport, it is the oldest settlement in the valley where James Devore and Joseph Parkinson operated a ferry. Parkinson also built a mill one mile from Monongahela on Pigeon Creek, where the Van Voorhis homestead is. Whiskey Point at Main and Park avenues was the scene of a 1794 Whiskey Rebellion meeting of 226 insurgents.

Two important Indian trails traversed the county. The *Catfish Path* ran from below Amity past Braddock to Washington, thence east of Chartiers Creek to a crossing south of Canonsburg, and west of the stream toward Bridgeville. The *Mingo Path* ran across the county from Brownsville to West Alexander very close to the course of the old National Road (US 40).

In 1806 Congress authorized the construction of the National Road, which began at Cumberland, Md., in 1811 and was completed to Wheeling in 1818. It was a state toll road from 1835 to 1905. Authentic murals of the early history of this road have been preserved inside the George Washington Hotel in the city of Washington. These murals were painted by Malcolm Stevens Parcell, a native of Washington and an internationally known artist.

Among the noteworthy people who lived in the county during its early days were David Bradford, leader of the Whiskey Rebellion; William Holmes McGuffey, author of the renowned *McGuffey's Readers,* born south of Claysville (McGuffey's supposed birthplace was purchased for Henry Ford's Greenfield Village Museum in Dearborn, Mich.); James G. Blaine, who narrowly missed election as president, born in West Brownsville; Capt. Philo McGiffin, born in Washington and father of the modern Chinese navy; Col. George Morgan, Indian agent during the Revolution; John Doddridge, who erected a fort in 1773, and his son Dr. Joseph Doddridge, who wrote an outstanding account of pioneer life; Edward Acheson, an eminent American chemist; Elisha

McCurdy, the great revivalist; John McMillan, Presbyterian minister and political leader of the area; Governor and U.S. (Gen.) Senator Edward Martin; Governor John K. Tener, from Charleroi; J. B. Finley, mastermind of Monongahela coal mine consolidation; and David Reed, leader of the Covenanter squatters on lands owned by George Washington.

Washington has always been a prosperous agricultural section, and sheep-raising has remained important over the years. Its natural resources include bituminous coal, natural gas, petroleum, sand, and clay. Rich deposits of coal had been discovered before 1800, when it was mined near Canonsburg and Washington. Alexander McGugin owned the first natural-gas well (1882) in the county. The Gantz oil well was the first in the county, drilled in 1884 at West Chestnut Street and Brookside Avenue in Washington.

Washington and Charleroi produce glassware, while Canonsburg is noted for its pottery, china, and tin and terneplate. Donora was once one of the world's largest manufacturers of steel wire. Standard Industries (now defunct) in Canonsburg, visited in 1921 by Madame Marie Curie, co-discoverer of radium, was one of the largest early radium producers.

The county has preserved twenty-seven covered bridges. There are also a great number of early log, stone, and brick structures. National Register districts in the county include West Alexander, West Middletown, Taylortown, East Washington, and Marianna.

Landmarks

1. Washington, originally Catfish's Camp.

1A. Courthouse (stone), the county's fourth, was erected in 1900 for $1 million. The first courts were held in the home of David Hoge, and the first courthouse and jail were constructed of logs in 1787 and destroyed by fire in 1790. The second building was erected in 1791–94 and enlarged in 1819. In 1839–42 the third courthouse was built; it was enlarged in 1867. *Location:* South Main and West Beau streets.

1B. Washington Town Hall (painted brick) was begun in 1869. Land for the structure had been purchased in 1842. In 1868 Dr. Francis Julius Le Moyne had offered to give $10,000 for a public library provided the town would erect a suitable building with a fireproof vault. The cost was $31,518. President Grant and his wife were visiting their friends, Mr. and Mrs. William W. Smith (see *Trinity Hall Academy*), at the time of the cornerstone-laying and this honor was given to Grant. In 1870 the Citizens' Library Association was granted a charter, and the library was formally opened in the town hall in 1872. Originally the structure was built on the corner of Main Street and West Cherry Avenue, but it was moved in 1897–98 to make way for the present courthouse. The second floor was removed in 1932, and the building remodeled into a one-story structure. In 1965 the library was moved to a new location on South College Street. The hall now houses the city's police department. *Location:* West Cherry and Brownson avenues.

1C. Washington and Jefferson College was incorporated as Washington Academy on September 24, 1787, and chartered March 28, 1806. Classes were first held in the courthouse in 1789 with Rev. Thaddeus Dodd serving as principal. In 1790 or before, Benjamin Franklin donated fifty pounds to the college for the purchase of books. From 1827 to 1833 the Washington Medical College of Baltimore functioned under the charter of this school. In 1852 by an agreement between its board of trustees and the synod of Wheeling, the school became a synodical college of the Presbyterian church. On March 4, 1865, Washington merged with Jefferson College (see *McMillan's Log Cabin School*) at Canonsburg, and by 1869 all classes were held in Washington. *Location:* Wheeling, Lincoln,

1D. Academy Building

East Maiden, East Beau streets, and College Avenue.

1D. Academy Building (stone), originally 30 by 35 feet, was erected as Washington Academy in 1793 on land donated by William Hoge. In 1816 wings were added to this structure, which now houses the administrative offices of Washington and Jefferson College. *Location:* On W&J campus.

1E. McIlvaine Hall (brick) was originally Washington Female Seminary, founded November 26, 1835, on land purchased from Alexander Reed. It now houses the English department of Washington and Jefferson College. *Location:* On W&J campus.

1F. East Washington Historic District is known for one of the finest sections of Queen Anne houses in western Pennsylvania, together with Italianate, Colonial Revival, and shingle style architecture. The town grew out of the oil boom and the introduction of interurban streetcars in the 1890s. There are over two hundred historic structures in this district. *Location:* East Washington, adjacent to Washington and Jefferson College.

1G. First Presbyterian Church (painted brick) was formally organized in 1793, with Matthew Brown its first regular pastor from 1805 to 1822. First services were held in the old administration building of Washington

Academy. The third and present church was built in 1868 on lot no. 102 of David Hoge's original plan of Washington, one of two lots presented by Hoge to George Washington. The chapel was built in 1886. *Location:* Southeast corner of Wheeling and College streets.

1H. Trinity Episcopal Church Rectory (brick) was built about 1840, and beginning in 1887 it was the city's first hospital. It is now used as church offices. *Location:* North College Street near East Beau Street.

1I. Boyle Gristmill (frame), originally operated by steam and constructed of hewn timbers, was built in 1844 by millwright Daniel Boyle. It was run by Samuel Hazlett and Daniel Dye until 1849. Later owned by the Zelt family from 1885 to 1910, it stopped functioning as a mill in 1915. At present it is used as a woodwork shop and auction center. *Location:* Corner of Oregon and West Wheeling streets.

1J. Sackville House (frame), a three-story Queen Anne Victorian structure (shingle style and Romanesque), was built in the late 1800s. *Location:* 309 East Wheeling Street.

1K. Le Moyne House (cut stone), a fine example of early Greek Revival architecture, was built in 1812 by Dr. John Julius Le Moyne, a French physician who came to America during the French Revolution and settled in Washington in 1797 after four years of prac-

1K. Le Moyne House

tice in Gallipolis, Ohio. In 1823 his only son, Dr. Francis Julius Le Moyne, bought the property, which remained in the family until 1943 when it was inherited by the Washington County Historical Society. While Francis Julius, an ardent abolitionist, lived here, the house became one of the first stops on the underground railroad. As many as twenty-six slaves were concealed in a secret room on the third floor of what appears to be a two-story house. *Hours:* Monday, Wednesday, and Friday, 9:30 A.M.–2:30 P.M. *Location:* 49 East Maiden Street.

Note: The Duncan Miller Glass Museum is located on the second floor of this house. The brick home directly across the street was built in 1826 and was also a Le Moyne house.

1L. Le Moyne Crematory (brick), the first in the United States, was constructed in 1876 at a cost of $1,500. Built under the direction of Dr. Francis Julius Le Moyne, the one-story structure is divided into two rooms—a reception room and a furnace room. Because of the controversial nature of the building, it had to be erected at night. Between 1876 and 1900 there were at least forty-two bodies cremated here. The first cremation was of Baron de Palm, a Bavarian nobleman, with Dr. Le Moyne the third on October 16, 1879. A granite monument, a memorial to the founder, is located in the front yard. Le Moyne's philanthropies included Le Moyne College, Washington's Citizens' Library, and a school for blacks in Memphis, Tenn. *Location:* South Main Street, opposite Presbyterian Home.

1M. Paul-Linn House (brick) was built in 1838 by the Houston Paul family on land pur-

chased in 1825. The same family that owned the Linn house on Brehm Road (q.v.) were later occupants of this home. *Location:* 1004 Redstone Road.

1N. Martin House (brick), easily identified by the words "Governor's House" written above the door, was the home of Maj. Gen. Edward Martin, who was a U.S. senator, governor, and veteran of the Spanish-American War, Mexican-border campaign, and of World Wars I and II. *Location:* Corner of Le Moyne Avenue and Lockhart Street.

1O. Baird-Acheson House (brick with round corner), built about 1825, was the birthplace of Edward Acheson, an eminent American chemist born here in 1856. He was awarded many medals for his invention of Carborundum, artificial graphite, and other valuable products of the electric furnace. The house, also owned at one time by Thomas Baird, has an outstanding curved stairway. *Location:* Southwest corner of Maiden and Main streets.

1P. Waynesburg & Washington Railroad Station (brick), now occupied by a builders' firm, is within sight of the Washington stone depot and a frame one, both on the same side of the street—a unique situation, for within one block are three railroad depots of three different types of construction and on their original sites. The "Waynie" was a narrow-gauge road, with so many curves that a wag wrote of it:

It doubles in and doubles out,
And leaves the traveler in doubt
Whether the snake that made the track
Was going out or coming back.

Location: Main Street at railroad yards.

1Q. Maurer House (brick) was built in the late 1800s and was occupied by Dr. Joseph Maurer. *Location:* South Franklin and West Wheeling streets.

1R. Bradford House (stone), of early Federal design, was built in 1787–88 by David Bradford, a successful lawyer, businessman, deputy attorney general (district attorney of the county), and leading figure of the Whiskey Rebellion. Bradford lived here from 1788 to 1794 when, according to legend, he jumped from a rear window of this house to escape from a cavalry detachment sent by President Washington to subdue those protesting against high excise taxes. (These taxes fell especially hard on the grain producers of western Pennsylvania.) Bradford fled to Span-

1R. Bradford House

ish West Florida and sold his house in 1803. One of the later owners was Rebecca Harding Davis, a well-known author who was born in the house in 1831. The structure was used for a store at one time. In 1959 the Pennsylvania Historical and Museum Commission assumed control of the building and restored the front to its original appearance. The interior still retains the beautiful mahogany staircase. A well discovered on the property has been reopened near the house. *Hours:* Wednesday–Saturday, 11 A.M.–4 P.M.; Sunday, 1–4 P.M. Closed December 20–April 1. *Admission charge. Location:* 175 South Main Street.

1S. Blaine's Temporary Residence (painted brick) was the home of James G. Blaine, congressman, party leader, secretary of state, and presidential candidate, while he attended Washington College in 1843–47. In 1854 he moved to Maine. The house can be identified by a glass-covered plaque on the side of the building, which now houses a glass company. *Location:* 331 South Main Street, near South Street.

1T. Trinity Hall Academy (brick) was established by William Wrenshall Smith at his estate in the fall of 1879. Smith had purchased this house, built about 1857, and twenty-five acres of land from Joseph McKnight in 1876 for $16,500. This Victorian Italianate home, with a large cupola, contained twenty-five rooms and was one of the best built in the United States at that time. R. M. Copeland of Boston landscaped the property, which was said "to be the most beautiful of any private residence in the state." It was called Spring

Hill until 1879 when Trinity Hall was established. At that time, Smith, a widower, decided to open his house as a school for the convenience of his two sons. Although Bishop John B. Kerfoot had originally selected the Swearingen-Cook house (q.v.) for a military boarding school of the Protestant Episcopal church, the Smith estate was chosen instead. The church later gave up the project, and Smith financed the school until his death in 1904. Ulysses S. Grant often visited the Smiths (see *Washington Town Hall*); and Smith's son, who was named for Grant, managed the school later. He made it a financial success, preparing men for Annapolis and West Point. In 1904 William McKennan Smith, Smith's other son, rented it to Charles Eckels and Finis Montgomery, and the school continued until 1907. The building was then vacant until 1913 when it was used as an armory. In 1925 it became Trinity Joint High School, later Trinity High School, said to have been the largest vocational school of its kind east of the Mississippi, with the largest agricultural department in Pennsylvania at that time. A fine rural stone gateway is in the rear, and the present gymnasium houses one of the exhibit buildings of the Buffalo World's Fair brought here by the elder Smith. *Location:* Just south of Washington, on SR 0018 (Park Avenue).

1U. The Granary (frame), now a restored barn converted into a restaurant by the present owner Steve Del Corso (1970s), was built 125 or more years ago. This bank barn, with oak beams some sixty feet long, is situated on property that belonged to the Harleys in the 1920s and 1930s. At that time it was used for storing roller coasters for the adjacent Mapleview Amusement Park. It was also part of a dairy farm and apple orchard. At one period the Luttons owned the barn. *Location:* About 1 mile north of The Meadows racetrack at US 19, 1180 Mapleview Drive.

2. West Alexander, is now, in part, a restored historic business district. Many early brick houses (along the Old Pike and near the site of the last tollgate west) have been converted into craft and gift shops.

2A. Three Ridges Church (brick) was erected in 1840. A plaque on a tree stump in the churchyard bears the following inscription: "1785–1936 Site of oak tree under which the first religious services were held in community by the congregation of Three Ridges by Dr. John McMillan, Rev. John Brice and others, as early as 1785." In 1795 land was purchased for the first church, and three houses of worship were built on the same site. The first pastor, Brice, is buried in the cemetery. *Location:* Old US 40 (Main Street).

2B. Murray Brothers Store (brick) belonged to J. W. and William M. Murray, who started a business in this early building in 1871. It was later occupied by the Vensel family and is still a store. *Location:* Main (old US 40) and Liberty streets.

Note: Next to the store is a long frame structure which is reputed to have been a ladies' seminary at one time. There are many old buildings in this town, which was laid out by Robert Humphreys in 1796 and named for his wife Martha Alexander.

2C. Morgan's Tavern (frame) was built on the National Road and is still operating as a tavern. *Location:* 1 mile west of West Alexander, on US 40.

2D. Valentine Tavern (frame), one of the area's favorite wagon stands, was built about 1812 and kept by John Valentine, whose brother Daniel was a tavern keeper in Washington. A second brother, Charles, was a wagoner on the National Road. *Location:* 1 mile east of West Alexander, on north side of US 40 (old National Road).

3. Wheeling Hill Church (frame) was built in 1866. The structure, with a fieldstone foundation, has two front entrances. It was an early United Presbyterian church. The "C P" on the building apparently resulted from confusion with the old Windy Gap Cumberland Presbyterian Church nearby. *Location:* Near Good Intent, on SR 0231, 6.3 miles south of Claysville.

4. Claysville was named for Henry Clay, champion of the National Road, and founded by John Purviance in 1817. Because the National Road went through Claysville on Main Street, there were numerous early taverns. The four houses below could have been operated as taverns by the following proprietors in stagecoach days: John Purviance (first tavern keeper), James Sargent (1821, at sign of Black Horse), Basil Brown (1836), James Dennison (1840), David Bell, John Walker, James Kelley, Stephen Conkling, John McIlree, a Walkins, a Walker, and the widow Callahan.

4A. Miller's Fort Memorial and Cemetery, site of one of the last Indian border raids of the Revolutionary War, March 31, 1782.

Jacob Miller's gravestone is in the adjacent cemetery near Claysville. *Location:* North of US 40, 3.5 miles west of Claysville.

4B. Brick House at Cooper's Corner was once owned by D. M. Campsey. *Location:* Corner of Main and Greene streets, adjacent to insurance office which faces Main Street.

4C. Painted Brick House was built about 1818, the time of the opening of the National Road. *Location:* Corner of Bell Street (SR 0231 south) and Main Street (old US 40).

4D. Old Brick Tavern. *Location:* 139 Main Street (old US 40).

4E. Brick Tavern with a front gable. *Location:* Corner of Main Street and Highland Avenue, next to market.

4F. T. C. Noble House (frame), with a cupola and captain's walk on top, was built prior to 1876 and is pictured in an old atlas of that date. *Location:* West Main Street (old US 40) on same side of street as Methodist church and across from antique shop.

4G. Porter-Montgomery House (frame), a Victorian gingerbread house with an unusually ornate tower, was built in 1879–80 by a contractor and carpenter, Robert Porter. His love for fancy woodwork is reflected in the style of this house, which was owned at a later date by the James Montgomery family. *Location:* West Main Street (old US 40) next to Catholic church.

Note: Next to this building is the Margaret Derrow house, a nineteenth-century structure with Gothic windows.

4H. S. White's Sons Building (frame) is believed to be the nation's oldest firm of monument makers, founded by Alexander White as early as 1800, although the first documented date is 1811. In early years stone from the old quarry at the nearby Finley farm was used. Among the noteworthy memorials made here is one for the famous racehorse Adios at The Meadows racetrack and the miner statue at Fairmont, W.Va., representing coal miners of ten counties who lost their lives in the mines. *Location:* North Alley.

5. Dutch Fork Christian Church (frame), built in 1863, was an outgrowth of the movement founded by Alexander Campbell. This congregation was established about 1830. Its first church was erected in 1836. *Location:*

Budaville, northeast of Claysville, near Rice's Fort site on SR 3004.

6. Caldwell's Tavern (brick and stone ruins) was built by James Caldwell about the time the National Road opened in 1818 and was operated by him until his death in 1838. His widow Hester continued the business until 1873. It was later owned by J. A. Gordon, also a tavern keeper, who kept his house as one of the favorite resorts along the way. At one time it was a children's home. In later years it was called the Rosemire until it was destroyed by fire. It was partially reconstructed but never completed due to the operation of an illegal still on the premises. This tavern inspired J. N. Matthews to write the poem "The Old Country Inn." Claire Elliot was the last owner of the tavern. *Location:* On old US 40 (south side of road), west of S-Bridge (no. 7) and across from McGuffey High School.

Note: Across the road is another old brick house, built after the tavern. It was an antique shop owned by a Mr. Ullom and later purchased by Recco Luppino.

7. S-Bridge (stone), completed in 1818 and so named for its double-curve design, was built to carry the National Road over a branch of Buffalo Creek. At one time there was an S-Bridge post office located nearby, and taverns operated at both ends of the structure during the height of travel. Today there are two early buildings on the west end and one near the east end which may have been taverns. When U.S. 40 was relocated, the bridge was no longer used, and the west end was demolished, although pedestrians may yet walk over it. *Location:* 4 miles southwest of Washington, at junction of SR 0221 and US 40.

Note: Nearby is Taylorstown, a one-time oil-boom village.

8. John Miller Tavern (brick) was built in 1812 with a fanlight in the front entrance. It was kept before 1836 by Levi Wilson, who entertained the first wagoners on the road. In 1836 John Miller moved here from a wagon stand east of Cumberland, Md. His daughter married a son of Levi Wilson, and the couple lived here after the establishment was no longer operating. *Location:* About 4.5 miles west of Washington, on north side of US 40, east of S-Bridge at top of Mounts Hill.

9. Martin's Tavern (brick) was a popular hostelry with twelve rooms and a spacious front porch. It was built in 1825 on the National Road by Jonathan Martin. Andrew Jackson and the celebrated theologian Alexander Campbell both stopped here. Martin operated the tavern until business closed on the road, except for a brief time when J. W. Holland managed it in the 1840s.

The community where the tavern is located was first called Pancake for George Pancake, who kept a tavern here as early as 1800. Prior to being named Laboratory, the village was also called Martinsburg in honor of Jonathan Martin. *Location:* Laboratory, 1871 East Maiden Street extension.

Note: The Nadar homestead (painted stone with frame addition), across the street, was built in 1818.

10. Little Tavern (brick), with an earlier brick house behind the main building, was kept by a Mr. Little. Today a modern tavern is located next to it. *Location:* About 4 miles east of Washington, near junction of US 40 and Myers Road.

11. Weaver House (brick) has a signature stone that reads, "Adam & M. Weaver, June 14, 1837," and is one of the few on which the owner included at least his wife's initial. This house, with a double porch in front of half of it and a cut-stone foundation, is still in the same family. *Location:* Near Scenery Hill. 2.5 miles south of US 40 on Weaver Run Road (SR 2053, also called Scenery Hill–Marianna Road).

12. Charley Miller's Tavern (painted brick) has a signature stone over the front door which reads, "For G. & S. Tombaugh, 1832." Later it was operated as a tavern by Henry Taylor followed by Charley Miller. At this time parties of young people drove ten miles from Washington to eat and dance at Miller's. His meals were sumptuous, and peach brandy was his specialty. After Miller's death the house was purchased by David Ullery. *Location:* About 1 mile west of Scenery Hill on south side of old US 40 (T 449). (Old US 40 is immediately in front of house and parallel with new US 40, next to it.)

13. Scenery Hill, originally Hillsboro, resulted from the building of the National Road in 1819, although its first name came from a tavern that antedated that highway by a quarter century. The town was almost exactly halfway between Brownsville and Washington.

13A. Century Inn (stone) was originally Hill's Tavern, one of the oldest on the National Road, and has been in continuous use as a

13A. Century Inn

14. Madonna of the Trail Monument

public house since 1794. It was first kept by Stephen Hill, for whom the tavern and town were named, and later by his nephew Thomas Hill. When Thomas retired, Samuel Youman, a stage driver, took over. Succeeding proprietors were John Hampson, John Gibson, William Dawson, and Oliver Lacock. In 1825 General Lafayette and Andrew Jackson were among its celebrated guests. It was for a number of years the leading tavern in the area and continues to exist today as a well-known inn. In later years Dr. Gordon F. Harrington bought the building and restored it, uncovering a large fireplace with the original hand-forged crane and utensils intact. (The paymaster station when US 40 was being built is nearby, now owned by Larry Pastories. Like this one, other early houses in Scenery Hill have been turned into gift shops.) *Location:* Near center of town, on north side of US 40.

13B. Wilson Tavern (brick) was possibly kept by John Wilson and later operated by Stephen Phelps and David Powell. *Location:* On south side of US 40, across from Century Inn.

13C. Riggle Tavern (brick) was founded about 1820 by Zephania Riggle, who owned taverns at several locations on this highway (see *Zephania Riggle Tavern*). Later a Dr. Clark owned this house. *Location:* On south side of US 40, about 1 block east of Century Inn.

14. Madonna of the Trail Monument is one of twelve memorials "to the pioneer mothers of the covered wagon days" erected by the National Society of the Daughters of the American Revolution. The statue is ten feet high, weighs five tons, and has a six-foot-high base weighing twelve tons. Created by the sculptor A. Leinbach, this is the only one of these monuments in Pennsylvania and the tenth to be unveiled (on December 8, 1929). It depicts a pioneer woman with a baby in her arms and a boy clutching her skirt. *Location:* 3.9 miles east of Scenery Hill, on US 40, at eastern edge of Beallsville and opposite Nemacolin Country Club.

15. Beallsville

15A. National Hotel (brick), also known as Greenfield Stand, was kept by William Greenfield until his death. This famous inn on the National Road was a stop where a traveler could always get a good cup of coffee, a rare thing in a tavern at that time. Greenfield was not only an innkeeper but a banker as well. His bank, known as the Beallsville Savings Bank, was operated in his tavern with the safe being his pocket. The pressure was too much for the proprietor to withstand, and his banking business did not last long. The famous Ringgold Cavalry started from this hotel for the Civil War. The building, with a wooden balustrade surrounding the second-story porch, is now used as a store and residence. *Location:* Southwest corner of junction of US 40 and SR 2041.

15B. Miller's Tavern (brick) was kept as early as 1830 by Charley Miller and subsequently by a Mrs. Chambers, who ran "a quiet, orderly, and aristocratic inn." Following this ownership, Moses Bennington occupied the tavern. It was later operated by Benjamin Demen and Charles Guttery, the last old-time tavern owner at this site. *Location:* Junction of US 40 and SR 2041 (on southeast corner across from National Hotel).

16. Van Voorhis Hill House (brick) is a Victorian house built in the late 1800s. *Location:* 1 mile west of Beallsville on hillside overlooking old National Pike.

17. Martindale House (brick) was built in 1861, with an addition in 1976. A log cabin was built on the property in 1794. The estate was once called Lindenhurst for the linden trees at the site, which were brought from England. *Location:* On Martindale Road, at Beallsville-Marianna Road.

18. Marianna, a coal mine "patch," includes about two hundred fifty mostly identical shotgun-style yellow brick buildings, now owned and operated by Bethlehem Steel Company (also a school and mine buildings). The bricks were manufactured by the Joneses, who founded this model mining town. The town was established when the Pigeon Creek Branch railroad connecting the Pennsylvania Railroad at Monongahela City was built. One of the worst mine disasters occurred here; the explosion killed about one hundred fifty men. *Location:* Marianna (West Bethlehem Township).

Note: St. Nicholas Old Believer church in Marianna is one of four remaining churches of this denomination in the United States.

19. Sibbits House (fieldstone) has a signature stone on the gable end which reads, "S.S 1807," the first initial standing for Solomon. A fine springhouse stands in the back yard. The property is now part of a dairy farm. *Location:* Between Lone Pine and Marianna. Go 0.3 mile south of bridge on Lone Pine-Marianna Road (SR 2011); turn east on T 728 at dairy sign; thence 0.2 mile to house.

20. Ten Mile Brethren Church (brick), a Dunkard congregation said to have met as early as 1775 at the Spohn home, was organized about 1800 by a clergyman named Bruist. It was built in 1832 and, until a recent reconstruction, had a fireplace with an iron kettle and crane. On March 14, 1905, it was incorporated as the German Baptist Church of the Brethren. *Location:* North of Marianna. Go 1.5 miles north on Lone Pine-Marianna

Road (SR 2011); turn east on a red-dog road. Church is at top of hill (0.3 mile).

21. Gantz House (cut stone) has a signature stone which reads, "John & Anna Gantz 1814." The Gantz family owned the first oil well in the county. *Location:* Between Lone Pine and Marianna, 0.8 mile below bridge on Lone Pine-Marianna Road (SR 2011).

22. Martin's Mill (frame) was built before 1850. *Location:* 1.5 miles east of Ten Mile Village, on SR 2020.

23. Joseph Ross House (brick) has on its gable end a signature stone which reads, "Joseph S. & Elizabeth Ross, 1835." *Location:* 0.5 mile from Glyde, on Glyde-Lone Pine Road (second house on right from Glyde).

Note: On a hill, one-half mile to the south of the Ross house and on SR 2013, is an old log cabin behind the Bethlehem Lutheran Church. The church was founded in 1787, with the present building erected in 1906.

24. Victorian House (brick), with seven bays, built in the late 1800s, is an impressive country home having two rose windows and brackets under the eaves. *Location:* East of Washington near Glyde, corner of Rainey Road and SR 0519.

25. Methodist Church (frame) was built in 1867. *Location:* Glyde, US 40 at SR 0519.

26. Zollarsville

26A. Ulery Gristmill (brick), a large structure with a stone foundation, was built in 1835 by the Ulery family on the bank of the north fork of Ten Mile Creek. Originally operated by water, the mill was later converted to steam power. After ceasing to function as a mill, it became a grocery store. *Location:* 0.3 mile off SR 2011, on Beallsville-Marianna Road.

26B. Ulery House (brick) has a signature stone which reads, "This Building was erected by Jacob Ulery & Israel in the [year] of our Lord 1838." Once operated as a hotel it is now a private residence and is located near the Ulery gristmill (see above). In the past, this mill and house have erroneously been described as being constructed of stone. *Location:* 0.2 mile off SR 2011 on Ten Mile Creek, Beallsville-Marianna Road.

26C. Ulery Homestead (fieldstone and brick) was the old Ulery farmhouse across the creek from the mill and Ulery brick house. At the rear of the stone section is an attached two-story brick ell. A large barn with a cut-stone foundation is on the property. *Location:* Near Zollarsville, SR 2011, on Beallsville-Marianna Road (West Bethlehem Township).

26D. Ten Mile Methodist Church (brick) has a front signature stone which reads, "Ten Mile 1842 Methodist Episcopal Church erected by Stephen Ullery [old spelling] for use of the Methodist Society." The building, which has two front entrances, is adjacent to the old cemetery. *Location:* SR 2022, on Beallsville-Marianna Road (West Bethlehem Township).

26E. Crumrine House (covered log and stone) dates back to the early 1800s. The log section was built by George Crumrine in 1801 and the stone section in 1810. George was the father of Daniel Crumrine, who was an uncle of Boyd Crumrine, the historian. Signed masonry work on the front steps reads:

Virtu, Liberty & Independence
Rebuilt by Daniel & Margaret Crumrine
June 22, 1847
Francis Fogler

Location: Near Zollarsville, on Plum Run Road, 0.2 mile off SR 2011.
Note: Nearby is a fine log barn built in 1805.

27. Wise House (fieldstone), an unusually constructed house with a narrow front, was built before 1815. It was almost certainly erected by Jacob Wise, an early stonemason. *Location:* Halfway between Marianna and Beallsville, at junction of SR 2024 and SR 2011.

28. Kinder Stone Gristmill, now ivy covered, was erected before 1780 by George Kinder (see below), and was reputedly the site of a Whiskey Rebellion meeting. Valentine Kinder, George's son, was killed in 1781 while operating the mill. The business later became a woolen mill, followed by a distillery run by Samuel Thompson at this location, still known as Thompsons Corners. This business, which made the well-known Sam Thompson rye whiskey, was later taken to West Brownsville (see *Sam Thompson Distillery*). *Location:* 3 miles south of Beallsville on SR 2011, Barnard and Martinsdale roads.

29. George Kinder House (fieldstone), one of the earliest houses west of the Alleghenies, was built in 1783. A smaller stone section was erected even earlier. A solid, bulletproof (for that time) door was discovered in the house by the latest owners, and there are portholes in the third floor of the house. The basement

ceiling is constructed of heavy beams placed within inches of one another. Sheep were raised in this house for twenty years. It was restored into a lovely home by the Charles Appel family. *Location:* 3 miles south of Beallsville, on SR 2011.

30. Welsh-Emery House (stone) was built about 1815 on a 1781 land grant by William Welsh, son of John Welsh, a fine cabinet-maker, and his wife Eleanor, both of whom came from Ulster County, Ireland. The Welshes named their land Enniskillen for their former home, and at first lived in a log cabin about two hundred yards behind the present house. William, one of seven justices of the county in the early days, had an office in the front of this dwelling. He was also president of the first library west of the Alleghenies and the father of eight daughters and two sons, all of whom were well educated for that period.

The kitchen was a one-story addition of stone on the east side of the house, which was later enlarged to two stories. In 1878 William's son Joseph Bud Welsh remodeled the house; and in 1909 Geraldine and Helen Emery remodeled it completely, enlarging rooms and adding a two-story portico in the front with an iron railing. The house is now owned by Joseph B. Welsh's daughter, Mrs. C. W. Theakston. The Rankin Playhouse Olde Trail Players operate in the barn next to the house. *Location:* Halfway between Centerville and Madonna of the Trail monument, on old US 40 (now called Emery Road) 0.2 mile south of its junction with new US 40.

31. Centerville, laid out in 1821 halfway between Uniontown and Washington, has many interesting old buildings.

31A. Rogers Tavern (brick covered with siding) was the first tavern in the village kept by John Rogers, father of Joseph Rogers of Bridgeport. John's other son Robert succeeded his father in the business and died in possession of the house, with his son-in-law Solomon Bracken and a Mr. Wilson occupying it at intervals. The tavern was known as a quiet, orderly, well-kept establishment. *Location:* Junction of old US 40 and SR 0481 (north side of road), house no. 902.

31B. Zephania Riggle Tavern (brick) was the leading wagon stand in the village with a wagon yard in the rear. It was destroyed by fire but promptly rebuilt while Riggle owned it. He was succeeded in 1845 by Peter Colley (see *Peter Colley Tavern*, Fayette County), Henry Whitsett, Jacob Marks, William Garrett,

Jesse Quail, and Joseph Jeffreys. John Strathers was the last to operate the tavern; it closed in the 1930s. *Location:* Old US 40, house no. 935.

31C. Hiram Smith House (frame), with the original front porch removed, was built in 1830. *Location:* Old US 40, house no. 947.

31D. Taylor-Linton House (quarried fieldstone) was begun in 1797 by a Mr. Taylor. The second section, constructed largely of fieldstone, was built by Samuel Taylor in 1843. Taylor, who established a bank in Brownsville, owned this property until about 1870, when Malin Linton and his wife Elizabeth bought it. The third and present owner is William Spray, who bought and restored the house in 1949. The large front porch was added in 1909, with another addition made to the house in 1912. Large triangular stone fireplaces with six flues help support the house. Nearby is a stone springhouse, and on the road leading to the house is a fence of fine old Osage orange (hedge apple), typical of early pioneer plantings. *Location:* From old US 40 in Centerville, turn north on unmarked road opposite Vestaburg Clinic sign, and continue about 0.5 mile to house.

32. Wheeler-Taylor House (fieldstone and brick) dates back to before 1808. The original stone section was built by Dr. Charles Wheeler. When Bishop Asbury visited Taylor Methodist Church (q.v.) in 1808, he stopped here to see Dr. Wheeler, who had fallen from a horse. The Oliver Knight Taylor family built the front Victorian brick addition in the 1870s. *Location:* About 0.5 mile east of Centerville, on north side of US 40, across from restaurant.

33. Taylor Methodist Church (brick) was founded between 1772 and 1784 as Hawkins Chapel on the William Hawkins property, later owned by William Taylor. Early circuit riders in the area were Eli Shickle, John Cooper, and Solomon Breeze. In 1786 Robert Ayers preached here. The congregation has had four buildings: the first of log (reputedly 1772), the second of stone (1810), the third of brick (1857, destroyed by fire in 1872), and the present building (1872, remodeled in 1904, 1928, and 1959). The chair that Bishop Francis Asbury sat in when visiting here in 1808 is preserved in a glass case inside the church with other historical memorabilia. The earliest gravestone in the cemetery is that of Joseph Woodfil (1754–98), who according to his descendants preached his first sermon here in 1772 at the age of eighteen. His sister,

who was killed by Indians, is also buried at the site. Nearby in the cemetery is the McCutcheon monument (q.v.). *Location:* 1.4 miles east of Centerville, on old US 40.

34. McCutcheon Monument, often referred to as the "spite monument," is a granite memorial ordered built by James Shannon McCutcheon (1824–1902), a miserly farmer who made his money in coal land. Because of a family feud he left his entire estate to buy as expensive a monument as could be erected, with any money left over going toward the construction of four granite columns around the obelisk. His two brothers were paid $1,000 each for the construction. McCutcheon died before its completion and is buried in front of the structure. The eighty-five-foot memorial, with a base over forty-five feet square, blew over in a 1936 storm (the winds also taking off the roof of the Taylor Church, q.v.), and today only eighteen feet of the original structure remain in the cemetery. *Location:* 1.4 miles east of Centerville, on old US 40 (in Taylor churchyard).

35. Jeffreys House (quarried stone), with a frame addition and alterations, was built before 1820 by the father of Joseph Jeffreys, a tavern owner (see *Zephania Riggle Tavern*). The old family cemetery is near the house. *Location:* East of Centerville. Go 1.5 miles east on US 40 and 1 mile north on Daisytown Road.

36. Isaac Morris House (fieldstone) has a signature stone which reads, "E I & M 1811." In 1804 the Morris family, who were Quakers, built a log barn near the house. The Binns family later bought the property. *Location:* About 2 miles southeast of Centerville, on Ridge Road.

37. Theakston House (stone) has a stone springhouse on the property. Another early stone house of this family is the Welsh-Emery house (q.v.). *Location:* 2 miles southeast of Centerville, turn off Ridge Road onto Binns Road and continue about 1 mile to house; Binns Road is almost directly across from Isaac Morris house.

38. Malden Inn (stone), a large impressive building with H chimneys and a court in the back, was built as Kreppsville Inn, since John Krepps, the builder, assumed that a village of this name would grow up around the inn. The town was called Malden, reportedly from emigrants encamping nearby who imagined that the area reminded them of their native town

38. Malden Inn

by that name in Massachusetts. The western and original section of the tavern was built in 1822 and the eastern in 1830. The second part bears a unique stone tavern sign built in the front portion. It reads "Kreppsville, 1830" above a moldboard plow; beside the plow is an eagle with "Liberty" inscribed between the wings, and beneath it are sheaves of wheat. Another signature stone in the gable end of the first section is also engraved with an eagle and three sheaves of wheat.

The tavern was first kept by Bry Taylor. His daughter Kizzie was accidentally killed in this house by a gun fired by her brother James, who in later years was shot by a U.S. marshal. Following Taylor, Samuel Acklin, Samuel Bailey, William Pepper, William Garrett, and James Britton operated the inn.

A stone barn, where a large wagon yard had been, is west of the inn. Once a residence, it later became a restaurant. *Location:* 1.5 miles west of Brownsville, junction of old US 40 and SR 2073.

39. West Brownsville

39A. Sam Thompson Distillery (brick) was the site where the famous Sam Thompson whiskey was made. The business first started at Kinder's mill (see *Kinder Stone Gristmill*) and was later transferred to West Brownsville. Some of the distillery warehouses are in use by various firms. *Location:* Junction of SR 0088 and old US 40.

39B. Krepps Tavern (stone) was built before 1800 and operated by Vincent Owens, a Revolutionary War soldier, followed by Samuel Acklin, John Krepps (see *Malden Inn*), and Morris Purcell. The father of Vincent Owens was murdered in this house while his son ran the tavern. Krepps ferry was operated here in conjunction with the inn until 1845. The house

was later used for the Sam Thompson Distillery office and is still an office building. A fill on the highway has obscured the first story on the side away from the river. *Location:* Near Sam Thompson Distillery buildings, junction of SR 0088 and old US 40 (now fronts on Monongahela River).

39C. St. John's Episcopal Church (frame) was built in 1860–70 in Carpenter Gothic design. It began with Sunday school work in 1850. The parish was organized in 1860, the same year a lot was donated to the congregation by John Cock. The church took ten years to build due to the Civil War. It is now a Methodist church. *Location:* 124 Pittsburgh Street.

39D. Old High School (brick) was built at the turn of the century and has now been adapted for use as a municipal building. *Location:* Main Street near Blaine historical marker.

40. Chambers Mill House (stone) was built in 1823 by William and Robert Chambers on Banes Fork of Ten Mile Creek. Their father, James Chambers, came from Downpatrick, Ireland, and took up land here between 1795 and 1797. The mill, built in 1832 on the site of a former one, is in ruins near the house. A later addition to the home has been removed. A fine stone smokehouse is in the front yard. *Location:* Chambers, 6.7 miles on SR 2007 off SR 0018 (in Gabby Heights).

41. Bane House (fieldstone), built by one of the original five Bane brothers who settled in Amwell Township in 1769, is a small cottage that was later stuccoed. Located beside Bane Run, it is one of the oldest houses in the county. The crossroads where it is located was originally called Pleasant Sunset. *Location:* Baker Station, junction of SR 2007 and SR 2009.

Note: The brick house that sits across the road was the home of the stationmaster for the Waynesburg & Washington Railroad at Baker Station. It is more than a century old.

42. North Ten Mile Baptist Church (brick) is now called Mt. Hermon Baptist Church. The first services were held in the home of Enoch Enoch of Little Ten Mile Creek in 1773. The first log meeting house was built in 1786 and replaced by a larger hewn-log structure in 1794. The present building was erected in 1840, with an addition in 1975. A later brick church of the divided congregation, built in 1904, is located at Lone Pine. *Location:* About

1.5 miles south of Baker Station, junction of SR 2007 and SR 3020.

43. Upper Ten Mile Presbyterian Church (brick) and Lower Ten Mile Presbyterian Church (q.v.) were organized together August 15, 1781, by Thaddeus Dodd (Dod). Dr. Dodd, who first preached in the community about 1777, continued to serve the congregation until his death in 1793. The first church building, of log, was erected in 1792 followed by two wooden structures of 1818 and 1854. The present church was built in 1860 on land donated by Demas Lindley and remodeled in 1894. *Location:* Prosperity, about 0.2 mile off SR 0018 at Lindley Fort marker.

44. Bethel Cumberland Presbyterian Church (brick) has a round signature stone above the front entrance which reads, "Bethel C. P. Church, Fiftieth anniversary celebration May 20th 1883." A bell tower is in the front yard, and in the rear of the church is a cemetery containing the cut-stone family vault of H. B. Lindley (see *Lindley Fort Site House*) erected in 1883. *Location:* 3 miles south of Lagonda, at corner of SR 0018 (Park Avenue) and Bethel Church Road.

45. Lindley Fort Site House (brick) was built about 1840 by Isaac Connett, whose father James had bought the land in 1801 from the Lindleys. Demas Lindley had settled on this tract, known as Mill Seat, in 1773 and patented it in 1785. In 1928 the descendants of the Lindley family erected a monument on the lawn of this property at the site of the Lindley fortified blockhouse, which was built in 1774–75. *Location:* About a quarter mile south of Prosperity, on SR 0018.

46. Old Concord, founded in 1826, has a number of noteworthy landmarks, all in view of one another.

46A. Mansion House (frame) was built by Elias Day in 1837. In the 1920s, when the property was owned by the Rogers family, a group of ministers and laymen decided to establish an Institute of Practical Arts for immigrant boys here. It operated for over twenty years and was closed in 1943. The Mansion House restaurant was opened here in 1947 by the James Simpson family and features family-style dinners.

46B. Concord Cumberland Presbyterian Church (frame) was organized in 1831, a year after missionaries from Cumberland College in Kentucky held meetings on the camp-grounds. The picturesque country church has an interesting interior with designs painted by construction employees building the Waynesburg & Washington Railroad.

46C. Old Concord Gristmill (frame) has remained in the Earnest family for years. It was run first by steam and then by a gasoline engine for the nearby farmers. A village blacksmith shop operating on the grounds from Civil War days until the 1920s has been converted into a garage.

Note: About one mile from Old Concord on SR 0018 is a sawmill built by E. L. McCormick, who invented and patented one of the fastest wedge-shaped cap-cutting machines.

46D. General Store and Post Office (frame) was once the halfway hotel between Waynesburg and Washington. Also a drovers' stand, it accommodated many cattlemen driving their stock through the village. This house, now restored, belonged to the Parkinsons, the same family that owned an 1830 yellow frame house on SR 0018 near the north edge of town.

47. Dunn's Station (frame) was a depot on the old Waynesburg & Washington Railroad. It is now being used for storage along the abandoned track, which carried the last train in 1965. After 1931 there had been only one run a year, to keep the franchise alive. *Location:* Dunns Station, on SR 0221.

48. Thomas Ross House (brick covered with stucco) first belonged to Thomas Ross. In 1833 he contracted with John Andrew to build the house, originally having six rooms, at a cost of $500. Ross hauled the logs for the basement beams with an ox team, and Andrew burned the bricks on the property. The house, with a fieldstone foundation, was built between March and November of 1834. Ross lived in this house only about a month when he died of pneumonia. (Andrew took his pay, went to Ohio, and built a blacksmith shop on one corner, a general store on another, and his home on a third. This crossroads formed the nucleus of Alliance, Ohio.) The Ross house was stuccoed in 1867. Ezra Hoge bought the property from Timothy Ross in recent years. *Location:* Near Dunns Station, on SR 0221, 4.5 miles west of US 19.

49. Amity was founded in 1797. The village has been most widely acclaimed as the home of Rev. Solomon Spaulding, long erroneously supposed to be the real author of the *Book of Mormon*. (His book, discovered some years

313

ago, bears no resemblance to that work.) He is buried in the cemetery at the Lower Ten Mile Church.

49A. Lower Ten Mile Presbyterian Church (brick) was organized at Jacob Cook's house in 1781 at the same time that the Upper Ten Mile Presbyterian Church (q.v.) was formed. From 1805 to 1817 Cephas Dodd served these congregations, following his father Thaddeus. This church has had four buildings: the first of log (1785), the second of brick (1832), the third of brick and frame (after 1842), and the present church (1875). Another church evolved from this one when some of the members moved away (see *Fairfield Presbyterian Church,* Mercer County).

A monument commemorating the life and service of Thaddeus Dodd, organizer of the church, is in the front yard on the exact site of the first log church. Thaddeus Dodd also established the first Latin school west of the Allegheny Mountains in 1782–85. Dodd's Classical Academy was the forerunner of Washington Academy (see *Washington and Jefferson College*). *Location:* On US 19.

49B. Amity Hotel (painted brick) has a large porch running full length across two of its sides. It is now a machine shop. *Location:* On US 19.

Note: Across the road is an early stone house.

49C. Methodist Protestant Church (frame), organized in 1832, first met in the original log church belonging to the Lower Ten Mile Presbyterian Church, which adjoined its land. The building, later moved to the location of the present church, was replaced in 1851 with a frame structure, rebuilt in 1867. *Location:* On US 19.

50. Cumberland Presbyterian Church (brick), now United Presbyterian, has a signature stone which reads, "This building dedicated to the worship of God by the C.P. Church A.D. 1840." A later addition is adjacent to the church. *Location:* Millsboro, on SR 0088.

Note: The brick Methodist church in the community was built in 1855. This river town has many old structures.

51. Fredericktown

51A. Bower House (stone) was built on a tract called "Apple Bottom" which was patented by David Blair on May 14, 1789. It is reputed that Blair, a gunsmith, built the small portion of the house with the large chimney. He sold the property for $1,000 on August 8, 1801, to John Bower, who built the larger part. A signature stone has an engraved flower on it and reads, "J. and E. Bower, 1806." Bower came to western Pennsylvania from York County in 1796 and married Elizabeth Rex. He was a miller, distiller, justice of the peace, school director, potter (patenting a type of clay pipe in 1814), and boat builder (among his craft the *Fancy* and the *Ariadne*). His sons Andrew and Benjamin also lived in the house. In the late 1800s it was sold but was returned to the family in 1972 when John Bower's great-great-grandson, W. Scott Bower, purchased it from the Russell Bane family. *Location:* North end of Fredericktown, on SR 0088.

51B. Buckingham House (brick) was built in the early to middle 1800s with a later frame addition. The initials E.K. are on the facade. A stone smokehouse is also on the property. *Location:* Northwest of Fredericktown, at Deemston on SR 2024 just east of SR 2041.

51C. Fredericktown Ferry, the area's last operating ferry, runs between Fredericktown and East Fredericktown (Fayette County). It is believed to be the only inland river ferry in Pennsylvania. The property was purchased as a joint venture between the two counties in 1972 at which time it was refurbished. *Hours:* Monday–Friday, 6:00 A.M.–10:00 P.M. Weekends by request to Fayette County commissioners' office. *Location:* Off SR 0088 at river, Water (Front) Street.

51D. Old Stone Parsonage has a plaque on the front that reads, "Old Stone Parsonage, 1803." The community where this house is located was not founded until 1817. *Location:* SR 0088 next to First Methodist Church.

52. Regester Log House, built about 1830, is an L-shaped double log structure. *Location:* On SR 2063, 3 miles north of Fredericktown.

53. Dorsey House (fieldstone with dressed stone corners) was built in 1787 by James Dorsey, who migrated from Baltimore and lived here until his death. The house, with a beautiful doorway, faces the Monongahela River and Brownsville. A stone story-and-a-half addition, reputedly built by slave labor, is on the south side of this Georgian house. The woodwork in the house is cherry. *Location:* Denbo Heights, 113 Cherry Avenue, opposite Maxwell locks and near SR 0088.

54. California and area

54A. Old Main (brick), the oldest existing building on the California University campus, was constructed in 1868. Originally California State College, it was founded in 1852. *Location:* North end of town.

54B. Museum of Southwestern Pennsylvania opened in 1988. The university also includes an archeology department that deals with local historical sites. *Location:* Reed Arts Building on California University campus.

54C. Lilley House (stone) has on its signature stone:

L
T X R
1810

The property also includes a stone barn, a springhouse, and a washhouse. Now owned by California University, it is used as a dormitory for the tennis team. *Location:* Near University stadium (off SR 0088).

54D. Large Stone House, with four sizable chimneys and a later addition on the left rear half, in recent years was purchased by a physician. There is a stone springhouse on the property. *Location:* SR 2079, 0.6 mile off Blaine Road.

54E. Pittsburgh, Virginia & Charleston (PVC) Railroad Station (brick), later the Pittsburgh & Lake Erie Railroad, has a tile roof and keystone windows. It has been converted into a library. *Location:* California, First and Wood streets.

55. The Poplars (painted stone) has an inscription over the door that reads, "The Poplars 1831–1906." The building is at present a California University fraternity house. *Location:* North of California, just south of Coal Center on SR 0088.

56. Coal Center, originally known as Greenfield, was laid out in 1814. Its name was changed in the 1880s due to the concentrated coal industry in the area. Here a bridge abutment can be seen in the center of the river where a bridge was planned but never built. *Location:* SR 0088 and SR 2036, east of California.

57. Greenfield Bend is one of the most spectacular views in western Pennsylvania. From High Point one can see the entire hairpin bend of the Monongahela just downriver from

59A. Charleroi Chamber of Commerce Building

California, Coal Center, Newell, Allenport, and Roscoe. In the early 1980s the movie *Maria's Lovers* was filmed here. *Location:* SR 0088.

58. Speers House (brick) was built in 1806 by Henry Speers, Jr., a brother of Noah Speers who founded Belle Vernon (meaning "beautiful green"). The Speers family operated a ferry in the area for over 100 years. Joseph and Sally Pappalardo rescued this house from demolition and restored it as a restaurant, which opened as The Back Porch in 1975. *Location:* Speers, almost under bridge which spans Monongahela River between Speers and Belle Vernon.

59. Charleroi, called the "Magic City," was founded in 1890 along the Monongahela River on land originally the McKean, Redd, and McMahon farms. In recent years this city has made extensive progress in city development and restoration. The Charleroi-Monessen Bridge, numerous houses and business buildings, some designed by R. L. Barnhart (inventor and proprietor of "The Electric Theater," the fourth motion picture house to open in the United States, in 1905), are now on the National Register of Historic Places. Rego's Old Hotel has been readapted as a youth hostel. (For more information regarding these structures, contact Charleroi Main Street Program.)

59A. Charleroi Chamber of Commerce Building (brick) was originally the old freight house for the Charleroi, Pittsburgh Plate Glass Company, the largest of three glass companies established in the town (1891). They became famous for their Carrara Glass, solid colored glass panels resembling Italian Carrara marble, used for covering earlier facades of buildings. The glass company was located here until 1930. In 1949 the Chamber of Commerce moved into the building, which temporarily also serves as a collection center for a glass museum. *Location:* 1 Chamber Plaza, between railroad and river.

59B. Charleroi Glass (Corning Plant), erected in 1893, became the largest producer of lamp chimneys by the following year. In 1899 it merged with Thomas Evans Co. and became Macbeth-Evans Glass Co., which made automobile headlight lenses. The company purchased the American Lamp Chimney Co. and rights to the Owens glassblowing machine in 1900. In 1918 it acquired the Hamilton Bottle Works adjacent to the plant. The company, in 1930, pioneered an automatic pressing department for making "Depression glass," as well as developing opal glass. Six years later it merged with Corning Glass works, specializing in opal tableware and illuminating glassware. This plant also pioneered the manufacture of glass block, originally made solid. *Location:* Near Chamber of Commerce.

59C. Coyle Theater was built in the early 1900s for live drama and vaudeville. Entertainers arrived by horse and buggy, and a nearby funeral parlor provided their dressing rooms. The theater was remodeled in 1927 and again in the 1940s when modern equipment was installed. The present owners bought the property in 1982 and reopened the old house of entertainment the following year. Once again it presents live stage shows as well as movies. *Location:* North of Water Street.

59D. Holy Ghost Byzantine Catholic Church, built in 1970, is one of the few churches in America adorned in the ancient, full iconographic style. There are over two hundred fifty icons covering the entire ceiling and wall surfaces of the sanctuary, presenting the history of salvation. This spiritual art was executed by iconographer Mila Mina of Goleta, Calif., assisted by Judy Lauderbaugh and a staff of parishioners over a two-year period. Mina, who fled from Czechoslovakia when it came under Communist control, studied in Paris. Group tours are welcome. *Location:* 828 Meadow Avenue and Eighth Street.

59E. Elks Club, in neoclassical style, is perhaps the best-preserved club building in the Monongahela Valley. *Location:* Downtown.

60. Donora, founded about 1890 by William H. Donner, takes its name from his own and that of Nora Mellon, wife of Andrew Mellon, his friends. Donora made news in 1948 when poisonous fumes from a zinc-smelting plant caused the death of twenty-three persons.

60A. Cement City, composed of about one hundred concrete two-story houses built in 1916, was developed for the middle management of Donora Mill. The houses are all poured-in-place concrete, based on a Thomas Edison patent. The moulds were reused from lot to lot, as the houses were cast. This was the first time that slag by-products of coal from mills were mixed with cement instead of gravel, for building purposes. *Location:* Wall, Chestnut, Bertha, Ida, and Modisette streets (among others).

60B. Hell Stretch is a bend in the Monongahela River where riverboat captains have had to face the dangers of smog, a pier (now gone) in the middle of the river, and dangerous curves. *Location:* At Westmoreland-Washington County bridge.

60C. Baker-Gruessmer House (rubble stone) is an early five-bay house with an added porch. Across the road is another stone (stuccoed) house of about the same vintage. *Location:* 2 miles west of Donora on SR 0837.

61. Monongahela City, also called Monongahela or Mon City, on the Monongahela River, was originally called Parkinsons Ferry and later Williamsport. It was laid out in 1792 by Joseph Parkinson, incorporated as a borough in 1837, and chartered as a city in 1873. It is Pennsylvania's second smallest city. (For more information contact Monongahela Valley T.O.U.R.)

61A. Headwaters District River Museum, in Italianate style, is operated by Monongahela Valley River Buffs. It features exhibits of river memorabilia, photographs, and scale models of stern wheel riverboats. This is the only museum in Pennsylvania devoted to inland rivers: Allegheny, Monongahela, and Ohio. It is located in the former Odd Fellows Building, erected in 1869, site of the first Monongahela High School commencement (1878). *Location:* Main and Second streets.

61B. Monongahela Area Historical Society Musem (brick) originally was the Kerr house, built in 1889 and designed by architect John Blythe. It was added onto an existing house (Layman house) which dates from about 1830. The museum features changing exhibits of local history, including architecture, quilts, and industrial histories. *Hours:* Tuesday–Thursday, 6–8 P.M.; Saturday–Sunday, 1–4 P.M. *Location:* 717 West Main Street between Seventh and Eighth streets.

61C. Commercial Buildings (brick) were built about 1876. They were later converted into apartments and an insurance business. *Location:* Fifth Street and West Main Street.

61D. Chess Park, with a picturesque gazebo built in 1987, was the property of Mary Wickerham Chess Miller, whose house later became the civic clubhouse (demolished in 1920). This park is the site of the community's annual midsummer Town and Country Arts Festival, as well as its Christmas in the Park. *Location:* West Main Street and Seventh Street.

61E. Monongahela City Trust (tile and granite over steel), in neoclassical style, was built in 1927. It closed four years later at the time of the Depression and has for the most part been vacant ever since. It was designed by architects Morgan and French of New York. The original president was Joseph A. Herron, a state senator and millionaire. *Location:* West Main Street at Second Street.

61F. Van Voorhis House (brick) was built in 1834 or earlier by Isaac Van Voorhis whose father, Daniel, recorded that he moved his family to this area in 1786 from what is now New York City. According to *McFarland's History of Washington County,* "one of the first brick houses in the county was built by James Parkinson in 1785 on Pigeon Creek and is yet known as the Vanvoorhis Homestead." This early house has many fine features including double-hung twelve-pane windows and a bracketed cornice. A porch with a mansard roof was added about 1880. *Location:* SR 0481 (First Street) at West Main Street.

61G. Sampson House (brick) was built about 1850 by the founder of the Monongahela City Trust Company. Part of it served as Scott's Academy, Monongahela's "prep school," which commenced in 1887. In the 1920s the architect Frederick G. Scheibler, Jr., remodeled the house. *Location:* West Main Street at Fifth Street.

61H. Wickerham House was built in 1834 by William Wickerham on land his father, Adam, had laid out in 1807 as the town of Georgetown which in 1816 he annexed to Williamsport. In the 1870s the house was enlarged, and in the 1920s was remodeled in neo-

colonial style. *Location:* West Main Street between Fifth and Sixth Streets.

61I. Keenan House (brick), with a fanlight door, was built prior to the Civil War. This house and the other Greek Revival house along West Main Street between Fifth and Sixth streets are the last remaining buildings of Adam Wickerham's Georgetown. *Location:* 525 West Main Street at Sixth Street.

61J. Longwell House (brick) was the home of David Longwell, a riverboat captain. His original house, barn (behind present house), and the basement of the Bethel A.M.E. church were used as an underground railway station during the Civil War. The old barn and early house are gone. The architect John Blythe, who designed and built the present structure, is responsible for changing the architectural style of the town from Greek Revival to Italian villa, including this house. *Location:* West Main Street near Seventh Street.

61K. Anawalt House was built prior to 1850, with a later addition about 1872. A former barn and house behind this property (now gone) were believed to have been used as an underground railway station during the Civil War. *Location:* Next to Longwell house on West Main Street.

61L. St. Paul's Episcopal Church (stone) was built during the Civil War era as a chapel, constructed by members of the congregation. The marble baptismal font is from St. Thomas (Old West) Episcopal Church. *Location:* Main section of town.

61M. First Methodist Church, built in 1864–73, was designed by a Philadelphia architect, Joseph C. Hoxie. John Blythe, then a young carpenter, was on the building committee. The original wooden steeple was removed in 1925 when the present belfry was constructed—reputed to be the closest to Pittsburgh of any full carillon outside the city. *Location:* Main section of town.

61N. Presbyterian Church, built in 1873 in neo-Gothic style, was designed by John Blythe (a patternbook-style architect). The congregation was founded in 1785. *Location:* Main section of town.

61O. Bethel African Methodist Episcopal Church (brick), designed in Norman Gothic style by John Blythe, was organized in 1834 by Samuel Clingman, the first pastor. The construction of the original building began in

1842. It was partly burned in 1849 and rebuilt in 1858. The present building, a handsome structure, was begun in 1871 and completed after 1882. It now serves as an educational facility for the black community. *Location:* 715 Chess Street.

61P. Hiker Monument was erected at the present post office in 1915, commemorating soldiers from Monongahela who fought in the Spanish-American War. It was placed at the site by the Col. Alexander Hawkins Encampment of the United Spanish War Veterans. The inscription reads: "Copyright 1904, Allen G. Neuman (sculptor)"; and on the reverse, "Jno. Williams., Inc., Founders, N.Y. 1915." It is the former site of a high school (1853). *Location:* Chess Street.

61Q. Monongahela Cemetery, established in 1863, was designed in part by John Chislett, a Pittsburgh architect and native of England. (See also *Allegheny Cemetery,* Allegheny County.) The chapel in this outstanding cemetery was designed by Frank Keller. The newer Catholic section was planned by Hare & Hare, designers of Arlington Cemetery in Washington, D.C. Here is located the mausoleum of John Barclay Finley, Monongahela millionaire banker. *Location:* SR 0088 near Monongahela Valley Country Club.

61R. Robinson Model Home (brick) was built in the 1930s by the Robinson family as a promotional project for their newspaper, inspired by the "Home of Tomorrow" at the 1939 World's Fair. R. H. Robinson was also a director of the First National Bank. The house was designed by Frederick G. Scheibler, Jr., "regarded as Pittsburgh's most distinctive regional architect." *Location:* 522 Fourth Avenue.

61S. Stewart House (brick), with three bays, was built in the early 1800s by Joel Butler whose family member, Benjamin Butler, had migrated from Chester County in 1805. The Butlers stayed at a local tavern and Benjamin became ill. A local man, professing to be a doctor, gave him a powder which turned out to be brick dust. Benjamin died but his family decided to settle here instead of continuing on to their destination. The Stewart family owned the house during most of the nineteenth century; and about 1885 a Second Empire mansard roof and Queen Anne stained glass windows were added. (Most of the present windows are original.) The house was moved from Main Street and altered about

1909 when it was threatened by the erection of a new bridge. *Location:* Off Fourth Street at 900 Lawrence Street.

61T. Keller House (brick), built in 1910, was designed by Frank P. Keller, whose children were pioneers in the movie industry in Hollywood. Keller apprenticed another local architect, George Yohe, who designed the Odelli Building on Third Street and West Main and the Stahlman Apartments on Marne Avenue and Seventh Street, among other buildings. *Location:* Lockhart Plan (Third Ward).

Note: The Lockhart Plan was laid out at the end of the Civil War with streets named for generals of that war. But building was not common until the turn of the century when the Alexander Heron families, a banking dynasty, started to build in this section.

61U. Bridge Abutment is the last remaining structure of a 900-foot-long covered bridge built in 1838 to replace the river ferry. The bridge burned in 1883.

61V. Aquatorium, the first theater of its kind in the state and one of the most unusual in Pennsylvania, was built in commemoration of the two hundredth anniversary of the Monongahela area. This 75-by-300-foot open-air stage was constructed over the Monongahela River and opened July 10, 1969, with a seating capacity of 3,500. It is the site of an annual July 4th fireworks display. *Location:* On SR 0837.

61W. James and John Blythe Houses were built in the 1870s. The one on the right was the residence of John Blythe, an architect and builder. The other later became a Christian Science Church. *Location:* Between Eighth and Ninth streets.

62. Campbell House (stone) was built by Robert Campbell in 1837–39. Before it was completed, Campbell was killed by a team of horses while working on his farm. His wife had the construction finished. Campbell's father John, a native of Ireland, bought this farm and Robert was born near here in 1790. *Location:* Near Finleyville, close to Mineral Beach, on SR 0088, 0.8 mile northwest of Hidden Valley Road.

63. Barr House (stone) was constructed by the Barr family in 1803 around a log cabin. *Location:* 2 miles south of Finleyville, on SR 0088 at Airport Road (T 834).

64. James Chapel Methodist Church (stone) was organized as Peter's Creek Methodist Episcopal Church in 1810. The congregation erected this building in 1817 on land donated by the James family (see *James House*), and stones for the building were quarried on the James property. In 1876 the interior was remodeled and stained glass windows installed. *Location:* Near Gastonville, on Stone Church Road. Go 1.5 miles northeast on SR 1008 from its junction in town with Elrama-Finleyville Road (SR 1006).

Note: Near the church is the site of Gabriel Cox's stockaded fort.

65. Holcroft-Story Home (stone) is better known for the original owner of the land than for the man who built this early residence. A log house formerly at this site belonged to John Holcroft, one of the most active insurrectionists of the Whiskey Rebellion and reputedly known as "Tom the Tinker." He bought this property, called "Liberty Hall," from Robert Henderson in 1795. Holcroft, who lived in the log house until 1818, had eight sons and eight daughters. T. Story purchased the property in 1832 and built the present house. A signature stone bears the date. *Location:* Near Finleyville, on SR 1006, 2.4 miles west of its junction with SR 0837 in Elrama.

66. Mingo Creek Presbyterian Church (brick) was organized by August 1786, but the congregation had no regular pastor until 1796. At this time Samuel Ralston was installed and served until 1836. The first meetinghouse was a log structure 50 by 55 feet erected before 1794. This was the meeting place of the Mingo Society, which was active in the Whiskey Rebellion. Opposing an excise tax, about forty men gathered at this church and went to Bower Hill to bring John Neville, the internal revenue inspector, back for punishment. James McFarlane was killed at Bower Hill and is buried in this cemetery (see *Ginger Hill House*), along with other insurrectionists who outlived the troubles (one was John Holcroft; see *Holcroft-Story Home*). The present church was built in 1831. A monument near its front marks the site of the log meetinghouse. *Location:* About 1.5 miles south of Finleyville, on SR 1061 at its junction with SR 0088.

67. Mineral Beach, a swimming pool originally filled with filtered mineral water, was built in 1925. The owner, Willis Abel, also has a large collection of steam engines preserved in a building nearby, where the Tri-State Historical Steam Engine Exhibition is held annually. *Location:* SR 0837.

68. Limetown Bend is the site of about forty early coal mines dating from the 1830s and 1840s, many of which are now part of Mathies Mine. It includes the Cincinnati Mine where 100 men were killed in a disaster in 1913. *Location:* SR 0837, between New Eagle and West Elizabeth.

69. Longwood Farms, covering 150 acres, includes an 1840 private residence and the Sumney log house, built in 1800. Restored by the Long family in recent years, the log house is furnished with period antiques, and the surrounding grounds are kept as they were in pioneer times, supplying herbs and wild greens to the present occupants, Mariana Long and her son Philip Long. The frame house, once a tavern, was built by "Dutch" John Kammerer. *Location:* Mingo Creek Park, Eighty Four, near Venetia, SR 0136 at Kammerer Road.

70. Ginger Hill House (ruins) was the home of James McFarlane, who was killed while carrying a flag of truce to the soldiers guarding John Neville's home at Bower Hill. When McFarlane was shot, the insurrectionists burned Neville's house. McFarlane's home at Ginger Hill, a landmark for many years and later owned by the George family who expanded it about 1900, was destroyed by fire in 1974. *Location:* Near Mingo Creek Park, junction of SR 0136 and Mansion Road.

71. Dusmal House (brick), a three-bay late Georgian house, is a variation of western Pennsylvania Post-Colonial architecture. *Location:* Gastonville (Union Township).

72. Gaston House (brick with cut-stone foundation), built by Samuel Gaston, is reputed to date from 1800, but its architectural design denotes a later time. John Gaston came from New Jersey and purchased a tract of land called "Belmont" from John Cox in 1790. Before his death he divided the property among his four sons. An 1807 mill stood below the house where a later mill, now a residence, is located. *Location:* Gastonville, junction of McChain and Stone Church roads (Union Township).

73. James House (cut stone) was built in 1800 by Robert James. In 1786 his father Richard had purchased land from Gabriel Cox on a tract called "Coxbury." In 1793 Richard James divided some of the land between

319

his sons Robert and William. Robert built a log house and later this stone one, where he lived until his death in 1834. The house, with exterior native chestnut trim, was used for seven years as a meeting place for Peter's Creek Methodist Episcopal Church (later James Chapel Methodist Church, q.v.). The James family donated the land for the church. Near the house is a stone smokehouse. *Location:* Near Gastonville, on Stone Church Road.

74. Wright House (brick), now a museum operated by the Peter's Creek Historical Society, was built with wings on both sides of a center section about 1815. Joshua Wright and his brother James came from Cumberland and settled on Peter's Creek about 1765, buying a tract of over one thousand acres. Joshua married Charity Sauns, daughter of John Harris, for whom Harrisburg was named. In 1776 he was one of the justices of the peace in Yohogania County and ex-officio judge of the court. In 1783 he was captured and burned at the stake by Indians. Enoch Wright, born at the homestead, participated in the 1794 Whiskey Rebellion. *Hours:* By appointment. *Location:* East edge of Venetia, on SR 1006.

75. Eighty Four, so named because the post office was founded there in 1884.

75A. Spring House is a family-owned farm and country store featuring fresh dairy products and home cooking. *Location:* SR 0136.

75B. Samuel Brownlee House (brick) was built in 1846. It has an impressive Greek Revival verandah. *Location:* SR 0519.

76. Pigeon Creek Church (brick), one of the oldest congregations in the region, was the first meeting place of the Redstone Presbytery, the first organized west of the Allegheny Mountains. Both this church and the Chartiers (Hill) Church (q.v.) were organized in 1776. According to legend James Power preached to the settlers on Pigeon Creek in 1774, and documented services were held there in 1775 by Dr. John McMillan, who served the congregation from 1776 to 1794. A log and then a stone church were used until 1829 when the third and present 56-by-70-foot structure was erected. The signature stone reads, "A.D. 1829." A porch was added later. *Location:* Near Eighty Four. Go east 2 miles on SR 0136 from its junction with SR 0519; turn south on SR 1055 and continue about 1 mile; turn left on Church Road.

77. Early Church Campgrounds, including small frame cottages, an outdoor worship center, and a covered pulpit area (all built in the 1860s), is now operated by the Union Holiness Association. *Location:* Bentleyville, SR 2030 across from Mary Street.

78. Newkirk Methodist Church (brick) was built about 1868 by John and James Blythe. Although a landmark for years, its original architecture has been destroyed. It is now a commercial building. *Location:* Near Bentleyville, junction of SR 0917 and I-70.

79. Ellsworth was founded in 1915 by James W. Ellsworth, a native of Chicago who had been a director of the Columbian Exposition in 1893. This model town's Georgian and Welsh-style miners' cottages had their prototypes in some of the best mining towns of Great Britain. Nearby are Cokeburg (with mine patch houses) and other mine towns, the results of the Pigeon Creek Branch Railroad. *Location:* SR 2019.

80. Stechers Old German Lutheran Church (log, covered) was built in 1784–87, a two-story structure with a loft. In 1800 Christopher Stecher sold this building and the land to the church, and twelve years later the first conference of the Lutheran church west of the Alleghenies was established here. A granite marker to the right of the old church relates this history. In 1846 a new (brick) church was built (see *Mt. Zion Church*). After the German ("Dutch") congregation moved to the new church, Frederick Cooper bought the log structure and converted it into a dwelling. The settlement around this church, once called "Weygandt's Choice," was made up of the following families: Stechers, Weygandts, Yohes, Coopers, Irwins, and Hamiltons. In 1986 the first three families held a reunion at this site, known in later years as the Locust Dairy Farm. *Location:* Near Bentleyville on Glades Road (SR 0136), off Crackerjack Road (SR 1067) at T 846; 1.2 miles from Mt. Zion Church.

81. Mt. Zion Church (brick), a one-story, Greek Revival structure, was built in 1846 on land donated by Christopher Stecher, across from his home, the property of which was purchased in 1781. The builder, Michael Yohe, added Victorian brackets to the eaves, which were criticized by early parishioners as being too ornate. *Location:* Corner of Crackerjack Road (SR 1067) and Ridge Road, 0.25 mile from SR 0917 near Ginger Hill.

80. *Stechers Old German Lutheran Church*

83A. *McMillan's Log Cabin School*

82. James Scott House (brick), built in 1842 with a signature stone on the gable end, has been completely restored inside and out. It has a two-column portico in front and H chimneys. A restored smokehouse is in the rear, and the Scott family cemetery is nearby. *Location:* North Strabane Township, 710 Waterdam Road (off US 19).

83. Canonsburg was named for John Canon, who founded it in 1787.

83A. McMillan's Log Cabin School, the oldest existing school building west of the Alleghenies and the forerunner of Jefferson College, was founded in 1785 by Dr. John McMillan. McMillan, who organized many of the churches in the region and was closely associated with Washington Academy, Washington College, Canonsburg Academy, and Jefferson College, first instructed a group of young men in Latin and Greek who had studied with Rev. Thaddeus Dodd and Rev. Joseph Smith until shortly after the academy was opened at Canonsburg. In 1895 the log cabin was moved to the grounds of the present Canonsburg Junior High School from its site at the McMillan farm, where a great oak still stands near the site of the old manse (go 0.4 mile on SR 1006—off US 19 at Hill Church—to road leading north; thence 2.3 miles on this road to farm and McMillan oak).

The old brick Jefferson College building is gone, but the noteworthy Franklin literary social room and the library of that structure have been restored inside the junior high school building behind the log school. Jefferson College began in 1794 as the Academy and Li-

brary Company of Canonsburg; a stone school building was erected in 1796 and chartered in 1802 as Jefferson Academy. Dr. McMillan was appointed president in 1798. In 1824 the college chartered Jefferson Medical College in Philadelphia. *Location:* College Street near North Central Street.

83B. Canonsburg Pottery Company (brick) was founded (as Canonsburg China Company) between 1899 and 1900 due to the abundant availability of coal and natural gas in this area. W. S. George, Jr., a pottery manufacturer from East Palestine, Ohio, supervised the construction of this building by Taylor and Crawford. *Location:* South edge of town.

83C. Roberts House (stone and brick) was built in 1804 by John Roberts, with later brick and stone additions. The Georgian house has a fanlight and pedimented doorway with fine woodwork on the interior. *Location:* 225 North Central Avenue.

83D. Morganza State Training School (brick) for disturbed boys and girls between the ages of ten and twenty-one opened in Allegheny County in 1854 as a reform school and was removed to Morganza, a farm named by Col. George Morgan, in 1876. The land was patented by Alexander and Matthew McConnell.

Colonel Morgan's house, now razed, was built in 1796 by John Morgan, his oldest son, and the colonel lived here until his death in 1810. He was an Indian agent during the Revolution and later was noted for his scientific work in farming. The home site is marked by a monument made from the foundation stones and erected in 1928. The former penal institution is now a school and mental hospital. *Location:* Near Canonsburg, on SR 0519 (0.2 mile northeast of roadside marker at east gate of industrial school).

84. John Hegarty House (fieldstone and frame) was built in 1805 with a later frame addition. *Location:* Edge of Houston, corner of East Pike Street and Fairmount Avenue.

85. Swearingen-Cook House (painted brick with H chimneys) was built on land originally purchased by Andrew Swearingen, a captain in McIntosh's campaign of 1778. It was later owned by his daughter Sally, who married John Cook. The old Cook family cemetery is near the house. The wife of Alfred Creigh, a Washington historian, is buried here. The house is now the Washington Country Clubhouse. *Location:* Near Meadow Lands, on Country Club Road (SR 1045) off Locust Road, at Washington Country Club (can be seen on hill from I-79).

86. Octagonal Barn (frame) was built in 1888 by Robert D. Wylie. *Location:* North of Washington, at Octagon Acres on west side of US 19, about 1 mile south of The Meadows racetrack.

Note: Next to this structure is a colonial brick house built in 1823.

87. Meadow Lands Harness Racing Museum, founded and operated by Albert and Delvin Miller, is housed in a Union Pacific business car and a Norfolk & Western caboose located on the grounds of the racetrack. Nearby is the Adios champion pacer monument (see *S. White's Sons Building*). *Location:* Near Washington, on Race Track Road (off US 19).

88. Linn House (brick), with H chimneys and a one-story portico of Greek Revival architecture, was built in 1848. *Location:* Near Washington, on Brehm Road (T 631), 0.7 mile off US 19 at Conklin Road, almost beside racetrack.

89. William M. Quail House (brick), with an unusual two-story portico for that period, was built in 1837 with H chimneys. It is now a restaurant. The Quail, Linn, and James Scott houses appear to have been designed by the same person. *Location:* Near Washington, at Quail Acres, on US 19 on Race Track Road (SR 1041).

90. Arden Trolley Museum

90. Arden Trolley Museum, located on the site of an original trolley line, was founded and is operated by the Pennsylvania Railway Museum Association. It features visual aids and conducted tours. Included in the museum is the famous trolley, the streetcar named "Desire" from New Orleans. *Hours:* July 4–Labor Day: 12 noon–5 P.M.; May, June, September: Weekends and holidays, 12 noon–5 P.M. *Admission charge for trolley rides. Location:* 2 miles from downtown Washington, in Arden Downs Industrial Park, on North Main Street extension. (The trolley line extends from the museum to county fairgrounds.)

91. Chartiers (Hill) Church (brick) dates from the time when Dr. John McMillan, on his first missionary tour of the West in 1775, preached at John McDowell's on Chartiers Creek. Dr. McMillan took charge of the Chartiers and the Pigeon Creek congregations in 1776 and served Chartiers until 1830. The first log church was built in 1778 and was used until 1800, when it was replaced by a stone structure, enlarged in 1832. The third and present church was erected in 1841 and remodeled in 1909, with a tower addition in 1912. Dr. McMillan and his wife are buried in the walled-in cemetery adjacent to the church. Woodrow Wilson's father was one of the pastors of this congregation. *Location:* Hill Church, on US 19 at junction of SR 0980 (5 miles northeast of Washington).

92. McConnell House (stone) was built by Alexander McConnell in 1805 and is still owned by the family. *Location:* Near Bishop. Take Muse Road (SR 1005) off SR 0050 in Bishop for 0.4 mile; then turn left on Hickory Grade Road (T 793) and continue 0.5 mile to house.

93. Millers Run Church (brick) was founded in 1793. The present church was built in 1835. An early cemetery is adjacent to it. The old manse is next to the church, which is only used for anniversary services. *Location:* Near Venice. At its junction with SR 0050, go south on SR 0980 for 0.7 mile; turn right on Swihart Dairy Road (T 771); thence 0.4 mile and church is on right.

94. Bigger House (cut stone) was built in 1848 by the Bigger family on the Glenlock tract. Thomas Bigger was the original property owner. For years it has been owned by a Thomas Bigger, of the same family, which has provided the only occupants of this house since its construction. The first Bigger-house, a log cabin, which Thomas found half-finished upon his arrival here from Philadelphia in 1774, was located nearby on Raccoon Creek. There is a later log house still standing on the property. *Location:* 0.9 mile from edge of Murdocksville, on SR 4002.

Note: Matthew Dillow's fort site, built in 1779, is somewhere in the vicinity of this property, in the fork of Dillow Run off SR 4002 just west of Murdocksville.

95. Seminary-Academy House (painted brick), built prior to 1832 on land owned by Philip Jackson, became Mrs. Lambden's Seminary in 1832. Between 1833 and 1848 the building housed an academy founded by Robert Fulton in 1832 in a log building on land that turned out to have a title defect. Fulton, a cousin of the famous steamboat builder, was a teacher in this school from 1832 to 1839. William Burton succeeded Fulton in 1839 and continued until 1848. The house was later purchased by the Thomas Moore family. *Location:* Florence, near corner of old US 22 and SR 0018 (between gasoline station and cemetery).

Note: This community was once called Bricelands Crossroads. Next to this house is the burial site of Elisha McCurdy, first pastor of Crossroads Church across the street, where the "Great Revival" began in 1802. A new church now stands on the site.

96. Raccoon Presbyterian Church (brick) dates from Dr. John McMillan's first visit to the Raccoon Creek settlement in 1778. In his journal Dr. McMillan recorded that he preached at Raccoon also in 1779, 1780, 1782, and 1785. The first regular pastor was Joseph Patterson, who served from 1789 to 1816. The congregation's first house of worship was a rough-log meetinghouse built in 1781. This was followed by a hewn-log church of 1785, a brick church of 1830, and the present structure, built in 1872–73. The early pews and original pipe organ have been preserved inside the church. In the front churchyard, about one hundred yards southeast of the church, is the site of Beelor's blockhouse, built by Capt. Samuel Beelor, who came to this region around 1774. On his second trip to Raccoon Creek, Dr. McMillan preached at this blockhouse. *Location:* Candor, on SR 4009, which leads off US 22 near Allegheny-Washington County line.

Note: An early log house, now covered with siding, is next to the Fort Beelor site at a spring.

97. Cross Creek village

97A. Cross Creek Presbyterian Church (brick) was organized in June 1779 by Dr. John McMillan. James Power preached the first sermon under an oak tree at nearby Vance's Fort in 1778. Joseph Smith served as the first pastor from 1779 to 1792. There have been five churches here: the first of unhewn logs (1781), one of hewn logs (1784), the third of stone (1803), an 1830 brick structure, and the present one built in 1864. A cemetery is across the road. *Location:* Main Street (SR 4029).

97B. Vance House (brick) was erected in 1830 by Col. Joseph Vance, builder of Vance's Fort (site on Ridge Road, one mile north of Cross Creek Presbyterian Church, q.v.). The house has always been a private residence. *Location:* Main Street (SR 4029) next to Cross Creek Church.

97C. Wilkin-Stockton House (brick) was built in 1821 by David Wilkin, who sold the property in 1827 to John Stockton, minister of the Cross Creek Presbyterian Church. Dr. Stockton kept bachelor's hall in this house for about two years. Later he married, and his five sons and one daughter were born in the home. Stockton lived here until his death in 1882. At the turn of the century, William H. Allen bought the house, which is one of the oldest in the area. At one time it was considerably larger than it is now. *Location:* Main Street (SR 4029) near church and across from cemetery.

98. Russell House (brick), built in 1875 by Andrew Russell, was called Mt. Pleasant Valley Farm. Alexander Russell was an early settler, and William M. Russell was the last of that family to live in this house, which overlooks the reservoir. The Russells were breeders of

Durham cattle, hogs, and sheep. *Location:* About 2.5 miles north of Hickory, on SR 4015 at Cherry Valley Reservoir.

99. Langeloth Zinc Mine Town was built by the American Zinc and Chemical Co., a subsidiary of American Metal (AMAX), over the great Pittsburgh coal seam, a ready source of fuel. It began operating in 1914 and closed in 1947. Immigrant labor came mostly from Eastern and Southern Europe, Spain, and Cuba. The zinc ore originated in the Midwest, then came from South America. Once having Hegeler-type furnaces, the site is now an industrial ruin in the vicinity of occupied company houses (sold at a later date to private owners). The company town was named for Jacob Langeloth, chairman of American Metal. (Donora's zinc plant, no longer running, began two years after Langeloth.) *Location:* Langeloth, south of Burgettstown.

100. Hickory, named for a local hickory tree landmark.

100A. Johnson House (log), one of the oldest houses in the area, was owned in 1876 by M. Johnson. Once covered with siding, it was recently restored by the McChesney family. *Location:* SR 0050 across from post office.

100B. Hickory Academy (frame) was built late in 1892. It was an academy for ten years and later the Hickory High School. At present it is a plumbing store. The stage of the school is still intact inside the rear part of the building. *Location:* SR 0050.

100C. McElroy House (frame), with large columns in the front, was the home and office of Dr. J. McElroy in 1876 and is at present an antique shop. *Location:* SR 0050.

100D. Kline House (brick), with a large front porch, was owned by W. H. Kline in 1876. It was later purchased by Jacob Stewart about 1900. It is at the supposed site of the hickory tree from which the town acquired its name. *Location:* SR 0050 and Washington Avenue.

101. Shady Elms Farm, a restored colonial mansion, is now a bed and breakfast inn. *Location:* 3 miles from Hickory (4 miles from Cross Creek Lake Park).

102. Meadowcroft Village, opened in 1969, was developed by Albert and Delvin Miller on their old farm property originally settled by their great-great-grandfather, George Miller,

102. Schoolhouse at Meadowcroft Village

Sr., in 1795. The original patent dating back to the 1780s was a Virginia grant. The land, now comprising more than eight hundred acres, had been since the early 1880s a harness and racehorse farm, where many champion trotters and pacers were bred.

The name "Meadowcroft" is derived from a combination of Meadow Lands (formerly Delvin Miller's horse farm) and Bancroft Farm (the original Miller holdings). Operated as an educational and historical museum by the Meadowcroft Foundation, a nonprofit corporation, this early nineteenth-century village started with the Miller schoolhouse built about 1834, the Miller log house of 1795, and a 100-year-old covered bridge. It has grown to include more than thirty structures, many of which house permanent exhibits.

A University of Pittsburgh archeology team uncovered at Meadowcroft Village the earliest documented evidence of inhabitants in the eastern United States dating back to about 16,225 B.C. *Hours:* May 1–October 31: Wednesday–Saturday, 10 A.M.–5 P.M.; Sunday, 1–6 P.M. Closed Monday and Tuesday. *Admission charge. Location:* 3 miles west of Avella, on SR 0050.

103. Cross Creek Valley Wool Mill is the only mill in Pennsylvania using traditional methods for processing wool. Tours by appointment. *Location:* Avella.

324

104. Patterson's Mill House (painted brick) was built in 1820 by W. J. Patterson. Gen. Thomas Patterson built a mill on land purchased from his father William in 1793–94. Thomas enlarged his business in 1812 by building a fulling mill. (The mill scars can be detected along Cross Creek near this house.) He was also a member of Congress (1817–25) and a member of the electoral college (1816). Materials from the stone ancestral home of the Pattersons, built in 1794 on a hill above the mill, have been used to build another house in Ligonier (Westmoreland County). The barn was relocated at Meadowcroft Village (q.v.). *Location:* About 1 mile northeast of Avella, on SR 0231.

Note: A later brick house built in 1838 by T. M. Patterson, grandson of Gen. Thomas Patterson, has been restored. It is on a dirt road 0.5 mile north of SR 4029 at the west end of Cedar Grove. Another early brick house, built by Robert Perrine, is in Cedar Grove.

105. Independence

105A. Old Independence Hotel (brick) was built in 1803 and is the oldest building in the village, which was laid out the same year and originally called Williamsburg. *Location:* SR 0844.

Note: This community has many old log (covered) and brick houses.

105B. Plumer House (brick) was built in 1831 by Jerome Plumer, a prosperous farmer. (The date was discovered on a locally fired brick from the house.) The DiPietro family bought the house in 1930. *Location:* On SR 0844 near old hotel on opposite side of street.

Note: Another of Plumer's houses, a log structure built in the early 1800s, is visible off SR 0844.

106. West Middletown, once active in the underground railroad, is a charming community of early historic buildings too numerous for most to be listed. Miraculously just about every dwelling on the picturesque main street has been preserved in its original exterior condition. The community is worth visiting if only to stroll along its sidewalks and see the quaint structures. Laid out in 1796, the town became a borough in 1823. (Robert Fulton, of steamboat fame, owned land in this area, on which his mother and sister lived.)

106A. The McKeever Study (frame polygon) is a reconstructed copy of the original one erected at Pleasant Hill Seminary by and for Thomas Campbell McKeever during the 1860s. McKeever was a grandson of Thomas Campbell, nephew of Alexander Campbell, and son of Matthew and Jane Campbell McKeever, founders of the seminary about 1845. Thomas became the first teacher in the seminary and later took over the job of principal, which his mother had held. This building is an almost exact replica of the original study, which was patterned after the study of Alexander Campbell at Bethany, W.Va., and was moved to West Middletown following the close of the seminary. In the 1930s it was torn down. The present structure, erected under the sponsorship of the borough council, was built by Rea Dunkle and Homer Denning, among others, and now houses historical and genealogical records as well as a circulating library. The center is a good source of information about the historic buildings in West Middletown. *Location:* West Main Street (SR 0844).

106B. McKeever House (brick) was built prior to the Civil War by Thomas Campbell McKeever, who, in addition to being a seminary teacher and principal, was a justice of the peace, associate county judge, noted abolitionist, early associate of John Brown, and a leader of the underground railroad. His home has been used as a hat factory, a store, a post office, and a community club. It was purchased in recent years by the King family. *Location:* Main Street, across from post office and down street.

106C. Old McClure Log House is believed to be the oldest log house in West Middletown. At the time of its construction people from miles around came to see a two-story house being built. James Hardy had a blacksmith shop on the property, and from 1860 to about 1876 it was the home of Robert B. McClure, who operated a machine shop (which stood next to the house) for the manufacture of threshing machines, an invention of Andrew Ralston of Hopewell Township in 1842. About five hundred machines were produced here until 1859 when many farmers went bankrupt because of a disastrous frost and McClure's business was ruined. That year he had shipped a large number of machines to St. Louis, but they rusted on the wharf since there was no demand for them. *Location:* 61 Main Street (SR 0844), next to Ralston Thresher historical marker.

106D. First Christian Church (brick) dates back to about 1830 when members of the Disciples group began worshiping in a McKeever school at the east end of town, with formal organization taking place in 1837 at Pleasant Hill Seminary. The original Disciples church at Brush Run was organized in 1811 several miles southeast of here. The present building was erected in 1848. (The congregation sold it in 1861 and erected another church, which stands one-half mile east of this point.) The older building is now used for commercial purposes. Alexander Campbell, founder of Bethany College in W.Va., was ordained here. *Location:* Main Street, not far from Ralston Thresher historical marker.

106E. Henderson House (brick), erected in 1798, is the oldest brick building in town. In the 1850s and 1860s it was occupied by T. Lane who had a chair factory here with a horse-driven lathe. It became the home of Milton Hemphill, who served as deputy sheriff, and later was owned by the Henderson family. *Location:* 43 East Main Street.

106F. McNulty-France Hotel (frame) was built in 1804. From 1856 to 1861 W. W. McNulty conducted a hotel here. Later R. M. Garrett operated the establishment. Prior to his death in 1929 John D. France operated it. In 1903 Samuel Ferguson, a contractor for the Wabash Railroad, lived at the France Hotel. Funeral services were conducted here for him after he was murdered at the foot of Seminary Hill that same year. A brick addition to the building is believed to have been built by Samuel Urie. The building is now a residence and antique shop owned by William Huston. *Location:* Main Street.

106G. Lindsey Hotel (frame), the first in town, was built by James Lindsey in 1801 and at one time was the finest tavern between Baltimore and the Ohio River. Traveling circuses at various times were on exhibit at this drovers' tavern. Here Henry Clay and Philip Doddridge debated the issue of the proposed National Road. *Location:* Main Street, next to France Hotel antique shop.

106H. African Methodist Episcopal Church (frame) was built about 1860 by a Wesleyan Methodist congregation on the former site of a blacksmith shop owned by J. W. Smith. The A.M.E. church had met in the old Doddridge chapel located about three miles west of town. When the Wesleyan Methodist congregation disbanded, the A.M.E. took over its building. *Location:* Main Street.

106I. Grove United Presbyterian Church (brick) was built in 1859. Samuel Taggart, who lived in a stone house in West Middle-town, was pastor of this church for fifty years. *Location:* Main Street.

106J. Stewart House (brick), an outstanding residence, was built in 1859–60 by Galbraith Stewart. *Location:* 1 West Main Street.

106K. Armour House (log covered with siding) was built in the early 1800s. It is situated on a bank next to a soldier's and sailor's monument at the west end of town. *Location:* Main Street.

107. Tucker Church (stone) was built in 1824 on land owned and set aside for the church by John Tucker. Stonemasons named Minesingers constructed this building for less than ninety dollars. The congregation first met in the home of James Holmes. In 1965 an addition was built on the front from stones taken from the foundation of the old Cross Roads Church that was destroyed by fire and replaced by a brick structure. *Location:* Halfway between Paris and Florence, on old US 22, 2 miles west of SR 0018.

108. Tucker House (stone) reportedly was built by Wesley Tucker, son of Jonathan II. Pioneers, John and Henrietta Tucker, came to Hanover Township in 1775, raising their children on a tract called "Grace." Their first son, Jonathan, was born in Fort Vance ten miles away during an Indian raid. John Tucker was a Quaker and a leader of Methodism in the area (see *Tucker Church*). He died in 1830 at the age of one hundred. Both he and his wife are buried in the church cemetery. A depression in the ground marks the original log cabin, and the frame Mansion House built by John Tucker in 1825 (now covered with siding) is nearby. *Location:* 1.8 miles west of Florence, turn north 0.2 mile on unmarked road off old US 22, east of Tucker Church.

Note: Another stone house in the area is the Black house on T 352, 1.7 miles off US 22 northwest of Tucker Church. The Hanlin-Phillips stone house is on T 853 near its junction with T 350. Also in this area is the King's Creek Cemetery which has been restored in recent years (on T 867 north of Tucker Church).

109. Livingston House (stone), a long one-story structure, was built on the old James Livingston farm. This early house served as a Boy Scout cabin in later years. *Location:* 1.4 miles south of Florence. Turn off US 22 on Harmon Creek Coal Road for 2.3 miles. House can be seen from I-70, 1.5 miles east of Florence interchange.

110. Paris

110A. McCabe Store (frame) was built prior to the Civil War and was operated by James C. McCabe in 1856 when he moved his business here from Florence. McCabe dealt extensively in wool and other farm items. The old ledger from this store has been preserved in the market across the street (formerly the Seceder Church, q.v.). This long building, covered with shingles, has been converted into apartments. *Location:* Off old US 22, across from market.

110B. Seceder Church (brick) was built in 1843–44 on the Pittsburgh-Steubenville Pike. In 1858 this denomination merged with the Associate Reformed church, and the building was used as a house of worship until 1927. In 1931 the Longs bought the church and converted it into a grocery store. *Location:* Across road from McCabe store.

111. Wallace House (stone and brick) was obviously a tavern, but little is remembered about this remarkable structure. It has probably been in its present form since 1830. The stone section of the house has a fine arched doorway with a fanlighted entranceway. The home was owned a century ago by J. Harper Wallace and was later purchased by Michael Pollock. *Location:* About 1 mile north of Florence, on SR 0018 at Purdy Road (SR 4003).

112. Standish House (cut stone) marks the area where in 1793 Levi Dungan, first settler in the county, obtained a patent for 306 acres, naming it Turkey Plains. A later owner, Henry Hayes, sold the land in 1823 to Miles Standish (reputed descendant of the Mayflower immigrant), who built the house on the property. *Location:* From SR 0018, 3.1 miles south of Frankfort Springs, turn west on Purdy Road (SR 4003) 4 miles; turn right across small bridge at creek 0.1 mile; make sharp left on unmarked road for 0.5 mile.

113. Ramsey House (cut stone), sometimes referred to as the "still house," was erected by Miles Standish (see *Standish House*). It is reputed that a still was operated in the attic. The heirs of Lee Ramsey, who was born in the house, sold it to Mrs. Bea Carmody, who has had the house restored. There is another smaller stone building on this property. *Location:* 5.7 miles northwest of Florence, on Purdy Road (SR 4003) at Little Brook Farm.

114. Freshwater House (brick) was built about 1811 with a double front porch and a

116. Plantation Plenty

large fireplace in the basement. *Location:* Across Irwin Road from Ramsey house.

115. Cross House (stone) was constructed in 1832 by James Cross, whose family came from Ireland in 1793, settling on 300 acres of land called Haywood. This house, which replaced a log home, was built on the property with stones hauled from the Levi Standish farm. Susannah Cross, the granddaughter of James Cross, lived in the house until 1913. After standing vacant for eighteen years, the house was bought by James Sutherin, who planted honeysuckle vines around it. Started from sprouts in the woods, these vines now cover much of the house. *Location:* From Freshwater house go 0.9 mile on Irwin Road to unmarked road. Turn right 0.7 mile.

116. Plantation Plenty (brick), the ancestral home of the Manchesters, was finished in 1815 by Isaac Manchester. While he was traveling to Kentucky from his home in Newport, R.I., in 1796, he came across this land and liked it so much that he brought his family to settle here. Manchester purchased a 380-acre tract of land, originally called "Plenty," from Capt. Samuel Teeter and built a home of post-Colonial architecture, similar to houses in Newport. The interior, trimmed in native black cherry, was completed by an experienced cabinetmaker whom Manchester brought from Philadelphia. This beautiful mansion, in its original condition with a captain's walk, window shutters, and classic doorway, is the private residence of the great-great-grandson of Isaac Manchester. In the front yard of the house is the site of Samuel Teeter's fort. Teeter, a relative of John Doddridge, had come to the area after 1773 and took up this tract of land patented in 1785 and situated off the old Buffalo Trail. There are numerous outbuildings on the property including a smokehouse, a workshop, a spring-house, and a barn built in 1803. *Location:* West of West Middletown, on SR 0844, 0.6 mile northeast of its junction with SR 0231.

117. Upper Buffalo Presbyterian Church (brick) was organized in 1779, with Joseph Smith the first pastor, serving from 1780 to 1792. Smith, who is buried in the cemetery, founded an academy of languages and sciences in 1785. Among those who received their training there were John Brice, James McGready, James Hughes, Samuel Porter, and Joseph Patterson. The first two churches were log, one built in 1779, which stood in the northwest corner of the present cemetery, and the other in 1798. The third and present building was constructed in 1872. *Location:* Buffalo, one square south of SR 0844.

118. Buffalo Associate Presbyterian Church (brick), now the North Buffalo United Presbyterian Church, was founded in 1775 with Matthew Henderson the first pastor in 1782. It was one of the oldest congregations of this sect in the county. Another early minister was Thomas Campbell, father of Alexander Campbell, who founded Bethany College in West Virginia. The first hewn-log church was built in 1811, at the time the members divided into the North and South Buffalo congregations. It served the North Buffalo Associate group until 1848, when the present brick church was erected. It was remodeled and enlarged in 1896. *Location:* 1.8 miles west of Wolfdale. Turn south off SR 0844 onto SR 4055 for 0.6 mile to SR 4024; thence west 0.5 mile.

Previous Sites Now Lost

Harrison House, burned
Hickory Associate Presbyterian Church, demolished
Hickory Hotel, demolished
Irwin House, demolished
Keys Hotel, demolished
Samuel Ross House (near Glyde), demolished

Covered Bridges

Bailey Bridge over Ten Mile Creek, SR 2020, Amwell Township
Brownlee Bridge over Wheeling Creek, T 414, East Finley Township
Crawford Bridge over Wheeling Creek, SR 3037, West Finley Township
Danley Bridge over Wheeling Creek, T 379, West Finley Township
Davis Bridge (1889) over Ten Mile Creek, T 325, West Bethlehem Township to Morgan Township, Greene County
Day Bridge over Short Creek, T 339, Morris Township
Ebenezer Bridge over Maple Street, SR 1016, Fallowfield Township
Erskine Bridge over Middle Wheeling Creek, T 314, West Finley Township
Hawkins (Rainey) Bridge (ca. 1890) over Ten Mile Creek, Deemston to Morgan Township, Greene County
Henry Bridge across Mingo Creek, T 822, Nottingham Township
Hughes Bridge over Ten Mile Creek, SR 2020, Amwell Township
Jackson Mill Bridge over Kings Creek, T 853, Hanover Township
Krepps Bridge over Raccoon Creek, T 799, Mt. Pleasant Township
Leatherman Bridge over Pigeon Creek, T 449 North Bethlehem Township
Longdon Bridge over Wheeling Creek, T 414, West Finley Township
Lyle Bridge over Raccoon Creek, T 861, Hanover Township
McClurg Bridge over Kings Creek, T 346, Hanover Township
Martins Mills Bridge over Ten Mile Creek, T 323, Amwell Township
Mays Bridge over Middle Wheeling Creek, T 423, Donegal Township
Pine Bank Bridge, moved to Meadowcroft Village, Avella
Plants Bridge over Wheeling Creek, T 408, East Finley Township
Ralston Bridge (1915) over Kings Creek, T 352, Hanover Township
Sawhill Bridge (1915) over Buffalo Creek, T 426, Blaine Township
Sprowls Bridge over Wheeling Creek, T 450, East Finley Township
Wilson Bridge over Cross Creek, T 486, Cross Creek to Hopewell Township
Wright Bridge over Pigeon Creek, T 802, Somerset Township
Wyit Sprowls Bridge over Wheeling Creek, T 360, West Finley Township

Note: The Washington County Covered Bridge Festival is held annually during the third week of September.

Pennsylvania Historical and Museum Commission Markers

Augusta Town US 40, 3 miles southwest of Washington

Bradford House Washington, at property, 175 South Main Street (2 markers)

Capt. Philo McGiffin Washington, US 40, Main and Beau streets

Col. George Morgan SR 0519 south of Morganza

Cross Creek Church Cross Creek, SR 4029

David Reed Venice, north of SR 0050, Brown's Orchard

Doddridge's Fort SR 0844, 2.5 miles west of West Middletown

Edward Acheson Washington, southwest corner of Main and Maiden streets

Elisha McCurdy Florence, US 22

Gantz Oil Well Washington, West Chestnut Street at Brookside Avenue

George Washington Venice, SR 0050, Brown's Orchard

Globe Inn Washington, 155 South Main Street

Hill Church US 19, 5 miles northeast of Washington at Hill Church

Hill's Tavern Scenery Hill, US 40

James G. Blaine West Brownsville, 238 Main Street

John McMillan US 19, 5 miles northeast of Washington

Le Moyne Crematory Washington, SR 2001 South Main Street

Le Moyne House Washington, 49 East Maiden Street

McGugin Gas Well SR 0018 northwest of Washington

Miller's Blockhouse US 40, 3.5 miles west of Claysville

Monongahela On main highways leading into city

The Mounds Monongahela, Memorial Park, Mound and Decker streets

National Road US 40 southeast of Washington near Scenery Hill; US 40, 3.6 miles southwest of Washington; and US 40 west of Claysville

Ralston Thresher West Middletown, SR 0844

Rice's Fort US 40, 3.5 miles west of Claysville

S-Bridge US 40, 5 miles southwest of Washington

Washington On main highways leading into city

Washington and Jefferson College Washington: East Maiden Street at gateway; East Beau Street opposite gymnasium; and College Avenue at main entrance

Washington County Washington, at courthouse, South Main and West Beau streets

Whiskey Point Monongahela, SR 0481 at Park Avenue

William McGuffey Claysville, intersection of US 40 and SR 0231

Wolff's Fort US 40, 3.3 miles southwest of Washington

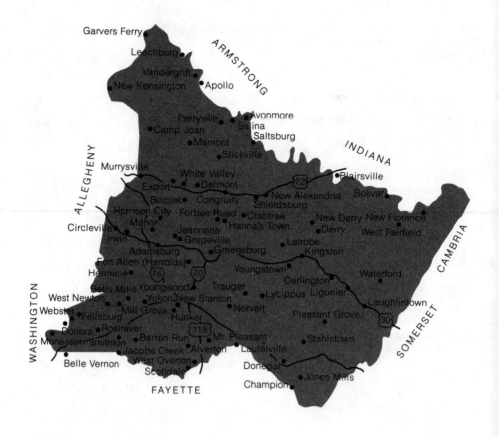

Westmoreland County

Capsule History

Westmoreland, the eleventh and last county founded by the colony, was the first English-speaking one in the nation established west of the Allegheny Mountains. "Land of the western moors," named for a county in England, it was called "star of the west" by eastern politicians in the 1800s. More often referred to as "mother of the western counties," it embraced all the land west of Laurel Mountain. Its original area, erected from Bedford County on February 26, 1773, comprised the counties which are now Westmoreland, Greene, Fayette, and Washington together with parts of Alle-

330

gheny, Armstrong, Beaver, and Indiana. Today the county has 1,033 square miles (the same land area as Rhode Island) and a population of 392,184.

The military road cut by Brig. Gen. John Forbes in 1758 became a well-worn highway, following the general course now taken by US 30. Many Indian trails and trader paths traversed the county. The *Catawba Path* ran from New Florence past Fort Palmer, Ligonier, Pleasant Grove, Stahlstown, and Acme, exiting near Laurelville. The *Glades Path* ran almost along the course of present-day SR 0031 by Acme, Mt. Pleasant, and West Newton. *Nemacolin's Path* entered east of Prittstown, passing through or near Mt. Pleasant, Hunker, and Madison, and exited on a ridge near Greenock. It was followed by Braddock on most of his way through Westmoreland County. The *Raystown Path* followed approximately the course of the Lincoln Highway (US 30) in this area, passing Laughlintown, Big Bottom, St. Vincent's (College), Luxor, Hannastown, Harrison City, and Trafford. Forbes swung northward after passing present-day Forbes Road, turning south of Export, and passing along the ridge near Murrysville. The *Salt Lick Path* left the Catawba Path near Laurelville, following the Glades to Mt. Pleasant and Braddock's Road to Hunker. The *Sewickley Old Town Path* joined two Indian towns of the same name, one near West Newton, the other near New Kensington. It passed Trafford, New Texas, and Logans Ferry.

In 1763 Col. Henry Bouquet and his troops defeated the Indians at Bushy Run, thus raising the siege of Fort Pitt and checking attacks on British posts and settlements during Pontiac's Rebellion. From 1777 to the end of the Revolutionary War, the militia of Westmoreland County manned a chain of many forts and blockhouses from Fort Reed on the Allegheny to Fort Ligonier at the western base of Laurel Ridge on the banks of the Loyalhanna Creek, which had been the depot for Brig. Gen. John Forbes's expedition against Fort Duquesne in 1758.

Hanna's Town (historic village not to be confused with nearby Hannastown mining town) became the first county seat in 1773. Courts were held here until Greensburg, originally called Newton (New Town) but later named for Revolutionary War hero Nathanael Greene, took the honor. On May 16, 1775, the settlers of Hanna's Town drew up resolves somewhat similar to the Declaration of Independence, which was written the following year, and formed the Westmoreland County Association and the First Battalion under Col. John Proctor, whose regiment in the Revolution carried the famous rattlesnake flag with the motto "Don't Tread on Me" (preserved in the state museum at Harrisburg). In 1782 the settlement was destroyed by the Seneca Indians.

Among the noteworthy people in the early days of the county were Gen. Arthur St. Clair, president of the Continental Congress and governor of the Northwest Territory; Henry Clay Frick (1849–1919), who made the manufacture of coke a large-scale industry in the county; William Freame Johnston (1808–72), eleventh governor of Pennsylvania, from 1848 to 1852; John White Geary (1819–73), sixteenth governor of Pennsylvania, from 1867 to 1873; Frederick Pershing, an ancestor of Gen. John J. Pershing, who settled on a tract called Coventry in 1769; and Erskine Ramsey, a noted steelmaker.

Flax-scutching, an early pioneer method for preparing flax for linen, has been revived at an annual festival (since 1907) at Stahlstown, first settled by Leonard Stahl. Other early products of the county included iron, bituminous coal, coke, glass, salt, and gas. Westmoreland had sixteen stone blast furnaces, with Westmoreland furnace (1792) the first in the county and the third west of the Alleghenies.

Today New Kensington, the largest city in the county, is one of the most extensive producers of aluminum in the world, while Arnold and Jeannette have large window-glass plants. Mt. Pleasant and Grapeville are noted for glass manufacture, and Monessen is important for iron and steel. Latrobe is widely known in industry as the "tool steel capital," and here are manufactured some of the world's largest casting molds. It is the home of golf pro Arnold Palmer and also the site of the world's first all-pro football team of 1897.

Landmarks

1. Greensburg and environs. Greensburg was laid out as a town in 1782, incorporated as a borough in 1799, and became a city in 1926–28. It was sometimes called Truby's Town for the pioneer Christopher Truby.

1A. Courthouse (stone) was erected in 1906–08 in French Renaissance style. After the county seat was moved from its location in Robert Hanna's log tavern at Hanna's Town, another log courthouse was built in Greensburg. The first court was held at the new county seat January 7, 1787. This structure was replaced by a brick building in 1798. In 1854–56 the third courthouse in Greensburg was built, a stone Roman-porticoed building that looked like a temple. The bell from the brick building of 1798, later placed in the old jail tower, has been preserved by the county historical society. *Location:* North Main Street.

1B. Westmoreland Museum of Art (brick) is located in a Georgian-style building with a large columned portico. It opened in 1959, the gift of Mary Marchand Woods, the widow of Cyrus Woods, who was minister to Portugal and ambassador to Spain and Japan. The museum's permanent collection has a concentration on American art, with an emphasis on Pennsylvania, and more specifically, works from the southwestern area of the state. Throughout the year there are frequent special exhibitions as well as a concert, lecture, and film series. It also has an extensive antique toy collection which is featured during each Christmas season. *Hours:* Sunday, 1–5 P.M;. Tuesday–Saturday, 10–5 P.M. Closed Mondays and holidays. *Location:* 221 North Main Street.
Note: Westmoreland County Historical Society (located at the Greensburg Garden Center, 951 Old Salem road) exhibits local historical displays and includes a research and genealogical library. *Hours:* Tuesday–Friday, 9 A.M.–5 P.M.; Saturday, 10 A.M.–1 P.M.

1A. Courthouse

1C. Brown House (brick), built about 1896 by Samuel Brown, is a fine late Victorian–Queen Anne house having a tower with a finial-topped cone. It has always been owned by the Brown family whose ancestors came to Greensburg in the late 1700s. (See also *Sindorf-Brown House.*) *Location:* 402 North Main Street.

1D. Masonic Temple (brick, stone facade), with Corinthian capitals on its columns, ornamental brackets, and egg-and-dart cornice molding, has a High Venetian Renaissance facade. Masonic symbols are integrated in the plan of the structure. This early Italianate structure was built about 1872 with a matching fourth floor added in 1896. Stained glass windows are in the rear. *Location:* 132–34 South Main Street.

1E. Coulter House (brick), in late Second Empire style with a mansard roof, was built in 1881 by the Coulters, an early Greensburg family, and was later used as a library. *Location:* 249 South Main and Third streets (northeast corner).
Note: at 331 South Main Street at Fourth Street is the A. E. Troutman house. Troutman's Department Store was built after 1918 at 200 South Main Street. (See also *Troutman House,* Butler County.)

1F. Merchants and Farmers National Bank (stone) was built in the late 1800s. It was chartered in 1881. Lewis Trauger was the first president; W. H Markel, vice-president; and D. W. Shryock, cashier. *Location:* 39 North Main Street.

1G. (Most Holy) Blessed Sacrament Catholic Church (stone) was built in 1925–28. The architects were Comes, Perry, and McMullen of Pittsburgh. This English Gothic-style church has a modern-day addition. The windows were made by Franz Maier and Co. of Munich, Germany. Stations of the Cross were carved by Anton Schmitt of Cologne. *Location:* 300 North Main Street.

Note: To the right of the church is the brick parochial school built in 1904.

1H. First Presbyterian Church (granite with sandstone trim), built in 1916–19, was designed by Ralph Adams Cram (and Ferguson). Several windows were by Charles J. Connick. The church was founded in 1788; its first minister was William Speer. The Sunday school, founded in 1816, was one of the first organized west of the Alleghenies. The present church, with a 1966 addition, is in adapted early English Gothic style. *Location:* 300 South Main Street.

1I. Tribune Review Building (concrete block), on property originally the estate of Congressman George F. Huff, was designed by the architect Louis Kahn, of Philadelphia. The newspaper began publication here in 1961. *Location:* North Main Street at Cabin Hill Drive.

1J. YWCA Building (brick), in Jeffersonian neoclassical style with Ionic columns and a large portico, was built in 1900 for the William A. Huff family. The architect was Ralph Adams Cram (1863–1942). It included a freestanding spiral staircase. A porte-cochere was added later. The house was also owned by the John M. Horn family. In 1970 it was donated to the YWCA by Katherine Huff Horn. In 1910 the smaller building behind it was moved from across the street at 419 North Main Street to its present site (12 O'Hara Street) by the Huff family for their daughter as a wedding gift. Former owners were the Armstrong family. In 1975 the mansion was sold to the YWCA for a program building. *Location:* North Main and O'Hara streets.

1K. Otterbein Evangelical United Brethren Church (stone and brick), in neoclassical style with a polygonal interior and central dome, was built in 1908. (The first church was built in 1857 followed by another in 1881.) The present church (United Methodist) was designed by Winkler & McDonald of Pittsburgh. Prior to a YMCA or a Boy Scout program in the community, this church had its own gymnasium and Boys' Brigade. *Location:* West Otterman Street and College Avenue.

1L. Kinderhook, in German meaning "children's corner," is a historic district originally settled by Germans. The houses are mostly frame Victorian in style. One house (at East Fourth Street and Maple Avenue) is the last original log house remaining in the downtown area of Greensburg. There are two fine brick Victorian houses at the entrance (South Maple Avenue at South Main Street). *Location:* South Maple Avenue.

1M. St. Clair Theater (brick), built by George W. Good, opened in 1903 with the German character comedian John W. Ransome playing in *The Prisoner of Pilsen.* It originally seated 1600 with a large orchestra section, balcony, and gallery. This was the site of silent movies, "talkies," and other entertainment until a fire in 1915. It later served as a garage for the Westmoreland Motor Car Co. It is now an office building. *Location:* 218 Maple Avenue.

1N. St. Clair Monument marks the site where Maj. Gen. Arthur St. Clair and his wife Phoebe Bayard are buried, having died within eighteen days of each other. St. Clair (1734–1818) was a lieutenant in the Sixtieth Royal American Regiment in 1759, commander at Fort Ligonier from 1767 to 1769, major general in the Revolution in 1777 (the only officer from Westmoreland County who attained this rank during the war), president of the Continental Congress in 1787, first governor of the Northwest Territory in 1789, and commander of the U.S. Army at the battle of the Wabash in 1791. In 1832 the Masonic Society of Greensburg erected a sandstone monument over the double grave; it was replaced with a granite one in 1913. (See also *Fort Ligonier* and *Arthur St. Clair Homes.*) In this cemetery (incorporated in 1856) is also the site of the first Presbyterian church organized in Greensburg in 1788 and built in 1816. A monument with an engraved picture of the church stands at the site. A reconstructed log structure today represents the early schoolhouse/church (German Lutheran and Reformed, ca. 1783). It was dedicated in this park in 1976. *Location:* St. Clair Park, Maple Avenue and Otterman Street.

1O. Seton Hill College was founded by the Sisters of Charity, mainly through the efforts of Mother Aloysia Lowe, who procured the 200-acre Jennings farm August 7, 1882. Seton Hill remained the motherhouse until 1969 when nearby Ennis Hall became the novitiate and convent. (Ennis Hall on Mt. Thor Road was once the stone mansion of Henry Coulter. Another old brick mansion, once the Margaret Coulter house, is on the same road.)

On this property St. Joseph's Academy (1883–89), St. Mary's Preparatory School for boys (1889–1927), a conservatory of music, and an art school were located at various times. In 1889 the present administration building was erected. Seton Hill became a junior college in 1914 and was chartered in 1918 as a four-year liberal arts college. In 1975 Mother Elizabeth Seton (1774–1821), founder of the order of Sisters of Charity at Emmitsburg, Md., in 1809, became the first American-born saint.

The Stokes House (brick), which housed the academy and preparatory school and presently is the home economics department, was the former home of Col. William A. Stokes, chief counsel for the Pennsylvania Railroad. (This land was claimed in 1784 by Ludwig Otterman, and it remained in his family until George Otterman sold it in 1817. Stokes acquired title in 1850 and sold it to John Jennings in 1868.) In 1853, Andrew Carnegie, who at the time was a seventeen-year-old telegraph operator for the Pennsylvania Railroad, visited this home and was so impressed by Major Stokes's private library that he was inspired not only to have one of his own but to build public institutions as well. Carnegie later donated more than two thousand libraries to communities across the country. *Location:* College Avenue.

1P. Hawksworth House (brick) was built by the Hawk family a few years after receiving a 1790 land grant. This family was the sole possessor of the property until 1955 when the Roy Barclays purchased it and redesigned the interior in French, German, and English decor. *Location:* North side of Greensburg, at 111 Hawksworth Drive off Main Street.

1Q. Coulter Mansion (stone) was built by Gen. Richard Coulter, who served in the Spanish American War and World Wars I and II. His father, Gen. Richard Coulter, Sr., was an officer in both the Mexican and Civil wars. The elder Coulter's uncle, Richard Coulter (1789–1852), was an eloquent orator and first of three members of the Westmoreland County bar who became justices of the Supreme Court of Pennsylvania. Now owned by the Roman Catholic Diocese of Greensburg, the building is a convent, the Regina Coeli Missionary Cenacle. *Location:* College Avenue near Hawksworth Drive.

1R. Kepple House (brick) was built between 1799 and 1807 on the Kepple farm later owned by the Rughs. In the front yard of this property is the site of the Kepple blockhouse erected in 1774, where some of the settlers fled during the 1782 attack on Hanna's Town by the Indians and British. An account written by historian George Dallas Albert describes the incident as follows:

> Across the country, at a little block-house, the remains of which are still to be seen about a mile and a half north of Greensburg on the Salem road, lived Kepple, a brother-in-law of Michael Rugh, Sr. Kepple was in the field with his team, his dog running towards him, frisking and barking with all signs of fear, and the sound of the far-off crack of the guns made him on the instant strip the gear from his horses and hasten back to the house, built for war and peace, and barricade the openings.

Some of the logs from this blockhouse were later used in the construction of a corn crib on the property. In more recent years the house was purchased by the Dom family. *Location:* North of Greensburg, off SR 0066, 135 Locust Valley Road.

1S. West Penn Trolley Freight Station (buff brick) was built in the 1920s. Constructed in typical railway architecture, with overhanging eaves, this building, owned by the city, used to house the Firemen's Museum. (Their firefighting memorabilia are now in storage and a new location for a more permanent museum is needed.) *Location:* Pennsylvania Avenue, behind City Hall on Main Street.

Note: Nearby City Hall used to be the West Penn Passenger Station. Later the local office for West Penn Power, it was built in 1927. An addition was erected in the late 1980s.

1T. Pollins House (frame) and barn represent the only rural farm complex remaining in the city. The house has a mansard roof with a wrought iron "captain's walk" decor. It was built in the late 1800s and has been in the John Pollins family for many years. *Location:* 319 Pennsylvania Avenue at Fourth Street.

1U. Pennsylvania Railroad Station (brick), built in 1909–12 in French Renaissance style, has a fine Jacobean clock tower. The archi-

1U. Pennsylvania Railroad Station

tect was William H. Cookman. (When he was seventeen, Andrew Carnegie worked as a telegraph operator at an earlier building at this site.) There are plans to readapt this fine landmark for other usage. *Location:* Pennsylvania Avenue, at the tracks.

Note: An early railroad freight station (red brick), now owned by Conrail, is located on Depot Street at North Washington Avenue.

1V. Palace Theater (brick), originally the Rialto, owned by Michael Manos, was rebuilt in 1926–27 by the Manos family. This was a center for vaudeville, big bands, and eventually motion pictures. The Manos family sold the building to RKO of Hollywood, which in turn sold it to the Cinemette chain of Pittsburgh (in 1930 it was sold to Warner Brothers' studios). It continued as a movie house until 1970. In 1976 Carl Marinelli purchased and restored it. It is one of the few theaters in the area providing live entertainment, including the Westmoreland Symphony Orchestra and is worthy of preservation. (It is at the site of the 1899 Victorian house of Dr. H. G. Lomison and later Tavern Hotel.) *Location:* Courthouse Square, Otterman Street and Pennsylvania Avenue.

1W. Rialto Tavern and Stark Block (brick complex). The original building at the corner was erected by William Barnes, a noted innkeeper, in 1796. This was a well-known wagon stand between Philadelphia and Pitts-

burgh, built of stone (rebuilt of brick in 1889). It was later owned by John Stark, who manufactured the first stagecoaches west of the Allegheny Mountains, according to tradition. Stark also built Dearborn wagons here. His son, C. H. Stark, learned the trades of silver plating and carriage building, and was appointed by the U.S. government as wagon inspector for Pittsburgh. In 1888 he constructed one of the finest brick business blocks in the town. Stark Block is adjacent to the old wagon stand site which again is an inn, known as Rialto's (owned by the Montuori family for over fifty-five years). *Location:* 25 West Otterman Street at Pennsylvania Avenue.

1X. Cope Hotel and Building (brick). The earlier section is on the site of the former log Grant house, bought by Cyrus P. Cope, a cattle dealer, in 1884. He became the proprietor of this public house with the dining room in the rear and the bar at the upper left side. The Cope Hotel was expanded in 1893 when Cope removed the right side of the building and erected what is known as the Cope Building (brick and stone), in Richardsonian style. Its five stories and turret tower over the three-story adjacent building. *Location:* West Pittsburgh Street and Pennsylvania Avenue.

1Y. Germano's and The Baggy Knee restaurants (brick) occupy a fine Italianate commercial building with eyebrow windows, built in the late 1800s. Once Teddy O'Keefe's, it continues to serve as a public house. Another Victorian brick building, at the corner to the right of Germano's, is the B.P.O.E. (Elks) Lodge, erected at about the same time. *Location:* 9 East Pittsburgh Street (B.P.O.E. at corner of East Pittsburgh Street and Maple Avenue).

1Z. Jamison Mansion, once called "East Gate" for the nearby tollhouse, is on property owned by the coal operator Robert S. Jamison (1835–1903) in 1872. It was originally part of the Philip Kuhns farm and the old stone Eicher tavern (now gone) where Robert's son, John M. Jamison, and his family lived while their house was being built. This brick mansion was purchased by the Roman Catholic Diocese of Greensburg in 1957. The carriage house in the rear is the newspaper and communications office for the diocese. To the left of this house is another brick Jamison residence, now painted white. John M. Jamison built it for his mother, Mrs. John Jamison, but she died before it was completed, around 1913. It was finished by the Robertshaw family and later owned by T. Lynch III. This residence and its carriage house in the rear are now apartments and an office building, respectively. *Location:* 711–23 East Pittsburgh Street (diocese house to the right of it).

1AA. Tollhouse Inn (stone) was the David Eicher house built in 1827. David's son, Henry Reed Eicher, used the sand bank at this site as a source for his sand company. This house along the old Greensburg-Stoystown Turnpike was constructed within a mile of one of the original tollhouses and has for years been associated with the early Peter Eicher tavern (see *Jamison Mansion*). In recent years, with stone additions, this house has been converted into apartments, offices, and now a restaurant. *Location:* US 30, just east of Davis Market and David Weis store, at Tollhouse Apartments.

1BB. Stoneybrooke (stone), originally "Melrose Farm," was built in 1895 by Henry Clay Buchman. (A stone in the chimney reads "Melrose Inn—1899.") Originally the land belonged to William Jack, followed by Andrew Row(e), (see *Rowe House*). Joseph Coulter Head purchased the property in 1910, followed by L. J. Fierst in 1956. During Prohibition, Head, after he had retired as president of the Latrobe First National Bank, hid 20,000 bottles of bourbon in a bank vault in his basement, with access through a trap door in the living room. The house has forty-seven rooms

1AA. Tollhouse Inn

and the carriage house, which once housed servants, has twenty-three rooms. In recent years a 300-year-old oak was struck by lightning; it is believed to have shaded Indians meeting at this site. The estate was purchased by Patrick McArdle who converted the mansion into an inn (now adapted for other use). *Location:* Unity Township, east of Greensburg at the top of a long winding lane off US 30 near the Hempfield Township line.

Note: On the lane leading to the house is the Yeneral barn, an outstanding structure, beside a stone house.

1CC. Rowe House (brick), reputed to have been a tavern, was built on the old McCausland farm and purchased in 1872 by Andrew Rowe, who came from Germany and operated a blanket mill. His granddaughter later lived here. *Location:* About 2.3 miles east of Greensburg on old US 30, 0.4 mile east from its junction with new US 30 (near Greendale Drive and early brick schoolhouse).

1DD. Hough-Crissinger House (fieldstone), dating back to the early 1800s or before, is a noteworthy landmark in the area and an important link to the area's pioneer history. It was formerly owned by Polly Hough and later by the Crissinger family. *Location:* About 2.3 miles east of downtown Greensburg on old US 30, 0.4 mile east from its junction with new US 30 (near Greendale Drive.)

1EE. Hillview One-Room Schoolhouse (brick, originally frame), once a neighborhood school, now serves as Laurel Design Center and Art Gallery. The building was erected in the late 1800s. It is owned and operated by Mary Ann and Joe Cigich. *Location:* About 0.5 mile east of Westmoreland Mall, old US 30 near Greendale Drive.

1HH. Old Republic Insurance Co., on T. Lynch Estate

1FF. Alex Fletcher Memorial Art Center (brick). This one-story, 30-by-45-foot structure was built in 1883 as the Todd Schoolhouse on land donated by Frank Shearer. It was constructed by J. F. Sinlord, and the building committee consisted of M. G. Blank, David Highberger, and a Mr. Long. Its first teachers were W. N. Stahl and J. A. Zundel. The building was purchased in 1955 at public auction and became the home of the Greensburg Art Club, organized in 1935 with Alex Fletcher as its first president. (Its forerunner was the Kinderhook Art Club, 1929). *Location:* Todd School Road and Fernway Drive, outskirts of Greensburg, off US 30 east.

1GG. Overly Mansion (stone) was built in 1904 and at one time was a nursing home. The owner, William Fisher Overly, was the founder of an architectural sheet metal works on Depot Street. *Location:* West Newton and Spring Streets.

1HH. T. Lynch Estate (brick) is situated on property which in 1887 consisted of a block belonging to F. Y. Clopper, the Greensburg Seminary, and Thomas Lynch, in about equal portions. Thomas Lynch (1854–1914) built his first house here in 1888–89, the present apartment house south of the Georgian mansion. The larger Georgian house, erected by Lynch in 1905, is occupied by the Old Republic Insurance Co. Architects were Rutan & Russell of Pittsburgh. Henry Schenke & Co. of

Erie was the contractor. A Tiffany window depicting Lynch's homestead in Ireland was added to the original design. The stable was converted to a garage in 1910. The Lynch heirs sold the property to the Coal Operators Casualty Co. in 1945. *Location:* 414 West Pittsburgh Street, at Seminary Avenue.

1II. Burrell-Brunot-Fogg House (brick) was built about 1840 by Judge Jeremiah Burrell. This Greek Revival-Victorian home also belonged to Hilary J. Brunot (founder of the *Daily and Weekly Press*—one of the country's leading papers in 1883). The house was later purchased by Joseph B. Fogg whose father, Charles H. Fogg, and W. W. Jamison founded a civil and mining engineering company in Greensburg. *Location:* 133 Morey Place.

1JJ. Mt. Odin Park was once the estate of Dr. Frank Cowan (1844–1905), Westmoreland County's eccentric genius who was a lawyer, medical doctor, horticulturist, scientist, author, poet, scholar, printer, and editor of a journal which he called *Frank Cowan's Paper.* An extensive world traveler, he served as secretary to a U.S. Senate committee, as a private secretary to President Andrew Johnson, and as county district attorney. Interested in Norse tradition and mythology, he gave his estate and everything involved with it Norse names, such as Mt. Odin. He loved trees and plants and had 2,000 different varieties planted on his property, together with over 220 kinds of grapevines. Cowan wanted to be buried in a Viking boat, burned with quicklime, but his wish was thwarted. However, one of his dreams did come true. To the citizens of Greensburg he willed Mt. Odin Park "for the sole and exclusive use of the people thereof and adjacent boroughs, as a place for play, recreation and social enjoyment." Today the park is a public golf course. The log cabin on the property was moved from downtown Greensburg to this site (former Williams house). The great stone pillars at the entrance to the park are reproductions of the original ones which Cowan had built with round tops, symbolic of the two hemispheres and in keeping with the Egyptian rules of proportion. *Location:* On old US 30, at top of Grapeville Ridge about 1.3 miles west of center of town.

1KK. C. M. Lynch House (brick), in English Tudor style, was built in 1923 with a 1929 addition on a former dairy farm. The house was designed by Paul A. Bartholomew and Brandon Smith. It was called "Starboard Light." the owner, Charles McKenna Lynch (1884–1963) was a graduate of the U.S. Naval Academy in Annapolis, Md. Lynch helped establish the Pittsburgh brokerage firm of Moore, Leonard and Lynch (now Paine Webber). The Home, called Lynch Hall since 1964, houses the administration offices of the University of Pittsburgh's Greensburg campus. *Location:* Mt. Pleasant Road near Greensburg and US 30 bypass.

Note: At the entrance to the campus is the home of Mary Quinn (C. M. Lynch's daughter), a 1940 Sears, Roebuck house of historical significance.

1LL. Lynch Homestead (log) is an outstanding landmark, well preserved. It belonged to the prominent Lynch family. One member, Thomas (see *T. Lynch Estate*) was active in the coke business, and his son Charles (see *C. M. Lynch House*) was a partner in a Pittsburgh brokerage. *Location:* Near Lynch Hall (University of Pittsburgh Campus, Greensburg), on Airport Road not far from Mt. Pleasant Road.

Note: There are also noteworthy McKenna houses from the Latrobe and Kennametal steel family. One is at St. Joseph's Hall on US 30 in Unity Township near the Hempfield Township line, and the other is now the senior citizen (McKenna) center near the Greensburg Garden and Civic Center on Old Salem Road (old PA 66).

1MM. White Horse Tavern (frame). This old wagon tavern later served as a candy factory and is now once again a tavern. It has been in the Logan family for many years. *Location:* 528 Mt. Pleasant Road.

2. Kelly and Jones Company, purchased by the Walworth Company of Boston in 1925, was established in 1887–89 with 300 employees. At one time this world-renowned company made valves, fillings, and equipment for handling steam, liquids, and chemicals. The Stilson wrench was invented at this site, according to report. Although most of the original buildings were razed in recent years, one structure, now an office building, remains *Location:* South Greensburg, US 119.

3. Fishel (Fishell) House (log and stone) was erected by Henry Fishel, a carpenter who constructed the log section in 1817 and the first stone part in 1830. In 1936 another stone addition was erected. This home was later purchased by the Wakefield Murray family. *Location:* Near Greensburg, on SR 0130, 1 mile southeast of US 30 (Hempfield Township).

4. White Stone House (stone and log), now Springhill Country Furniture and Gifts, was built of log before 1782 with a later addition of stone by the White brothers. During the attack by the Indians on Hanna's Town, these men helped rescue the settlers in the fort. A group of neighbors rode their horses back and forth over a bridge to deceive the Indians into believing there were many troops arriving during the night. (See *Hanna's Town.*)

In more recent years the Charles Cunningham family bought the house, which had fallen into disrepair, and has completely restored it. During the remodeling a note from an indentured servant was found concealed behind a stone in an interior wall, and a door with the date 1776 was discovered under many layers of paint. *Hours:* Monday–Saturday, 10 A.M.–5 P.M. (Friday to 8 P.M.) *Location:* Just east of Greensburg turn off US 30 onto SR 0130 and go 3 miles toward Pleasant Unity (2 miles beyond Fishel house).

5. Shaffer House (log) was built before 1859 with a later log addition. The parlor and two bedrooms were the original home. In 1903 Margaret Shaffer willed the property to the George Schaeffer family. William Haines purchased it in 1959 and restored the house. *Location:* 4.5 miles east of Greensburg, 0.5 mile off Mt. Pleasant Road on SR 2015.

6. Frans House (stone) was built in 1796 by Jacob Frans, according to the signature stone in the gable end of the house. Although its interior has been modernized, the house still retains the original plank floors. The basement, once used for a barn, has a large double door. At present this dwelling is the home of the country club greens keeper. *Location:* Greensburg, on old Jeannette Road at Greensburg Country Club.

7. Lefevre Log Cabin is believed to have been built in the 1760s by the Andrew Byerly family. (Andrew Byerly ran the earliest tavern on the old Forbes Road near Bushy Run Battlefield.) In later years this two-section log structure was owned by the Croushure family, followed by J. Rappe Myers, proprietor of the General Greene Hotel (a National Register landmark in Greensburg, now demolished). The log house was Myers's summer estate where he raised vegetables and flowers for his city hotel and where he kept horses and carriages for the hotel trade. As a young man, while in Europe, Myers was inspired by a thirty-five-room stone villa in Florence, Italy, which he copied in miniature for his carriage house (now garage) on his log-cabin property. It is over 100 years old, unusual architecture for this country at that time. In 1941 Ernest and Thelma Lefevre bought the estate and it is still owned by this family. Both the log cabin and stone villa used to have thatched roofs. The stone springhouse at this location was built from the remains of the old flour mill at the village of Bouquet. The millstone forms the step for the structure. *Location:* Pleasant Valley Road, SR 4002, Hempfield Township (property borders SR 0130), near Greensburg Country Club.

Note: Nearby, near the junction of Pleasant Valley Road and North Greengate Road, is another early log house (in the bend of the road).

8. Alwine School House (painted brick), named for the Samuel Alwine family, was built in 1874 and still has the original bell in its belfry. The first classes were taught by Lawrence Strump at the Shuster home until this school was erected. Bell Young was the first teacher in the new building. In 1949 it was incorporated as the Alwine Community Civic Association. It is located on the old Forbes Road. *Location:* From SR 0066, 3.2 miles north of Locust Valley Road (near Greensburg), turn east onto old SR 0066 and continue 0.2 mile to right. School can be seen from new SR 0066.

9. Bair (Bierer) House (brick) was built in 1838 by Frank Bair, who was from an old German family. Signature stones are in the gable ends of the house. A fine brick barn is also on the property. The house was later purchased by the Heinnickel family. This area has yielded an abundance of Indian artifacts. *Location:* Near old Hanna's Town, junction of US 119 and SR 1032.

10. Steele (Steel) House (brick) was built in 1861 by William Steel. The structure retains its original woodwork and has had few alterations. A rose-glass entranceway is directly across from the stairway where seven brides of this family have descended to be married at various times. The property, still owned by the Steels, includes a brick complex consisting of a springhouse, smokehouse, and various other structures. A fine stone stile is in the front yard. *Location:* Near Hannastown, junction of SR 1055 and Fire Station Road.

Note: Other early Steel houses are on this road also.

11. St. Walburga Wayside Chapel (glass and frame), dedicated in 1974, was designed by architect Francis Church at St. Emma's Convent. Incorporated in its walls are twelve stained glass windows depicting the life of the Benedictine nun and missionary, St. Walburga, patron of the order's motherhouse in Eichstaett, Bavaria. Over fifty years ago St. Walburga's Roman Catholic Church (German) at the corner of Lincoln and Campania avenues in Pittsburgh was constructed with these windows, made in Munich. When the parish was dissolved, the church was sold to a Baptist congregation. At that time the windows were dismantled and sent here to be used in the walls of this star-shaped chapel as a gift of Bishop Leonard of Pittsburgh. (St. Emma's, built in 1931 next to where the chapel now stands, was originally John Robertshaw's residence. It was bought by the Sisters in 1943 after Emma, the young daughter of this family, had died, and was named in her honor. The property itself dates back to a land deed of 1789 and was first owned by John Brownlee.) *Location:* Northeast of Greensburg, on Five Points Road (SR 0819) near Glenmeade Drive.

12. Kepple-Rial House (log) was built about 1812. The remains of a stone barn foundation contain a cornerstone that reads, "J S 1847." Behind the home is a stone springhouse. The property, once owned by the Kepple and Rial families, was later purchased by Matthew Doyle, followed by Jack Zaharias. *Location:*

Northwest of Greensburg, junction of Stony Springs Road and SR 1022.

13. Ringle House (stone) was built in 1797 and is the oldest structure in the area. *Location:* Madison, near junction of SR 3016 and SR 0136.

Note: Nemetz Barn (frame, altered) is situated on the early property of Mathias Ringle (see *St. James Reformed Church,* near Salina). Ringle had bought the land from J. Cavett in 1797. Upon Ringle's death in 1811, John Kintigh acquired the property. He willed it, in 1889 to his stepson, Thomas B. Brown, a horse dealer. The brick house at the site was said to have been "the finest in Westmoreland County" at one time. In 1941 Jozsef A. Nemetz purchased this site. In recent years he converted the barn into a restaurant. *Location:* Madison, at the crossroads of PA 0136.

14. Old Tavern (stone) is a survivor of the early inns of western Pennsylvania. This nineteenth-century building continues to serve as a public house. *Location:* Arona, SR 0136.

15. Old Zion Lutheran Church (brick), the first church of this denomination organized west of the Allegheny Mountains, was erected in 1884. At first this congregation and St. John's (below) worshiped in the same church. Balthasar Meyer, the schoolmaster, had baptized children as early as 1772, since the congregation did not have a pastor at that time. A log schoolhouse, built that year, had been its original place of worship. The Pittsburgh Synod of the Evangelical Lutheran Church erected a monument on the site of the log schoolhouse to celebrate the one hundred fiftieth anniversary of the congregation. The marker stands in the cemetery, directly across the road from this church, which is now the Hempfield Township Maintenance Building. *Location:* Harrolds area, 0.2 mile south of SR 0136 on SR 3097 in Fort Allen School district (about 3 miles southwest of Greensburg).

16. St. John's Evangelical and Reformed Church (brick) is one of this denomination's oldest congregations in western Pennsylvania. In 1783 Rev. John William Weber (see *Milliron Church*) organized this church and also the Brush Creek–Salem church (q.v.). Originally, this Reformed congregation and the Old Zion Lutheran congregation held joint ownership of the building, but today they are separate churches, with cemeteries, beside each other.

17. Courthouse-Tavern at Hanna's Town

The first Reformed church building was erected in 1829. Its cornerstone is now located in the present structure, built in 1892, which is now the United Church of Christ. In the front churchyard stands a monument erected by the Pennsylvania Historical and Museum Commission in memory of the German settlers from Harrolds who petitioned for the erection of a fort in 1774 at the time of Indian attacks. The actual fort site is marked by another monument about 150 yards to the south of the church. *Location:* Next to Old Zion Lutheran Church.

17. Hanna's Town, the first county seat from 1773 to 1787, held its first court April 6, 1773, at the house of Robert Hanna, who kept a log tavern on the Forbes Road. During Dunmore's War over the Virginia-Pennsylvania boundary in 1774, Arthur St. Clair recommended the erection of a fort here. John Connolly, an agent of the governor of Virginia, who had stirred up trouble between the Indians and Pennsylvania settlers, was arrested and put in jail in Hanna's Town. Instead of appearing for trial after being released on bail, he became the leader of 150 Virginia militiamen and returned, barring the Pennsylvanians from entering their own courthouse.

Hanna's Town became the principal outpost for defense in 1776 when Kittanning was abandoned. On July 13, 1782, the village was attacked by a party of Seneca Indians and British rangers—one of the last border raids of the Revolution. At this time Peggy Shaw, a young girl, lost her life rescuing a child. The town was burned, all except the fort and two houses. The Indians also attacked Miller's blockhouse several miles away. Joseph Brownlee was captured at this time; and while the Indians were taking the prisoners from Miller's to Canada, he and his child were tomahawked. A lone marker on a hillside farm indicates the place where they were buried (off US 119 near its junction with Luxor-Bovard Road). Some histories read "John" instead of "Joseph." Hanna's Town, which had consisted of nearly thirty dwellings, was never rebuilt.

The Steel family, which bought the land in 1826, sold 183 acres to the county in 1969, when the restoration project of the Westmoreland County Historical Society began with archeological excavations under the direction of Jacob Grimm, curator of Fort Ligonier (q.v.). In 1973 during the county's bicentennial the log courthouse-tavern was rebuilt by contractor Carl Schultz. Reconstruction of the stockaded fort and storehouse was completed in 1976 at its exact site (69 by 122 feet). In 1986 the Klingensmith House was completed. This was an 1802 log structure moved from Armstrong County. An original Conestoga wagon, used to transport whiskey in the 1794 Whiskey Rebellion, is also on display. *Hours:* Summer: Tuesday–Sunday, 1–5 P.M.; Spring and Fall: Saturday and Sunday, 1–5 P.M. Closed in winter. Tours given by costumed hostesses and hosts. A field museum is also open to the public. *Admission charge. Location:* Hanna's Town, about 3 miles northeast of Greensburg, junction of SR 1055 and SR 1032 (Forbes Road).

18. Hannastown Coal Patch once contained 500 brick beehive coke ovens, built about 1860 or before. They were closed down with the development of modern by-product coke production. The ovens have been dismantled, but the company houses remain. *Location:* Hannastown, off US 119, northeast of Greensburg.

19. Humes House (stone and log) is an early structure on Crabtree Creek. In 1867 T. Humes owned the property, which was occupied by D. McGowan by 1876. In more recent years it was purchased by Charles Urcheck. This house is located in the area of the Cook stone house where Judge Thomas Mellon lived as a boy with his parents and grandparents when first coming from Ireland. The mines of the area probably demolished the old Captain Cook homestead. *Location:* Old Crabtree, SR 1022 near SR 1032 (Unity Township).

20. Oliver Perry Smith House (brick) was built about 1850. It has been restored by the J. H. Malkames family. *Location:* Near village of Forbes Road, on SR 0819 near Carasea Drive.

21. Ross House (stone), built by Thomas Alexander Ross in 1832, has remained in this family for at least seven generations. Alexander Ross died in 1873, at age eighty-three. His wife Elizabeth died in 1846, at age fifty-four. They are buried in St. Clair Park, Greensburg. *Location:* Near old Hanna's Town, off US 119, 2.3 miles on SR 1032 (about 3 miles northeast of Greensburg).

22. Sindorf-Brown House (brick) was built by George Sindorf in 1850. This L-shaped building has a double porch and original interior woodwork, and is a fine example of Asher Benjamin architecture. At a later date William Brown, a Greensburg druggist, acquired the property, consisting of about 127 acres, from Lucinda Sindorf Ehrle. After it had changed hands several more times during the coal-mining era, George Barnhart sold the house (which had been owned by W. R. Barnhart in 1876) and much of the land to Stowell Mears, who refurbished the exterior in 1959. The restored brick springhouse is now a tack shop. In recent years the old log tavern from Jones Mill was rebuilt by the Amish as a residence above this property. *Location:* Northeast of Greensburg, on US 119, 0.5 mile from SR 1028.

23. Blank Farmhouse (brick with shutters) was built before 1850 by the Blank family. In 1876 J. Blank, Sr., owned the property. The woodwork in this pre–Civil War home is all original. A third floor was added in 1890, and several porch additions were built in 1920. This farm was the site of the first Westmoreland Hunt Steeplechase in October 1926 (later the Rolling Rock races at Ligonier). The Weidlein family purchased this house from the McNareys in 1919. It is now called "Huntland Farm" and serves as a bed and breakfast inn. *Location:* Northeast of Greensburg, on US 119 at SR 1028.

24. Crabtree Beehive Coke Ovens are located in this mining town, which was laid out about 1890. These ovens were discontinued about 1932. The area is honeycombed by coal-mine tunnels, with the entry at Hannastown several miles west. *Location:* Turn south on US 119 at Crabtree, near fire hall, and go 0.8 mile; turn left across bridge and go 0.2 mile to remains of ovens.

Note: Company-owned houses and the large frame company store, later Neilson's general store, can be seen from US 22 just west of New Alexandria.

25. New Alexandria, once known as Denniston's Town, was laid out by Alexander Denniston. Its first post office was established in 1804, and it became a borough in 1834. Numerous early structures are located here.

25A. Gallagher Store and House (both brick) were built in the 1840s by J. E. Gallagher. His first store, which connects the long store building and the adjacent house, was erected earlier. The house has an interesting metal signature plate on its front near the roof. A bell tower, since removed, used to grace the store. Gallagher Hall, where dances, concerts, and other entertainment took place, was located on the top floor of this store. *Location:* On Main Street across from bank.

25B. Turnbull House (frame) was the former home of Agnes Sligh Turnbull, well-known western Pennsylvania novelist who wrote, among other works, *The Day Must Dawn* and *The Rolling Years* which concern the area where she grew up. The house later became a private convalescent home. *Location:* On Church Street across from New Alexandria Presbyterian Church (q.v.).

25C. New Alexandria Presbyterian Church (brick) was organized in 1837 with Adam Torrance serving as first pastor until he took a fourteen-and-a-half-month leave of absence to serve as chaplain during the Civil War. The present church, now Community Presbyterian, was built in 1858. Gen. Arthur St. Clair's daughter Jane Jarvis, who lived in a log house in New Alexandria, is buried in this church cemetery. *Location:* On Church Street.

Note: Adam Torrance's brick house is on U.S. 22 just west of New Alexandria and situated on a bank overlooking the highway.

26. Craig House (brick) was built by Gen. Alexander Craig (1755–1832) who married Jane Clark. "A. Craig" is inscribed on a stone at the foot of the front steps of this home. In 1793 Craig purchased the farm on Loyalhanna Creek from Samuel Wallace, who had bought it from Loveday Allen in 1769. An early barn at this site burned in 1974. Craig was commissioned lieutenant colonel of the state militia in 1793, and brigadier general in 1807 and again in 1811. Samuel Craig, Sr., and his three eldest sons, John, Alexander, and Samuel, all served in the Revolution. (The father, Samuel, was killed while defending the Pennsylvania border. He had served with Washington in the 1777 campaign.) This family

preserved the original rattlesnake flag of Col. John Proctor's battalion. In 1914 it was presented to the state and is in the museum at Harrisburg. *Location:* Near Shieldsburg, across east side of creek from New Alexandria Presbyterian Church (near private Craig cemetery).

27. Alter's Halfway House (log with weatherboards) was built during the 1830s as a tavern halfway between Johnstown and Pittsburgh, overlooking Spruce Run and situated on the Northern Pike. The first known proprietor was Jacob Alter of Berlin, Pa., who in 1829 also built the Henry Hotel (run by John Henry for a number of years at the corner of East Market and Brady streets in Blairsville). "Jockey" McLaughlin also kept a tavern at this halfway house. Jacob Alter, Jr., lived in the house during the 1890s, when it became known as "Alter's Voting Precinct." Some think it may have served as a tollhouse. This rare landmark is in need of preservation. *Location:* Between Blairsville and New Alexandria, on US 22 on hillside (4.6 miles east of junction of US 22 and SR 0981 at New Alexandria).

28. Simpson-Giffen Stone House Tavern, once called "The Stone Jug," was built on the old Northern Pike, possibly as a stagecoach tavern, about 1820. Stagecoaches operated along this road between Pittsburgh and Philadelphia as early as 1805. In 1866 Joseph Simpson purchased the property. His granddaughter Mrs. John E. Giffen operated a tearoom in this house in the early 1920s and later an antique showroom. Her ancestor Dorcas Miller was taken captive during the Hanna's Town (q.v.) raid of 1782. *Location:* Just east of New Alexandria, 1.4 miles east from junction of US 22 and SR 0981. House is situated on old US 22 but can be seen from new US 22.

29. Stoney Run Ferry House (painted brick) was built about 1802. It is reputed to have been a ferry hotel near the Conemaugh River at one time. In 1840 the Burkley family purchased the property. In later years, a descendant, Dr. George Burkley, owned this house and restored it. In recent years it was converted into a convalescent home. *Location:* On old US 22 along Stoney Creek. Just west of US 22 bridge before reaching Blairsville exit, turn northeast. House is 0.1 mile from present US 22.

30. Baird House (stone), with a signature stone on the right front side, was built in 1834 by William Baird, brother of James Baird who founded the village of Bairdstown on the west side of the Conemaugh River across from Blairsville (in Indiana County). *Location:* On SR 0016 just west of bridge at Blairsville between Indiana County and Westmoreland County.

31. Pennsylvania Canal Tunnel and Aqueduct (stone), western division, were completed in 1829. The 412-foot aqueduct with elliptical stone arches spanned the Conemaugh River on the western side of the tunnel, which was cut through limestone. The tunnel was 817 feet long, 22 feet wide, and 14 feet high. Its builders were Alonzo Stewart, Hart Stewart, and Thompson Neel. It was the third canal tunnel in the United States, built before any railroad tunnel in the nation. Due to danger of falling rocks, a Gothic stone arched ceiling was added to the tunnel in 1831. The tunnel has been closed since the dam was built, for it would have drained the reservoir. *Location:* About 1.5 miles up Conemaugh River from Tunnelton at Conemaugh Dam, near former railroad bridge now used as access road. (From US 22 take SR 1029.) Western portal is visible at foot of hillside and in line with remnants of aqueduct piers in water. Eastern portal is accessible over old Pennslyvania Railroad bed only at times when water in dam reservoir is low.

The canal, as it crossed the Conemaugh to the left bank, followed the course of the Conemaugh and Kiskiminetas rivers in alternate sections of canal and slackwater navigation to Freeport, thence via canal on the right bank of the Allegheny River to Pittsburgh. (The bridge at this location was demolished in the 1889 Johnstown flood. At that time it straddled the Conemaugh River, which forms the southern border between Westmoreland and Indiana counties.) An Indian village site is north of US 22 at west end of the bridge over the Conemaugh River. *Location:* Conemaugh Dam, T 312 (Derry Township).

According to the National Park Service, in the area between Bolivar and Blairsville, along the south bank of the Conemaugh River, are the best-preserved remains (including well-preserved Lock no. 5, a fine cut-stone structure) of the Pennsylvania Main Line Canal to be found anywhere between Harrisburg and Pittsburgh.

32. Torrance State Hospital (brick), covering 375 acres of woodlands, was founded in 1919 at a remodeled dairy farm where five patients were transferred from the Danville State Hospital. The first permanent structure, named for Senator W. F. Graff, was completed in 1921. A new administration building was erected in 1977. This complex provides in-patient care for the adult emotionally ill and serves Armstrong, Indiana, Butler, and Westmoreland counties. It is now being considered for veterans' housing, since many of its buildings are vacant. *Location:* Derry Township, across the Conemaugh River from Blairsville.

Note: Northwest of Torrance are coke ovens and an early stone barn, near an old railroad grade to Blairsville.

33. West Schoolhouse (brick) was built in 1910–12. It was later jointly owned as a summer retreat. *Location:* In curve of road on SR 0259 southeast of Torrance near T 984.

34. Derry area. Derry Township was organized in 1775.

34A. Derry Fire Museum includes antique fire-fighting equipment, memorabilia, and displays. Tours are available through the volunteer fire department in the borough building. *Location:* Derry, 116 East Second Avenue.

34B. Fisher Building (brick) is one of the early landmarks of the community and still in its original condition. *Location:* Derry, South Chestnut and Seventh streets.

34C. Riggs House (log), later covered and built as a saltbox, sits down in a hollow and is one of the earliest houses of the area. An early barn is adjacent to the house. Several other log and stone houses are in this area near the center of town. *Location:* New Derry, near a corner market.

34D. Hoskinson House (ashlar stone), with five bays, was built in 1848 by R. M. Hoskinson (date stone in gable). It is situated along the railroad tracks in rear. *Location:* Hillside, near Ridge View Park, T 846 and SR 0217.

35. Old Salem Presbyterian Church (brick) was founded in 1786. The first "tent" church (early outdoor pulpit boarded up and roofed) was located in a depression of Sugar Loaf Hill. Later a small log building was erected and given the name of Salem. Before the close of the century another log structure (70 by 40 feet) was erected and renovated in 1832. This church was destroyed by fire in 1848, the same year that the present church was built. It was remodeled in 1963. Early ministers were James Power, Robert McPherrin, and Thomas Moore. An adjoining cemetery contains graves of Revolutionary War soldiers. *Location:* North of New Derry, on Derry Road (SR 0982), 2.2 miles south of US 22.

36. Pomeroy House (brick) stands on the Fort Pomeroy property. The fort site is directly across the road from the house, which was built about 1835. At one time it was owned by the late John C. Walkinshaw. *Location:* Near New Derry, at Bergman's Dairy about 0.7 mile on SR 1039 (which is 0.2 mile east of SR 0982).

Note: Nearby on the same road is the Skacel brick farmhouse, formerly owned by the Atlantic Coal Company and also built in the middle 1800s.

37. Gilson Farmhouse (brick) is a mid-nineteenth-century home at the site of Fort Barr on the old Gilson farm. In 1769 Robert Barr, one of the first settlers who came to the region, established the New Derry settlement. A barn across from this house has the name Fort Barr written on it. Old coke ovens are in view from the house and barn. *Location:* Atlantic, 0.6 mile off SR 0982, 1 mile northwest of New Derry.

Note: Fort Barr House (log and stone) used to be at the Fort Barr site near New Derry (Atlantic). It was dismantled in 1969 and restored in 1973 at a new location by the Lamolinaro family. Fort Barr was a frontier fort built in 1774. *Location:* Derry Township, about 2 miles north of Elks Golf Club on Lee Valley Road.

38. Rugh Home (brick with shutters) was built in 1860 by the Rugh family. Now on the Turner dairy farm, it overlooks several ponds. *Location:* Near Slickville, on SR 0819.

39. Congruity, a small village, has grown up around the church of this name in Salem Township.

39A. Congruity Presbyterian Church (brick) was organized in 1789. On September 22, 1790, Samuel Porter and John McPherrin were ordained at a tent on James McKee's farm. Porter, the first pastor, was followed by W. K. Marshall and Edward R. Geary. The first brick church, erected in 1830, was badly damaged by wind. The second and present structure was built in 1855 and damaged by fire in 1953. *Location:* On old US 22 between Delmont and New Alexandria, at Congruity.

39B. Congruity Tavern (stone) was built about 1820 and opened as a tavern the same year. At this time the owner planned a party for the young people of the area. However, Rev. Samuel Porter (see *Congruity Presbyterian Church*) in a sermon discouraged the congregation from attending the open house, which was then canceled. The second story has a large dormitory room where male guests stayed overnight. A small room off this one was for occasional women travelers. Early owners of this house were the David Kirkpatricks and the Stewarts. In 1976, during restoration, it was badly damaged by fire and rebuilt. It is now an antique shop and home. *Location:* Near junction of US 22 and SR 1055, at Congruity.

39C. Stagecoach Inn (painted brick) was built in the early 1800s and has had an interesting history. First operated as an inn on the Northern Pike, it was a recruiting station for Civil War soldiers, later a glove factory, and now contains a stained glass studio (Silianoff's) as part of a private residence. *Location:* At Old William Penn Highway (Northern Pike) and SR 1063, Congruity.

40. Sloan Log House. This nearly 200-year-old house is in remarkable condition. It was built by the Sloan family at what was once known as Sloan's Crossing. *Location:* Slickville, on SR 0819.

41. Latrobe, which owes its existence to the railroad, was laid out by Oliver J. Barnes in 1851 and was incorporated as a borough in 1854. It was named for J. H. B. Latrobe, a prominent civil engineer associated with the Baltimore & Ohio Railroad. Three of the early houses are located at 401 Depot Street, 208 Lloyd Avenue at Unity Street, and corner of Ligonier and Thompson streets (1868 Dickie house). Latrobe is also known for the first professional football player, Dr. John K. Brailler (1895); the first official airmail pickup in the world (1939); and the first banana split.

41A. Sloan House (stone), believed to have served as a frontier fort, was built in the late 1700s by Samuel Sloan, who was one of the county's first justices. The Daily family purchased the property at a later time, followed by the Palmers. *Location:* 1909 Raymond Avenue at Cedar Street (next to shopping center).

41B. Pennsylvania Railroad Station (brick), recently restored and readapted for use as a restaurant, was built in 1903. The chief engineer was William H. Brown. *Location:* McKinley Avenue and Depot Street.

41D. Mozart Hall

42. Carney Station

Note: The brick trolley depot (ca. 1915) is located at the Latrobe Airport (SR 0981 south of US 30). At one time it was used as an airport terminal. Nearby on a lane off US 30 is a fine early stone house.

41C. Bitner Mansion (brick) was built in 1890 by Samuel Miller. It has Tiffany windows, eyebrow windows of Italianate design, and an oval tower. *Location:* 414 Baker Hill.

Note: The home of Latrobe's Burgess, Joseph E. Peebles (1918–25 and 1930–33) was called "The Castle." This Victorian house was bought by funeral director M. S. Hartman in 1964. *Location:* 1500 Ligonier Street.

41D. Mozart Hall (brick), with twin German onion domes colorfully painted, was built in 1890 by George Seiler. Erected in the style of the grand opera houses of Germany, it now serves as a restaurant. *Location:* 340 Main Street.

42. Carney Station (log), 33 by 33 feet, was built in 1790 (date on beam). It was an old drovers' stand which later served as a stagecoach stop. The original family spelled their surname Kearney. In recent times James Bator purchased this house as a surprise birthday gift for his wife Susan. They moved it to the present location where it is a private residence and country gift shop. *Hours:* Saturday, 11 A.M.–5 P.M. January–March by appointment only. *Location:* T 898 (Lightcap

School Road) near Latrobe (Unity Township). Follow signs.

43. Selders House (fieldstone), on property called "Wild Wind Farms," has a gable stone that reads, "G & AS 1792." This landmark was built by George Selders, who had been burned out by Indians in three successive log houses. Selders was born in Hanover, Germany, about 1724. At the age of ten he was kidnaped and taken to Ireland and then to America where he was indentured to a Mr. Baird of Philadelphia. From there he moved to Hagerstown, Md., in 1744 and married Ann Leeper in 1763. They had ten children. Their property, according to report, adjoined that of Gen. Arthur St. Clair. Selders lived to be about 104 years old. In recent years the house was purchased by Joseph Frola. *Location:* On a dirt road off SR 2033 near Westco Highlands in area of Baggaly (Unity Township).

Note: Another stone house, built in the early 1800s, reputedly on the site of a flour mill, is on T 860 about one mile northeast of T 898.

44. Unity Presbyterian Church (brick) was founded in 1774, when the Penns granted the congregation seventy acres of land for a burial ground and a meetinghouse. Before the house of worship was built on this land, known as "Unity," James Power and John McMillan preached in "Proctor's Tent," so called because it was on John Proctor's property and consisted of a pulpit covered by a roof. Power was conducting a preparatory communion service in Unity Church the afternoon that Hanna's Town was raided in 1782, at which time the congregation upon hearing the news dispersed and the pastor hastened to his home near Mt. Pleasant. (See *Hanna's Town*.)

The present brick church was built in 1874. Remodeling, spearheaded by the late James

44. *Unity Presbyterian Church*

47. *Mill at St. Vincent Archabbey*

H. Rogers of Latrobe, began in 1937 with money provided by the Mellons and the McFeely-Rogers families (the family of TV's Mr. Rogers). The red, white, and blue art glass in the windows at the front are Tiffany glass from the old East Liberty Presbyterian Church, previously donated by the Mellons in memory of early members of their family who worshiped here and are buried in the cemetery.

The congregation was dissolved in 1921, and the building now belongs to the Unity Church Cemetery Association. A champion for the preservation of this historic site was Charles H. Townsend, director of the New York Aquarium (in Battery Park) for thirty-five years. He was one of the world's leading marine naturalists and conservationists. While working on President Cleveland's commission for the preservation of seals and at Galapagos Island, he was responsible for saving animals from extinction. Townsend was also a great benefactor of the Latrobe Library. *Location:* Near Latrobe, behind St. Vincent College, off US 30. Turn west off SR 0981 in Latrobe at Unity Street (SR 1026); thence 0.6 mile to its junction with SR 1024 and travel 1.2 miles west on that road.

45. Baldridge House (stone) was built in 1777 by Joseph Baldridge. This spacious structure was remodeled in 1933 and added on to in 1960. Baldridge erected a mill nearby on the Loyalhanna in 1804, laid out part of the village of Youngstown, and, according to historian G. D. Albert, "died in 1840, a very wealthy man for his day." *Location:* North of Youngstown, south edge of Latrobe, on SR 0982, 0.4 mile north of US 30.

46. St. Clair House (log) was built in 1777 by Daniel St. Clair on property originally belonging to his father (the general). In 1959 it was

moved 125 feet to its present site. *Location:* Near Youngstown, on US 30 at its junction with SR 0982.

47. St. Vincent Archabbey (brick) was the first abbey in America founded by the Benedictine order of the Roman Catholic Church. In 1790 Father Theodore Brouwers, a Franciscan, bought a 350-acre tract, called "Sportsman's Hall," and built a log cabin on it. Father Brouwers died before his dream of an abbey came true, but in 1846 a monastery was founded here by Boniface Wimmer, O.S.B., a monk of St. Michael's Abbey in Metten, Bavaria. It became a priory in 1852 and an abbey in 1855. The church of St. Vincent de Paul, built in 1835, became the students' chapel in 1846, and the college was incorporated April 18, 1870. From here ten abbeys and colleges in eight states were founded. The basilica was built in 1905 of Rhenish Romanesque style. A multi-million-dollar fire destroyed many of the buildings, including the chapel, in 1963. A new monastery was completed in 1967 and a science center opened two years later.

An old gristmill built in 1854, still used for grinding grain, is open to the public. St. Vincent's museum contains a large exhibit, including Indian relics and a fossil and mineral collection. (*Hours:* Tuesday and Thursday, 1:30–4 P.M. and by appointment.) The college also has a fine library with rare handwritten volumes dating back hundreds of years before the invention of printing. Religious art and stained glass windows are in the crypt of the basilica. *Location:* 7.7 miles east of Greensburg, on US 30, near Latrobe.

Note: Close by and closely related to St. Vincent's is the site of St. Xavier's Academy, the first Roman Catholic academy in western Pennsylvania, opened by the Sisters of Mercy in 1845. Although it was demolished, there is

346

still a nineteenth-century brick house on the property. *Location:* US 30, just west of St. Vincent's.

48. Ferguson Farm includes a small stone house and a later frame house. Across from these are two early barns, one constructed of logs. The frame barn now serves as a clubhouse. All the structures are over 100 years old. The farm was at one time owned by the Fergusons and later bought by the Statlers, who operate a golf range here. *Location:* 0.7 mile west of Beatty Crossroads (SR 2017 and US 30), on old US 30 but visible from new US 30.

Note: Just east of Beatty on a hillside on the north side of US 30 is the early M. Keough brick tavern, now a residence.

49. Youngstown, one of the oldest communities in the area, was a turnpike town about halfway between Ligonier and Greensburg. Named for Alexander Young, it was incorporated as a borough in 1831.

49A. Cunningham Barber Shop and Jewelry Store (weatherboard), the former home of John Cunningham, is one of the oldest houses in town. Construction underneath the siding is believed to be log. *Location:* On Main Street.

Note: A log house built in 1812 was owned by David Small in 1835. On Forbes Road leading to Darlington, 0.5 mile from Youngstown.

49B. Youngstown Borough School (frame), built in 1873, was the third school in the area. In recent years it was converted into a community center. *Location:* Latrobe Street.

Note: Next to the communtiy center is St. James Evangelical Lutheran Church (brick), built in 1867 with a 1966 addition.

49C. Washington House (painted brick) was once an inn along the Forbes Road, later the Pittsburgh-Philadelphia Turnpike. This eight-bay tavern, built in the late 1700s, later became the Barrett Hotel and continues to operate as a tavern. *Location:* 506 Main Street, near Latrobe Street.

49D. Youngstown Hotel (brick), in recent years the Tin Lizzie Restaurant. According to report, this property was purchased in 1895 by Dave McAtee who built the hotel (with a turret) on an existing stone foundation which was part of a 1750s stagecoach stop on the Ligonier-Pittsburgh road, near the Old Forbes Road (later old US 30). However, a signature

stone on the facade reads "S. AMER 1905." In 1980 John Powlosky bought the property and restored it for use as a tavern and restaurant. The old tavern foundation is now the rathskeller. *Location:* Main and Latrobe streets.

49E. Catholic Church (log) was formerly the house of Bayton Myers. *Location:* 429 Main Street.

49F. McAtee House (brick) was built about 1825 by the Patrick McAtee family. *Location:* 519 Main Street.

49G. G. Pershing House (log) was built in 1792. Members of this family were ancestors of Gen. John J. Pershing, America's first six-star general since George Washington. In 1769 Frederick Pershing settled on a tract called "Coventry." A monument in Frederick's honor is located at the Lincoln Highway (US 30) less than one mile west of Youngstown. *Location:* Unity Township, off SR 0982 between T 872 and T 579.

50. Ligonier is located in a picturesque valley along the Loyalhanna Creek. It became a borough in 1834. The historic Ligonier Diamond, with a newly constructed bandstand at the same location as an 1894 one, is the site of a corral where stagecoaches and horses on the Philadelphia-Pittsburgh Turnpike used to stop. This area has many interesting buildings.

50A. Fort Ligonier (restoration), "Key to the West," was constructed, on Col. Henry Bouquet's recommendation, near the site of Loyalhanning Indian Town. In the fall of 1758 the fort served as a staging area for Brig. Gen. John Forbes. The structure was but partially finished when the men, under Col. James Burd, withstood an attack by the French and Indians a month before Forbes took Fort Duquesne. (This battle has been re-enacted over the years.) The fort also withstood a siege during Pontiac's Rebellion in 1763. Following the Indian wars, it was abandoned in 1765. During the Revolution, since the old fort had fallen into decay, another stockade called Fort Preservation was built on property below the first.

In 1949 the Fort Ligonier Memorial Foundation began a fund-raising campaign for the reconstruction of the original fort, and ground was broken in 1954. Excavations have yielded many artifacts from the French and Indian War which may be viewed in the museum on the property. Authentically dressed mannequins depict scenes in the restored

50A. Fort Ligonier

buildings. The main or inner fort was a 200-foot square with four bastions. There are four outlying redoubts, a hospital, and a blacksmith's forge.

The administration building and museum (stone) contains an annex furnished in Georgian style. It includes the Lord Ligonier room, which has an original painting of Ligonier by Joshua Reynolds, and an original room from Maj. Gen. Arthur St. Clair's home, Hermitage (see *Arthur St. Clair Homes*). *Hours:* April 1– October 31: Daily, 9 A.M.–dusk. *Admission charge. Location:* Junction of SR 0711 and US 30 (South Market Street).

50B. Ligonier Valley Train Station (granite), which closed in 1952, later became the southwest division headquarters of the Pennsylvania State Game Commission. The engine house and locomotive repair shop across the street was converted into a Roman Catholic church in 1957, and the ticket office became an apartment building. *Location:* Loyalhanna Street.

50C. Arthur St. Clair Homes include "Hermitage," built in 1802 when Major General St. Clair (1734–1818) retired as governor of the Northwest Territory. The house was dismantled in 1962 and one room moved to Fort Ligonier where it was rebuilt as an annex to the museum. Only the chimney of this house remains on the original property. A historical plaque marks the site. *Location:* 1.8 miles north of Ligonier, on SR 0711.

St. Clair's "Cottage" site still has an early springhouse on it. This property was the last home of Arthur St. Clair and his wife Phoebe

Bayard St. Clair (1743–1818). They operated an inn here, after they had unfortunate financial losses. *Location:* Chestnut Ridge, on SR 2016 (old Forbes Road) 2.3 miles from Youngstown. Pennsylvania Historical and Museum Commission marker is directly over ridge from house site and is on US 30 near Sleepy Hollow Restaurant, a log, mid-twentieth-century landmark.

50D. Town House (frame) was built as an inn in 1870 by Jacob and Nancy Frank. For years it was a small hotel and boarding house. In 1915 it was acquired by Mrs. Agnes Frye, mother of the former owner, Mrs. June Millison. They reopened it as the Town House restaurant in 1951. A fine collection of antiques is on display here. Now owned by the Richard Olson family, it is a bed and breakfast inn. *Location:* 201 South Fairfield Street.

50E. McFarland House (brick) was built in 1830 by Col. John McFarland, a contractor for the West Penn Railroad and a state senator. This property was purchased by John H. Frank in 1886. At this time a front bay window was added, together with side porches and an iron fence. It was later purchased by the Fairfield family. *Location:* South Fairfield and Loyalhanna streets.

Note: A cottage in the rear was the ticket office for the Ligonier Valley Railroad about 1900 and at one time was an ice cream parlor.

50F. Ivy Manor (brick) was built in 1850 as a home by Noah M. Marker, "prominent merchant, legislator and civic leader." This building, with much of the original woodwork, was developed as a restaurant by the Brant family, followed by other owners, including the Mellons. *Location:* Corner of East Main and South St. Clair streets.

Note: Marker built another brick house, for his son, on 108 South Market Street.

50G. Shaw House (brick) was built before 1830 by Bales McColly, who operated a harness shop next to his home. *Location:* 204 East Main Street.

50H. Clark House (frame) was built about 1796 by William Ashcom. The building was originally a cobbler's shop. *Location:* 230 East Main Street.

50I. Robb Shop (frame), known as the "crooked house," is over 150 years old. It was a cabinet- and coffin-maker's shop. *Location:* 243 East Main Street.

50J. Graham House (brick) was built before 1860, probably by Robert Graham. Later owners were William Houston, Edmond Kibble, Reuben Wilt, and the Menoher family. *Location:* 131 West Main Street.

50K. Miller House (frame) was built by the Miller family about 1850 and was later occupied by C. F. Cairns. An outdoor bake oven, smokeshop, and workshop are also on the property. *Location:* 216 East Church Street.

50L. Stitt Jewelry Store (brick) was built in the 1840s and at one time belonged to the Stecks. Conrad George, a cabinetmaker, also lived here. *Location:* 111 South Market Street.

50M. Cook Insurance Office (brick) was built in the 1830s, probably by the Steck family, descendants of John Michael Steck, first Lutheran minister west of the Alleghenies. The Noah Marker family also lived here at one time. *Location:* 115 South Market Street.

50N. Bunger Spring, originally known as Bonjour Spring, was named for Andrew Bonjour, a wagoner with Brig. Gen. John Forbes's army and a tavern keeper in 1771. Andrew's wife Barbara owned this land, which was later purchased by Arthur St. Clair. The saying about this spring, which is still in use, is, "Once you drink from Bunger Spring, you will always return to Ligonier Valley." *Location:* Near Bunger Street, northwest section of town.

50O. Pioneer Presbyterian Church (brick) was built in 1876. *Location:* West Main Street near Hemlock Avenue.

51. Speedwell Carding Mill (stone) was operated by Abraham Brant and produced yarn, blankets, and cloth until 1896. The mill, originally built of logs and rebuilt with stone quarried nearby, was closed after Abraham's death, and his son John A. Brant sold the property to Edward S. Carne in 1906. It was restored in 1917 and used as a gristmill. The mill, part of the Rolling Rock property, functions today as a pumping station, sending water from McGinnis Run to Rolling Rock Club at the top of the hill. Stones from the millrace were used to build the small bridge nearby. The brick house next to the mill was erected before 1800. *Location:* 5 miles southeast of Ligonier, off SR 0381 near Rolling Rock Racetrack on private road (wildlife preserve) at Rector.

52. Powdermill Nature Reserve Museum, a gift of Alan Scaife and Gen. Richard K. Mellon, is a field station of Carnegie Museum in Pittsburgh. It contains displays of mounted birds and mammals, wax flowers, and models of amphibians and reptiles at an 1,800-acre sanctuary devoted to the study of the flora and fauna of the Ligonier Valley. At one time the property included an early powder mill on the nearby run. Although the sanctuary is closed to the public in order to maintain undisturbed environmental conditions, the small roadside museum and a bird-banding laboratory are open. *Hours:* April–October: Saturday and Sunday, 9 A.M.–5 P.M. *Location:* Southeast of Ligonier, on SR 0381, about 3 miles south of Rector.

53. Robbins House (log) was built before 1800. William (Billey) Robbins had a shoe shop in this house in the early 1800s. The second story was added early in the nineteenth century by a soldier who was later killed in the Civil War. *Location:* South of Ligonier on SR 0381, near Rolling Rock Club.

54. Boucher-Beebe House (brick) is believed to have been built by the family of historian John Newton Boucher. This home at one time had white pillars. It was later owned by Mrs. Amanda Smith. *Location:* Near Ligonier, on SR 0711 about 0.5 mile south of its junction with US 30.

Note: Across the road is another brick house built in 1830 by the Boucher family. It was later owned by Gen. John Ramsey, who laid out the town of Ligonier.

55. Forbes Road Gun Museum (brick) contains a wide collection of more than 500 firearms dating from the year 1450 to models of the present day. The museum is operated by Russell Payne, third in a line of gunsmiths who have worked in the area for more than 100 years. *Hours:* 9 A.M.–5 P.M. *Admission charge.* Special group rates. *Location:* 4 miles north of Ligonier, on SR 0711, near Oak Grove village.

56. Naugle Covered Bridge (steel beams supporting wood frame) was built in 1963 by Richard K. Mellon who patterned it after the Burr truss Rockwood Bridge (Somerset County) that was destroyed in 1954 by hurricane Hazel. It is nearly forty-seven feet long and twelve feet wide, crossing Rolling Rock Creek. Permission to visit this bridge may be obtained at the administration building at Rolling Rock. *Location:* Ligonier, near Rector, Rolling Rock Farms.

57. Jones House (log) was built in 1840 near an Indian spring and is reputed to be the oldest log cabin in Ligonier Township. It was originally a schoolhouse, later converted into a honeymoon cottage for a settler's daughter. It was purchased by the Ralph Jones family in 1931. *Location:* Old Forbes Road, about 1 mile off US 30 (Ligonier Township).

58. Brandt-Todd House (brick), with five bays, one of the earliest houses in Ligonier Township, was the home of the Brandt family. In the late 1700s John Brandt (Brant) migrated to America from Amsterdam. Shortly after settling at this site he discovered an Indian hiding in his bake oven and killed him with a fence rail. He was a Revolutionary War soldier (d. 1802), and his son, John Brandt, Jr. (d. 1844), who also lived on this property, fought in the War of 1812, Both are buried in a private cemetery at this location. According to tradition, two daughters were killed here during an Indian raid. Also on the property is one of the earliest (brick) schoolhouses in Ligonier Valley. It was called the Dutch Meeting School. *Location:* SR 0711, 3.5 miles south of Ligonier, on T 595 (Barren Road).

59. Keffer-Mellon House (stone and frame) was built, in part, about 1800. An enormous cantilevered barn with an ashlar stone foundation is also on the property. *Location:* On lane off SR 1021 (Ligonier Township).

Note: An Andrew Mellon log and stone house is on SR 2017 at T 687. The Carr-Stewart log and stone house is on SR 0130 just west of S 2017. It was built in 1827.

60. Methodist Church (brick), one story, is now a bank. *Location:* Bolivar, Washington Street between Second and Third streets (Fairfield Township).

Note: Other Bolivar landmarks include an early pharmacy and brick works.

61. Camp Henry Kaufmann (log and brick) represents an early structure, reminiscent of pioneer days, now readapted for other use. *Location:* Off SR 1011 (Fairfield Township).

62. Kingston House (stone) was built by Alexander Johnston in 1815 and named after his tract of land patented under the name Kingston. Johnston, who came to this country from Ireland, settled in western Pennsylvania and became engaged in a Pittsburgh business. Later he bought Kingston and built a forge (which proved unsuccessful) on Loyalhanna Creek in 1811. About the same time he began keeping a tavern in his home. His son

William was governor of Pennsylvania from 1848 to 1852. The stone mansion is now a private residence owned by the Victor Smith family. *Location:* Kingston, on US 30 across from Kingston Dam.

63. Idlewild Park is believed to be the oldest continuously operated amusement park in the United States. It was originally the end-of-the-line picnic area created by the Ligonier Valley Rail Road. The rail line that first served this area was the Ligonier & Latrobe Rail Road, a narrow-gauge lumber hauler, started in 1853, that ran from the coal mines at Fort Palmer five miles north of Ligonier to Latrobe where it connected with the main line of the Pennsylvania Railroad. In 1871, Judge Thomas Mellon bought the lumber train, and in 1878 land for the 410-acre park was acquired from William M. Darlington. The narrow gauge had been changed to standard in 1877, and trains transported people to and from the park. Later West Penn provided trolley service here. *Hours:* Daily, 10 A.M.–9 P.M. Closed Mondays (except holidays). *Location:* 2.5 miles west of Ligonier, on US 30.

Note: A carousel with forty-eight wooden horses, one of the last of its kind, was built between 1928 and 1931.

64. Fisher Mansion House (log and stone), originally known by this name, was at one time used for shelter from Indians. It was built in 1773 by Abel Fisher on the Forbes Road. It is believed that this house at one time served as an inn. The stone addition is over 100 years old. *Location:* Near Darlington, SR 2045 and Dickey Road (Ligonier Township).

Note: Nearby on the same road is another log house which was a former school, moved to this location at an uncertain date. A smaller, earlier log house in the area of these two structures was reconstructed at Fort Ligonier.

65. St. Boniface Catholic Church (brick) was built in 1847. Next to the church a stone and brick structure, originally a farmhouse for the monks, now serves as a retreat building. *Location:* Between Stahlstown and Lycippus, turn north on private road off SR 0130 (0.25 mile west of new St. Boniface Church).

Note: A weatherboarded log building, a former post office, is located across the road.

66. St. Mary's Catholic Church (brick) was built about 1843 and remodeled in 1855. *Location:* New Florence.

Note: A frame mill, built in the late 1800s, is on Eleventh Street.

68. Compass Inn

67. Pleasant Grove Presbyterian Church (stone), formerly called Old Donegal, was organized in April 1785. George Hill became the first pastor in 1792. The name of the church was changed from Old Donegal to Pleasant Grove between 1856 and 1859. The first two meetinghouses, which stood south of the present church, were built of logs. The present church was built in 1832 and rebuilt in 1892. *Location:* 4.2 miles north on SR 0711 from its junction with SR 0130 in Stahlstown; thence 0.3 mile on private road from "church arrow" on SR 0711.

Note: At this location are two early one-room structures: a schoolhouse and an 1857 Evangelical United Brethren church (later Methodist).

68. Compass Inn (stone and log) was built in 1799 by Philip Freeman, whose license is preserved in the inn. Frederick Meyers operated it until it was taken over by the Robert Armor family in 1814. Seven generations of Armors occupied the building until the Ligonier Valley Historical Society acquired it in 1966.

The inn accommodated drovers and later stagecoach travelers coming over the Philadelphia-Pittsburgh Turnpike (now US 30). In 1820 a stone addition was completed. Among its early guests were Daniel Webster, Henry Clay, Andrew Jackson, William Henry Harrison, and Zachary Taylor—who held a political reception here in 1849. One guest, Sally Hastings, wrote in her diary in 1808 that the inn

had "one large, unfinished and unfurnished room, with a Kitchen of equal dimensions."

The building is now completely furnished with authentic nineteenth-century items. A newly constructed log barn, cook house, and blacksmith shop behind the inn contain other interesting exhibits. *Hours:* May–September: Tuesday–Sunday, 12 noon–4 P.M. (June, July, August, 10 A.M.–4 P.M.) Candlelight tours are arranged on weekends during November until December 14. *Admission charge. Location:* Laughlintown, on US 30, 3 miles east of Ligonier, at the foot of Laurel Hill (Main Street).

Note: Across the road at 137 West Main Street is the Ligonier Tavern, built by Burgess William J. Potts in 1895. It has been a public house since 1935.

69. Naugle Inn (weatherboard), sometimes called "the Yellow House," was built near the end of the eighteenth century by William Curry. It was later purchased by Joseph Naugle and for years was owned by descendants of this family. The structure, with a double balcony or drovers' porch and a special wine cellar, was the only tavern in the area in continuous use from 1830 to 1885. *Location:* Laughlintown, on US 30, east end of town.

70. Warden House (fieldstone), possibly built before 1789, has chestnut beams and hand-forged iron hinges. This restored struc-

72. Jacob Kinsey Memorial Museum

ture at one time was a store. *Location:* Stahlstown, on SR 0711.

71. Unity United Methodist Church (brick) is the site of the annual Flax-scutching Festival (since 1907), when dried flax is broken, combed, spun, and woven into linen. Second Saturday and Sunday in September. *Location:* Stahlstown, SR 0711.

72. Jacob Kinsey Memorial Museum (log), authentically furnished, consists of four early buildings that have been moved to the site from other locations. The largest is a log house of mortise and tenon construction which had been the earliest schoolhouse in Juniata County. The washhouse was formerly used by a third-generation Kinsey family and contains a beehive oven. Another structure contains a collection of primitive tools, and the fourth is a small smokehouse. The museum is a nonprofit organization operated by a family whose ancestors, Jacob and Eliza Kemp Kintzy, migrated from Germany to Bedford County in 1795. *Hours:* Memorial Day–Labor Day: Saturday, Sunday, and holidays, 2–7 P.M. *Admission charge.* Special group rates. *Location:* Waterford, on SR 0271 northeast of Ligonier.

73. McKelvey House (brick) was built in 1851 by Reuben McKinley McKelvey. This property in 1777 belonged to Capt. Robert Knox, commander of Fort Preservation. Known as the Reliance Tract, it was originally owned by Maj. Gen. Arthur St. Clair. A later owner was Rev. Scroggs. *Location:* Between Oak Grove and Waterford, on SR 0271.

74. Jones Mill (frame), for which the town was named, was built before 1800 and was originally powered by water. The present mill has the name of Matthews on it. *Location:*

Jones Mills, on SR 0031 about 3 miles north of Champion.

75. Little Church (frame), formerly a Mennonite meetinghouse (or the Church of the Brethren), is now a county craft and gift shop owned by Eugene Coon, sheriff of Allegheny County. *Hours:* Weekends only, 10 A.M.–8 P.M. *Location:* Champion, SR 0711 south.

76. Mt. Pleasant Borough, settled as early as 1793 and incorporated in 1828, has many early buildings still preserved. Among the noteworthy ones are those at 729 and 644 West Main Street. In the town square on Main Street at Diamond Street is a World War I doughboy statue.

76A. First Baptist Church (brick and frame) was built in 1869. *Location:* 709 West Main Street.

76B. Memorial Presbyterian Church (brick) was built in 1870 and dedicated in 1873. At that time all members of the old mother church (see *Middle Presbyterian Church*) were organized into a separate society known as Re-union Presbyterian Church of Mt. Pleasant. The early pastor of this congregation was Rev. John McMillan. *Location:* 720 West Main Street.

Note: Good Shepherd Lutheran Church, Mt. Pleasant Chapel (brick), was built in 1884. *Location:* West Main Street at Jordan Street.

76C. Church of God (brick) was built in 1891. *Location:* West Main Street and Braddock Road Avenue.

76D. Wesley United Methodist Church (brick), originally the Methodist Episcopal Church, was built in 1856. It was remodeled in 1892. *Location:* 720 West Main Street.

76E. Polish Catholic Church (brick) has a signature stone above the door which reads, "Kościół Przemienienia Panskiego built in 1899" (Church of the Transfiguration). Across the street is a brick Polish Catholic school erected in 1906. The church was remodeled in 1986. *Location:* Hitchman and Smithfield streets.

Note: Also in Mt. Pleasant is the Tree of David Synagogue (brick), built in 1871 as a Presbyterian church (South Church Street and Stand Pipe Alley).

76F. Pritts Feed Mill (frame), formerly the O. P. Shupe mill, was built in 1847 (the prior building was constructed in 1828). The Wil-

74. Matthews Mill at Jones Mill

liam E. Pritts' family homestead, a Victorian frame house built in the late 1800s, is now Brown's Candy Shop, to the left of the mill. *Location:* 26 East Main Street at West Main Street and railroad.

76G. E. C. Brownfield House (brick) was built in 1860. *Location:* 729 West Main Street.

76H. Overholt Store (brick) is now the Gregor Apartments. Here Henry Clay Frick (1849–1919) began his financial career as a clerk in the store of his uncle, Martin Overholt. *Location:* 751 West Main Street.

76I. Hitchman House (brick), with a small brick outbuilding in the rear, was later purchased by Robert Blum. It was built in 1810 or later. The Hitchman family were bankers and also owned the Hitchman Coal & Coke Co. *Location:* 353–55 West Main Street at Hitchman Street.

76J. Bryce Brothers Glass Company, was founded by James Bryce and his brothers (from Scotland) in 1882 in Pittsburgh. (As early as 1850 he was in the glass business with James and Fred McKee.) In 1896 the firm moved to Mt. Pleasant on Depot Street (the building is now a furniture warehouse). The company was bought out by the Lenox China Company in 1965 and moved to the present location in 1970. Nationally known, it is the largest American manufacturer of lead crystal

glass. *Location:* East Mt. Pleasant, Lenox Road, SR 0031.

76K. L. E. Smith Glass Company was founded in 1907 by L. E. Smith and features hand-crafted glass. A boardinghouse (brick), now used as a gift shop and visitors' center, was built at the same time for out-of-town employees. In the early days, before child-labor laws, eleven- to fourteen-year-old boys worked in factories such as this. The company had its own football team between 1911 and 1916. Henry Ford visited the plant and brought a lens as a sample of those to be made for Model T Ford headlights. It may be seen in the showcase in the visitors' center. This company was acquired by Owens-Illinois in 1975. Visitors are welcome. *Factory tours:* Monday–Friday, 9:30 A.M.–3 P.M. *Store hours:* Monday–Saturday, 9 A.M.–5 P.M.; Sunday, 12 noon–5 P.M. *Location:* On Factory Street and Liberty Street off SR 0031.

77. Middle Presbyterian Church (brick) was the last of four buildings erected by this congregation. As early as 1772 David McClure preached at Jacob's Swamp or Mt. Pleasant, and James Power preached there two years later. Power organized the church in 1776, one of the first established in western Pennsylvania. He became the first regular supply minister from 1776 to 1779, and then pastor until about 1817. He died in 1830 and is buried in the church cemetery. (See also *Sewickley Presbyterian Church* at Bells Mills.)

In 1781 the trustees purchased the church property, a tract of more than six acres. The first two houses of worship were built of logs, the last two of brick. The present church, built in 1854, replaced the one built in 1830.

The Middle Church Cemetery Association administers the cemetery, which has been the church burial plot since 1773. It is here (across the highway from the church) that Peggy Shaw, heroine of the 1782 Indian raid at Hanna's Town, is buried. *Location:* North of Mt. Pleasant, at junction of SR 0981 and SR 2007.

78. Fisher-Fitch House, "Century Farm" (brick), is built on property that in earlier times belonged to Mathias Ringle, wainwright for Gen. George Washington. (See *St. James Reformed Church.*) The present house was built in the middle 1800s. Also at this site are a bake oven, coopers shop, and other outbuildings. Nearby is the old family cemetery. *Location:* Brinkerton Road near Tulip Drive (T 988) (Mt. Pleasant Township).

79. Plank Road School (frame), built in 1901 on a plank road, has not been a school for years. This two-room structure has been renovated for use as a community center. *Location:* Acme, on Three Mile Hill (Mt. Pleasant Township).

Note: a fine Victorian brick house is located near the junction of SR 3004 and SR 3081.

80. Norvelt, with a few one-story white frame houses left from the original community, was a social experiment during the administration of Franklin D. Roosevelt. Led by Eleanor Roosevelt (the town's name is adapted from hers), this project provided housing for many families who were in need following the decline of the great coal industry. *Location:* Mt. Pleasant Township.

81. Pollins House (brick) was built by David S. Pollins in 1852. This farm was part of Sewickley Manor, one of the manor lands of the Penns, and was called the garden spot of Westmoreland County. The overshot of the barn, built in 1849, is supported by nine black walnut columns turned by a horse-powered lathe. Mrs. Calvin E. Pollins, who resides in this house and owns the farm, is of the seventh generation of the same family to own it. Her husband's ancestor who acquired it from the Penns in 1769 was Abraham Leasure (LeSueur), who lived on this land until his death in 1805. *Location:* Turn east on

Greensburg–Mt. Pleasant Road at County Fairgrounds entrance on SR 2017 toward Pleasant Unity; then turn right on first road (T 830).

82. St. Paul's Reformed and Lutheran Congregations were organized in 1782 by John William Weber, first Reformed minister to serve west of the Alleghenies. Their church was first known as "Ridge Church" or "Frey's." The land for the first meetinghouse was purchased in 1796. The second log church had two stories with a balcony on three sides. A brick church was built in 1846; it was considered unsafe in 1896, at which time the Reformed and Lutheran congregations agreed to separate. A new Reformed church (brick) was built, and the Lutherans purchased six acres on the opposite side of the road. The Lutherans' present church (brick) was dedicated in 1904. They are known as the twin churches since they are across the road from each other. The cemetery adjoins the older Reformed church. *Location:* Trauger (Mt. Pleasant Township).

83. Lobingier House (stone) was built about 1804 by John Lobingier, who was a member of the 1776 Pennsylvania Constitutional Convention. He erected a stone mill here at the same time, replacing a log one built by Ralph Cherry before 1772. The Lobingier mill, operated by three generations of the same family, is no longer here. (The site is across the road from the house, where a gasoline station now stands.) Lobingier also built a tannery which was just over the Fayette County line on a site now occupied by another gasoline station.

A private cemetery, surrounded by a stone wall, is about 300 yards behind the house. The residence and a nearby stone springhouse have been completely restored. *Location:* Laurelville, on SR 0031.

84. Hurst House (brick) was built in 1812 by Nathaniel Hurst, who settled in the area in the late 1700s. His name appears on a 1789 tax list and in 1780 he owned four slaves. In 1790 he had patents for 1,000 acres of land. Lydia Hurst, born in 1811, married John Irwin, of Irwin. A log house next to the main home was moved from Lone Pine, Washington County, and rebuilt as an antique shop. *Location:* Near Norvelt, vicinity of Hurst High School; off Mt. Pleasant Road at corner of Hecla Road and Astor Drive.

85. Alverton Coke Company. This company's brick beehive ovens were the last operational structures of their kind in the world.

The H. C. Frick Coke Company at one time operated 35,000 coke ovens from Latrobe to Brownsville. *Location:* Alverton (formerly Stonerville).

86. Lycippus Hardware and Museum (brick) looks much as it did over 100 years ago when Joseph Kloss opened his store in this same building, starting out as a feed store with an adjacent blacksmith shop. The building was later owned by Ed Kloss, Joseph's son, later by Bill Chicks, and since 1965 by Chuck Mozingo. The hardware museum contains many items that were sold when the original owners had it, such as buggy top material, miners' buckets, wagon parts, early windmill blades, and handles for a one-horse plow. The front part of the building was once used as a buggy showroom. *Location:* Lycippus, Main Street.

87. S. Dillinger and Sons Distillery (brick) was built by Samuel Dillinger, who married Sarah Loucks. One building, featured in the 1876 Westmoreland County Atlas, was rebuilt in the 1940s. Another original building remains. *Location:* Ruffsdale, near SR 0031 and US 119.

88. Scottdale, incorporated as a borough in 1874 (originally Fountain Mills), was laid out by Peter and Jacob Loucks (grandsons of Peter Loux, or Loucks). It was named for Col. Thomas A. Scott, president of the Pennsylvania Railroad, after a spur was extended to the town in 1873. Many Victorian houses built by the officials of the H. C. Frick Company are open to the public during the annual Coal and Coke Festival on the third weekend in September.

In addition to those listed below, the borough's early buildings include: J. R. Stauffer-Zellers House, 201–03 North Chestnut Street; Brennen-Burns House, South Broadway Street at Moyer Avenue; Glasgow-Grabiak House, 701 Loucks Avenue; Klinerman House, 409 Arthur Avenue; and St. Bartholomew Episcopal Church (frame), South Chestnut Street at Mulberry Street.

88A. Loucks House (brick) was built in 1853 by Jacob S. Loucks, eldest son of Rev. Martin Loucks, the year he married Mary Saylor. Their eleven children were born here. On the property is a brick building containing a bake oven, washhouse, springhouse, and fuel shed. Their son Aaron was a Mennonite minister at the Pennsville meetinghouse (Fayette County) in 1892. *Location:* Near corner of Walnut and Broadway avenues.

88B. Scottdale Mennonite Church (brick) was built in 1939 and is the oldest church of this sect in the county. It replaced a church of 1893. Prior to this the Mennonite church for the area was at Alverton; it had been built in 1841. The old cemetery is on the former site of East Huntingdon Township High School. This land formerly belonged to Jacob Loucks.

The first minister of the present church was Aaron Loucks. Next to the church is a frame parsonage, built in 1895. It was first occupied by another minister, Jacob Ressler. It is possibly the first Mennonite Church manse in the United States. The church was incorporated in 1898, reportedly the first in the country. Aaron Loucks (1864–1945) was the first ordained minister. *Location:* Grove and Market streets.

Note: Mennonite Publishing House (brick and tile) nearby was dedicated in 1922 with a minor addition in 1949. It is directly related to the Mennonite church and the Loucks family history.

88C. "Green Acres" (brick) was built by Martin Loucks in 1833 and remodeled in Victorian style in the 1900s. It replaced a stone house belonging to Martin's father, Peter Loucks (son-in-law of Henry Overholt). Martin, a Mennonite preacher, married Nancy Stauffer, the daughter of the Mennonite bishop, Abraham Stauffer. In later years this house was inherited by Peter S. Loucks. One of the original outbuildings still sits to the right of the house. "Green Acres" is now the home of Nancy Loucks Rogers and her husband, Donald Rogers. Also on the property are a springhouse, smokehouse, and summer kitchen complex. A carriage way connects the main house to the springhouse. *Location:* 527 North Chestnut Street.

88D. Reed's "Graystone" (stone) was built in 1900 by E. H. Reed, a banker. It now houses the Chamber of Commerce (old Presbyterian church property). *Location:* Mulberry and North Chestnut streets.

Note: North Chestnut Street has many fine early mansions. Across the street from "Graystone" is the brick house of the Loucks family, now attached to Trinity Church.

88E. Trinity United Church of Christ (brick and stone) was built in 1873. *Location:* Mulberry and Hickory streets.

88F. Michael Mulroy House (brick) was built in 1855. *Location:* 115 Walnut Avenue.

89. Henry Clay Frick Birthplace

89. Abraham Overholt House, Henry Clay Frick Birthplace

89. Henry Clay Frick Birthplace (rubble stone) includes a two-room springhouse, the three-story brick home of Frick's Mennonite grandfather, Abraham Overholt, and the latter's distillery. In 1800 Abraham's father, Henry Overholt, had acquired the land. Here Abraham established a six-story brick distillery/gristmill where Old Farm pure rye whiskey was made. (It was originally called "Monongahela"; after Abraham's death it was marketed as "Old Overholt".) In 1838 he built a brick mansion next to the springhouse.

Abraham's daughter Elizabeth was the mother of millionaire Henry Clay Frick, born in 1849 at the springhouse "cottage." Henry, a pioneer in the manufacture of coke, organized the Henry C. Frick Coke Company in 1871 and later became a partner of Andrew Carnegie, the steel magnate. Frick died in 1919, the same year the distillery was closed due to Prohibition.

The estate, which includes a brick flour mill, brick barn, and distillery erected in 1859, has been a museum since 1929 and contains local artifacts and other items; it also houses the headquarters of the Westmoreland-Fayette Historical Society, founded by Helen Clay Frick. A tablet over the museum's doorway lists the names of the builders. The estate is owned by the Helen Clay Frick Foundation. (See also *Clayton* [*Frick House*], Allegheny County.) *Hours:* May 15–October 15: Tuesday–Saturday, 10 A.M.–4 P.M.; Sunday, 1–5 P.M. October 16–May 14: Open by appointment. *Admission charge. Location:* West Overton, on SR 0819, 1 mile north of Scottdale (Frick Avenue).

Note: There are a number of early brick buildings once used for Overholt employees at West Overton and numerous one-room schoolhouses in the Scottdale area.

90. Espey Water-Powered Mill (ruins) is across from the early miller's stone house. *Location:* North of Wesley Chapel, 3 miles west of Scottdale-Smithton Road.

Note: Another old cut-stone house is beyond the mill site toward Reagantown.

91. Olive Branch Baptist Church (brick) was built in 1857. It is situated next to a stone barn. *Location:* 1 mile east of Twin Coaches, on SR 3027 near junction of Smithton and East McClain roads.

92. Stoner House (brick) was built in 1842 by John Stoner (1784–1865), the son of Christian Stoner who came to Westmoreland County in 1799. The lumber was prepared by "Sawmill" Joe Stoner at his mill near Hawkeye. According to legend Christian paid $1,000 and a metal plow point for nearly 600 acres. John's son Adam later lived here. In 1926 George Kintigh purchased the farm, which includes a springhouse, smokehouse, and bake oven. *Location:* Near Alverton, on T 670 about 0.5 mile off Smithton Road from Mt. Nebo.

93. Smithton, incorporated as a borough in 1901.

93A. Jones Brewing Company (brick) was started in 1907 by William Jones, a Welsh immigrant known as Stoney. The Eureka Brewing Company, as it was then called, became known for making "Stoney's" beer. The company is now run by William Jones II with William Jones IV as the brewmaster. One member of the family, Paul Jones, was the father of movie actress Shirley Jones. She attended the old South Huntingdon High School and later acted in the Pittsburgh Playhouse where she was discovered for her lead role in *Oklahoma. Location:* Second Street.

93B. Thomas Universalist Church (frame) has had several buildings. The first, a brick structure erected in 1872 at the north edge of Smithton on SR 0981 and Dutch Hollow Road, was taken over by the Waverly Coal Company the following year. (This company, headed by the Mellons and Coreys of Pittsburgh, ceased to operate in 1923.) The old church, used as a stable for the coal company, was later converted into a garage. The present church was built in 1887. *Location:* Second Street, about 100 yards from the brewery.

93C. Winnet (Winnett) Methodist Church (frame) was built in 1885 with a new front addition in recent years. *Location:* Third Street.

94. Albright School (stone) was built by George Albright in the early 1800s. *Location:* Mendon, SR 0031 (South Huntingdon Township).

95. Plumer House (frame and brick) was built by John Campbell Plumer (1788–1873) in 1814 soon after his first marriage. In 1846 a four-bay brick addition of two-and-a-half stories was made to the gable end of the house.

Plumer was the son of Congressman George Plumer and his wife Margaret Lowrey Plumer. He acquired his name in honor of Col. John Campbell, who had rescued George Plumer from drowning at Fort Pitt when he was a boy. John bought a gristmill and sawmill near his property from his brother Alexander and William Clark. About 1820 he erected a new stone mill, which at the time was one of the largest in western Pennsylvania, and sold it in 1866.

Plumer was superintendent in the erection of the bridge across the Youghiogheny at Robbstown (West Newton's former name) and in 1819 was commissioned justice of the peace by Governor William Findley. In 1830 Plumer was elected to the state legislature and in 1839 to the state senate, serving from 1840 to 1842. Resembling Andrew Jackson in appearance and being of the same party, he was nicknamed "Old Hickory." In addition, he was a member of the Sewickley Presbyterian Church and burgess of West Newton in 1847–49. This house is now a museum. *Location:* West Newton, 131 Water Street at Vine Street (South Huntingdon Township).

Note: West Newton is the site of Simrall's ferry where a group of Revolutionary War veterans from New England, with their leader Gen. Rufus Putnam, arrived in 1788. Here they built a fleet of five boats and started out for Ohio, founded Marietta, and became the first permanent settlers in the Northwest Territory. This original trek was re-created in 1938 by modern-day pioneers, who built replicas of Putnam's boats for their journey.

96. Salem Regular Baptist Church (brick) was organized in 1792 and is the oldest of this denomination in the county. Land for the first church was donated by Joseph Budd, Sr. The second and present church was built in 1842. The cemetery is adjacent to the church. *Location:* West of West Newton, on SR 3021, 1.3 miles northeast of its junction with SR 0051.

97. Rehoboth Presbyterian Church (brick), also known as the "Upper Meetinghouse in the Forks of the Yough," was organized in 1778. Before the first meetinghouse was built, the congregation met at the home of Col. Edward Cook (see *Cook Mansion,* Fayette County). Dr. John McMillan preached here in 1784, the same year that James Finley was installed as the first regular pastor. The congregation has built two churches: a log meetinghouse and the present brick one erected in 1899–1900. Colonel Cook (1725–95) is buried in the cemetery that adjoins the property. *Location:* Near Belle Vernon, 0.2 mile on SR 3011 from its junction with SR 0981.

98. Barren Run School (brick) was held in this one-room schoolhouse built by William Crise in 1871. Nearby stood an old molasses mill, owned and operated by John Baird, which the schoolchildren used to visit at noon for samplings. The school's first teacher was W. H. McBeth and the last was Grace Hoenshel. In 1959 the school was vacated and returned to the original landowners. The school and property were sold in 1962 for $1,500 to the Evangelical United Brethren Church (now United Methodist) next door. (This frame church was built in 1883.) *Location:* Near Jacobs Creek, on SR 3033.

Note: There are several early log houses in this area.

99. Church of Hope (Hoffman Cemetery Chapel) (brick) was built in 1813 as Hoffman's Evangelical Lutheran Church. Henry Hoffman, a settler in 1794 when the congregation was organized, donated the land and funds for this church in his will. Prior to 1842 all services were conducted in German. Services are held here once a year. *Location:* Jacobs Creek, on hillside (Smithton area near Barren Run School).

100. Concord School

Note: Jacobs Creek Methodist Church, built in 1865, on the John Strickler farm, was formerly called "The Meeting House." At the mouth of Jacobs Creek.

100. Concord School (stone), built in 1830 of local materials, is the oldest stone schoolhouse still standing in the county. It was erected from the subscription of land, money, and labor, and used as a school until 1870. Later it became a dwelling, a store, a storage shed, and a stable. In 1947 it was restored by the schoolchildren of Rostraver Township. *Location:* Rostraver, on SR 0051.

101. Cedar Creek Gorge is a beautiful natural landmark deeply cut out by Cedar Creek, which cascades down shale steps surrounded by forested slopes rising from the 50- to 100-foot-wide plain. *Park hours:* 8 A.M.– dusk. *Location:* Cedar Creek Park, 1 mile north of I-70 and SR 0051 cloverleaf (Rostraver Township).
Note: The offices of Cedar Creek Park are in an early brick house off McKee Drive (formerly Finley house). Another well-preserved early house, Robinson-Betters, is at the junction of SR 0031 and SR 0136 (Rostraver Township).

102. Fells Methodist Church (stone), organized in 1785, was known as Teal's, since worship services were held in the home of Edward Teal. Robert Ayers conducted the first services here, one of the original meetingplaces on the Redstone circuit. In 1787 Benjamin Fell donated land to the society, and the first meetinghouse was built between 1792 and 1804. In 1835 the original log church was replaced by the present stone one, which has log beams in the basement. *Location:* Fellsburg, junction of SR 3008 and SR 3109.

103. Daily House (brick) was built in 1797 and used as a store by John Daily. The front door of this Georgian style house has a remarkable fanlight. *Location:* Near Webster, junction of SR 0051 and SR 3019.

104. Black Horse Tavern (brick), built by the Donaldsons about 1800, has been in the same family ever since. The house has beams in the cellar with the bark still intact and fireplaces in every room. The present living room is located where the bar was. *Location:* 2 miles east of Donora, junction of SR 0051 and SR 3021 (near Daily house).

105. Donner House (brick) was built by William H. Donner, who founded the tin-plate mill in Monessen (named for "Essen"—the steel center in Germany) on the Monongahela. He was a partner of Andrew Mellon in the Donner mill across the river, which gave part of its name, "Don," along with "Nora" (Mellon's wife), to the town of Donora. *Location:* Monessen, 435 McKee Avenue.

106. Dillinger's House (stucco) was a private hospital that handled minor surgery. It was founded and headed by G. A. Dillinger. At this house plans were formulated for the construction of the Charleroi-Monessen Hospital, now of major importance, serving the Monessen Valley and located in Charleroi. *Location:* Monessen, 657 McKee Avenue.
Note: Next to this house (at 653 McKee Avenue) is a frame one, the former home of Colonel Derrickson, an aide to President Lincoln.

107. Yukon Mine Buildings (stone) were built during the coal mining boom in western Pennsylvania. They comprise the only stone mine building complex in the western half of the state. Unfortunately, mine and industrial pollution have ruined this site. *Location:* Yukon, off I-70 (Sewickley Township).

108. Markle Plantation was settled in 1770 by Gaspard Markle who two years later founded an enterprise which continued for almost 100 years. Markle built one of the first gristmills in the area in 1772 and retired in 1799. It was here that Col. Archibald Lochry and his militia, en route to join George Rogers Clark's expedition, camped overnight in 1781. Mill Grove, Markle's frame mansion with an arched doorway, was built here by him before 1800. In 1811 Markle's son Gen. Joseph Markle and Simon Drum built a paper mill, the third to be established west of the Allegheny Mountains. Later the Markles es-

110. Bells Mills Bridge, near Sewickley Presbyterian Church

tablished paper mills at West Newton and woodpulp mills in Somerset County.

Gaspard Markle's second home was built of stone in 1818. The mansion stands between the site of the old blockhouse and the family burial ground known as Mill Grove Cemetery. Today one may see Markle's first home, an old stone smokehouse, the stone mansion (on the H. W. Branthoover farm), the cemetery, and remnants of the millrace and the foundation of the paper mill. *Locations:* Mill Grove and ruins: near Turkeytown, along SR 0136 at bridge over Little Sewickley Creek. Stone mansion and cemetery: follow SR 3059 (also T 449) leading northwest off SR 0031 at Turkeytown. Turn off SR 3059 to no-outlet road which leads past cemetery to Branthoover farm.

109. Sewickley Presbyterian Church (stone) was organized in 1776 by James Power, who had preached in the area on his first missionary tour in 1774. During the first service it is said that the men in the congregation had to stand with rifles in their hands to guard against Indian attack. In 1782 the Redstone Presbytery was formed, but the first meeting, which was scheduled at Sewickley, was canceled due to an insufficient number of members because of threatened Indian incursions near the homes of the Washington County members.

The first log meetinghouse, built during Dr. Power's pastorate (1776–87) was about one-and-one-half miles north of the present church on the road leading from Markle's mill toward Pittsburgh. The second log church

was erected on the present church site. The third church, built of stone in 1831, is one of the few remaining stone churches of the area. This structure is next to the county's only remaining covered bridge (built in 1850). *Location:* Bells Mills (west of Yukon), on SR 3012 off SR 0136 near covered bridge over Big Sewickley Creek.

110. Bells Mills Covered Bridge was built in 1850 by Daniel McCain. It is the only original early covered bridge left in the county. This Burr-arch truss structure spans Big Sewickley Creek. *Location:* Bells Mill, SR 3012 off SR 0136, about halfway between West Newton and Madison.

111. Hepler's Gristmill (brick), designed by William Pollock, was built by Israel Painter in 1853. The mill, operated by the Stantons, was later run by the Heplers. With a private rail siding, it is situated on Jacks Run. *Location:* New Stanton, at bridge on US 119.

112. Martin Wertz House (brick), built in 1869, was constructed with an open court in the rear of the house. A signature stone is above the front entrance. *Location:* South of New Stanton, on US 119 (1.1 miles north of junction with SR 0031).

113. Krause Farmhouse (brick), built by a Dr. Krause in 1875, has been remodeled with new brick and windows. The interior woodwork has been restored. It is on the Donald Funk farm. *Location:* South of New Stanton, on US 119 (1.9 miles south of automobile assembly plant and near Martin Wertz house).

114. St. Paul's Reformed Church (Seanor's) (brick) was founded before 1816. The first meetinghouse of both the Lutheran and Reformed congregations was built of logs on the Seanor property. The Reformed group was part of the First Greensburg Reformed congregation from 1829 to 1867, when it became attached to the Second Greensburg charge. A brick church was built in 1837 and replaced in 1875 by the present one. Among the congregation's first ministers were John William Weber, William Weinel, Nicholas Hacke, H.E.F. Voigt, and John Love. *Location:* South of Hunker, on Seanor's Church Road toward Yukon.

Note: About 1.5 miles from Seanor's Church is the old Errett cemetery on the present Miller property.

115. Youngwood area. The town was incorporated as a borough in 1902.

115A. Milliron Church (Mühlisen) (frame) was built in the 1890s on the original foundation of a former log church. At first a Reformed church, this congregation later became the United Church of Christ (now Weber Memorial Center, Penn West Conference). John William Weber (1735–1816), one of the first Reformed missionaries in western Pennsylvania, is buried in the adjacent cemetery. A rose marble obelisk erected in 1874 marks his grave. Inside the church, now used as a chapel in the summer, is the original octagonal wineglass pulpit, which was formerly at St. John's Evangelical and Reformed Church (q.v.) and was in recent years discovered under a porch. It is now located on a tree stump in the front interior of the sanctuary, next to an altar table made from early cemetery stones whose epitaphs had been obliterated. *Location:* West of Youngwood. On US 119 at first traffic light in town, turn west on Depot Street; thence 1.5 miles where SR 2012 continues on to Whitehead Road; church is situated off road to left.

115B. Youngwood Railroad Station (brick), now a railroad museum, also contains shell fossils from the area across the railroad tracks. Open by appointment. *Location:* Depot and First streets.

116. Means (Mains) House (stone) was built in 1840. Along with the date on the signature stone are the initials "F. M." This home, at one time owned by Linley Means, has two hex signs carved on stones in one gable end of the house. One stone depicts an eight-shafted design and the other an eagle. The house, now in disrepair, is used as a barn. *Location:* Near Herminie, 0.2 mile from junction of SR 3045 and SR 3016.

Note: A Quaker cemetery is nearby (on SR 3045, 0.1 mile from its junction with SR 3016).

117. Circleville

117A. Long Run Church (brick) dates from a service led by missionaries David McClure and Levi Frisbie in 1772. Three years later at the same location Dr. John McMillan preached. In 1791 Rev. William Swan became the pastor, serving until 1821.

A log meetinghouse was built on property donated by William Marshall, who with his family was massacred by the Indians in 1780. This edifice was destroyed by fire about 1782. In 1800 the first brick church was built. It was replaced in 1865 by the third church, also of brick, which is now the Christ United Presbyterian Church. Many soldiers of the Revolutionary War, War of 1812, Civil War, and other past conflicts are buried in the adjacent cemetery, as is John Scull of Brush Hill (q.v.). *Location:* 2 miles west of Irwin just south of US 30.

117B. Larimer Mansion (part log, and frame) was built in the 1790s by William Larimer (of the Mellon family), who died in 1838 at the age of sixty-seven. Larimer entertained William Henry Harrison and Aaron Burr at his home, known as Mansion Farm. According to tradition, Larimer sold a slave girl by mistake to Harrison before he realized that the Pennsylvania law forbade it. Larimer's son, Gen. William Larimer, Jr., became a coal baron in the area, and the town of Larimer and a county in Colorado were named for him. This house was later purchased by James Leach. It is now a gift shop. *Location:* 50 Maus Drive, at its junction with Clay Pike.

117C. McIntyre's Hotel (frame), operated by a Mrs. McIntyre, served as a stagecoach stop and voting place for the community. *Location:* Old Lincoln Highway (US 30) near Southside Road.

Note: Jacktown (Jacksonville), between Irwin and Circleville, was laid out in 1810 by James Irwin and Humphrey Fullerton.

117D. Fullerton Inn (stone) was built in 1798 by William Fullerton and later purchased by J. E. White. *Location:* 11029 Old Trail Road, corner of Old Lincoln Highway and Southside Road (opposite side of road from McIntyre's).

117E. Jacktown Stagecoach Tavern (painted brick), built in 1826, is now the Ride and Hunt Club. In the rear is an early 1800s log building. In later years this property was purchased by John Serro. *Location:* Old Lincoln Highway, behind Jacktown Motel.

Note: Jacktown Hotel (log) was built in 1810. Enlarged and remodeled, this landmark was a well-known inn until it burned down in 1966. A modern Jacktown Motel is on the property.

117F. Braddock's Trail Park is the site where George Washington and Maj. Gen. Edward Braddock's army camped during the French and Indian Wars. The 148-acre property contains hiking trails. *Location:* Circleville.

118. Irwin, once known as Irwin Station on the Pennsylvania Railroad, was laid out in 1853 by John Irwin and incorporated as a borough in 1864. It was the western terminus

118C. Brush Hill

of the original Pennsylvania Turnpike. Many of the early Scotch-Irish settlers in this area during the late 1700s were active in the Whiskey Rebellion of 1794, and the town was called Tinker Run (derived from "Tom the Tinker," a name given to those who destroyed the stills of the farmers who paid the whiskey excise tax).

118A. Irwin Inn (painted brick) was built at Tinker Run in 1836 by John Irwin, the nephew of Col. John Irwin of Brush Hill (q.v.). In addition to the inn, which served as a stagecoach stop for travelers on the Pittsburgh and Greensburg Pike, there originally were servants' quarters, a smokehouse, a washhouse, and a bake oven on the estate. The barroom used to be in the present living room. Irwin also ran a canal freight line between Pittsburgh and Philadelphia about 1830 with his partner, William Larimer, Jr., and was one of the first coal operators in the area. In 1834 he married Lydia Hurst (see *Hurst House*). This house, later occupied by his granddaughter Lydia Irwin Altman, has remained in the same family since its erection. *Location:* Pennsylvania Avenue and Main Street (old US 30).

118B. Irwin House (weatherboarded log) was built about 1783 when James Irwin, brother of Col. John Irwin, came to America from northern Ireland. He served as justice of the peace in 1810 and helped lay out the area known as Jacktown. James Irwin married Jane Fullerton. His house was later purchased by Charles McIntyre. *Location:* 141 Verdant Boulevard.

118C. Brush Hill (stone) was built in 1798 and owned by Col. John Irwin, founder of Irwin. It was the third house he built on his Penglyn estate. The first was a log fur-trading post which was burned by Indians in 1782. The second house, a frame dwelling, was

struck by lightning and burned to the ground. When he built his third dwelling, he was quoted as saying, "I'll build a house that neither the Indians nor the Devil can destroy." Colonel Irwin was an associate judge of Westmoreland and a representative in the General Assembly.

Brush Hill, as it is known today, consisted of 700 acres in 1782. Along with the house were slave quarters and a gristmill on Brush Creek. The dwelling faced the pike and originally had a beautiful tree-lined driveway leading up to it.

John Scull, founder of the *Pittsburgh Gazette* in 1786 and son-in-law of Colonel Irwin, lived here after Irwin died in 1856. (Irwin's grave is in Irwin Unity Cemetery—originally his property.) In 1972 the LaSalles restored this home. *Location:* 1 mile east of Irwin, 651 Brush Hill Road off Pennsylvania Avenue (Lincoln Highway).

118D. Stern's Antique Restoration Motor Museum includes in its collection the first mail car in Pittsburgh, a 1903 Marble-Swift runabout, a 1915 Pierce Arrow model 48 limousine, a 1915 locomotive, and other classic and special interest vehicles. By appointment only. *Location:* 10316 Center Highway (old US 30).

118E. Sears "Magnolia" House (brick), featured in *Smithsonian* magazine (November 1985), was a top-of-the-line mail order house, the only one of this model recorded for Pennsylvania. The kit sold for $5,140 from the Sears, Roebuck catalog and was shipped by West Penn Railroad to Jerome Runt, who assembled the ten-room, southern style mansion in 1926. *Location:* 1800 Penn Avenue.

118F. Nemec House (stone, brick, shingle) is a fine Victorian house with stained glass windows. *Location:* 412 Main Street.

Note: Other historic houses are: Klingensmith House (brick), 510–512 Main Street; Mitchell House (brick), 808 Pennsylvania Avenue.

118G. Adams House (frame), a Queen-Anne-style house with shingles and a slate roof, built about 1900, was the home of Dr. Lytle S. Adams, a dentist who lived in Irwin from the late 1920s until 1951. He died in 1970. Dr. Adams established America's first airmail pickup station at Jacktown (Jacksonville) between 1934 and 1939. (The first scheduled airmail service was in Latrobe, May 12, 1939.) In the late 1930s Adams had conceived the idea of making airmail more convenient for smaller towns by using planes to pick up and drop mail bags where they made no stops. In 1939 he was given an experimental contract to provide such service for fifty-two towns in Ohio, Pennsylvania, and West Virginia. In the succeeding nine years this operation, named All American Aviation, increased its circuit to include more than two hundred towns. Much of the equipment used in this air service was made at Dr. Adams's workshop on this property. (Prior to his move to Irwin, Adams and William E. Boeing experimented with airmail pickup in Seattle, Wash.) Adams acquired Charles Lindbergh's help in promoting the system. His aviation service later became known as Allegheny Airlines, today USAir. *Location:* Penglyn (development), 1911 Pennsylvania Avenue.

119. Kunkle-Mills House (stone) was built in the mid nineteenth century on property named "Baldock Acres." *Location:* 8760 Barnes Lake Road (North Huntingdon Township).

120. Ludwick House (brick) was the first stagecoach stop in the borough. The site of an old mill is across from the house. *Location:* Manor, 55 Race Street.

121. Walthour House (brick), the front now altered, was built in the early or middle 1800s by the Walthour family. Michael Walthour operated a gristmill in Manor in 1785 at the junction of Brush Creek and Bushy Run. Fort Walthour was at Strawpump, east of Irwin. *Location:* Near Manor, on Manor–Pleasant Valley Road.
Note: There are also several early log houses on this road.

122. Taylor Plantation (brick), originally consisting of 320 acres, was owned from 1820 to 1855 by Samuel and Sarah Black Taylor, who were Irish immigrants from Virginia. Slaves reputedly helped build the Georgian-style house, which has a winding cherry staircase, original woodwork, and plank floors. A fine springhouse is also on the property. *Location:* 3210 Pine Hill, at Colonial Manor Road (North Huntingdon Township).
Note: Nearby on the same road is the Manor East Restaurant (next to White Barn Theater), a remodeled mansion about one hundred fifty years old.

123. Brush Creek–Salem Church (brick) was first jointly owned and used by the Evangelical Lutheran and Evangelical and Reformed congregations. It now belongs to the

123. Brush Creek–Salem Church

United Church of Christ. John William Weber was the first pastor, beginning in 1783, and early services were held at the Loutzenheiser and Davis homes. After obtaining their church property in 1797 (founded in 1773), the congregations built a log meetinghouse. The cornerstone of the present church was laid in 1816 (finished in 1820). This brick edifice, still in use, has a fine interior with original pews and other outstanding features. The woodwork was hand carved by Jacob Dry. The pipe organ, purchased in the 1870s, is still in use. Four churches in Iowa are reputed to have begun from this congregation. *Location:* 651 Brush Hill Road, near Adamsburg, on spur 120 off old US 30.

124. Penn Methodist Church (frame) was built in 1866–67 as part of the Irwin circuit with George W. Cranage as pastor. First services were conducted in a school every other week by William F. Lauck. On December 22, 1865, organization took place in the home of Alexander Watson, a preacher who came to Penn as foreman of the coal pits. The charge was changed to Penn in 1870. *Location:* Penn (just west of Jeannette), on Emma Street.

125. F. C Hockensmith Company was started in Irwin in 1874 by a German (the name means "hoe maker") from Franklin County. A foundry blacksmith, he purchased the firm's equipment when it went into bankruptcy and started his own company. In 1902 it was moved to Penn under the name Hockensmith Wheel and Mine Car Company. *Location:* Penn.

126. Westmoreland Glass Company, founded in 1889, produced glass made by hand using the same methods employed three centuries ago. The location was chosen because of a successful gas well drilled in the area in 1885. (In 1887 President Cleveland and his bride stopped nearby at the Grapeville station, and local citizens set the gas well on fire, the flame leaping forty feet into the air.) The company was under the management of the Brainard family for three generations on the same factory site. No longer in business. *Location:* Grapeville, along Pennsylvania Railroad about 0.5 mile east of Jeannette.

127. Jeannette was incorporated as a city in 1938. It was named for the wife of the major glass industrialist, H. Sellers McKee.

127A. Painter House (stone), located at Monsour Hospital, was built by John and Tobias Painter in 1783 on a tract of land called "Paintership" deeded by Gov. Thomas Mifflin. The house was constructed about sixteen years before the deed, pursuant to a warrant dated June 2, 1755. The building, once a stagecoach tavern, was later occupied by the Gordon family. In 1952 Monsour Hospital and Clinic had its beginning in this house, where the first X-ray room was located in the so-called Indian Room, constructed with narrow windows. By 1958 plans were made to enlarge the hospital, and it was moved to an adjacent structure. The old stone house is now the administration building. *Location:* Junction of US 30 and SR 4008.

Note: Another early stone house is at 291 Locust Street.

127B. Tiberi House (stone), one of the oldest houses in Jeannette, may have been built by the same stonemason who constructed the early Monsour Hospital building, originally the Painter House. *Location:* 301 Lafferty Street.

127C. Jeannette Glass Company Row Houses (brick) housed employees of the nearby glass factory on Chambers Street near Cuyler Street.

Note: Jeannette has numerous old glass plants which provided its main industry years ago. McKee glass produced the first Ford headlight lenses and was the only U.S. manufacturer able to make eye pieces for World War I gas masks.

127D. Oakford Park, purchased by the Greensburg, Jeannette, & Pittsburgh (trolley)

Railway in 1896 from W. F. Sadler, became a well-known recreational area with a lake. (The dam on Bush Creek broke in 1903 causing twenty-one deaths.) Fred Waring's band used to play at the dance pavilion here. *Location:* Oakford Park Road near PA 0130, near Jeannette.

128. Claridge, a coal mine "patch" (town) north of Jeannette, is the home of the Slovene Cultural Group (Slovenska Narodna Propna Jednota, SNPJ), singers and "button box" players who organized in 1980 to preserve, advance, and promote the cultures brought to the area by European immigrants. They perform in authentic ethnic costumes. *Location:* Claridge.

129. Bushy Run Battlefield is the site where an army under a Swiss-born British colonel, Henry Bouquet, defeated the Indians in a two-day action on August 5 and 6, 1763, raising the siege of Fort Pitt and marking a decisive victory for the British which ended Pontiac's Rebellion. On the first day of battle Bouquet's army was surrounded and attacked by four to five hundred Indians. The British quickly threw up a breastwork of flour bags and other provisions. (Bouquet had started from Carlisle on July 18 with 500 regulars and 340 horses loaded with supplies for the starving troops of Fort Pitt.) Feigning withdrawal of his advance guard on the second day, the colonel drew the enemy into the open, and ambushing troops caught the Indians in crossfire.

In 1930 Bushy Run Battlefield State Park was created and a monument erected to mark the site of the "flour-bag fort," arranged in an emergency to protect the wounded. On the hill to the west another marker shows the approximate location of graves of fifty soldiers who died in the battle. A museum on the property is administered by the Pennsylvania Historical and Museum Commission. *Hours:* Tuesday–Saturday, 9 A.M.–5 P.M.; Sunday, 12 noon–5 P.M. Grounds open until 8 P.M. during Daylight Saving Time. Closed Mondays and holidays except Memorial Day, July 4, and Labor Day. *Admission charge. Location:* Bushy Run State Park, on SR 0993, north of Greensburg and just east of Harrison City, Bushy Run Road.

Note: A log house built by the Busch family in 1803 at Bushy Run (later converted into a barn) was purchased in recent years by the Robert and Greg Connell families who rebuilt it in Peters Township, Washington County.

130. Gongaware-Lazar House (brick) was built in 1871. Formerly owned by Lewis

Gongaware, this property was later purchased by William Lazar. The first day's fighting during the battle of Bushy Run in 1763 took place on part of this farm (see *Bushy Run Battlefield*). *Location:* Near Harrison City on the road to Bushy Run Battlefield Park (SR 0993).

131. Whiskey Bonding House (cut stone), purchased in more recent years by John Beacom, was erected about 1818 as a whiskey storage plant. Later, Sanford Beck constructed a gristmill across the road from the house. *Location:* Bouquet, on SR 4024.

132. Denmark Manor Church (brick) was built on the tract reserved by the Penns under this name. Originally it was composed of members of the Evangelical Lutheran and Evangelical and Reformed churches. Rev. John Steck of the Lutheran congregation and Rev. John William Weber of the Reformed shared the first services. In 1811–15 the first church was built. A log school served as a meetinghouse until this brick structure was erected. The present church was built in 1888, and is now the United Church of Christ. *Location:* Near Harrison City, on Harrison City Road, next to Manor Valley Country Club.

133. Murrysville, formerly Franklin Township, was erected between 1785 and 1788. Named for Benjamin Franklin, who signed the patent issued to Jeremiah Murry, founder of Murrysville, it became a borough in 1975 and was renamed in 1976. It is the only community in Pennsylvania governed by home-rule charter and the birthplace of the natural gas industry.

133A. Oldest Producing Gas Well, no. 1 of Peoples Gas Company, is the oldest well in the United States, and perhaps the world, that was drilled commercially for gas and is still producing. It was struck in the 1880s. *Location:* On Old William Penn Highway near its junction with North Hills Road (at Presbyterian church property).

133B. Haymaker Gas Well was struck in 1878 by Michael and Obadiah Haymaker, grandsons of Justice Jacob Haymaker, an early settler (see *Rugh House* and *George Haymaker House*). Gas suddenly exploded when they had drilled down 1,400 feet in search of oil. It caught on fire and burned out of control for about a year and a half, the flame seen from a distance of up to eighteen miles away. A large lamp-black works operated here for some months until its building burned in 1881.

After the Haymaker gas-well riot of November 26, 1883, when Obadiah was murdered defending his enterprise from a Chicago promoter who tried to claim the well, it was finally bought by Joseph Newton Pew, founder of the Sun Oil Company. This well was the first in the county and one of the world's most productive. *Location:* On bank of Turtle Creek near community clubhouse and library at end of Carson Street on Norbatrol Avenue.

133C. Rugh House (stone) was built by Michael and Phoebe Hawkins Rugh. Their first house, a log cabin (site on adjoining golf course) was burned by Indians in 1778. The family members were captured and taken to a camp near Oil City and then to Canada. They eventually returned to their property, where it is believed they built a second log structure in 1798 (date found on foundation stone) followed by this stone house constructed from plans which Michael brought from Philadelphia. (He served in the Pennsylvania House of Representatives and died on his farm in 1820. His father, also Michael Rugh, lived in Rughtown near Greensburg.) George, the son of Michael, Jr., died during captivity; his wife died in 1809. Michael's daughter, Mary (Polly, a common nickname for Mary at that time), married Jacob Haymaker in 1794 (see *Haymaker Gas Well*). The Haymakers lived in this house and built a mill nearby. At one time the house was called the Philadelphia Mansion. In 1916 the Meisters bought it and served Sunday dinners here from 1923 to 1947. Now owned by the Richard Miller family, it is being restored. *Location:* Sardis Road near Bulltown Road at Meadowink Golf Course.

Note: The nearby brick house at the golf course on Bulltown Road was built in 1837 for Catherine (daughter of Michael Rugh, Jr.) and William Meanor, a descendant of the first settler in the area.

133D. Murrysville Tree Sign (pine and spruce tree formation), covering an area 800 by 300 feet, spells the name of the community it overlooks. Originally planted in 1932 by a local Boy Scout troop under the direction of F. Morse Sloan, who owned the land, this sign should be in the Guinness Book of Records and is one of the world's largest man-made (natural) signs. Years ago, Arthur Godfrey, a radio and TV celebrity, used to mention this sign on his program after having flown over it. Before the use of radio beams, this sign gave pilots a fix on their location. *Location:* Adjacent to Duff Park, between Pleasant Valley Road and Trafford Road, south side of US 22.

133E. Glunt House (log) was built before 1818. Early owners were Jane Glendy and James Elliot. In 1826 John Heddinger purchased the property, followed by Lewis Glunt and his son Frank, who between them owned it for fifty-two years. It was later purchased by the Hay family. *Location:* 3752 Windover Road.

133F. Wallace House (cut stone) was built in 1854 by Samuel Hilty for George Wallace. A signature stone on one gable is inscribed with "G. W." and the date. George Evans and the Shields family were later owners. This house, which has interior chestnut beams, was restored in the 1930s by Stephen Ondish, and Adelaine Hunter purchased it shortly afterward. A gas well on the property still supplies energy for the house. *Location:* 5011 Hunter Lane.

133G. Staymates House (log), on property originally belonging to James Hoy, was owned in 1852 by William Staymates. This was the home of Staymates' granddaughter Bessie Iola Staymates, a teacher in the area for fifty years. (Nearby Girl Scout Camp Iola is named for her.) She died here in 1972 and willed this house to the Boy and Girl Scouts. *Location:* On Round Top Road at Staymates Road.

Note: About 0.5 mile on the same road and beyond Staymates Road is another log structure, now weatherboarded. It was built by the Moore family in 1829 on property formerly belonging to Jeremiah Murry.

133H. Amity Hill Farmhouse (painted brick) was built about 1820 by the Ramaley family. The owner, "Doc" Ramaley, continued to make house calls until he was in his nineties. This interesting house was remodeled and later purchased by the James Ackerman family. *Location:* On Harrison City Road near junction with Round Top Road.

133I. George Haymaker House (painted brick), of late Greek Revival architecture, was built in 1860 by George Haymaker, a grandson of Stoffel Haymaker, a German immigrant. George's father was Jacob Haymaker and his two sons were Michael and Obadiah (see *Haymaker Gas Well*). This mansion, which has a cupola on top, was used by the Trinity Episcopal Cathedral of Pittsburgh for a girls' summer vacation retreat, which became Trinity Manor—Girls' Friendly Society Holiday

House. It later became a duplex, and in the early 1940s George Haymaker's great-granddaughter, Mrs. Lee (Margaret) Simmons, and her husband bought the property. In 1950 the surrounding acreage was sold and it became Marlee Acres, in honor of Mr. and Mrs. Simmons. The house is still owned by this family. *Location:* On Haymaker Farm Road (Marlee Acres), off US 22.

133J. McCall House (brick) was built in 1825 by John McCall, whose grave stone is outside the kitchen door of the homestead. It reads, "John McCall, died April 30, 1836, age 67." John's son Robert built the log barn (covered with siding) near the house. The signature stone on the barn's foundation reads, "R. McCall 1826." Below the farmhouse, near a spring, is a smaller brick house with two front entrances. This was the so-called honeymoon house where John and his wife lived before 1825, when they first moved to the property. It has the original woodwork and cupboards. Behind it is a log springhouse. *Location:* Haymaker Farm Road (Marlee Acres), off US 22 just east of Murrysville (southeast of George Haymaker House).

133K. Ryckman House (log and brick) was built in 1868 by Levi Ryckman. (At a later date the logs were completely concealed by brick.) Both Levi and his father, Alonzo, served in the Civil War. They were taken as prisoners to Andersonville, Ga., and later transferred to Florence, S.C. *Location:* Junction of Old William Penn Highway and Sunset Drive.

133L. McAlister Stagecoach Tavern (frame) was built in the early 1800s. A veteran of the Civil War, Duncan McAlister, operated a post office here at one time. *Location:* 5380 Logans Ferry Road.

133M. Mellon House (weatherboarded log) was built in 1825 by Andrew Mellon, who had come with his father Archibald to the United States from Ireland in 1816. Their first house in this area was near the present property, along a stream where the family had a still. The Mellons bought the farm that had belonged to John Hill and later to a man named Shaeffer. Thomas, Andrew's son, helped haul the logs for this house and the stones for the chimney. He later became judge of the Court of Common Pleas of Allegheny County, was the founder of the Mellon fortune, and was the father of Andrew W., secretary of the treasury from 1921 to 1932; Richard B.; W. L.; and James. This house was purchased by Peter

133M. Mellon House

133O. Tollhouse

Pifer after the Mellons moved to Allegheny County in 1841. It was weatherboarded about 1856 for Pifer's wife, Catherine Cline Pifer. It is still owned by a member of this family, Mrs. Edgar Marts. In 1975 the county historical society erected a marker here. A replica of the house has been constructed at the Mellon homestead in Ireland. *Location:* Corner of Cline Hollow and Hills Church roads.

133N. Hill's (Emmanuel Reformed and Lutheran) Church (brick) dates back to 1828 when Peter Hill and Philip Drum, who had served in the Revolutionary War, donated the land, at which time a log church was built. This union church (now United Church of Christ) was enlarged in 1845 by sawing out the eastern end and adding fourteen feet to its length. In 1858 it was replaced by a brick church which was rebuilt in 1884. Near this site in about 1782 white settlers were attacked by Indians, and the unmarked graves of both groups are located near the church. Before their church was erected, the members traveled to Brush Creek–Salem Church (q.v.). The first Reformed pastor was William Weinel, and the first Lutheran minister was John Michael Steck. *Location:* Hill's Church Road.

133O. Tollhouse (log) was built on the Northern Pike, which was opened in 1818 and reached this area the next year. Simeon Clark was the last to operate the tollhouse, and his daughter Nancy was its final resident. It is now owned by the Emanuel Viola family. This rare structure, now in disrepair, has a huge chimney with an exterior fireplace. It formerly had a balcony and a pike, or pole, for stopping travelers in order to collect the toll. *Location:* Corner of Kistler Road and West Pike Street.

Note: The one-room Clark schoolhouse (brick), built in 1908, is across the road.

134. Export

134A. Duff's (McIlduff's) "Tent" Church Site, now the Seceder Church cemetery, is next to a former Lutheran church (white frame), now a thrift store. It contains the grave of the first settler of Franklin Township, John McIlduff. The community later became a coal boom town. *Location:* Church Street.

134B. Krushinski House (yellow brick) was the home of the seven Krushinski brothers who formed their own band and became the first to broadcast on KDKA radio in Pittsburgh in 1921. They later joined Wesley Barry, an actor who made one of the earliest sound films in America, and toured the vaudeville circuit with his "Hollywood Harmony Hounds." With brother Ed as leader and pianist-composer, and calling themselves "Lee Crossley and His Orchestra," they auditioned for Mae West's first show (she liked them but their fee was too high) and were booked in such places as Boston Symphony Hall and Roseland Cabaret on Broadway. *Location:* Old William Penn Highway, south side of road, east end of town.

134C. St. Nicholas Russian Orthodox Church (frame) was originally the Berlin family home. One church member, Andrew

Drnjevich, Sr., built a front addition with a steeple. Its membership was described as being "a veritable United Nations of Serbian, Russian, Slav, Italian and other nationalities." *Location:* Hamilton Street (old US 22).

135. Delmont was laid out in 1814 and incorporated as a borough in 1833. Originally called Salem Crossroads or New Salem, it was a well-known stopping place, with as many as five lines of stages passing through on the Northern Pike between Pittsburgh and Philadelphia until 1853. The main street of Delmont has become a preservation area, and many early houses are being restored to the 1830–70 period. At least seventy houses are included in this historic district, mostly on Pittsburgh and Greensburg streets.

135A. Watering Trough (wooden) was restored in 1972 at the original spring where travelers stopped to refresh themselves and their horses. *Location:* On East Pittsburgh Street, near SR 0066.

135B. Trinity Reformed Church (brick) was built about the end of the Civil War. This congregation together with a Lutheran one had worshiped in the Union Church built in 1849. The first pastor was S. H. Giesy, followed by Thomas G. Apple in 1855. In 1864 the old Union Church was in disrepair, and the Reformed congregation built its present structure in 1866–67. It is now the Salem Crossroads Christian Museum. *Location:* On East Pittsburgh Street.
Note: The Lutheran church, built in 1868–70, is also located on East Pittsburgh Street.

135C. Old Tannery (log) was owned in the 1830s by John Hutton, followed by Robert Shields. *Location:* On East Pittsburgh Street next to Trinity Church.

135D. Lutheran Hill Home (brick), built between 1830 and 1840, was one of the first restored buildings in the community. It is owned by the Donald Sparkenbaugh family. *Location:* 100 East Pittsburgh Street.

135E. Kepple House (frame) was the home of Anna Martha McQuilkin Kepple (1880–1969), daughter of Jacob and Hettie Leightner Kepple. A talented musician who later in life became an eccentric recluse, she left her entire fortune to schools in Switzerland. It was not known until her death that she was a millionaire and that she had invested in the New York stock market. Her home, on the property of one of the original lots in town,

contained a museum and was the Salem Crossroads Historical Society headquarters. In recent years this house was moved to a nearby site. *Location:* 39 East Pittsburgh Street, next to Trinity Church.

135F. Old Wagon Shop (brick) is now an office building owned by Frank Piper. It was built in 1830 with another section added about five years later. *Location:* 19 West Pittsburgh Street.

135G. Delmont Central Hotel (brick), built between 1814 and 1830s by Robert Black as an inn, has been restored and is now a commercial building. *Location:* Corner of Pittsburgh and Greensburg streets.

135H. Thompson House (brick) was built before the Civil War. It has been restored by the Peter Muse family. *Location:* On Mark Drive.

135I. Christy House (brick) was built by David Christy and later owned by his son. This family at one time owned much of the land which is presently Delmont. *Location:* On Vrbanic farm on Rock Springs Road.
Note: Beyond this house is another brick house, once owned by the Vrbanics, that has been completely restored.

135J. Grain Mill (frame), once operated by steam, was built in the late 1800s and continues to serve the community as a feed store. *Location:* SR 0066 and old US 22.

135K. Steinmatz House (brick), now called "Tollgate," with five bays, was built about 1825 by J. Phillip Steinmatz, a stonemason who constructed numerous houses in the area. He was born in 1776 (one of ten children), the son of Phillip Von Steinmatz, a soldier of fortune during the Revolution. (See *Staymates House;* she was a descendent, the name anglicized.) In later years Rev. J. C. Carson, founding minister of the United Presbyterian church in Delmont lived here, followed by Dr. Levi Hoffman. A two-room tollhouse used to stand nearby on the Northern Turnpike. Here, too, is the source (behind house) of the Turtle Creek which flows into the Monongahela River at Braddock. The house is now used commercially for offices and shops. *Location:* Delmont, old US 22, west, across from Monticello Drive.

135L. Anderson's Cave site in the late 1800s was the hiding place for the loot of a highway robber on the old Northern Pike. In more recent times it was blown up by a farmer trying to rid the area of predators. *Location:* Off old US 22, in vicinity of R. J. Shield's farm, now owned by Salem Crossroads Historical Society.

135M. Apple Hill Playhouse (frame), now used as a summer theater, is a good example of the numerous early barns of the area. Another is on Church Street. *Location:* Manor Road.

136. Bush House (log), built shortly after Hanna's Town was burned by the Indians (1782), is perhaps the most original and most authentic log house in this region. The house has never had plumbing; over the years a spring has supplied water to the family which has owned the property ever since the house was built. It was owned by John G. Bush in 1857 and in 1867–76 by Josiah Bush. The German-built central fireplace still provides heat. The house has never been altered or covered and has no additions. *Location:* Green Drive off Beaver Run Road (SR 1057) between SR 0819 and SR 0066 (Salem Township).

137. Seanor Lime Kiln (stone), on private property, is one of the only three of its kind in existence in the region. Once owned by Marcus Seanor, it later was purchased with the property by Charles P. Bowman. *Location:* Lone Maple Drive (T 881) (Salem Township).

138. Fennell-Wolf-Reynolds House (stone) is a noteworthy house that has been well preserved over the years. Inscribed on the barn, built in the late 1800s, is the rebuilding date "1932" with the initials "W.J.W." This property was once a resort. *Location:* Wolf Lake Road (T 929) (Salem Township).

139. Loyalhanna Dam, constructed in 1942 to provide flood protection for Pittsburgh and towns along the lower Allegheny and Kiskiminetas rivers, controls 95,300 acre feet of water. The concrete gravity dam, with a central spillway with five crest gates, is 114 feet high, 88.5 feet wide, and 760 feet long. Discharge through the dam involves four hydraulically operated conduits. *Location:* Loyalhanna Lake (Loyalhanna Township).

Note: Nearby Beaver Run Reservoir was built in 1950.

140. Pioneer Landmark (log), now covered with frame, was, according to tradition, a station house where the early settlers retreated during times of Indian attack. It has an ex-

137. Seanor Lime Kiln

ceedingly large stone chimney. A log outbuilding is located next to the house (few of the early log outbuildings have survived in western Pennsylvania). *Location:* Northmoreland County Park, in view of SR 0356 and SR 4030 (Allegheny Township).

141. Glen Karns (Cairn) Estate (River Forest Golf Course) originally belonged to Stephen Duncan Karns, one of the largest producers of oil in the Armstrong-Butler oil region. In 1866 he drilled his first well at Parkers Landing. He founded Karns City, built a pipeline from that place to Harrisburg and a railroad from Karns City to Parkers Landing, and was controller of several banks. In 1880 this oil king, who owned numerous racehorses, operated a ranch in Colorado. He returned to his home in the middle 1880s, practiced law, and ended his career as manager of a Populist newspaper in Pittsburgh. When Coxey's Army came through that city, he marched at the head of the parade.

This estate, including eighteen farms, was purchased in 1902 by Andrew Carnegie, and in 1957 Allegheny Ludlum Company bought it. In 1964 it became a golf course, and a shelter was erected on the site of the $35,000 mansion built by Karns in 1873. The original cistern was restored and is in use today. *Location:* 0.7 mile south of Garvers Ferry, 0.2 mile off T 662.

Note: Site of Massa Harbison Log Cabin (q.v.).

142. Zimmerman House (brick) was built in 1830 by Daniel Zimmerman, a tailor. His son Jacob was a Lutheran clergyman who in 1841

140. Pioneer Landmark

took charge of Klingensmith's church near Leechburg and Hill's and Hankey's in Franklin Township. This house is one of the few remaining structures that still retain the original spring in the interior of the home. The building has in recent years been converted into a furniture and gift shop. *Location:* Near Leechburg, junction of SR 0356 and SR 0056.

143. Fort Hand Marker (stone) was erected by the Fort Hand Chapter, DAR. According to G. B. Albert's *Frontier Forts of Pennsylvania* (1896), "Fort Hand was erected [between 1777 and 1779] near the house of John McKibben, whose 'large log house' had been the refuge and asylum of a number of people whither they had fled at times." It was named for Maj. Gen. Edward Hand and served as a refuge from Indian attack from 1779 until 1791. In 1779 "during the night the Indians were there they fired a deserted house near the fort—the old building of McKibben's." Albert continues: "Fort Hand was located on what is now the farm owned by Jacob M. Kearns. . . . Francis Kearns, the father of Jacob M. Kearns, purchased and occupied the farm in 1835. At that time the signs of the ditch which marked the course of the palisade—the earth having been thrown up against it from the inside—were to be seen distinctly. This line included nearly an acre, and would have enclosed the ground which is now occupied by the [brick] farm house, garden and spring." *Location:* Near Apollo, on Pine Run Church at Watt Road, 0.8 mile off SR 0066, 3 miles south of the Kiskiminetas River.

144. Jack House (log) is believed by the owners to have been the John McKibben house (see *Fort Hand Marker*). John McKibben in 1799 sold his house to James Hamilton. The Jack house, in sight of Fort Hand, is a fine link to the past and has been restored

completely by the family. *Location:* Pine Run near Fort Hand (Washington Township).

145. Pine Run German Reformed Church (frame) was organized in 1861. In the beginning, members worshiped at "Yockey's Schoolhouse." This large rural church was built in 1875 with Henry Bain as the first pastor. *Location:* Near Fort Hand on Pine Run Church Road off SR 0066 near Apollo (Washington Township).

146. Poke Run Presbyterian Church (brick), built by Matthew Callen and John Paul, was organized in 1785. John McMillan was the first supply minister, and Samuel Porter was the first regular pastor from 1790 to 1798. It was originally known as "Head of Turtle Creek" and in 1780 as "Poke Run." A log structure, 70 by 30 feet, was built in 1789–90 by a spring near the present building. A brick church was erected in 1836. (According to tradition, ladies' riding skirts and saddles were stored in the basement of this structure during services. The choir sat in the back, and the pulpit was in the center. The floor was covered by a red carpet, the only one in the area at that time.) From 1835 to 1869 David Kirkpatrick served as minister here. The present building was constructed in 1881. *Location:* Near Mamont, on SR 0066, 0.4 mile north of its junction with SR 0366.

Note: David Kirkpatrick's home, built in 1840, is nearby just off SR 0286 on a dirt road leading from Evans Road. This restored brick house was later purchased by the Potts and Krokosy families. Also in Mamont are the 1848 brick Metzgar house, off SR 0066 (east of its junction with old PA 66), and the weatherboarded log George house, owned by the Ferdinand Garbin family on George Drive.

147. McKown House (brick) was built in 1834 by Robert McKown, Sr., who came to this area from Ireland in 1791 and seven years later bought this property. A smaller stone section was built in 1800, later replaced by brick. His son, Robert, Jr., married Rebecca Callen, the sister of Theophilus Callen who fought in the Civil War with the Kiski Squad of ten farm boys in Company E of the 155th Pennsylvania Regiment. (All ten came from the region lying between Puckety Creek and the Kiskiminetas River, from which the group took its name.) Only one—J. King Alter—lived to return. Theophilus, age eighteen, was shot one night while on picket duty. His friend, Sgt. John M. Lancaster, wrote the Callens to tell them of their son's death. Lancaster fell in love with Callen's sister, Louisa, but she died before he had a chance to marry her. Lancaster and Mr. Callen brought back the body of Theophilus from the Shenandoah Valley in Virginia, and today his burial site is in the cemetery of Poke Run Presbyterian Church (q.v.), along with those of his sisters. A monument to Theophilus and some of the others who fought in the same squad is in the Sardis Methodist Church cemetery. *Location:* Near Mamont, on Pfeffer Road at Lover's Lane, just off SR 0066 near Poke Run Presbyterian Church.

Note: Robert McKown's grandson, Jacob Haymaker McKown, built a frame house, still finely preserved, near the junction of SR 0066 and SR 0356. Jacob married Caroline Callen. Another fine late 1800s brick house is off SR 0066 at Kistler Drive, nearby.

148. Walter House (brick) was built in 1848 by John Walter and his wife Bithynia. John operated a blacksmith shop for thirty-seven years across from this property. The house has been restored and retains much of its original woodwork. *Location:* SR 0066 at Mamont Drive (Washington Township).

149. Kiski Valley Free Methodist Church Camp consists of numerous white frame buildings, typical of the Bible camp conference buildings that were built at the turn of the century. *Location:* SR 0066, about 2 miles south of Apollo, opposite Washington Elementary School (Washington Township).

150. Kiskiminetas Springs School, founded in 1888, is still functioning as a private boys' school. The site had first been known as Stewart's Grove, including land where the Pennsylvania National Guard held its encampments in the 1850s and 1860s. The grove became known as Mineral Springs Grove in the latter part of the 1870s, at which time it was a hotel and health spa for the elite. In 1888 Andrew Wilson, Jr., and R. W. Fair purchased the resort property and founded the school.

Old Main (frame), which burned in 1955 and was restored, is now the admissions office. A picturesque walk from the campus along the wooded hillside below follows an old Indian trail to the springs, now dry. *Location:* On hill across Kiskiminetas River from Saltsburg (Indiana County).

151. "Greystone" (stone), a five-bay colonial, was built in the 1830s by the Robinson brothers. In later years it was owned by Anna Wilson Daub, daughter of Col. John Daub, a prominent teacher at Kiski Prep School. In re-

cent times this landmark served as an antique shop. *Location:* SR 0286 between Mamont and Saltsburg near county line (Loyalhanna Township, across from Kiski School).

152. Chambers House (frame), with five bays, was built in 1868 by William Chambers, whose grandfather was a Revolutionary War soldier captured by Indians. The house is still in the Chambers family. One grandson, John B. Chambers, built the canal boat *Apollo Packet. Location:* Oklahoma (south of Vandergrift), Orr Avenue (formerly Chambers Road).

153. Haggs House (log) in more recent years has been owned by Joseph Haggs. This three-bay structure is one of the earliest and one of the few pioneer houses of the area. *Location:* Mamont, SR 0286.

154. Lockport Hotel (frame) was in business during the heyday of the Pennsylvania Canal. The canal crossed the Conemaugh River near here on a cut-stone aqueduct, most of which was removed in 1893. The remaining piers are now a part of the Pennsylvania Railroad bridge. *Location:* Go north 1.9 miles on SR 1011 from its junction with SR 1006 (SR 1006 leads northwest off SR 0711 north of West Fairfield, beside railroad tracks).

155. Updegraff House (brick), with a fine cupola, was built by Uri Updegraff. It is featured in the 1876 Westmoreland County atlas. *Location:* South of Bolivar, SR 0259 at SR 1013 (Fairfield Township).

156. Avonmore was incorporated as a borough in 1893. This community was first settled by a Dutchman, Stephen Rinebolt, who came to this area in order to escape from religious and political persecution in the mid 1700s. He later returned to Holland and brought back with him ten families of relatives and friends. He died in 1815 at the age of 105.

156A. Avonmore Area Historical Society Museum (frame) is a small Victorian office building having a charming decorative bargeboard. It was built in the 1890s by the Avonmore Land and Improvement Company. At one time this building was used by the town's first physician, Dr. Mordecai Alvah Sutton. *Location:* 209 Fifth Street.

156B. Hine Graveyard, the proposed site for St. James Lutheran and Reformed Church congregations around 1800 when a log church was begun but never finished. Here are buried Revolutionary War Veterans and early settlers such as Simon Hine (1750–1838), a blacksmith who owned this land. *Location:* Along abandoned roadway in the woods, at top of hill above Avonmore, next to the reservoir (Bell Township).

156C. Avonmore Homestead (brick), now a museum, was built about 1850 by Simon Hine, grandson of the first Simon Hine who came with Stephen Rinebolt as an early settler. About 1890 the Eugene Morenus family of the German Glass Works lived in this house, later occupied by the Harry Wilson family. In subsequent years Dr. Robert Yockey (whose father owned the house previously and operated a funeral home there) adapted the structure for use as a personal care home. A springhouse still exists on the property. *Location:* 512 Indiana Avenue.

156D. West Penn Foundry and Machine Company, founded in 1894, was bought by National Roll and Foundry Company in 1909 under the leadership of A. J. Baird from Canton, Ohio. In 1945 it received an Army-Navy Production Award of Excellence from the U.S. government. In 1957 the foundry became the National Roll Division of General Steel Industries, Inc. *Location:* Fourth and Third Streets, at river.

157. St. James Reformed Church (brick), in Greek Revival style, was originally known as Yockey's Meetinghouse. It was founded on land donated by Simon Hine (in Avonmore) for a Lutheran and German Reformed Church. The first pastor was John William Weber. The present church was erected in 1838–39 by Matthew Callen and John Paul. (Some of the log beams may have come from an earlier, unfinished church.) In the adjoining cemetery of the present church is the grave of Mathias Ringle, a wainwright for George Washington at Valley Forge. *Location:* Near Salina (Bell Township), off SR 0380. From Perryville (Perrysville) turn right on Church Road near Kiskiminetas River.

158. Carnahan's Blockhouse Site. A marker indicates the site of Adam Carnahan's blockhouse of 1774, where Col. Archibald Lochry assembled his troops for his ill-fated expedition down the Ohio River in 1781. John Carnahan, Adam's brother, and an Indian were buried here in 1777 after a skirmish on this property. *Location:* From Perryville, 0.2 mile from the junction of SR 0380 and SR 0819 (Carnahan Road).

159. Kier Fire Brick Company (brick) is an early brickworks, once an important and productive industry in this area. It is a significant industrial archeological site. *Location:* Salina (Bell Township).

160. Vandergrift, a famous late-nineteenth-century industrial community, was called "A Worker's Paradise" by Ida M. Tarbell, the celebrated writer at the turn of the century. The town was founded in 1895 by George G. McMurtry (1837–1915), a Scotch-Irish mill owner and president of the Apollo Iron and Steel Company (later part of United States Steel Company). It was planned and laid out by the firm of landscape artist Frederick Law Olmsted (1822–1903) who at that time was near retirement. (Olmsted's plan received a gold medal at the 1904 St. Louis Exposition.) The younger members of Olmsted, Olmsted and Eliot carried out most of the work. The town was named for McMurtry's friend and financial backer, Capt. Jacob Vandergrift (1827–99), an outgoing riverboat captain and industrialist. It has been said that the round-cornered buildings and streets were inspired by riverboat navigation. McMurtry studied millworker housing in Europe such as the Krupp installations at Essen, Germany.

160A. St. Gertrude's Roman Catholic Church (brick) was built in 1911 in Romanesque style with twin campaniles that can be seen for miles from their site on a high hill overlooking Vandergrift and East Vandergrift. The architect, John Theodore Comes, was inspired by Carnegie Library and Music Hall in Pittsburgh (Oakland), which in turn was inspired by the Palais de Trocadero from the 1878 Paris Exposition. *Location:* 303–11 Franklin Avenue.

160B. SS. Constantine and Eleni Greek Orthodox Church (brick) was built in 1916 at a cost of $50,000. It is the first chartered church built in Pennsylvania for the "purpose of perpetuating the Orthodox faith to its members." The architect and craftsmen for the building all came from Greece to carry out the project. Interior paintings are by George Costakis. The church's first priest, Father Avramopoulos, was brought from Greece by the congregation. *Location:* Lincoln Avenue.

160C. Vandergrift Methodist Church (brick) was organized September 4, 1896. The cornerstone of the present church was laid July 1, 1897, and the building was remodeled in 1958–59. This church is one of the first in Vandergrift, a model community that was laid out in 1896 by the Apollo Iron and Steel Company at a point known as Townsend Station and named in honor of Capt. J. J. Vandergrift. The Vandergrift Land and Improvement Company had offered to any church denomination sufficient ground upon which to erect church buildings and a donation of $7,500 provided the church membership would subscribe a similar amount and build a church worth at least $15,000. The First United Methodist congregation agreed to these conditions; J. D. Allison of Pittsburgh designed the church, and Kennedy, Hamilton, and Fair of Blairsville built the structure for $17,240. The first pastor was Noble G. Miller, who served in 1896–97. *Location:* Between Thirteenth Street and SR 0056.

160D. Edward Bush House is perhaps the least changed of all the community's early houses in exterior appearance. *Location:* 200 Washington Avenue.

160E. Casino (brick), once a playhouse and theater, is now, in part, the community library. This Greek Revival building was built in 1901–04 during the administration of Burgess George A. Hunger. An addition was constructed in 1927. This outstanding theater, inspired and supported by G. G. McMurtry, is worthy of preservation. *Location:* Washington and Grant avenues.

160F. Vandergrift Railroad Station (brick), with a tile roof, is now a commercial building. *Location:* Washington Street, at railroad.

161. East Vandergrift, incorporated in 1901, was originally a workingman's community along the Kiskiminetas River where many employees from Apollo settled. A stone wall separated this town from adjacent Vandergrift years ago. It ran from Ninth Street to Hamilton Street for about a quarter of a mile. Numerous ethnic churches and clubs, as well as a stone store on the corner of Jackson Street and McKinley Avenue, were built here during the peak of the steel mills.

161A. Holy Trinity Catholic Church (buff brick) was built in 1915–16. This Slovak church has the following inscription on its facade: "Skola SV. Tojice." *Location:* McKinley Avenue at Chambers Street.

161B. Lithuanian Club (stone). Inscribed on the facade are the dates "1908" and "1915." *Location:* McKinley Avenue.

162. Arnold House

161C. St. Casimir's Church (buff brick) is Lithuanian (Szv. Kazimiero) and is located across from the Lithuanian club. it was built shortly after the 1936 flood. *Location:* McKinley Avenue.

161D. All Saints Polish Church (brick) was built in 1924. *Location:* McKinley Avenue.

161E. Polish Corporation (buff brick), a Polish club, has the following dates on its facade: "1917" and "1921." *Location:* McKinley Avenue at Chambers Street.

161F. Polish National Alliance (buff brick) was a club house built in 1910. *Location:* 791 McKinley Avenue between Read and Chambers streets.

162. Arnold House (frame), in Italianate style, constructed of board and batten, was built in the mid 1800s by Capt. Robert Parks Arnold, the first to ship large quantities of oil down the river to Pittsburgh. In 1862 Arnold, for whom the nearby town was named, was in the 15th Pennsylvania Cavalry. In the 1870s he helped lay out Arnold. Next to the house is St. Margaret Mary's Church, which opened in 1925 as a mission church to Mt. St. Peter's in New Kensington (q.v.). *Location:* Braeburn, off Braeburn Road on Wickes Drive.

163. Markle Normal Academy (frame) was built by the Miller family in the 1830s as a wood shop for grain cradles and coffins. According to one owner, a navy seaman in the Civil War named Robert Miller moved the building on log rollers to its present site in 1870. Here he established the academy, which charged $4 for a student to attend a semester. The song "Moon Over Markle" was written by one of the academy's alumni. Teachers' institutes were held here and participants came from as far away as Harrisburg and Grove City. After the death of Robert (1909) and his wife Sara (several years later), a local church purchased the property. The building was later occupied by a blacksmith. In recent years Edward and Carole Salyer restored the building which is now the Old Academy Country Shop. *Location:* Markle, near junction of SR 4034 and SR 4073 (Allegheny Township).

164. New Kensington was incorporated as a borough in 1892 and a third-class city in 1934. Home of Willie Thrower, first black quarterback to play in the NFL (Chicago Bears, 1953).

164A. Mt. St. Peter's Church (stone), constructed of red Michigan sandstone in 1942, was built with materials from the former Richard K. Mellon house at Shady and Fifth avenues in Pittsburgh (see *Pittsburgh Center for the Arts*, Allegheny County). The building materials were donated to the members of the church who, with the aid of volunteers, built the church themselves. The contractor was Charles Camarata. The church includes a beautiful Tiffany stained glass window, alabaster chandeliers, granite balustrades, and bronze stair railings from the original mansion. *Location:* Seventh Street.

164B. Massa Harbison Log Cabin (log) was moved to this park setting from Butler County, where Massa Harbison, once an Indian captive, lived briefly in later life. *Location:* Massa Harbison Park, SR 0056 bypass and Oats Road.
Note: Massa Harbison's earlier home site is at River Forest Golf Course near Garvers Ferry.

164C. Parnassus Presbyterian Church (frame) was founded in 1842. The present white frame structure, with a bell tower, was built in 1889. John W. Logan donated the church property. To the right of the church is the site of Fort Crawford, built by Colonel William Crawford, whose home was near Connellsville (Fayette County). The fort is recorded as being in existence in 1777 and mentioned in official correspondence as late as 1792. *Location:* Parnassus (New Kensington), Main and Church streets.

164D. Beale House (fieldstone) was built about 1805 by John Beale, who came to this area from Juniata County. He gave the property to the Puckety Church for its house of worship and cemetery. The old church is now gone, but its foundation and a monument in the cemetery mark the site on Puckety Church

Road. *Location:* East of New Kensington, in Lower Burrell on Puckety Church Road, 0.3 mile off SR 0056. House sits out of view on dirt road off Puckety Church Road.

164E. Logan House (brick), built before 1876, in later years became the community's first hospital. This Victorian house was originally owned by J. W. Logan. *Location:* Sixth Avenue between Fourth and Fifth streets.

164F. United States Aluminum Company (Alcoa) Offices (brick and limestone), a three-story structure of English Tudor style, now called Kensington Towers Apartments, was built in 1914. It was designed, with turrets topped by gargoyles and copper finials, by the architect J. H. Giesey of Pittsburgh. This was headquarters for the Aluminum Cooking Utensil Company, manufacturers of Wear-Ever implements, which was dissolved in 1952. (One employee had become a partner with J. P. Morgan.) About 1960 the building was donated to the city and five years later it was converted into apartments. *Location:* Eleventh Street between Fourth and Fifth avenues.
Note: The Aluminum Company of America's laboratories were established in New Kensington and Upper Burrell. One of them, built in 1929, was the site of research for all-metal aircraft.

165. Thompson House (stone) was built by George Thompson in 1849 at the site of an early tannery. The tannery mill stone is still on the property. *Location:* Near New Kensington, Merwin Road, in sight of junction of SR 0366 and SR 0380.

166. Early Log House. *Location:* Kinlock, Wills Avenue near Dugan Way, off SR 0366, about 2 miles east of New Kensington.

Previous Sites Now Lost

Bossart-Osterman House, demolished by bank for parking lot
Earhart Museum, burned
East Huntingdon High School, demolished
Dible Log House, removed to Boyce Park, Allegheny County
Geiger Inn, demolished
Ludwick House, demolished
McHenry Hotel, burned
Obadiah Haymaker House, demolished
Old Murrysville Presbyterian Church, demolished by bank for parking lot
Old Stone Inn, demolished by bank for parking lot

Laurel Hill Iron Furnace

Saint Xavier's Academy, demolished
Silvis Blacksmith Shop, in disrepair
Strand Theater, demolished
Waugaman House, demolished

Iron Furnaces
(originally sixteen)

Baldwin Furnace (1810), built by James Stewart and Henry Baldwin. On State Game Lands No. 42, on SR 1003, 2 miles south of New Florence. Requires walk of 1.3 miles from game lands parking lot.

California Furnace (1853), built in by J. D. Mathiot and Dr. S. P. Cummings. About 3 miles south of Laughlintown (at restaurant) on an unmarked road.

Fountain Furnace (1810), built by J. Mayberry; rebuilt by Gen. R. K. Mellon. On old lane about 1 mile northeast of starting point (Laughlintown) at SR 0381, 0.75 mile north of SR 0031.

Laurel Hill Furnace (1845–46), with four arches, built in 1845–46 by Hezekiah Reed, Gallagher, and Hale. In later years it was owned by Judge J. T. Hall from Centre County. It went out of blast sometime between 1855 and 1860. In the best condition of any furnace in the county. From SR 0711 (1.1 miles). Go to New Florence and at eastern edge of town turn south onto SR 1003 to first road to the left. Follow road across creek and bear right at the forks in the road. The stack is close to the road.

Ross Furnace (1815), built by J. D. Mathiot, Isaac Meason, and James Paull. On golf course, Ross Mountain Park. (Furnace owned by Western Pennsylvania Conservancy. The ruins of Hannah [Unity] Furnace are about a mile from Ross Furnace.)

Valley (Hillsview) Furnace (1850), built by L. C. Hall. On SR 1009, 0.25 mile from SR 0711, 5 miles north of Ligonier.

Washington Furnace (1809), built by Johnson and McClurg, operated until 1826; rebuilt in 1848 by John Bell, and abandoned in 1854. About half a mile north of US 30, 1 mile east of Laughlintown (turn left through stone pillars just east of Washington Furnace Inn).

Pennsylvania Historical and Museum Commission Markers

Arthur St. Clair US 30, 6.5 miles northwest of Ligonier

Bushy Run US 30 at Jeannette; Adamsburg, US 30 at SR 3077; Delmont, old US 22 and SR 0066; and at property on SR 0993, 1 mile east of Harrison City

Dagworthy's Camp US 30, 8.3 miles east of Greensburg

Forbes Road US 22, 1.2 miles east of Murrysville; and US 22 east of Murrysville

Fort Allen SR 0136 southwest of Greensburg

Fort Ligonier Ligonier, Main and Marker streets

Hanna's Town SR 0819 north of Greensburg

Henry Clay Frick US 119 north of Scottdale

John W. Geary SR 0031 east of Mount Pleasant

Johnston House US 30, 7 miles northwest of Ligonier

Loyalhanning US 30 southeast of Ligonier

Murrysville Gas Well Murrysville, US 22

St. Vincent US 30, 6.6 miles east of Greensburg at entrance to college

St. Xavier's US 30. 6 miles east of Greensburg at Saint Xavier

Tollhouse Greensburg, at Mount Odin Park

Tollhouse Greensburg, East Pittsburgh Street east of Stark Street

Twelve Mile Camp US 30, 7.1 miles east of Greensburg

Westmoreland County Greensburg, at courthouse, North Main Street

West Newton SR 0136 at bridge

Bibliography

No attempt will be made to list manuscript collections, theses, monographs, and other specialty items applicable to one or two sites. These are more in the realm of the researcher than the historical pilgrim to whom this book is addressed. (A fair listing of these—at least for the early period—may be found in Mulkearn and Pugh's *A Traveler's Guide to Historic Western Pennsylvania,* available in most libraries. For a fuller listing of published works up to 1957 the reader may consult Norman B. Wilkinson's *Bibliography of Pennsylvania History* (Harrisburg: Pennsylvania Historical and Museum Commission, [1957]). For the same reason, we are not including maps or atlases, although helpful material may be found by the researcher in atlases published for various counties and in the warrantee atlas maps of original land grants, available in Harrisburg and in some county courthouses and large libraries. Much material, especially for Allegheny County, is to be found in the Western Pennsylvania Historical Magazine and in publications of several other county and regional historical groups. The titles listed here are limited to those most likely to be available and helpful to the person seeking more information on some of the sites in this work.

General Works

Agnew, Daniel. *A History of the Region of Pennsylvania North of the Ohio and West of the Allegheny River.* Philadelphia, 1887.

Albert, George Dallas. *Report of the Commission to Locate the Site of the Frontier Forts of Pennsylvania.* Vol. 2. Harrisburg, 1896.

Botsford, Harry. *The Valley of Oil.* New York, 1946 [?].

Day, Sherman. *Historical Collections of the State of Pennsylvania.* Philadelphia, 1843.

Egle, W. H. *An Illustrated History of the Commonwealth of Pennsylvania.* Harrisburg, 1876.

Esbenshade, A. H. *Pennsylvania Place Names.* State College, Pa., 1925.

Godcharles, Frederic A. *Daily Stories of Pennsylvania.* Milton, Pa., 1924.

———. *Pennsylvania, Political, Governmental, Military and Civil.* New York, 1933.

Guidebook to Historic Places in Western Pennsylvania. Pittsburgh, 1933.

Haas, Henry A. *Guide to the Historical Markers of Pennsylvania.* Harrisburg, 1975.

Jenkins, H. M., ed. *Pennsylvania, Colonial and Federal. . . .* Philadelphia, 1903.

McKnight, W. J. *A Pioneer Outline History of Northwestern Pennsylvania.* Philadelphia, 1905.

McLaurin, Jon J. *Sketches in Crude Oil.* Harrisburg, 1896.

Montgomery, Thomas L., ed. *Report of the Commission to Locate the Site of the Frontier Forts of Pennsylvania.* Vol. 1. Harrisburg, 1896.

Mulkearn, Lois, and Pugh, Edwin V. *A Traveler's Guide to Historic Western Pennsylvania.* Pittsburgh, 1954.

Pates, Mrs. William S., ed. *Historia.* Tarentum, Pa., 1972.

Pennsylvania Historical Commission. *Marking the Historic Sites of Early Pennsylvania.* Harrisburg, 1926.

Pennsylvania Writers Project. *Pennsylvania Cavalcade.* Philadelphia, 1942.

———. *Pennsylvania, A Guide to the Keystone State.* New York, 1940.

Ray, J. W. *A History of Western Pennsylvania.* Erie, Pa., 1941.

Rieseman, Joseph. *History of Northwestern Pennsylvania.* New York, 1943.

Rupp, I. D. *Early History of Western Pennsylvania.* Pittsburgh, 1846.

Searight, T. B. *The Old Pike.* Uniontown, 1894.

Sharp, Myron, and Thomas, William H. *Guide to Old Stone Blast Furnaces in Western Pennsylvania.* Pittsburgh, 1966.

Stevens, S. K. *Pennsylvania, Birthplace of a Nation.* New York, 1964.

Stewart, Nora M. *The Achieving Student and Local History.* Shippenville, Pa., n.d.

Stotz, Charles Morse. *The Architectural Heritage of Early Western Pennsylvania.* 1936. Reprint, Pittsburgh, 1966.

Swank, J. M. *Progressive Pennsylvania.* Philadelphia, 1908.

Swetnam, George. *Pennsylvania Transportation.* 2d ed. Gettysburg, Pa., 1968.

———. *Pittsylvania Country.* New York, 1951.

Van Atta, Robert B. *Guide to Allegheny Power System Service Area Communities' Cultural, Historic, and Recreation Attractions.* Greensburg, Pa., 1970.

Walkinshaw, L. C. *Annals of Southwestern Pennsylvania.* New York, 1939.

Wallace, Paul A. W. *Indian Paths of Pennsylvania.* Harrisburg, 1965.

Zacher, Susan M. *The Covered Bridges of Pennsylvania: A Guide.* Harrisburg, 1982–86.

Allegheny County

Baldwin, L. D. *Pittsburgh: The Story of a City.* Pittsburgh, 1937. Reprinted in paperback, Pittsburgh, 1970.

Borkowski, Joseph A. *Historical Highlights and Sites of Lawrenceville Area.* Pittsburgh, 1969.

———*Miscellaneous History of Lawrenceville.* Pittsburgh, 1989.

Botset, Elizabeth K., and Waldrop, George B. *Fox Chapel: The Story of a District.* Pittsburgh, 1954.

Boucher, J. N. *A Century and a Half of Pittsburgh and Her People.* New York, 1908.

Cushing, Thomas, ed. *History of Allegheny County, Pa.* Chicago, 1889.

Fleming, G. T. *History of Pittsburgh and Environs.* New York, 1922.

Group for Historical Research. *Annals of Old Wilkinsburg and Vicinity.* Wilkinsburg, Pa., 1940

Harper, F. C. *Pittsburgh of Today: Its Resources and People.* New York, 1931.

Johnston, W. G. *Life and Reminiscences.* Pittsburgh, 1901.

Kidney, Walter C. *Landmark Architecture: Pittsburgh and Allegheny County.* Pittsburgh, 1985.

Lambing, A. A., and White, J. W. F. *Allegheny County: Its Early History and Subsequent Development.* Pittsburgh, 1888.

Lorant, Stefan. *Pittsburgh: The Story of an American City.* New York, 1964. Reprint, Lenox, Mass., 1975.

Parke, J. E. *Recollections of Seventy Years.* Boston, 1886.

Swetnam, George. *Where Else but Pittsburgh!* Pittsburgh, 1958.

Thompson, Noah. *Early History of the Peters Creek Valley and the Early Settlers.* N.p., 1974.

Thurston, G. H. *Allegheny County's Hundred Years.* Pittsburgh, 1888.

Van Trump, James D., and Ziegler, Arthur P., Jr. *Landmark Architecture of Allegheny County, Pennsylvania.* Pittsburgh, 1967.

Wilson, Erasmus, ed. *Standard History of Pittsburg.* Chicago, 1898.

Armstrong County

Beers, J. H., & Co. *Armstrong County, Pennsylvania. . . .* Chicago, 1914.

Smith, R. W. *History of Armstrong County.* Chicago, 1883.

Wiley, S. T. *Biographical and Historical Cyclopedia of Indiana and Armstrong Counties, Pennsylvania.* Philadelphia, 1891.

Beaver County

Bausman, J. H. *History of Beaver County, Pennsylvania.* New York, 1904.

History of Monaca. Monaca, Pa., [1940].

Hoover, G. L. *Historic Stone Houses on the South Side of Beaver County.* N.p., 1969.

Richard, J. F. *History of Beaver County, Pennsylvania. . . .* Chicago, 1888.

Bedford County

Blackburn, E. H., and Welfley, William H. *History of Bedford and Somerset Counties, Pennsylvania.* Vol. 1. New York, 1906.

Garbrick, Winona, ed. *The Kernel of Greatness.* State College, Pa., 1971.

Hall, William M. *Reminiscences and Sketches.* Harrisburg, 1890.

History of Bedford, Somerset and Fulton Counties, Pennsylvania. Chicago, 1884.

Jordan, William, ed. *Bedford County Pennsylvania, Historical Background.* Bedford, Pa., 1973.

Rupp, I. D. *History of Bedford, Somerset, Cambria and Indiana Counties.* Lancaster, Pa., 1848.

Schell, W. P. *The Annals of Bedford County.* Bedford, Pa., 1907.

Blair County

Adams, P. G. *History of Hollidaysburg, 1790–1870.* State College, Pa., 1939.

Africa, J. S. *History of Huntingdon and Blair Counties.* Philadelphia, 1883.

Clark, C. B. *A History of Blair County, Pennsylvania, 1846–1896.* Altoona, Pa., 1896.

Davis, T. S., ed. *A History of Blair County, Pennsylvania.* Harrisburg, 1931.

Ewing, J. H. *A History of the City of Altoona and Blair County.* Altoona, Pa., 1880.

Sell, J. C. *Twentieth Century History of Altoona and Blair County, Pennsylvania.* Chicago, 1911.

Wolt, G. A., ed. *Blair County's First Hundred Years.* Altoona, Pa., 1945.

Butler County

Brown, R. C., ed. *History of Butler County, Pennsylvania.* Chicago, 1895.

Butler County Pennsylvania. . . . Butler, Pa., 1950.

History of Butler County, Pennsylvania. Chicago, 1883.

McKee, J. A., ed. *20th Century History of Butler and Butler County, Pennsylvania.* Chicago, 1909.

Sipe, C. H. *History of Butler County, Pennsylvania.* Indianapolis, 1927.

Cambria County

Connelly, Frank, and Jenks, G. C. *Official History of the Johnstown Flood.* Pittsburgh, 1889.

McLaurin, J. J. *The Story of Johnstown. . . .* Harrisburg, 1890.

Rupp, I. D. *History of Bedford, Somerset, Cambria and Indiana Counties.* Lancaster, Pa., 1848.

Storey, H. W. *History of Cambria County, Pennsylvania.* New York, 1907.

Swank, J. M. *Cambria County Pioneers. . . .* Philadelphia, 1910.

Cameron County

Leeson, M. A., ed. *History of the Counties of McKean, Elk, Forest, Cameron and Potter, Pennsylvania.* Chicago, 1890.

Clarion County

Caldwell, J. A. *Caldwell's Illustrated Historical Combination Atlas of Clarion County Pennsylvania. . . .* Condit, Ohio, 1877. Reprint, with supplemental data, Rimersburg, Pa., 1964.

Clarion County Centennial. [Clarion, Pa.], 1940.

Davis, A. J. *History of Clarion County, Pennsylvania.* Syracuse, N.Y., 1887. Reprint, with historical supplement, Rimersburg, Pa., 1968.

Niece, B. F., ed. *Souvenir Book of Clarion, Pa.* N.p., n.d.

Clearfield County

Aldrich, L. C. *History of Clearfield County, Pennsylvania.* Syracuse, N.Y., 1887.

Barrett, H. G. *History of Clearfield County, Pennsylvania.* Altoona, Pa., 1896.

McCreight, M. I. *Memory Sketches of Du Bois, Pennsylvania.* Du Bois, Pa., 1938.

Pentz, W. C. *The City of Du Bois.* Du Bois, Pa., 1932.

Swoope, R. D. *Twentieth Century History of Clearfield County, Pennsylvania.* Chicago, [1911].

Wall, T. L. *Clearfield County, Present and Past.* Clearfield, Pa., [1925?].

Crawford County

Bates, S. P. *Our County and Its People.* N.p., 1899.

Brown, R. C., et al. *History of Crawford County, Pennsylvania.* Chicago, 1885.

Huidekoper, Alfred. *Incidents in the Early History of Crawford County.* Philadelphia, 1850.

Miller, F. G. *Our Own Pioneers.* Meadville, Pa., 1929.

Reynolds, J. E. *In French Creek Valley.* Meadville, Pa., 1938.

Elk County

Leeson, M. A., ed. *History of the Counties of McKean, Elk, Forest, Cameron and Potter, Pennsylvania.* Chicago, 1890.

Schout, C. J. *Early St. Marys and Some of Its People.* Clearfield, Pa., 1952.

Erie County

Federal Writers Project. *Erie: A Guide to the City and County.* Philadelphia, 1938.

Miller, John. *A Twentieth Century History of Erie County, Pennsylvania.* Chicago, 1909.

Reed, J. E. *History of Erie County, Pennsylvania.* Indianapolis, 1925.

Robbins, D. P. *Popular History of Erie County, Pennsylvania.* Erie, Pa., 1895.

Sanford, L. G. *The History of Erie County, Pennsylvania.* Philadelphia, 1894.

Spencer, Herbert R., and Jack, Walter. *Roaming Erie County.* Erie, Pa., 1958.

BIBLIOGRAPHY

Whitman, Benjamin, and Russell, N. W. *History of Erie County, Pennsylvania*. Chicago, 1884.

Fayette County

Ellis, Franklin. *History of Fayette County, Pennsylvania*. Philadelphia, 1882.
Hadden, James. *A History of Uniontown*. . . . Akron, Ohio, 1913.
Hart, J. P., ed. *Hart's History and Directory of Brownsville, Bridgeport and West Brownsville*. Cadwallader, Pa., 1904.
McClenathan, J. C. *Centennial History of the Borough of Connellsville, Pennsylvania, 1806–1906*. Columbus, Ohio, 1906.
Nelson, S. B. *Nelson's Biographical Dictionary and Historical Reference Book of Fayette County, Pennsylvania*. Uniontown, Pa., 1900.
Wiley, S. T. *Biographical and Portrait Cyclopedia of Fayette County, Pennsylvania*. Chicago, 1889.

Forest County

Irwin, S. D. *History of Forest County*. Tionesta, Pa., 1876.
Leeson, M. A., ed. *History of the Counties of McKean, Elk, Forest, Cameron and Potter, Pennsylvania*. Chicago, 1890.

Greene County

Bates, S. P. *History of Greene County, Pennsylvania*. Chicago, 1888.
Evans, L. K. *Pioneer History of Greene County, Pennsylvania*. Waynesburg, Pa., 1941.
Hanna, William. *History of Greene County, Pennsylvania*. . . . N.p., 1882.
High, Fred. *Waynesburg, Prosperous and Beautiful*. Waynesburg, Pa., 1905.

Indiana County

Caldwell, J. *A History of Indiana County, Pennsylvania*. Newark, Ohio, 1880.
Rupp, I. D. *History of Bedford, Somerset, Cambria and Indiana Counties*. Lancaster, Pa., 1848.
Stewart, J. T., ed. *Indiana County Pennsylvania*. . . . Chicago, 1913.
Trexler, R. O. *History of Armagh, Pennsylvania*. N.p., 1950.
Wiley, S. T. *Biographical and Historical Cyclopedia of Indiana and Armstrong Counties, Pennsylvania*. Philadelphia, 1891.

Jefferson County

Elliott, W. C. *History of Reynoldsville and Vicinity*. Punxsutawney, Pa., 1922.
McKnight, W. J. *Jefferson County, Pennsylvania*. . . . Chicago, 1917.
———. *Pioneer History of Jefferson County, Pennsylvania*. Philadelphia, 1898.
Scott, K. M., ed. *History of Jefferson County, Pennsylvania*. Syracuse, N.Y., 1888.
Smith, W. O. *Punxsutawney, 1772–1909*. Punxsutawney, Pa., 1909.

Lawrence County

Book of Biographies: Sketches of Leading Citizens of Lawrence County, Pennsylvania. Buffalo, N.Y., 1897.
Durant, S. W. *History of Lawrence County, Pennsylvania*. Philadelphia, 1877.
Hazen, A. L., ed. *20th Century History of New Castle and Lawrence County, Pennsylvania*. Chicago, 1908.
Wood, W. W. *Historical Review of the Towns and Business Houses of Lawrence County*. New Castle, Pa., 1887.

McKean County

Hatch, V. A., ed. *Illustrated History of Bradford, McKean County, Pennsylvania*. Bradford, Pa., 1901.
Henretta, J. E. *Kane and the Upper Allegheny*. Philadelphia, 1929.
Leeson, M. A., ed. *History of the Counties of McKean, Elk, Forest, Cameron and Potter, Pennsylvania*. Chicago, 1890.
McDonnell, F. M., ed. *The Book of Bradford*. . . . Bradford, Pa., 1897.
Stone, R. B. *McKean, the Governor's County*. New York, 1926.

Mercer County

Dayton, David M. *'Mid the Pines*. Grove City, Pa., 1971.
Durant, S. W. *History of Mercer County, Pennsylvania*. Philadelphia, 1877.
History of Mercer County, Pennsylvania. Chicago, 1888.
History of Sharpsville, Pennsylvania. Sharpsville, 1949.
White, J. G., ed. *A 20th Century History of Mercer County, Pennsylvania*. New York, 1909.

Somerset County

Blackburn, E. H., and Welfley, William H. *History of Bedford and Somerset Counties, Pennsylvania.* Vol. 2. New York, 1906.

Cassaday, J. C. *The Somerset County Outline.* Scottdale, Pa., 1932.

Doyle, Frederic. *Early Somerset County.* Somerset, Pa., 1945.

Hause, Mary. *A Somerset County Historical Notebook.* Somerset, Pa., 1945.

Rupp, I. D. *History of Bedford, Somerset, Cambria and Indiana Counties.* Lancaster, Pa., 1948.

Venango County

Babcock, C. A. *Venango County, Pennsylvania: Her Pioneers and Her People.* Chicago, 1919.

Bell, H. C., ed. *History of Venango County, Pennsylvania.* Chicago, 1890.

The Historical Album. Franklin, Pa., 1968.

Newton, J. H., ed. *History of Venango County, Pennsylvania. . . .* Columbus, Ohio, 1879.

Warren County

Bristow, Arch. *Old Time Tales of Warren County.* Meadville, Pa., 1932.

Putnam, Mary, and Putnam, Chase, eds. *Historic Buildings in Warren County.* 3 vols. Warren, Pa., 1971–74.

Schenck, J. S., ed. *History of Warren County, Pennsylvania.* Syracuse, N.Y., 1887.

Smith, B. A., ed. *Historical Collections of Sheffield Township, Warren County, Pennsylvania.* Warren, Pa., 1943.

Warren Library Association. *Warren Centennial.* Warren, Pa., 1897.

Washington County

Baker, W. A. Jr., ed. *Canonsburg, Pennsylvania, 1773–1936.* Canonsburg, Pa., 1936.

Campbell, June, and Slasor, Kathryn, comps. *So Firm a Foundation: A History of the Tucker Methodist Church.* N.p., 1965.

Commemorative Biographical Record of Washington County, Pennsylvania. Chicago, 1893.

Creigh, Alfred. *History of Washington County. . . .* Washington, Pa., 1870.

Crumrine, Boyd. *History of Washington County, Pennsylvania.* Philadelphia, 1882.

Forrest, E. R. *History of Washington County, Pennsylvania.* Chicago, 1926.

"Historical Stops in Washington County." Typescript, Washington Area Community Resources Workshop. Washington, Pa., 1959.

McFarland, J. F. *20th Century History of the City of Washington and Washington County. . . .* Chicago, 1910.

Preserving Our Past. Washington, Pa., 1975.

Reader, F. S. *Some Pioneers of Washington County, Pennsylvania.* New Brighton, Pa., 1902.

Thompson, Noah. *Early History of the Peters Creek Valley and the Early Settlers.* N.p., 1974.

Westmoreland County

Albert, G. D. *History of the County of Westmoreland, Pennsylvania.* Philadelphia, 1882.

Altman, G. P., and Agnew, Thomas. *Tales from Tinker Run.* Irwin, Pa., 1972.

Biographical and Historical Cyclopedia of Westmoreland County, Pennsylvania. Philadelphia, 1890.

Bomberger, C. M. *Brush Creek Tales.* Jeannette, Pa., 1950.

————. *A Short History of Westmoreland County. . . .* Jeannette, Pa., 1941.

Boucher, J. N. *History of Westmoreland County, Pennsylvania.* New York, 1906.

————. *Old and New Westmoreland.* New York, 1918.

Foley, Helene M., and Berger, Marion L. *This Is Murrysville.* Murrysville, Pa., 1959.

History of Greensburg. . . . Greensburg, Pa., 1899.

History of Our City, Monessen, Pennsylvania. Columbus, Ohio, 1902.

Laughlintown, Pennsylvania, 1797–1947. Laughlintown, Pa., 1947.

Pollins, John W. *Dr. Frank Cowan: A Biographical Sketch.* Greensburg, Pa., 1950.

Sesqui-Centennial Corporation. *The History of Greensburg.* Greensburg, Pa., 1949.

Smith, Helene. *Export: A Patch of Tapestry out of Coal Country America.* Greensburg, Pa., 1986.

Studer, Gerald C., ed. *Over the Alleghenies.* Scottdale, Pa., 1965.

Woman's Club of Ligonier. *Our Heritage in Ligonier Valley.* Ligonier, Pa., 1963, 1965, 1976.

Index

Page numbers in bold refer to illustrations. An Index of Site Locations listing the towns and cities where the sites are located begins on page 407.

Index of Site Locations

408